P9-DCH-105

Smith, Currie & Hancock LLP's
COMMON SENSE CONSTRUCTION LAW

A Practical Guide for the Construction Professional

THIRD EDITION

General Editor
Thomas J. Kelleher, Jr.

CHAPTER EDITORS

Thomas E. Abernathy, IV
William L. Baggett, Jr.
David H. Bashford
Philip E. Beck
James K. Bidgood, Jr.
Harry R. Bivens
James F. Butler, III
Sarah E. Carson
Robert C. Chambers
Rolly L. Chambers
Aubrey L. Coleman, Jr.
James W. Copeland
Karl F. Dix, Jr.
Mark E. Farrell, Jr.
Eugene J. Heady
Reginald M. Jones

S. Gregory Joy
Thomas J. Kelleher, Jr.
S. Elysha Luken
John E. Menechino, Jr.
Eric L. Nelson
Frank E. Riggs, Jr.
Ronald G. Robey
Gregory L. Shelton
C. Michael Shull
Kent P. Smith
Joseph C. Staak
Charles W. Surasky
George D. Wenick
Steele B. Windle, III
Brian A. Wolf
Daniel T. Young

WILEY

John Wiley & Sons, Inc.

This book is printed on acid-free paper ∞.

Copyright © 2005 by John Wiley & Sons, Inc. All rights reserved.

Published by John Wiley & Sons, Inc., Hoboken, New Jersey
Published simultaneously in Canada

No part of this publication may be reproduced, stored in a retrieval system, or transmitted in any form or by any means, electronic, mechanical, photocopying, recording, scanning, or otherwise, except as permitted under Section 107 or 108 of the 1976 United States Copyright Act, without either the prior written permission of the Publisher, or authorization through payment of the appropriate per-copy fee to the Copyright Clearance Center, Inc., 222 Rosewood Drive, Danvers, MA 01923, (978) 750-8400, fax (978) 750-4470, or on the web at www.copyright.com. Requests to the Publisher for permission should be addressed to the Permissions Department, John Wiley & Sons, Inc., 111 River Street, Hoboken, NJ 07030, (201) 748-6011, fax (201) 748-6008, e-mail: permcoordinator@wiley.com.

Designations used by companies to distinguish their products are often claimed as trademarks. In all instances where John Wiley & Sons, Inc. is aware of a claim, the product names appear in initial capital or all capital letters. Readers, however, should contact the appropriate companies for more complete information regarding trademarks and registration.

Limit of Liability/Disclaimer of Warranty: While the publisher and author have used their best efforts in preparing this book, they make no representations or warranties with respect to the accuracy or completeness of the contents of this book and specifically disclaim any implied warranties of merchantability or fitness for a particular purpose. No warranty may be created or extended by sales representatives or written sales materials. The advice and strategies contained herein may not be suitable for your situation. You should consult with a professional where appropriate. Neither the publisher nor author shall be liable for any loss of profit or any other commercial damages, including but not limited to special, incidental, consequential, or other damages.

For general information on our other products and services or for technical support, please contact our Customer Care Department within the United States at (800) 762-2974, outside the United States at (317) 572-3993 or fax (317) 572-4002.

Wiley also publishes its books in a variety of electronic formats. Some content that appears in print may not be available in electronic books. For more information about Wiley products, visit our web site at www.wiley.com.

Library of Congress Cataloging-in-Publication Data

Smith, Currie & Hancock LLP's common sense construction law / general editor, Thomas J. Kelleher, Jr.; chapter editors, Thomas E. Abernathy, IV...[et al]—3rd ed.
    p.cm.
    Rev. ed. of: Smith, Currie & Hancock's common sense construction law, second edition / editors, Robert B. Ansley, Jr....[et al.]. c2001
    Includes bibliographical references and index.
    ISBN 0-471-66209-7 (cloth: alk. paper)
    1. Construction contracts—United States. 2. Construction industry—Law and legislation—United States. I. Title: Smith, Currie and Hancock LLP's common sense construction law. II. Title: Common sense construction law. III. Kelleher, Thomas J. IV. Smith, Currie & Hancock. V. Title: Smith, Currie & Hancock's common sense construction law.

KF902.S63 2005
346.73'078624—dc21

00-026832

Printed in the United States of America

10   9   8   7   6   5   4

In the first edition of *Common Sense Construction Law*, we recognized Overton A. Currie and Luther P. House, Jr., for their leadership and mentoring of the firm and its construction law practice. Consistent with the tradition established by the founders of this firm, we dedicated the second edition of *Common Sense Construction Law* to our clients, whose confidence and trust are essential to our practice and success. With this third edition, we recall with fond memories our deceased partners, G. Maynard Smith (1907–1992), E. Reginald Hancock (1924–2004), and Bert R. Oastler (1933–2002), who devoted their professional lives to the practice of our profession at the highest level of excellence and set the standard for future generations of lawyers in the firm.

CONTENTS

18 Construction Insurance   439

PREFACE

The attorneys of Smith, Currie & Hancock LLP have practiced construction law, government contracts law, and employment law for over four decades. During that time, we have conducted hundreds of construction and government contract law seminars and employment law seminars for clients, trade associations, colleges and universities, and professional groups. Throughout those efforts, our consistent goal has been to provide a practical, commonsense perspective to the legal issues affecting the construction industry. In many respects, this book reflects a culmination and refinement of those educational endeavors and the practical approach they entail.

Construction law and employment law are essential to the construction industry, as they provide the theories, principles, and generally established rules that contribute to the smooth running of the construction process. When that process falters and disputes arise that involve the construction contract or employment issues, a variety of procedures can be used to resolve these differences. These procedures vary in their legal formalities; however, an appreciation of these processes and principles should not be limited to lawyers. Individuals in responsible positions in the industry must be cognizant of what the law requires of them and what they can expect and require from others. Nor can lawyers focus on legal rules and procedures to the exclusion of the *business* of construction and expect to effectively represent and assist their clients. Construction and employment law and the business of construction are inextricably intertwined. We hope this book reflects this interrelationship in the topics that it covers and the various perspectives and approaches it employs.

Claims and disputes are addressed throughout this edition of *Common Sense Construction Law*. They must be in any complete and competent analysis of the construction environment. This book, however, is about much more than just preparing claims and resolving disputes once they arise. Rather, our goal is to help provide the kind of insight and understanding needed to *avoid* claims and disputes. Reasonable recognition of the contractual allocation of rights, risks, and legal responsibilities, coupled with a spirit of communication and teamwork in the execution of the work, is far more likely to culminate in a successful project than an atmosphere rife with confrontation and dispute. Practical knowledge of the general rules governing employment-related issues can have the same beneficial result. Of course, the possibility of claims and disputes cannot be ignored. Careful attention and planning is required to avoid disputes and to deal effectively with them when they become inevitable.

The third edition of *Common Sense Construction Law* is a general teaching tool and is not a substitute for the advice of your attorney. Specific concerns and problems require the timely attention of legal counsel familiar with construction law, government contracts, and employment law. Nevertheless, this book will help you to expand your knowledge and awareness of the issues in construction that may affect you at any time. It may not provide all the answers, but you will be well equipped to ask the right questions. To make these materials more useful to you, we have included checklists, sample forms, and summary "Points to Remember" for each chapter.

We thank our clients who have shared their insights and concerns and provided the opportunities for experience and learning that are shared in this book. We also owe much gratitude to the construction industry as a whole for allowing us as construction attorneys to participate in the challenges of the industry to avoid and resolve problems. We hope this work will contribute to the worthy goals of the industry. We also hope that this book helps its readers pursue their interests in and commitments to construction from concept to completion.

SMITH, CURRIE & HANCOCK LLP

Atlanta, Georgia

SMITH, CURRIE & HANCOCK LLP

A Firm Concentrating Its Practice on the Construction Industry

For over four decades Smith, Currie & Hancock LLP, with offices in Atlanta, Georgia; Charlotte, North Carolina; Fort Lauderdale and Tallahassee, Florida, has developed a nationally recognized practice focused on the construction industry and the variety of legal issues facing those in that industry. The firm represents private and public clients working or located in all fifty states, as well as Mexico, Canada, Central and South America, Europe, Asia, and Africa.

After developing construction and employment law practices in the context of a general service firm, G. Maynard Smith, Overton A. Currie, and E. Reginald Hancock formed this firm in 1965 to concentrate their practices in those areas in order to provide more effective service to the firm's clients. Having trained and practiced law in the culture created by those three outstanding professionals, the current members of the firm remain committed to a tradition of providing quality, cost-effective legal services to clients ranging from small, family owned concerns to multibillion-dollar corporations.

In representing the many participants in the construction industry and government contracting, we are necessarily involved in a wide variety of legal and business related issues. The breadth of these issues is reflected by the topics addressed in the third edition of *Common Sense Construction Law*. From bidding questions to environmental risk evaluation to employment law questions, the spectrum of the potential legal issues and risks affecting those working in the construction industry is varied and complex. The goal of this book is to provide an informative discussion of many of these topics for the construction professional without all of the specific details of a multi-volume legal treatise. To accomplish that task in a practical and meaningful manner, this book reflects the collective efforts of many attorneys drawing on over five hundred years of experience in the areas of construction law, government contracts law, and employment law.

Many of the firm's attorneys have engineering degrees in addition to their legal education, and several worked in the construction industry prior to pursuing their law degrees. Others joined this firm after military service as government contracts legal counsel or have extensive training in public procurement. Three members of Smith, Currie & Hancock LLP have served as Chair of the Public Contract Law

Section of the American Bar Association, and another partner has served as the Chair of the American Bar Association Forum Committee on the Construction Industry. Many members of the firm are arbitrators and mediators for the American Arbitration Association.

Smith, Currie & Hancock LLP has represented clients from the entire spectrum of the construction industry: contractors, subcontractors, construction managers, owners (public and private), architects, engineers, sureties, insurance companies, suppliers, lenders, real estate developers, and others. They include multinational and Fortune 500 companies and trade associations representing billion-dollar industries, as well as local and regional clients doing business on a smaller scale. While our attorneys have appeared in numerous reported court decisions and even more arbitrations, our traditional goal has been to achieve resolution of differences by communication and agreement rather than formal litigation. Consequently, we have assisted in the amicable resolution of many more matters than these reported decisions over the last four decades.

In addition to serving clients nationwide, Smith, Currie & Hancock LLP attorneys have published numerous articles in trade magazines and other periodicals and have authored or co-authored dozens of books in construction and public contract law. Our lawyers maintain a heavy schedule of lectures and seminars sponsored by various trade associations, colleges, and universities, including the U.S. Army Corps of Engineers, Georgia Institute of Technology, Auburn University, the American Bar Association, the Practicing Law Institute, The Associated General Contractors of America, and the Associated Builders & Contractors, Inc.

ATLANTA OFFICE

THOMAS E. ABERNATHY, IV: Born, Chattanooga, Tennessee; Vanderbilt University, B.A. 1963 and J.D. 1967; Fellow and member of Board of Governors, American College of Construction Lawyers; Past Chairman, American Bar Association, Section of Public Contract Law; American Arbitration Association National Roster of Arbitrators; listed in the 2003–04 Chambers USA Directory of America's Leading Business Lawyers in the practice area of construction; listed in the Top 100 of Georgia Super Lawyers; co-author, *Changed Conditions/Edition II, Construction Briefings,* West Group (2000); contributing author, *Construction Business Handbook* (2004).

WILLIAM L. BAGGETT, JR.: Born, Birmingham, Alabama, A.B., Dartmouth College, 1984 (magna cum laude); Phi Beta Kappa; J.D., Vanderbilt University, 1987. Articles Editor, *Vanderbilt Law Review,* 1986–1987. Law Clerk to the Honorable Albert J. Henderson, Senior Circuit Judge, United States Court of Appeals for the Eleventh Circuit, 1987–1988. Member: American Bar Association; Tennessee Bar Association; State Bar of Georgia; State Bar of Tennessee.

PHILIP E. BECK: Born, Salisbury, North Carolina; Univ. of Tennessee, B.S. 1978 (high honors), M.B.A. 1981, J.D. 1981; Order of the Coif; Moot Court Board; Omicron Delta Kappa; Beta Gamma Sigma. Law Clerk to Hon. Houston Goddard, Tennessee Court of Appeals, 1980–1981. Listed in the 2003–2004 *Chambers USA Directory of America's Leading Business Lawyers* and in *Law & Politics* and *Atlanta Magazine*'s 2004 Georgia

Super Lawyers, in the area of construction law. Frequent author and lecturer on various aspects of construction law; experienced litigator, arbitrator & mediator. Member, Associated General Contractors of America Board of Directors, 2002–2007.

HUBERT J. BELL: Born, Elberton, Georgia; B.A., Davidson College, 1966; M.A., Pacific Lutheran University, 1974; J.D., University of Georgia, 1981 (cum laude); Order of the Coif. Co-author: "The Economic Loss Rule; A Fair Balancing of Interests," *Construction Lawyer*, Volume II, Number 2, April 1991; *Alternative Clauses to Standard Construction Contracts*, Second Edition (contributing author), John Wiley & Sons, Inc., 1998.

JAMES K. BIDGOOD, JR.: Born Dublin, Georgia; B. Civil Engineering, Georgia Institute of Technology 1974; M.B.A. Phillips University 1980; J.D. Emory University (1983) (with distinction). Order of Coif, Member Emory Law Journal. Pilot, Instructor Pilot, Captain, USAF, 1974–1980. Experience in variety of construction and environmental-related matters in arbitration, litigation, and mediation. Member, American Arbitration Association Panel of Neutrals. Frequent lecturer on topics of construction law.

JAMES F. BUTLER, III: A.B., Duke University, J.D., University of Kentucky. Member: State Bars of Georgia, Florida, Kentucky, Texas, and Washington. His practice is concentrated in the negotiation, arbitration, and litigation of construction contracts and hazardous waste issues. He has experience with a variety of projects and sites, including petrochemical plants, dams, power plants, tunnels, water/wastewater systems, airports, office buildings, casinos, semiconductor facilities, food-processing facilities, schools, condominiums, prisons, highways, hospitals, Superfund sites, and government facilities.

SARAH E. CARSON: Born, Columbia, South Carolina; B.A., Emory University, 1996. J.D., Catholic University, Columbus School of Law, 1999; Moot Court Team, Moot Court Association. Member: State Bar of Georgia, American Bar Association, Litigation Section; Atlanta Bar Association.

ROBERT C. CHAMBERS: Born, Cornelia, Georgia; B.S.C.E., 1979 (high honors); M.S.C.E., 1980 (Study Emphasis—Geotechnical Engineering), Georgia Institute of Technology; J.D., University of Georgia, 1985 (magna cum laude); Order of the Coif. Co-Author: "Changed Conditions, (1984); Changed Conditions/Edition II (2000)," *Construction Briefings* Federal Publications. Frequent lecturer on environmental issues affecting the construction industry, including environmental liability.

AUBREY L. COLEMAN, JR.: Born, Little Rock, Arkansas; Senior Partner of Smith, Currie & Hancock LLP, B.A., Tulane University, 1964 (cum laude); LL.B., Vanderbilt University, 1967; Order of the Coif; Managing Editor, *Vanderbilt Law Review*, 1966–1967; Phi Beta Kappa. Co-author: *Georgia Construction Law,* Professional Education Systems, 1986. Author and lecturer on various aspects of construction law and construction claims, including participation in programs presented by Georgia State University, Professional Education Systems, Inc., and Federal Publications, Inc.

JAMES W. COPELAND: Born, Durham, North Carolina; B.E., Vanderbilt University, 1988; J.D., Duke University, 1995. Member: Atlanta and American Bar Associations, State Bar of Georgia.

KARL F. DIX, JR.: Born, Iron Mountain, Michigan; B.S., Economics (magna cum laude), Wharton School of Finance and Commerce at the University of Pennsylvania (1980); J.D., with Specialization (cum laude) in International Law from Cornell University (1983). Captain, U.S. Army Corps of Engineers, Attorney Advisor (1983–1987); Chief Counsel's Honors Program. Member of the State Bars of New York and Georgia, U.S. Court of Appeals for the 11th and Federal Circuits and U.S. Court of Federal Claims.

MARK E. FARRELL, JR.: Born, Dayton, Ohio; B.A., University of Notre Dame, 1996 (magna cum laude); M.A., Teaching, University of Portland, 1998; J.D., University of Notre Dame Law School, 2002. Dean Konop Legal Aid Award. Member of the State Bar of Georgia.

ROBERT O. FLEMING, JR.: Born, Greenville, North Carolina. B.S. with honors, North Carolina State University, 1972; J.D., with distinction, Duke University, 1977. Co-author: *Deposition Strategy, Law and Forms: Building Construction*, Matthew-Bender, 1981. Approved Arbitrator for Construction Contract Disputes, American Arbitration Association. Member of the Atlanta and American Bar associations; State Bar of Georgia.

PHILIP L. FORTUNE: Born, High Point, North Carolina; B.A., University of North Carolina at Chapel Hill, 1967, Gamma Beta Phi; J.D., University of Toledo, 1970. Comments Editor, *University of Toledo Law Review*. Author and lecturer on construction law, bonds, liens, and preparation of claims. Lecturer on various aspects of the hazardous waste and environmental protection laws and regulations, including Superfund.

EUGENE J. HEADY: Born, Poughkeepsie, New York; University of Hartford, BSE 1981 (Kappa Mu Honorary Engineering Society); Texas Tech University, J.D., 1996 (cum laude); Editor-in-Chief, *Texas Tech Law Review*, 1995–1996; Editor, *Texas Tech Legal Research Board*, 1995–1996. Listed in *Who's Who in American Law*, 2000 and *Georgia Super Lawyers*, 2004. Contributing author to numerous professional publications, including chapters *in Alternative Clauses to Standard Construction Contracts*, Aspen Law & Business, 1998. Public Contract Law Section, Vice Chair, Region IV, Georgia, 1999–2004. State bars of Georgia, Texas, Colorado, and Florida.

CATHERINE M. HOBART: Born, Buffalo, New York; B.A. 1988, State University of New York at Albany; J.D. 1991, Washington and Lee University. Catherine practices labor and employment law, representing management before all courts and government agencies. Catherine is a frequent speaker at seminars and conferences on all topics of labor and employment law, with a primary emphasis on sexual harassment training.

CHRISTOPHER B. HOLLEMAN: Born, Columbus, Mississippi; B.A., Vanderbilt University, 1999; J.D., Vanderbilt University, 2002. 2001 Mock Trial Tournament Semi-finalist; 2000 Lightfoot Franklin & White Best Oralist Award, Appellate Advocacy; Phi Delta Phi Malone Inn President, Historian. Member, American Bar Association, Atlanta Bar Association, Cobb County Bar Association.

REGINALD M. JONES: Born, Alexandria, Virginia; B.A, College of William & Mary, 1991. J.D., University of Georgia, 1999 (cum laude); Editorial Board, *Georgia Law Review*, Omicron Delta Kappa; Captain, United States Army; Author, "Lost Productivity: Claims for the Cumulative Impact of Multiple Change Orders," *31 Public Contract Law Journal 1* (Fall 2001); Author, "Update on Proving and Pricing Inefficiency Claims," *23 The Construction Lawyer 19* (Summer 2003); Lecturer on Construction Delay, Acceleration & Inefficiency Claims for Federal Publications Seminars, LLC.

S. GREGORY JOY: B.A (with high distinction), Univ. of Virginia, 1981; Phi Beta Kappa, Raven Honor Society; J.D., University of Virginia, 1984; Editor or co-author of four books and over 50 seminar manuals and speaker at over 70 seminars on construction and government contract law issues, and author of articles on international and environmental law issues. He has represented owners, contractors, subcontractors, and/or suppliers regarding construction projects throughout the United States, in the Caribbean, Latin America, and the Middle East. Member: American Bar Association; State Bar of Georgia; ABA Section on Public Contract Law; ABA Forum Committee on the Construction Industry.

RAMSEY KAZEM: Born, Nijmegen, Netherlands; B.S., Farleigh Dickinson University, 1996 (magna cum laude); M.B.A., Goizueta Business School, 2000; J.D., Emory University School of Law, 2000. Member, Atlanta Bar Association, State Bar of Georgia.

THOMAS J. KELLEHER, JR.: Born, Malden, Massachusetts; Managing Partner and Senior Partner of Smith, Currie & Hancock LLP. A.B., Harvard College, 1965 (cum laude); J.D., University of Virginia, 1968. Co-author, "Preparing and Settling Construction Claims," *Construction Briefings,* Federal Publications, Inc., December 1983; *Construction Litigation: Practice Guide with Forms*, Aspen Law & Business; "Development in Federal Construction Contracts," *Wiley Construction Law Update,* Wiley Law Publications (1992–1999). Member: American College of Construction Lawyers; American Bar Association, State Bars of Georgia and Virginia; Associated General Contractors of America, Board of Directors (2000–2004); Chair: Federal Acquisition Regulation Committee.

MAURA KRAUSE: Born, Pittsburgh, Pennsylvania; B.B.A., University of Notre Dame, 1991; M.A.L.S., Valparaiso University, 1992; J.D., Emory University School of Law, 1996. Member, American Bar Association, Atlanta Bar Association, State Bars of Georgia and South Carolina.

STEPHEN I. LINGENFELTER: Born, Terrell, Texas; B.A., Texas Christian University, 1965; J.D., University of Texas at Austin, 1969; LL.M, George Washington University, 1970 (summa cum laude); Retired in 2002 with 33 years of federal service; Assistant Division Counsel, U.S. Army Corps of Engineers, Missouri River Division, 1970–1973; District Counsel, U.S. Army Corps of Engineers, San Francisco District, 1973–1983; Division Counsel, U.S. Army Corps of Engineers, South Atlantic Division, 1983–2002; 1988–1989, participant, President's Commission on Executive Exchange."

ANDREW R. McBRIDE: Born, Whitby, England; B.A., History, Rutgers College, 1992; J.D., Emory University School of Law, 1996.

JOHN E. MENECHINO, JR.: Born, Islip, New York; B.A., Political Science and Economics, University of South Carolina, 1986 (magna cum laude, Phi Beta Kappa); J.D., University of South Carolina College of Law, 1989 (American Inns of Court). Contributing author, *Construction Subcontracting: A Legal Guide*, John Wiley & Sons, 1991; *Alternative Clauses to Standard Construction Contracts*, John Wiley & Sons, 1991, supplements 1992, 1997, second edition 1999. Member, ABA Forum on the Construction Industry; ABA Tort and Insurance Practice Section, Fidelity and Surety Law Committee.

ERIC L. NELSON: Born, Los Angeles, California. B.A., California Polytechnic State University at San Luis Obispo; J.D., Washington & Lee University. Co-author: "Delay Claims Against the Surety," *The Construction Lawyer,* July 1997. Lecturer on construction claims for various professional organizations. Member, American Bar Association, Section of Public Contract Law (Chair, Construction Division, Insurance and Bonding Subdivision, 2001–Present; Vice-Chair, Subcontracting Subdivision (2000–2001), Forum on the Construction Industry; Associated General Contractors of America, Inc. (Young Leadership Council 1998–2000); State Bar of Georgia.

FRANK E. RIGGS, JR.: Born, Hattiesburg, Mississippi; B.A., University of Southern Mississippi, 1971 (with honors); J.D., University of Virginia, 1974; Omicron Delta Kappa; Phi Delta Phi. Author: *Georgia Construction Law*, a co-authored layman's handbook; "The Owner's Damages," presented to the ABA Forum Committee on the Construction Industry; "Practical Recommendations on Documenting and Demonstrating Extra Work Costs," *Financial Management and Accounting for the Construction Industry,* Construction Financial Management Association; "Default Termination Checklist," State

Bar of Texas Construction Law Newsletter. Member: Atlanta and American Bar associations, Public Contract Law Section, Litigation Section; Forum Committee on the Construction Industry; the American Arbitration Association Panel of Arbitrators; state bars of Georgia and Colorado.

RONALD G. ROBEY: Born, Savannah, Georgia; B.A., Centre College and University of Kentucky, 1974 (with distinction); J.D., University of Kentucky, 1977; Order of the Coif, Lead Articles Editor, *Kentucky Law Journal*, 1976–1977. Author: "Construction Management—Avoid Being a Fiduciary," *Contractor Profit News,* October 1986; co-author: "Winning Strategies in Construction Negotiations, Arbitration and Litigation," *Construction Contracts,* Practicing Law Institute, 1986. Chair of CLE Construction Seminars in Atlanta, Orlando, and Law Vegas. Member, American Bar Association, Forum on the Construction Industry and Public Contract Law Division, state bars of Georgia, Florida and Kentucky.

C. MICHAEL SHULL: Born, Owensboro, Kentucky; B.S., Civil Engineering, University of Kentucky, 1996 (cum laude); J.D., University of Kentucky, 2000. Moot Court Board; Student Bar Association; American Society of Civil Engineers; Chi Epsilon Civil Engineering Honorary; Kentucky Society of Professional Engineers; President, University of Kentucky Engineering Student Council; Contributing Author: "Changed Conditions," *Construction Briefings,* No. 84-12, Federal Publications, Inc. Member, State Bar of Georgia.

KENT P. SMITH: Born, Alva, Oklahoma; B.A., Northwestern Oklahoma State University, 1963; J.D., Washburn University School of Law, 1966 (cum laude); Washburn Law Journal Editorial Board, Alumni Fellow in Law, 1992. Law clerk to the U.S. Court of Appeals for the Tenth Circuit (1966–1967); attorney for the United States Atomic Energy Commission (1967–1968). Author: "Contractor Default: How to Recognize It, What to Do About it, and How to Finish the Project," *The Florida Bar* (5th Annual Construction Contract Litigation Seminar), 1981; "Changed Conditions in Dredging Contracts," *World Dredging & Marine Construction,* Vol. 14, No. 4, 1978; Guest lecturer, Georgia Institute of Technology, Legal Aspects of Architecture, Engineering and Contracting. Member, State Bars of Georgia and Kansas.

JOSEPH C. STAAK: Born, Philadelphia, Pennsylvania; B.S. Civil Engineering, Georgia Institute of Technology, 1974; J.D., University of Georgia, 1981 (cum laude); Member, *Georgia Law Review* 1979–1981. U.S.A.F. 1974–1978 (Engineering Officer). Co-Author: *Georgia Construction Lien and Public Contract Bond Law,* Lorman Education Services; Co-Author: *Practical Construction Law for Florida Contractors.* Member, State Bar of Georgia, District of Columbia Bar, Florida State Bar, ABA Public Contracts Law Section. Associate Member, American Society of Civil Engineers (Georgia Section).

CHARLES W. SURASKY: Born, Columbia, South Carolina; B.A., University of South Carolina, 1973 (cum laude); J.D., Georgia Washington University, 1978 (with honors). *George Washington Law Review,* 1976–1978. Member, state bars of Georgia, Florida, South Carolina, and the District of Columbia.

GEORGE D. WENICK: Born, Belle Vernon, Pennsylvania; B.S., University of Pittsburgh, 1972; J.D., University of Pittsburgh, 1975. Senior Claims Attorney, Office of Chief Counsel, Pennsylvania Department of Transportation, 1975–1984. Member, American Bar Association, Section on Litigation, Public Contract Law; Forum Committee on the Construction Industry; State Bar of Georgia.

CHARLOTTE OFFICE

DAVID H. BASHFORD: Born, Wilmington, North Carolina; B.A., Davidson College, 1998; J.D., University of North Carolina, 2002 (with Honors); Member, State Bar of North Carolina.

HARRY R. BIVENS: Born, Memphis, Tennessee; Of Counsel to Smith, Currie & Hancock LLP. B.S. Civil Engineering, University of Tennessee, 1976; J.D. University of the Pacific, 1990 (Highest Honors); Order of the Coif. Licensed in North Carolina and California. Prior to entering law school, employed as Construction Engineer; licensed Civil P.E. (California). Member of the Construction Law and Litigation sections of the North Carolina and American Bar associations. Practice concentrated in construction counsel, litigation, mediation, and arbitration.

ROLLY L. CHAMBERS: Born, Aurora, Illinois; B.A., University of North Carolina at Chapel Hill, 1975 (with honors); J.D., Marshall-Wythe School of Law of the College of William & Mary, 1984. Contributor, *William & Mary Law Review,* 1982–1984; contributing author, *North Carolina Law for Design Professionals* and *Construction Management/ Design-Build in North Carolina,* Lorman Educational Services. Member, American Bar Association (Litigation Section and Construction Industry Forum), North Carolina Bar Association (Construction Law Section and Litigation Section), State Bar of North Carolina.

GREGORY L. SHELTON: Born, Tallahassee, Florida; B.S., Florida State University; J.D., Florida State University, College of Law. Author: "In Search of the Lost Amendment," *23 Fla. St. U.L. Rev. 105* (1995). Member, Florida Bar and North Carolina Bar Associations; Mecklenburg County Bar Association; Young Lawyer's Division of the Florida Bar.

STEELE B. ("AL") WINDLE, III: Born, Charlotte, North Carolina; B.S. Finance, University of Virginia, 1978; J.D. Wake Forest School of Law, 1981. North Carolina Bar Association Construction Law Council Director, 1978–1980 and 1986–1988. Co-author, "North Carolina Construction Law, Design Build Contracting in North Carolina," "The Use of Special Masters in Construction Litigation and Arbitration, "Working with the AIA Standard Construction Contracts," "Construction Management in North Carolina and North Carolina," *LienLawOnLine.* Member, American Arbitration Association Panel of Arbitrators. Member: State bars of North Carolina and Georgia.

TALLAHASSEE / FT. LAUDERDALE OFFICES

F. ALAN CUMMINGS: Born, Mobile, Alabama; J.D., Florida State University School of Law; B.S., Auburn University. During his 28 years of practice, he has practiced in the area of contract litigation and counseling and has handled all aspects of construction disputes from preconstruction and postaward bid disputes to construction litigation on behalf of contractors, owners, subcontractors, design professionals, and sureties. He has extensive experience in litigating delay claims on major construction projects throughout the Southeast. He also has authored numerous articles and is a frequent lecturer on the subjects of risk avoidance and construction claims preparation.

S. ELYSHA LUKEN: Born, San Diego, California; B.A., University of Florida, 1996; J.D., Florida State University, 1999 (magna cum laude). Legislative Editor and Editorial Board Member, Florida State University Law Review. Member, American Bar Association and the State Bar of Florida.

BRIAN A. WOLF: Born, Farmington, Michigan. B.S.B.A., University of Florida, 1990. J.D., Stetson University College of Law, 1993; *Stetson Law Review*; Intern, Honorable Judge Elizabeth A. Kovachevich, United States District Court M.D. Florida. Member: Construction Law Committee, Florida Bar R PPTL Section; Construction Law and Government Contracts Sections, Associated Builders & Contractors. Co-Author *Florida Lienlaw Online*, Construction Publications, Inc. Lecturer on various aspects of construction law and construction claims.

DANIEL T. YOUNG: Born, Tallahassee, Florida; B.A., Florida State University, 1989; J.D., Florida State University, 1991 (with honors). Member: Golden Key National Honor Society, Florida State University. Member: Journal of Land Use and Environmental Law, 1990–1991; State Bar of Florida.

1

THE LEGAL CONTEXT
OF CONSTRUCTION

1.1 INTRODUCTION

Construction projects are complex and multifaceted. Likewise, the law governing construction is complex and multifaceted. Aside from questions of what one *can* do in construction, there looms also the question of what one *may* do—that is to say, what the law of construction allows. So what is the law of construction?

For practical purposes, the law applicable to construction projects falls into three major categories: contract, tort, and statutory/regulatory. Contract law seems intuitively logical, at least on the surface. Tort law may not seem logical in application, but it is an omnipresent influence on any construction project. Statutory or regulatory law generally applies to construction simply because some governing body has said it should, whether the application is logical or not.

This book discusses in detail these legal bases of construction law. In this first chapter, each theory is introduced in concept.

1.2 CONTRACT LAW

Contracts are the threads from which the fabric of commerce is woven. A contract may be as simple as an agreement to pay for food ordered in a restaurant, or so complicated that no legion of lawyers could hope to decipher the real intent, or somewhere in between. Whatever their character, contracts govern the transactions that permeate our existence.

Contracts and contract law dominate construction. What is a contract, and what is contract law?

A contract has traditionally been defined as "a promise or set of promises, for the breach of which the law gives a remedy, or the performance of which the law in some way recognizes as a duty."[1] Thus, a contract is basically a set of promises made by one party to another party, and vice versa. In the United States, contract law reflects both the common law of contracts, as set forth in court decisions, and statutory law governing the terms of certain transactions. An example of the latter is the Uniform Commercial Code (UCC), adopted by every state except Louisiana. *See* **Chapter 6**.

Parties with capacity to contract may generally agree to whatever they wish, as long as their agreements do not run afoul of some legal authority or public policy. So it is that an owner and a contractor may agree to some risky undertaking in a construction project, but they may not agree to gamble on the project's outcome. The former agreement reflects a policy of freedom-of-contract; the latter violates prohibitions on gambling transactions.

1.3   Breach of Contract

A "breach of contract" results when one party fails in some respect to do what that party has agreed to do, without excuse or justification.[2] For example, a contractor's failure to use the specified trim paint color, or its failure to complete the work on time, constitutes a breach of contract. Owners may likewise breach their contract obligations. Many contracts expressly provide, for example, that the owner will make periodic payments to the contractor as portions of the work are completed. If the owner unjustifiably fails to make these payments, this failure constitutes a breach. Similarly, an owner may be held in breach for failing to meet other nonfinancial contractual obligations, such as timely review and return of shop drawings and submittals. In short, any failure to live up to the promises that comprise the contract is a breach.

Whenever there is a breach of contract, the injured party has a legal right to seek and recover damages. In addition, if there has been a serious and "material" breach—that is, a breach that, in essence, destroys the basis of the parties' agreement—the injured party is justified in treating the contract as ended.[3]

1.4   Implied Contract Obligations

Express contract obligations are those that are spelled out in the agreement or contract. Less obvious than the express duties under a contract, but just as important, are those obligations that are implied in every contract. Examples of these duties include the obligations of good faith and cooperation.

In the context of a construction project, one of the most important of these implied duties is the obligation that each of the contracting parties cooperate with

---

[1] Williston, Contracts § 1 (1957).

[2] *See* Restatement (Second) of Contracts §§ 235, 236.

[3] *See generally* 13 Am. Jur. 2d Contracts § 446 (1964).

the other party's performance.[4] The fact that this obligation is implied rather than express is not reflective either of its importance or of the frequency with which it forms the basis for breach actions. Rather, the obligation to cooperate forms the very basis of the agreement between the parties.

The obligations to coordinate and cooperate are reciprocal and apply equally to all contracting parties. By way of illustration, an owner owes a contractor an obligation to allow the contractor access to the site in order to perform its work; a prime contractor has a similar duty not to hinder or delay the work of its own subcontractors; and one prime contractor is obligated not to delay or disrupt the activities of other parallel prime contractors to the detriment of the owner. Each example demonstrates that a contracting party owes an obligation of cooperation to the other party, whether owner-contractor or contractor-subcontractor. See **Chapters 5** and **8**.

In addition to the obligation of cooperation, the owner and the contractor have other implied obligations, such as warranty responsibilities. The owner's implied warranty of the adequacy of plans and specifications is of great importance to the contractor, and the breach of this warranty forms the basis for a large portion of contractor claims. The existence of an implied warranty in connection with owner-furnished plans and specifications was recognized in *United States v. Spearin.*[5] The so-called Spearin Doctrine has become well established in virtually every American jurisdiction that has considered the question of who must bear responsibility for the results of defective, inaccurate, or incomplete plans and specifications. In layman's language, the doctrine states that when an owner supplies the plans and specifications for a construction project, the contractor cannot be held liable for an unsatisfactory final result attributable solely to defects or inadequacies in those plans and specifications. The key in this situation is the allocation of the risk of the inadequacies of the design to the contracting party, which furnished the design. Thus, in a design-build project, the design-build contractor, not the owner, may bear the risk for a design error or deficiency. See **Chapters 2, 5,** and **9**.

Similarly, contractors have other warranty responsibilities with regard to the results of their performance. For example, when the owner of a newly built structure or the purchaser of construction-related goods or services is justifiably dissatisfied with the facility, goods, or services, the owner may have a cause of action against the general contractor based on a breach of construction warranties. The nature of that action and the remedies available to the owner would, in large measure, depend upon the provisions of the contract.

Even where there are no express warranties in the contract, most courts, under applicable state law, will imply a warranty for workmanship and materials, provided there is no contract provision to the contrary. This implied warranty may, in some instances, be operative regardless of the presence in the contract of express warranties of limited duration that would appear to restrict the scope of the contractor's warranty liability.

---

[4] *See* 11 Williston, Contracts § 1296 (1968).

[5] 248 U.S. 132 (1918).

1.5 TORTS

A tort is a "civil wrong, other than a breach of contract, for which the court will provide a remedy in the form of an action for damages."[6]

A tort is not the same thing as a crime, although the two areas overlap to some extent. A crime is an offense against the public at large and is prosecuted by public officials. In contrast, a tort action is a civil action commenced and maintained by the injured party itself. Such an action seeks to recover compensatory and even punitive damages from the wrongdoer (tort-feasor).

The law of torts changes as societal norms change, because one important consideration is: Who must bear the burden of a loss? Torts are generally divided into three basic categories: intentional torts, negligent torts, and strict liability.

1.6 Intentional Torts

An "intentional" tort is just what the name suggests: a tort where the wrongdoer either expressly or by implication intended the act that resulted in the injury. Assault and battery falls into this category, though this tort rarely occurs in a construction dispute. Fraud and misrepresentation, by contrast, may appear in a construction case, as with a claim that the contract documents "misrepresented" some material fact or condition upon which a contract was based.

In *Robert E. McKee, Inc. v. City of Atlanta,* the United States District Court for Georgia discussed the application of the theory of misrepresentation in the context of a changed condition claim.[7] The city of Atlanta had supplied the contractor with inaccurate information concerning the rock excavation required for the project. The court noted that a mere showing by the contractor of subsoil conditions unexpected by either party would not automatically release the contractor from its obligations under the contract. Moreover, the court noted that the contract placed the burden of uncertainty on the contractor. Nevertheless, the court held that the city could be held liable if the contractor could show (1) that it was not reasonably able to discover the true facts through investigation, and (2) that the misrepresentation was material. Thus, the theory of misrepresentation may be available to a contractor even if it has assumed the risk of changed conditions by contract.

Another example of an intentional tort is conversion. Conversion refers to an interference with some property right, so serious as to effectively force a "judicial sale" of the property item to the defendant in the form of damages. Conversion may come into a construction project where a project participant is alleged to have received but not distributed (i.e., kept for itself) contract proceeds for the work of a lower-tier contracting party.

Economic relations are entitled to protection against unreasonable interference. Interference with economic relations, which has been regarded by the courts as a

---

[6] W. Prosser, The Law of Torts 2 (1974).

[7] 414 F. Supp. 957 (N.D. Ga. 1976).

separate tort—and which is of particular interest to contractors—is inducement to breach of contract, or interference with contract rights.

The area where this tort comes into play most often is in labor disputes. Interference with contract rights was, at one time, a fertile field for labor union liability. The common law quite strictly curtailed union activities (such as secondary boycotts and picketing) that prevented the performance of existing contracts. However, over the years, the tort liability of labor unions has been radically affected by federal legislation affecting industries involved in interstate commerce. The existence of a contract, in itself, is no longer the exclusive consideration. The effect of labor legislation (such as the Norris-LaGuardia Act, the National Labor Relations Act, the Wagner Act, and the Taft-Hartly Act) on common law liability of unions is beyond the scope of this section, but should be analyzed in connection with the effects of strikes and boycotts on a contractor's performance.

1.7 Negligence

Negligence in the popular sense is the lack of due diligence or care.[8] It is a second branch of the law of torts, and may be distinguished from intentional torts by the fact that no specific intent need be proven for the imposition of liability.

The traditional elements of a claim for negligence are:

> (1) *A duty, or obligation, recognized by the law,* requiring the actor to conform to a certain standard of conduct, for the protection of others against unreasonable risks.
>
> (2) *A failure on its part to conform to the standard required.* These two elements go to make up what the courts usually have called negligence.
>
> (3) *A reasonably close causal connection between the conduct and the resulting injury.* This is what is commonly known as "legal cause," or "proximate cause."
>
> (4) *Actual loss or damage resulting to the interests of another.*[9] Typically, there would be the claimant's economic or monetary damages.

Negligence as a theory of recovery against the project architect or engineer is important for contractors because their lack of contractual privity with the design professional makes a breach action impossible. Third-party beneficiary arguments (i.e., where the contractor asserts that it is an intended beneficiary of the contract between the owner and the design professional, and is thus entitled to recover damages for negligent breach of contract) are accepted in some jurisdictions; however, traditional negligence arguments probably stand a greater chance for success.[10]

The standard of conduct applied to the design professional is not that of the reasonable person, but rather that of the "reasonable design professional." The

[8] *See* 57 Am. Jur. 2d Negligence § 1 (1971).

[9] W. Prosser, The Law of Torts § 30, at 143 (1971) (emphasis added).

[10] W. Prosser, The Law of Torts 161.

usual requirement is that the design professional must have the skill and learning commonly possessed by members, in good standing, of its profession. It will be liable for the harmful results if it does not meet that standard.[11]

This duty of competence is owed to anyone, including the contractor, who could *foreseeably* be injured by the design professional's negligence. It is not dependent on any contractual relationship between the parties. The duty of competency also extends to both the design and supervisory functions of the design professional (to the extent that it is obligated by the contract with the owner to function in a supervisory capacity).

The contractor, like the architect or engineer, may be held liable for negligence that results in injury to third parties—whether that negligence is attributable to unsafe construction methods while the work is in process or to defects in the completed structure. According to 13 Am. Jur. 2d Building and Construction Contracts § 132 (1964), during the course of construction, a contractor may be liable for its negligence that results in personal injury or property damage to persons rightfully on the premises, occupants of adjacent premises, and persons lawfully using a street or highway abutting the construction site. Subcontractors, likewise, are liable to third parties where their negligence results in personal injury or property damage. This liability extends to the owner, when a subcontractor negligently damages the building during construction, even though there is no contractual privity between the owner and the subcontractor.

1.8 STRICT LIABILITY

Strict liability is liability without fault. Contractors generally encounter strict liability when they become involved in highly dangerous activities such as blasting or demolition. In general, if a party is aware of the abnormally dangerous condition or activity, and has voluntarily engaged in or permitted it, that party accepts the fact that it will be liable for resulting damage even though it has taken every possible precaution, was not negligent, or was not at fault in any moral sense.

1.9 STATUTORY AND REGULATORY LAWS AFFECTING CONSTRUCTION

The contract and tort bodies of law discussed above trace their origins to historical dealings of peoples in organized society. They reflect, rather than dictate, the customs, values, and expectations of society's members. As society evolves, so do the customs, values, and expectations of its members, followed in short order by the development and evolution of the common law of contracts and of torts. This

---

[11] *Erlich v. First National Bank of Princeton*, 505 A.2d 220 (N.J. 1984); *see Vonasek v. Hirsch & Stevens, Inc.*, 221 N.W.2d 815 (Wis. 1974); W. Prosser, The Law of Torts 162.

evolution occurs principally through the mechanisms of court decisions of actual cases and controversies between members of society. In short, contract and tort law reflect society.

Statutory and regulatory law, by contrast, do not necessarily evolve from any aspect of society. These laws become laws because some governing body with authority to do so declares that they should be laws. This is not to suggest that statutes and regulations are less significant or valuable than common law concepts of contract and tort; it is merely to observe that statutes and regulations derive from a different source and in a different manner.

Anyone with passing familiarity with construction and the construction process will be able to name any number of such statutes and regulations, and may at some time have had occasion to deal with these statutes, such as:

Licensing statutes for designers and contractors;

Statutes governing qualifications to conduct business in the jurisdiction of a state or local government;

Building codes;

Environmental laws and regulations;

Statutes and ordinances governing the procurement process in public construction at the federal, state, and local levels;

Regulations governing the public procurement process, such as the Federal Acquisition Regulation and comparable state and local government contracting procedures and regulations;

Regulations governing the issuance of building permits;

Statutes governing workplace safety;

Statutes governing wages and benefits paid to construction workers;

Statutes governing social policies such as equal opportunity laws;

Statutes governing labor relations in construction;

Insurance statutes such as workers' compensation laws and regulations;

Lien and bond statutes;

Bankruptcy laws; and

Dispute resolution procedures, such as those that prescribe the disputes process on contracts with the United States.

The list could go on and on. This book, in subsequent chapters, will address each of these topics, which frequently present themselves in construction projects. In this effort, neither this book nor any book could be exhaustive; hence, it is imperative that those involved in the construction process obtain competent and timely counsel and advice about construction-related laws pertinent to their particular project. The objective here is simply to give the reader an overview of some of the more commonly presented statutes, as well as the interpretation of the principles governing the duties and obligations of the parties to a construction project.

➤ **POINTS TO REMEMBER**

- The rights and obligations of the parties to a construction project are, in general, first defined by their contracts.
- In general, parties are free to contractually allocate the risks, duties, and obligations associated with a construction project, so long as the parties do not violate public policy.
- An understanding of any contract often requires analysis of the written terms and conditions, as well as the application of the common law of contracts and any statutes governing that particular contract transaction.
- Contract obligations and duties are also subject to implied obligations, such as the duty of good faith.
- In addition to contract law principles, the conduct of the parties to a construction project will also be evaluated in light of the applicable law of torts.
- Tort liability can be based on conduct amounting to an intentional tort, negligence (breach of the applicable standard of care), or strict liability reflecting public policy.
- In every jurisdiction, the construction project and the parties' obligations are also subject to myriad federal, state, and local laws and regulations.

2

ALTERNATIVE CONTRACTING METHODS: MULTIPRIME CONTRACTING, CONSTRUCTION MANAGEMENT, AND DESIGN-BUILD

Construction projects have traditionally been designed, bid, built, and paid for within a framework of strictly defined roles, relationships, and procedures. The traditional structure for construction contracting has proved effective overall, but perceived weaknesses or opportunities for improvement have led to consideration and use of new, alternative methods. These alternative methods include multiprime contracting, construction management contracting, and design-build contracting. While these new methods have provided many advantages, they raise new questions about the altered roles, relationships, and procedures involved in these options.

Under some of these alternative approaches to construction, the classic relationship between the general contractor and its subcontractors can be dramatically changed or eliminated altogether. Although the subcontractor's actual work in the field may be precisely the same as under the traditional approach, the subcontractor's relationship with the owner, the design professional, and other subcontractors may be fundamentally changed. Indeed, the term "subcontractor" may no longer apply. A subcontractor in the traditional model may become a trade contractor under a construction management approach or a parallel prime contractor under a multiprime contracting approach. Fast-track construction introduces additional uncertainties and ambiguities about the roles of subcontractors and the rights and responsibilities of various parties in the altered contractual structures.

The manner in which these alternative contracting methods diverge from traditional practices and roles requires careful attention, to make certain that the advantages sought through their employment are not lost through unanticipated problems and disputes. Despite significant use of these alternative methods, questions remain about how they affect otherwise established theories of liability among project participants. Consequently, it is difficult and perhaps dangerous to make generalizations about the impact of the alternative methods on the role of the project participants.

2.1 TRADITIONAL APPROACH TO CONSTRUCTION: ADVANTAGES AND DISADVANTAGES

The traditional method of project delivery, like the family minivan, is dependable, practical, and familiar. Construction industry professionals are familiar with the traditional construction contract structure and the roles of the parties under that structure: owner, design professional, independent general contractor, and subcontractors. In the traditional structure, design and construction proceed sequentially, with construction commencing only after the design is complete.

The process is initiated by the owner's recognition of a need or an opportunity for construction. The owner then contracts with a design professional to transform the owner's general concept ultimately into a complete set of plans and specifications for the entire project—from site preparation to finishes. The prepared plans and specifications are then used to solicit bids or proposals from general contractors, who rely on the scope of work defined by the plans and specifications as the basis for their pricing and to solicit subcontractor quotes. Ultimately, the construction contract is awarded to one general contractor, usually the one with the lowest price. The general contractor then procures subcontractors for those divisions of the work that the general contractor will not perform with its own forces. After the owner makes the site available and issues a notice to proceed, construction starts. The general contractor's work is financed by regular monthly progress payments from the owner. The designer generally maintains a review and inspection role throughout construction, but the owner continues to maintain control over both the design professional and the general contractor.

The traditional approach and sequencing for construction are reflected in and reinforced by industry customs and practices, by statutes, and by standard contract documents. Although not welcome, the problems that arise are fairly predictable and can be resolved through established procedures and remedies. It is well established, for example, that the owner will generally be liable to the general contractor for additional costs associated with defects in the project plans and specifications. The subcontractors are responsible to the general contractor for their work, but also look to the general contractor, or through it to the owner, for resolution of problems. The familiarity and predictability arising from long use of this traditional approach to construction has generated standard procedures for obtaining insurance and bonding, dealing with unexpected conditions, making changes, and generally resolving unforeseen contingencies. A well-defined model of rights, duties, and remedies is in place.

The traditional mode affords many advantages. It provides the owner with a complete design and a stated maximum price before construction begins. Also, the owner maintains exclusive control over the design professional and the contractor throughout construction. The traditional approach to construction has generally proven reliable and satisfactory.

Conversely, there are certain disadvantages to the traditional approach. The sequence of completing the design before construction arguably is not the most effective use of time and money. Waiting for a complete design before obtaining price commitments from contractors or starting any construction may expose the owner to inflation and delayed occupancy. That long lead time also denies the owner the ability to react quickly to changing market conditions and revised needs. Use of completed plans and specifications to generate competition solely on a price basis may also be counterproductive. The practice tends to encourage contractors to employ the lowest acceptable standards, and it frequently generates disputes as to what is acceptable under the plans and specifications, and what is an "extra," requiring additional payment. The manner in which the traditional approach to construction relies so heavily on the owner's management of the design professional and the general contractor often presumes far greater expertise than some owners may possess.

Certainly, none of these or other perceived shortcomings are fatal flaws. The general success and effectiveness of the traditional approach to construction is evident. Nonetheless, new approaches do suggest ways around those shortcomings. As new approaches are tested and applied, the roles and relationships of subcontractors and others can change dramatically.

2.2 MULTIPRIME CONTRACTING AND FAST-TRACKING

Multiprime contracting, sometimes referred to as "parallel prime contracting," differs from the traditional method of construction by displacing the general contractor. The owner no longer contracts directly with one general contractor who, in turn, subcontracts out portions of the work to various subcontractors. In multiprime contracting, the owner contracts directly with a number of specialty or trade contractors who would otherwise be the first-tier subcontractors in the traditional system. Each trade contractor is responsible for the performance of a discrete portion of the work.

Cost saving is frequently cited as a justification for a multiprime contracting approach. One source of savings is the elimination of the general contractor's markup and profit from construction costs. Further savings may be available by employing multiple prime contractors in conjunction with other alternative approaches to construction, such as fast-track construction.[1] The hope is that the compressed time frames associated with these techniques will save borrowing costs, blunt the impact of inflation on the construction budget, or allow for earlier utilization of the facility by the owner.

---

[1] There is some ambiguity in the literature and in the trade about whether *fast-track construction* is the same as *phased construction*. In this chapter, the terms are used synonymously.

Multiprime contracting is often employed with fast-track construction. The goal of fast-track construction is to phase the design and construction so that construction can begin on preliminary items of work, such as site work, foundations, and even the structure, as design of mechanical and electrical systems, interior partitions, and finishes continues. The goal of this phasing is to constrict the time required to complete a project from commencement of design to final completion by overlapping the end of the design process with the beginning of construction.

In many instances, however, the use of multiprime contracting is unrelated to reducing the time of construction. Instead, the sequence of design and construction may be the same as under the traditional approach, with no bidding or construction on any of the work commencing until the entire design is complete. For example, North Carolina public projects, which are delivered under the multiprime system, must be divided into at least four categories:—(1) heating, ventilation, and air-conditioning, (2) plumbing, (3) electrical, and (4) general work relating to erection, construction, alteration, or repair—and all aspects of the construction proceed largely contemporaneously.[2] Regardless of the lack of any time savings, this approach to multiprime contracting is promoted by subcontractors, who emphasize the cost benefit of increased competition on multiple contracts and the elimination of the general contractor's markup and profit.

Although there are certainly benefits to be gained by the use of multiprime contracting, experience over the last 20 years counsels caution on the part of all parties. The most significant hazard is the coordination problem that multiprime contracting seems to create. Without a general contractor who has clear responsibility for coordination for the entire project, some other party must fill that void and provide essential management, administrative, and scheduling functions. As the party bringing the trade contractors together on the project, the owner, by implication, assumes the coordination duties and the liability that flows with them, just as the general contractor does with its subcontractors. Scheduling and coordinating trade contractors on a major project is a formidable task that most owners are ill equipped to handle. The owner who does not possess the requisite expertise and resources must recognize the need to pay someone else to perform the required services. The owner's employment of a construction manager can largely offset a lack of ability and expertise on the part of the owner.

Unfortunately, some owners refuse to acknowledge the need for a single person or entity with the expertise and authority to provide essential coordination in a multiprime approach. Instead, these owners simply seek to shift the responsibility and liability for coordination to unwary trade contractors, who may not recognize the scope of the undertaking. Owners have succeeded in shifting coordination responsibilities by designating one of the multiprime contractors as being responsible for management and control of the project[3] or simply by expressly requiring the trade contractors to coordinate with each other.[4] The owner is not always successful,

---

[2] N.C. Gen. Stat. § 143-128(b) (2004).

[3] *Broadway Maintenance Corp. v. Rutgers,* 447 A.2d 906 (N.J. 1982).

[4] *Hanberry Corp. v. State Bldg. Comm'n,* 390 So. 2d 277 (Miss. 1980).

and can be exposed to significant liability if it fails even to make an effort to coordinate.[5]

The coordination problems that accompany multiprime contracting are not limited to the private sector. Until recently, North Carolina required public entities to employ multiprime contracting as the default delivery system for public building contracts. This rigid system was unsatisfactory because many qualified general contractors, who would otherwise fill the "general work" division under the North Carolina model, wanted no part of the coordination problems that plagued North Carolina public projects. In order to attract qualified general contractors to participate in public projects, North Carolina amended its public procurement law in 2001 to allow traditional, construction management, construction management-at-risk, and other delivery systems to be used.

The amount of litigation over this issue of responsibility for coordination in a multiprime contracting approach to construction demonstrates that there is great uncertainty about where ultimate responsibility will rest. The litigation also suggests that uncertainty on a project about who has the responsibility for coordination will likely breed problems with coordination. Experience also shows that even if a particular party is designated as being responsible for coordination, that party must possess a "big stick" for enforcement, usually in the form of some authority or substantial influence on key management, scheduling, and payment issues. Without such enforcement mechanisms, a project can quickly descend into chaos.

2.3 CONSTRUCTION MANAGEMENT

Construction management departs from the traditional model of construction contracting by replacing the general contractor with a construction manager who typically offers diverse expertise in design, construction, and management. Construction management emerged as a method of project delivery in the late 1960s, though it did not gain industrywide approval or broad use and support until the late 1970s. While there has been a tremendous growth in the use of construction management since its inception, construction management appears to have leveled off in recent years. According to Design-Build Institute of America (DBIA) projections, construction management has and will continue to hold steady at approximately 10 percent of the construction market.[6]

Ironically, although construction management is used very much as a term of art, it means different things to different people. The term actually describes a broad range of services and contractual frameworks that may be applied to a particular project. Consequently, great caution must be exercised when discussing construction management, either in abstract terms or in terms of its use and impact on a particular

---

[5] *Id.*; *Broadway Maintenance Corp.*, *supra* note 3.

[6] These statistics are reflected in a chart entitled "Market Penetration of Major Project Delivery Systems," available online at www.dbia.org.

project, to make certain everyone is clear about the specific parameters of the concept being discussed.

The construction manager's (CM) role will be as diverse and extensive as the expertise the individual or entity brings to the project, and as determined by the owner's needs on a particular project. The CM may be a general contractor hired to supervise and coordinate work of specialty contractors during construction. The CM may also be a multifaceted team—supervising design; having important input into site selection, financing, and accounting; providing expertise in the areas of cost control, constructability reviews, value analysis, contract interfacing, and quality control; and serving as supervisor and coordinator of construction activities. The CM may act exclusively as the owner's agent, having responsibility without risk, or may have to assume some of the risks borne by the general contractor in the traditional model, such as guaranteeing a maximum price for the project. Within these two extremes, there are any number of variations or combinations of services provided, or roles filled by the CM. Because general principles regarding construction management are lacking, and because someone operating under a title and position designated as CM performs many and varied roles, it is always necessary to examine the specific contractual obligations undertaken by the CM and the owner through the contract at issue.

Generally, the role of the CM appears to depend on whether the CM most closely resembles the architect or the general contractor in traditional construction. CMs are usually either architects or general contractors, but their approaches to construction management are different. The key distinction is whether the risk of completion of the project on time and within budget has been shifted from the owner to the CM.

2.4   Agency Construction Management

The definition employed when a CM is described from an architect's perspective usually involves construction management in its purest form—the CM is acting solely as the owner's agent. In this pure form, generally referred to as "agency construction management," the CM takes no entrepreneurial risk for costs, timeliness, or quality of construction, and all subcontractors contract directly with the owner.

The agency CM acts as the owner's agent in supervising and coordinating all aspects of the construction project from the beginning of design to the end of construction. Because management expertise is being provided by the agency CM, the role of the general contractor is typically eliminated. However, because the agency CM assumes no financial risks of construction, the owner will directly enter into contracts with the trade contractors. The agency CM may execute those contracts, but does so only as an agent of the owner.

As discussed above in the context of multiprime contracting, the owner's direct contractual relationship with the specialty contractors, required in the agency CM approach, changes the owner's relationship to the construction process by creating increased owner responsibility for coordinating and solving problems among the contractors. Although the CM assumes some of this responsibility, the owner may ultimately be liable to the specialty contractors if lack of coordination generates claims. The owner may pursue rights against the agency CM for such extra costs based on the agency CM's failure to coordinate, but the owner's ability to succeed in such a claim is impeded by the fact that the agency CM generally does not guarantee a maximum price for the construction; thus the owner bears the risk of cost overruns.

Contract documents produced by the Associated General Contractors of America (AGC) and the American Institute of Architects (AIA) provide some degree of standardization of the agency CM system. Under the AGC's 500 Series of documents,[7] an owner's separate contracts with the architect, trade contractors, and agency CM take into account the agency CM's role in assisting the owner in the design and construction phases of construction. The AIA's CM Adviser Family of construction management documents is based upon a similar premise, where the owner has direct privity with the architect, agency CM, and contractors.[8]

Construction management continues to evolve. Program management is a rapidly emerging delivery model that arose out of the agency CM model. Program management is most frequently used where an owner, such as a school board, requires multiple projects to be constructed within a certain period of time. The program manager's role is tailored to the needs of the owner and, as of yet, is not defined by standard contract forms. The program manager may provide design services; manage budgets; assist in selecting architects, engineers, contractors, and subcontractors; monitor and oversee multiple projects; and play a significant role in planning the owner's program. The program management model benefits from the institutional knowledge, experience, and synergies that result from overseeing an entire building program. However, program management is relatively new, and some owners may not be comfortable with the lack of objective and time-tested performance and contracting standards.

2.5 Construction Manager/General Contractor

At the other extreme from the agency CM is the CM that offers its services during the design phase and then also acts as the general contractor during the construction phase—the construction manager/general contractor (CM/GC). This variation makes the CM/GC's duties, rights, and risks ultimately resemble those of a typical general contractor.

The CM/GC will frequently become involved early in the design of the project. Although a design professional remains solely responsible for the design in this form of construction management, the CM/GC will offer its practical construction expertise to suggest more effective approaches to the design and methods to save costs. Frequently, the CM/GC immediately begins estimating and scheduling functions, both to expedite the design process and to provide the owner and design professional

---

[7] The AGC 500 Series includes: AGC Document No. 510; AGC Document No. 520; AGC Document No. 525; AGC Document No. 530.

[8] The AIA Construction Manager-Adviser Family includes: AIA Document A101 Cma-1992; AIA Document A201 Cma-1992; AIA Document A511 Cma-1993; AIA Document B141 Cma-1992; AIA Document B801 Cma-1992.

with feedback about the construction cost and time implications of the evolving design.

Once construction is ready to commence, the CM/GC, very much like a general contractor, will enter into fixed-priced subcontracts on its own behalf and not on behalf of the owner. These subcontract prices, together with the CM/GC's costs of performance and markups, will be the basis of the CM/GC's guaranteed maximum price (GMP). It is these two features—that the CM/GC binds itself to subcontracts and to a GMP—that are the principal distinctions from the agency CM approach.

Although the CM/GC may be the party entering into the subcontracts, it is common for the owner to be afforded considerable involvement in the selection of subcontractors. In addition, cost-reporting requirements often found in the CM/GC's contract with the owner in turn require the subcontractors to provide more job cost information and reporting than a fixed-price contract usually requires. Finally, consistent with the CM/GC's more extensive dealings with the design professional and owner, subcontractors may perceive that the CM/GC is much more closely aligned with the owner than is the case with a general contractor.

Once construction begins, the coordination duties owed to the subcontractors by the CM/GC are virtually identical to those owed by a general contractor. Indeed, as part of its contractually defined services, the CM/GC may assume even greater coordination and scheduling responsibility than would a typical general contractor, although these additional services would primarily be for the benefit of the owner.

2.6 DESIGN-BUILD CONTRACTING: WHAT WORKS TO AVOID DISPUTES

2.7 The Design-Builder's Perspective

The "master builder" is again becoming prominent on the construction scene. An increasing number of owners, both public and private, are turning to the design-build method of project delivery in order to fast-track the project and reduce overall project costs. Although the traditional checks and balances that come with using a separate designer and builder are sacrificed to some extent, the design-build method provides the owner with a single point of responsibility for project design and construction. In addition, the owner is relieved from responsibility for the potential delays and costs associated with design errors and omissions. To this extent, the method protects the owner; but where does it leave the design-builder?

The design-builder is liable for both design problems and construction defects. The design-builder warrants the adequacy of the design and agrees that the finished project will meet certain performance specifications. At first glance, this level of risk would seem unacceptable to most contractors and design professionals, but careful project selection and definition, contract formation, and project control enable the risks to be minimized and managed.

Obviously, projects must be selected that are within the expertise of the design-builder. There are specialized design-build firms, as well as contractors and design firms owned by the same companies, that work as a team on design-build projects.

However, a contractor without design capabilities should not automatically shy away from design-build opportunities. Design-builders take a variety of forms, and often the design professional part of the organization is a subcontractor or joint venture partner of the contractor. Similarly, the design professional can retain the contractor as a subcontractor, or both the design professional and the contractor can act as subcontractors to the construction manager.

Regardless of the form chosen by the design-builder, the single most important step in the project is to arrive at a mutually understood and agreed definition of the project with the owner. Once the project definition, parameters, and requirements are established, the contract documents must be prepared consistent with the mutual expectations of the owner and the design-builder.[9] The design-builder can then limit its risk with contract clauses limiting or fixing damages to a specific amount—say, the amount of the design-builder's fee—or excluding certain types of damages such as lost revenues or consequential damages. In addition, a contingency fee can be used as a component of the guaranteed maximum price, to be used to absorb unanticipated cost growth. Cost overruns or savings can be addressed in such a way that all parties have an incentive to ensure cost-effective results.

If the design-builder is composed of different design and construction entities, it is important that the respective roles, responsibilities, and liabilities are clearly established. Often, a breakdown of the design-builder costs and fees between designer and contractor will be necessary for licensing and insurance purposes. The design professionals will want to limit their risk to the design portion of the work, where they can obtain errors and omission insurance. Likewise, the contractor will need to restrict its exposure to completion of the project in accordance with the design so it can obtain any necessary performance bonds. Finally, design-build team members may wish to provide for cross-indemnification of each other for any claims arising out of the other team member's work.

Careful contract formation with anticipation of the possible areas of exposure allows contractors or design professionals to again assume the role of master builder. An understanding of what design-build is, how it works, and how the various parties can protect their interests can result in more, and hopefully more profitable, opportunities.

Every proposed project should be methodically reviewed in order to assess the proposed possible risk. Issues to be addressed by the design-builder include:

(1) Selection of the owner
(2) Project definition and performance expectations
(3) Qualifications and experience of team members
(4) Contractual relationship of team members
(5) Licensing concerns
(6) Insurance and bonding

---

[9] Industry standard forms can provide a starting point for drafting or tailoring appropriate contract documents. For example, the AGC's DocuBuilder® version 3.0 is a comprehensive software package of contract documents, bond forms, and related forms for project management for both traditional and alternative contracting methods.

(7) Responding to the request for proposals (RFP)

(8) Innovativeness of the proposal

(9) Flexibility of contract with owner

(10) Design review

(11) Handling of tenant or user input

(12) Scheduling

(13) Trade contractors

(14) Cost control

(15) Quality control

(16) Changes to the contract

(17) Differing site conditions

(18) Environmental remediation risks

(19) Contingencies

(20) Allowances

(21) Shared savings

(22) Responsibility for cost overruns

(23) Design errors and omissions

(24) Construction defects

(25) Limitations of liability

(26) Delay damages

(27) Preventing and resolving disputes

The design-builder also needs to understand the owner's approach and perspective on the design-build project.

2.8 The Owner's Viewpoint

To the owner, there is no better method of project delivery than design-build. Since the design-builder is responsible for both design problems and construction defects, the owner can avoid the traditional trailer battles between its design professional and its contractor. Free at last of the dreaded Spearin Doctrine and its implied warranty of fitness of the plans and specifications, the owner can sit back and enjoy a viewer's perspective on its project as it moves from design through construction to completion. Finally, design-build provides a method of designing and constructing a project that permits the owner to avoid the three dreaded plagues of projects: changes, claims, and litigation.

The design-build method is so enticing that the dollar volume of design-build projects has nearly tripled in the last five years. An increasing number of public and private owners have elected to go design-build because it allows for the fast-tracking of projects without the risk of cost and time impacts due to defective or untimely completion of design elements. Design-build works! Sometimes.

Design-build works when the owner knows what the desired end product is and adequately communicates that information to the design-builder. The single most important aspect of a successful design-build project is the preparation of the scope of work for the project. The owner must adequately define the project. If a comparable project can be identified, the owner should specify this in the scope of work in order to give the design-builder a better idea of the owner's project definition. Although this description is too general for construction, it allows the design-builder to obtain an understanding of the nature of the project.

If the owner does not have in-house capability or consulting professionals, the required clarity of scope may be lacking. The owner must have pre-established and definitive design criteria identifying the project requirements before the project can evolve toward design and construction. Adequate project definition at this stage represents the best opportunity for the owner to protect itself on the project.

If the owner is going to obtain competitive proposals on a design-build project, it must establish a clear program of requirements and performance specifications. This is commonly done through an RFP. Guidelines should be established that allow an apples-to-apples comparison of the proposals received. The RFP should set out the scope of work and the criteria to be used for selection of the design-builder. It helps both the owner and design-builder if the RFP includes: the size and character of the project; the technical scope of work; budget and financial considerations; schedule requirements; requirements and timing for establishing the price; provisions for value engineering and alternates; performance standards and guarantees; quality control/quality assurance requirements; operations, maintenance, and life cycle considerations; requirements in the areas of liability, warranty, licensing, and bonding; clarification of the consequences of nonperformance or late delivery; and clear guidelines for selection of the successful proposer.

Thoroughness in the preparation of the RFP allows the owner to define the project and to develop overall priorities in terms of spatial and system requirements, cost, design excellence, size, construction quality, schedule, and life-cycle costs. The more specifically the scope of work and priorities are set out in the RFP, the better the completed project. The evaluation criteria should be clearly set out in the RFP. If the evaluation criteria are weighted or are set up in priority order, make sure the proposal is structured to emphasize the owner's priority items. Make sure a clear scope of work is provided to the design-builder.

Inadequate or erroneous information in the RFP is one of the more common sources of disputes and can be costly to the design-builder. In *United Excel Corp.*,[10] the Veterans Affairs Board of Contract Appeals (VABCA) rejected a design-builder's claim for $120,000 that it incurred as a result of conflicting HVAC specifications in the RFP. The design-builder, United Excel Corp. (UEC), knew that some portions of specifications called for aluminum ceiling diffusers, and other portions called for more expensive stainless steel diffusers. UEC did not raise the conflict with the Department of Veterans Affairs (VA) when UEC submitted its response to the RFP.

When it came time to install diffusers, the VA insisted that UEC install the more expensive stainless steel diffusers. UEC performed the work under protest and filed an appeal seeking equitable adjustment for the difference in cost between stainless steel and aluminum diffusers. The VA argued that UEC was barred from recovery because UEC knew of, but failed to inquire about, the aluminum/stainless steel discrepancy. The VA's defense was based on the *contra proferentum* rule, where ambiguous specifications are construed against the government unless the contractor knew of the ambiguity or the ambiguity was so glaring or obvious as to be a "patent" ambiguity. A corollary of this rule is that a contractor will be barred from recovery if the contractor knew or should have known of the ambiguity but failed to inquire about it. UEC argued that the *contra proferentum* rule did not apply in the

---

[10] *United Excel Corp.*, VABCA No. 6937, 04-1 BCA ¶ 32,485.

design-build context. The RFP drawings and specifications, argued UEC, established only "design parameters" and UEC was therefore entitled to choose aluminum diffusers as the most economical way to achieve the design intent.

The VABCA rejected UEC's argument, holding that UEC was not relieved of its obligation to inquire about the discrepancy. The VABCA was not persuaded by UEC's design-build argument, stating that "a design build contract shifts risks to a contractor that a final design will be more costly than the bid price" and that the traditional rules of contract interpretation apply to design-build contracts.

✔ 2.9   DESIGN-BUILD PROJECT CHECKLIST FOR OWNERS

These are some of the considerations an owner should make in preparing to use a design-build approach to a project:

- Exculpatory language and risk-shifting clauses are potentially helpful to the owner. However, the best way for an owner to protect itself on a design-build project is through complete and precise project definition. Develop that definition with input from design professionals, construction professionals, operational personnel, maintenance personnel, tenants, and users.

- If there are no statutory restraints, prequalify the potential design-builders and develop a shortlist of the most qualified teams. Establish clear guidelines for selecting the design-builder and adhere to those guidelines.

- Structure the RFP so that the proposers can understand the project definition, including all important elements of the project.

- Include the contract documents in the RFP. Inform the proposers that selection will be based on qualifications, technical quality of proposal, and responsiveness to invitation (including proposed contract documents).

- Tailor the contract documents to the particular project. Each project is unique, and this should be recognized during contract formation. Do not use any standard-form contract without modification.

- There is no justifiable reason for the design professional to disclaim its professional responsibility to the owner on a design-build project. For example, AIA Document A191 purports to extinguish any professional obligation of the designer to the owner. Modify this standard-form language to specifically provide that the owner is an intended third-party beneficiary of all contracts for design or engineering services, all subcontracts, purchase orders, and other agreements between the design-builder and third parties.

- Limit the owner's obligations under the contract. Modify the contract, if practical, to require that the design-builder obtain all permits, conduct all geotechnical testing, and perform any environmental assessments. If the owner retains responsibility for the site conditions, the old problems—extra costs and delays—caused by inaccurate information can again plague the design-build project. The design-builder is supposed to be the single point of responsibility. Therefore any responsibilities, aside from payment, that remain with the owner tend to vitiate the desired "one-stop shopping."

- Require adherence to the contract timetable, including milestones established by the owner. Eliminate any standard-form language inconsistent with the design-builder's obligation to complete its work in strict accordance with the contract requirements.
- Structure the payment terms so that the owner is given an adequate time to verify, process, and fund any application for payment. Establish the procedures that will be used for payment and allow for any anticipated slippage in payment due to lender, grantor, or third-party involvement. Also, specify the rate of interest that will be assessed for any late payments.
- Set out the owner's termination rights, specifically establishing the owner's right to terminate the design-builder for default or at the owner's election (convenience). Limit the owner's liability in the circumstances of a termination even if a default termination is later determined to have been improper.
- Require the design-builder to include all its costs within the guaranteed maximum price or lump-sum price. Eliminate separate reimbursable items, contingencies, or allowances that are not included within the contract price.
- Design-build projects are scope-driven. Tailor exculpatory language to the particular project. Include a no-damages-for-delay clause for general application, but also specifically tie anticipated delays to any remaining owner responsibilities. Similarly, clearly establish the design-builder's responsibility for the performance of equipment, process, and components. Require the design-builder to verify the appropriateness of any equipment, process, or component for achieving the desired performance criteria.
- Do not allow the design-builder's proposal to become a contract document unless it contains no qualifications, no exceptions, no ambiguities, no exclusions, no limitations, and no language contrary to the contract documents. Instead, set out the specific scope of work—that is, technical specifications; drawings by drawing number and date; and other pertinent equipment, material, component, and finishes information. Too often the proposal and killer contract documents that have so lovingly been created will be contradictory or create ambiguities in the owner's desired contractual scheme.
- Require the design-builder to provide all insurance, including payment and performance bonds, and a design professional project policy with an extended discovery period. The advantage of the project policy is that it reserves coverage for that particular project, so that coverage will not be reduced by other claims or be subject to cancellation when the project is completed.
- Set out a procedure for any change orders on the project. Establish a strict timetable for notice to the owner, and require contemporaneous submission of cost and time impact documentation. Control the change order process with procedures that are actually implemented.
- Do not allow the design-builder to limit its liability, disclaim guarantees or warranties, or otherwise vitiate its responsibility as the single-source responsible party. If anything, the design-builder's responsibility (and liability)

should be greater than the sum of the contractor's construction responsibility and the designer's design responsibility.

- Do not meddle with the design after the guaranteed maximum price has been established, unless absolutely necessary. After the guaranteed maximum price has been established, any modification of the design puts the owner at risk in terms of cost and time to complete.
- Do not allow the owner's program consultant, staff personnel, or users to alter or modify the scope of work. To the extent the program consultant requires any change in quantity, quality, means, methods, techniques, sequences, or procedures, the owner is potentially liable.
- Do not provide any equipment, materials, or components. If the owner does, then to the extent late deliveries are experienced, the single-source responsibility of the design-builder is lost, and potential exposure to changes, claims, and litigation returns.
- Once the owner has the design-builder indeed performing as the single-source responsible entity, the owner should provide some incentive to the design-builder. Shared savings, with 25 percent going to the design-builder and/or bonuses for early completion, should be considered. That way owners can demonstrate that they are being fair.

2.10   The Successful Design-Build Project

What works to avoid disputes on design-build projects is what works to avoid disputes on traditional projects: a fair allocation of risk, reasonable interpretation of the contract, a clear scope of work, acknowledgment of responsibility, acceptance of change, and good-faith cooperation between the parties. The design-build method of project delivery is not a panacea for the perceived ills of the construction marketplace, nor is it a substitute for adequate design and sound construction management. The design-build method is simply an alternative manner of providing the owner with a high-quality project, on time and within budget—if the project participants are willing to commit the necessary time and resources to project definition, definitization, and actualization.

2.11   DESIGN-BUILD ASPECTS OF TRADITIONAL CONSTRUCTION

Even within the traditional "design-bid-build" approach, contractors must be aware of the extent to which they can assume design-build responsibility through performance specifications, the shop drawing process, and clauses that impose design review responsibilities on the contractor.

2.12   Performance Specifications

Specifications fall into two general categories: performance specifications and design specifications. Design specifications precisely describe the work the contractor is to accomplish, including dimensions, tolerances, and materials. The design specifications are the "recipe" the contractor is required to follow in constructing the work. Performance specifications do not tell the contractor how to accomplish the result, but only dictate what the result must be. This distinction is of critical importance, because design liability under performance specifications is generally allocated as it would be if the entire project were design-build. The contractor is responsible for all the costs associated with achieving the end result described in the performance specifications.

Often, a specification is not exclusively a performance specification. Instead, the desired end result is described; but at least some design information is offered. When problems result from the contractor's inability to meet the performance criteria using the design data provided, liability for the design defect is unclear.[11] Liability may ultimately be allocated on the basis of which party had superior knowledge. A contractor, on its own or through some specialty subcontractor or supplier, may be deemed to have sufficient knowledge to recognize the conflict between the design outlined and the performance required, so that the defect constituted a patent defect. In that case, the contractor is, at a minimum, required to call the defect to the attention of the owner. In *Brunson Associates, Inc.*,[12] the owner's lack of superior knowledge was a factor in holding the design-build contractor liable for a design defect that caused two fabric buildings to collapse simultaneously.

In *Regan Construction Co. & Nager Electric Co.*,[13] the project specifications included performance criteria for air-handling units. At trial, the contractor proved that the only air-handling unit on the market that met the performance criteria was the one provided by the contractor. Unfortunately, that unit did not fit into the space allotted for the air-handling unit in the overall design. Thus, although the contractor was able to establish that the performance specification was defective within the context of the overall design, the contractor was nonetheless found liable for the extra cost associated with accommodating the unit because the contractor should have discovered the conflict earlier and called it to the attention of the owner.

Contractors need to be aware of the risk of performance specifications that may take somewhat unconventional forms. *Florida Board of Regents v. Mycon Corp.*[14] involved what appeared to be a "brand name or equal" specification for architectural concrete. Under the specifications, the contractor was to "provide a skin plate with a smooth, non-corded 'true-radius' forming surface, equal to that manufactured by Symons." The contractor used the referenced Symons system not only for the "skin plate" but also throughout the project, thinking that a Symons forming system would provide a suitable result. The owner concluded, however, that the concrete work failed to achieve the required tolerances. The contractor argued that its use of the specified Symons system was subject to the owner's implied warranty of the

---

[11] For an example of how limited information can cause an owner trouble even in a design-build context, *see M. A. Mortenson Co.*, ASBCA No. 39978, 93-3 BCA ¶ 26,189 (owner forced to pay for extra structural concrete and steel despite contract status as design-build project, because owner provided conceptual design for project).

[12] ASBCA No. 41201, 94-2 BCA ¶ 26,936.

[13] PSBCA No. 633, 80-2 BCA ¶ 14,802.

[14] 651 So. 2d 149 (Fla. Dist. Ct. App. 1995).

adequacy of the specifications so that the contractor could not be liable if the finished product did not meet specifications. The Florida Court of Appeals disagreed.

The court initially noted that if only one brand of product was specified so that the contractor had no discretion but to use that one product, then the owner's implied warranty of the specifications would apply and the contractor would be entitled to relief. Moreover, the court recognized that if there were true "or equal" language in the contract, the contractor would be able to meet the contract by proposing a system equal to the brand specified. In this case, however, the court pointed out that the "or equal" references in the specifications related solely to the "skin plate" portion of the work, not to the entire steel concrete forming system that would need to be used on the project. While the court appeared to agree that there was an implied warranty of the plans by use of the Symons system in connection with the "skin plate," the contractor nevertheless had to meet the specific tolerances for other concrete surfaces, and there was no representation in the contract that the Symons forming system would be adequate.

2.13   Shop Drawings

Shop drawings are an essential element of construction, bridging the gap between the design set forth in the plans and specifications and the details and specifics necessary to fabricate material and install the work in the field. There is the ever-present risk that in translating the design to shop drawings the contractor may intentionally or unintentionally alter the design. If that occurs and the change results in a design defect that impacts construction, the contractor assumes the liability for that defective design even if the design professional generally approved the shop drawing incorporating the change.

Most construction contracts contain a shop drawing clause that states that the design professional's approval does not relieve the contractor from responsibility for complying with the plans and specifications.[15] Unless there is some basis to argue an ambiguity in the plans and specifications, this clause will likely shift responsibility to the contractor for any changes to the design in the shop drawing process, at least as between the owner, contractor, and designer.[16] The design liability for such changes can, however, be shifted back to the owner and designer if they are clearly identified and called to the attention of the owner or the designer who reviews and approves the shop drawing.[17] Standard contract clauses state that changes in or deviations from the plans and specifications must be specifically identified in writing as changes and deviations and must be specifically approved.

The numerous factual issues involved in what constitutes a change or deviation, whether it was sufficiently highlighted as such to the designers and whether there was specific acceptance and approval, are all fertile grounds for disagreement and

---

[15] *See* AIA Documents A201 (1997 ed.), ¶¶ 3.12.6 and 3.12.8, Engineers Joint Contract Documents Committee (EJCDC) No. 1910-8, ¶¶ 6.27 and 6.25.1.1.

[16] *See, e.g., Fauss Constr. Inc. v. City of Hooper*, 249 N.W.2d 478 (Neb. 1977).

[17] *See, e.g., Montgomery Ross Fisher & H. A. Lewis*, GSBCA No. 7318, 85-2 BCA ¶ 18,108.

litigation. Structural steel shop drawings, including the detailing of fabrication, erection plans, and welding details, as compared to information contained in the structural drawings and specifications, generate a tremendous number of disputes because the stakes are so high and the technical issues so complex. Steel fabricators and erectors frequently feel an unreasonable amount of design responsibility is being shifted to them, as they perceive that structural drawings omit much critical detail that is necessary to fabricate and install the structural steel frame.

The extent of the problems and pressures described by steel fabricators is not imagined. The seriousness of the problem is highlighted by the infamous Kansas City Hyatt disaster. In litigation arising from the disaster, the Missouri Court of Appeals held that the design of a structural steel connection could not be delegated to the steel fabricator. To have done so was grounds for revoking the license of the professional engineer, who was deemed to be grossly negligent for making only a cursory review of the involved shop drawings.[18]

Another area of frequent dispute in the shop drawing process involves dimensional errors in the plans and specifications. The standard shop drawing clauses require the contractor to verify field dimensions when preparing shop drawings. A failure to verify existing field conditions can therefore transfer liability for dimensional errors on the plans from the owner to the contractor even if the owner's designer included the erroneous dimensions in the original design and approved the shop drawing that repeated the erroneous dimension.[19]

2.14   Secondary Design Review

Compliance with performance specifications and providing details in the shop drawing process are affirmative acts that hopefully alert the contractor to potential design liability. There are other standard contract clauses, however, that seek to shift design responsibility to the contractor. These clauses are based not upon the contractor's actions, but upon the contractor's failure to take affirmative action to identify and correct defects in the design. Such boilerplate language is generally unnoticed and often not even an issue. Unfortunately, if there is a major design bust, and more than enough damages and blame to go around, the contractor is likely to hear arguments about how it assumed some of that liability through these stealthy risk-shifting clauses.

2.15   The Interpretations Clause   Plans and specifications often lack all the details and specifics necessary to translate the design into construction—hence the need for shop drawings and material and equipment submittals. The requirement for the contractor to detail the design for construction purposes may also require the contractor to "fill in the gaps" of the design. Recognizing that all details cannot be addressed, many construction contracts contain a catchall clause that requires the

---

[18] *Duncan v. Missouri Bd. for Architects, Professional Eng'rs & Land Surveyors*, 744 S.W.2d 524 (Mo. Ct. App. 1988).

[19] *KAM Elec. Enters.*, VABCA No. 2492, 89-1 BCA 21,558.

contractor not only to supply and construct the work specifically set forth in the plans and specifications, but also to furnish all necessary labor and materials that may be "reasonably inferred" from the plans and specifications in order to achieve a complete and functional project.[20] Disputes over the coverage of this clause frequently involve responsibility for piping and control wiring and whether the contractor is responsible to provide them at no additional cost. The stakes can be considerably higher than simply the cost of the omitted detail, if the omission of the procurement or installation creates a major delay to the project or requires completed work to be torn out.

What the contractor is required to provide is tied to the circumstances of the project and what a reasonable contractor would do. If a reasonable contractor would have included the work in its bid, or at least should have inquired about it, then the contractor will generally be responsible for the cost of providing the work, regardless of the fact that the work was not detailed in the plans and specifications.

2.16   *Identification of Patent Defects*   Even the most carefully designed and engineered project is not going to be perfect. The plans and specifications are too voluminous to not contain some errors. In recognition of this reality, many construction contracts attempt to impose upon the contractor the responsibility to review the design and to call to the attention of the owner or design professional any errors or omissions it finds.[21] Failure to disclose such errors renders the contractor potentially liable for them. Under AIA Document A201, the contractor's liability extends only to those errors that the contractor knowingly fails to report. Similarly, under AGC Document No. 200, the contractor is not liable for errors, omissions, or inconsistencies unless the contractor "knowingly fails to report a recognized problem to the owner." The Engineers Joint Contract Documents Committee (EJCDC) Document, on the other hand, imposes liability on the contractor for errors that the contractor knew or should have known.

These clauses basically shift the liability for defective design for patent or obvious design defects to the contractor, while maintaining the owner's liability for hidden defects. What is patent or obvious will depend on the specific circumstances of the project and the relative expertise of the contractor.

2.17   *Compliance with Permits, Codes, and Regulations*   It is the responsibility of the design professional to design the project in accordance with applicable building codes and regulations. In most construction contracts, the contractor also assumes a separate and additional duty to obtain necessary permits and comply with applicable building codes and regulations.[22] These clauses are primarily intended to hold the contractor liable for the means and methods of construction. However, they can also be used to hold the contractor liable for design defects arising from conflicts with building codes. As a practical matter, however,

---

[20] *See* AIA Document A201 (1997 ed.), ¶ 1.2.1 and EJCDC No. 1910-8 ¶ 3.2.

[21] *See, e.g.,* AIA Document A201, ¶ 3.2.1; EJCDC No. 1910-8 ¶ 2.5.

[22] *See, e.g.,* AIA Document A201, ¶ 3.7; EJCDC No. 1910-8 ¶¶ 6.13-6.14.

the contractor will be unlikely to assume that liability unless the design defect was patent and the contractor failed to notify the owner.

2.18 CONTRACTOR LIABILITY ISSUES

In the traditional system, the design professional is responsible for design deficiencies. However, as the single point of contact for the owner, the design-build contractor may be required to bear not only its own costs incurred because of a defect, but also those extra costs incurred by the owner or other parties arising out of the design defect.

Some owners are attracted to design-build contracts for the very reason that they relieve the owner from being caught between its design professional and its contractor with respect to design disputes.[23] In addition to assuming the risks of defects and design, the design-build contractor also assumes the risk that construction will cost more than originally anticipated. As long as the performance criteria provided by the owner are not impracticable, a design-build contractor may be forced to bear the extra cost of its performance due to extended construction time.[24]

Owners are not completely immunized from design liability by entering into a design-build contract. An owner may be subject to liability for design defects depending on the level of the owner's technical expertise, the owner's active direction of the design process, or the information provided by the owner at the outset of the project. Because the design-build project delivery regime deviates from the traditional allocation of design risks, owners, contractors, and design professionals must carefully scrutinize the contract language.

One way in which a contractor performing under the traditional design-bid-build delivery scheme may also assume a degree of design liability is by the owner's use of performance specifications or criteria. Although performance specifications dictate the results to be achieved by the contractor, they do not tell the contractor how to accomplish the desired results. Consequently, the contractor is responsible for the costs associated with achieving the end result specified. Also, the AIA's General Conditions, A201—1997 § 3.12.10, invite the design professional to delegate design responsibility to the contractor. Since standard-form documents allow for such delegation, a contractor must take great care to (1) perform with competence any design tasks it assumes; (2) account for the added costs and exposure related to assumption and performance of professional duties; and (3) make sure that the risks represented by such exposure are insured or otherwise managed.

Conflict may exist between design and performance specifications. If the contractor recognizes (or should recognize) such a conflict among the performance specifications, the contractor must notify the owner and the design professional in order to avoid potential liability due to the conflict. For example, in *Regan*

---

[23] *Mobile Hous. Env'ts v. Barton & Barton*, 432 F. Supp. 1343 (D. Colo. 1977) ("turn-key" contractor and replacement both responsible for design liability).

[24] *Ruscon Constr. Co.*, ASBCA No. 39586, 90-2 ¶ 22,768.

Construction Co. & Nager Electric Co.,[25] performance criteria provided by the owner for air-handling units could be met only by one particular unit on the market, which the contractor incorporated into the construction. The unit, however, did not fit into the space allotted for it with the design. As a result, the contractor incurred extra costs associated with accommodating the unit. In an action against the owner, the board of contract appeals held that the contractor assumed the risk of extra costs, reasoning that the contractor could have calculated that the specified unit would not fit in the space provided, based upon the contract drawings, before it ordered the air-handling unit.[26]

Another specification issue that may give rise to contractor design liability involves the use of a "brand name or equal" specification by the owner. Use of the specified brand-name product by a contractor does not necessarily or automatically relieve the contractor of liability for noncompliance with applicable performance criteria. In other words, a design defect that results from a contractor's use of a brand name as specified in a "brand name or equal" specification does not necessarily fall within the owner's implied warranty of the adequacy of the specifications. If the contractor has a choice of products, the contractor may bear the burden of compliance.[27]

As noted above, one of the common duties of a design professional is to review and approve contractor submittals, including shop drawings. However, if shop drawings prepared by the contractor require a change to the original design, the contractor may still be held responsible for impacts to the overall construction caused by problems with that change even though the change has been approved by the design professional.[28] It may, however, be possible for the contractor to effectively reduce the risk of this type of design liability by immediately bringing any shop drawing-related design modifications to the attention of both the owner and the design professional.

Sometimes the limits of risk shifting related to substitutions are established by statute so that an architect's approval of the contractor's suggested substitution may not relieve the contractor of some warranty obligations. In *Leisure Resorts, Inc. v. Frank J. Rooney, Inc.*,[29] a contractor suggested the substitution of an air-conditioning unit on a condominium project. The substitution was approved by the architect and the engineer. When many of the units failed to perform, several condominium unit owners filed a class-action lawsuit against the developer who, in turn, sought indemnity from the contractor in a third-party action. The court held that while developers are subject to statutory "warranties of fitness or merchantability for the purposes or uses intended," the contractor's statutory warranty is to provide work and materials that "conform with the generally accepted standards of workmanship and perform-

[25] *Supra* note 13.

[26] *See also D.C. McClain, Inc. v. Arlington Co.*, 452 S.E.2d 659 (Va. 1995) (contract documents not allowing adequate room on-site for installation of post-tensioning apparatus did not relieve contractor of obligation to obtain easements necessary to install apparatus).

[27] *Florida Bd. of Regents v. Mycon Corp.*, 651 So. 2d 149 (Fla. Dist. Ct. App. 1995).

[28] *See generally Fauss Constr., Inc. v. City of Hooper*, 249 N.W.2d 478, 481 (Neb. 1977).

[29] 654 So. 2d 911 (Fla. 1995).

ance of similar work."[30] In short, though the contractor had a duty to provide accept-able materials, it did not have a duty to evaluate broader issues of suitability of those materials for the purpose intended. Presumably, that would fall to the developer and the developer's architect or engineer.

Finally, contractors should be wary of standard contract clauses that expose the contractor to potential liability for design defects. Many contracts contain catchall clauses, which, for example, could require the contractor to supply any and all labor and materials that can be reasonably inferred from the plans and specifications as being necessary to achieve a complete project. If the contractor fails to provide such labor or materials, and a defect results, the contractor may be held liable.

2.19   ARCHITECT/ENGINEER LIABILITY ISSUES IN A DESIGN-BUILD PROJECT

In many design-build projects, the architect or engineer enters into a subcontract with the design-builder. The fact that the design professional is one step removed from the owner does not mean the design professional is off the hook for design defects. In fact, the design professional must exercise a greater deal of caution when venturing into the less settled realm of design-build.

One source of unanticipated or increased risk to the design professional is the con-struction contract itself. For example, under the DBIA's Subcontract Between the Design-Builder and Designer,[31] the design professional may be held to performance standards that exceed the standard of care for the industry. The DBIA Subcontract also requires the design professional to make site visits to "determine if the construc-tion is proceeding in accordance with the Construction Documents."[32] If this require-ment is not altered, the design professional could face liability for defective work.

The design professional must also be cognizant of tort liability. In many jurisdic-tions, the design professional may be liable not only to the party with whom it con-tracted, but with third parties (such as the owner) who could foreseeably be injured by the professional negligence. Consequently, it is possible for an owner to bring a claim directly against the design professional even where there is no privity of con-tract. The net result is the same as under the traditional system: the design profes-sional may be liable both to the owner and to the builder.

Licensing laws present another source of liability for architects or engineers involved in design-build projects. Licensing laws are a simpler matter in the tradi-tional delivery system, where the functions of the contractor and the architect/engi-neer are neatly compartmentalized. However, in design-build, the design professional may wear one of many hats. For example, the architect or engineer might form a joint venture with a contractor to act as the design-builder and, in turn, subcontract its design services to the joint venture. The design professional might

---

[30] *Id.* at 914.

[31] DBIA Document 540, ¶ 2.2.1.

[32] *Id.* at ¶ 2.7.6.

lead the design-build team by contracting directly with the owner and then subcontracting the construction portion of the work to one or more contractors.

Under each of these scenarios, the design professional must check the state licensing laws governing architects, engineers, contractors, and subcontractors. State laws governing the formation and authority of business organizations, such as joint ventures and professional corporations, must also be checked if the design professional intends to form a joint venture or other entity as part of the design-build plan. The language of the design-build contract should also be analyzed to ensure that the design professional does not promise to perform services that would violate licensing laws.

➤ POINTS TO REMEMBER

- The traditional approach to construction of design-bid-build has many strengths, but also weaknesses that have prompted pursuit of other approaches to the construction process.
- The manner in which alternative contracting methods divert from clearly defined and accepted practices and roles requires careful attention to avoid unanticipated problems and disputes.
- Multiprime contracting, particularly when employed with fast-track construction, can offer opportunities to reduce the time and cost of construction.
- All parties to a multiprime project must recognize that with the elimination of the general contractor, another party with appropriate power should be designated to assume the coordination responsibilities generally fulfilled by the general contractor. Without some express disclaimer, the owner assumes the duty to coordinate in the multiprime setting.
- Construction management generally entails involving an entity with diverse expertise in design, construction, and management in the design and construction process. The precise role of a construction manager on any project, however, can be determined only by reference to specific contract language.
- The role of the construction manager can range from that of a traditional general contractor, who provides some estimating and constructibility input during the design phase but is still required to guarantee time and price of performance, to a traditional design firm, which simply provides a higher level of construction administration and scheduling services for a fixed fee, without any guarantee of time or cost of performance.
- Design-build contracting represents the most radical departure from the traditional approach to construction by vesting all design and construction responsibilities and resulting liabilities in one party. The dramatic alteration of the traditional roles of the parties in design-build requires special attention to make certain the contract sets out the mutually understood and specific rights and responsibilities of each party.

- Even in the traditional build-to-design approach, contractors can assume discrete design liability as the result of performance specifications, the shop drawing process, and where secondary design review responsibility is imposed by standard contract clauses.
- Many states have passed laws allowing alternative methods of project delivery. However, it is important for architects, engineers, contractors, and subcontractors to check state laws governing licensing and the formation of business entities before signing on the dotted line.

3

PREPARING TO WORK IN A NEW STATE: PREPROPOSAL AND PERFORMANCE CONSIDERATIONS

The challenges facing industry firms on a new construction project are inherently difficult. When a construction firm attempts to do business in a new state for the first time, or without adequate experience in that jurisdiction, the potential stumbling blocks to success increase significantly. In order to meet those challenges, construction firms must arm themselves with information about the political climate, the labor market, and the laws affecting construction projects in that new jurisdiction. To assume that the laws and the construction climate in a new jurisdiction are identical, or even similar, to those in a home state can be very dangerous. Therefore, in this chapter, some of the fundamental preparations for doing business in a new state are identified.

Consider these guidelines as a first step, not as an all-encompassing road map, as you prepare to avoid legal land mines while doing business in an unfamiliar jurisdiction.

3.1 QUALIFYING TO DO BUSINESS

Any foreign corporation that does business or obtains, possesses, or disposes of property in any state must first obtain a certificate of authority from that state.[1] The performance of construction work generally constitutes "doing business" as the term

---

[1] Ala. Code § 10-2b-15.01; O.C.G.A. § 14-2-1501; Haw. Rev. Stat. § 414-431; Ky. Rev. Stat. Ann. § 271b.15-010; N.C. Gen. Stat. § 55-15-01; S.C. Code Ann. § 33-15-101; Wis. Stat. Ann. § 180.1501.

is used in foreign corporation statutes.[2] By requiring a foreign corporation to obtain a certificate of authority, a state is able to maintain a record of the foreign corporation, require the appointment of a registered agent to accept service of legal process, and obtain revenue, generally in the form of taxes. To ensure conformity with these requirements, most states, either through specific language in a statute or by common law, will not allow the foreign corporation to bring disputes to the state's courts until the foreign corporation has obtained the necessary certificate of authority.[3] A foreign corporation's failure to acquire the certificate of authority, however, generally will not damage the validity of any contract entered into by the unregistered foreign corporation.[4]

Since the failure to obtain a certificate of authority often may be corrected at any time to allow the filing of a lawsuit, a failure to obtain the required certificate of authority typically will cause a substantial problem only when the time required to obtain the certificate of authority precludes the timely taking of some action necessary to preserve claim rights. For example, a foreign contractor can lose its mechanics' lien rights due to its failure to obtain the certificate of authority before the expiration of the time frame to foreclose the lien.[5]

Most construction work within a state does not constitute a single or isolated transaction.[6] This is important to note because a foreign corporation is not required to obtain a certificate of authority if its work constitutes only an "isolated transaction" in the foreign state. There are a number of factors to consider when determining whether a contractor's work constitutes an isolated transaction. The typical analysis to determine whether the nature of the construction work constitutes an isolated transaction is illustrated by a decision of the Maryland Court of Appeals in *Tiller Construction v. Nadler.*[7] The court in *Tiller* held that Maryland law did not hold that any single act of construction constitutes "doing business" in that state. Rather, the determination depends upon the facts of each individual case, and rests not on a single factor, but rather on the nature and extent of the business and activities that occur in that state. As most construction work does *not* constitute an isolated transaction, very little business activity is necessary to constitute "doing business" in another state.

---

[2] *A.H.L. Inc. of Delaware v. Star Ins. Co.*, 10 F.Supp.2d 1216 (D. Kan. 1998) (holding "the majority rule is that the performance of construction work by a foreign corporation in a state is generally considered 'doing business' in the state . . ."); *S&H Contractors v. A.J. Taft Coal Co.*, 906 F.2d 1507, 1509 (11th Cir. 1990) (holding that a "foreign corporation doing construction work within a state is held to be 'doing business' in that state").

[3] *St. Paul Fire & Marine v. Paw Paw's Camper City, Inc.*, 346 F.3d 153 (5th Cir. 2003); *Northfield Ins. Co. v. Odom Industries, Inc.*, 119 F. Supp.2d 631 (S.D. Miss. 2000).

[4] *Springwall, Inc. v. Timeless Bedding, Inc.*, 207 F.Supp.2d 410 (M.D. N.C. 2002); *Quarles v. Miller*, 86 F3d 55 (4th Cir. 1996).

[5] *Space Planners Architects, Inc. v. Frontier Town–Missouri, Inc.*, 107 S.W.3d 398 (Mo. App. 2003); *In re Branson Mall, Inc.*, 970 F.2d 456 (8th Cir. 1992) (holding unregistered architectural firm could not enforce mechanics' lien even though firm registered with board after work was complete).

[6] 17A Fletcher Encyclopedia of the Law of Private Corporations, § 8469.

[7] 637 A.2d 1183 (Md. 1994). *See also S.A.S. Personnel Consult. v. Pat-Pen*, 407 A.2d 1139, 1143 (Md. 1979).

3.2 STATE REGISTRATION REQUIREMENTS: BONDS TO SECURE PAYMENT OF TAXES

A foreign corporation interested in doing construction work in a foreign jurisdiction must determine if a bond is required to provide security for any costs or taxes payable to the state as a consequence of the proposed construction activities. Many states require that an out-of-state contractor post a bond to provide security for the payment of sales and use taxes. This type of bond may be required even though the work is performed pursuant to a federal government contract.[8] While a state may recover the tax from the contractor that posted the tax bond, it cannot, however, recover such taxes from the federal government, which may be a party to the construction contract.[9]

A nonresident contractor's surety that has provided a performance bond also can be held liable for the sales and use taxes.[10] This rule has a long history, first receiving the blessing of the United States Supreme Court in 1827 and remaining a tenet of law recognized by a majority of the states.[11]

As most states have unique requirements regarding the issuance and necessity of these tax bonds, a contractor must identify and comply with the requirements prior to starting any construction in a foreign jurisdiction. For example, Alabama requires every nonresident contractor to register with the Department of Revenue before engaging in any work.[12] At the time of registration, the nonresident contractor must deposit with the Department of Revenue 5 percent of the contract amount or provide a surety bond to provide a guarantee of payment for the applicable taxes.[13] Early identification of, and compliance with, state law requirements for bonds to secure payment of taxes will avoid costly problems in the future, since the failure to comply with a state's requirements may prevent the assertion of contract or claim rights in the courts of that state.

3.3 STATE LICENSING AND QUALIFICATIONS

In an effort to protect the public from potential problems associated with poor-quality construction, state and local governments have passed laws and regulations requiring licensure of certain construction professionals. To ensure strict adherence to these licensing laws, most states' laws will prevent an unlicensed individual or company

---

[8] *United Pacific Ins. Co. v. Wyoming Excise Tax Division, Dpt. of Revenue and Taxation*, 713 P.2d 217 (Wy. 1986); *C.R. Frederick, Inc. v. State Board of Equalization*, 38 Cal. App.3d 385, 120 Cal. Rptr. 434, 440 *cert. denied*, 419 U.S. 1120, 95 S. Ct. 802, 42 L. Ed.2d 819 (1974).

[9] 4 U.S.C. § 107(a); *Washington v. U.S.*, 460 U.S. 536, 103 S. Ct. 1344, 75 L. Ed.2d 264 (1983).

[10] *Tri County Electrical Association, Inc. v. City of Gillette*, 584 P.2d 995 (Wyo. 1978).

[11] *Ogden v. Saunders*, 25 U.S. 213, 6 L. Ed. 606 (1827).

[12] Ala. Code § 39-2-14.

[13] *Id.*

from recovering any monies owed due to services performed, as such a mistake is generally not curable.[14]

In some states, it is not safe to delay the completion of the licensing process until after you determine that you will be awarded the contract. For example, a failure to have the required license when a bid is submitted may be a violation of the licensing requirements in some states. In addition, any contract entered into by an unlicensed contractor may be found invalid or void in some jurisdictions. In California, however, a licensing failure at the time of the contract signing will not invalidate the contract—at least where the lack of a license does not implicate the safety concerns underlying the license requirement. In that state, the contractor can recover for work performed after a license is obtained, even if the license was not obtained until after the start of the contractor's work.[15]

While all states have an interest in regulating the licensure of construction companies and professionals, each state has unique licensing requirements. For example, only about half the states require contractors to be licensed.[16] In Florida, contractors must possess a license, and certain corporations involved in construction[17] and architecture[18] must maintain specific certifications. In Maryland, a nonresident contractor must obtain a construction license,[19] as well as pay an additional fee to perform the work in the state,[20] unless the nonresident contractor's home state does not require a license of Maryland contractors, in which case the additional fee is waived. While there is no state law requiring that a contractor be licensed in Kansas, a water well contractor must be licensed by the Kansas Department of Health and Environment.[21] The lesson to be learned, of course, is that it is unsafe to make assumptions about the licensing requirements in a foreign jurisdiction. The requirements vary greatly from state to state.

While a state may or may not require the licensure of contractors, all states have laws that regulate the practice of design professionals.[22] For example, in West Virginia, architects must register with the West Virginia Board of Architects[23] and engineers must register with the West Virginia Board of Registration for Professional Engineers.[24] In Missouri, the failure of a person involved in architecture or engineering

---

[14] Nev. Rev. Stat. § 624.700.

[15] *MW Erectors, Inc. v. Niederhauser Ornamental and Metal Works Co., Inc.*, Nos. G030681, G030825, 2004 WL 179360 (Cal. App. 4th Dist. Jan. 30, 2004).

[16] NM Stat. Ann. § 1978.

[17] Fla. Stat. § 489.119.

[18] Fla. Stat. § 481.219.

[19] Md. Code Ann., Bus. Reg. §§ 17-601, 17-602, 17-603.

[20] Md. Code Ann., Bus. Reg. § 17-603(b).

[21] Kan. Stat. Ann. § 82a-1206(a).

[22] Ind. Code § 25-4-1-26.

[23] W. Va. Code § 30-12-11.

[24] W. Va. Code § 30-13-13.

to obtain the necessary license constitutes a misdemeanor and makes all contracts entered into by the unlicensed person void and unenforceable.[25]

Compliance with licensing requirements, like compliance with code provisions, is greatly influenced by the sometimes-subjective interpretations of those who are charged with the enforcement of licensing provisions. Contractors are well advised to get to know not only the letter of the licensing laws but also the manner in which those regulations are applied by the licensing board or staff members.

3.4   PUBLIC CONSTRUCTION AWARDS

It is paramount that any contractor interested in performing work in another state become knowledgeable of the procurement laws of local government entities, as well as the regulations at the state level. Compliance with local construction project regulations may require more than knowledge of applicable code requirements. Local permits or licenses may be necessary in many counties and municipalities. For example, Baltimore County, Maryland, requires a special building permit for the removal and disposal of asbestos shingles.[26]

Depending on the type of construction or the government entity involved, a variety of procedures may be used to award a contract. For example, the Georgia Department of Transportation has its own authority to plan, designate, improve, manage, control, construct, and maintain a state highway system.[27] In 1986, Alaska enacted a procurement code for contracts entered into by the state, but the procurement code does not apply to 41 categories of procurement, including certain contracts for the Alaska Marine Highway system and the Alaska Industrial Development and Export Authority.[28] Similarly, the municipality of Anchorage has its own regulations for procurement.[29]

State statutes governing contracts awarded by certain state agencies may contain requirements that add to, or take away, contract rights of the parties, even though the contract itself is silent on the particular issue. For example, the statutes governing Georgia Department of Transportation contracts purport to insulate the state from liability for delay damages, although no such limitation is apparent from the face of the parties' contract. If you are doing business with a state agency, you cannot simply read your contract and be certain that you understand your contract rights and risks. You also must examine the state statutes and regulations affecting contracts with that state agency.

The use of design-build contracts has increased in popularity in recent years, with some states passing specific legislation to address and encourage its use. The

---

[25] Mo. Rev. Stat. §§ 327.111; 327.201; 327.461.

[26] Baltimore Cty., Md. Dept. of Environmental Protection & Resource Management, www.co.ba.md.us/directory/constructionandlanduse/directory_construction_buildingpermits.

[27] O.C.G.A. §§ 32-2-1, et seq.

[28] Alaska Stat. § 36.30.850(b).

[29] Anchorage Mun. Code § 7.20.010, et seq.

Colorado legislature has recognized the advantages of design-build contracts and has enacted specific laws to encourage these contracts for highway construction.[30] Contracts for design-build are awarded in Tennessee if the use of design-build is addressed in the invitation for proposals or other bid information.[31] Some states are wary of awarding the design and construction of a project to the same entity and have limited design-build contracts to certain agencies.[32]

3.5 STATE STATUTES AND POLICIES AFFECTING CONTRACT TERMS AND CONDITIONS

Each state has specific statutes and policies affecting the enforcement and validity of language in a construction contract. The three areas that these regulations most often address are: (1) subcontractor/general contractor relationships, (2) contract award preference policies, and (3) public policy limitations on contract terms and clauses.

3.6 Subcontractor/General Contractor Relationships

One of the elementary tenets of construction law, promissory estoppel arises when a general contractor relies on and incorporates into its bid a subcontractor's quote. When a subcontractor's quote is incorrect, because of a mathematical error or otherwise, or when a subcontractor refuses to provide the goods at the cost quoted, the doctrine of promissory estoppel is triggered. Depending on the laws of the particular state, a subcontractor may be estopped from changing or withdrawing its quote because the general contractor has reasonably relied on the subcontractor's price in submitting its bid to the owner.[33] Other states, in contrast, view the subcontractor's quote as simply an offer to perform, not an act that creates a binding contract;[34] thus, the doctrine of promissory estoppel is not triggered. The subject of promissory estoppel is treated in more detail in **Chapters 4 and 8**. Subcontractors doing business in a new jurisdiction should understand that state's treatment of subcontractor bids.

A common issue involving subcontractor bidding is whether a state has any subcontractor listing requirements for contractors bidding on a project. Some states have specific statutes that require a contractor to list its intended subcontractors when the general contractor submits its bid.[35] Other states, such as Louisiana, do not have a statutory requirement to list the subcontractors; but if such information is

---

[30] Colo. Rev. Stat. §§ 43-1-1401, *et seq.*

[31] Tenn. Code Ann. § 12-10-124(c).

[32] Wash. Rev. Code § 39.10.051.

[33] *Olson v. Synergistic Tech. Bus. Sys.*, 628 N.W.2d 142 (Minn. 2001).

[34] *Ark Const. Co. v. Indian Const. Services*, 848 P.2d 870 (Az. Ct. App. 1993).

[35] Ca. Public Contract Code § 4100 et seq. (requires bidders to submit names of subcontractors whose work constitutes at least ½ percent of the total contract amount).

requested in an owner's request for bids or request for proposals, the failure to provide such information can cause a bid or proposal to be rejected.[36]

A subcontractor issue that has received much attention in legislatures and courts in many states is the timing of subcontractor payments. To ensure subcontractors are paid in a timely manner, several states have adopted laws that define the contractor's burden of payment to the subcontractor, the time period for issuing such payments, and the penalties for noncompliance.[37] Other states, such as Kentucky, have not adopted a statute addressing subcontractor prompt payment rights, but courts in Kentucky hold that a contractor must pay a subcontractor within a reasonable time period.[38]

Contractors and subcontractors may find their contract performances in a strange jurisdiction affected by criminal as well as civil regulations. For example, some states have enacted "trust fund" statutes to encourage the proper application of payments by contractors to subcontractors, laborers, and materialmen.[39] Construction contract proceeds paid by an owner to a contractor, and which are then diverted for purposes other than the proper payment for construction services and materials, may result in civil and criminal liabilities for the contractor, and perhaps for the individual members of the contracting company who actively or passively permitted the diversion of construction proceeds.[40]

In another form, a state trust fund statute may provide that if a contractor or subcontractor fraudulently obtains an "advance" of contract payments with a promise to perform construction work, and fails to do so, the contractor, or the principals of the contracting firm, may be guilty of larceny.[41] A similar Oklahoma statute provides that managing officers of a corporate contractor can be found guilty of embezzlement for trust fund statute violations.[42] And in Wisconsin, the courts have allowed civil suits against officers of corporate contractors for diverting funds protected by trust fund statutes.[43]

3.7   Contract Award Preference Regulations

States, for socioeconomic reasons or otherwise, may choose to have certain groups or companies receive preferential treatment when awarding a contract. Many states have a stated preference for contractors who are residents of that state; thus, rewarding those resident contractors who contribute to the funding of the public improvements

---

[36] *Boh Bros. Const. v. DOT*, 698 So.2d 675 (La. Ct. App. 1997) (citing *C.R. Kirby Contractors, Inc. v. City of Lake Charles*, 606 So.2d 952 (La. App. 1992)).

[37] Arkansas Code Ann. § 19-4-1411; Fla. Stat. §§ 218.70; 255.071.

[38] *Thomas J. Dyer Co. v. Bishop International Engineering Co.*, 303 F.2d 655 (6th Cir. 1962).

[39] *McMahon v. State*, 574 S.E.2d 548 (Ga. App. 2002).

[40] *Doyle Dickerson Co. v. Durden*, 461 S.E.2d 902 (Ga. App. 1995).

[41] Va. Code § 18.2-200.1; *Holsapple v. Commw.*, 587 S.E.2d 561 (Va. 2003); *State v. Cohen*, 783 So. 2d 1269 (La. 2001).

[42] *See* Okla. Stat. Ann. Title 42, Section 153; Title 21, Section 1451.

[43] *Tri-Tech Corp. of America v. Americomp Services, Inc.*, 646 N.W.2d 822 (Wisc. 2002).

through payment of taxes.[44] This residency preference, however, has been eliminated by court decisions in some states, finding that the preference violates competitive bidding objectives and the "privileges and immunities" clause of the United States Constitution.[45]

Because a preference for resident contractors has obvious benefits, an issue may arise as to a firm's status as a "resident." This question most often arises when a joint venture contractor bids on a contract and proclaims itself a resident poised for preferential treatment. What happens if one party to the joint venture resides in the state but the other is a nonresident? In Alaska, a joint venture is entitled to a residency preference so long as one of the coventurers is an Alaska resident.[46] Louisiana, however, requires that each coventurer be a Louisiana resident to receive the residency preference.[47]

The federal government[48] and many state and local governments[49] allow a statutory preference to "small business" contractors in the form of a "set-aside": a percentage of a public contract designated specifically for contractors qualifying as a "small business." A "small business" is defined as a business having average employment/average annual revenues below certain stated limitations.[50] A contractor that bids on a contract with a set-aside provision must ensure that a qualified small business provides the work.

Preferences also may be granted to minority- or women-owned enterprises[51] in the award of a public contract. The definition of "minority" varies from state to state, but generally includes African Americans, Native Americans, and females.[52] Even if a state does not have a specific requirement for such a preference, a state may encourage the use of these minority- or women-owned contractors in its request for bids.

Battles continue in courts across the United States about whether these contract award preferences constitute inappropriate discrimination against those companies not falling within the definition of minority- or women-owned enterprises. The United States Supreme Court, in *City of Richmond v. J.A. Croson Company*,[53] sought to clarify when and how these preference policies can be used. The Court set out four major requirements that must be met when formulating these preferences:

(1) A high, "strict scrutiny" standard of review;
(2) The discrimination must be particularly linked to the market area of the implementing agency;

[44] 41 U.S.C.A. §§ 10a to 10d.

[45] *C.S. McCrossan Construction Co. v. Rahn*, 96 F.Supp.2d 1238 (D.N.M. 2000).

[46] *Irby-Northface v. Com. Elec. Co.*, 664 P.2d 557 (Ala. 1983).

[48] *Bristol Steel & Ironworks, Inc. v. State Dept. of Transp. & Development*, 507 So.2d 1233 (La. 1987).

[48] F.A.R. §§ 19.00, *et seq.*

[49] 2000 Model Procurement Code for State and Local Governments § 11-101–11-301.

[50] 13 C.F.R. §§ 121.101-108; 121.201.

[51] N.J. Stat. Ann. § 52:32-20.

[52] NC Gen. Stat. § 143-128.2.

[53] 488 U.S. 469, 109 S.Ct. 706 (1989).

(3) The government organization must evaluate race-neutral remedies prior to adopting race-conscious requirements; and

(4) The plan must be carefully tailored and must be in place only for the amount of time required to reverse the effects of past discrimination.

Despite this guidance, the debate continues on whether race, ethnicity, and gender should be used as criteria for awarding contracts.

3.8   Public Policy Limitations on Contract Clauses

The enforceability of certain popular risk-shifting clauses in a construction contract may vary from state to state. A number of these clauses address the risk associated with project delay. One of the most often used and debated clauses is the no-damages-for-delay clause. This clause can be used by a contractor to avoid paying additional costs associated with a delay. Some state legislatures have found the clause to be an unfair shifting of a big-dollar construction risk and prohibit the use of no-damages-for-delay clauses, at least in certain contracts.[54] Other states will allow the parties to negotiate at arm's length the terms of a contract, including the use of the no-damages-for-delay clause, as long as concealment, misrepresentation, or fraud was not at issue.[55]

Pay-when-paid and pay-if-paid clauses have long been the topic of heated negotiations in the construction industry. General contractors attempt to insert the pay-when-paid clause into their contracts with subcontractors to allocate the risk of an owner's nonpayment from the general contractor to the subcontractor. Subcontractors generally view enforcement of the clause as unfair, as they may have satisfactorily completed their work yet not have been paid because the owner refuses to pay the general contractor for its unsatisfactory work. Some courts hold that a pay-when-paid clause establishes an absolute commitment to pay by the general contractor, but simply affords the general contractor a reasonable amount of time to make the payment.[56] Other courts, however, have interpreted the pay-when-paid clause as a condition precedent, thereby making the subcontractor's right to payment dependent upon the general contractor's receipt of payment from the owner.[57] Courts in these states, however, have held the pay-if-paid language must be clear, to avoid an argument that the provision cannot be enforced due to ambiguity. For example, "Subcontractor is paid *only if* the general contractor is paid." On federal projects, some courts also require a specific waiver of the subcontractor's Miller Act bond rights complying with the terms of the Miller Act since failure to do so would effectively nullify most pay-when-paid provisions.[58] (*See* **Chapter 14.**)

---

[54] NC Gen. Stat. § 143-134.2; Or. Rev. Stat. §§ 279.063; 279C.315.

[55] *Pasty & Fuhrman v. Housing Authority of City of Providence*, 68 A.2d 32 (RI 1949).

[56] *Koch v. Construction Technology, Inc.*, 924 S.W.2d 68 (Tenn. 1996).

[57] *Printz Services v. Main Electric*, 949 P.2d 77 (Colo. App. 1997).

[58] *United States for the Use and Benefit of Walton Technology, Inc. v. Weststar Engineering, Inc.*, 290 F.3d 1199 (9th Cir. 2002).

The cost of delay also may be addressed in a construction contract in terms of liquidated damages. Most often, the liquidated damages are a set amount that accrues on a daily basis after a specified date of completion is surpassed. In South Carolina, a liquidated damages clause is allowed if a party can prove a breach of contract,[59] but not if the liquidated damages clause is found to act as a penalty.[60] A liquidated damages clause is enforceable in Colorado if it is written at a time when the damages were difficult to ascertain, it represents an accurate reflection of the costs that might occur, and it reflects an agreement by all parties to liquidated damages.[61]

The meaning of certain payment terms and conditions may be impacted when a construction contract involves foreign entities. On an international construction project, there is a unique risk when defining and valuing the payment terms. Losses from currency fluctuations can result when a contractor's home currency is different from the currency in the country where the work was performed. Depending on how and when payments are to be made, as dictated by the contract, a U.S. company that receives a local currency for construction services provided in a foreign country runs the risk that, between the time the service is rendered and payment is made, the value of the local currency, relative to the U.S. dollar, may fall. Construction contractors performing services and receiving payments in a foreign country with a soft currency should address the possibility of and solution for devaluation in the construction contract to ensure a fair and negotiated value is received for the contractor's services.

3.9 PRESERVATION OF LIEN/BOND RIGHTS

For the contractors, subcontractors, suppliers, and owners involved in construction projects in more than one jurisdiction, the navigation of the lien laws in those "foreign" states presents a significant challenge.

Lien law requirements are frequently confusing; nonetheless, failure to precisely meet these requirements can be fatal to a company's lien rights.

3.10 Preconstruction Knowledge of Lien Law Peculiarities Is Essential

Far too often, contractors (as well as owners) first think about investigating the lien law requirements in a particular jurisdiction only when there is an immediate need to file a claim of lien or, from the owner's perspective, after the lien has been filed.

In too many jurisdictions, if steps are not taken very early in the project to either preserve lien rights or, in the case of the owner, to limit lien obligations, those rights will be lost forever.

In some states, actions must be taken before the project even begins, or lien rights may be lost. In Alabama, a "full price" lien (as opposed to a lien on just the unpaid

---

[59] *Carolinas Cotton Growers Ass's v. Arnotte*, 371 F.Supp. 65 (D.S.C. 1974).

[60] *Benya v. Gamble*, 321 S.E.2d 57 (S.C. App. 1984).

[61] *Rohauer v. Little*, 736 P.2d 403 (Colo. 1987).

balance of the owner/GC contract) is available only to those who have a direct contract with the owner or to materialmen who give notice to the owner prior to furnishing materials.[62] Also in Alabama, an owner receiving a "Notice to Owner" from a material supplier may avoid responsibility for the supplier's materials altogether by giving a "Pre-Delivery Notice" back to the supplier stating that the owner will not be responsible for the price of the materials being furnished.[63]

In other jurisdictions, lien rights may survive the start of construction, but are quickly in jeopardy if some action is not taken very soon after starting work. In Michigan, within 20 days after first furnishing labor or materials to a construction project (and if a "Notice of Commencement" has been filed and properly posted by the owner), a subcontractor or supplier wishing to preserve its lien rights must serve a "Notice of Furnishing" on the general contractor and on the owner's designated recipient of project notices.[64] In addition, a "Notice of Commencement" must have been filed and properly posted by the owner.[65] Thus, a delay in providing the owner with notice of the intended lien claim may result in a complete forfeiture of lien rights.

3.11   Lien Law Protections and Procedures Vary Greatly from State to State

Do not assume that familiarity with your state's lien laws will equip your company to protect its rights under the lien laws of another jurisdiction. Lien laws—perhaps more than any other statutory scheme affecting the construction industry—vary widely from state to state. For example, in North Carolina, the fact that a contractor is performing punchlist or warranty work is unlikely to extend the time for filing a lien claim. In contrast, in South Carolina, remedial or warranty work may qualify as a reason to extend the time for filing a claim of lien.[66]

3.12   "Almost Right" Is Almost Always Not Good Enough

In many areas of contract law, parties are not penalized when they are "almost right" or when they have "substantially complied" with the contract or other legal requirements.

For example, contractors and subcontractors that fail to observe contract notice requirements may be excused by the owner's actual knowledge of the circumstances requiring the contract notice. On the other hand, the failure of a contractor, subcontractor, supplier, or owner to *exactly* satisfy lien law requirements is very often fatal to that party's rights under the lien statute. Even the slightest noncompliance can be costly. For example, the Maryland lien statute provides that a "Notice of Intent to Claim a Lien" must be served within 120 days of the claimant's last work. This does not mean that the notice can be sent four months after the last work. There is a

---

[62] Ala. Code §§ 35-11-210 *et seq.*

[63] Ala. Code §§ 35-11-210; 35-11-218.

[64] MCL §§ 570.1101–570.191.

[65] MCL §§ 570.102; 570.1108-570.1301.

[66] NCGS § 44A-7 *et seq.*; SC Code Ann. § 29-5-10 *et seq.*

difference between 120 days and four months, and this difference can be fatal to a company's lien rights.[67]

3.13 A Valid Claim of Lien Does Not Guarantee Payment

Even if your company is able to navigate the lien law maze in the jurisdiction in which it is working, the exercise of its mechanics' lien right may fall short of the payment guarantee it seeks.

The inadequacy of lien right as payment security may result from several causes: The lien may be subordinate to other security interests that consume all of the funds from which liens otherwise might be satisfied; or the lien may not cover all of the damages or costs for which your company is entitled to be paid.

From the contractor's and supplier's perspective, the limited scope of the damages covered by most lien law statutes is a frequent problem. For example, delay damages (the extended job site and home office overhead attributed to a project's delay) are one of the "big-dollar" consequences of a troubled construction project.

The existence of lien rights, however, is no substitute for the exercise of "good financial management," which includes systems and procedures to prequalify those with whom your company intends to do business. Obtain preproject proof of adequate project financing, and avoid contracts that require that your company continue to work during payment disputes.

3.14 Arm Yourself Early with Accurate Lien Law Information

Your company's ability to exactly satisfy the lien requirements—and to avoid the many pitfalls that await it in the lien laws of foreign jurisdictions—begins with the gathering of reliable lien law information. A number of sources are available to the construction industry. For example, mechanics' lien filing services (as well as various contractor associations) have pamphlets, handouts, and other publications available that cover basic—and even more sophisticated—lien law information. Courts have often construed statutory language defining lien rights in ways that make a literal reading of the lien statute unreliable. Similarly, statutorily mandated lien forms may be misleading to those who are unaware of the manner in which the lien statutes define the terms used in the lien form. Investing time in preparing yourself to take full advantage of the lien laws and other payment protections available to you in any new project jurisdiction is priceless.

✓ 3.15 RISK ASSESSMENT CHECKLISTS

The process of identifying general construction project risks, as well as risks unique to the state where construction is planned, is crucial to the success of a construction project. Owners, construction managers, designers, contractors, subcontractors, and materialmen cannot afford to wait until a problem arises

---

[67] Md. Code Ann. Real Prop. Title 9, Subtitle 1.

to assess the peculiar risks inherent in doing business in an unfamiliar state. The risk assessment process must start early, and it should be a systematic approach to risk identification. If your firm does not have such a systematic approach to risk identification, implement one. Borrow from the numerous checklists and guidelines created by industry participants and adapt that system to meet the particular operational style of your firm. Preserve the information gathered during your risk assessment so that it can be of benefit to the project management team. The following checklist can be used as a start to an early and thorough evaluation of the issues to be considered before performing work in a new state:

1. **Qualifying to Do Business**
   a. Unless the planned construction work constitutes an isolated transaction, obtain a certificate of authority.
   b. Establish whether the state has any additional requirements for nonresident bidders; for example, filing with the state's Department of Revenue a statement of a contractor's tangible property.
   c. Ascertain and satisfy required registration fees.
   d. Establish a registered agent/office.

2. **State Revenue Department Requirements**
   a. Ascertain whether the state requires a bond to ensure payment of taxes.
   b. Identify the bond amount and renewal requirements.
   c. Identify any sales or use tax liability.
   d. Plan for *ad valorem* or other taxes.

3. **Licensing Requirements**
   a. Identify any need for contractor or subcontractor licenses.
   b. Determine whether the state requires a contractor to obtain a license *prior to* bidding on a construction project or performing work.
   c. Confirm conformance with architect and engineer licensing requirements.
   d. Determine whether a license is required for other construction professionals or specific trades, such as plumbers, electricians, fire alarm installers, individuals involved in asbestos or lead abatement, and others.
   e. Review unique requirements of city or county licensing or permit requirements.
   f. Review building code requirements.
   g. Identify any required environmental permits or requirements.

4. **Evaluating the Effect of a State's Laws on Contracts Terms**
   a. Subcontractor issues:
      (1) Must subcontractors be listed on the bid or prior to performance?
      (2) Is there a state prompt payment statute?
      (3) Can parties contract for payment terms that vary from the prompt payment act?

    b. Contract award preference regulations:

       (1) Determine whether the jurisdiction allows an award preference for "residents."

       (2) Determine whether the state has a specified small business preference.

       (3) Determine whether the state or bid requires a certain amount of the work to be performed by a minority- or a woman-owned business.

    c. Contract term laws or regulations:

       (1) Determine the existence/validity of no-damages-for-delay clauses.

       (2) Determine the existence/validity of pay-if-paid clauses.

       (3) Does a state statute affect the enforceability of indemnity clauses?

       (4) Does the contract adopt the laws of another jurisdiction?

       (5) Are there other public policy limits on exculpatory clauses?

       (6) Does a state statute affect the validity of a provision specifying a choice of venue for court actions?

5. Special Insurance Requirements

    a. Identify the nature of required insurance coverages.

    b. Is an additional rider required for work in this jurisdiction?

    c. Identify filing/reporting requirements.

6. Preservation of Lien/Bond Rights

    a. Is the project public or private?

    b. Verify the existence of lien rights.

    c. Gather property legal description/owner information.

    d. Verify the existence and coverages of payment bonds.

    e. Identify any precontract filing requirements.

    f. Identify preliminary/early notice requirements.

    g. Verify postperformance notice requirements.

    h. Determine any limitations on lien/bond recovery.

    i. Make an early request for bond/lien information.

    j. Identify any need to use mandatory lien waiver forms.

7. Payment Security Verification

    a. Verify the adequacy of project financing.

    b. Identify notice-to-lender requirements.

    c. Are lender approvals required for change orders or other actions?

    d. Identify any extra work payment limitations.

    e. Identify change order authority limitations.

    f. Verify the existence and impact of a state prompt payment statute.

    g. Identify trust fund/retainage requirements.

8. Labor, Equipment, and Material Issues

a. Verify the adequacy of available local labor.

b. Is the locale primarily a union or nonunion labor market?

c. Determine materials/equipment availability.

d. Identify applicable sales or use taxes.

e. Verify applicable labor rates/fringes.

f. Is the project affected by project/union agreements?

9. Political Climate Assessment

a. Identify special political ties/circumstances.

b. Identify other business climate considerations.

3.16 INFORMATION SOURCES

In the pursuit of obtaining a state's requirements for performing construction work, the Internet can provide a plethora of information. Each state maintains a Secretary of State Web site that provides information for obtaining a certificate of authority.[68]

For an overall review of a state's construction contracting requirements, the state chapters of the Associated General Contractors of America (AGC)[69] or the Associated Builders and Contractors (ABC)[70] organization can provide valuable information. For example, on the AGC's Web site, a State Law Matrix may be purchased that offers a comprehensive listing and review of laws that influence the construction process in all 50 states, the District of Columbia, and Puerto Rico.

Some states have organizations unique to the state and the construction professional. For example, in New York, the General Building Contractors of New York State is an organization of more than 150 general contractors and construction managers.[71] Contacting these local organizations can provide additional familiarity with each state's unique requirements, as well as legislation in the state's legislature that may affect a contractor's practice.

Other construction industry trade associations (e.g., the Construction Financial Manager's Association) publish magazines, newsletters, and books that provide valuable information. Construction law seminars that focus specifically on the laws of a particular state can be found in most states. Several publishing companies sell books that detail construction law issues for a particular state or that focus on how all 50 states handle a particular construction law issue (e.g., LienLaw Online, a subscription Web service providing information regarding the lien laws in all 50 states and the District of Columbia).[72]

---

[68] www.state.in.us.sos/.

[69] www.agc.org.

[70] www.abc.org.

[71] www.gbnys.org.

[72] www.lienlaw.com.

If you are bidding for work to benefit one of the state's governmental entities, it is important to review the requirements unique to each department, such as the Department of Transportation[73] or the Department of Administration,[74] as these requirements may vary from those at the state level.

➤ POINTS TO REMEMBER

- As construction work generally constitutes "doing business" in a state, a contractor preparing to work in a new state must first obtain a certificate of authority from the Secretary of State's office.
- Most states require a bond from out-of-state contractors to ensure prompt and full payment of any taxes that become due as a function of performing construction work in the state.
- While not every state requires that a contractor obtain a license prior to bidding or performing construction work, all states require that architects, engineers, and other design professionals obtain a license.
- State lien and bond law statutes often impose early filing or notice requirements. Identify those requirements before you start work on a new project.
- The manner by which public construction projects are awarded varies by state and should be understood and followed to ensure proper consideration of the bid.
- State and local regulations regarding general contractor relationships with subcontractors, contract award preferences, and the enforceability of contract terms vary greatly from one jurisdiction to another. Do not assume that the laws in your home jurisdiction will be identical to, or even similar to, those in a foreign jurisdiction.
- A comprehensive risk assessment should be made prior to bidding on a construction project, and that assessment should be preserved and revisited throughout the project duration to minimize potential problems.

---

[73] www.state.hi.us/dot.

[74] www.in.gov/doa.

4

COMPETING FOR
THE CONTRACT

4.1 INTRODUCTION: SEALED BIDS TO NEGOTIATED BEST-VALUE AWARDS

The bidding process is often the general contractor's first exposure to the particular project and the owner of that project. Bidding procedures vary widely depending on whether the owner is public or private. The vast majority of federal, state, and municipal contracts are awarded pursuant to public bidding. Competitive bidding, although less prevalent in the private sector, is used by many private owners as a means of obtaining an advantageous price while maintaining some degree of control over the quality of the successful awardee. Although private owners are rarely, if ever, "required" to use competitive bidding procedures, for those private owners who do choose to solicit competitive bids for a project, both the owner and potential bidders should pay close attention to general principles of public bidding, because many of the same considerations are present whether the project is public or private.

4.2 GENERAL CONSIDERATIONS IN BIDS FOR PUBLIC CONTRACTS

The essential characteristics of public contracts at all levels are similar. Public contracts generally are awarded to the contractor presenting the "lowest responsible and responsive" offer or the "lowest and best offer." In other words, a successful bid will usually be the one that represents the lowest price from a responsible bidder and that meets the specifications provided by the owner or contracting agency. The following materials discuss in greater detail the elements of the typical successful bid.

4.3   THE RESPONSIBLE BIDDER

The terms "lowest responsive and responsible" and "lowest and best" bidder, as used in statutes, are not confined to the lowest-dollar bid. Indeed, the words "responsible" and "best" are often as important as the word "lowest."

Responsibility determinations focus on whether the contractor has the necessary technical, managerial, and financial capability and integrity to perform the work. A "responsible" bidder is a contractor that is capable of undertaking and completing the work in a satisfactory fashion. Public contracting authorities will consider a number of factors in determining whether a contractor is responsible. These factors, falling into two general categories, are also relevant to a private owner's evaluation of prospective contractors.

First, a contractor must have the ability to perform the work required by the solicitation. In determining the ability of a contractor to perform, public contracting authorities will take into account the contractor's financial resources, facilities and equipment, experience, and licenses and permits. The second general category of responsibility standards addresses the contractor's desire and reliability to perform the contract. In this category, procurement officials will consider the ethical integrity of the contractor and the contractor's ability to perform and complete previous projects.

In federal procurement, Federal Acquisition Regulation (FAR) § 9.104-1 specifies that a contractor must demonstrate the following qualifications in order to be considered responsible:

(1) Have adequate financial resources to perform the contract, or the ability to obtain them;

(2) Be able to comply with the required or proposed delivery or performance schedule, taking into account all existing commercial and governmental business commitments;

(3) Have a satisfactory performance record;

(4) Have a satisfactory record of integrity and business ethics;

(5) Have the necessary organization, experience, accounting and operational controls, and technical skills, or the ability to obtain them;

(6) Have the necessary production, construction, and technical equipment and facilities, or be able to obtain them; and

(7) Be otherwise qualified and eligible for award under applicable laws and regulations.

The determination of responsibility is based on the contractor's ability to perform the specified work as of the time work is to commence, not at the time of bidding. Therefore, a bidder does not have to demonstrate the ability to perform at the time the bid is submitted. Rather, a bidder will be deemed responsible if the bidder has or can obtain the apparent ability to perform the work as of the date work is to begin.[1]

A contractor's "ability to obtain" certain elements listed in the FAR can be particularly important for small contractors. The General Services Board of Contract Appeals (GSBCA), deciding a protest involving automated data processing engineering services, held that the Federal Aviation Administration (FAA) had improperly determined that an offeror was not responsible.[2] The FAA cited the small business offeror's lack of in-house general and administrative (G&A) service personnel. According to the board, the FAA was required to consider whether the services could be obtained through alternative means as permitted by FAR § 9.104-1. In this case, the offeror demonstrated its ability to provide G&A services through a subcontract arrangement.[3]

All available facts, whether or not submitted with the bid, should be submitted by the contractor and considered by the government to resolve responsibility questions. Since a public official is making a quasi-judicial decision when determining whether a bidder is "responsible" within the meaning of the governing statute, the bidder is entitled to the prerequisites of due process. Therefore, a finding by a public body that a bidder is not responsible should be supported by a record establishing (1) the facts upon which the decision was based, (2) details of the investigation that disclosed these facts, and (3) the opportunity that was offered to the bidder to present its qualifications.

Generally, the contractor will be entitled to an informal hearing on the matter, although a formal hearing may be prescribed by statute. The contractor is normally entitled to present evidence in its own behalf. Once a decision is made, however, the courts generally will not reverse the agency's decision and will require award of the contract, except where there has been a clear violation of the law. In *Ward La France Truck Corp. v. City of New York*,[4] for example, the court found that requirements of a fair hearing had not been observed. The court, however, did not order award of the contract to the affected bidder; instead, it returned the matter to the public body for reconsideration.

In the federal procurement setting, the Comptroller General has limited challenges to responsibility determinations to those involving serious concerns that the contracting officer failed to consider available relevant information or otherwise violated a statute or regulation. The result has been the acceptance of agency determinations in the vast majority of cases.[5] However, where an agency determination of nonresponsibility is so unreasonable as to be arbitrary and capricious, the affected bidder will be permitted to recover its bid preparation costs.[6]

---

[1] Comp. Gen. Dec. B-176227, 52 Comp. Gen. 240, 1972 CPD ¶ 97.

[2] *Universal Automation Leasing Corp.*, GSBCA No. 11268-P, 91-3 BCA ¶ 24,255. (The GSBCA no longer has jurisdiction over any form of bid protests.)

[3] *Id.* at 121,271.

[4] 160 N.Y.S.2d 679 (Sup. Ct. 1957).

[5] 54 Comp. Gen. 66 (1974); 4 C.F.R. § 21.5(c).

[6] *L. A. Anderson Constr. Co.*, GSBCA No. 6235, 82-1 BCA ¶ 15,507.

4.4   THE RESPONSIVE BIDDER

Public contract bids usually will not be successful unless the bids comply with all material requirements of the solicitation. Responsiveness differs from responsibility, as it focuses on whether the bid, as submitted, is an offer to perform the exact tasks spelled out in the bid invitation and whether acceptance will bind the contractor to perform in strict conformance with the invitation.[7]

Failure of a contractor to carefully comply with all the requirements for competitive bidding may result in the bid being declared "nonresponsive," or if an award has been made, may render the contract voidable or prevent the contractor from recovering full compensation for work performed. In determining the responsiveness of bids, the bidder's intent must be clearly ascertainable from the face of the bid.[8] However, in order to rise to the level of nonresponsiveness, the deviation must be considered material.

A deviation is considered material if it gives one bidder a substantial competitive advantage that prevents other bidders from competing equally. A deviation is also material if it goes to the substance of the bid or works prejudice upon other bidders. The deviation goes to the substance of the bid if it affects price, quantity, quality, or delivery of the items offered.[9] A contractor bidding on public work must generally take the contract as presented. Thus, any qualification of a bid that limits or changes one or more of the terms of the proposed contract subjects the contractor to the risk of being held nonresponsive. For example, in *Lift Power, Inc.*,[10] a contractor was found to be nonresponsive where it reserved the right in the bid to change the price if costs should increase.[11] Obviously, such a qualification, if accepted by the owner, could have given the contractor an unfair price advantage over other bidders.[12]

The contractor's inclusion of reservations or conditions in its bid generally renders the bid nonresponsive. According to the Federal Acquisition Regulation, a bid is nonresponsive if it includes conditions such as:

(1) Protecting against future changes in conditions, such as increased costs, if total possible costs to the government cannot be determined;

(2) Failing to state a price and indicating that price shall be "price in effect at time of delivery";

(3) Stating a price but qualifying it as being subject to "price in effect at time of delivery";

---

[7] *Prestex, Inc. v. United States*, 320 F.2d 367 (Ct. Cl. 1963); *East Side Constr. Co. v. Town of Adams*, 108 N.E.2d 659 (Mass. 1952).

[8] *Jarke Corp.*, Comp. Gen. Dec. B-231858, 88-2 CPD ¶ 82.

[9] FAR § 14.404-2; 48 C.F.R. § 14.404-2.

[10] Comp. Gen. Dec. B-182604, 75-1 CPD ¶ 13.

[11] *See also Kipp Constr. Co.*, Comp. Gen. Dec. B-181588, 75-1 CPD ¶ 20.

[12] *See also Chemtech Indus., Inc.*, B-186652, 76-2 CPD ¶ 274.

(4) Conditioning or qualifying a bid by stipulating that it is to be considered only if, before date of award, the bidder receives (or does not receive) award under a separate solicitation when that is not authorized by the invitation;

(5) Requiring the government to determine that the bidder's product meets applicable government specifications; or

(6) Limiting rights of the government under any contract clause.[13]

The majority of rules concerning bid responsiveness are aimed at preventing a contractor from having "two bites at the apple." In other words, the concept of "bid responsiveness" is used to guard against a low bidder having the opportunity, after bids are opened and all prices are revealed, to accept or reject an award based on some contingency that the bidder created itself, and which only applies to, and works to the advantage of, that bidder.

The prohibition against a bidder having "two bites at the apple" applies most often when a defect in the bid or an ambiguity in a solicitation subjects the intended bid to differing interpretations. For example, in *Caprock Vermeer Equipment, Inc.*,[14] a bidder for an equipment supply contract included in its bid descriptive literature upon which was written the word "optional." The Comptroller General found that there were two interpretations of the bid, at least one of which rendered the bid nonresponsive. The Comptroller General, therefore, upheld the government's rejection of the bid.

A bid will also be considered nonresponsive if the bidder attempts to make the bid contingent upon some act or event. In *HewlettPackard*,[15] the Comptroller General found a bid to be nonresponsive where the bidder sent a transmittal letter stating that the bid was contingent upon the removal of a contract clause. The Comptroller General found that the contingency rendered the bid nonresponsive because the bidder sought to change the terms of the contract to the bidder's sole advantage.

A bid will also be considered nonresponsive where the bidder deviates from the bidding requirements by failing to acknowledge addenda, particularly where the addenda contain a statutorily required provision.[16] Also, an oral, rather than written, acknowledgment of an amendment is unacceptable.[17]

According to the Comptroller General, nonresponsive bids also include bids that fail to acknowledge an amendment that would impose a new legal obligation (even if it would have no effect on price)[18] and that fail to certify that a small business product will be provided.[19]

A determination that a bid was nonresponsive because it was materially unbalanced was upheld by the Comptroller General even though the bidder contended the

---

[13] FAR § 14.404-2(d); 48 C.F.R. § 14.404-2(d).

[14] Comp. Gen. Dec. B-217088, 85-2 CPD ¶ 259.

[15] Comp. Gen. Dec. B-216530, 85-1 CPD ¶ 193.

[16] *Grade-Way Constr. Co. v. United States*, 7 Cl. Ct. 263 (1985).

[17] *Alcon, Inc.*, Comp. Gen. Dec. B-228409, 88-2 CPD ¶ 114.

[18] *American Sein-Pro*, Comp. Gen. Dec. B-231823, 88-2 CPD ¶ 209.

[19] *Delta Concepts, Inc.*, Comp. Gen. Dec. B-230632, 88-2 CPD ¶ 43.

"unbalancing" resulted from allocated technical evaluation and preproduction costs to first articles.[20] The Comptroller General said that, where costs necessary to produce the first articles also are a necessary investment in the production quantity, the costs should be amortized over the total contract rather than allocated solely to the first articles. The reason for rejecting "front-loaded" bids is that the greatly enhanced first-article prices will provide funds to the firm in the early period of contract performance, and will be, in essence, an interest-free loan to which the contractor is not entitled.[21]

Rejection of a bid for nonresponsiveness may also be proper when the principal on the bid bond submitted by the bidder is not the same legal entity as the offeror on the bid form. Generally, a surety can be obligated on a bid bond only if the principal named in the bond fails to execute the contract. The refusal of another entity to contract with the awarding authority does not result in a forfeiture of the bid bond. Defective bid bonds constitute a substantial deviation, ordinarily requiring rejection of the bid as nonresponsive because such bonds do not protect the public body and enable bidders to get out of contracts with impunity.[22]

While many deviations such as those noted above may be considered "material," minor irregularities may be waived by the awarding authority.[23] This long-established policy permitting waiver of minor irregularities or informalities preserves the focus of competitive bidding on lowest price by discouraging questions over matters not affecting the substance of the bid.[24]

The basic rule observed in connection with minor irregularities is that the defect or variation in the bid must have trivial or negligible significance when contrasted with the total cost or scope of the invitation for bids. Deviations affecting price, quantity, quality, delivery, or completion are generally material and merit especially stringent standards to protect against any bidder obtaining a competitive advantage.[25] For an irregularity in a bid to be waived, it must be so inconsequential or immaterial that the bidder does not gain a competitive advantage after all bids have been exposed. Thus, a minor irregularity may be found where the bidder fails to initial a price change in its bid before bid opening;[26] fails to mark its bid envelope with the solicitation number, date, and time of bid opening;[27] or fails to provide incidental information requested by the invitation.[28]

The determination of what constitutes a minor informality generally is left to the discretion of the contracting officer,[29] and courts often give contracting officers

---

[20] *M. C. General, Inc.*, Comp. Gen. Dec. B-228334, 87-2 CPD ¶ 572.

[21] *Fidelity Technologies Corp.*, Comp. Gen. Dec. B-232340, 88-2 CPD ¶ 511.

[22] *See Yank Waste Co.*, Comp. Gen. Dec. B-180418, 74-1 CPD ¶ 190; *but see* Comp. Gen. Dc. B-178824 (Aug. 16, 1973).

[23] 51 Comp. Gen. 62 (1971).

[24] 41 Comp. Gen. 721 (1962); *Faist v. Hoboken*, 60 A. 1120 (N.J. Sup. 1905).

[25] *See Prestex, Inc.*, *supra* note 7; 40 Comp. Gen. 321 (1960); FAR § 14.405; 48 C.F.R. § 14.405.

[26] Comp. Gen. B-211870, 31 CCF ¶ 71,615 (Aug. 23, 1983).

[27] Comp. Gen. B-210251, 30 CCF ¶ 70,804 (Jan. 24, 1983).

[28] Comp. Gen. B-215162, 64 Comp. Gen. 8 (1984).

[29] *Excavation Constr., Inc. v. United States*, 494 F.2d 1289 (Ct. Cl. 1974).

broad discretion as to what constitutes a minor irregularity. For example, one court in Maryland held that a bidder's failure to furnish a bid bond was not a material irregularity necessitating bid rejection.[30] In that case, the court characterized the governing considerations as follows:

> Of course, bidders should make every effort to comply as strictly as possible with specifications. On the other hand, *it is the duty of an administrative agency to secure the most advantageous contracts possible for the accomplishment of its work.* A bidder's variation from specifications will not exclude him from consideration for the award of the contract unless it is so substantial as to give him a special advantage over the other bidders. In judging whether or not the omission or irregularity in a bid is so substantial as to invalidate it, the court must be careful not to thwart the purpose of competitive bidding by declaring the lowest bid invalid on account of variations that are not material.[31]

As noted previously, however, the court's conclusion that a bid without a bid bond did not constitute a "special advantage over the other bidders" is inconsistent with the great majority of such decisions.[32]

Another far-reaching example of a procuring agency's exercise of discretion to award to the low bidder despite a potential bid irregularity arose in *Pullman Inc. v. Volpe.*[33] There, the court upheld "clarifications" made by the low bidder after bid opening on the ground that the clarifications demonstrated that the bid conformed to and did not alter the specifications.

In contrast to the two cases just cited, a number of Comptroller General decisions have helped define what are more typically considered to be minor informalities, including the following:

(1) The omission of unit prices under circumstances where they could be calculated by dividing total prices by estimated quantities;[34]

(2) The insertion of the wrong solicitation number on a bid bond;[35]

(3) The omission of a principal's signature on a bid bond when the bond is submitted with a signed bid;[36]

(4) An ambiguous bid price if the bid is low under all reasonable interpretations;[37]

(5) A failure to include required information on affiliates;[38]

---

[30] *Board of Educ. of Carroll County v. Allender*, 112 A.2d 455 (Md. Ct. App. 1955).

[31] *Id.* at 460, *citing George A. Fuller Co. v. Elderkin*, 154 A. 548 (Md. 1931). (Emphasis added.)

[32] *Thorp's Mowing*, Comp. Gen. Dec. B-181154, 74-2 CPD ¶ 37; *George Harms Constr. Co. v. Ocean County Sewerage Auth.*, 394 A.2d 360 (N.J. Super. 1978).

[33] 337 F. Supp. 432 (E.D. Pa. 1971).

[34] *GEM Eng'g. Co.*, Comp. Gen. Dec. B-231605.2, 88-2 CPD ¶ 252.

[35] *Kirila Contractors, Inc.*, Comp. Gen. Dec. B-230731, 88-1 CPD ¶ 554.

[36] *P-B Eng'g. Co.*, Comp. Gen. Dec. B-229739, 88-1 CPD ¶ 71.

[37] *NJS Dev. Corp.*, Comp. Gen. Dec. B-230871, 88-2 CPD ¶ 62.

[38] *A & C Bldg. & Indus. Maintenance Corp.*, Comp. Gen. Dec. B-229931, 88-1 CPD ¶ 309.

(6) A failure to acknowledge an amendment to the solicitation that would not have a material impact on price[39] or only a trivial impact on price;[40]

(7) A failure to acknowledge an amendment reducing the quantity of items to be ordered where the amendment imposed no obligations not already in the original invitation and had no impact on the bid price;[41] and

(8) A failure to provide equipment description information when the solicitation did not make it clear a failure would result in bid rejection.[42]

Finally, the GSBCA classified as minor informalities a bidder's failure to include with the bid evidence of an agent's authority and the failure to set out the corporate name on each page on which an entry had been made.[43]

4.5 THE "LOWEST AND BEST" BIDDER

Some who engage in competitive bidding assume that an owner has the legal obligation to award the construction contract to the lowest bidder. This belief, however, is only partially accurate in public contracting, and generally is not true in private contracting. A contractor's bid, in a legal sense, is simply an offer to perform work; until that offer is accepted by the owner, no enforceable obligation arises.[44] Highlighting this idea that the bid itself is only an offer to perform, the owner's Invitation for Bids (IFB) will usually contain a provision to the effect that "the owner reserves the right to reject any or all bids." This provision is designed to put contractors on notice in the bidding documents that the owner may choose not to "accept" any of the bid "offers."[45]

While the federal government must take into account factors other than price in the evaluation process, the relative pricing of bids is of great importance in federal procurement. Federal agencies are obligated to accept the bid that is the most financially

---

[39] *Adak Communications Sys., Inc.*, Comp. Gen. Dec. B-228341, 88-1 CPD ¶ 74.

[40] *Star Brite Constr. Co.*, Comp. Gen Dec. B-228522, 88-1 CPD ¶ 17 ($2,000 out of a $118,000 difference between low and second low bid).

[41] *Automated Datatron, Inc.*, Comp. Gen. Dec. B-231411, 88-2 CPD ¶ 137.

[42] *Houston Helicopters, Inc.*, Comp. Gen. Dec. B-231122, 88-2 CPD ¶ 149.

[43] *Federal Sys. Group, Inc.*, GSBCA No. 9548-P, 88-3 BCA ¶ 21,021.

[44] As stated in 1 Williston on Contracts (4th ed., Lord, 1990), at § 4:10:

> Often tenders or bids are advertised for by public corporations, municipalities, counties or states or private corporations. The rules governing such bidding are analogous to the rules governing auction sales. Thus, an ordinary advertisement for bids or tenders is not itself an offer, but the bid or tender is an offer which creates no right until accepted.

[45] However, some courts have found that a "reservation of right to reject all bids" clause will not permit an arbitrary rejection of bids, particularly when the bids meet the terms of the solicitation and the rejection is intended primarily to avoid a bid protest. *See Pataula Elec. Membership Corp. v. Whitworth*, 951 F.2d 1238, 1243–44 (11th Cir.), *overruled on other grounds sub nom. Flint Electrical Membership Corp. v. Whitworth*, 68 F.3d 1309 (11th Cir. 1995), *corrected decision*, 77 F.3d 1321 (11th Cir. 1996); *Cianbro Corp. v. Jacksonville Transp. Auth.*, 473 So. 2d 209 (Fla. Dist. Ct. App. 1985).

advantageous to the federal government, so long as that bid is responsive to the terms of the solicitation and the bidder is a responsible contractor. According to 10 U.S.C. § 2305(b)(1)(3), agency heads are to award contracts "to the responsible bidder whose bid conforms to the solicitation and is most advantageous to the United States, *considering only price and the other price-related factors included in the solicitation*" (emphasis added).

The federal concern for securing the most financially advantageous bid is well illustrated by the evaluation of bids responding to solicitations with multiple items. Bids presented on this type of solicitation generally must be evaluated based both on the unit price offered by a bidder as well as the total price. In *S. J. Groves & Sons Co.*,[46] the Comptroller General stated that "where awards on a combination of schedules is contemplated the award made must result in the lowest cost to the Government to carry out the mandate of 10 U.S.C. § 2305(c). . . ."[47] As a result, a federal agency may actually be required to make multiple awards if different bidders offer the lowest unit price on different specific items or if the value of prices of individual items is lower than the total price offered by another bidder.

Even though the relative prices offered by bidders are of great importance to federal procurement officials, a contractor submitting the low bid generally has no vested interest in the award of that contract.[48] Nevertheless, that contractor cannot be denied the contract unless the denial would be in the best interest of the public. A further qualification to the importance of price is that even if the bidder on a federal contract does not present the lowest bid, the bid is entitled to fair consideration.[49] Where a federal agency fails to consider adequately a bidder's proposal, the bidder may be entitled to recover bid preparation costs.[50]

Most state and local governments are also bound to award their contracts to the lowest and best bidder. Most states and many localities have enacted statutes or ordinances mandating award to the lowest bidder whose bid meets the technical requirements of the solicitation.[51] Some courts addressing state and local public competitive bidding statutes, regulations, ordinances, and guidelines have held that such provisions can create a protected property interest in favor of the lowest responsible, responsive bidder in the expectation of award if the solicitation is subject to competitive bidding requirements protected by federal and/or state law.[52] Other courts

---

[46] Comp. Gen. Dec. B-184260, 76-1 CPD ¶ 205.

[47] *Id.* at 23.

[48] However, courts in some jurisdictions have found that the contractor submitting the lowest, responsible responsive bid does have a protected interest under state or local law in contract award. *See Pataula Elec., supra* note 45.

[49] *Keco Indus., Inc. v. United States*, 428 F.2d 1233 (Ct. Cl. 1970); *Heyer Prods. Co. v. United States*, 140 F. Supp. 409 (Ct. Cl. 1956).

[50] *Continental Business Enter., Inc. v. United States*, 452 F.2d 1016 (Ct. Cl. 1971).

[51] *See, e.g.,* Fla. Stat. Ann. §§ 255.29 and 337.11; Ga. Code Ann. § 36-91-5.

[52] *See, e.g., Pataula Elec., supra* note 45; *L & H Sanitation, Inc. v. Lake City Sanitation, Inc.*, 585 F. Supp. 120 (E.D. Ark. 1984), *aff'd on other grounds,* 769 F.2d 517 (8th Cir. 1985); *Teleprompter of Erie, Inc. v. City of Erie*, 537 F. Supp. 6 (W.D. Pa. 1981); *Three Rivers Cablevision, Inc. v. City of Pittsburgh*, 502 F. Supp. 1118 (W.D. Pa. 1980).

interpreting state and/or local competitive bidding requirements have found that the lowest responsible, responsive bidder does not have a protected property interest in the award of the contract.[53] The determination of whether a protected property interest exists turns on the nature of the state or local law, regulation, or ordinance.[54]

If a protest is contemplated, the contractor should first determine whether a competitive bidding statute or regulation governs the state's or locality's procurement, and, if so, what the regulation permits or requires.

4.6 NEGOTIATED "BEST VALUE" SELECTION PROCESS

Traditionally, the preferred method of contracting in the federal government system was through formal advertising with the government issuing an IFB (Invitation for Bids). Bids were received on the date specified in the solicitation, and award was made to the lowest-dollar bid from a responsive, responsible bidder. Negotiated procurement was another method of contracting, but was only used under specific circumstances set forth in statue and regulations. Under negotiated procurement procedures, the federal government issued a request for proposals (RFP). Generally, once proposals were received, the government and the offerors entered into negotiations under the terms of the solicitation, with award being made to the offeror that ultimately submitted the lowest negotiated price.

The negotiated "best value" procurement process is authorized under Part 15 of Title 48 of the Code of Federal Regulations (CFR).[55] Under this procedure the government is not required to award to the lowest-priced offeror; but through a trade-off evaluation process as specified in the RFP, the government makes an award to the offeror whose proposal provides the "best value" to the government. Title 48 C.F.R. 15.101-1 provides:

(a) A tradeoff process is appropriate when it may be in the best interest of the Government to consider award to other than the lowest priced offeror or other than the highest technically rated offeror.

(b) When using a tradeoff process, the following apply:

(1) All evaluation factors and significant subfactors that will affect contract award and their relative importance shall be clearly stated in the solicitation; and

(2) The solicitation shall state whether all evaluation factors other than cost or price, when combined, are significantly more important than, approximately equal to, or significantly less important than cost or price.

(c) This process permits tradeoffs among cost or price and non-cost factors and allows the Government to accept other than the lowest priced proposal. The perceived benefits of the higher priced proposal shall merit the additional cost, and the rationale for tradeoffs must be documented in the file in accordance with 48 C.F.R. 15.406.

---

[53] *See, e.g., Key West Harbour Dev. Corp. v. City of Key West*, 987 F.2d 723 (11th Cir. 1993); *Corner Constr. Corp. v. Rapid City Sch. Dist.* No. 51-4, 845 F. Supp. 1354 (D.S.D. 1994).

[54] *See, e.g., Pataula Elec., supra* note 45.

[55] 48 C.F.R. § 15.

The negotiated "best value" procurement process has been the subject of numerous appeals to the boards of contract appeals, as well as to the United States Court of Federal Claims and the United States Court of Appeals for the Federal Circuit. The boards and federal courts will give substantial deference to the discretion of the government in determining which offer is the most advantageous to the government. However, the ultimate standard or test applied by both the boards of contract appeals and the federal courts is whether or not the government complied with (a) the CFR and FAR requirements for negotiated best-value procurements, and (b) whether or not the agency followed the selection and evaluations procedures set forth in the RFP.[56]

4.7 ELECTRONIC BIDS: REVERSE BID AUCTIONS

Electronic commerce is in place, or scheduled to come online in the very near future for virtually all of the states and federal government. However, there is no particular pattern among the states. Many have passed enabling legislation that allows state officials to establish procurement programs for electronic commerce, while others provide only electronic solicitation notices. Some states allow online bidding as an alternative method, and still others will accept electronic bids for selected agencies. The federal government has procedures in place for electronic procurement practices, and Section 15 of the Federal Acquisition Regulation (FAR), which governs the conduct of negotiated procurement, has been rewritten to allow federal agencies to use online auction technology. Still prohibited is conduct that "favors one offeror over another," "reveals an offeror's technical solution," or "knowingly furnishes source selection information" contrary to regulatory or statutory requirements.[57] Online reverse auctions are also used by the federal government. In a reverse auction, prospective contractors bid down the price to provide the products or services sought by the government.

However, four decisions from the Comptroller General are indicative of problems that e-bidding for federal contracts presents. In *PM Tech, Inc.*,[58] a contractor bidding online attempted to take all steps necessary to timely submit its bid, but failed to get anything other than the cover sheet for its proposal in by the time responses to the solicitation were due. It was only the next day that PM Tech's bid was completely submitted, and it was thereafter rejected as untimely. PM Tech protested to the Comptroller General, and the Comptroller General rejected PM Tech's arguments. The Comptroller General's decision stated, in part, "We view it as an offeror's responsibility, when transmitting its proposal electronically, to insure the proposal's timely delivery by transmitting the proposal sufficiently in advance of the time set

---

[56] *Widnall v. B3H Corp.*, 75 3d 1577 (Fed. Cir 1996). *See also Grumman Data Systems Corporation v. Dalton*, 88 F.3d 990 (Fed. Cir. 1996); *TRW Inc. v. Unisys Corp.*, 98 F.3d 1329 (Fed. Cir 1996).

[57] FAR 15.306(e).

[58] Comp. Gen. Dec. B-291082, 2002 CPD ¶ 172.

for receipt of proposals to allow for timely receipt by the agency."[59] In a decision similar to those involving late delivery of bids or late delivery of faxes, the Comptroller General concluded that PM Tech took a certain amount of risk when it waited until only 13 minutes before the deadline for receipt of proposals to begin to attempt to transmit its proposal. Similarly, in *Sea Box, Inc.,*[60] the Comptroller General held that while the bid was received by the federal government's e-mail system before the deadline, it was untimely because it failed to reach the specified e-mail box by the stated deadline. In the *Sea Box* decision, the Comptroller General pointed out that the protestor sent its bid, consisting of seven e-mails, approximately 11 minutes before the stated deadline. Seven e-mails reached the agency's initial point of entry for e-mail before the deadline and were held for a period of time, then were sent to a virus-scanning server and subsequently arrived 7 to 24 minutes late at the e-mail box. The agency rejected the bid as late, and the Comptroller General agreed.

In *Tischman Construction Corp.,*[61] the prospective contractor submitted identical bids electronically and on paper, as was required by the RFP for construction management services. The paper version of the bid was received by the contracting activity approximately 73 minutes after the stated deadline, while the electronic version of the bid was received approximately 50 minutes prior to the time for receipt of bids. The agency rejected the bid as untimely. The Comptroller General disagreed and sustained Tischman's protest, relying on a prior decision in which a bidder submitted its bid at two separate locations, as required by the solicitation, but only one was timely.[62] In that earlier decision, the Comptroller General found that the contractor did not obtain a competitive advantage, as the agency had a complete copy of the bid in a timely manner, and no competitive advantage was obtained. Under those circumstances, the late bid at the second location was considered a minor informality by the Comptroller General.

Finally, in *VSA Information Sys. Inc.,*[63] the Comptroller General denied a protest where the solicitation materials were available only on the Internet. The procuring agency had posted an amendment to the solicitation with a short response time and did not specifically advise the protestor of the amendment. The Comptroller General found that the protestor had not taken reasonable steps to have been made aware of the amendment, such as registering for e-mail notification or checking the Internet site, and it was for those reasons the protestor had insufficient time to protest the terms of the solicitation.

Clearly, the basic and longstanding rules regarding timeliness of the submission of bids or proposals should be as strenuously adhered to by firms submitting their bids electronically as they would be if they were submitting those same bids in a paper format.

---

[59] *Id.* at 3.
[60] Comp. Gen. Dec. B-291056, 2002 CPD ¶ 181.
[61] Comp. Gen. Dec. B-292097, 2003 CPD ¶ 94.
[62] *ABT Associates, Inc.,* Comp. Gen. Dec. B-226063, 87-1 CPD ¶ 513.
[63] Comp. Gen. Dec. B-291488, 2002 CPD ¶ 205.

4.8 GENERAL CONSIDERATIONS WHEN COMPETING ON PRIVATE CONTRACTS

Few rules exist in private contract bidding that obligate the owner to award to a particular contractor. While a private owner is not bound by statute to operate under the "lowest responsible, responsive bidder" approach, the owner is likely to consider many of the same factors when reviewing the bids. The private owner may select a contractor based on any criteria it deems appropriate. The private owner is generally under no obligation to make award to the lowest bidder, and might attempt to negotiate an even lower price once the low bid has been determined. Moreover, private owners are generally under no duty to disclose the bases for their decisions. Private owners may open bids outside the presence of all bidders. The private owner may require the bidders to provide a wide variety of information concerning the contractor's ability to perform the project. In addition, the private owner may or may not require the contractor to provide a bid bond or payment and performance bonds to guarantee performance.

As with public bidding, the contractor will want to present itself as a responsible business that is responsive to the owner's needs and that will perform at a reasonable price. The contractor should also be careful to determine whether the owner will be able to meet payment obligations and to provide promised logistical support. The private owner presents a much greater financial risk than a public body with its tax base. Additionally, the contractor should carefully review all specifications and plans presented by the owner, because the private owner may not have the resources to provide the review necessary to find and eliminate potential, and costly, design problems.

4.9 EFFECT OF PAST PERFORMANCE EVALUATIONS ON AWARD PROCESS

In 1994, Congress passed the Federal Acquisitions Streamlining Act (FASA).[64] In so doing, Congress acknowledged that a contractor's past performance should be evaluated during a current acquisition process to ascertain whether or not that contractor should receive future work. Section 1091 of FASA provides that "past contract performance of an offeror is one of the relevant factors that a contracting official of an executive agency should consider in awarding a contract." As a result of the passage of FASA, all federal departments and agencies have initiated procedures to record contractor performance contemporaneous with that performance on all contracts over $100,000, and to use the contractor's past performance during future acquisition processes. The federal government believes that the use of past performance evaluations will sufficiently motivate contractors to perform at the highest standards, or to the extent they are not, to improve their performance before they are again rated by an agency or department. Past performance evaluations are a significant factor in

---

[64] P.L. 103-355 (Oct. 13, 1994).

the agencies' determinations of a "best value" selection. Procuring agencies are better able to predict the quality of the contractor's performance and, therefore, the associated customer's satisfaction.

The primary theory behind the evaluation of contractors' performance and its use in future procurements is twofold. First, Congress believes that an active dialogue between the contractor and the government during performance will result in better current performance by the contractor. Second, as contractors are made aware that their performance evaluations will be used by other procuring activities on future procurements, it will enable procuring activities to better select high-quality contractors for new contracts.

The federal government has been careful to limit the scope and content of past performance evaluations to matters related to a contractor's actual contract performance. In April 2002, the Office of Federal Procurement Policy issued a governmentwide memorandum providing that contractors could not be given "downgraded" past performance evaluations for availing themselves of their rights by filing protests and claims or for deciding not to use alternative dispute resolution (ADR) to resolve disputes. That same memorandum also provided that contractors could not be given more "positive" past performance evaluations for refraining from filing protests and claims or agreeing to use ADR.

Several decisions from the Comptroller General have addressed the relevance of past performance information and the use of past performance information in current procurements. In *C. Lawrence Construction Company, Inc.,*[65] the Comptroller General found that the Army Corps of Engineers' requirement to provide at least five past performance references for relevant contracts, which were defined in the RFP as similar construction contracts in the $5 to $10 million range, was not unduly restrictive and was consistent with the Army's position that evaluating at least five projects provided a "comfort zone" with respect to a prospective contractor's overall performance trends.

The Comptroller General has also ruled that it is reasonable for an agency to consider the *specific* experience of a contractor to which award was being made more favorably than the *general* experience of the protesting company.[66] Similarly, agencies have the right to look at the contractor's performance on contracts other than those similar to the one for which the past performance is being evaluated, and can, in fact, look to see how a firm has carried out all of its contractual obligations, as that provides the agency with a prediction of whether or not the contractor will satisfactorily perform the new contract.[67] A smaller dollar value does not render the previous contract performance irrelevant for past performance purposes.[68] Agencies may also consider negative past performance comments even though those comments have not been documented contemporaneously with the occurrence of the past performance.[69]

---

[65] Comp. Gen. Dec. B-289341, 2002 CPD ¶ 17.

[66] *M&W Construction Corporation*, Comp. Gen. Dec. B-288649.2, 2002 CPD ¶ 30.

[67] *The Standard Register Company*, Comp. Gen. Dec. B-289579, 2002 CPD ¶ 54.

[68] *Dan River, Inc.*, Comp. Gen. Dec. B-289613, 2002 CPD ¶ 80.

[69] *Kathpal Technologies, Inc.*, Comp. Gen. Dec. B-291637.2, 2003 CPD ¶ 6.

4.10 Past Performance Evaluation Procedures

As part of the overall evaluation process for a current procurement, the procuring agency should confirm the accuracy of any prospective offeror's past contract information and assign a performance risk rating. Final past performance ratings may be reflected in a color, adjective rating, a number, or some other means, depending on the particular agency policy for indicating the relative ranking of offerors. In a prospective contractor's performance risk assessment, the number and severity of problems in its overall work record should be considered, as should demonstrated effectiveness of corrective action taken. In instances where good or poor performance is noted, it should be related to a specific solicitation requirement. When a prospective contractor's past performance reflects problems, the procuring agency must evaluate the extent to which the government played a part in that poor performance. Naturally, the procuring activity should look for the areas of performance that are most critical to the procurement and seek instances of excellent or exceptional performance by contractors in related areas on previous procurements.

When a procuring activity is drafting past performance evaluation criteria, the Office of Federal Procurement Policy has provided the following guidance for drafting past performance evaluation factors:

(1) *Use Past Performance as a Distinct Factor.* The past performance factor should be distinct and identifiable, in order to reduce the chances of its impact being lost within other factors and to ease the evaluation process. However, if integrating past performance with other noncost/price factors provides a more meaningful picture, each agency should use its own discretion. The key is to not dilute the importance or impact of past performance when determining the best-value contractor.

(2) *Choose Past Performance Subfactors Wisely.* Tailor the subfactors to match the requirement and to capture the key performance criteria in the statement of work. Carefully consider whether subfactors add value to the overall assessment, warrant the additional time to evaluate, and enhance the discrimination among the competing proposals.

a. *Quality of Product or Service.* The offeror will be evaluated on compliance with previous contract requirements, accuracy of reports, and technical excellence, to include quality awards/certificates.

b. *Timeliness of Performance.* The offeror will be evaluated on meeting milestones, reliability, responsiveness to technical direction, deliverables completed on time, and adherence to contract schedules, including contract administration.

c. *Cost Control.* The offeror will be evaluated on the ability to perform within or below budget; use of cost efficiencies; relationship of negotiated costs to actuals; submission of reasonably priced change proposals; and providing current, accurate, and complete billing timely.

d. *Business Relations.* The offeror will be evaluated on the ability to provide effective management, meet subcontractor and SDB [Small Disadvantaged Business] goals, cooperative and proactive behavior with the technical representative(s) and contracting officer, flexibility, responsiveness to inquires, problem resolution, and customer satisfaction. The offeror will be evaluated on satisfaction of the technical monitors with the overall performance, and final product and services. Evaluation of past performance will be based on consideration of all relevant factors and circumstances. It will include a determination of the offeror's commitment to customer satisfaction and will include conclusions of informed judgment. However, the basis for the conclusions of judgment should be substantially documented.

(3) *Subcontractor, and Teaming, and Joint Venture Partner's Past Performance.* For the purpose of evaluation of past performance information, offerors shall be defined as business arrangements and relationships such as joint ventures, teaming partners, and major subcontractors. Each firm in the business arrangement will be evaluated on its performance under existing and prior contracts for similar products or services.[70]

Procuring activities using the guidance set forth above in evaluating the past performance of prospective contractors should first determine how well a prospective contractor has performed and how relevant that performance is to the instant procurement. That final rating is then used along with other rated evaluation factors, such as price, in a comparative assessment to ascertain the most highly rated offeror. That offeror is the one most likely to be awarded the contract. If the procuring activity identifies negative findings that translate to high performance risk ratings, the agency should determine the extent to which the government may have played a part or contributed to the negative finding and the extent of that contribution. Finally, procuring activities are required by the Office of Federal Procurement policy to be cautious not to downgrade or penalize offerors "for the judicious use of the contract claims process."[71]

4.11 Challenges to Past Performance Evaluations

FAR 42.1503 provides that contractors have the opportunity to respond to performance evaluations after the contracting officer has signed the final assessment. The initial assessment of the contractor's performance is made by the program and contracting office and is typically signed by the program office person most familiar with the contractor's performance. The contracting officer initials the initial assessment and signs the final assessment. Once the final assessment has been signed, it should be sent to the contractor for the contractor's comments. The contractor has at least 30 days to respond, and the contracting officer may extend the response time on an as-needed basis. The contracting officer is encouraged to call the contractor and initiate discussions on the performance assessment, even if the contractor fails to respond by the established deadline. If the contractor fails to respond at all, then the government's comments will stand alone. On the other hand, if the contractor provides a rebuttal for a part of or all of the ratings, then the contracting officer and

---

[70] Best Practices for Collecting and Using Current and Past Performance Information, Office of Federal Procurement Policy, Office of Management & Budget, Executive Office of the President, May 2000, pp. 19-20.

[71] *Id.* p. 21.

lead assessor must work with the contractor to see if an agreement can be reached on the contractor's ratings. When the contracting officer and lead assessor meet with the contractor to ascertain whether or not an agreement on the ratings can be reached, these meetings should be face to face. If no agreement can be reached, the contractor may seek review at least one level above the contracting officer.

Any rebuttal statements provided by the contractor and agency review thereof must be attached to the performance evaluation and provided to any acquisition officials evaluating the contractor for future contracts. Contracting officers are required to send a copy of the government's assessment to the contractor once it is complete, and in no event later than the point in time when the assessment is input into any automated Past Performance Information System (PPIS). Any interim assessment should be retained until the completion of the contract and included as part of the final assessment in the contract file, but not entered in the PPIS. Finally, no assessments may be retained in any PPIS longer than three years after completion of contract performance. Any assessment storage system should provide an individual contractor access to only its own assessments.

Other than discussed above, challenges to a contractor's past performance are normally in the context of either challenges following the government's terminating a contract for default based upon a contractor's unacceptable performance, or alleged failures of the government to comply with the CFR, FAR, and/or agency regulations regarding use of past performance information in the evaluation of bids (*See* **Section 4.9** *supra*).[72] See also *In the matter of Aerospace Design & Fabrication, Inc.*[73]

However, neither the boards nor the courts have jurisdiction under the Contract Disputes Act (41 U.S.C. §§ 601-613) to hear an appeal by a contractor contesting only its final performance evaluation under a government contract. As stated by the Armed Services Board of Contract Appeals (ASBCA) in *TLT Construction Corp*, wherein TLT sought to "appeal the decision to issue a final unsatisfactory performance rating, . . . [a] performance evaluation under a contract is an administrative matter not a Government claim, and a contractor's request that a contracting officer change an evaluation is not a contractor claim."[74]

4.12   CONTRACTOR BID MISTAKES

Bid mistakes are a fairly common occurrence in the rush of competitive bidding situations. Contractors do not work under ideal conditions in the hurry to meet the deadline for submitting bids. Most courts recognize that honest, sincere people, even in the exercise of ordinary care, can make mistakes of such a fundamental character that holding the contractor to the bid would be fundamentally unfair.[75]

---

[72] *Widnall v. B3H Corp; Grumman Data Systems Corporation v. Dalton; TRW Inc. v. Unisys Corp.*, *supra* note 56.

[73] Comp. Gen. Dec. B-278896.3, 98-1 CPD ¶ 139.

[74] *TLT Construction Corp.*, ASBCA 53,769, 02-2 BCA ¶ 31,969.

[75] *Kenneth E. Curran, Inc. v. State*, 215 A.2d 702 (N.H. 1965).

The rationale behind allowing a contractor to withdraw an erroneous bid lies in the principle that, in most cases where performance has not yet commenced, the owner can be returned to the status quo, and will suffer no injury if withdrawal of the bid is permitted. The mere fact that the owner will have to accept a bid at a higher price generally is not viewed as the type of "injury" that would justify holding the contractor to its mistaken bid. If the contractor is low due only to a mistake, the owner would get an unearned windfall if it could force the contractor to perform at the mistakenly low price.[76]

4.13 Elements for Relief from Bid Mistake

Despite the general availability of equitable relief, not every bid mistake will entitle a contractor to retract its bid. To justify the court's intervention, a contractor generally must satisfy the following criteria:

(1) The mistake is of such consequence that enforcement would be unconscionable;

(2) The mistake must relate to the substance of the consideration, that is, a "material" feature;

(3) The mistake must have occurred regardless of the exercise of ordinary care; and

(4) It must be possible to place the other party in status quo.[77]

This test has been adopted in a number of cases.[78] For example, the Arizona Court of Appeals held, in *Marana Unified School District No. 6 v. Aetna Casualty & Surety Co.*,[79] that a contractor would be allowed to withdraw its bid containing a bid mistake in excess of $300,000 without forfeiting its bid bond because the mistake: (1) was large; (2) related to a material matter; (3) resulted from an honest mathematical error; and (4) did not seriously prejudice the owner.

Other cases suggest a fifth requirement: timely notice. When there has been a unilateral mistake, prompt notification to the other party concerning the error may be crucial in determining whether the contractor will be allowed to withdraw its bid.[80] Relief from a bid mistake is most easily obtained where notification of the mistake is given before the bid has been accepted.[81]

Even if award has already been made, relief may be available if the contractor acts promptly. In *School District of Scottsbluff v. Olson Construction Co.*,[82] a public owner

[76] *M.F. Kemper Constr. Co. v. City of Los Angeles*, 235 P.2d 7 (Cal. 1951).

[77] *Kenneth E. Curran, supra* note 75.

[78] *Dick Corp. v. Associated Elec. Coop., Inc.*, 475 F. Supp. 15 (W.D. Mo. 1979); *Clinton County Dep't of Pub. Works v. American Bank & Trust Co.*, 268 N.W.2d 367 (Mich. Ct. App. 1978), *rev'd on other grounds*, 276 N.W.2d 7 (Mich. 1979); *Puget Sound Painters, Inc. v. State*, 278 P.2d 302 (Wash. 1954).

[79] 696 P.2d 711 (Ariz. Ct. App. 1984).

[80] *M. F. Kemper Constr. Co., supra* note 76.

[81] *Clinton County Dep't of Pub. Works, supra* note 78.

[82] 45 N.W.2d 164 (Neb. 1950).

sued a contractor and its bonding company because the contractor refused to enter into a school facilities contract. The contractor had submitted a bid of $177,000, and its bid had been accepted and the award made. The only other bid was $203,700. When the contractor's vice president learned of the discrepancy in the two bids, he immediately suspected an error. He examined the estimate sheets and found that a clerk, though experienced in preparing bids, had inadvertently entered an amount of $2,628 instead of $26,289 for the structural steel, resulting in an error of approximately $23,000. The owner was notified at once of the error, but insisted on compliance with the bid. Only four days had elapsed between the bid opening and notification of the mistake.

The court held that the contractor was entitled to retract the bid. Although the contractor's bid had been accepted and the contract awarded to it, the contract had not been signed and performance had not started.

If a contractor waits too long to request relief, courts may be reluctant to allow the mistake to be corrected. For example, a contractor who made a $317,000 arithmetical error in its $15.8 million Florida state highway bid was not entitled to an increase in its contract price, despite the Florida Department of Transportation's knowledge of a possible error. The contractor did not sue for correction of the mistake until 21 months after bid opening, with the project three-quarters complete.[83]

Courts regularly emphasize the requirement that the bid mistake must not have resulted from any culpable negligence on the part of the contractor.[84] The burden is placed on the contractor to establish the absence of such negligence in bid preparation.[85] In addition, courts often make a distinction between (1) errors of a mathematical, typographical, or clerical nature (e.g., incorrect transposition of figures to the bid sheet); and (2) errors in judgment (e.g., incorrectly estimating the amount of steel required for the project). Generally, relief will be available in the courts for clerical errors, but not for errors in judgment.[86]

An example of the application of this concept is found in a Comptroller General decision, *Matter of Continental Heller Corp.*[87] Continental Heller submitted the apparent low bid on a contract for construction of a Navy training building. Prior to contract award, Continental Heller notified the Navy it had made a mistake in its bid by including only $50,000 for profit rather than the intended $500,000. In support of its claim, Continental Heller submitted, among other things, its bid preparation worksheets showing the $500,000. The Comptroller General sustained Continental Heller's bid protest because its bid preparation documents provided clear and convincing evidence of a clerical error and the specific amount of the intended bid. Continental Heller was thus allowed to receive the contract at the corrected price.

[83] *Department of Trans. v. Ronlee, Inc.*, 518 So.2d 1326 (Fla. Dist. Ct. App. 1987). *See also Chris Berg, Inc. v. United States*, 426 F.2d 314 (Ct. Cl. 1970); *Dick Corp., supra* note 78; *C.N. Monroe Mfg. Co. v. United States*, 143 F. Supp. 449 (E.D. Mich. 1956).

[84] *See Kenneth E. Curran, supra* note 75; *Liebherr Crane Corp. v. United States*, 810 F.2d 1153 (Fed. Cir. 1987).

[85] *See, e.g., State Bd. of Control v. Clutter Constr. Corp.*, 139 So. 2d 153 (Fla. Dist. Ct. App. 1962); *Ex parte Perusini Constr. Co.*, 7 So. 2d 576 (Ala. 1942).

[86] *Balaban-Gordon Co., Inc. v. Brighton Sewer Dist.*, 342 N.Y.S.2d 435 (App. Div. 1973).

[87] Comp. Gen. No. B-230559, 88-1 CPD ¶ 571.

A contractor that realizes prior to award that the bid contains a material error should take certain steps to safeguard its chances of obtaining relief. First, the contractor should immediately notify the owner or public contracting official awarding the contract of the error, preferably in writing; but if time will not permit, then orally, followed promptly by a written request for modification or withdrawal with documentation supporting the assertion of a mistake.[88]

Once the owner has been notified, an informal conference should be requested to discuss the bid mistake, at which time the contractor needs to present evidence supporting its request for modification and withdrawal. This evidence should include statements (preferably affidavits) explaining the mistake, copies of the bid, original worksheets, subcontractor quotations, published price lists, and any other data used in preparing the bid that establishes (1) the existence of the error, (2) the manner in which it occurred, and (3) the intended bid. The contractor should gather this information as quickly as possible and secure it until the presentation to the owner.[89]

If the error is detected after award, the contractor faces greater difficulty in modifying or withdrawing its bid. An error discovered after award should be brought to the owner's attention immediately in the same manner as if discovered prior to award. However, the likelihood of successfully reforming the bid is much more remote.[90]

Some states have enacted laws regarding the withdrawal of bids containing mistakes. For example, in Georgia, a bid on a public project (other than a Georgia Department of Transportation project) containing a bid mistake may be withdrawn after bid opening, without forfeiture of the bid bond if: (1) the bidder has made an appreciable error in the calculation of the bid that can be documented by clear and convincing evidence; (2) such errors can be clearly shown by objective evidence drawn from inspection of the original work papers or other materials used in preparing the bid; (3) the bidder serves written notice on the public entity that invited the proposals prior to award of the contract and not later than 48 hours after the opening of bids, excluding Saturdays, Sundays, and legal holidays; (4) the bid was submitted in good faith and the mistake was due to calculation or clerical error, an inadvertent omission, or a typographical error, as opposed to an error in judgment; and (5) the withdrawal of the bid will not result in undue prejudice to the public entity or other bidders by placing them in a materially worse position than if the bid had never been submitted.[91] If the bid is withdrawn, the other bids will be considered as if the withdrawn bid had not been submitted.[92] If the project is relet for bids after the bid is withdrawn, the withdrawing bidder cannot submit a bid on the resolicitation, and the withdrawing bidder cannot supply any material or labor to the project for compensation and cannot subcontract work on that project.[93]

---

[88] 38 Comp. Gen. 218 (1958); Comp. Gen. Dec. B-167649 (3 Oct. 1969).

[89] *Matter of Continental Heller Corp.*, *supra* note 87.

[90] *Edgemont Constr. Co.*, ASBCA No. 23794, 80-2 BCA ¶ 14,468.

[91] O.C.G.A. § 36-91-52; *see also* O.C.G.A. § 32-2-69.

[92] O.C.G.A. § 36-91-52(c).

[93] O.C.G.A. § 36-91-52(c)-(d).

In private contracting, a contractor has no vested right to withdraw an erroneous bid. However, a contractor's right to retract its bid, when equitable criteria are met, is not affected by a statutory prohibition or restriction against withdrawal of public bids. Similarly, when equitable conditions are satisfied, a bidder may be entitled to recover its bid deposit.[94]

4.14   Owner's Duty If Bid Mistake Is Suspected

The owner may also have a duty to notify the contractor that there may be an error in the bid if the circumstances are sufficient to place the owner on notice of a possible error. For example, in *Hudson Structural Steel Co. v. Smith & Rumery Co.*,[95] a contractor's bid for steel roof framing was so much less than the actual cost of furnishing framing for two buildings that the owner, who was also an experienced contractor, knew immediately that the bidder had interpreted the specifications as covering only one building. The *Hudson* court found the facts sufficient to have put the owner on notice, and to impose upon it the additional duty to inform the contractor of the suspected bid mistake. As a general rule, the existence of a wide range between the low bid price and the other bid prices is generally sufficient to put the recipient of the bid on notice of a possible error. Similarly, a substantial variation in the bid from the owner's estimate of the approximate cost can also put the owner on notice of a possible error.[96]

4.15   Withdrawal versus Reformation of Bid Mistake

While the right to withdraw a mistaken bid is recognized under most states' laws, the right to correct is often not available. The courts of some states have recognized that an erroneous bid should be reformed where the bid was the lowest bid before and after reformation.[97] Other courts have held that a bid is properly rescinded where the bidder makes a unilateral mistake.[98]

The right to withdraw and the opportunity to correct a mistaken bid are more well established under federal law. Section 14.407 of the Federal Acquisition Regulation (FAR) describes in detail the procedures for dealing with bid mistakes and the circumstances in which a bid may be withdrawn or corrected. To guard against mistakes, the contracting officer must review all bids and must notify a bidder if an apparent mistake is found or if there is a reason to believe there is a mistake.[99]

---

[94] *See Rushlight Automatic Sprinkler Co. v. Portland*, 219 P.2d 732 (Or. 1950).

[95] 85 A. 384 (Me. 1912).

[96] *See, e.g., Moffett, Hodgkins & Clark Co. v. City of Rochester*, 178 U.S. 373 (1899); Comp. Gen. Dec. B-170190 (July 21, 1970).

[97] *Chris Berg, Inc.*, *supra* note 83; *Dick Corp.*, *supra* note 78; *C.N. Monroe Mfg. Co.*, *supra* note 83.

[98] *See Clinton County Dep't of Pub. Works*, *supra* note 78; *Wil-Fred's, Inc. v. Metropolitan Sanitary Dist. of Greater Chicago*, 372 N.E.2d 946 (Ill. App. Ct. 1978); *Baltimore County v. John K. Ruff, Inc.*, 375 A.2d 237 (Md. 1977).

[99] FAR § 14.407-1; 48 C.F.R. § 14.407-1; *BCM Corp. v. United States*, 2 Cl. Ct. 602 (1983).

Even if the bidder verifies the accuracy of its bid, relief for mistake may still be allowed where the government's request for verification does not alert the bidder to the basis for the government's belief that the bid is erroneous.[100] If a contractor's mistake is known or should have been known by the contracting officer, then award of a contract is tantamount to bad faith and constitutes overreaching. Under such circumstances, relief may be appropriate if the contracting officer does not properly verify the contractor's price.[101]

In federal procurement, bidders are permitted to alter their bids to correct mistakes so the government can enjoy the cost benefits of a downward correction.[102] If a downward correction would displace the low bid, the bidder must present clear and convincing evidence, ascertainable substantially from the invitation and the bid itself,[103] that establishes both the existence of the mistake and the dollar amount of the bid actually intended by the contractor.

Where the low bidder seeks to increase its bid and still remain low, it must also present clear and convincing evidence of the mistake and its actual intended bid. However, the evidence it presents is not limited to the solicitation and the bid itself, and can include statements, a file copy of the bid, original worksheets, subcontractor quotations, and published price lists.[104] However, even if there is evidence to support such a correction, the correction may be disallowed if it brings the low bidder too close to the second low bidder.

Finally, federal statutes and regulation expressly provide for relief from mistakes after award. The Contract Disputes Act of 1978 authorizes contracting officers and the boards of contract appeals to grant relief to contractors that allege a mistake in bid after award. The contractor's claim for relief is handled by the contracting officer like any other claim.[105] Under the regulations, the contracting officer has the authority to rescind a contract or to modify the contract by deleting the item involved in the mistake or increasing the price.

As noted previously, some state laws permit the withdrawal of bids in limited circumstances, although the reformation of bids after bid opening is rarely allowed.[106]

4.16 BID PROTESTS

The federal government, as well as virtually all other governmental entities, primarily uses either sealed bidding or competitive best-value proposals in the award of

---

[100] *P. T. Service Co.*, GSBCA No. 7589, 85-3 BCA ¶ 18,430.

[101] *Chemtronics, Inc.*, ASBCA No. 30883, 88-2 BCA ¶ 20,534.

[102] FAR § 14.407-3; 48 C.F.R. § 14.407-3; *P K Contractors, Inc.*, Comp. Gen. Dec. B-205482, 82-1 CPD ¶ 368.

[103] FAR § 14.407-3; 48 C.F.R. § 14.407-3.

[104] FAR § 14.407-3(g)(2); 48 C.F.R. § 14.407-3(g)(2); *Coleman Indus. Constr. Co.*, Comp. Gen. Dec. B-207682, 82-2 CPD ¶ 213.

[105] *See* FAR § 14.407-4; 48 C.F.R. § 14.407-4.

[106] *See* notes 92 and 93.

public construction contracts. The historical preference for the competitive bid system is rooted in the reasoning that sealed bids, independently submitted, result in the lowest cost to the owner and best protect the public interest. The issue of bid protests arises almost exclusively in connection with sealed bids (IFBs) or competitive proposals (RFPs)—predominantly at the federal level, but to an increasing degree at the state and local government levels. In bidding or proposing on projects for public owners, contractors must rely not only upon their own evaluation of the invitation for bids, but also on a proper application of competitive bidding procedures by the owner. Increased competition for contracts, combined with economic cycles that reduce the total volume of contracts available for bidding, have forced both contractors and their attorneys to become knowledgeable about the rules governing competitive procurements, the enforcement of rules governing sealed bids or competitive proposals, and related bid protest rules and regulations. Whether the procurement is conducted using sealed bids or competitive proposals, challenges to the public agency's conduct of a particular procurement action are labeled "bid protests."

The nature and degree of formality of competitive procurement procedures varies greatly among states and localities and with the type of owner involved. However, some general guidelines, primarily developed from federal competitive bidding procedures, are applicable to many situations. Increased use of competitive bidding at state and local levels has resulted in the development of the American Bar Association Model Procurement Code for state and local government. This proposed Code attempts to further standardize competitive bid procedures for public construction contract awards.

The guiding principle in bid protests is quick action, since most regulations specify that such action must be taken within a few days. In addition, under some circumstances, the contracting authority may award the contract while the protest is still pending. Once the award is made, the reviewing body can be expected to be reluctant to reverse the decision of the awarding authority. Thus, obtaining a favorable ruling on the merits of a bid protest may prove to be an empty victory if the contract itself has already been awarded to another bidder.

4.17   Protests on Federal Government Contracts

When a contractor that has submitted a bid or proposal on a public contract believes that the rules and regulations applicable to the particular procurement have not been followed, it may want to protest award of the contract. The protesting contractor generally will base the protest on the successful offeror's or bidder's failure to meet one or more of the requirements previously discussed: lowest bid, responsibility, and responsiveness to the solicitation, or the agency's failure to evaluate the offer consistent with the evaluation criteria in the solicitation.

In the federal contract arena, a protester has many options for filing a bid protest. A bid protest may be filed with:

(1) The contracting agency responsible for the procurement;
(2) The Comptroller General of the Government Accountability Office, formerly the General Accounting Office (GAO); and
(3) The United States Court of Federal Claims.

4.18   Protests before or after Receipt of Bids or Offers

A disappointed bidder may initially submit a bid protest to the agency that is involved in the procurement. Federal regulations do not discuss in detail the procedures for agency protests, but some general guidelines are discussed at FAR Subpart 33.1.

Agency protests may be filed before or after contract award by a bidder/offeror or a prospective bidder/offer if its direct economic interest is affected by the award.[107] The protester must submit the protest in writing.[108] The agency receiving the protest must respond using a method that provides evidence of receipt.[109]

The interested parties and agency are to use their best efforts through open and frank discussion to try to resolve concerns raised by an interested party before the submission of a protest.[110] However, there are time limits for agency protests. Protests based on alleged apparent improprieties in the solicitation shall be filed before bid opening or the closing date for the receipt of proposals.[111] In all other cases, protests are to be filed not later than 10 days after the basis for the protest is known or should have been known, whichever is earlier.[112] An agency can consider an untimely protest if the agency determines that the protest raises issues significant to the agency's acquisition system.[113] (In general, the protester should submit a protest as soon as it becomes aware of the basis for the protest, because the likelihood of success declines significantly once the award has been made.)

4.19   Protests to the Contracting Agency

Protests to the agency must be addressed to the contracting officer or other official designated to receive protests.[114] It is probably advisable to submit a protest at a level within the contracting agency or contracting entity higher than the contracting officer if allowed by the agency's rules, because decisions of the contracting officer may be the very decisions in question. The agency is required to provide a procedural mechanism for the protester to request an independent review above the contracting officer level, either as an initial review of the protest or as an appeal from the contracting officer's decision.[115]

The protest needs to be concise and logically presented, and needs to include the following: (1) the name, address, and fax and telephone numbers of the protester; (2) the solicitation or contract number; (3) a detailed statement of the legal and factual grounds for the protest, including a description of the resulting prejudice to the protester; (4) copies of relevant documents; (5) a request for ruling by the agency;

---

[107] FAR § 33.101; 48 C.F.R. § 33.101.

[108] *Id.*

[109] FAR § 33.103(h); 48 C.F.R. § 33.103(h).

[110] FAR § 33.103(b); 48 C.F.R. 33.103(b).

[111] FAR § 33.103(e); 48 C.F.R. § 33.103(e).

[112] *Id.*

[113] *Id.*

[114] FAR § 33.103(d)(3); 48 C.F.R. § 33.103(d)(3).

[115] FAR § 33.103(d)(4); 48 C.F.R. § 33.103(d)(4).

(6) a statement of the form of relief requested; (7) all information establishing that the protester is an interested party; and (8) all information establishing the timeliness of the protest.[116]

Upon receipt of a protest before award, the contract may not be awarded, pending agency resolution of the protest, unless the award is justified in writing for urgent and compelling reasons or determined in writing to be in the government's best interest.[117] The justification must be approved at a level above the contracting officer.[118] If the award is withheld pending agency resolution of the protest, the contracting officer is to notify the other bidders/offerors whose bids or offers may become eligible for award and, if appropriate, request that the bidders or offerors extend the time for acceptance.[119] If an extension cannot be obtained, the agency should consider proceeding with the award.[120] Upon receipt of a protest within 10 days after contract award or within five days after a debriefing date offered to the protester under a timely debriefing request (whichever is later), the contracting officer shall immediately suspend performance pending resolution of the protest by the agency, including any review at a higher agency level, unless continued performance is justified, in writing, for urgent and compelling reasons, or is determined, in writing, to be in the government's best interests.[121] That justification or determination must be approved at a level above the contracting officer, or by another official, pursuant to agency procedures.[122] An agency protest will not extend the time for obtaining a stay from the GAO; agencies must include in their protest procedures a voluntary suspension period when the agency protest is denied and the protester subsequently protests to the GAO.[123] Agencies are to use their best efforts to resolve protests within 35 days after the protest is filed.[124]

Bidders are often reluctant to protest to the contracting agency because the agency is being asked to judge the actions of its own employees. Protests to the GAO or in the United States Court of Federal Claims provide more of an opportunity for a "neutral, third-party review" of the agency's actions and positions. Furthermore, agency protests are likely to be less successful than protests to the GAO if the basis for the protest involves an unusual issue or one that is not a clear violation of applicable laws or regulations. The contracting agency is likely to ratify the actions of its employees if there is any basis for such actions.

However, there are circumstances in which an agency protest may be advantageous to a bidder. An agency protest may be less costly and time-consuming if the

---

[116] FAR § 33.103(d)(2); 48 C.F.R. § 33.103(d)(2).

[117] FAR § 33.103(f)(1); 48 C.F.R. § 33.103(f)(1).

[118] *Id.*

[119] FAR § 33.103(f)(2); 48 C.F.R. § 33.103(f)(2).

[120] *Id.*

[121] FAR § 33.103(f)(3); 48 C.F.R. § 33.103(f)(3).

[122] *Id.*

[123] FAR § 33.103(f)(4); 48 C.F.R. § 33.103(f)(4).

[124] FAR § 33.103(g); 48 C.F.R. § 33.103(g).

protest is unquestionably valid, because the agency may act quickly to correct any deficiency so as not to delay the commencement of work on the particular project.

Additionally, agency protests may be useful where the protest is filed well before bids are to be received. In such a situation, the protester may have the opportunity to attempt to obtain a quick decision from the contracting agency; and, if that decision is adverse to the protester's position, the protester may then seek relief in another forum, such as the GAO. However, the protester needs to be mindful that if the agency protest is unsuccessful, then the protester has 10 days from the actual or constructive knowledge of the initial agency decision to file a protest to the GAO.[125]

4.20   Protests to the Comptroller General (GAO)

The following is a summary of the important initial time constraints and factors to consider in filing a protest with the GAO. Keep in mind that these regulations are subject to change (including the initial deadline for filing a protest) and the current bid protest regulations as published in the Federal Register and the Code of Federal Regulations must be followed to assure a valid protest.[126]

Any "interested party" may file a protest with the GAO alleging an irregularity in the solicitation or award of a federal government contract to which a federal agency is a party. An "interested party" is an actual or prospective bidder or offeror whose direct economic interest would be affected by the award of a contract or by the failure to award a contract.[127] In several cases, protesters who did not even submit offers were, nevertheless, held to be interested parties. For example, protesters precluded from submitting a proposal because of short response time and restrictive specifications,[128] or otherwise denied the opportunity to compete,[129] have been allowed standing to protest.[130]

Protests based upon alleged improprieties in a solicitation that are apparent prior to bid opening must be filed prior to bid opening or the time set for receipt of initial proposals.[131] As a result, the Comptroller General has held that protests regarding improprieties that were apparent prior to bid opening are untimely even if submitted with a bid[132] or proposal.[133] Generally, other protests must be filed not later than 10

---

[125] 4 C.F.R. § 21.4(a)(3); FAR § 33.103(d)(4); 48 C.F.R. § 33.103(d)(4).

[126] *See* 4 C.F.R. § 21.0, *et seq.*; *see also* 31 U.S.C. § 3553.

[127] 4 C.F.R. § 21.0(a).

[128] *Vicksburg Fed. Bldg. Ltd. Partnership*, Comp. Gen. Dec. B-230660, 88-1 CPD 515.

[129] *Afftrex, Ltd.*, Comp. Gen. Dec. B-231033, 88-2 CPD ¶ 143; *REL*, Comp. Gen. Dec. B-228155, 88-1 CPD ¶ 25.

[130] Until August 1996, the General Services Board of Contract Appeals (GSBCA) had jurisdiction with the GAO to hear and decide protests involving procurements under the Brooks Act (40 U.S.C. § 759) for automatic data processing equipment (ADPE) software, maintenance services, and supplies. The GSBCA's jurisdiction for such protests was eliminated in 1996 and the GAO now has jurisdiction over such protests. 40 U.S.C. § 759, *et seq.*

[131] 4 C.F.R. § 21.2 (a)(1).

[132] *Fredrico Enter., Inc.*, Comp. Gen. Dec. B-230724.2, 88-1 CPD ¶ 450.

[133] *Darome Connection*, Comp. Gen. Dec. B-230629, 88-1 CPD ¶ 461.

calendar days after the basis of the protest is known or should have been known, whichever is earlier, except protests challenging a procurement conducted on the basis of competitive proposals under which a debriefing is requested and, once requested, is then required. If the debriefing is required and the basis for the protest is known before or as a result of the debriefing, the protest must be filed after the debriefing but within 10 calendar days of the debriefing.[134] The GAO must notify the contracting agency of the protest within one working day after receipt of a protest.[135] Under most circumstances, a contracting agency cannot award a contract after the agency has received notice of the protest and while the protest is pending.[136] The head of an agency may authorize award of a contract notwithstanding a protest upon a finding that (1) urgent and compelling circumstances that significantly affect the interests of the United States will not permit waiting for the Comptroller General's decision (as long as the award was otherwise likely to occur within 30 days after the making of the finding), and (2) after the Comptroller General is advised of the finding.[137]

If a protest is appropriate and is filed, within 10 calendar days after the award (or five calendar days after the date offered for a required debriefing), and the agency is notified of the protest, the contracting officer may not authorize performance to begin while the protest is pending, or the contracting officer shall immediately direct the contractor to cease performance and suspend related activities.[138] The head of the contracting agency can authorize performance of the contract notwithstanding the protest (1) upon a written finding that the performance is in the best interest of the United States, or urgent and compelling circumstances that significantly affect the United States will not permit waiting for the Comptroller General's decision, and (2) after the Comptroller General has been notified of the finding.[139]

Under 4 C.F.R. § 21.1(b), a protest must be in writing and addressed to General Counsel, Government Accountability Office, 441 G Street, NW, Washington, D.C. 20548, Attention: Procurement Law Control Group. The protest must include the name, address, and telephone number of the protester and be signed by the protester or its representative. It must also identify the contracting activity and the solicitation and/or contract number and include a detailed statement of the legal and factual grounds of the protest, including copies of all relevant documents. Finally, the protest must set out all information establishing that the protester is an interested party, set out the information establishing the timeliness of the protest, specifically request a ruling by the Comptroller General, and state the form of relief requested.[140]

A protest shall not be deemed filed unless it is actually received by the GAO within the time for filing and is accompanied by a certificate that a copy of the protest, together with relevant documents not issued by the contracting agency, was

[134] 4 C.F.R. §§ 21.0(e) and 21.2(a)(2).

[135] 4 C.F.R. § 21.3(a).

[136] 4 C.F.R. § 21.6 and 31 U.S.C. § 3553(c)(1).

[137] 31 U.S.C. § 3553(c)(2) and (3).

[138] 31 U.S.C. § 3553(d)(3)(A).

[139] 31 U.S.C. § 3553(d)(3)(C).

[140] 4 C.F.R. § 21.1 (c).

concurrently served upon the contracting agency and the contracting activity (a contracting activity is the subelement of the contracting agency that actually issued the solicitation and/or contract).[141] No formal briefs or other technical forms of pleadings are required.[142]

The Comptroller General has held that a protest received in the GAO's Office of Congressional Relations within the time required for protests to the GAO (but four days before receipt in the GAO's Document Control Section) was timely filed.[143] The Comptroller General said the protest was timely since it was actually received by the GAO in accordance with GAO regulations. However, it is highly advisable to make sure your protest is timely delivered to the Procurement Law Control Group.

The GAO's regulations permit consideration of untimely protests raising significant issues. For example, the Comptroller General invoked its discretion to consider an untimely protest under the "significant issue" exception in *Reliable Trash Service Co.*,[144] since the record clearly indicated that bids could not have been evaluated on a common basis. In *Associated Professional Enterprises, Inc.*,[145] however, the Comptroller General held that the "good cause" exception to the timeliness rule will be limited in future cases to circumstances in which a compelling reason beyond the protester's control prevents timely filing.

The protest may initially be filed with the contracting agency and a subsequent protest to the GAO may be filed within 10 calendar days of actual or constructive knowledge of initial adverse agency action (unless the contracting agency imposes a more stringent time for filing).[146]

In most cases, the protested agency is to issue an agency report regarding the bases for the protest within 30 days of telephone notice of the protest to the agency from the GAO.[147] The protester may submit comments to the GAO on the agency report within 10 calendar days of receipt of the report, with a copy to the agency and other participating parties.[148]

The Comptroller General is required to render a decision within 100 days after the protest is filed.[149] If the Comptroller General finds that the protested solicitation, termination of the contract, proposed award, or award does not comply with statute or regulation, it can direct the agency to refrain from exercising options under the contract, terminate the contract, recompete the contract, issue a new solicitation, award a contract consistent with the law, or make other recommendations as deemed appropriate.[150] If the Comptroller General determines that applicable statutes or

---

[141] 4 C.F.R. §§ 21.0(g) and 21.1(e).

[142] 4 C.F.R. § 21.1(f).

[143] *McLaughlin Enter., Inc.*, Comp. Gen. Dec. B-229521, 88-1 CPD ¶ 232.

[144] Comp. Gen. Dec. B-234367, 89-1 CPD ¶ 535.

[145] Comp. Gen. Dec. B-235066.2, 89-1 CPD ¶ 480.

[146] 4 C.F.R. § 21.2(a)(3).

[147] 4 C.F.R. § 21.3(c).

[148] 4 C.F.R. § 21.3(i).

[149] 4 C.F.R. § 21.9(a).

[150] 4 C.F.R. § 21.8(a).

regulations have not been followed, it may find the protester entitled to bid preparation costs, protest costs, and reasonable attorneys' fees.[151] However, the Comptroller
General, in *Princeton Gamma-Tech, Inc.,*[152] has held that costs incurred in connection with the agency-level protest cannot be reimbursed under the GAO's rule
permitting reimbursement of costs for a prevailing protester.

Comptroller General decisions are technically advisory only due to separation of
powers considerations.[153] However, the Competition in Contracting Act requires
an agency to provide a full report on any refusal to follow a Comptroller General
decision.[154]

4.21 Bid Protests in Court

One of the most important aspects of bid protests is quick action. From the standpoint of the protester, it is imperative to prevent the award or performance of the
disputed contract to go any further than it has at the time the decision to pursue a
protest is made. The farther along the award and/or performance on the contract, the
less likely that a court will be willing to grant injunctive relief to suspend any further performance.

Often, a contractor will want to obtain a temporary restraining order and injunction to prevent the award to and/or commencement of the contract by another bidder. This is particularly true on state and local projects where award is not
automatically stayed and in federal contracts where the agency has indicated it
intends to award despite the automatic stay regulation[155] or because the agency
claims award and performance is in the agency's best interests and urgent and compelling reasons exist to start performance.

An injunction suspends any further activity on the contact, whether award or performance, while the court or appropriate agency has the opportunity to decide the merits of the protest. Although the automatic stay provisions of the Competition in
Contracting Act diminish the need for injunctive relief in federal government procurements, there will still be situations in which such relief is required. In addition,
although federal courts give substantial deference to Comptroller General decisions,[156]
a protester may want the court involved to review the administrative decision rendered
by the Comptroller General. Most important, court action may provide the only vehicle to pursue a protest beyond "agency level" in state and local procurements.

The U.S. Court of Federal Claims is the appropriate court for the protesting bidder seeking injunctive relief against a federal agency or activity. The Federal Court

---

[151] 4 C.F.R. § 21.6.

[152] Comp. Gen. Dec. B-228052.5, 89-1 CPD ¶ 401.

[153] *Ameron, Inc. v. U.S. Army Corps of Eng'rs*, 809 F.2d 979, 995 (3d Cir. 986), *cert. granted,* 485 U.S.
958, *cert. dismissed,* 488 U.S. 918 (1988).

[154] 31 U.S.C. § 3554(e)(1).

[155] 4 C.F.R. § 21.4(b).

[156] *Honeywell, Inc. v. United States*, 8 FPD ¶ 46 (Fed. Cir. 1989), 31 GC ¶ 135; *Shoals Amer. Indus., Inc. v.
United States*, 877 F.2d 883 (11th Cir. 1989).

Improvement Act of 1982 (FCIA), created the U.S. Claims Court (now the Court of Federal Claims) and Court of Appeals for the Federal Circuit to replace the U.S. Court of Claims. In addition, the FCIA granted the U.S. Claims Court (Court of Federal Claims) "exclusive jurisdiction" to decide preaward federal contract disputes.[157] Previously, only federal district courts had jurisdiction over bid protests. The district courts' jurisdiction was based upon the Scanwell Doctrine, named for the first case in which the federal courts took jurisdiction over a federal bid protest.[158]

Until 2001, federal district courts had concurrent jurisdiction over postaward bid protests.[159] However, as of January 1, 2001, Congress ended the U.S. district courts' concurrent jurisdiction over protests regarding federal government procurements,[160] leaving the U.S. Court of Federal Claims as the exclusive judicial forum for such actions.

The most a contractor can expect in the way of damages in a court action is the cost of bid or proposal preparation, but not anticipated profits.[161] The protester may also recover bid protest costs under the Equal Access to Justice Act.[162] Additionally, a protester can be required to post a bond for security, if a restraining order is issued.[163]

4.22 Bid Protests on State and Local Public Contracts

For state or local projects, absent specific procedures, a bid protest similar to that described above should be delivered to the awarding authority and other involved parties. For example, in connection with federally funded projects at the local level (such as EPA sewage treatment projects), notice of the protest should be sent to the grantor as well as the grantee, usually the local awarding authority. Also, the protestant should consult any pertinent federal statutes or regulations governing protests of federally funded state or local contracts (such as the EPA Construction Grant Regulations for EPA treatment projects).

Thereafter, it is essential to prepare as quickly as possible a comprehensive statement with supporting documentation stating the detailed basis for the protest. This presentation should be submitted to all concerned parties.

In some states, a disappointed bidder may be able to seek bid protest relief on public (state and/or local) contracts through administrative procedures and/or court. Many state and local agencies have administrative protest procedures.[164]

---

[157] 28 U.S.C. § 1491(a)(3).

[158] *Scanwell Lab., Inc. v. Shaffer*, 424 F.2d 859 (D.C. Cir. 1970).

[159] *In re Smith & Wesson, Inc.*, 757 F.2d 431 (1st Cir. 1985); *Coco Bros. v. Pierce*, 741 F.2d 675 (3rd Cir. 1984); *see also American Dist. Tel. v. Department of Energy*, 555 F. Supp. 1244 (D.D.C. 1983).

[160] Pub.L. No. 104-320, 110 Stat. 3870.

[161] *Rockwell Int'l Corp. v. U.S.*, 8 Ct. Cl. 662 (1985); *Heyer Prod. Co. v. U.S.*, 140 F. Supp. 409 (Ct. Cl. 1956).

[162] 28 U.S.C. § 2412(d)(1)(A); *Crux Computer Corp. v. U.S.*, 24 Ct. Cl. 223 (1991).

[163] Fed. R. Civ. P. 65(c).

[164] *See, e.g.,* Georgia Dep't of Admin. Services, Georgia Vendor Manual, Art. III, § 9; City of Atlanta, Procurement and Real Estate Code §§ 5-5111 to 5-5116 (Supp. No. 50, 3-91).

Additionally, judicial relief may be available for disappointed bidders in some states.[165] However, federal courts have been reluctant to entertain bid protests on state or local contracts on the basis of a violation of procedural due process rights under 42 U.S.C. § 1983.[166]

4.23 BID BONDS

In connection with public contracts in particular, agencies frequently require that each bidder provide security with the bid that will guarantee execution of the contract in the event that the bidder is awarded the contract.[167] In some instances a cash deposit is required. More commonly, the security called for is in the form of a "bid bond."[168] These bonds commonly provide that if the contractor does not execute the contract, the surety will be liable to the owner only to the extent of the difference between the contractor's bid and the lowest amount for which the owner may be able, in good faith, to award the contract within a reasonable time. A further limit generally is the penal sum of the bond.[169]

Federal contracts usually require that a bid bond (also known as a "bid deposit") be provided to guarantee contractor performance. As the Court of Claims noted in *Anthony P. Miller, Inc. v. United States*, "[i]t is well established that in the event of a default by a bidder the United States may retain the bid deposit as liquidated damages unless the amount is so large or disproportionate as to constitute a penalty."[170]

States may require bid bonds on their construction contracts as a matter of law or public policy. While not all states have statutory provisions requiring bid bonds, the power of public agencies to require such bonds is not generally dependent upon statute. Thus, it is generally conceded that a municipal corporation or other public agency or body that has been empowered to let a contract, as well as the state itself, may require the contractor to furnish a surety bond, although express statutory authority for such a requirement is lacking.[171]

In addition to requiring bid bonds, some states require posting of separate bonds as part of the process to qualify to conduct business or obtain licenses. These bonds may exist to secure payment of taxes (sales, worker's compensation, etc.) and are distinct from those associated with a particular project's bid bond. The State Law

---

[165] *See, e.g., Amdahl Corp. v. Ga. Dep't of Admin. Servs.*, 398 S.E.2d 540 (Ga. 1990).

[166] *Flint Elec. Membership Corp. v. Whitworth*, 68 F.3d 1309 (11th Cir. 1995), *corrected decision,* 77 F.3d 1321 (11th Cir. 1996).

[167] *See Diamond Int'l Corp.*, Comp. Gen. Dec. B-180426, 74-2 CPD ¶ 139.

[168] *See, e.g., Bolivar Reorganized Sch. Dist. No. 1 v. American Sur. Co.*, 307 S.W.2d 405 (Mo. 1957).

[169] *See Brown v. United States*, 152 F. 964 (2d Cir. 1907); *Bd. of Educ. of Union Free Sch. Dist. No. 3 v. Maryland Casualty Co.*, 98 N.Y.S.2d 865 (App. Div. 1950) (in the context of the difference in cost exceeding the penal sum of the bond).

[170] 161 Ct. Cl. 455, 468 (1963).

[171] *Union Indem. Co. v. State*, 114 So. 415 (Ala. 1927); *Foster v. Kerr & Houston*, 179 A. 297 (Mass. 1907); *Southwestern Portland Cement Co. v. Williams*, 251 P. 380 (N.M. 1926).

Matrix of the Associated General Contractors of America *DocuBuilder* publication contains references to state laws addressing bidding laws, requirements for bid bonds, as well as other bonds, which contractors may be obligated to post in order to conduct business in that jurisdiction.

In addition, a summary of the major provisions of all state laws concerning public bonds may also be found in the *Credit Manual of Commercial Laws*, published by the National Association of Credit Management and updated annually. Although the practice is perhaps more common in connection with public contracts, bids on private contracts are also occasionally required to be accompanied by bid bonds.

The extent of liability under a bid bond is usually a fixed sum specified in the bond or the difference between the bid submitted by the defaulting contractor and the next-lowest bidder or the price at which the owner is forced to contract.[172] For example, in *Board of Education of Community United School District No. 303 v. George S. Walker Plumbing & Heating, Inc.*,[173] summary judgment was awarded the owner for the difference between the lowest bidder's bid and the second bidder's contract price because the lowest bidder, whose bid was accepted, refused to enter into a contract. With respect to the contractor's risks, it should be noted that the surety also received summary judgment against the contractor for indemnification at the same time. Indemnification between the contractor and surety usually arises out of the express obligations in the bond itself. In addition, the master surety agreements executed between contractors and their surety almost invariably provide for similar indemnification of the surety.

Courts have given various treatments to the limit of the surety's liability to the owner pursuant to the bond. In *A. J. Colella, Inc. v. Allegheny County*,[174] the amount of recovery was limited to the penal sum of the bid bond, although the difference between the amount of the bid and the amount at which the county ultimately let a contract greatly exceeded the penalty of the bond.

Other cases have held that the penal amount of the bid bond is, in effect, a liquidated damages provision. Thus, upon failure of the low bidder to enter into a contract, the owner was entitled to recover the penal sum of the bond, even though the difference between the defaulting contractor's bid and the eventual contract price was less.[175]

Several defenses have been argued by a defaulting contractor and its bid bond surety when the contractor has refused to enter into a contract and there has been a call on the bond. Under appropriate facts, the contractor may successfully argue that there has been a material change in the contract upon which the bid was submitted. Such was the case in *Northeastern Construction Co. v. City of Winston-Salem*,[176] when, after bid opening, the municipal authority eliminated approximately 15 percent

---

[172] *Brown v. United States*, 152 F. 964 (2d Cir. 1907).

[173] 282 N.E.2d 268 (Ill. App. Ct. 1972).

[174] 137 A.2d 265 (Pa. 1958).

[175] *See Bellefonte Borough Auth. v. Gateway Equip. & Supply Co.*, 277 A.2d 347 (Pa. 1971); *City of Lake Geneva v. States Improvement Co.*, 172 N.W.2d 176 (Wis. 1969).

[176] 83 F.2d 57 (4th Cir. 1936).

of the work. Furthermore, the contractor and its surety may also be released when the contractor made a material mistake in its bid, as well as when bid conditions are not met.[177]

In some circumstances, contractors may have claims against their sureties if, after execution of the bid bond and before award, the surety refuses to execute the necessary payment and performance bonds for the contractor that is the low bidder. While the giving of the bid bond ordinarily does not obligate the surety to furnish additional bonds, some contractors have claimed against their bid bond surety for the surety's refusal to issue the other bonds necessary for the contractor to accept award.

In attempting to assert such a claim against the surety, the contractor might use an estoppel argument if sufficient facts can be presented to indicate that words or conduct on the part of the surety were relied upon by the contractor to the contractor's detriment.[178] In addition, even though the surety company, where a standard form of application is used, is not obligated to furnish payment and performance bonds upon the furnishing of the bid bond, the contractor might be able to introduce evidence tending to show that the writing of payment and performance bonds is customary after the writing of the bid bond.[179]

4.24 "BID SHOPPING": WHAT IS THE OBLIGATION OF THE PRIME CONTRACTOR TO THE SUBCONTRACTOR WITH THE LOWEST PRICE?

One of the most emotional issues connected with the prime contractor/subcontractor relationship involves "bid shopping" by the prime contractor. "Bid shopping" refers to actions taken by the prime contractor after award of the prime contract to reduce subcontractor prices by "shopping" the lowest bid in a particular craft from subcontractor to subcontractor. One court has referred to such postaward conduct as "bid chiseling," and defined "bid shopping" or "bid peddling" as those actions occurring before award of the prime contract.[180]

Although "bid shopping" has been described as "the purest form of competition," virtually all subcontractors and suppliers categorically reject the possibility of any virtue in the practice.[181] Bid shopping has been condemned by The Code of Ethical Conduct of the Associated General Contractors of America (Pub. 1947, reprinted 1970). However, it remains present in the industry, and the difficult position of the subcontractor is magnified by the lack of available legal theories to bind the prime.

While much of the attention is focused on allegations of such conduct by general contractors, the practice can occur at any tier in the chain of subcontracts, for

---

[177] *See* David B. Harrison, Annotation, Right of Bidder for State or Municipal Contract to Rescind Bid on Ground That Bid Was Based upon His Own Mistake or That of His Employee, 2 A.L.R.4th 991 (1980).

[178] *See generally Reynolds v. Gorton*, 213 N.Y.S.2d 561 (Sup. Ct. 1960).

[179] *Commercial Ins. Co. v. Hartwell Excavating Co.*, 407 P.2d 312 (Idaho 1965).

[180] *People v. Inland Bid Depository*, 44 Cal. Rptr. 206 (Cal. Ct. App. 1965).

[181] *See* Orrick, "Trade Associations Are Boycott Prone—Bid Depositories as a Case Study." 19 Hastings L.J. 505 (1968).

example, subcontractor and sub-subcontractor, subcontractor and supplier, and so on. While the issues in this section are addressed in the context of general contractors and their prospective subcontractors, the analysis has equal application to all tiers of the contracting process.

As a result of the various criticisms that have been leveled at bid shopping, several measures have been taken to eliminate, or at least minimize, the practice. The first of these measures has been the establishment of local bid depositories for subcontractor bids. However, a number of depository (by law) provisions necessary for the effective operation of bid depositories have been held to violate state and federal antitrust laws because of their restrictive effect on competition among both subcontractors and general contractors. In *Mechanical Contractors Bid Depository v. Christiansen*,[182] treble damages were awarded the plaintiff for antitrust violations by use of a bid depository.[183]

A second measure to combat bid shopping (addressing any postaward bid shopping) has been the statutory or contractual requirement that the prime contractor list in its bid the subcontractors it intends to use.[184] Where listing is required, there may be a statutory prohibition on changing subcontractors.[185] Only when a subcontractor is unable or unwilling to perform will substitution be permitted, and the prime contractor must seek consent to substitute from the awarding authority.[186] The requirement of subcontractor listing has in some instances resulted in actions by subcontractors against prime contractors.[187]

Federal regulations requiring subcontractor listing have been abandoned. The General Services Administration employed a subcontractor listing requirement for several years but eliminated the requirement in 1984.

In the absence of organized measures such as bid depositories or subcontractor listing requirements, what measures are available to subcontractors to counteract the effects of bid shopping? Subcontractors bringing suits against "shopping" prime contractors generally base their actions on two theories of recovery:

(1) That the prime contractor through its acts (principally by using the subcontractor's bid in its own bid to the owner) has "accepted" the bid of the subcontractor, and has thereby entered into a subcontract; and

(2) That the conversations and negotiations between the subcontractor and the general contractor have created an oral agreement for performance of the subcontracted work.

---

[182] 352 F.2d 817 (10th Cir.), *cert. denied,* 384 U.S. 918 (1965).

[183] *Id., but see Cullum Elec. & Mechanical, Inc. v. Mechanical Contractors Ass'n of S.C.*, 436 F. Supp. 418 (D.S.C. 1976), *aff'd,* 569 F.2d 821 (4th Cir.), *cert. denied,* 439 U.S. 910 (1978) (four-hour bid plan approved).

[184] *See, e.g.,* California Subletting and Subcontracting Fair Practices Act, Cal. Pub. Cont. Code § 4100, *et seq.*

[185] *Id. at* § 4107.

[186] *See Southern Cal. Acoustics Co. v. C. V. Holder, Inc.*, 456 P.2d 975 (Cal. 1969).

[187] *Id.*

Such subcontractor actions have generally not met with great success.

The first theory of recovery set out above was rejected in *Williams v. Favret*[188] and in *Merritt-Chapman & Scott Corp. v. Gunderson Bros. Engineering Corp.*[189] The *Gunderson* court found that there had never been the requisite "meeting of minds" in negotiations between the prime and subcontractor to create a contract, even though the subcontractor's bid had been listed as a part of the bid on the prime contract. The naming of Gunderson, the subcontractor, in the prime contractor's bid made no difference in the result. Correspondingly, the argument for an oral contract is generally defeated by the Statute of Frauds, which requires that certain types of contracts be in writing in order to be enforceable.

The general lack of success of subcontractors in proving that a contract exists with the prime contractor prior to execution of a formal written subcontract or purchase order should not, however, leave the impression that there is no possibility of a prime contractor being contractually obligated to a subcontractor under appropriate circumstances. One of the common problems in proving a contract is to establish that there is a sufficiently specific agreement between the parties.

A sufficiently specific agreement is necessary for enforcement. However, detailed items such as the precise scope of the work to be performed, the period of performance, and so on, are subjects that may not be discussed in preliminary negotiations. Nonetheless, many such details can be supplied from various sources. For example, certain items will be contained in the general and special conditions of the prime contract, the specifications, and in the drawings as set out in the bid documents. These details may be adopted by reference. Contract terms can also be proved by reference to custom and usage. Terms defining exactly what work is included in the contract, and establishing a price for that work, may be confirmed in writing without an elaborate document. A one-page letter or memorandum may succinctly encompass the few remaining details sufficient for a contract, and, if signed by the general contractor, might serve as an enforceable contract.

4.25 HOLDING SUBCONTRACTORS/VENDORS TO THEIR BIDS

Prime contractors can be faced with the unfortunate situation of having relied on a low subcontractor bid only to discover after award of the prime contract that the subcontractor is unwilling to perform at the price originally bid. Although the prime contractor's formal, written bid has been accepted, and the prime contractor is bound to the owner, the prime contractor has no contract with the subcontractor and is faced with making up the shortfall. Similar to the discussion of bid shopping in the prior section of this chapter (**Section 4.24**), this analysis of a contractor's ability to hold a subcontractor or vendor to its bid applies to any tier in the contracting process.

---

[188] 161 F.2d 822 (5th Cir. 1947). A subcontractor was successful, when compelling facts were present, in *Electrical Constr. & Maintenance Co. v. Maeda Pac. Corp.*, 764 F.2d 619 (9th Cir. 1985).

[189] 305 F.2d 659 (9th Cir.), *cert. denied,* 371 U.S. 935 (1962).

Under the doctrine of promissory estoppel, however, the subcontractor may be bound to the prime contractor as if a subcontract had actually been executed.[190]

4.26 DOCTRINE OF PROMISSORY ESTOPPEL

The doctrine of promissory estoppel is set forth in Section 90 of the Restatement (Second) of Contracts (1981) as follows:

> A promise which the promisor should reasonably expect to induce action or forbearance on the part of the promisee (or a third person) and which does induce such action or forbearance is binding if injustice can be avoided only by the enforcement of the promise. The remedy granted for breach may be limited as justice requires.

The leading case regarding the application of the doctrine of promissory estoppel to subcontractors' bids is *Drennan v. Star Paving Co.*[191] Drennan, a general contractor, was preparing to bid on a school project in California. Star Paving Company submitted to Drennan a bid on the paving portion of the school job. Star's bid was submitted by telephone on the day that Drennan had to submit its bid to the school district. Because Star's bid was the lowest received on the paving work, Drennan included Star's price in its computation of the overall costs of the project and submitted the total as its bid to the school district. Drennan was awarded the contract, as it had submitted the lowest general bid.

The next day, a representative of Drennan visited the offices of Star, and before he had the opportunity to do more than introduce himself, an officer of Star informed Drennan that Star was revoking its bid. Drennan indicated that it had used the bid in computing its own overall bid, and that it expected Star to carry out the work in accordance with the terms of Star's bid. Upon Star's refusal to do so, Drennan was forced to obtain a contract for the paving work from a different company at an increase in the price. Drennan sued Star for the amount of the price increase. The court applied the doctrine of promissory estoppel to rule that Star had become bound to the terms of its offer as a result of Drennan's detrimental reliance on the promises contained in the offer.

Indeed, subcontractors may be bound not only by the price given in their quote but also to subcontract terms deemed to be standard in the industry. For example, in *Crook v. Mortenson-Neal*,[192] a subcontractor whose bid was accepted balked at the scheduling and bonding requirements in the subcontract prepared by the general contractor. The court stated that:

> At the time [the subcontractor] bid on its subcontract, it should have expected to be bound by reasonable additional terms governing standard conditions implicit in the

---

[190] *See* O. Currie and N. Sweeney, "Holding Subcontractors to Their Bids," Construction Briefings, No. 86-3, February 1986, Federal Publications, Inc.

[191] 333 P.2d 757 (Cal. 1958).

[192] 727 P.2d 297 (Alaska 1986).

relationship between subcontractor and general contractor. Both industry custom, as expressed in standard form subcontracts, and the circumstances surrounding the particular project, dictate the kinds of provisions [the subcontractor] should reasonably have expected in its final subcontract.

The majority of courts now hold that a contractor may enforce a subcontractor's bid under a promissory estoppel theory.[193] However, other courts have rejected the *Drennan* reasoning. For example, in *Home Electric Co. v. Underdown Heating & Air Conditioning Co.*,[194] a North Carolina court ruled as a matter of law in that state that a subcontractor was not bound to its bid. The court was disturbed by the one-sided arrangement caused by promissory estoppel, since the prime is allowed to enforce the subcontractor's price while the subcontractor has no recourse if it is not awarded the subcontract. The court reasoned that prime contractors can avoid the problem by securing a contract with a subcontractor at the outset, conditioned on a successful bid to the owner.[195]

4.27   Elements of the Doctrine of Promissory Estoppel

In order to hold a subcontractor to its bid under the doctrine of promissory estoppel, the contractor must show:

(1) A clear and definite offer by the subcontractor to perform the work at a certain price;
(2) A reasonable expectation by the subcontractor that the prime contractor will rely on the subcontractor's price in preparing the prime contractor's bid;
(3) Actual reliance by the prime contractor on the subcontractor's bid; and
(4) Detriment to the general contractor as a result of reliance on the subcontractor's bid and the subcontractor's subsequent refusal to perform.[196]

4.28   Clear and Definite Offer   Generally, a lower-tier subcontractor or supplier submits its price to the upper-tier firm as an offer to do the work at a specific price. However, the requirement that there be a clear and definite offer to perform a certain part of the work for a particular price prevents the application of the doctrine of promissory estoppel where a subcontractor or supplier offers only an estimate of the

---

[193] *See Allen M. Campbell Co. Gen. Contractors, Inc. v. Virginia Metal Indus., Inc.*, 708 F.2d 930 (4th Cir. 1983); *Hoel-Steffen Constr. Co. v. United States*, 684 F.2d 843 (Ct. Cl. 1982); *Jenkins & Boller Co. v. Schmit Iron Works, Inc.*, 344 N.E.2d 275 (Ill. App. Ct. 1976); *E. A. Coronis Assocs. v. M. Gordon Constr. Co.*, 216 A.2d 246 (N.J. 1966); *James King & Son, Inc. v. Desantis Constr. No. 2 Corp.*, 413 N.Y.S.2d 78 (Sup. Ct. 1977).

[194] 358 S.E.2d 539 (N.C. App. 1987), *aff'd*, 366 S.E.2d 441 (N.C. 1988).

[195] *See also Anderson Constr. Co. v. Lyon Metal Prods.*, Inc., 370 So. 2d 935 (Miss. 1979).

[196] *Preload Technology, Inc. v. A.B. & J. Constr. Co.*, 696 F.2d 1080 (5th Cir. 1983); *E.A. Coronis Assocs.*, *supra* note 193.

cost of the work, without intending to make a definite offer to perform the work at that price.[197] Likewise, where the bid is made expressly revocable or subject to revision, there is no clear and definite offer.[198]

4.29 Subcontractor Expects Reliance In order for the doctrine of promissory estoppel to apply to a subcontractor's bid, it must be reasonable for the subcontractor to have expected the firm receiving the bid to rely on the subcontractor's bid in the preparation of the prime contractor's overall bid. In order to prove that this was the expectation of the subcontractor, or else that it reasonably should have been its expectation, the courts have, in cases like *Constructors Supply Co. v. Bostrum Sheet Metal Works, Inc.*,[199] allowed the prime contractor/upper-tier firm to introduce testimony as to the ordinary customs and practices of the construction industry in this regard. Of course, evidence may also be presented to demonstrate a subcontractor's actual knowledge that its quotation would be used in submitting a bid for the overall project.[200]

4.30 Reliance Must Be Reasonable Another fundamental requirement for the application of promissory estoppel is that the reliance on the subcontractor's bid must have been reasonable. Again, ordinary customs and practices of the construction industry can be relied on to establish the reasonableness of such reliance. Where the allegedly mistaken bid does not differ substantially from the other bids received and there is no obvious mathematical error in the bid, then the reliance will normally be considered reasonable.

However, it may be necessary in some cases to refute the contention of the subcontractor that its bid reflected an obvious mistake that should have been evident to the general contractor or upper-tier firm and, therefore, that its reliance upon the bid was unreasonable. Thus, if the subcontractor's bid is much lower than other subcontract bids received on the same work, any reliance upon that bid may be unreasonable.[201] Furthermore, reasonable reliance is not established where the general contractor misleads an inexperienced subcontractor into believing that the subcontract work can be performed at a price suggested by the general contractor but, in fact, that price underestimates the true cost of performance.[202]

If a prime contractor or upper-tier contractor is confronted with an unusually low bid that it did not suggest, and verifies this bid with the subcontractor or supplier, the resulting reliance may be shown to be reasonable.[203]

---

[197] *See N. Litterio & Co. v. Glassman Constr. Co.*, 319 F.2d 736 (D.C. Cir. 1963).

[198] *Preload Technology, Inc., supra* note 196.

[199] 190 N.W. 2d 71 (Minn. 1971).

[200] *Debron Corp. v. National Homes Constr. Corp.*, 493 F.2d 352 (8th Cir. 1974).

[201] *Edward Joy Co. v. Noise Control Prods., Inc.*, 443 N.Y.S.2d 361 (Sup. Ct. 1981); *Anderson Constr. Co., supra* note 195.

[202] *Architects & Contractors Estimating Serv. Inc. v. Smith*, 211 Cal. Rptr. 45 (Cal. Ct. App. 1985).

[203] *H.W. Stanfield Constr. Corp. v. Robert McMullan & Son, Inc.*, 92 Cal. Rptr. 669 (Cal. Ct. App. 1971); *Preload Technology, supra* note 196.

Even if it can be established that the subcontractor's bid was mistaken, the subcontractor may be bound. In *Constructors Supply Co. v. Bostrum Sheet Metal Works, Inc.*,[204] the court found that a bid that was 10 to 11 percent lower than the other subcontract bids was not self-evidently mistaken, and the general contractor was reasonable in relying upon it.[205]

4.31   STATUTE OF FRAUDS ISSUES

It is common in the construction industry for a general contractor to receive subcontract bids on the date that the general contract bid is required to be submitted. Often these subcontract bids or supplier quotes will be given over the telephone at the last minute, because the subcontractors wish to prevent general contractors from engaging in preaward "bid shopping." As a result, the general contractor is often in a position where it must rely upon these oral bids, with the possibility of substantial financial exposure should the subcontractors refuse to perform. The question therefore arises whether a general contractor, which is invoking the doctrine of promissory estoppel to enforce a subcontractor's bid, is barred by the Statute of Frauds if the subcontractor's or supplier's bid is oral.

The courts have split as to whether the Statute of Frauds defense is overcome by the promissory estoppel argument. In numerous cases, the Statute of Frauds has been held not to apply to subcontractor bids enforced under the doctrine of promissory estoppel.[206] However, in *Anderson Construction Co. v. Lyon Metal Products, Inc.*,[207] the court ruled that a prime contractor was barred by the Statute of Frauds from recovering damages for a subcontractor's failure to honor its oral bid.

4.32   DAMAGES

Assuming that the contractor has established all the elements of an action based upon promissory estoppel, what is the measure of damages it may receive from the subcontractor or supplier? In most cases, the measure has been the difference between the price at which the original subcontractor bid the work and the price the general contractor has had to pay to obtain a replacement subcontractor.[208]

A somewhat different formulation of damages was used in *Constructors Supply Co. v. Bostrum Sheet Metal Works, Inc.*[209] In that case, the court found that the

---

[204] *Constructors Supply Co.*, *supra* note 199.

[205] *See also Saliba-Kringlen Corp. v. Allen Eng'g Co.*, 92 Cal. Rptr. 799 (Cal. Ct. App. 1971).

[206] *See, e.g., Allen M. Campbell Co.*, *supra* note 193; *Ralston Purina Co. v. McCollum*, 611 S.W.2d 201 (Ark. Ct. App. 1981).

[207] 370 So. 2d 935 (Miss. 1979).

[208] *See, e.g., C & K Eng'g Contractors v. Amber Steel Co.*, 587 P.2d 1136 (Cal. 1978); *James King & Son, Inc.*, *supra* note 193.

[209] *Supra* note 199.

general contractor had not attempted to bid shop the defendant subcontractor. As a result, the general contractor was held entitled to recover its damages from the sub-contractor. However, the court found that the general contractor had engaged in bid shopping on other subcontracts for the same project and, as a result, had saved a certain amount of money. The damages awarded to the general contractor for the difference in cost between the defendant subcontractor's bid and the cost of obtaining a replacement subcontractor were reduced by the amount that the general contractor had saved by bid shopping on other subcontractors. This case illustrates the extent to which some courts dislike the practice of bid shopping and the danger that bid shopping poses to a general contractor that may want to use promissory estoppel to obtain damages from a subcontractor that has withdrawn its bid and refused to perform.

➤ POINTS TO REMEMBER

Competitive Bid Public Contracts

- Generally awarded to low bidder that is financially, technically, and historically responsible to perform the work.
- Past performance or evaluations may be critical to the determination of a bidder's responsibility.
- The bid must be responsive to the solicitation.
- Minor irregularities in the bid can be waived.
- Material irregularities may not be waived.
- Online offerors or bidders will be held to the same strict rules regarding timely submission.

Competitive Proposals on Public Contracts

- Generally awarded on a "best value" trade-off basis.
- Low price may not be the controlling factor.
- Past performance evaluations may be a significant factor in the technical evaluation of the offeror's proposal.

Bidding on Private Contracts

- Owners may restrict eligible bidders.
- Owners generally have broad discretion in selecting contractor.

Elements of a Mistaken Bid

- The error must be large in comparison to overall bid price.
- The mistake must relate to an important or "material" aspect of the work.
- The mistake cannot be the product of the bidder's own negligence.
- Relief is more likely for mathematical error.
- Relief is less likely for estimating/subjective error.
- The owner must be capable of being returned to the status quo.
- Timely notice of the mistake must be given.

Potential Relief from Bid Mistakes (Maximizing the Mistaken Bidder's Potential for Success)

- Notify the owner or public contracting official immediately upon discovery of the mistake.
- Request modification or withdrawal of bid in writing.
- Request immediate conference with owner or public contracting official to discuss the mistake.
- Put together evidence of the mistake to present to owner or public contracting official, including:
  - Affidavits of those individuals involved in bid preparation explaining the mistake
  - Copies of the bid
  - Original worksheets
  - Subcontractor quotes
  - Published price lists or trade catalogues
  - Any other data used to prepare the bid.
  - Gear presentation to prove:
    - The existence of the mistake
    - How the mistake happened
    - The bid that was intended

Efforts to Relieve Bid Shopping

- Bid depositories—limited success.
- Subcontractor listing requirements—infrequently used.

Holding the Subcontractor to Its Bid—Promissory Estoppoel: Summary of principles

- There is a clear and definite offer from the subcontractor.
- Subcontractor or lower-tier sub-subcontractor expects the recipient of the bid to rely upon it.
- There is actual reliance on the bid from the lower-tier firm.
- The reliance on the bid is reasonable.
- A party may not rely on obviously mistaken bid.
- A contractor may not mislead a lower-tier bidder into an unfairly low price.
- Damages, if subcontractor or lower-tier bidder refuses to perform in accordance with bid, include difference between the bid and ultimate price for that scope of work.

5

INTERPRETING THE CONTRACT

5.1 THE IMPORTANCE OF CONTRACT INTERPRETATION

The "contract" is the foundation of virtually every relationship in the construction industry. "Contract interpretation" is the process of determining what the parties agreed to in their contract. It involves deciding the meaning of words, filling in gaps, and resolving conflicts. The more familiar you are with the basic rules of contract interpretation, the better your chances of avoiding the numerous problems that frequently arise during the negotiation and performance of construction contracts.

5.2 WHAT IS A "CONTRACT"?

A "contract" may be defined succinctly as a set of promises. If a contract is enforceable, the law requires the performance of these promises and provides a remedy if they are not performed. Every contract must satisfy the following conditions to be enforceable:

(1) There must be a real agreement between the parties—that is, a true "meeting of the minds" on the subject matter of the contract;

(2) The subject matter must be lawful;

(3) There must be consideration for each promise;

(4) The parties must have the legal capacity to contract; and

(5) There must be compliance with legal requirements regarding the form of the contract (for example, some contracts must be made in writing).

The law will not enforce a contract that fails to meet any of these requirements. Practical considerations, however, require recognition. For example, even if an oral contract is enforceable as a matter of law, the complexities of the construction business make reliance on an oral agreement a risky proposition.

The promises that constitute a contract may do more than just impose duties on the promisor and grant rights to the promisee. They may also operate to allocate certain risks that would ultimately make performance by one party more difficult or expensive. Thus, a court, when interpreting a contract, may speak not only in terms of contractual duties and rights, but also in terms of which party assumed the risk of certain contingencies.

5.3   THE GOAL OF CONTRACT INTERPRETATION

The goal of contract interpretation is to ascertain and enforce the intent of the parties at the time of contracting. It is rarely possible to determine what was in the minds of the parties at the time of contracting. Therefore, courts rely upon the objective manifestations of the parties.

A primary contract interpretation rule, which has several facets, is that the *reasonable, logical meaning* of the contract language will be presumed to be the meaning intended by the parties. This reasonable and logical meaning rule overrides all other rules of contract interpretation.[1]

According to this rule, contract language is interpreted as it would be understood by a reasonably intelligent and logical person familiar with the facts and circumstances surrounding the contract. Courts use two sources of information in determining this objective intent: (1) the language used by the parties in the contract; and (2) the facts and circumstances surrounding contract formation.

5.4   DEFINING CONTRACT TERMS

Contract interpretation starts by defining the contract's terms. These definitions come from three sources. First, the parties may have defined the terms within the contract. Second, technical terms are given their meaning within various industries and trades. Third, general terms are given their widely accepted meanings. Each of these sources of definitions is discussed below.

5.5   Terms Defined by the Parties

It is common practice for parties to define the terms they use in a contract. These agreed-upon definitions are the clearest manifestation of the parties' intent. Therefore, courts will generally abide by the parties' definitions.[2]

---

[1] *Sprucewood Inv. Corp. v. Alaska Housing Finance Corp.*, 33 P.3d 1156 (Alaska 2001); *Alvin Ltd. v. United States Postal Serv.*, 816 F.2d 1562 (Fed. Cir. 1987).

[2] *See, e.g., Hayden Corp. v. Glacier Park Co.*, 134 Or. App. 604, 896 P.2d 604 (1995); *Guy F. Atkinson Co.*, ENGBCA No. 4891, 86-1 BCA ¶ 18,555.

5.6 Technical Terms

Terms may acquire nonstandard or technical meanings in certain industries or trades. These meanings may differ substantially from the meanings generally associated with those terms. Technical meanings will override generally accepted meanings when circumstances indicate that the parties intended to use the technical meaning of the term.[3]

5.7 Generally Accepted Definitions

Terms will be given the meanings generally ascribed to them unless the parties have defined a term otherwise or intended for a term to have a technical meaning.[4]

5.8 Interpreting the Language of the Contract

The following sections examine the legal rules generally applicable to interpreting the language of a contract once its individual terms have been defined in accordance with the principles discussed in the prior sections.

5.9 *The Contract Must Be Considered as a Whole* A fundamental principle of contract interpretation is that a contract must be considered as a whole, giving effect to all of its parts.[5] Each part of the agreement should be examined with reference to all other parts, because one clause may modify, limit, or illuminate another.[6] Similarly, where several documents form an integral part of one transaction, a court may read these together with reference to one another even where the documents involved do not specifically refer to one another. A similar rule applies to documents annexed to the contract or incorporated by reference. Therefore, an interpretation that leaves portions of the contract meaningless will generally be rejected. Likewise, because the contract is to be read as a whole, its provisions should, if possible, be harmonized.

5.10 *Order of Precedence* It may be impossible to interpret a contract without resolving a conflict between different terms. Construction contracts are complex and frequently contain numerous sections drafted by different people or organizations. When two or more conflicting provisions cannot be harmonized, the rules of contract interpretation establish an order of precedence that may resolve the conflict.

---

[3] See, e.g., *L.K. Comstock & Co., Inc. v. Becon Construction Co.*, 932 F.Supp. 948 (E.D. Ky. 1994); *P.J. Dick Contracting, Inc.*, PSBCA No. 1097, 84-1 BCA ¶ 17,149.

[4] *Lodge Corp. v. Assurance Co. of America*, 775 N.E.2d 1250 (Mass. App. 2002); *Atlas R.R. Constr. Co.*, ENGBCA No. 5972, 94-3 BCA ¶ 26,997; *see, e.g., Sauter Constr. Co.*, ASBCA No. 22338, 78-1 BCA ¶ 13,092.

[5] *Downey v. Clauder*, 811 F. Supp. 338 (S.D. Ohio 1992); *New Valley Corp. v. United States*, 119 F.3d 1576 (Fed. Cir. 1997); *McDevitt Mechanical Contractors, Inc. v. United States*, 21 Cl. Ct. 616 (1990).

[6] *T. Brown Constructors, Inc. v. Pena*, 132 F.3d 724 (Fed. Cir. 1997); *Plaza Dev. Serv. v. Joe Harden Builders, Inc.*, 365 S.E.2d 231 (S.C. Ct. App. 1988).

The general conditions of many contracts include an "order of precedence" clause expressly stating which provisions control over others in case of conflict.[7] For example, the order-of-precedence clause may state that the specifications generally take precedence over the drawings, special conditions take precedence over general conditions, and so on. However, in federal government contracts, provisions required by law generally cannot be altered by such a clause.

In the absence of an order-of-precedence clause, general common-law rules of precedence will apply. For example, it is a basic rule of contract interpretation that general terms and provisions in a contract yield to specific ones.[8] It is also a general rule of contract interpretation that when specific requirements or definitions are itemized and spelled out, anything not expressly included is deemed to be excluded.[9] Additionally, handwritten terms take precedence over typewritten terms, and typewritten terms take precedence over printed terms.[10]

5.11   THE FACTS AND CIRCUMSTANCES SURROUNDING CONTRACT FORMATION

Courts frequently interpret a contract based upon the facts and circumstances surrounding the contract's formation. This evidence comes in three forms: (1) evidence of discussions and conduct; (2) evidence of the parties' prior dealings; and (3) evidence of custom and usage in the industry.

5.12   Discussions and Conduct

The parties' discussions and conduct can be persuasive when interpreting a contract. For example, a contractor may become aware of a possible ambiguity at a prebid conference and request a clarification. Such a clarification may serve as proof that the parties agreed upon the resolution of a possible ambiguity and upon a common interpretation of the contract.

Similarly, one of the parties may make its interpretation of the contract known to the other party. This can be done expressly through discussions or impliedly by its actions. If the other party, knowing this interpretation, remains silent or does not object, this interpretation will be binding.

---

[7] *See, e.g., General Engineering & Mach. Works v. O'Keefe,* 991 F.2d 775 (Fed. Cir. 1993), citing *Hensel Phelps Constr. v. United States,* 886 F.2d 1296 (Fed. Cir. 1989).

[8] This rule is generally known as *ejusdem generis. See Smith Barney, Inc. v. Sarver,* 108 F.3d 92 (6th Cir. 1997); *see also* 17A C.J.S. Contracts § 313.

[9] This rule of contract law is generally known as *expressio unius est exclusio alterius* (the express mention of the one is the exclusion of the other). *See* 17A C.J.S. Contracts § 312.

[10] *Authentic Architectural Millworks, v. SCM Group,* 586 S.E.2d 726 (Ga. Ct. App. 2003); *Patellis v. 100 Galleria Parkway Assoc.,* 447 S.E.2d 113, 115 (Ga. Ct. App. 1994); *see also Wood River Pipeline Co. v. Willbros Energy Servs. Co.,* 738 P.2d 866 (Kan. 1987).

Evidence of the parties' discussions and conduct before, and at the time, a written contract is signed ("parol evidence") may not, however, be admissible as evidence to resolve a dispute regarding the interpretation of a contract. Reducing a contract to writing has legal consequences. Traditionally, the law has imposed rules that limit the use of external or parol evidence to vary or contradict the terms of a written contract. This is often called the "parol evidence rule."[11]

The first question that must be answered to determine the admissibility of parol evidence is whether the contract is a final and complete expression of the parties' agreement. Parol evidence may be used to make this determination. If the contract is final and complete, normally parol evidence cannot be used to vary or contradict its unambiguous terms.[12] For example, a contractor was not allowed to rely upon an oral, prebid extension of time to establish an acceleration claim when that evidence would have contradicted the express provisions of the written contract.[13] However, if a term is ambiguous, courts may hear extrinsic evidence concerning the parties' negotiations to ascertain the intent of the parties at the time of contracting.[14]

5.13   The Parties' Prior Dealings

If parties have dealt with each other previously, courts may look at their earlier behavior and practices to help interpret their current contract. Although evidence of an established pattern of prior dealings may be offered to aid a court, it cannot be used to vary or modify the clear, express terms of a written contract. The parol evidence rule prevents such a use of extrinsic evidence.

The admission of prior dealings serves the purpose of showing what the parties intended by the language in the contract. For example, a Pennsylvania court interpreted an ambiguity in a contract as to the meaning of the term "positive shielding" in favor of the contractor based on the "conduct of the parties" throughout a prior project. The court allowed extrinsic evidence as to the parties' conduct to determine the parties' intent in using the term.[15]

As previously stated, extrinsic evidence is not generally admissible to show intent entirely different from what is clearly stated in the contract. A prior course of dealing may, however, show that the contract is not the final and complete agreement of the parties.[16]

---

[11] *S & B Mining Co. v. Northern Commercial Co.*, 813 P.2d 264 (Alaska 1991); *see also Lower Kuskokwim Sch. Dist. v. Alaska Diversified Contractors, Inc.*, 734 P.2d 62 (Alaska 1987).

[12] *Fidelity and Deposit Co. v. ROTEC Ind.*, Case No. 01 C 5829 (N.D. Ill. 2004); *Rothlein v. Armour and Co.*, 377 F. Supp. 506, 510 (W.D. Pa. 1974). *See also Fuller Co. v. Brown Minneapolis Tank & Fabricating Co.*, 678 F. Supp. 506 (E.D. Pa. 1987).

[13] *See Lower Kuskokwim Sch. Dist.*, *supra* note 11.

[14] *Hickman v. Kralicek Realty and Const. Co.*, 2003 WL 22723484 (Ark. App. 2003); *Teleport Communications Group, Inc. v. Barclay Fin. Group*, 176 F.3d 412 (7th Cir. 1999); *Judge v. Wellman*, 403 S.E.2d 76 (Ga. Ct. App. 1991).

[15] *Department of Transp. v. IA Constr. Corp.*, 588 A.2d 1327 (Pa. Commw. Ct. 1991).

[16] Restatement (Second) of Contracts §§ 209-210.

Prior conduct may also amount to waiver or estoppel. A party may be prevented from enforcing an explicit contract requirement if in its prior dealings it did not require compliance with the requirement.[17]

5.14   Custom and Usages in the Industry

Evidence of customs within a particular industry may be used to show that the parties intended for an ordinary word to have a specialized meaning.[18] However, courts are divided on the role of such evidence.[19] One line of cases holds that evidence of trade practice and custom may be admitted to show the meaning of an ambiguous contract term, but not to override a seemingly unambiguous term.[20] The second line of cases maintains that evidence of trade practice and custom may be introduced to show that a term, which appears on its face to be unambiguous, has, in fact, a specialized meaning other than that of its ordinary meaning.[21]

A party seeking to assert a trade custom or practice must present evidence that the custom is well established.[22] One method of establishing trade custom is to show the interpretations of other bidders on the contract.[23]

Similarly, a technical word will be given its ordinary meaning in the industry unless it is shown that the parties intended to use it in a different sense. The appropriate meaning of ambiguous technical terms may also be clarified by the introduction of extrinsic evidence. For example, in a classic case, a Texas appellate court allowed the introduction of evidence of custom to establish the intended meaning of the contract term "working days" as it related to the owner's right to assess liquidated damages for delay in completion.[24] More recently, the United States Claims Court relied on trade practice to interpret patently ambiguous pipe-wrapping requirements in a federal government construction contract.[25]

5.15   RESOLVING AMBIGUITIES

The rules of contract interpretation discussed above may not resolve every ambiguity in a contract. If an ambiguity remains, courts will apply one of the following two

---

[17] *James v. Zurich-American Ins. Co. of Illinois*, 203 F.3d 250 (3d Cir. 2000); *Sperry Flight Sys. v. United States*, 548 F.2d 915 (Ct. Cl. 1977).

[18] *See, e.g., Rosenberg v. Turner*, 98 S.E. 763 (Va.1919).

[19] *Metric Constructors v. National Aeronautical & Space Admin.*, 169 F.3d 747 (Fed. Cir. 1999).

[20] *R. B. Wright Constr. Co. v. United States*, 919 F.2d 1569 (Fed. Cir. 1990); *George Hyman Constr. Co. v. United States*, 564 F.2d 939 (Ct. Cl. 1977); *WRB Corp. v. United States*, 183 Ct. Cl. 409 (1968).

[21] *Western States Constr. Co., Inc. v. United States*, 26 Cl. Ct. 818 (1992); *Haehn Management Co. v. United States*, 15 Cl. Ct. 50 (1988), *aff'd*, 878 F.2d 1445 (Fed. Cir. 1989); *Gholson, Byars & Holms Constr. Co. v. United States*, 351 F.2d 987 (Ct. Cl. 1965).

[22] *W. G. Cornell Co. v. United States*, 376 F.2d 299 (Ct. Cl. 1967).

[23] *See Eagle Paving*, AGBCA 75-156, 78-1 BCA ¶ 13,107.

[24] *Lewis v. Jones*, 251 S.W.2d 942 (Tex. Ct. App. 1952).

[25] *Western States Constr. Co., Inc. v. United States*, 26 Cl. Ct. 818 (1992).

risk-allocation principles to resolve the conflict: (1) the ambiguity should be construed against its drafter; or (2) the ambiguity should be construed against the party that failed to request a clarification of the ambiguity. These principles are discussed below.

5.16 Construction Against the Drafter

The risk of ambiguous contract language generally belongs to the party responsible for drafting the ambiguity unless the nondrafting party knew of, or should have known of, the ambiguity.[26] Several requirements must be met for this principle to apply.

First, there must truly be an ambiguity—that is, the contract must have at least two reasonable interpretations. A nondrafting party's interpretation need not be the only reasonable interpretation for this principle to apply.[27] Second, one of the two parties must have drafted or chosen the ambiguous contract language. Third, the nondrafting party must demonstrate that it relied on its interpretation.[28]

5.17 Duty to Request Clarification

A obviously ambiguous contract provision will not be construed against its drafter if the nondrafting party fails to clarify an obvious, or patent, ambiguity prior to bidding.[29] Ambiguities are either obvious (*patent*) or *latent*. An obvious, or patent, ambiguity is one that is readily apparent from the wording of the contract.[30] In contrast, language containing a latent ambiguity initially appears to be clear and unambiguous but actually contains an underlying ambiguity that becomes apparent only after a close examination or presentation of extrinsic facts.[31]

A bidder generally has an obligation to seek clarification of patent ambiguities or inconsistencies that appear in the bid documents.[32] Typically, government construction bid documents contain an express provision imposing an affirmative duty on a contractor to seek clarification of patent ambiguities.[33] However, the lack of such a provision does not relieve a contractor of its duty to request clarification of obvious ambiguities. For example, the United States Court of Federal Claims held that, when a provision in the solicitation conflicts directly and openly with a provision in a

---

[26] The technical name for this interpretive rule is *contra proferentem*. See *Freeman & Co. v. Bolt*, 968 P.2d 247 (Idaho App. 1998); *United States v. Turner Constr. Co.*, 819 F.2d 283 (Fed. Cir. 1987).

[27] *Infoconversion Joint Venture v. United States*, 22 Cl. Ct. 497 (1991); *Bennett v. United States*, 371 F.2d 859 (Ct. Cl. 1967); *Gall Landau Young Constr. Co.*, ASBCA No. 25801, 83-1 BCA ¶ 16,359.

[28] *Interstate Gen. Govt. Contractors v. Stone*, 980 F.2d 1433 (Fed. Cir. 1992); *Fruin-Colnon Corp. v. United States*, 912 F.2d 1426 (Fed. Cir. 1990).

[29] *Kiska Const. v. Washington Metro Area Tran. Auth.*, 321 F.3d 1151 (D.C. Cir. 2003); *Triax Pac., Inc. v. West*, 130 F.3d 1469 (Fed. Cir. 1997).

[30] *See Big Chief Drilling Co. v. United States*, 15 Ct. Cl. 295 (1988).

[31] *See AWC, Inc.*, PSBCA No. 1747, 88-2 BCA ¶ 20,637.

[32] *White v. Edsall Constr. Co.*, 296 F.3d 1081 (Fed. Cir. 2002); *Newsom v. United States*, 676 F.2d 647 (Ct. Cl. 1982).

[33] *Blount Bros. Constr. Co. v. United States*, 346 F.2d 962 (Ct. Cl. 1965).

referenced handbook, a contractor has an obligation to clarify such an obvious ambiguity.[34] Because the contractor in that case did not alert the contracting officer to the glaring discrepancy, the court barred the contractor from recovering any damages caused by the conflicting provisions within the solicitation and handbook.[35]

The difficulty arises in determining whether an ambiguity was obvious prior to bidding. One factor used to make this determination is whether other bidders requested a clarification prior to bidding.[36] Ultimately, the question of whether the ambiguity was obvious will depend on "what a reasonable man would find to be patent and glaring."[37]

5.18   IMPLIED CONTRACTUAL OBLIGATIONS

The law includes implied obligations in every contract, in addition to the obligations that are expressly agreed upon by the parties.[38] Implied obligations can allocate risk and responsibility between contracting parties with the same force as terms that are negotiated and reduced to writing in a signed written agreement. Two of the most important implied obligations for the construction industry are briefly discussed below.

5.19   Duty to Cooperate

From the contractor's perspective, the owner's implied duty to cooperate is probably the most important of all the implied contractual obligations. In one old but often cited case where a contractor obtained damages for owner-caused delays, the United States Court of Claims reviewed several generally accepted legal authorities supporting the duty to cooperate, and concluded:

> [I]t is however, an implied provision of every contract, whether it be one between individuals or between an individual and the Government, that neither party to the contract will do anything to prevent performance thereof by the other party or that will hinder or delay him in its performance.[39]

The owner can breach its duty to cooperate either by taking action that has the effect of hindering or delaying the contractor, or by failing to act when action by the owner is necessary to avoid hindrance or delay.[40]

---

[34] *Nielsen-Dillingham Builders, J.V. v. United States*, 43 Fed. Cl. 5 (1999).

[35] *Id.; see also Big Chief Drilling Co., supra* note 30.

[36] *See W.M. Schlosser Co.*, VABCA No. 1802, 83-2 BCA ¶ 16,630.

[37] *Max Drill, Inc. v. United States*, 427 F.2d 1233 (Ct. Cl. 1970).

[38] *See, e.g.,* Restatement (Second) of Contracts, § 231.

[39] *George A. Fuller Co. v. United States*, 69 F. Supp. 409 (Ct. Cl. 1947). *See also Coatesville Contractors v. Borough of Ridley*, 506 A.2d 862 (Pa. 1986).

[40] *CEMS v. United States*, 59 Fed. Cl. 168 (2003).

The owner's implied duty to cooperate includes an implied duty to exercise care to coordinate the activities of the various entities with which the owner has contracts, such as parallel prime contractors.[41] Although sophisticated owners often attempt to avoid their duty to coordinate through the use of contract clauses that obligate parallel prime contractors to coordinate directly with each other, courts have recognized that when an owner retains the right of control over its contractors, it cannot absolve itself of all responsibility for the coordination of their work.[42]

When an owner fails to provide the necessary coordination, it must generally respond by paying delay or disruption damages to the impacted contractor.[43] These principles also apply to general contractors, which have implied duties to cooperate with and coordinate the work of the subcontractors and trade contractors under their control.[44]

5.20   Warranty of Plans and Specifications

Another important implied obligation is that the party responsible for furnishing the completed design impliedly warrants its adequacy and sufficiency.[45] This rule was first pronounced by the United States Supreme Court in the case of *United States v. Spearin,* as follows:

> [I]f the contractor is bound to build according to plans and specifications prepared by the owner, the contractor will not be responsible for the consequences of defects in the plans and specifications.[46]

Often referred to as the Spearin Doctrine, this implied duty has been recognized by the courts in nearly every state. The owner impliedly warrants the adequacy and sufficiency of the completed plans and specifications to the contractor, even when the design is prepared by the owner's independent architect or engineer.[47] Generally,

---

[41] *Baldwin-Lima-Hamilton Corp. v. United States,* 434 F.2d 1371 (Ct. Cl. 1970); *Snyder Plumbing & Heating Corp. v. State,* 198 N.Y.S.2d 600, 604 (Ct. Cl. 1960).

[42] *Amp-Rite Electric Co., Inc. v. Wheaton Sanitary District,* 580 N.E.2d 622 (Ill. Ct. App. 1991); *Shea-S&M Ball v. Massman-Kiewet-Early,* 606 F.2d 1245 (D.C. Cir. 1979); *Eric A. Carlstrom Constr. Co. v. Independent School District No. 77,* 256 N.W.2d 479 (Minn. 1977).

[43] *Freeman Contractors, Inc. v. Central Sur. & Ins. Corp.,* 205 F.2d 607 (8th Cir. 1953); *L. L. Hall Constr. Co. v. United States,* 379 F.2d 559 (Ct. Cl. 1966); *Gasparini Excavating Co. v. Pennsylvania Turnpike Commission,* 187 A.2d 157 (Pa. 1963).

[44] *United States f/b/o Wallace v. Flintco, Inc.,* 143 F.3d 955 (5th Cir. 1998); *Allied Fire & Safety Equipment Co. v. Dick Enterprises, Inc.,* 886 F. Supp. 491 (1995); *Crawford Painting & Drywall Co. v. J.W. Bateson Co, Inc.,* 857 F.2d 981 (5th Cir. 1988).

[45] *Big. Chief Drilling Co. v. United States,* 26 Cl. Ct. 1276 (1992); *Ordnance Research, Inc. v. United States,* 609 F.2d 462 (Ct. Cl. 1979); *State Highway Dep't v. Hewitt Contr. Co.,* 146 S.E.2d 632 (Ga. 1966).

[46] *United States v. Spearin,* 248 U.S. 132, 136 (1918).

[47] *Greenhut Constr. Co.,* ASBCA No. 15192, 71-1 BCA ¶ 8845.

in federal construction contracts, all delays caused by defective design specifications are compensable.[48]

In "performance specifications," an owner specifies the performance characteristics that are to be obtained by the contractor, and leaves the details of the design to the contractor's judgment. Although the Spearin Doctrine does not apply to performance specifications, an owner can still be liable for a contractor's unanticipated difficulties under a performance specification if the contractor shows that the owner-furnished performance specification was impossible or commercially impracticable to achieve.[49] A performance specification is commercially impracticable if it can be performed only at an excessive and unreasonable cost.[50]

In design-build contracts, the designer-builder has the implied duty to furnish an adequate and sufficient design, instead of the owner, because the designer-builder is responsible for furnishing the design.[51]

The Spearin Doctrine can serve as both a shield and a sword for a party that is not responsible for furnishing the design. When the owner furnishes the design, the contractor will not be liable to the owner for an unsatisfactory final result if the contractor performs in accordance with owner-furnished plans and specifications. If an inadequacy in an owner-furnished design results in delay, disruption, or additional cost to the contractor, the contractor may use the Spearin Doctrine as the basis for claims for additional time and recovery of the additional costs incurred.[52] For example, in a recent case arising from the construction of two helicopter hangers, the Federal Circuit Court of Appeals affirmed a board decision awarding a contractor additional costs under the Spearin Doctrine, where the government's design called for the hangar doors to be constructed and rigged with three "pick" points, which would not work.[53] In another recent case, the Seventh Circuit enforced the Spearin Doctrine under Illinois law, holding that a city impliedly warranted the suitability of a specified quarry to produce adequate armor rock.[54]

A contractor cannot recover under the Spearin Doctrine if it knew, or through the exercise of reasonable care should have known, of the defective nature of the design prior to submitting its bid.[55] Thus, when the solicitation documents direct

---

[48] *Daly Constr. Inc. v. Garrett*, 5 F.3d 520 (Fed. Cir. 1993); *American Line Builders, Inc. v. United States*, 26 Cl. Ct. 1155 (1992); *Chaney & Jones Constr. Co. v. United States*, 421 F.2d 728 (Ct. Cl. 1970).

[49] *Int'l Elec. Corp. v. United States*, 646 F.2d 496 (Ct. Cl. 1981).

[50] *Oak Adec, Inc. v. United States*, 24 Cl. Ct. 502 (1991); *W. F. Magann Corp. v. Diamond Mfg. Co.*, 775 F.2d 1202 (4th Cir. 1985); *Keller Constr. Corp. v. George W. Coy & Co.*, 119 So. 2d 450 (La. 1960).

[51] *Mobile Hous. Env't v. Barton & Barton*, 432 F. Supp. 1343 (D. Colo. 1977).

[52] *USA Petroleum Corp. v. United States*, 821 F.2d 622 (Fed. Cir. 1987); *Felton Constr. Co.*, AGBCA No. 406-9, 81-1 BCA ¶ 14,932; *R. M. Hollingshead v. United States*, 111 F. Supp. 285 (Ct. Cl. 1953).

[53] *White v. Edsall Constr. Corp.*, 296 F.3d 1081 (Fed. Cir. 2002).

[54] *Edward E. Gillen Co. v. City of Lake Forest*, 3 F.3d 192 (7th Cir. 1993).

[55] *Blount Bros. Constr. Co. v. United States*, 346 F.2d 962 (Ct. Cl. 1965).

the bidders to conduct a prebid site inspection, the contractor will be deemed to have prior knowledge of any inaccuracies in the design that could have been discovered through a reasonable site inspection, even if the contractor never inspects the site.[56] In addition to site inspection clauses, sophisticated owners often attempt to avoid liability under the Spearin Doctrine by including clauses in their contracts that disclaim the sufficiency of the plans and specifications. However, when owners provide design information with the intent that contractors rely upon it when formulating their bids, the Spearin Doctrine should prevail over a disclaimer clause, unless it expressly and specifically shifts the risk of the design flaw to the contractor.[57]

5.21 No Damage for Delay Clauses and Implied Duties

There are numerous factual scenarios in which contractors have sought delay damages for owner breaches of express and implied contract duties.[58] As a result, many owners routinely include "no-damage-for-delay" clauses in their contracts in an attempt to avoid liability for delay damages attributable to certain specified causes. Sophisticated no-damage-for-delay clauses typically provide that in the event of a delay, the contractor will be entitled to a time extension only.

No-damage-for-delay clauses can have harsh consequences for contractors and subcontractors, and as a result, several states have enacted statutes limiting or banning the

---

[56] *Stuyvesant Dredging Co. v. United States*, 834 F.2d 1576 (Fed. Cir. 1987); *Johnson Controls, Inc. v. United States*, 671 F.2d 1312 (Ct. Cl. 1982); *Allied Contractors, Inc. v. United States*, 381 F.2d 995 (Ct. Cl. 1967).

[57] *See Spearin, supra* note 46; *White v. Edsall Constr. Co, Inc.*, 296 F.3d 1081 (Fed. Cir. 2002); *Sherman R. Smoot Co. of Ohio v. Ohio Dep't of Admin. Services*, 736 N.E.2d 69 (Ohio Ct. App. 2000); *Morris, Inc. v. State ex rel. South Dakota Dept. of Transportation*, 598 N.W.2d 520 (S.D. 1999).

[58] *See, e.g., Celeron Gathering Corp. v. United States*, 34 Fed. Cl. 745 (1996) (government failed to candidly disclose vital information to contractor during project); *SIPCO Servs. & Marine, Inc. v. United States*, 41 Fed. Cl. 196 (1998) (owner imposed excessive supervision and testing procedures); *Lewis-Nicholson, Inc. v. United States*, 550 F.2d 26 (Ct. Cl. 1977) (government failed to properly stake work site); *Gulf M. & O. R.R. v. Illinois Cent. R.R.*, 128 F. Supp. 311, *aff'd*, 225 F.2d 816 (5th Cir. 1955) (railroad that asked Interstate Commerce Commission to order the abandonment of a certain route could not later rely on that order as an excuse); *Great Lakes Constr. Co. v. United States*, 96 Ct. Cl. 378 (1942) (contractor may recover for unwarranted delays in construction of federal building caused by government); *Griffin Mfg. Co. v. Boom Boiler & Welding Co.*, 90 F.2d 209 (6th Cir. 1937), *cert. denied*, 302 U.S. 741 (1937) (plant owner had duty to not delay equipment seller's installation of equipment); *Triple R Paving, Inc. v. Broward County*, 774 So.2d 50 (Fla. Dist. Ct. App. 2000) (owner withheld vital information); *Clifford R. Gray, Inc. v. City School District of Albany*, 716 N.Y.S.2d 795 (App. Div. 2000) (owner breached fundamental obligation to supervise and coordinate contractors); *Pennsylvania D.O.T. v. Gen'l Asphalt Paving Co.*, 405 A.2d 1138 (Pa. Cmwlth. Ct. 1979) (owner directly interfered by failing to act expeditiously in negotiating relocation of water main).

use of no-damage-for-delay clauses on public projects.[59] In jurisdictions where they have not been prohibited by statute, courts strictly construe no-damage-for-delay clauses against the parties that seek to benefit from them.[60] The courts also recognize several exceptions in which no-damage-for-delay clauses will not prevent a contractor from recovering its delay damages. The exceptions vary from state to state. In many states, no-damage-for-delay clauses are not enforceable as to any delay that: (1) is not contemplated by the parties to be within the scope of the clause at the time of contracting; (2) results from fraud, misrepresentation, or other bad faith on the part of the party seeking the benefit of the clause; (3) has extended for such an unreasonable length of time that it either amounts to an abandonment of the contract by the delaying party or would have justified abandonment by the nondelaying party; or (4) is not within the specifically enumerated delays as to which the no-damage-for-delay clause applies.[61]

> **POINTS TO REMEMBER**

- A contract should be entered into and performed with an awareness and understanding of the principles of contract interpretation.
- Contracts should be written.
- Contracts should fully allocate risks between the parties and embody the parties' entire agreement.
- Important contract terms should be defined.
- A contract should include an order-of-precedence clause.
- Reliance upon prior or contemporaneous discussions and conduct, prior dealings, and industry usages is risky. The terms of the contract itself should address these issues explicitly.

---

[59] Ariz. Rev. Stat. § 41-2617; Cal. Pub. Cont. Code.§ 7102; Colo. Rev. Stat. § 24-91-103.5(1)(a); Mass. Gen. Laws. Ch. 30, § 39O; Mo. Rev. Stat. § 34.058; N.J. Stat. Ann. § 2A:58B-3 (2002); N.C. Gen. Stat. § 143-134.3; Ohio Rev. Code Ann. § 4113.62; R.I. Gen. Laws § 37-2-42; Va. Code Ann. § 2.2-4335; Wash. Rev. Code § 4.24.360.

[60] *Mississippi Transp. Commission v. SCI, Inc.*, 717 So.2d 332 (Miss. 1998).

[61] *See United States f/b/o Wallace v. Flintco, Inc.*, 143 F.3d 955 (5th Cir. 1998) (contractor actively interfered with subcontractor's performance); *Allied Fire & Safety Equipment Co. v. Dick Enterprises, Inc.*, 886 F. Supp.491 (E.D. Penn. 1995) (subcontractor alleged that contractor affirmatively hindered subcontractor's performance); *Bovis Lend Lease LMB, Inc. v. GCT Venture, Inc.* (N.Y.S.2d), 2004 N.Y. Slip. Op. 02679 (N.Y. App. Div. April 13, 2004) (unreasonable delays and design changes); *Clifford R. Gray, Inc. v. City of Albany*, 716 N.Y.S.2d 795 (N.Y. App. Div. 2000) (owner breached fundamental duty to supervise and coordinate subcontractors); *U.S. f/b/a Williams Electric Co. v. Metric Constructors, Inc.*, 480 S.E.2d 447 (S.C. 1997); *Triple R Paving, Inc. v. Broward County*, 774 So.2d 50 (Fla. Dist. Ct. App. 1991) (owner willfully concealed information); *Newberry Square Dev. Corp. v. Southern Landmark, Inc.*, 578 So.2d 750 (Fla. Dist. Ct. App. 1991); *Castagna & Son, Inc. v. Bd. of Education*, 570 N.Y.S.2d 286 (App. Div. 1991); *Corinno Civetta Constr. Corp. v. State*, 502 N.Y.S.2d 681 (1986); *DAL Constr. Corp. v. City of New York*, 485 N.Y.S.2d 774 (App.Div. 1985).

- The drafter of the contract must be aware that when both parties to a construction contract submit a reasonable interpretation of an ambiguous provision, in most cases the contract language will be construed against the drafter.
- Contractors have an obligation to inform owners of patent ambiguities or inconsistencies in bid documents.
- Every contract imposes an implied duty of cooperation on both parties to the contract.
- Owners have an implied duty to coordinate the work of their contractors, and contractors have an implied duty to coordinate the work of their subcontractors.
- The party responsible for furnishing the completed design has an implied duty to furnish an adequate and sufficient design.
- No-damage-for-delay clauses are enforceable in many jurisdictions, but they are strictly construed, and in most jurisdictions, the courts recognize several exceptions to the general rule of enforceability.

6

THE UNIFORM
COMMERCIAL CODE AND
THE CONSTRUCTION
INDUSTRY

6.1   THE UNIFORM COMMERCIAL CODE

The Uniform Commercial Code (UCC or Code) is a set of laws governing a wide range of business transactions and commercial instruments. These include the sale of goods, negotiable instruments, bulk transfers, letters of credit, and certain credit transactions involving security interests, among others. In the construction context, the UCC will primarily affect transactions involving the sale of materials or equipment.

The Code was developed by a group of legal scholars and practitioners to rationalize and lend uniformity to the state laws governing commercial matters. Uniformity was considered important because commercial transactions often involve parties in two or more states. Forty-nine states, the District of Columbia, and the Virgin Islands have fully adopted the UCC. The sole exception is Louisiana, which has adopted seven of the nine articles but not Article 2 (concerning the sale of goods) and Article 9 (concerning secured credit transactions). The states that have adopted the UCC have done so in substantially the same form, with only minor variations, resulting in considerable uniformity. In addition, some federal courts have applied the UCC to federal government supply contracts, although the UCC has not been enacted as federal statutory law.[1]

6.2   APPLICABILITY OF THE UCC TO CONSTRUCTION

Article 2 is the UCC article that has the greatest importance for the construction industry. That article governs the sale of "goods," which the Code defines as "all

---

[1] *See Padbloc Co. v. United States*, 161 Ct. Cl. 369 (1963).

102

things (including specially manufactured goods) that are movable at the time of identification to the contract for sale."[2] Because of this broad definition of goods, it might seem that the UCC would apply to nearly all construction contracts, but determining UCC applicability can be difficult. The UCC does not apply to many construction contracts because it does not cover contracts for the provision of labor or other services, as opposed to the sale of goods.

Many construction contracts involve a mixture of goods and services. For such mixed, or "hybrid," contracts, courts have adopted several approaches for determining UCC applicability. Most courts have adopted the rule that UCC applicability depends on the contract's primary or predominant purpose. If the contract's primary purpose is the sale of goods, with labor or other services incidentally involved, then the UCC will apply.[3] Otherwise, the UCC will not apply.

A few courts have taken a different approach. They apply the UCC to the portion of the "hybrid" contract pertaining to goods but not to the rest of the contract, even where the contract's primary or predominant purpose is to provide services.[4] This approach is more likely if the goods are supplied separately and the buyer could have purchased them off the shelf.[5]

Even under the predominant purpose approach, no litmus test is available for determining UCC applicability because of the difficulty of identifying a contract's predominant purpose, although a few rules of thumb provide guidance. The UCC is more likely to apply to a hybrid construction contract that does not require the performance of labor or other services at the job site. The UCC is also more likely to apply where the hybrid contract is a purchase order rather than a subcontract. Conversely, the UCC is less likely to apply to a prime contract with an owner, which

---

[2] § 2-105.

[3] *See, e.g., Dakota Gasification Co. v. Pascoe Building Systems, A Division of Amcord, Inc.*, 91 F.3d 1094 (8th Cir. 1995) (holding that contract to supply and service structural steel was governed by the UCC); *United States v. City of Twin Falls, Idaho*, 806 F.2d 862 (9th Cir. 1986), *cert. denied*, 482 U.S. 914 (1987) (contract to furnish and install sludge-control equipment governed by Article 2); *Pittsburgh-Des Moines Steel Co. v. Brookhaven Manor Water Co.*, 532 F.2d 572 (7th Cir. 1976) (sale and installation of million-gallon water tank governed by Article 2); *Bonebrake v. Cox*, 499 F.2d 951 (8th Cir. 1974) (sale and installation of bowling alley equipment governed by Article 2); *Town of Hooksett Sch. Dist. v. W.R. Grace & Co.*, 617 F. Supp. 126 (D.N.H. 1984) (Code applied without discussion of sale and installation of asbestos insulation); *Standard Structural Steel Co. v. Debron Corp.*, 515 F. Supp. 803 (D. Conn. 1980), *aff'd*, 657 F.2d 265 (2d. Cir. 1981) (sub-subcontract to design and fabricate steel was contract for sale of goods with services incidentally involved); *Gulf Coast Fabricators, Inc. v. Mosley*, 439 So. 2d 36 (Ala. 1983) (sale and erection of prefabricated metal building governed by Article 2); *Port City Constr. Co. v. Henderson*, 266 So. 2d 896 (Ala. Civ. App. 1972) (contract for sale of concrete and "all labor to pour and finish" held to be a sale of goods); *Colorado Carpet Installation, Inc. v. Palermo*, 668 P.2d 1384 (Colo. 1983) (installation of carpet a sale of goods); *Mennonite Deaconess Home & Hosp., Inc. v. Gates Eng'g Co.*, 363 N.W.2d 155 (Neb. 1985) (installation of one-ply roof membrane governed by Article 2); *Meyers v. Henderson Constr. Co.*, 370 A.2d 547 (N.J. 1977) (contract to supply and install overhead doors governed by Article 2).

[4] *See, e.g., Foster v. Colorado Radio Corp.*, 381 F.2d 222 (10th Cir. 1967).

[5] *Anthony Pools v. Sheehan*, 455 A.2d 434 (Md. 1983) (supply of diving board governed by UCC even though construction of swimming pool was not).

courts usually find to be a contract primarily for services. Because of the many exceptions, these rules of thumb cannot predict with certainty whether the UCC will apply to a particular transaction.

6.3   MODIFYING UCC OBLIGATIONS

Even when the UCC applies, buyers and sellers may alter most UCC provisions, by agreement. UCC Section 1-102(3) expressly permits parties to make alterations in its provisions and obligations, except where specifically limited. In addition, other Code sections expressly authorize parties to "contract out" of that section.

The parties cannot limit or disclaim certain obligations under the Code, however, even when they agree. These unwaivable obligations include the obligations to act in good faith, with diligence, with due care, and in a reasonable manner, all of which are implied in all transactions covered by the UCC. Section 102(3) provides, however, that the parties may determine by agreement the standards by which performance of these obligations is to be measured.

6.4   CONTRACT FORMATION UNDER THE UCC

The traditional, common-law rules of contract formation provide that a contract is formed when there is an offer and an acceptance of that offer. Under those traditional rules, an offer is rejected unless the acceptance is its "mirror image." For example, if the response to an offer includes terms that add to or differ from the terms in the original offer, then the response is considered to be a rejection of the original offer and a counteroffer, based on the additional or different terms. If the parties proceed to perform, a contract is formed that includes the terms of the counteroffer.

Article 2, governing the sale of goods, changed the common-law rule to bring the process of contract formation into line with the perceived realities of business practices relating to contracts for the sale of goods. The basic principles governing the formation of a contract for the sale of goods are outlined below.

6.5   Total Agreement on All Terms and Conditions Is Not Required

Departing from the common-law "mirror image" rule for offer and acceptance, Article 2 focuses on the practical conduct of the parties. That article permits formation of a contract any time the parties show a sufficient intent to form a contract, by their words or conduct.[6]

Under § 2-207, an acceptance is not required to be a "mirror image" of the offer. Instead, an acceptance may contain different or additional terms, so long as it is coupled with a definite expression of acceptance or a written confirmation sent within a

---

[6] *See* § 2-207(3).

reasonable time, unless the acceptance is expressly made conditional upon the original offeror's acceptance of the additional terms. Additional terms are treated as proposals for additions to the contract. They will become part of the contract unless the offer limits acceptance to its terms or the offeror timely objects to the additional terms. Finally, as mentioned above, the parties' conduct may be sufficient to establish a contract despite major unresolved conflicts in the written offer and acceptance. Complete agreement between the parties on all terms is not required. In the absence of complete agreement, the contract will consist of the terms upon which the parties agreed, along with the implied terms (price, time, etc.) provided under other provisions of Article 2, which are discussed below.

6.6 The Requirement for a Written Contract

Section 2-201 provides that contracts for the sale of goods with a value of more than $500 are unenforceable unless there is a written document that is "sufficient to indicate that a contract for sale has been made between the parties and signed by the party against whom enforcement is sought." This rule has several exceptions and can be satisfied in several ways. For example, the requirement of a written document may be satisfied where one party, within a reasonable time, sends a written confirmation of the contract to the other party, and the receiving party has reason to know of the contents of the confirmation and fails to give written notice of objection to its contents within 10 days after receipt.[7] The writing requirement does not apply when:

(1) The goods are specially manufactured for the buyer, and the seller has started manufacturing or procuring the goods;

(2) The opposing party admits in court papers the existence of the contract; or

(3) The buyer has received and accepted the goods or made payment that the seller has accepted.

The best way to ensure compliance with the requirement for a written contract is to formalize the contract in a document signed by both parties. This may not be customary or it may be impractical, such as where one is ordering supplies or materials by telephone. In such cases, either party may be able to back out if none of the above exceptions apply.

6.7 Withdrawal of an Offer

In another departure from the common law, the Code allows a buyer or seller to hold an offer open even if the other party does not pay to keep it open. Section 2-205 provides that a written offer to buy or sell goods that gives assurances that the offer will be held open is irrevocable for the stated period or, if no period is stated, for a reasonable period not exceeding three months.

---

[7] *See Atlas R. Constr. Co. v. Commercial Stone Co.*, 33 Pa. D. & C.3d 477 (Ct. Comm. Pl. 1984) (contractor's lawyer's demand letter sent to stone supplier three and one-half months after breach of oral contract held timely written confirmation of oral contract).

6.8   Filling Gaps in Essential Contract Terms

Ideally, parties to a contract for the sale of goods will agree in writing to all essential contract terms after careful negotiations, during which the terms are openly presented and discussed. The UCC recognizes, however, that a contract may be formed without such negotiations and that gaps in the contract may result. To resolve problems arising from such gaps, § 2-204(3) provides that a contract will not be unenforceable because of indefiniteness, merely because the parties left one or more terms open. This only applies, however, where the parties clearly intend to make a contract, and a reasonably certain basis exists for formulating a remedy in the event of a breach.

Under the UCC, the quantity of goods bought and sold is usually the only essential contract term. If the parties agree on those terms, courts will enforce a contract even if they have to imply a reasonable price.[8] Courts will also enforce a contract by filling in other "gaps." For instance, if the delivery date is missing, courts will imply a reasonable date based on the circumstances. Except in the case of a "requirements" or "output" contract, if the quantity of goods is missing, the courts will not fill in the "gap" by implying a "reasonable" quantity of goods.[9]

In addition to implied terms, a court enforcing a contract may also take notice of customary industry practices and other factors. Section 2-208 provides that express terms of the contract may be interpreted in light of the parties' conduct, course of dealing, trade usage, or course of performance. This Code section recognizes that the parties themselves know best what they meant by their agreement and that their actions under the agreement are the best indication of what was meant.

6.9   RISK OF LOSS

The Code provides a comprehensive scheme for allocating risk of loss between the parties while the goods are in transit or storage. In doing so, it provides greater certainty and enables the party that bears the risk of loss to arrange for appropriate insurance.

---

[8] *D.R. Curtis Co. v. Mathews*, 653 P.2d 1188 (Idaho App. 1982); *Irby Constr. Co. v. Shipco, Inc.*, 548 F. Supp. 1023 (D. La. 1982) (place of delivery); *Beiriger & Sons Irrigation, Inc. v. Southwest Land Co.*, 705 P.2d 532 (Colo. App. 1985) (time of delivery).

[9] A "requirements" contract is one in which the buyer expressly or implicitly agrees to obtain all of the requirements for a certain kind of goods from the seller. In certain circumstances, a "requirements" contract may be useful to a contractor purchasing construction materials. Where it would be difficult to estimate accurately the quantity of material required, the supplier may simply agree to meet the contractor's requirements—that is, to supply all the material the contractor needs to perform the contract. Should the quantity exceed that which was reasonably contemplated, the courts limit the quantity, at the contract unit price, to a reasonable amount. If the buyer does not in fact require any of the goods, there is no obligation under a requirements contract to take or pay for any quantity. An "output" contract calls for the buyer to purchase all of the seller's output of a certain kind of goods. In the construction setting, the "output" contract is rarely encountered. *Brem-Rock, Inc. v. A. C. Warmack*, 624 P.2d 220 (Wash. Ct. App. 1981) (sand and gravel requirements contract upheld despite being "harsh bargain"); *Atlantic Track & Turnout Co. v. Perini Corp.*, 989 F.2d 541 (1st Cir. 1993) (sale of salvaged materials on railroad rehabilitation project); *R. A. Weaver & Assocs., Inc. v. Asphalt Constr., Inc.*, 587 F.2d 1315 (D.C. Cir. 1978) (subcontract to supply and install crushed limestone).

Where neither party is in breach of contract, Section 2-509(1) allocates the risk of loss as follows:

(1) If shipment is by a carrier, risk of loss passes to the buyer upon delivery to the carrier, unless the contract requires delivery at a particular destination, in which case the risk of loss passes to the buyer when the carrier tenders delivery at that destination.

(2) If a third party is to hold the goods in a bailment, the risk of loss passes on tender of documents of title or when the bailee acknowledges the buyer's right to possession. Thus, the risk of loss may pass to the buyer for construction materials that are stored off-site in a warehouse over which the buyer has no control.

(3) In all cases not covered by (1) and (2), the risk of loss passes to the buyer upon receipt of the goods if the seller is a merchant, or on tender of delivery if the seller is not a merchant. For example, where a supplier ships in its own trucks, the risk of loss passes upon the buyer's receipt of the goods.

The Code allows any of these provisions to be changed by agreement of the parties.[10] A contract that specifies "F.O.B. (free on board) place of shipment," also known as a "shipment" contract, places the risk of loss on the buyer as soon as the goods are placed in the possession of a common carrier.[11] Conversely, a contract that specifies "F.O.B. place of destination," also known as a "destination" contract, leaves the risk of loss on the seller until the delivery of the goods is tendered at the named destination.[12]

6.10   INSPECTION, ACCEPTANCE, AND REJECTION

6.11   Inspection of the Goods

Where the seller is required or authorized to send the goods to the buyer, the Code gives the buyer the right, before acceptance, to inspect the goods at any reasonable time and place and in any reasonable manner.[13] The parties may agree to modify the time, place, or even the right of inspection by inserting appropriate terms in the contract.[14]

Inspection and payment are linked under the Code, although the parties may agree otherwise by contract. Where the buyer is to pay on or after delivery of the goods, the buyer has the right to inspect before payment. Absent an opportunity to inspect, the buyer has no obligation to pay. The buyer may lose the right of inspection, however, by agreement or by conduct showing waiver.

---

[10] In a typical purchase order or sales order form, the risk of loss is covered by delivery terms, such as FOB.
[11] § 2-319(1)(a).
[12] § 2-319(1)(b).
[13] § 2-513(1).
[14] *Id.*

The buyer may contract away its right of inspection by agreeing to cash on delivery (C.O.D.) payment terms or other similar terms. C.O.D. effectively requires payment before delivery, which precludes inspection.[15] Where the contract requires payment before inspection, payment does not necessarily constitute acceptance or defeat the buyer's right to a later inspection and assertion of its rights and remedies.[16] Denial of the right of inspection is a breach of contract. Consequently, if the contract does not allow the seller to ship C.O.D., the seller breaches the contract by shipping C.O.D. because this denies the buyer its right to inspect.[17]

The buyer may waive the right of inspection by unreasonably delaying inspection.[18] Whether an inspection delay is reasonable or so unreasonable as to amount to a waiver depends on the facts and circumstances of the transaction. The buyer must also give notice of any defect within a reasonable time after inspection or it will likewise waive any remedy.[19]

The right of inspection includes the right to test the goods, which may include tests that must destroy a small amount of the goods. Use of the goods for destructive or nondestructive testing does not constitute acceptance of the goods as long as the testing is necessary and reasonable.

Initially, the buyer bears the expenses of inspection and testing. It may recover those expenses from the seller, however, if the buyer properly rejects the goods as a result of the inspection and testing.[20]

6.12   Rejection of Goods

If the goods themselves or the seller's manner of tending their delivery do not meet the contract requirements, the buyer has the option of accepting or rejecting the goods or any part of them.[21] If the buyer rejects some or all of the goods, the buyer must do so within a reasonable time and give notice to the seller.[22] If the buyer fails to notify the seller of the reason for rejection, the buyer cannot rely on that reason to justify rejection if the seller could have cured the defect after reasonable notice.[23]

6.13   Acceptance and Notice of Breach

Section 2-606 defines "acceptance" of goods. It provides that a buyer "accepts" goods by knowingly taking nonconforming goods or by doing any act inconsistent with the

---

[15] § 2-513(3).

[16] § 2-512.

[17] 4 Anderson, Uniform Commercial Code § 2-513:13 (1983).

[18] *Michael M. Berlin & Co. v. T. Whiting Mfg., Inc.*, 5 U.C.C. Rep. Serv. 357 (N.Y. Sup. Ct. 1968).

[19] § 2-607; *see* discussion *infra* **Section 6.12**.

[20] § 2-513(2).

[21] § 2-601.

[22] § 2-602(1).

[23] § 2-605(1).

seller's ownership.[24] For example, a buyer may accept construction materials by using them to perform work because such use is inconsistent with the seller's continued ownership of those materials.

Section 2-607 governs the buyer's conduct upon acceptance of goods and is one of the most important Code sections for construction projects. Section 2-607(a) provides that the buyer must pay for all accepted goods. This may seem obvious because, in the absence of problems with quantity, quality, or timeliness, the buyer usually pays for the goods in the ordinary course of business. Section 2-607(a) has important implications, however, because of the Code definition of "acceptance." For instance, where the buyer contends that there are problems with the goods but it fails to give the seller notice or otherwise protect its interests, the buyer may still have to pay for the goods because it may be deemed to have accepted them.[25]Another aspect of § 2-607 that merits attention is its notice requirement. The buyer cannot sit idly by while defective goods are being used. Section 2-607(3) requires the buyer to give the seller notice of any breach within a reasonable time to preserve any remedy.[26] Failure to give notice bars any remedy.[27] For the notice to be "reasonable," the buyer must give it within sufficient time to afford the seller a chance to remedy the breach and minimize the resulting damages.[28]

6.14 WARRANTIES UNDER THE UCC

The Code identifies three kinds of warranties to protect buyers of goods. The first and most obvious is the express warranty, which is a written explanation of the goods' capabilities or limitations of the goods.[29] The second is the implied warranty of merchantability, which is the warranty that the goods will be fit for ordinary use.[30] This warranty is "implied" because it is part of a contract regardless of whether it is written in the contract. The third is the implied warranty of fitness for the intended purpose. This warranty is also part of a contract, whether or not written in the contract, but only where the seller has or should have knowledge of the buyer's specific needs and sells goods to satisfy those needs. In that situation, the seller warrants that the goods are suitable for meeting such specific needs.[31]

---

[24] See *Meland v. Intermountain Sys., Inc.*, 712 P.2d 1295 (Mont. 1985) (buyer accepted goods by erecting entire building after discovering incorrect lengths in parts of prefabricated metal building).

[25] *Economy Forms Corp. v. Kandy, Inc.*, 391 F. Supp. 944 (N.D. Ga. 1974), *aff'd*, 511 F.2d 1400 (5th Cir. 1975) (general contractor was obligated to pay for concrete forms despite alleged defects).

[26] *Smith-Wolf Constr., Inc. v. Hood*, 756 P.2d 1027 (Colo. Ct. App. 1988) (subcontractor gave reasonable notice of breach of warranty of methods and rates of application of waterproofing product).

[27] *Town of Hooksett Sch. Dist.*, *supra* note 3 (school failed to give notice of breach of implied warranty after learning about problems associated with asbestos installed 25 years earlier).

[28] *Metro Inv. Corp. v. Portland Rd. Lumber Yard, Inc.*, 501 P.2d 312 (Or. 1972) (notice of siding defects not untimely although given two years after the defect was discovered).

[29] § 2-313.

[30] § 2-314.

[31] § 2-315.

6.15 Warranty Disclaimers and Limitations

The Code includes rules governing a seller's attempt to limit or disclaim warranty coverage.[32] Generally, a seller's disclaimer language must conform to the wording suggested by the Code. Case law addressing this subject has developed to the point that sellers have little trouble including enforceable disclaimer provisions in their contracts. The disclaimer provisions commonly state that "there is no implied warranty of merchantability or any other implied warranty that extends beyond the express warranty included in this contract." This is not required, however. A seller need only state that the goods are "as is" or "with all faults" to disclaim all warranties.

Warranty limitations are often more important than warranty disclaimers.[33] Sellers typically seek to limit their exposure to buyers by limiting the buyers' damages or substituting an alternative remedy. For example, a seller may seek to limit the buyer's remedy to a return of the goods and repayment of the price, or to repair and replacement of the defective goods.[34] To be effective in barring consequential damages—that is, business losses other than those incurred to obtain conforming goods—the seller must provide that the alternative remedy is exclusive of all other remedies. If the alternative remedy is not expressly exclusive, then the stated remedy will merely be one of many forms of relief.[35] A UCC disclaimer may not be effective to eliminate tort liability—that is, for negligence or strict liability in tort—although a seller may obtain a waiver of tort claims through a properly drafted contract provision.

Finally, § 2-719(2) gives the buyer recourse to all other Code remedies when the exclusive, limited remedy fails of its essential purpose. In other words, the buyer is not restricted to an exclusive, limited remedy that fails to work. The most common limited remedy is repair or replacement of the defective goods. If the defect cannot be repaired or replaced within a reasonable time, however, that remedy may fail of its essential purpose and the buyer may be able to sue for damages.[36]

---

[32] § 2-316.

[33] §§ 2-718, 2-719.

[34] *Salt River Project Agric. Improvement & Power Dist. v. Westinghouse Elec. Corp.*, 143 Ariz. 368, 694 P.2d 198 (1984) (disclaimer of UCC contract remedies and limitation on damages upheld where $4.5 million turbine failed).

[35] *Id.*

[36] *Chatlos Sys., Inc. v. NCR Corp.*, 635 F.2d 1081 (3d Cir. 1980) *after remand*, 670 F.2d 1304 (3d Cir. 1982), *cert. dismissed*, 457 U.S. 1112 (1982) (ineffective repair of computer system over one-and-one-half-year period was failure of repair remedy); *Garden State Food Dist., Inc. v. Sperry Rand Corp.*, 512 F. Supp. 975 (D.N.J. 1981); *but see Kaplan v. RCA Corp.*, 783 F.2d 463 (4th Cir. 1986) (repair remedy did not fail where seller replaced defective antenna immediately); *Flow Indus., Inc. v. Fields Constr. Co.*, 683 F. Supp. 527 (D. Md. 1988) (late delivery of pump not necessarily a failure of essential remedy). *But see Middletown Eng'g Co. v. Climate Conditioning Co.*, 810 S.W.2d 57 (Ky. Ct. App. 1991) (126 days found to be reasonable; summary judgment granted for the seller). Even if the limited remedy fails and the buyer is entitled to sue for damages, a contract clause excluding consequential damages may still be effective.

6.16 STATUTE OF LIMITATIONS AND COMMENCEMENT OF THE WARRANTY PERIOD

Generally, tender of delivery triggers the start of the warranty period for the goods. Tender of delivery is "an offer of goods under a contract as if in fulfillment of its conditions even though there is a defect when measured against the contract obligation."[37] Similarly, tender of delivery triggers the right to sue, the cause of action, for delivery of defective goods. The statute of limitations begins to run when the cause of action arises.[38] In most, but not all states, the Code statute of limitations is four years from tender of delivery.[39]

There are several important exceptions, however, to these general principles. The most important exception permits the parties to alter by agreement the timing of both the commencement of the warranty period and the running of the statute of limitations. For example, they can agree to make both events contingent upon acceptance of the goods by the buyer after a reasonable period for inspection.

A second exception arises when the seller attempts repairs that ultimately prove unsuccessful. Sometimes such repair attempts are considered to "toll," or suspend, the running of the statute of limitations, but the rules governing this exception vary significantly from state to state. Some states hold that repair efforts do not suspend the running of the limitation period.[40] Other states hold that the limitation period does not run during the seller's repair efforts.[41] Often, the key factor in determining whether a seller's repair efforts toll the running of the statute is whether the seller made any promises or assurances to the buyer that the defects could be repaired. In such cases, a court will usually examine such promises or assurances to see if they caused the buyer to forbear from filing suit.[42]

A third exception arises where the seller makes a warranty of future performance. Some parties, seeking to avoid the running of the limitations period, have argued that this exception applies merely because they could not discover the defect until some point after tender of delivery. Courts have usually rejected this argument, however, unless the warranty required more in the way of future performance than merely meeting the contract specifications.[43] One example of a construction warranty that

---

[37] *Standard Alliance Indus., Inc. v. Black Clawson Co.*, 587 F.2d 813 (6th Cir. 1978), *cert. denied,* 441 U.S. 923 (1979).

[38] *South Burlington Sch. Dist. v. Calcagni-Frazier-Zajchowski Architects, Inc.*, 410 A.2d 1359 (Vt. 1980) (breach of contract to supply roof materials occurred on delivery).

[39] § 2-725.

[40] *See, e.g., K/F Dev. & Inv. Corp. v. Williamson Crane & Dozer Corp.*, 367 So. 2d 1078 (Fla. Dist. Ct. App.), *cert. denied,* 378 So. 2d 350 (Fla. 1979).

[41] *See, e.g., Ontario Hydro v. Zallea Sys.*, Inc., 569 F. Supp. 1261 (D. Del. 1983).

[42] *See Weeks v. Slavick Builders, Inc.*, 180 N.W.2d 503 (Mich. Ct. App. 1970), *aff'd,* 181 N.W.2d 271 (1970).

[43] *See Safeway Stores, Inc. v. Certainteed Corp.*, 710 S.W.2d 544 (Tex. 1986) (containing an extensive listing of cases supporting the "universal rule in other jurisdictions [that] an implied warranty does not fall under the exception in the Code because, by its nature, it cannot explicitly extend to future performance").

extends to future performance is the typical 10-year or 20-year roofing warranty. For instance, express language such as "bonded for up to 20 years" may provide a warranty of future performance.[44] In contrast, the statement that concrete forms will withstand specified loads was not a warranty of future performance, and breach of that warranty occurred upon tender of delivery, not upon use and failure of the forms.[45]

A special problem exists with regard to the statute of limitations where the purchase agreement provides that the seller will indemnify and hold the buyer harmless from claims and losses arising from the sale of, or the buyer's use of, the goods. The statute of limitations generally does not begin to run on a breach of an indemnification agreement until the seller refuses to honor it, even though delivery of the goods occurred much earlier.[46]

6.17 PERFORMANCE ISSUES

6.18 Anticipatory Repudiation/Adequate Assurance of Performance

When one party to a contract (the aggrieved party) has reasonable grounds for feeling insecure about the other party's ability or desire to fully perform in the future, the aggrieved party has a right to require the other party to provide adequate assurances of full performance.[47] The adequacy of the assurances is measured by commercial standards. The term "commercial standards," as well as the notion of insecurity, may be defined by agreement of the parties to avoid many of the problems of interpretation inherent in this section.

The aggrieved party may make a demand on the other party, which then has the duty to provide adequate assurance of performance within a reasonable time but not longer than 30 days. The failure to provide adequate assurances within a reasonable time is a repudiation of the contract. In case of repudiation, the aggrieved party is entitled to take action to mitigate its damages pursuant to § 2-610. The aggrieved party may: (1) await performance by the repudiating party for a reasonable time; (2) resort to any remedy for breach even though the aggrieved party has stated it will await performance; or (3) simply suspend its own performance. In practice, the aggrieved party cannot demand more than "adequate" assurances of performance. Otherwise, the aggrieved has none of these rights, even if the other party refuses to meet those demands.

The aggrieved party may also ask the other party to provide additional security, but not so much as to modify the essential terms of the contract. For instance, the

---

[44] *Little Rock Sch. Dist. of Pulaski County v. Celotex Corp.*, 574 S.W.2d 669 (Ark. 1978). *See Mittasch v. Seal Lock Burial Vault, Inc.*, 344 N.Y.S.2d 101 (N.Y. 1973) (warranty that a burial vault would provide "satisfactory service at all times" was a warranty of future performance).

[45] *Raymond-Dravo-Langenfelder v. Microdot, Inc.*, 425 F. Supp. 614 (D. Del. 1976).

[46] *See, e.g., Tolar Constr. Co. v. GAF Corp.*, 267 S.E.2d 635 (Ga. Ct. App. 1980), *rev'd on other grounds*, 271 S.E.2d 811 (Ga. 1980).

[47] § 2-609.

seller cannot demand payment in advance when the contract expressly or impliedly provides for a 30- to 60-day billing cycle and other security is offered. On the other hand, verbal assurances by a buyer that payment eventually will be made is not adequate when the seller is demanding that payment be made on time. Examples of adequate assurances by a buyer would include presentation of statements from its banker, submission of a letter of credit, establishment of an escrow account for future payments, or even offering a mortgage on other property.

6.19   Dealing with the Other Party's Insolvency

Under the UCC, a party is insolvent if it has ceased to pay its debts in the ordinary course of business, cannot pay its debts as they become due, or is deemed insolvent under federal bankruptcy laws.

Upon discovering the buyer's insolvency, the seller may:

(1) Stop delivery if the goods are still in transit;
(2) Refuse delivery unless the buyer pays cash for the delivered goods and all prior deliveries; or
(3) Reclaim the goods:
    (a) Within 10 days, if the buyer received the goods on credit while insolvent; or
    (b) At any time, if the buyer misrepresented its solvency in writing to the seller within three months prior to delivery.

The right to reclaim the goods is an important right under the Code, but it has certain limitations. The most important limitation is that the original seller's right to reclaim is lost if the original buyer has resold the goods to a good-faith purchaser. For example, in the construction context, a supplier may not recover goods from an insolvent subcontractor, even if the goods have not yet been incorporated into the project, if the prime contractor or owner has already paid the subcontractor for the goods.

A prime contractor or owner should be cautious about an attempt to use this exception to defeat a supplier's right to reclaim goods. First, payment to an insolvent subcontractor is generally unwise unless the subcontractor has already performed the work for which it is entitled to be paid, as opposed to merely purchasing supplies that it will later incorporate into the project. Second, this exception requires good faith by the prime contractor or owner and, therefore, may not apply if the subcontractor's insolvency is obvious. Unless the subcontract requires prompt payment and the contractor has made prior prompt payments for materials, a sudden hasty payment to a subcontractor may show that the prime contractor knew of the subcontractor's insolvency and was attempting in bad faith to impair the seller's ability to reclaim. In these circumstances, the better course of action would be to work directly with the seller to obtain possession and title to the goods.

The Code also addresses the opposite situation in which a buyer is faced with an insolvent seller. Under § 2-502, a buyer may take possession of goods for which it has contracted, but only where two conditions apply. First, the goods in question must be specially manufactured goods or goods specifically identified as intended for the buyer. Second, the buyer must have made at least partial payment for the goods and the seller became insolvent within 10 days after the first payment. Absent these special circumstances, the buyer may not obtain possession but may acquire a security interest in the goods under Article 9 of the Code.

6.20   Excuse of Seller's Performance by Failure of Presupposed Conditions

Purchase orders and sale agreements usually include a *force majeure* clause. A typical *force majeure* clause excuses nonperformance by either the buyer or the seller that is caused by an act of God, war, strike by a common carrier, and other causes beyond the control of the parties. Under the Code, a *force majeure* clause is lawful and enforceable.

Where the contract does not include a *force majeure* clause, the Code provides that a late delivery or nondelivery will be excused if the seller's performance has been made commercially impracticable by the occurrence of a contingency, the nonoccurrence of which was a basic assumption of the contract, or by good-faith compliance with a domestic or foreign governmental regulation.[48] Where the seller remains capable of partial performance, the seller must allocate production and deliveries among its customers.[49] In addition, the seller must notify the buyer of delay or nondelivery and the amount of any allocation of available deliveries.[50] If the impracticability affects the agreed manner of delivery, and a reasonable substitute is available, the buyer must accept the reasonable substitute.[51]

"Impracticability" under this Code section means "commercial impracticability." This is a more lenient standard for excusing performance than is available under the common law that typically applies to most construction contracts.[52] Consequently, contractors should bear this Code section in mind when purchasing goods, and should seek to impose by contract a greater obligation on the seller than the Code imposes.[53] Otherwise, the contractor may be required to perform while its suppliers—that are providing goods and, therefore, are governed by the Code—will be excused from performance.

Increased costs do not constitute commercial impracticability unless they result from an unforeseen contingency. Mere unexpected difficulties and expenses do not excuse performance unless they are so extreme that they are outside the contemplation of the parties.[54] A severe shortfall of raw materials or supplies due to a war

[48] § 2-615(a).

[49] § 2-615(b).

[50] § 2-615(c).

[51] § 2-614(a).

[52] *Helms Constr. & Dev. Co. v. State*, 634 P.2d 1224 (Nev. 1981).

[53] § 2-615.

[54] *Sachs v. Precision Prods. Co.*, 476 P.2d 199 (Or. 1970); *Resources Inv. Corp. v. Enron Corp.*, 669 F. Supp. 1038 (D. Colo. 1987).

embargo or unforeseen shutdown of a major source of supply that either causes a large increase in costs or prevents the seller from procuring basic supplies, however, may constitute commercial impracticability.[55]

6.21 Buyer's Remedies

If the seller delivers nonconforming goods or fails to make delivery, the buyer may either purchase replacement goods ("cover") or, in appropriate circumstances, obtain specific performance by forcing the seller to make delivery of conforming goods.

The measure of damages in the event of cover is the difference between the contract price and the amount actually paid for the substitute goods, plus incidental and consequential damages. An alternate measure of damages is the difference between the contract price and the market price, plus incidental and consequential damages. That latter measure may be used to establish that the buyer's actual cover price was unreasonably high or low. However, where the two measures of damages differ only marginally, the party seeking damages may recover by using the more favorable amount.

A buyer may obtain specific performance where the goods are otherwise unavailable or the price of replacement goods has increased so dramatically that it would be a poor business practice to cover. Specific performance is an extraordinary remedy that may be available from a court on an expedited basis.

The buyer must provide the seller with prompt notice of rejection or revocation of acceptance. Failure to provide prompt notice will almost always constitute wrongful rejection/revocation by the buyer.[56] Prompt notice is important because the seller has the right to cure the defects and tender the repaired goods as conforming to the contract as long as the time for performance has not yet expired.[57] Although the seller's right to cure does not extend to major repairs, the definition of "major" in the commercial construction context will vary, depending upon the cost and nature of the goods.

6.22 Seller's Remedies

Where the buyer wrongfully rejects goods, wrongfully revokes acceptance of goods, fails to make payment, or repudiates the contract, the seller may stop delivery, resell the goods and sue for losses from the resale, recover damages, or cancel the contract.[58] A seller's damages may also include incidental costs incurred in transportation, care, and custody of the goods involved in stopping delivery and any resale.[59]

---

[55] *Swift Textiles, Inc. v. Lawson*, 135 Ga. App. 799, 219 S.E.2d 167 (1975).

[56] § 2-601, 2-714(1).

[57] § 2-508.

[58] § 2-703.

[59] § 2-710.

➤ POINTS TO REMEMBER

The following key points should be noted:

- Article 2 of the Uniform Commercial Code (UCC) applies to virtually every construction project to some extent.

- Although Article 2 of the UCC does not apply to contracts for the sale of construction services, it does govern transactions involving the sale of "goods," which are defined as "all things . . . which are movable at the time of identification to the contract for sale."

- Where a contract involves the sale of both goods and services, most courts will look to the predominant nature of the contract to determine whether the UCC applies.

- Most of the terms imposed by the UCC may be modified by agreement of the parties.

- Some of the traditional common law rules governing contract formation do not apply under the UCC, making it easier to establish the existence of an enforceable contract.

- The UCC provides for three kinds of warranties for the protection of buyers of goods: express warranties; the implied warranty of merchantability; and the implied warranty of fitness for the intended purpose.

- Parties may disclaim or limit warranties, but the Code imposes limitations on the warranties that can be disclaimed and may require special language.

- The UCC grants certain rights if the buyer is insolvent:

- The UCC contains a comprehensive scheme for allocating the risk of loss between the contracting parties.

- Other issues expressly addressed by the UCC include the buyer's right to inspect the goods; the circumstances under which a buyer may reject the goods; the buyer's obligations and rights upon acceptance of the goods; the requirements governing notice of a breach; and a party's rights upon learning that the other party is not likely to perform ("anticipatory repudiation").

- Most purchase orders and sales agreements contain a *force majeure* clause; in the absence of such a clause, the UCC provides that late delivery or non-delivery will be excused if the seller's performance has been made impracticable by the occurrence of a contingency, the nonoccurrence of which was a basic assumption of the contract, or by good-faith compliance with a governmental regulation.

- The UCC sets forth the remedies that are available to a buyer or seller should the other party breach the agreement.

7

THE AUTHORITY AND RESPONSIBILITY OF THE ARCHITECT/ENGINEER

Design is (or should be) an integral part of the construction process, and many construction disputes have their genesis in real or perceived design problems. In addition to design responsibility, the project architect or engineer often plays a pivotal role in the administration of the construction project, with responsibility for contract interpretation, certifications of the contractor's applications for payment, inspections, contract compliance, and acceptance of the work.[1] Therefore, proper recognition of the relative rights and responsibilities of the design professional is essential to an understanding of the legal relationships involving the parties to construction projects and to the proper allocation of responsibilities and liabilities among those parties.

Professional services performed by architects and engineers overlap to such an extent that in many cases it is difficult to draw a distinction between them.[2] Frequently, the architect or engineer is primarily responsible for the design and contract documents. That entity or person, in turn, subcontracts specific responsibility to independent mechanical, electrical, structural, and plumbing engineers or other consultants.[3] However, many design firms provide both architectural and engineering

[1] Of course, there is no such thing as a "typical" construction project. However, for the sake of brevity, unless otherwise noted, comments in this chapter will presume project delivery by what Professor J. Sweet calls the "eternal triangle" (i.e., an owner contracting with a design professional and a contractor, each acting as an independent party). J. Sweet, *Legal Aspects of Architecture, Engineering, and the Construction Process*, 104 (5th ed. 1994).

[2] *Georgia Assoc. of the AIA v. Gwinnett County*, 233 S.E.2d 142 (Ga. 1977). Architects and engineers are generally licensed individually (not as corporations or partnerships) and must meet the standards for their particular profession. *Southern Eng'g Co. v. Central Ga. Electric Membership Corp.*, 389 S.E.2d 380 (Ga. Ct. App. 1989), *rev'd on other grounds*; *Kneip v. Southern Eng'g Co.*, 395 S.E.2d 809 (Ga. 1990).

[3] For the purposes of this chapter, the two professions will be considered interchangeable (or collectively as "design professionals"), as the principles discussed are in most cases applicable to both. *See generally* Abbett, *Engineering Contracts and Specifications* (Wiley, 4th ed., 1963). Unless otherwise noted, the term "design professional" will be used in this chapter to refer to licensed architects and engineers.

117

services. Federal government agencies use the term "architect/engineer" to refer to both types of services, and their contracts are generally similar in form and content.

7.1 STANDARD OF CARE AND PROFESSIONAL RESPONSIBILITY

The scope of the design professional's authority and responsibility on a particular project is often defined in the contract between the design professional and the owner.[4] Contractual privity is the direct relationship between parties to a contract. Contractual privity allows the owner to sue the design professional directly for damages attributable to a breach of contract, or the design professional to sue the owner if the owner breaches the contract.

Even if the design contract is between the owner and a design corporation, the individual design professionals can be personally liable to the owner, where their actions are negligent and the professionals reasonably knew or should have known that a client would be injured by the negligent performance of their services.[5] Moreover, certain obligations, such as a duty to perform the contract "skillfully, carefully, diligently, and in a workmanlike fashion," may be implied by law into a construction-related contract, so that the design professional is responsible for meeting that duty even if it is not specifically stated in the contract.[6]

More often than not, contractual privity is absent between the contractor and the design professional. Therefore, a contractor generally cannot sue a design professional engaged directly by the owner for breach of contract. A contractor seeking to recover directly against a design professional must resort instead to lawsuits based on legal theories such as negligence, third-party beneficiary, and breach of implied warranty, which are discussed later in this chapter.

Design professionals, like other professionals, are not required to be perfect. Whether a claim for professional negligence or malpractice is asserted by the project owner, the contractor, or some third party, the performance of the design professional

---

[4] For sample standard form contracts between architects and owners, see Associated General Contractors of America (AGC) Document No. 240 (2000 ed.) and American Institute of Architects (AIA) Form B141-1997. For sample standard form contracts between engineers and owners, see Associated General Contractors of America (AGC) Document No. 240 and Engineers Joint Contract Documents Committee (EJCDC) No. E-520. The design professional and the owner need to clearly identify the terms of their contract, particularly regarding the scope of the professional's standard of care, to avoid unintended consequences. In *Chesapeake Paper Products Co. v. Stone & Webster Eng'g Corp.*, 51 F.3d 1229 (4th Cir. 1995), the owner and engineer exchanged alternative contract forms, neither of which was signed by the other party. However, the owner's form was sent after the engineer's form and was not rejected by the engineer. The owner's contract form contained a higher standard of care providing "all materials and articles covered by this order . . . will be free from defects in material and/or workmanship, and merchantability." The owner and engineer later signed an amendment modifying the owner's contract form, even though that contract had not been signed by the engineer. When a dispute later arose concerning the engineer's standard of care, the jury found that the engineer had accepted the owner's contract and the higher standard of care as evidenced by the contract amendment that modified the owner's contract form.

[5] *Moransais v. Heathman*, 744 So.2d 973 (Fla. 1999).

[6] *Flintkote Co. v. Dravo Corp.*, 678 F.2d 942, 949 (11th Cir. 1982).

will be measured against the applicable professional standard of care. As one court explained,

> Architects, doctors, engineers, attorneys, and others deal in somewhat inexact sciences and are continually called upon to exercise their skilled judgment in order to anticipate and provide for random factors which are incapable of precise measurement. The indeterminate nature of these factors makes it impossible for professional service people to gauge them with complete accuracy in every instance. Thus, doctors cannot promise that every operation will be successful; . . . and an architect cannot be certain that a structural design will interact with natural forces as anticipated. [Instead,] the law has traditionally required, not perfect results, but rather the exercise of that skill and judgment which can be reasonably expected from similarly situated professionals.[7]

Thus, generally, the design professional is not liable for the occasional inconsequential error in judgment, and in order for a plaintiff to recover on a professional liability claim, the offense must typically rise to the level of a failure on the part of the design professional to exercise reasonable care and professional skill. If, before engagement, a representative of the design professional represents to the owner that he or she possesses specialization and experience in a particular area, that design professional may be held to a higher standard of care.[8] In addition, the description of the design professional's tasks or objectives may be so specific as to the final performance of the completed project that those representations can amount to an express warranty of the design (with the resulting contractual liability applied) in lieu of a professional negligence standard.[9]

7.2   THE AUTHORITY OF THE DESIGN PROFESSIONAL

During the design development phase, the design professional generally acts as an independent contractor to the owner. Thus, the design professional may not be deemed to be an agent of the owner, and, in such cases, the design professional may not have the power to bind the owner with regard to third parties. (Similarly, design consultants to the project architect or engineer are typically independent contractors, not agents of the project architect or engineer.[10])

However, when the design professional assumes inspection and supervisory responsibilities during construction (as often happens), that person becomes a "special" agent of the owner with limited authority to act on behalf of the owner.[11] Moreover, parties may, by their conduct during the course of a project, depart from the written terms of their contract, with the result being a modification of the parties'

---

[7] *City of Mounds View v. Walijarvi*, 263 N.W.2d 420, 424 (Minn. 1978).

[8] *See generally* J. Sweet, *Legal Aspects of Architecture, Engineering, and the Construction Process*, § 14.04, at 259–63 (1994).

[9] *Arkansas Rice Growers Cooperative Ass'n v. Alchemy Industries, Inc.*, 797 F.2d 565 (8th Cir. 1986).

[10] *Lagerstrom v. Beers Construction Co.*, 277 S.E.2d 765 (Ga. Ct. App. 1981).

[11] *See generally* J. Acret, *Architects and Engineers*, § 8.01 (Shepard's/McGraw-Hill 1993).

respective authority or responsibilities. In such circumstances, the limits of job-site supervisory authority of the design professional may be governed by application of the common-law agency principles of actual, implied, or apparent authority.

7.3   Actual Authority

"Actual authority" refers to that authority that an owner (i.e., the principal) expressly confers upon its agent (commonly the design professional) and that the agent accepts. As a "special agent," the design professional's actual authority is usually outlined in the contract with the owner and is limited to specific functions. For example, on a typical construction project (and in the absence of contract terms to the contrary), the design professional does not have the authority to make or modify contracts on behalf of the owner/principal,[12] or to materially change the scope of the work, the contract price, or the contract time.[13] The owner can, however, grant to the design professional the actual authority to take these actions by so providing in the applicable contracts. The Associated General Contractors of America's (AGC) Standard Form of Agreement Between Owner and Architect/Engineer (AGC Document No. 240, 2000 ed.) and Short Form Agreement Between Owner & Architect/Engineer (AGC Document No. 245, 2000 ed.) address the authority of the architect to act on behalf of the owner, as does the American Institute of Architects' (AIA) Standard Form of Agreement Between Owner and Architect with Standard Form of Architect's Services, Form B141-1997.[14]

The design professional's authority may also be established in documents to which the design professional is not a party. For example, it is common for the contract between the owner and the contractor to specify the extent of the design professional's authority to act as agent for the owner.

The AGC Document No. 200, Standard Form of Agreement and General Conditions Between Owner and Contractor (2000 ed.), provides that the project owner will provide professional services through the project architect/engineer and that the owner can direct the contractor to submit various documents to the project architect/engineer, including applications for payment, notice of unknown or concealed site conditions, shop drawings, samples, and submittals.[15]

The most recent edition of the standard-form General Conditions of the Contract for Construction, A201-1997, published by the AIA, describes with some specificity the authority of the architect to act in the owner's behalf.[16] Similarly, B141-1997, the AIA's standard-form owner/architect agreement, also addresses the architect's authority to act in the owner's behalf.[17] However, the limits set forth in the owner/architect agreement do not typically bind the contractor, who, in most cases, has not

---

[12] *Crown Constr. Co. v. Opelika Mfg. Corp.*, 480 F.2d 149, 151 (5th Cir. 1973).

[13] *See, e.g.*, A201-1997, § 4.1.2.

[14] AGC Document No. 240 (2000 ed.), ¶ 3; AGC Document No. 245 (2000 ed.); AIA B141-1997.

[15] *See, e.g.*, AGC Document No. 200 (2000 ed.), ¶¶ 3.15, 3.14, 3.16, 9.2.1.

[16] *See, e.g.*, A201-1997, Article 4.

[17] *See, e.g.*, B141-1997, §§ 2.6.1.6; 2.6.2.

even seen the owner/architect agreement. Moreover, both of these standard forms are often modified by the parties during precontractual negotiations. Therefore, to the extent that the various contracts and incorporated documents are not coordinated, disputes may arise due to the imposition of inconsistent obligations on the parties.

Similarly, language pertaining to a design professional's authority can often be found in different sections of the general conditions, in the specifications, and even on the plans, and many disputes arise because one or more of the parties failed to understand those limits. It is, therefore, essential that the design professional know the extent of the authority to act on behalf of the owner. Consequently, every participant in the construction process should be familiar with the design professional's actual authority as expressed in its contract with the owner and in the plans and specifications; and any inconsistencies should be resolved by the parties before disputes arise.

7.4 Implied Authority

The doctrine of "implied authority" is closely related to that of actual authority. Implied authority gives the design professional the means to act in ways that are incidental to the exercise of actual authority. In other words, implied authority allows the design professional to do those things that are considered reasonable and necessary for the exercise of the design professional's actual authority. The design professional acting under implied authority may bind the owner with those acts even though the authority to perform those acts is not expressly set forth in the contract. For example, if the contract makes the design professional responsible for the review and approval of pay requests, by implication, the design professional also receives the authority to reject pay requests. As this example illustrates, determination of the reasonableness and necessity of incidental acts is often a matter of common sense. However, this is not always the case.

Consider hypothetically the situation in which a contract expressly grants the design professional the actual authority to decide whether to require the contractor to post payment and performance bonds. Is, then, the design professional also granted the implied authority to represent to a potential subcontractor that a payment bond will be required? At least one court considering that question held that the design professional had the implied authority to make that representation, and thus the design professional's representation was binding upon its principal, the owner.[18]

7.5 Apparent Authority

"Apparent authority" differs from actual and implied authority. Apparent authority may arise when an owner acts in a way that leads a contractor (or other third party) to reasonably believe that the design professional has authority beyond the actual authority expressed in the contract. If a reasonably prudent third party would conclude from the owner's conduct that the design professional has been granted the

---

[18] *Bethlehem Fabricators, Inc. v. British Overseas Airways Corp.*, 434 F.2d 840 (2d Cir. 1970).

authority that the owner holds out to be reposed in the design professional, the owner will likely be bound by the design professional's acts. Thus, by their conduct, parties may unwittingly expand the authority of the design professional to act on the owner's behalf.

For example, suppose a contract expressly authorizes a design professional to issue change orders only if a written change order is signed by the owner. If a design professional subsequently issues written change orders without that signature (but with the owner's knowledge and consent), the owner will likely be bound by these change orders because the design professional had the apparent authority to issue them. However, a contractor must be particularly careful when relying upon the apparent authority of a design professional to approve changes or additional work without the owner's consent. It is always best to obtain the owner's signature on change orders or other contract modifications potentially impacting cost, time, or third parties.

The dilemma of apparent authority with respect to a design professional's issuance of change orders has been addressed in the evolution of the AIA General Conditions of the Contract, A201. Before 1976, the A201 indicated that the design professional had the authority to issue a written change order without the owner's signature if the design professional had written authority that could be furnished to the contractor upon request. In 1976, the AIA amended A201 to require that change orders be signed jointly by the owner and the architect. The 1987 edition of A201 went one step further by requiring that change orders be prepared by the architect and signed by the owner, architect, and contractor. Also, since 1987, a contract modification signed by only the architect and owner has been deemed to be a "Construction Change Directive."[19] In any event, with the exception of minor changes in the work that do not involve adjustment of the contract sum or the contract time, the AIA General Conditions limit the authority of the design professional to issue changes without the owner's signature.[20] This general scheme was not changed in the AIA's recent revisions, except that the architect is now responsible for making interim determinations of amounts to be paid for the purposes of the certification of the contractor's monthly pay applications where the parties dispute the cost impact of the scope changes related to Construction Change Directives.[21]

Similarly, the 2000 version of the AGC Document No. 200 does not provide for the project architect or engineer to issue changes, reserving that responsibility for the owner.[22] However, the AGC contract provides that the owner can direct the contractor to submit its pay applications to the architect/engineer.[23]

It has long been generally established that a design professional does not have authority to unilaterally modify the contract documents. For example, in *Smith v. Board of Education*,[24] an architect directed the original contractor to dispense with the specified wainscoting in the corridors of a building. Upon the completion of the

---

[19] *See* A201-1987, § 7.3.

[20] *See* A201-1997, § 7.4.

[21] *See* A201-1997, § 7.3.8.

[22] *See* AGC Document No. 200 (2000 ed.), Article 8.

[23] *See* AGC Document No. 200 (2000 ed.), § 9.2.1.

[24] 85 S.E. 513, 515 (W. Va. 1915).

building, the owner engaged a replacement contractor to install the omitted wainscoting and then deducted this cost from the amount paid to the original contractor. In the lawsuit that followed, the court held in favor of the owner, reasoning that the original contractor's reliance upon the architect's unilateral directive to omit the specified wainscoting was unreasonable. This principle generally applies today, unless the contractor can establish apparent authority of the design professional to alter the plans and specifications through the actions of the owner.

Disputes frequently arise in connection with a design professional's verbal orders for extra work or changes when the contract requires a written change order. Generally, the owner is not bound by such oral authorizations unless the owner waives the written change order requirement. In one case, for example, the design professional orally instructed the contractor to use a more expensive material than was originally specified. However, the contract provided that no changes resulting in added cost could be authorized by the architect, and that any such changes could be made only by a written order of the owner signed by the architect. The court held that the contractor was not entitled to recover any additional cost because the design professional did not have the authority to direct the change.[25]

A design professional who, without authority, issues orders or directives risks exposure to potential liability for the consequences. Modern courts have demonstrated an increased willingness to hold design professionals responsible for their actions and not let them hide behind concepts of agency, especially when a contractor has acted reasonably in relying on the design professional.[26]

7.6 Ratification of the Design Professional's Authority

Although contractual limits on a design professional's authority to act in an owner's behalf may afford some protection to owners where an agent acts outside the limits of its authority, the owner may undermine such protection by conduct or representations indicating the owner's ratification of the agent's acts or the owner's acceptance of the benefits related to them.

For example, in one case, the superintendent of the general contractor routinely signed delivery tickets presented by a concrete supplier. On the back of those tickets was a broad preprinted indemnification provision in favor of the concrete supplier. After a job-site accident, the concrete supplier sought enforcement of the indemnification provision. The general contractor defended by asserting that the superintendent was clearly without the authority to agree on behalf of the general contractor to indemnify the supplier. The court held that this defense, although it had some merit, did not overcome the fact that the general contractor had, without objection to the indemnity clause, routinely paid invoices based on the delivery tickets. Such conduct was deemed to have ratified the initially unauthorized conduct of the superintendent, and that ratification defeated the general contractor's agency-related defense.[27]

---

[25] *Iowa Elec. Light & Power Co. v. Hopp,* 266 N.W. 512 (Iowa 1936). *See also C.B.I. Na-Con, Inc. v. Macon-Bibb Water & Sewerage Auth.,* 421 S.E.2d 111 (Ga. Ct. App. 1992).

[26] *Prichard Bros., Inc. v. The Grady Co.,* 436 N.W.2d 460, 464–65 (Minn. Ct. App. 1989).

[27] *Pioneer Concrete Pumping Servs., Inc. v. T&B Scottdale Contractors, Inc.,* 462 S.E.2d 627 (Ga. Ct. App. 1995).

7.7   SUPERVISORY AND ADMINISTRATIVE FUNCTIONS OF THE DESIGN PROFESSIONAL

Although sometimes, particularly when the federal government is involved, responsibility for the supervision or administration of construction is placed with the owner or an independent construction manager, many contracts require the design professional to perform supervisory and administrative functions during the construction phase.

The following sections will focus on the five frequently occurring aspects of the design professional's construction-phase supervisory and administrative roles:

- Interpretation of the plans and specifications (§ 7.8);
- Review and approval of shop drawings and submittals (§ 7.9);
- Inspection and testing (§ 7.10);
- Issuance of certificates of progress or completion in connection with the contractor's applications for payment (§7.11); and
- Resolution of disputes between the owner and the contractor (§ 7.12).

7.8   Interpretation of the Plans and Specifications

The plans and specifications commonly generate many questions during the course of construction. Minor issues often arise because a specific element of work is inadequately detailed or specified in the contract documents. It is rare for every detail of the work to be expressly set forth in the plans and specifications. Thus, parties are often forced to interpret the contract requirements based on their prior dealings, industry practice, code requirements, and the conduct of the parties leading up to the point of dispute. However, simple contract interpretation is often inadequate to resolve disputes resulting from ambiguous or defective plans and specifications or oral change directives. During the course of a project, the parties' interests may conflict to the degree that it is difficult or impossible to distinguish between "interpretation" of the contract documents and "remediation" of those that are defective. Fortunately, most construction industry participants have historically employed reasonable judgment and open communication to resolve "informally" the great majority of interpretation issues and other disputes, relying on dispute review boards, arbitrators, or the courts only when necessary to resolve intractable problems related to defective documents.

Under most standard-form contracts and under many project-specific "custom" contracts, the supervising design professional is given the authority to interpret the plans and specifications. This authority theoretically gives the design professional some degree of control over the work as it progresses and establishes an initial framework within which to solve problems and maintain consistent project administration. However, the responsibility that accompanies this authority exposes design professionals to liability to owners for negligent interpretation of the plans and specifications. This may be true even when an owner uses the design of a separate design consultant. For instance, in one case, the architect was found liable for a faulty design that had been recommended to the owner by an expert engineer. In defense, the architect alleged that it was entitled to rely on the engineer's professional advice. The court viewed the architect's act of affixing its professional stamp on the plans as an implicit acceptance of an affirmative duty to review the plans to ensure that they were technically sound. In deciding against the architect, the court reasoned that, if the architect did not have the expertise to review the engineer's plans, the architect should have abstained from stamping the engineer's documents or should have withdrawn from the project.[28] In general, a design professional who seals drawings is assuming responsibility for those plans.[29]

As noted above, the design professional's authority to interpret the contract requirements does not include the authority to place additional burdens or liabilities upon the owner or the contractor by modifying contract terms. For example, a dispute arose on one project over a design professional's interpretation of the contractor's obligation to provide additional fill. Although the plans and specifications contained no reference to additional fill, the architect determined that the contractor was required to provide it without additional compensation. The court held that the architect did not have the power, express or implied, to add to or take away from the contractual rights or liabilities of either party under the contract.[30]

In addition to the literal wording of the contract documents, the design professional's discretion in interpreting the plans and specifications may be limited by general practice and trade custom in the construction industry. For example, in one case, a court held that a subcontractor was entitled to additional compensation for performing certain painting work beyond normal custom, despite a contrary interpretation of the subcontract by the architect. The court stated that although the architect had been given authority to make final decisions regarding the meaning of plans and specifications, the contract implied that the architect would render a reasonable decision that was consistent with industry custom or trade usage.[31]

This same principle applies in the federal arena. A contractor on a government project may be entitled to rely on industry custom and practice in the absence of any contractual provision to the contrary. In one case, the United States Court of Claims awarded damages to a contractor for costs incurred in meeting higher standards than required under a reasonable interpretation of the contract specifications. In that case, the contractor was directed to construct wooden concrete forms within tolerances that were not set forth in the specifications and that were more restrictive than necessary to meet the specified tolerances for the finished concrete. The contract merely specified that the "forms shall be true to line and grade." The court implied common

---

[28] *South Dakota Bldg. Auth. v. Geiger-Berger Assoc.*, 414 N.W.2d 15, 24 (S.D. 1987).

[29] *Ambassador Baptist Church v. Seabreeze Heating & Cooling Co.*, 184 N.W.2d 568 (Mich. Ct. App. 1970).

[30] *Tomlinson v. Ashland County*, 173 N.W. 300, 303–04 (Wis. 1919).

[31] *John W. Johnson, Inc. v. J.A. Jones Constr. Co.*, 369 F. Supp 484 (E.D. Va. 1973). *See also Batson-Cook Co. v. Loden & Co.,* 199 S.E.2d 591 (Ga. Ct. App. 1973) (general contractor liable for enforcement of architect's unreasonable rejection of slightly flawed bricks; rejection was inconsistent with industry practices but not technically violative of express contract terms).

trade practices to support an award to the contractor, reasoning that the federal government must state in clear and unambiguous language any intention to alter industry custom or trade usage with respect to required tolerances.[32]

The design professional's power to interpret contract requirements also carries with it the duty to render these interpretative decisions honestly and in good faith. Practically speaking, the design professional is working for the owner. Thus, it may be difficult at times for the design professional to exercise independent judgment. Furthermore, the design professional is often placed in the awkward position of being forced to judge the adequacy of the very plans and specifications produced by that firm. A sense of professional pride (combined with a reluctance to present the owner with a change order to correct an omission or mistake in the design) can sometimes influence a design professional's objectivity in the field. Courts faced with this situation often find that the failure of a design professional to perform its administrative duties honestly and in good faith diminishes or nullifies the authority to interpret contract requirements or arbitrate contract disputes.[33]

7.9 Review and Approval of Shop Drawings and Submittals

The design professional generally reviews data submitted by the contractor, such as samples, shop drawings, product data, and schedules. The primary purpose of shop drawings and submittals is for the owner and the architect to obtain an understanding of how the contractor intends to perform certain aspects of the work.[34] These submittals also inform the design professional and the owner of the processes, materials, and methods to be used by the contractor, and reflect the contractor's understanding of the contract requirements.

The design professional's review of submittals has legal consequences. One question that arises frequently is whether the design professional's approval of these processes and methods relieves the contractor of its responsibility to comply with the specifications. Generally, it does not.[35]

In one case, for example, a contractor with a design-build contract hired a design professional to do the design work and review shop drawings.[36] The contractor later awarded work to a subcontractor that was required to submit shop drawings prepared by the subcontractor to the contractor for review and approval. The contractor then forwarded the shop drawings to the design professional. The design professional approved them even though they contained errors. After the work had been performed in accordance with the shop drawings, problems were discovered and the subcontractor was forced to correct them. The subcontractor subsequently sued

[32] *Kenneth Reed Constr. Corp. v. United States*, 475 F.2d 583 (Ct. Cl. 1973).

[33] *See, e.g., State Highway Dep't v. Knox-Rivers Constr. Co.*, 160 S.E.2d 641 (Ga. Ct. App. 1968) (engineer's refusal to certify release of funds withheld did not excuse owner's payment where reason for refusal was based on engineer's erroneous interpretation of documents).

[34] *See* J. Sweet, *Legal Aspects of Architecture, Engineering and the Construction Process* 221 (5th ed.,1994).

[35] Community Science Technology Corp., ASBCA No. 20244, 77-1 BCA ¶ 12,352; *see also D.C. McClain, Inc. v. Arlington County*, 452 S.E.2d 659 (Va. 1995) (county's approval of shop drawings did not relieve the contractor of obligation to properly construct project).

[36] *Lutz Eng'g Co. v. Industrial Louvers, Inc.*, 585 A.2d 631 (R.I. 1991).

the design professional for its alleged negligence in approving the defective shop drawings. The court held in favor of the design professional, stating that the design professional owed no duty to the subcontractor, that the subcontractor was responsible for meeting all of the requirements of its subcontract, and that the subcontractor had no right to rely on the design professional's approval of its shop drawings because the design professional was hired to provide services only to the contractor, not to subcontractors.

When a design professional's performance of this review function goes beyond mere review and comment and the design professional attempts to change the contractor's scope of work, courts will likely deem such an attempt beyond the scope of its authority. In that situation and absent some ratifying act, the owner may not be bound by such approval.[37]

The 1987 AIA General Conditions were specific as to the design professional's liability for approving contractor submittals that change the specifications. The AIA's General Conditions relieve the contractor of responsibility for deviations from the contract documents contained in submittals, if and only if "the Contractor has specifically informed the Architect in writing of such deviation at the time of submittal and the Architect has given written approval to the specific deviation." Additional language in A201-1997 specifically excludes from the architect's indicated approval those revisions made by the contractor, its subcontractors, or suppliers to shop drawings and other submittals resubmitted without a specific graphic indication of each revised element.[38]

AGC Document No. 200, Standard Form of Agreement and General Conditions between Owner and Contractor, contains in subparagraph 3.14.1 similar requirements for the contractor's written identification of deviations, substitutions, or changes and express written approval from the "Owner" authorizing the deviation, substitution, or change. Subparagraph 3.14.5 contains an additional specific requirement for the approval of substitutions. One difference in the two industry forms is that the AGC form initially reserves to the owner, not the architect, the right to make such decisions or approvals.

However, courts can and do impose liability on design professionals for approving shop drawings that deviate from the contract documents. For example, in one case, the contract documents called for 10-gauge steel to be used for stair pans. The contractor submitted shop drawings showing 14-gauge steel, which the design professional approved. Workmen later walked onto the pans and were injured when the landing pan collapsed through the framework. The court held in favor of the workmen and against the design professional, finding that the contract language, ostensibly limiting the scope of the architect's review of shop drawings to "conformance with the design concept of the Project and for compliance with the information given in the Contract Documents," did not relieve the design professional of liability for its negligence in supervising the shop drawing process as evidenced by the architect's failure to detect the error.[39]

---

[37] *Fauss Constr., Inc. v. City of Hooper*, 249 N.W.2d 478, 481 (Neb. 1977) (enforcing contract terms limiting design professional's authority).

[38] A201-1997 § 3.12.9.

[39] *Jaeger v. Henningson, Durham & Richardson*, 714 F.2d 773, 776 (8th Cir. 1983).

Perhaps the most notable example highlighting professional responsibility related to the shop drawing process arose out of the 1981 Kansas City Hyatt Regency disaster in which a multistory interior hotel bridge collapsed, killing more than 100 persons and injuring 186. The cause of the collapse was a faulty structural steel detail that had been introduced into the process through shop drawings. The court discounted the engineer's attempt to avoid liability for negligence by asserting a defense that industry "custom and practice" allowed engineers to rely upon fabricators "to design certain structural steel connections." The court noted that, by affixing his professional stamp to the documents, the certifying engineer assumed responsibility for the entire engineering project and that his professional duties were "nondelegable."[40]

The design professional also has an obligation to review and act upon a shop drawing or submittal within a reasonable time. To the extent the contractor is delayed or hindered by the design professional's failure to approve or reject a submittal, the owner, and perhaps even the design professional, may be liable to the contractor.[41]

7.10   Inspections

Frequently the design professional is engaged by the owner to inspect work for conformity to contract requirements. In performing these inspection duties, the design professional acts as agent for the owner. The design professional, under these circumstances, typically has the implied authority to reject work. Disputes often arise when the design professional rejects work that the contractor believes complies with the contract. Factual disputes in this area cover every aspect of construction and generally turn on issues of contract interpretation, workmanship, and sufficiency of materials.

Improper rejection of work will generally not expose the design professional to liability to the contractor, because the design professional is usually acting on behalf of the owner.[42] However, incorrect or negligent inspections that result in improper rejection of the work or in the owner's liability to the contractor for damages may generate legal action by the owner against the design professional.

Additionally, problems often arise when a design professional fails to inspect work or fails to detect in a timely manner nonconforming work as the work proceeds. Contractors, believing their work to be satisfactory, may cover up or build upon nonconforming work, making corrections or remedial work more difficult. Who should be responsible when corrections to nonconforming work are more expensive because the problem is discovered too late: the contractor who improperly constructed the work or the design professional who failed to timely catch the error?

The 1987 AIA General Conditions, and most other construction contract forms, limit the scope of the owner's and design professional's responsibility to what can

---

[40] *Duncan v. Missouri Bd. for Architects*, 744 S.W.2d 524, 536–37 (Mo. App. 1988).

[41] *See, e.g., E. C. Ernst, Inc. v. Manhattan Constr. Co. of Texas*, 551 F.2d 1026 (5th Cir. 1977), *cert. denied*, 434 U.S. 1067 (1978); *Prichard Bros. Inc. v. Grady Co.*, 436 N.W.2d 460 (Minn. Ct. App. 1989).

[42] *See, e.g., Nannis Terpening & Assocs., Inc. v. Mark Smith Constr. Co.*, 318 S.E.2d 89 (Ga. Ct. App. 1984).

generally be described as inspection and contract compliance obligations.[43] However, the contractor's former and more general "study, compare, and report" obligations have been considerably expanded in A201-1997. The contractor is now required to take timely field measurements "related to that portion of the work" and to "observe any conditions at the site affecting it." Arguably, this imposes on the contractor an ongoing task-specific duty to confirm the constructability of the design. Reports of inconsistencies or omissions must be in a form "as the Architect may require." A201-1997 contains no model forms upon which a contractor is to report these problems. The prudent contractor, therefore, must determine exactly what form the architect requires, since these requirements have an onerous "club" attached. If a contractor fails to timely and properly observe, study, compare, and confirm the contract documents and field conditions, or to report potential conflicts and discrepancies, that contractor may be required to pay those resulting costs of correction that could have been avoided had the contractor done so. Similarly, under A201-1997, if a contractor fails to report promptly a discovered violation or deviation of the contract documents from "applicable laws, statutes, ordinances, building codes, and rules and regulations," that contractor may be liable for the related avoidable costs.

The scope of a design professional's potential liability for job-site accidents caused by unsafe working conditions continues to trouble many courts. Generally, the design professional's obligation to monitor the quality of the work is weighed against the contractor's responsibility to control the means and methods of its performance. The courts usually resolve this issue by closely examining the language of both the design professional's contract and the construction contract.[44] AGC Document No. 200 (2000 ed.), § 3.1.2 and A201-1997, § 3.3.1 are examples of standard-form means and methods clauses. Generally, the contractor retains the primary responsibility for contract compliance and for control of construction means, methods, and techniques.

In addition, the design professional is not deemed to be responsible for supervision or inspection of construction when not required to do so by the contract.[45] For example, in a Texas case, a supervising engineering firm was found not liable for a contractor's failure to use adequate supports when pouring a concrete slab that resulted in the death of a construction worker when the slab collapsed.[46] In its decision, the

---

[43] *See generally D.C. McClain, Inc.*, *supra* note 35 (contract required contractor to verify dimension at the site before commencing construction; owner not liable for elevation discrepancies discovered in contract documents during construction process).

[44] *Moore v. PRC Eng'g, Inc.*, 565 So. 2d 817 (Fla. 4th DCA 1990); *Shepherd Components, Inc. v. Brice Petrides-Donohue & Assoc. Inc.*, 473 N.W.2d 612 (Iowa 1991); *Marshall v. Port Auth. of Allegheny County*, 568 A.2d 931 (Pa. 1990).

[45] *Goette v. Press Bar & Café, Inc.*, 413 N.W.2d 854, 856 (Minn. Ct. App. 1987). *See also C.L. Maddox, Inc. v. Benham Group, Inc.*, 88 F.3d 592 (8th Cir. 1996) (design professional not responsible to guard contractor against construction defects and deficiencies despite contract requirement for design professional to keep contractor informed of quality and progress of the work because the contractor, not designer, was responsible for construction means and methods. Design professional was responsible to make site visits but not to ensure that contractor made no errors).

[46] *Rodriquez v. Universal Fastenings Corp.*, 777 S.W.2d 513, 516 (Tex. Ct. App. 1989).

court relied on the engineer's contract, which specified that the firm was not responsible for the contractor's construction means and methods or for safety at the job site.[47]

A means and methods clause, however, does not always absolve the design professional of liability. In another Texas case, the court held an architect liable for failing to adequately inspect a project despite exculpatory contract language stating that the architect would "not be responsible for the Contractor's failure to carry out the work in accordance with the contract documents." The court reasoned that an architect who is paid to protect the owner from construction defects should be held responsible for failing to detect defective work.[48]

In another case, a court considered whether a design professional could be held liable for a fire caused by the contractor's deficient performance.[49] The design professional had entered into a standard AIA design contract that provided the following:

> The Architect shall visit the site at intervals appropriate to the stage of construction . . .
> to become generally familiar with the progress and quality of the Work and to determine
> in general if the Work is proceeding in accordance with the Contract Documents.
> However, the Architect shall not be required to make exhaustive or continuous on-site
> inspections to check the quality or quantity of the Work. On the basis of such on-site observations as an architect, the Architect shall keep the Owner informed of the progress and
> quality of the Work, and shall endeavor to guard the Owner against defects and deficiencies in the Work of the Contractor.

The fire was apparently caused by the contractor's improper placement of insulation around light fixtures that the design professional had not detected. The court rejected the argument that the design professional was not obligated to catch such a defect. Despite the general disclaimers in the AIA standard contract, the court denied summary judgment to the design professional, reasoning that the design professional had a duty to be generally knowledgeable of the quality and quantity of work in order to evaluate payment applications. The design professional was not relieved from liability simply because the contractor had failed to perform its work correctly. While the design professional was not a guarantor of the contractor's performance, it still had the responsibility to keep abreast of the quality of work.[50]

The design professional is also obligated to take action when it discovers or should have discovered the contractor's defective workmanship. The design professional can be held liable to the owner for inspection and approval of a contractor's faulty and/or nonconforming work. For instance, an architect was found to have breached the duty to guard the owner against defects and deficiencies in the work and

[47] *See Davis v. Lenox School*, 541 N.Y.S.2d 814 (N.Y. App. Div. 1989). *See also Block v. Lohan Assocs., Inc.*, 645 N.E.2d 207 (Ill. Ct. App. 1993) (architect not liable for failure to supervise and coordinate work when subcontractor's employee fell from ladder; architect's contract was limited to design and design conformance, not worker safety).

[48] *Hunt v. Ellisor & Tanner, Inc.*, 739 S.W.2d 933 (Tex. Ct. App. 1987).

[49] *Diocese of Rochester v. R-Monde Contractors, Inc.*, 562 N.Y.S.2d 593 (N.Y. Sup. Ct. 1989).

[50] *Id.* at 596; *but see C.L. Maddox, Inc.*, *supra* note 45.

was therefore liable to the owner for the cost of repairing interior wall coverings damaged because of inadequate waterproofing observed and approved by the architect.[51]

In another case, a homeowner sued an architect for habitually neglecting its duties to inspect and approve the contractor's work.[52] The architect argued that while it was contractually obligated to perform "general supervision of the construction work," its fee did not include "the cost of superintendence by a full-time inspector or Clerk of the Works." The court, however, held for the homeowner, noting that:

> The term "general supervision," as used in the instant agreement, must mean something other than mere superficial supervision. Obviously, there can be no real value in supervision unless the same be directed toward securing a workmanlike adherence to specifications and adequate performance on the part of the contractor.[53]

Similarly, in *Central School District No. 2 v. The Flintkote Co.*,[54] the court required a trial on the issue of whether the design professional had properly inspected a roof. The owner had employed a "clerk of the works" to make inspections, and the design professional contended that this eliminated its duty to inspect the work. The court rejected this argument, holding that if the architect could rely solely on the clerk of the works in this regard, then:

> [T]he owner would be deprived of the professional judgment [which] he had the right to expect. The owner's retainer of a "Clerk of the Works" for full-time, on-site services, constituted a protection that is an addition to and not a substitute for the contractual and professional obligations of the architect.[55]

From the standpoint of the contractor, a design professional's periodic inspection of construction work and failure to object to nonconforming materials and workmanship may, under the right circumstances, establish a constructive acceptance of the work and preclude an owner from refusing to pay the contractor. Although no hard-and-fast rule applies in these situations, the contractor is more likely to prevail if it can show either a reasonable reliance on the design professional to detect nonconforming work or fault on the part of the design professional or owner.

For example, an architect (who in this case also happened to be the owner and the contractor) failed to inspect a subcontractor's repairs to work that the architect had originally found inadequate. The court held that the architect's failure to inspect the remedial work and to specify any additional corrections constituted a waiver of a condition precedent that work be performed to the satisfaction of the architect before payment, and that the owner-contractor was estopped from raising the condition precedent as a defense in a suit brought by the subcontractor for breach of contract.[56]

---

[51] *Dan Cowling & Assocs., Inc. v. Board. of Educ.*, 618 S.W.2d 158 (Ark. 1981).

[52] *Pancoast v. Russell*, 307 P.2d 719 (Cal. Ct. App. 1957).

[53] *Id.* at 722.

[54] 391 N.Y.S.2d 887 (N.Y. App. Div. 1977).

[55] *Id.* at 888.

[56] *Hartford Elec. Applicators of Thermalux, Inc. v. Alden*, 363 A.2d 135, 138 (Conn. 1975).

7.11   Issuance of Certificates of Progress or Certificates of Completion and Certificates for Payment

Design professionals are often engaged to issue certificates of progress or completion, which are generally related to the owner's duty to make payments to the contractor. This type of contract requirement is valid, despite the fact that the design professional acts as the agent of the owner.[57]

The AIA A201-1997 provides seven bases for which the architect may withhold a certificate for payment: (1) defective work not remedied; (2) third-party claims filed or reasonable evidence indicating probable filing of such claims; (3) contractor's failure to make payments properly to subcontractors or to pay for labor, materials, or equipment; (4) reasonable evidence that the work cannot be completed for the unpaid contract balance; (5) damage to the owner or another contractor; (6) reasonable evidence that the work will not be completed within the contract time and that the unpaid contract balance is not sufficient to cover actual or liquidated damages; and (7) persistent failure to carry out the work according to the contract documents.[58]

While contract language may provide the design professional with a broad range of bases on which to withhold a payment certification, the refusal to issue a certificate must be exercised carefully. Common issues that arise from this duty involve the acceptance of the work upon the design professional's approval of pay requests and the liability of the design professional for the improper failure to approve progress payments. As with issues relating to inspection of the work, the analysis of questions regarding progress payments is almost always fact- and contract-specific.

---

[57] *Friberg v. Elrod*, 296 P. 1061 (Or. 1931).

[58] A201–1997, § 9.5.1. In contrast, AGC Document No. 200 provides that the owner has the authority to adjust pay requests and sets forth the following bases entitling an owner to adjust or reject a contractor's pay request:

> 9.3   ADJUSTMENT OF CONTRACTOR'S PAYMENT APPLICATION   The *Owner* may adjust or reject a payment application or nullify a previously approved payment application, in whole or in part, as may reasonably be necessary to protect the *Owner* from loss or damage based upon the following, to the extent that the *Contractor* is responsible therefor under this Agreement:
>
> > the *Contractor's* repeated failure to perform the Work as required by the Contract Documents;
> >
> > loss or damage for which the *Owner* may be liable arising out of or relating to this Agreement and caused by the *Contractor* to the *Owner* or to Others;
> >
> > the *Contractor's* failure to properly pay Subcontractors and Material Suppliers following receipt of such payment from the *Owner;*
> >
> > Defective Work not corrected in a timely fashion;
> >
> > Reasonable evidence of delay in performance of the Work such that the Work will not be completed within the Contract Time, and
> >
> > Reasonable evidence demonstrating that the unpaid balance of the Contract Price is insufficient to fund the cost to complete the Work.
>
> The *Owner* shall give written notice to the *Contractor* at the time of disapproving or nullifying an application for payment of the specific reasons therefor. When the above reasons for disapproving or nullifying an application for payment are removed, payment shall be made for the amounts previously withheld. (Emphasis added)

A number of cases confirm the design professional's duty to use the care of one skilled in that profession when issuing payment certificates. As such, the design professional can be held liable for damages resulting from a failure to act accordingly. For example, in one California case, the owner asserted that the architect was negligent in issuing certificates of payment without first determining whether the contractor had fully paid its subcontractors and materialmen. The court held that the architect, under its contract, should have protected the owner by making certain that all bills were paid or by insisting on lien waivers from suppliers.[59]

The wrongful withholding of a payment certificate can also result in a design professional's liability directly to the contractor. For example, a Mississippi court found that an engineer that reduced a contractor's pay request contrary to an audit of the contractor's work, without consulting the contractor and without adequately checking the extent of the work, was directly liable to the contractor and was liable for bad-faith damages to the contractor.[60] Similarly, an engineer's failure to properly construe the contract requirements that resulted in withholding payment from the contractor entitled the contractor to release of the contract balance.[61]

The design professional's negligence in approving pay requests and issuing progress certificates may also expose it to liability to third parties that have a financial interest in the project, such as banks or sureties. For example, in *National Surety Corp. v. Malvaney*,[62] an architect was found liable to the contractor's surety for the negligent issuance of a substantial completion certificate. Under the contract, the architect could require the contractor to present evidence that payroll and material bills had been paid before releasing retained funds. The architect, however, failed to enforce this requirement. Consequently, the contractor collected its retainage and then defaulted, leaving the burden of completing the work and satisfying claims to the surety.

The court rejected the architect's argument that its lack of privity of contract with the surety insulated it from liability to the surety. The court relied on negligence theory, ruling that the design professional owed a duty to determine whether the contractor had paid the bills to both the owner and the surety for whose mutual benefit and protection contractor funds were retained. The surety's failure to take steps to ascertain whether outstanding bills were being paid by the contractor was not held to constitute contributory negligence, because the surety had a right to assume that the retainage would not be released until the contract was fully performed.

Furthermore, in *Peerless Insurance Co. v. Cerny & Associates, Inc.*,[63] the court determined that a surety was subrogated to any claim that the owner would have

---

[59] *Palmer v. Brown*, 273 P.2d 306 (Cal. Ct. App. 1954).

[60] *City of Mound Bayou v. Roy Collins Constr. Co.*, 499 So. 2d 1354 (Miss. 1986); *see also Magnolia Constr. Co. v. Miss. Gulf South Eng'rs*, Inc., 518 So. 2d 1194 (Miss. 1988) (recognizing that the contractor had a claim against the project engineer where engineer did not recommend that the owner pay the contractor).

[61] *Textor Constr. Co. v. Forsyth R-III School Dist.*, 60 S.W.3d 692 (Mo. Ct. App. S.D. 2001).

[62] 72 So. 2d 424 (Miss. 1954).

[63] 199 F. Supp. 951 (D. Minn. 1961).

against the architect for negligent certification of progress payments.[64] Similarly, in *Westerhold v. Carroll,*[65] the court confirmed that an architect can be held liable to the indemnitor of a contractor's surety for certifying payments in excess of the value of work performed.

In *Boren v. Thompson & Assocs.,*[66] a subcontractor on a public project was allowed to sue the project architect on claims that the architect negligently allowed the disbursal of funds without verifying that a payment bond had been provided by the contractor.

Contract language typically places responsibility for performing the requirements of the contract documents on the contractor. Thus, contracts usually state that payment to the contractor does not constitute acceptance of the work and does not waive the owner's right to demand contract compliance from the contractor. The AIA General Conditions attempt to foreclose the implication that the contractor has performed in accordance with the contract documents based solely upon the architect's approval of the contractor's payment applications:

> The issuance of a Certificate for Payment will constitute a representation by the Architect to the Owner, based on the Architect's evaluations of the Work and the data comprising the Application for Payment, that the Work has progressed to the point indicated; that, to the best of the Architect's knowledge, information and belief, the quality of the Work is in accordance with the Contract Documents . . . and that the Contractor is entitled to payment in the amount certified.[67]

Despite such wording to the contrary, the design professional's certification of progress or completion may still benefit the contractor. In one case, a breach-of-contract action was brought by the owner against the contractor for failure to comply with the plans and specifications.[68] The court held that the design professional's certificate of completion was an effective defense to the owner's claim of noncompliance unless there was proof of fraud, gross negligence, or bad faith on the part of the design professional in issuing the certificate.

The design professional's certification of progress payments has also been used by subcontractors as support for claims against the general contractor. In one case, the prime contractor terminated a subcontractor for deficient performance.[69] The subcontractor, however, argued that the general contractor had sought and obtained progress payments for the subcontractor's work and that the design professional's certification of the subcontractor's work was strong evidence that the work was satisfactory. The general contractor was placed in the difficult position of arguing either

---

[64] *See also Unity Telephone Co. v. Design Service Co.,* 201 A.2d 177 (Me. 1964); *but see Fireman's Fund Ins. Co. v. SEC Donohue, Inc.,* 679 N.E.2d 1197 (Ill. 1997) (surety's subrogation rights not sufficient to allow surety to sue project engineer; privity of contract required).

[65] 419 S.W.2d 73 (Mo. 1967).

[66] 999 P.2d 438 (Okla. 2000).

[67] A201-1997, § 9.4.2.

[68] *Fuchs v. Parsons Constr. Co.,* 111 N.W.2d 727, 734 (Neb. 1961).

[69] *Sweeney Co. of Md. v. Engineers-Constructors, Inc.,* 823 F.2d 805 (4th Cir. 1987).

that the payment applications were not representations that the work was acceptable or that the design professional's approval of the payments did not constitute a binding acceptance of the work. The court of appeals held that the trial court did not err in allowing the admission of the applications into evidence and in considering that evidence in the court's determination of the subcontractor's satisfactory performance.[70]

The requirement that the design professional issue a certificate prior to issuance of payment to the contractor may be excused or waived by the parties under certain circumstances. In one case, the court found that neither the owner nor the contractor had relied on a design professional's certificate as a basis for making or receiving progress payments for completed excavation work. Consequently, the provision in the contract requiring a certificate prior to final payment was deemed waived so that neither party could insist on strict compliance with the contract requirement.[71]

Furthermore, an architect cannot delegate the responsibility of certifying progress payments to another architect and thereby escape liability for a defective building. In *Sheetz, Aiken & Aiken, Inc. v. Spann, Hall, Ritchie, Inc.*,[72] the court found that the project architect's duty as inspecting architect was to verify that the contractor had performed the work in accordance with the plans and specifications, while the duty of the architect hired to certify progress was merely to determine the amount owed to the contractor for direct construction costs and not to ensure a defect-free building.

7.12   Resolution of Disputes between the Owner and the Contractor

Another important function that may be performed by the design professional pursuant to a contract provision is the evaluation of claims and disputes between the owner and contractor. For instance, the design professional is pivotal in the dispute-resolution process under the AIA General Conditions, which require that all claims be submitted initially to the architect and the owner in writing. The submission of claims is considered a "condition precedent to arbitration or litigation of a Claim between the Contractor and Owner as to all such matters arising prior to the date the final payment is due."[73]

In contracts requiring disputes to be referred to the design professional for decision, questions may arise as to whether the design professional's decision is binding, and, if not, at what point a party can initiate arbitration or litigation. Courts are reluctant to recognize final and binding power of a design professional to resolve disputes unless the contract is clear and unambiguous in assigning that power. This reluctance may be based upon a feeling that design professionals may be partial to the owner, or perhaps because such recognition would result in the waiver of a party's right to its day in court or arbitration.

---

[70] *Id.* at 808-11; *see also Magnolia Constr.*, *supra* note 60 (recognizing that third parties are entitled to rely on an architect's performance of its contractual obligations to the owner, including the architect's certification of work performed).

[71] *Palmer v. Watson Constr. Co.*, 121 N.W.2d 62 (Minn. 1963).

[72] 512 So. 2d 99 (Ala. 1987).

[73] A201-1997, § 4.3.2. (In contrast, AGC Document No. 200 (2000 ed.), Paragraph 12 does not require a role for the project professional in the dispute resolution process.)

More difficult issues tend to arise with contracts that require claims to be submitted to the design professional for decision prior to a party's initiating litigation. How long must a contractor wait for a decision from the design professional before litigation may be commenced? What if the design professional repeatedly asks for additional documentation to support the claim, thus delaying a decision? Courts typically will not consider initial referral of a claim to the design professional to be a condition precedent to litigation unless the contract clearly states that it is.[74]

If the contract requires the design professional to render a decision within a certain period of time, the commencement of litigation would be appropriate after the time for a decision has elapsed. For example, AIA A201-199, § 4.4.2 provides that the project architect will within 10 days of receipt of a claim (1) request additional supporting data, (2) reject the claim in whole or part, (3) approve the claim, (4) suggest a compromise, or (5) advise the parties that the architect is unable to resolve the claim if it does not have sufficient information or if it would be inappropriate for the architect to resolve the claim.

If no time is specified, a reasonable time is often assumed. Some courts have held that the design professional's role as arbitrator of disputes between owner and contractor ends once the architect is no longer responsible for supervising the contractor's performance.[75]

When a design professional assumes the role of an impartial arbitrator and the contract language deems the decision of the design professional to be "final," some design professionals have enjoyed limited immunity from arbitration or litigation brought by owners and contractors resulting from the professional's decision[76] because of the performance of a quasi-judicial function.[77] However, this immunity is limited to those acts performed in a "judicial" capacity. The crucial question in such situations is whether the challenged act was within the scope of the design professional's decision-making duties.

For example, in *Blecick v. School District No. 18*, the architect was not liable for its refusal to issue a final certificate because that refusal was within the architect's capacity as arbitrator. As such, the refusal did not amount to a failure to exercise care in the issuance of a final certificate.[78] In a contrasting case, after the contractor pointed out defects in the plans and specifications, the design professional who prepared them allegedly became enraged, intentionally and maliciously trying to bankrupt the contractor and attempting to interfere with the contract between the contractor and the owner. The contractor also claimed that the design professional issued contradictory instructions, changed the plans and specifications without regard to added cost or delay, interfered with the contractor's coordination of its subcontractors, and improperly withheld progress payments. The court found that the design professional's claim of immunity based on a status as an arbitrator was an

---

[74] *Shook of W. Va., Inc. v. York City Sewer Auth.*, 756 F. Supp. 848 (M.D. Pa. 1991).

[75] *Id.*; *Tsombikos v. Brager*, 559 N.Y.S.2d 460, 462 (N.Y. Sup. Ct. 1990).

[76] *Lane v. Geiger-Berger Assocs.*, 608 F.2d 1148 (8th Cir. 1979).

[77] *Lundgren v. Freeman*, 307 F.2d 104, 117 (9th Cir. 1962).

[78] 406 P.2d 750 (Ariz. Ct. App. 1965).

inadequate defense because so many of the challenged acts were clearly outside the architect's role as arbitrator.[79]

Distinguishing the design professional's protected functions from other duties can be difficult. The deliberate or negligent misuse of the design professional's powers as arbitrator may excuse a party's disregard of a design professional's decision. In one case, a state engineer's unreasonable behavior voided his authority to classify and quantify a contractor's excavation work.[80] The contractor had agreed to construct a bridge and reconstruct a section of state highway. All "unclassified excavation" was to be performed at one price while rock excavation was to be performed at five times that price. When the contractor unexpectedly struck rock and notified the state in accordance with the contract, the department's engineer, who was designated as the final arbiter of contract disputes, was noncommunicative and delayed visiting the job site to measure the extent of the rock encountered.

Although the court recognized the engineer's authority under the contract to determine the quantity of rock, it found that the parties were not bound by an engineer's decision "manifestly arbitrary or rendered in bad faith." On the basis of the engineer's intentional failure to conduct a timely inspection, the court awarded the contractor damages for the uncompensated rock excavation. The engineer's failure to exercise its powers as arbitrator in good faith rendered the resulting decision effectively meaningless.

7.13   OTHER DUTIES OF THE DESIGN PROFESSIONAL

The administrative duties of the design professional discussed above are found in many private construction contracts. They illustrate the design professional's basic responsibilities and obligations on a project. However, these general duties of the design professional may be supplemented by the inclusion of specific provisions in the specifications, such as the following:

(1) If soil conditions are such that, in the opinion of the Architect, yard hydrants cannot be secured, use bridles.

(2) Defects in the extension of existing gas lines must be repaired to the satisfaction of the Architect.

(3) The entire jacking and shoring procedure is subject to review by the Architect.

(4) Set manhole castings in fresh bed of mortar and carefully adjust elevation or as directed by the Architect.

(5) Concrete surfaces shall be finished to a true and even plane well within limits of best trade practice and to the satisfaction of the Engineer.

---

[79] *Craviolini v. Scholer & Fuller Associated Architects*, 357 P.2d 611, 614 (Ariz. 1960); *see also Laurel Race Course, Inc. v. Regal Constr. Co.*, 333 A.2d 319 (Md. 1975) (design professional's immunity lost when design professional fails to use reasonable care and good faith when acting as an arbitrator subjecting professional to liability to owner or contractor).

[80] *Brezina Constr. Co. v. South Dakota Dep't of Transp.*, 297 N.W.2d 168 (S.D. 1980).

7.14   THE DESIGN PROFESSIONAL'S LIABILITY TO THE CONTRACTOR

Under certain circumstances, the failure of the design professional to perform properly its supervisory or administrative responsibilities may result in liability for resulting damages to the owner. These same acts or omissions may also form the basis for an action by the contractor against either the owner or the design professional.

Design professionals are increasingly being held directly liable to contractors under various legal theories, with the most prevalent involving the design professional's negligent breach of a duty owed to the owner or the contractor.

7.15   Negligence and the "Economic Loss Rule"

The negligent breach of a duty by one person often injures another person. Such harm may include a bodily injury, an injury to property, or an injury to a financial or business interest of some type. The latter is often referred to as an "economic loss." It has long been established that a person may sue in negligence for personal injuries and property damage even where the person has no contractual relationship with the defendant.[81] However, courts have historically been more reluctant to allow parties to recover in negligence for purely economic loss where there is no contractual privity between the parties. This limitation on negligence actions is called the "Economic Loss Rule."

Some jurisdictions have rejected the Economic Loss Rule outright, reasoning that a person should not have to suffer personal injury or property damage in order to recover for damage caused by the wrongful acts of a licensed professional. Other jurisdictions have based rejection of the Economic Loss Rule on the theory that a person has a duty to avoid creating a foreseeable risk of harm—regardless of whether such harm is to property, person, or business interest.

Although the Economic Loss Rule is still recognized in many states[82] and was unanimously upheld in 1986 by the United States Supreme Court in an admiralty case,[83] the rule is less rigidly applied in many jurisdictions, particularly regarding design professionals.[84] The Rule is undergoing continuous modification as litigants argue for the demise of the Rule and the allowance of recovery for purely economic harms from persons with whom they are not in privity. Third parties have been allowed to recover damages for a design professional's (1) negligent preparation of

---

[81] *MacPherson v. Buick Motor Co.*, 111 N.E. 1050 (N.Y. 1916).

[82] *Fleischer v. Hellmuth, Obata & Kassabaum, Inc.*, 870 S.W.2d 832 (Mo. Ct. App. E. D. 1993); *2314 Lincoln Park West Condominium Ass'n v. Mann, Ginn, Ebel, & Frazier, Ltd.*, 555 N.E.2d 346 (Ill. 1990); *Floor Craft Floor Covering, Inc. v. Parma Community General Hosp. Ass'n*, 560 N.E.2d 206 (Ohio 1990).

[83] *East River S.S. Corp. v. Transamerica Delaval, Inc.*, 476 U.S. 858 (1986).

[84] *See, e.g.*, *Duffcy & Sons, Inc. v. BRW, Inc.*, 74 P.3d 380 (Colo. Ct. App. 2002); *Moransais v. Heathman*, 744 So.2d 973 (Fla. 1999); *Prichard Bros., Inc. v. Grady Co.*, 428 N.W.2d 391 (Minn. 1988); *Shoffner Industries, Inc. v. W. B. Lloyd Constr. Co.*, 257 S.E.2d 50 (N.C. Ct. App. 1979); *A. R. Moyer, Inc. v. Graham*, 285 So.2d 397 (Fla. 1973).

a soils report;[85] (2) negligent failure to prepare an environmental impact statement;[86] (3) preparation of defective plans and specifications;[87] (4) negligent performance of a water percolation test;[88] and (5) negligent evaluation of an existing building.[89]

Some courts recognize a duty on the part of the design professional toward the contractor based on the design professional's inherent power over the contractor. For example, in *United States ex rel. Los Angeles Testing Laboratory v. Rogers & Rogers,*[90] a contractor was delayed in completing the work because the architect negligently interpreted certain concrete tests. The court allowed the contractor to recover damages for delay directly from the architect, stating:

> Altogether too much control over the contractor necessarily rests in the hands of the supervising architect for him not to be placed under a duty imposed by law to perform without negligence his functions as they affect the contractor. The power of the architect to stop the work alone is tantamount to a power of economic life or death over the contractor.[91]

If a design professional has agreed to perform supervisory tasks on a construction project, the contractor on the project may have a right to rely on the competence of that supervision.[92] In one case, the contractor claimed that the architect inspected and approved certain roof trusses that were improperly designed and caused the roof to collapse. The court found that the contractor may sue the design professional directly for negligence when it is foreseeable that a contractor may sustain economic loss as a result of the design professional's negligent performance of its contractual duties to others. The court recognized that each participant in a construction project must rely on the performance of others, thus obligating each to perform its duties with due care. The contractor was allowed to recover from the architect the costs caused by the architect's negligence.[93]

At least some of the courts that have permitted recovery for economic losses by parties not in privity with one another under negligence theories have not distinguished between a design professional's duties that are "supervisory" and those that are "administrative." For instance, in *Dickerson Construction Co. v. Process Engineering Co.,*[94] the project architect's duties were defined by the contract as

---

[85] *Davidson & Jones, Inc. v. New Hanover County,* 255 S.E.2d 580 (N.C. Ct. App. 1979).

[86] *COAC, Inc. v. Kennedy Eng'rs,* 136 Cal. Rptr. 890 (Cal. Dist. Ct. App. 1977).

[87] *Dufficy & Sons, Inc., supra* note 84 (subcontractor allowed to sue project engineer for negligent misrepresentation); *Malta Constr. v. Henningson, Durham & Richardson, Inc.,* 694 F. Supp. 902 (N.D. Ga. 1988); *cf. Donnelly Constr. Co. v. Oberg/Hunt/Gilleland,* 677 P.2d 1292 (Ariz. 1984) (judgment dismissing architect/engineer reversed).

[88] *Southeast Consultants, Inc. v. O'Pry,* 404 S.E.2d 299 (Ga. Ct. App. 1991).

[89] *Robert & Co. v. Rhodes-Haverty Partnership,* 300 S.E.2d 503 (Ga. 1983).

[90] 161 F. Supp. 132 (S.D. Cal. 1958).

[91] *Id.* at 136.

[92] *See Day v. National U.S. Radiator Corp.,* 128 So. 2d 660 (La. 1961) (dictum).

[93] *Shoffner Indus., Inc. v. W. B. Lloyd Constr. Co.,* 257 S.E.2d 50, 55 (N.C. Ct. App. 1979).

[94] 341 So. 2d 646 (Miss. 1977).

administrative. The court concluded that the use of the word "supervision" in the jury instructions did not connote a higher or lower standard of duty than the use of the word "inspection." The court further held that the basic question was whether the design professional had exercised reasonable care in making the observations and inspections at the project. In another case, the architect admitted during testimony that "supervision" and "administration" at the job site constitute the same set of obligations.[95]

Even in jurisdictions that reject the Economic Loss Rule, design professionals have successfully defended against claims for economic damages by alleging contributory negligence on the part of the contractor. Also, a third party asserting the negligence claim against a design professional must be able to prove that the design professional's negligence proximately caused the injury or damage. For instance, a Florida court held that an architect was not liable to a subcontractor for negligently advising the owner to reject the subcontractor's request for a substitution. According to the court, the owner made the final decision on the subcontractor's request, and the architect therefore was not the "proximate cause" of the subcontractor's damages.[96]

In some cases, courts may be unwilling to allow a contractor to sue the design professional if the contractor could not sue the owner for the same claim. For example, a contractor sued an architect for delay damages caused by the architect's negligent failure to provide power to the site for more than a year during performance. The contractor could not sue the owner because its contract with the owner contained a "no-damages-for-delay clause," precluding recovery against the owner. The court held that the contractor could not circumvent the restrictions of the no-damages-for-delay clause by suing the design professional for negligence because the no-damages-for-delay clause was broad enough to include claims against the design professional.[97]

Even in jurisdictions that recognize a contractor's right to sue the design professional in negligence for economic loss, contractors face a tough battle to recover. In general, it is much easier to establish owner liability for defective design under contract and warranty theories than it is to prove professional negligence on the part of the design professional. Negligence is determined by evaluating the acts or omissions of the alleged wrongdoer according to a specific standard of care. Design professionals are required to exercise that degree of skill and diligence ordinarily exercised under like circumstances by design professionals in good standing in the same or similar communities.[98] This standard may vary according to local practice.[99] However, under some circumstances and in some jurisdictions, the "locality rule" does not apply.[100] A design professional's deviation from established standards of

[95] *Kleb v. Wendling*, 385 N.E.2d 346, 349 (Ill. App. Ct. 1979).

[96] *McElvy, Jennewein, Stefany, Howard, Inc. v. Arlington Elec., Inc.*, 582 So. 2d 47 (Fla. Dist. Ct. App. 1991). *See generally* Bell & House, *Current Status of Economic Loss Rule*, in 1992 Wiley Construction Law Update 239 (Currie & Sweeney, eds., 1992).

[97] *Bates & Rogers Constr. Corp. v. Greeley & Hansen*, 486 N.E.2d 902 (Ill. 1985).

[98] *Overland Constructors, Inc. v. Millard School. Dist.*, 369 N.W.2d 69 (Neb. 1985).

[99] *Id.* at 76; *see also Collins Co. v. City of Decatur*, 533 So. 2d 1127 (Ala. 1988).

[100] *See, e.g., Georgetown Steel Corp. v. Union Carbide Corp.*, 806 F. Supp. 74, 78 (D.S.C. 1992); *McMillan v. Durant*, 439 S.E.2d 829 (S.C. 1993); *Doe v. American Red Cross Blood Servs.*, 377 S.E.2d 323 (S.C. 1989).

care as announced in trade publications or industry manuals published by professional organizations such as the AIA, the National Society of Professional Engineers (NSPE), and the American Consulting Engineers Council (ACEC) can be considered evidence of negligence. Such evidence is not conclusive, however, and proof of professional malpractice usually requires expert testimony by someone in the same field. Moreover, some jurisdictions require parties suing a design professional for negligence to file with their complaints an affidavit from a professional in the same field substantiating the malpractice claim.[101]

Often, design firms are of relatively smaller size or financial strength than their clients and the contractors with which they work. Consequently, contractors and third parties with large claims often obtain a more satisfying recovery by suing the owner rather than the design professional. However, errors and omissions or professional liability insurance available to architects and engineers increases a party's prospects for recovery against a design professional while at the same time reducing the potential impact upon the design professional of a large judgment in a negligence action.

Questions often arise involving interpretation of the scope of coverage to determine whether the design professional is protected from the particular claims alleged. Errors and omissions insurance policies are very specific as to the negligent acts that are covered. For instance, if a design professional performs services outside its covered range of services, it may well risk exposure to a negligence claim arising out of those services that would not be covered under the typical malpractice liability policy. Also, some design professional liability policies expressly exclude from coverage certain acts that are not considered "insurable risks" because they involve conscious and deliberate conduct on the part of the professional. Such exclusions commonly include a design professional's failure to complete drawings or specifications on time or a professional's commission of intentional torts. Because professional liability insurance coverage is so limited, professional liability insurance policies often exclude coverage of claims for a design professional's general negligence in the performance of its duties.

7.16   Intentional Torts

Although undoubtedly less common than actions for negligence, lawsuits for intentional torts can also present problems for design professionals. However, the intentional tort theory is used much less frequently because negligence theories are now more widely recognized as tools for recovery of economic loss.

On occasion, however, lawsuits for an intentional tort against a design professional can be successful. In one case, a court held that an architect's unjustified and therefore arbitrary refusal to issue a certificate of performance subjected it to intentional tort liability.[102] In another case, an appellate court sent the matter back to the trial court for a determination of whether the architect was acting within its arbitral

---

[101] *See, e.g.,* O.C.G.A. § 9-11-9.1 (Georgia statute requiring an affidavit by a licensed professional averring at least one act of professional malpractice).

[102] *Unity Sheet Metal Works, Inc. v. Farrell Lines, Inc.,* 101 N.Y.S.2d 1000 (N.Y. Sup. Ct. 1950).

role or whether the architect had willfully and wrongfully interfered with a school construction contract by inducing the school district to default the contractor.[103] The court further held that the contractor could recover punitive damages in addition to compensatory damages if the contractor could demonstrate that malicious conduct on the part of the architect was unrelated to any arbitral contractual function.[104]

An architect will not necessarily be held liable for tortious interference with contractual relations merely because the design professional recommends that the contractor replace a subcontractor.[105] However, if the evidence shows that the design professional's actions were arbitrary or were undertaken specifically for the purpose of interfering with the subcontractor's business, a contractor may have a valid cause of action.

7.17 Third-Party Beneficiary Theory

Another theory that may be available to the contractor is the argument that the contractor is a "third-party beneficiary" of the contract between the owner and the design professional. This theory, for the most part, has been infrequently successful in the construction context.

A "third-party beneficiary" is a party who is not one of the original contracting parties but who may bring an action to enforce the provisions of the contract. To do so, however, the third party must have been an "intended beneficiary" of the parties to the contract. In other words, the parties to a contract must intend to confer a direct or immediate benefit on the third party who claims to be a beneficiary. In the absence of a written expression, that intent is difficult to prove because courts require a clear expression of intent to recognize a third-party beneficiary.[106] When a third party benefits by an agreement, but that benefit is not the specific object of the intended contractual obligation, they are referred to as "incidental beneficiaries." Incidental beneficiaries do not have a legal right to bring an action to enforce the provisions of the contract.[107]

As a practical matter, a contractor is more likely to succeed in a tort action than through a third-party beneficiary theory under the contract between the owner and the design professional. For example, in one case, a contractor claimed to be a third-party beneficiary to the design professional/owner contract.[108] The court reasoned that most provisions in the contract between owner and architect calling for supervision or administration by the architect are intended for the benefit of the owner,

---

[103] *Lundgren*, 307 F.2d at 119, *supra* note 77.

[104] *See also Craviolini, supra* note 79.

[105] *See generally John W. Johnson, Inc. v. Basic Constr. Co.*, 292 F. Supp. 300, 304 (D.D.C. 1968), *aff'd,* 429 F.2d 764 (D.C. Cir. 1970) (where unfair and unjust recommendation by an architect to terminate a subcontract was not heeded by the contractor, subcontractor's cause of action against architect was properly dismissed).

[106] *Peter Kiewit Sons' Co. v. Iowa S. Util. Co.*, 355 F. Supp. 376, 392–93 (S.D. Iowa 1973).

[107] *Engle Acoustic & Tile, Inc. v. Grenfell*, 223 So. 2d 613, 620 (Miss. 1969); *Valley Landscape Co. v. Rolland*, 237 S.E.2d 120, 124 (Va. 1977).

[108] *A. R. Moyer, Inc.*, 285 So. 2d at 402–03, *supra* note 84.

and the general contractor is only an incidental beneficiary. The court did, however, recognize that the design professional could be liable to the contractor for a negligence-based cause of action. Similarly, in a Louisiana case, the contractor sued a project architect under both tort and third-party-beneficiary theories. The contractor alleged that unreasonable delays were caused by improperly prepared plans, late delivery of plans and working drawings, untimely change orders, and improperly issued correction data by the design professional. The court found the tort claims supportable but dismissed the contractor's third-party beneficiary claims.[109]

Courts typically determine whether a contractor is a third-party beneficiary by examining the apparent intent of the contracting parties.[110] However, there may be circumstances in which the design professional assumes extra responsibilities to the contractor by its conduct. An example is where the architect has no contractual duty to the owner to make extensive and thorough on-site inspections but nevertheless does make such inspections.[111] Therefore, in some cases, damages that result from improper performance of assumed duties may be recovered through third-party beneficiary actions.

By carefully drafting the contract, a design professional can reduce or avoid third-party beneficiary claims. An example of this is A201-1997, § 1.1.2, which provides:

> The Contract Documents shall not be construed to create a contractual relationship of any kind (1) between the Architect and the Contractor, (2) between the Owner and a Subcontractor or Sub-subcontractor, (3) between the Owner and Architect or (4) between any persons or entities other than the Owner and Contractor.

Such clauses are usually judicially enforced.[112]

A court might be persuaded by a third-party beneficiary argument where it is needed to salvage a cause of action. In most cases, however, the same act that would constitute the basis for a third-party beneficiary action would also constitute a negligence action, which is a more likely basis for relief.[113]

7.18 STATUTES OF REPOSE

Often, injury and resulting liability relating to construction projects do not surface until many years after the work has been completed and accepted. With the increase in scope of liability for design professionals and the prospect of perpetual liability,

---

[109] *C. H. Leavell & Co. v. Glantz Contracting Corp. of La., Inc.*, 322 F. Supp. 779 (E.D. La. 1971).

[110] *See* 17A Am. Jur. 2d, *Contracts* § 440; *see also Malta Constr. Co. v. Henningson, Durham & Richardson, Inc.*, 694 F. Supp. 902, 908 (N.D. Ga. 1988) (upholding third-party beneficiary theory by a general contractor against supplier of shop drawings under contract with a subcontractor).

[111] *Krieger v. J. E. Greiner Co.*, 382 A.2d 1069, 1081 (Md. 1978) (Levine, J., concurring).

[112] *See, e.g., Sheetz, Aiken & Aiken, supra* note 72; *Michigan Abrasive Co. v. Poole*, 805 F.2d 1001 (11th Cir. 1986); *Federal Mogul Corp. v. Universal Constr. Co.*, 376 So. 2d 716, 724 (Ala. Civ. App. 1979). AGC Document No. 200 contains comparable no third-party beneficiary language in Subparagraph 2.2.

[113] *See, e.g., Engle Acoustic & Tile, supra* note 107.

courts and legislatures have limited the length of time during which a claim for damages may be brought against a design professional. The time limits set forth in these statutes are often triggered by the discovery of the act or omission giving rise to the claim. Conversely, statutes of repose establish an outer time limit beyond which the design professional cannot be held liable for design and construction defects. Thus, a party that discovers its claim after the expiration period provided in the statute of repose is barred from asserting that claim. The language of statutes of repose varies from state to state. Often, the statutes are broadly written, so as to bar claims against "any person performing or furnishing the design, planning, supervision, or observation of construction or the construction or repair of the improvement" that are brought after the specified time.[114] Therefore, a contractor suing a design professional for damages sustained in connection with the project must institute an action that complies with the applicable statute of repose. Most, if not all, statutes of repose apply to tort claims, such as those brought under negligence or intentional tort theories. Many of the statutes also time-bar contract claims. Thus a party suing a design professional on a third-party beneficiary theory must pay close attention to applicable statutes of repose.

Statutes of repose usually take one of two forms. The majority set a maximum time after completion of the construction, beyond which no claims may be brought that relate to the design or construction of the project.[115] The second type of statute also sets a maximum time after project completion for bringing a claim. However, the latter variety of statutes may also specify a shorter period of time after the cause of action accrues within which such action must be brought.[116] Statutes of repose will specify when the statute begins to run. Depending upon the jurisdiction, the statute may begin to run upon completion of the project, substantial completion of the project, termination of the design of the improvement, or termination of the construction services.[117] Furthermore, a few statutes can be triggered by other events, such as the date of actual possession by the owner of the improvement, the date of the issuance of a certificate of occupancy, or the date of completion or termination of the contract between the design professional or the contractor and the owner.[118] Unless a statute is triggered by the issuance of a particular document, such as a certificate of substantial completion or a certificate of occupancy, judicial interpretation of the facts and the statute may ultimately be required.

---

[114] *See* Ark. Stat. Ann. § 16-56-112 (West Supp. 1999).

[115] *See* Mo. Ann. Stat. § 516.097 (Vernon Supp. 1999).

[116] *See* Mass. Gen. Laws Ann. Ch. 260 § 2B (West Supp. 1999).

[117] *See, e.g.,* Fla. Stat. § 95.11(3)(c) (West Supp. 1999); Ga. Code § 9-3-51(a) (Michie Supp. 1998) (eight years after substantial completion); Mo. Ann. Stat. § 516.097 (Vernon Supp. 1999) (10 years after improvement complete); Mont. Code Ann. § 27-2-208 (1991) (10 years after completion of improvement to real estate); N.J. Stat. Ann. § 2A: 14-1.1 (West Supp. 1997) (10 years after substantial completion).

[118] *See, e.g.,* Fla. Stat. Ann. § 95.11(3)(c) (West Supp. 1999); Colo. Rev. Stat. § 13-80-104 (Supp. 1997).

7.19 ASSUMPTION OF DESIGN LIABILITY BY THE CONTRACTOR

Traditionally, the design professional is responsible for defects and other problems associated with the design of a project. There are several ways, however, that a contractor may assume design liability. When this happens, a contractor may be required to bear not only its own costs incurred by a defect, but also those extra costs incurred by the owner or other parties related to the defect.

The most common situation where a contractor assumes the risks of design defects is on design-build projects. A design-build contractor performs the tasks ordinarily assigned to the design professional in addition to its construction duties.[119] Some owners are attracted to design-build contracts because they ostensibly create a single source of responsibility. These contracts also relieve the owner from being caught between its design professional and its contractor with respect to design disputes.[120] In addition to assuming the risks of defects and design, the design-build contractor also assumes the risk that construction will cost more than originally anticipated. As long as the performance criteria provided by the owner are not impracticable, a design-build contractor may be forced to bear the extra cost of its performance due to extended construction time.[121]

Owners are not completely immunized from design liability by entering into a design-build contract. An owner may be subject to liability for design defects depending on the level of the owner's technical expertise, the owner's active direction of the design process, or the information provided by the owner at the outset of the project. Because the design-build project delivery regime deviates from the traditional allocation of design risks, owners, contractors, and design professionals must carefully scrutinize the contract language. For further discussion of the design-build method of project delivery, *see* **Chapter 2.**

One way in which a contractor performing under the traditional design-bid-build delivery scheme may also assume a degree of design liability is by the owner's use of performance specifications or criteria. Although performance specifications dictate the results to be achieved by the contractor, they do not tell the contractor how to accomplish the desired results. Consequently, the contractor is responsible for the costs associated with achieving the end result specified. Also, the AIA's General Conditions, A201-1997, § 3.12.10, invite the design professional to delegate design responsibility to the contractor. The implications of such delegation could be problematic if they are deemed to attempt to shift professional responsibilities in violation of state professional licensing and registration laws.

However, since standard-form documents allow for such delegation, a contractor must take great care to (1) perform any design tasks assumed with competence; (2) account for the added costs and exposure related to assumption and performance of

[119] *See* **Chapter 2** for a more detailed discussion of design-build projects.
[120] *Mobile Housing Env'ts v. Barton & Barton*, 432 F. Supp. 1343 (D. Colo. 1977) ("turn-key" contractor and replacement both responsible for design liability).
[121] *Ruscon Constr. Co.*, ASBCA No. 39586, 90-2 BCA ¶ 22,768.

professional duties; and (3) make sure that the risks represented by such exposure are insured or otherwise managed.

Conflict may exist between design and performance specifications. If the contractor recognizes (or should recognize) such a conflict among the performance specifications, the contractor must notify the owner and the design professional in order to avoid potential liability due to the conflict.

For example, in *Regan Construction Co. & Nager Electric Co.*,[122] performance criteria provided by the owner for air-handling units could be met only by one particular unit on the market, which the contractor incorporated into the construction. The unit, however, did not fit into the space allotted for it with the design. As a result, the contractor incurred extra costs associated with accommodating the unit. In an action against the owner, the board of contract appeals held that the contractor assumed the risk of extra costs, reasoning that the contractor could have calculated that the specified unit would not fit in the space provided based upon the contract drawings before it ordered the air-handling unit.[123]

Another specification issue that may give rise to contractor design liability involves the use of a "brand name or equal" specification by the owner. Use of the specified brand-name product by a contractor does not necessarily or automatically relieve the contractor of liability for noncompliance with applicable performance criteria. In other words, a design defect that results from a contractor's use of a brand name as specified in a "brand name or equal" specification does not necessarily fall within the owner's implied warranty of the adequacy of the specifications. If the contractor has a choice of products, the contractor bears the burden of compliance.[124]

As noted above, one of the common duties of a design professional is to review and approve contractor submittals, including shop drawings. However, if shop drawings prepared by the contractor require a change to the original design, the contractor may still be held responsible for impacts to the overall construction caused by problems with that change even though the change has been approved by the design professional.[125] It may, however, be possible for the contractor to reduce the risk of this type of design liability by immediately bringing any shop drawing-related design or modifications to the attention of both the owner and the design professional.

Sometimes the limits of risk shifting related to substitutions are established by statute so that an architect's approval of the contractor's suggested substitution may not relieve the contractor of some warranty obligations. In *Leisure Resorts, Inc. v. Frank J. Rooney, Inc.*,[126] a contractor suggested the substitution of an air-conditioning unit on a condominium project. The substitution was approved by the architect and the engineer. When many of the units failed to perform, several condominium unit owners filed a class-action lawsuit against the developer, who, in turn, sought

---

[122] PSBCA No. 633, 80-2 BCA ¶ 14,802.

[123] *See also D.C. McClain, Inc., supra* note 35 (contract documents not allowing adequate room on-site for installation of post-tensioning apparatus did not relieve contractor of obligation to obtain easements necessary to install apparatus).

[124] *Florida Bd. of Regents v. Mycon Corp.*, 651 So. 2d 149 (Fla. Dist. Ct. App. 1995).

[125] *See generally Fauss Constr., Inc., supra* note 37.

[126] 654 So. 2d 911 (Fla. 1995).

indemnity from the contractor in a third-party action. The court held that while developers are subject to statutory "warranties of fitness or merchantability for the purposes or uses intended," the contractor's statutory warranty is to provide work and materials that "conform with the generally accepted standards of workmanship and performance of similar work."[127] In short, though the contractor had a duty to provide acceptable materials, it did not have a duty to evaluate broader issues of suitability of those materials for the purpose intended. Presumably, that would fall to the developer and the developer's architect or engineer.

Finally, contractors should be wary of standard contract clauses that expose the contractor to potential liability for design defects. Many contracts contain catchall clauses that, for example, could require the contractor to supply any and all labor and materials that can be reasonably inferred from the plans and specifications as being necessary to achieve a complete project. If the contractor fails to provide such labor or materials and a defect results, the contractor may be held liable.

➤ POINTS TO REMEMBER

- Parties can avoid many construction contract disputes by understanding the authority, responsibility, and duties of the design professional on the project.
- Owners, design professionals, and contractors need to review carefully their contract documents to ensure that the authority, responsibilities, and standard of care of the design professionals are clearly stated.
- In any given case, a design professional may have authority to do certain things on the job site because:
    (1) It is expressly stated in the contract documents (actual authority);
    (2) It is incidental or necessary to the exercise of the design professional's actual authority (implied authority); or
    (3) The acts of the owner would lead a reasonable person to believe the design professional had such authority (apparent authority).
- During construction, the project design professional is generally responsible for:
    (1) The initial interpretation of the plans and specifications;
    (2) Reviewing and approving shop drawings and other submittals;
    (3) Inspection;
    (4) Reviewing the contractor's pay requests and certifying progress and completion; and
    (5) Arbitrating certain disputes between the owner and the contractor.
- On most jobs, the design professional does not have authority:
    (1) To make changes to the work;
    (2) To direct the operations of the contractor; or
    (3) To deviate from the requirements of the contract.

[127] *Id.* at 914.

- Remember that some contracts, such as the AIA standard-form contract documents, may emphasize the design professional's role as "administrative" and otherwise seek to insulate the design professional from potential liability to the contractor or the owner for interpreting, reviewing, inspecting, approving, and performing other functions set out in the contract documents.

- The design professional may be liable in some states to the contractor for economic losses suffered due to negligent performance of the design professional's duties and responsibilities, even though there is no contract between the design professional and the contractor. The applicable law on this issue must be reviewed in each case to determine if a cause of action is available and, if so, what damages are recoverable.

- The contractor may assume design liability in certain situations. To avoid such liability, the contractor should always notify the owner and the design professional about inconsistencies between the design and the performance specifications, as well as any changes to the design resulting from the shop drawings.

8

SUBCONTRACT ADMINISTRATION AND DISPUTE AVOIDANCE

Successful project performance depends on the legal and business relationship between the prime contractor and subcontractors and suppliers as much as any other factor. Although the prime contractor is responsible for the satisfactory and timely completion of the project, much of the work is performed by subcontractors and suppliers.

A subcontractor's unsatisfactory performance often generates disputes among the prime contractor, that subcontractor and the owner, and possibly other subcontractors. Disputes also arise between the prime contractor and the subcontractor from problems for which the owner may be responsible. Similarly, whenever the prime contractor fails to perform, everyone involved with the project is affected. These disputes are the things of which lawsuits are made. Unfortunately, litigation is costly and time-consuming, and it rarely produces a decision at the time the problem arises.

The focus of this chapter is dispute avoidance and contract administration among the prime contractor, subcontractors, and suppliers. In an effort to help identify and prevent problems from the outset, this chapter also concentrates on areas where prime contractor and subcontractor disputes often originate.

8.1 DISPUTE AVOIDANCE BEGINS AT THE BIDDING STAGE

8.2 The Importance of the Low Price

Price is *one* important consideration in selecting a subcontractor. However, the lowest-cost subcontract may turn out to be the most expensive one if the subcontractor is unwilling or unable to do the work.

A prospective subcontractor should consider the prime contractor's overall pricing strategy. Unfortunately, a subcontractor may never be completely sure how the prime contractor is pricing the project during the bid or proposal stage. However, history may provide a workable indication as to whether the prime contractor can be expected to underprice the contract with the expectation of negotiating even lower subcontract prices after the award, or of making up deficiencies on extras.

8.3   Know with Whom You Are Dealing

Dealing with irresponsible or unscrupulous contractors very likely will result in disputes. Avoidance of problems begins at the bidding stage, when both prime contractors and subcontractors identify potential contractors with whom they will bid and enter into contracts for the work.

All contractors should consider the following factors.

8.4   *Reputation*   A firm can avoid numerous headaches and possible losses simply by investigating the past performance record of a potential prime contractor or subcontractor. Unreliable contractors can be avoided at the outset by dealing with reputable individuals with a proven ability to perform, by running credit checks, and by inquiring about the experiences of other owners and contractors with that firm.

Even a cursory investigation may yield clues to potential problems. For example, engaging a subcontractor with a reputation for shoddy or defective work may force the prime contractor to remedy an unsatisfactory work-product at its own expense. A subcontractor may find that a prime has a history of slow performance at the initial phase of a project, forcing the subs to encounter extended schedules, frequent payment delays, or end-of-project acceleration. A particularly litigious contractor may refuse to negotiate a settlement in the event of a disagreement, disrupting the project schedule by refusing to work, and possibly forcing you to incur the expense of arbitration or a court battle.

8.5   *Financial Resources*   A contractor that lacks adequate working capital brings myriad problems to the project, even without a default. For example, suppliers concerned about the contractor's ability to pay may hold deliveries until they receive payment. Laborers may refuse to work because they are not timely paid. These problems can have an impact on the project.

The ultimate concern is the financial resources of the prime contractor, which may be called upon to finance part of the performance. For instance, the contractor may be forced to finance corrective work for defects caused by other subcontractors, or to continue performance in the face of differing site conditions or changes in the work while negotiations or litigation resolves ultimate entitlement to payment. If the prime contractor does not have sufficient financial resources to continue performance and pay its subcontractors and suppliers in the face of delayed payments from the owner, there is the potential of a prime contractor failure, affecting everyone involved with the project. That prospect warrants considerable attention to the reputation and resources of the prime contractors with whom subcontractors and suppliers do business.

A subcontractor with insufficient working capital may be encouraged to front-end load pay requests so that payment may be made for more than the work actually performed is worth or for work not yet performed. If an overpaid subcontractor defaults, the cost to complete the work, combined with the sum already paid to the defaulting subcontractor, may be substantially greater than the amount originally allocated by the prime contractor for the work. The difference, of course, may come out of the prime contractor's pocket.

8.6 *Experience and Qualifications* State and local laws may require licensing of general contractors and certain subcontractor trades. The licensing requirements provide minimal assurance of the contractor's competence, but the investigation should not stop there.

Inquiry should be made about the contractor's experience on projects of similar type and size to the one being bid. The best residential electrical subcontractor in the county is not necessarily the best subcontractor for a high-rise hotel project. That subcontractor's reputation may be built on his personal integrity and quality of his employees' work, which are laudable achievements. But they do not necessarily assure that the subcontractor has the experience to manage the work of 15 other electricians and coordinate with other trades, a requirement for a subcontractor's work on a high-rise hotel project.

The subcontractor may find through inquiry of other subcontractors and suppliers that a prime contractor has considerable experience in one type of project, but that experience is different from the requirements of the prospective project. The subcontractor may also learn that the prime contractor is already overcommitted on existing contracts, which may affect the prime contractor's performance on a new project.

Similarly, a prime contractor must explore the subcontractor's experience in light of special performance requirements for the particular project. For example, if the specifications give only performance criteria, the subcontractor must be able to produce engineering and design details to meet the criteria in a timely manner. If a subcontractor proposes to sub-subcontract out the engineering or design work, it is appropriate to investigate the credentials and experience of the proposed designer or engineer.

Some building product and component suppliers condition the warranty of their products upon installation or application by an approved (certified) subcontractor. In some cases, such requirements are not necessary and may serve to inflate the cost of the work. The applicable warranty and the legal basis to enforce that warranty must be reviewed before dismissing a supplier's or manufacturer's requirements. The prime contractor may find that its subcontractor is insolvent and that the supplier has no warranty obligation for failure of a roof or wall system because its product was installed by an unauthorized subcontractor. By contrast, if the work is performed by an approved installer, the prime contractor may be protected by both the supplier's periodic inspections and the warranties of the product and the installation.

8.7 *Union versus Nonunion Status* A prime contractor's choice of a union or nonunion subcontractor generally depends on its own union status. If a union subcontractor and a nonunion prime contractor contract for a project, the subcontract should contain provisions dealing with labor relations on the work site and give the prime contractor the right to terminate the subcontractor if labor problems delay or impede the progress of the work.

A subcontractor should carefully consider its contractual right to time extensions in the event the prime contractor or another subcontractor has labor problems that affect its work.

One option available to contractors, which has become more feasible in recent years due to favorable National Labor Relations Board (NLRB) decisions, is to operate "double-breasted."[1] In general, a double-breasted contractor is a union contractor that forms a second, separate company that operates "open-shop." In essence, there are two employers, one union, one nonunion. In order to establish a legally correct double-breasted operation, the contractor must conclusively establish that both entities (that is, the union operation as well as the open-shop operation) are distinct and separate business concerns and not merely convenient distortions, or alter egos, of each other. This form gives the contractor the advantage of being able to operate without a union where this is feasible, while at the same time continuing operation of the union company where the use of union labor sources is desirable or required.

Of course, double-breasted operations do not guarantee the freedom from labor problems, and the cost of maintaining two separate companies may be prohibitive for some organizations. Most importantly, the use of a double-breasted operation also requires careful adherence to very specific and technical labor law requirements. For example, the National Labor Relations Board has enumerated four criteria used to determine whether the two operations are truly independent in every conceivable aspect of their operation, including: (1) common management and supervision of operations; (2) common control of personnel policies and labor relations; (3) interrelation of operations; and (4) common ownership or financial control. Double-breasted operations can be an effective alternative for a contractor that wants to compete with open-shop contractors in some areas, while maintaining good relations with the union where union labor predominates. However, contractors are encouraged to seek the advice of a labor attorney prior to attempting to establish a double-breasted operation so as to ensure compliance with the requirements of all pertinent laws and regulations.

8.8   Problem Areas in Subcontract Bidding

When is there an enforceable agreement between a prime contractor and subcontractor? The simple answer is only when both parties have signed the subcontract agreement. But this simple answer may also be wrong.

For example, a prime contractor that has relied on a subcontractor's telephone bid may be entitled to enforce that bid even though the parties have not signed an agreement. A letter of intent, or a telephone conversation, may give rise to binding

---

[1] *Gerace Constr., Inc.*, 193 NLRB 645 (1971).

obligations such that a refusal to execute a subcontract agreement following a letter of intent or a telephone bid may itself constitute a breach.

Oral agreements can be binding, although they may be unenforceable in certain transactions. When a transaction involves primarily the sale of goods, a binding contract may arise under the Uniform Commercial Code (UCC). The UCC requires that the parties agree to material terms, even though disagreement may still exist with respect to other important terms of the "contract."[2]

8.9 Enforcement of Subcontractor Bids   Practically every prime contractor and subcontractor has had a subcontractor or supplier revoke its bid or proposal after the prime or sub has entered into a contract with a third party in reliance on the bid. This issue has generated as much litigation between prime contractors and subcontractors as almost any other problem facing the construction industry.

Many early cases held that the subcontractor was not bound to the prime contractor; or, similarly, the supplier was not bound to the subcontractor, unless the parties had actually signed a contract.[3] Therefore, bids and proposals could be withdrawn up until the point where the parties were bound by formal documents.

In recent years, many courts (but not all) have held that a subcontractor is bound to the prime, when notified within a reasonable time after award that the prime relied on the bid in obtaining the prime contract award and intends to use the subcontractor for the project.[4] What constitutes a reasonable time for acceptance of an offer depends on the circumstances.[5]

The trend toward binding subcontractors to the prime contractor based upon the bidder's proposal, even without a contract document, is a response to the hardship a contractor faces when it is awarded a contract based on the subcontractor's proposal, and the subcontractor is not obligated to proceed with performance. Many contractors seek to avoid this problem by requiring that companies that submit bids also agree that their proposal will not be revoked for the same period of time allowed for award of the prime contract in the owner's bid documents.

8.10 Subcontractor Rights against the Prime Contractor   Although subcontractors may be responsible to prime contractors that rely on their bid, prime

---

[2] *See* **Chapter 6** regarding the UCC.

[3] *See, e.g., Anderson Constr. Co. v. Lyon Metal Prods.*, 370 So. 2d 935 (Miss. 1979).

[4] *See, e.g., Allen M. Campbell Co. v. Virginia Metal Indus., Inc.*, 708 F.2d 930 (4th Cir. 1983); *Drennan v. Star Paving Co.*, 333 P.2d 757 (Cal. 1958); *Allied Grape Growers v. Bronco Wine Co.*, 249 Cal. Rptr. 872 (Cal. Ct. App. 1988); *Home Elec. Co. v. Hall & Underdown Heating & Air Conditioning Co.*, 366 S.E.2d 441 (N.C. 1987) (North Carolina Supreme Court refuses to follow *Campbell*); *Arango Constr. Co. v. Success Roofing, Inc.*, 730 P.2d 720 (Wash. Ct. App. 1986) (refusing to follow the *Anderson Const. Co. supra* note 3).

[5] *See Piland Corp. v. REA Constr. Co.*, 672 F. Supp. 244 (E.D. Va. 1987) (subcontractor not bound by telephone bid where general contractor failed to notify it of acceptance within industry's customary 30-day period); *cf. ATACS Corp. v. TransWorld Communications, Inc.*, 155 F.3d 659 (3rd Cir. 1998).

contractors are less frequently bound to the subcontractors whose bids were relied upon by the prime.[6]

The fact that the prime contractor used the sub's proposal in its bid to the owner does not ordinarily provide the subcontractor with rights equivalent to those that the prime contractor may have to bind the sub to a contract. However, each set of circumstances must be judged on its own merits. An argument has successfully been made that if the prime contractor sends the subcontractor a letter of intent or a clear statement that it intends to have the subcontractor perform the proposed work for a mutually acceptable price, and the subcontractor begins performance in reliance upon the prime's request, then there is a basis to find that the parties have entered into a contract, even though it is not completely reduced to writing. Under these circumstances, a subcontractor may be entitled to recover damages for breach of contract if the prime contractor later withdraws its commitment.

The fact that the parties have not executed a formal contract is not necessarily controlling. If the circumstances indicate that a sub intends to perform a specifically identified scope of work on mutually agreeable basic terms of price and time, and if the subcontractor begins performance pursuant to such terms, there is support for a finding that the prime and sub are bound to each other. Thus, the subcontractor may be entitled to a remedy for breach when it is not allowed to complete the work.

8.11   PREPARATION OF THE SUBCONTRACT AGREEMENT

The subcontract, for purposes of this discussion, refers to the contract between parties at any level below the prime contract where the owner is usually a party. The subcontract includes the contract between the prime contractor and a subcontractor and the contracts between a subcontractor and sub-subcontractor at all levels. Contracts with vendors that only supply materials or equipment and do minimal or no work on the project site are often subject to the principles of law in the Uniform Commercial Code, which are discussed in **Chapter 6**.

At the outset, a firm should decide whether to draft its own subcontract or use a standard subcontract form. Form subcontracts developed by The Associated General Contractors of America, Inc. (AGC), and the American Institute of Architects (AIA) are widely utilized in the industry. Form subcontracts have the advantage of being relatively inexpensive and fairly widely accepted.

In addition, the form developed by an industry group may offer the advantage of providing a series or family of documents, which address a variety of needs. For example, the AGC includes in its DocuBuilder software package of contract documents

---

[6] *See Williams v. Favret*, 161 F.2d 822 (5th Cir. 1947). *But see Electrical Constr. & Maintenance Co. v. Maeda Pac. Corp.*, 764 F.2d 619 (9th Cir. 1985) (reversing trial court's holding that general contractor not bound to accept subcontractor's low bid). *See generally, Steeltech Bldg. Prods., Inc. v. Edward Sutt Assocs., Inc.*, 559 A.2d 228 (Conn. Ct. App. 1989) (enforcing oral agreement against owner for benefit of contractor).

the AGC 600 Series of subcontracting documents, which includes a variety of forms such as:

AGC 601	Contractor/Subcontractor Agreement (Federal Construction)
AGC 603	Standard Short Form Agreement Between Contractor and Subcontractor (Where Contractor Assumes Risk of Owner Payment)
AGC 604	Standard Short Form Agreement Between Contractor and Subcontractor (Where Contractor and Subcontractor Share Risk of Owner Payment)
AGC 605	Invitation to Bid/Sub-bid Proposal
AGC 606	Subcontract Performance Bond
AGC 607	Subcontract Payment Bond
AGC 610	Subcontractor's Application for Payment
AGC 630	Standard Form of Agreement Between Contractor and Testing Laboratory
AGC 650	Standard Form of Agreement Between Contractor and Subcontractor (Where the Contractor Assumes the Risk of Owner Payment)
AGC 655	Standard Form of Agreement Between Contractor and Subcontractor (Where Contractor and Subcontractor Share Risk of Owner Payment)
AGC 650.1 /655.1	Standard Form Rider Between Contractor and Subcontractor for Storage of Materials at Subcontractor's Yard
AGC 660	Bid or Proposal Bond

Whenever standard forms are used, they still need to be carefully reviewed, as these forms may not address specific items of particular concern to the contracting parties. For that reason, some contractors may choose to develop their own forms. However, the software packaging of the modern standard forms also allows for modification or adaptation to address particular concerns or needs.

An adequate subcontract form should, at a minimum, accomplish the following:

(1) Define the exact undertakings of the subcontractor so that there can be no dispute about the scope of work the subcontractor is to perform, including standard of quality and performance time.

(2) Detail the terms and conditions of payment, including the method of computing progress payments, terms of payment for stored material, due dates for pay requests, handling of interim retainage, and the final payment.

(3) Anticipate the areas of trouble or dispute, and define the consequences if work is not properly or timely performed.

(4) Specify the relief that the innocent party is entitled to receive.

(5) Avoid favoring one party to such an extent that the other party will decline to sign the proffered form or refuse to perform under its terms. A subcontract should be tailored to fit the needs of a particular project. However, a collection of uncoordinated provisions from various unrelated form contracts can result in a "monster," which may create substantial unanticipated problems for both parties.

Such monsters are typically created in one of two ways. The first is a "cut-and-paste" operation by which various provisions are borrowed from different subcontracts and brought together in one document without being reconciled or analyzed for consistency. The second is an "inclusion" operation, by which the contractor includes (either expressly or by reference) in its subcontract the general and special conditions of the prime contract, the terms and conditions, which it has prepared specially, and perhaps some other standard-form document, such as the contractor's project procedures. The theory is that more is better. The result is often a hodge-podge of documents that are not consistent or coordinated.

A subcontract form should be prepared by someone competent for the task and be modified, as needed, for the conditions of each project. Also, it should be periodically reviewed in light of lessons learned through experience and changes in the law.

Unlike terms of many public contracts, which are set by law or regulation, there are no "standard" subcontract terms. The following points should be considered in drafting the terms of a subcontract.

8.12   "Flow-Down" Obligations

A flow-down clause, which contractually ties, for instance, the subcontractor to the prime in the same manner as the prime is bound to the owner, is imperative.[7] Since subcontractors at every level are bound together on the project by a series of contracts, all contracts should contain flow-down clauses. The absence of a flow-down clause can leave the contractor exposed to liability but unable to demand of the subcontractor the performance that it is required to undertake.

In return for this protection, the prime contractor is generally willing to provide the subcontractor with the same rights that the prime has against the owner up the contract ladder, including making claims, protesting, and providing notices to the owner. In other words, the rights and duties flow both ways—upward to the prime contractor, as well as downward to the subcontractors at each level. This tends to keep the parties on an even basis, even though there is no privity of contract between the owner and the subcontractors.

8.13   Scope of the Work

Every subcontract must set out as clearly and definitively as possible the work to be performed by the subcontractor. From a practical standpoint, it is very difficult to

---

[7] *See generally*, Hoe *et al.*, *Flow-Down Clauses in Subcontracts*, Briefing Paper No. 85-5 (1985).

define all of a subcontractor's work. Therefore, the subcontract form should refer to all contract documents between the owner and prime contractor.[8]

The general contract bid items are often too general to incorporate by reference into the subcontract as the basis for the definition of the scope of work. This practice should be avoided. Instead, the work description must explicitly define responsibilities for the scope of work and must also define the responsibilities each contractor assumes for its own activities.

✓ Scope of Work Checklist

The scope of work for a project is not simply the items of performance that are subcontracted out for a particular project. A scope of work provision also includes the responsibilities for the facilities and for contract administration. Therefore, a detailed description of the actual work to be performed by the subcontractor on a project, including incorporation of the owner's description of the work from the general contract, must be supplemented with revisions that address other contingencies, including:

(1) An explanation of items listed in the subcontract scope of work that may differ from the plans or technical specifications; for example:

    (a) items of work that appear in the specifications may be excluded by the subcontractor in its proposal;

    (b) items of work may be specifically listed to clarify a possible ambiguity as to which trade is responsible for performance; and

    (c) items may not be listed in the plans or technical specifications but are necessary for completion of work on the project and are included in the scope of work to be performed by the subcontractor.

(2) A clause that clarifies that the subcontractor agrees to furnish, without extra charge, all work, labor, materials, and equipment not mentioned or shown in the contract documents that are nonetheless generally included under a particular class of subcontract or fairly implied by the subcontract as necessary for the satisfactory completion of the project (including work necessary to conform to all laws, ordinances, orders, rules, regulations, and requirements).

(3) A clause that provides a method of interpretation of the subcontract document. This may include an agreement to allow the architect to resolve any conflicts between various subcontract provisions, plans, and specifications.

---

[8] *S. Leo Harmonay, Inc. v. Binks Mfg. Co.*, 597 F. Supp. 1014, 1024 (S.D.N.Y. 1984) (holding that incorporation by reference clause applies only to specifications and actual statement of work), *aff'd without opin.*, 762 F.2d 990 (2d Cir. 1985); *Turner Constr. Co. v. Midwest Curtainwalls, Inc.*, 543 N.E.2d 249, 251–252 (Ill. App. Ct. 1989) (holding that incorporation by reference clause binds the subcontractor to all terms and conditions of the prime contract); *Gibbons-Gravle Co. v. Gilbane Bldg. Co.*, 517 N.E.2d 559, 563 (Ohio Ct. App. 1986) (discussing incorporation by reference clauses with specific example); *Construction Subcontracting: A Legal Guide For Industry Professionals*, § 3.11 (Overton A. Currie *et al.*, eds., 1991); 1994 Wiley Construction Law Update, § 9.9 (Overton A. Currie *et al.*, eds., 1994).

The form of the contract may require the architect to resolve differences of interpretation under that contract, so a drafter may choose to carry that responsibility through into the subcontract.

If a general contractor elects to divide a certain item of work between subcontractors, two additional considerations arise. First, extreme care must be used to define each subcontractor's scope of work to assure that no aspect of the work is omitted. Second, the contractor must realize that responsibility for coordinating the efforts of these subcontractors will usually fall on the contractor that has divided the work. Efforts to avoid this responsibility through the use of subcontract disclaimers generally are ineffective because the necessary authority is not clearly and expressly delegated to make the assignment of responsibility effective.

8.14   Payment Obligations

The prime contractor's obligation to make progress payments or pay retainage to the subcontractor before the prime receives the corresponding payment from the owner is almost inevitably an area for disputes.

8.15   *The Case against the Paid-When-Paid Clause*   Article 11.3 of The AIA Standard Subcontract Form of Agreement (AIA Document 401, 1997 ed.) provides that if the prime contractor does not receive payment from the owner for any reason that is not the fault of the subcontractor, the prime contractor shall, upon demand, pay the subcontractor the amount computed for the progress payment in accordance with the contract. This provision places the risk of nonpayment by the owner on the prime contractor.

Paragraph 8.2.5 TIME OF PAYMENT of AGC Document No. 650 similarly places the risk of nonpayment by the owner on the prime (general) contractor. Both documents reflect an allocation of the risk of nonpayment consistent with rationale that the prime (general) contractor is in the best position to evaluate both the owner's willingness and ability to pay for the work within a reasonable period of time. In contrast, a "pay-when-paid" or "pay-if-paid" clause seeks to place the risk of nonpayment for its work on the subcontractor or supplier.

One example of a paid-when-paid clause is: "The total price to be paid to subcontractor shall be $ . . . no part of which shall be due until five (5) days after owner shall have paid contractor therefore. . . ."[9] The variations on this theme are almost unlimited. The prime contractor in the *Thomas J. Dyer* case was not released from its payment obligation even though the owner filed bankruptcy before final payment.

There are a number of reasons why the clause should not be applied to excuse payment under all circumstances. First, the intent of the parties must be examined. In most cases, the subcontractor is not in privity of contract with the owner, and usually has no opportunity to deal with the owner in the proposal or bid phase or at

---

[9] *Thomas J. Dyer Co. v. Bishop Int'l Eng'g Co.*, 303 F.2d 655 (6th Cir. 1962).

any time during performance. The subcontractor looks to the general contractor for coordination with other trades and for use of site facilities, for scheduling, for interpretation of the plans and specifications, and for payment for the work. If it is the intention of the parties that the subcontractor will look only to the owner for payment, that intention must be clearly expressed.

Second, the payment clause in the contract must be examined. Look for specific circumstances mentioned in the contract, such as the delay of progress payments because of default of the subcontractor in the AIA A401 contract, or a reference to the owner's insolvency as a condition excusing nonpayment. If the payment clause deals with the amount, timing, method of payment, and other essential provisions, without reference to specific conditions excusing payment, then it is likely that the court will decide that payment to the subcontractor is not conditioned on payment from the owner under all circumstances.[10]

Many courts have simply held that an interpretation of the contract terms that would require the subcontractor to wait for an indefinite period of time until the prime contractor has been paid by the owner, an event that may never occur, is simply an unreasonable construction. The subcontractor may be forced to wait for a reasonable period of time, but many courts have held that paid-when-paid provisions are unenforceable as against public policy when they require a subcontractor to wait indefinitely or forgo payment under circumstances that the subcontractor cannot control.[11] Finally, a small but growing number of states have statutes that declare the clauses to be unenforceable under mechanic's lien laws or as a matter of public policy.[12]

8.16   *The Case for the Paid-When-Paid Clause*   Some states have taken a stance more favorable to the prime contractor and upheld the subcontract payment provision making the owner's payment to the prime contractor a condition precedent to the prime's obligation to pay the subcontractor for work performed.[13]

As an example, a prime contractor was excused from the obligation to pay until it had received payment when the subcontract provided: "[P]ayments will be made [to the subcontractor] from money received from the owner only and divided pro rata [among] all approved accounts of subcontractors, labor and materials."[14] This

---

[10] *See Mrozik Constr., Inc. v. Lovering Assocs., Inc.*, 461 N.W.2d 49 (Minn. Ct. App. 1990).

[11] *See William R. Clarke Co. v. Safeco Ins. Corp.*, 938 P.2d 372 (Cal. 1997); *Southern States Masonry, Inc. v. J.A. Jones Constr. Co.*, 507 So. 2d 198 (La. 1987); *Kawall Corp. v. Capolino Design & Renovation*, 388 N.Y.S.2d 346 (N.Y. App. Div. 1976); *West-Fair Elec. Contractors v. Aetna Cas. & Sur. Co.*, 661 N.E.2d 967 (N.Y. 1995); *Certified Fence Corp. v. Felix Indus., Inc.*, 687 N.Y.S.2d 682 (N.Y. App. Div. 1999).

[12] *See* N.C. Gen. Stat. § 22C-2 (1991) and ILCS 770 60/121 (2003).

[13] *See Sasser & Co. v. Griffin*, 210 S.E.2d 34 (Ga. Ct. App. 1974); *A. A. Conte, Inc. v. Campbell-Lowrie-Lautermilch Corp.*, 477 N.E.2d 30 (Ill. App. Ct. 1985). Subparagraph 8.2.5 of AGC Document No. 655, Standard Form of Agreement Between Contractor and Subcontractor, contains a pay-when-paid provision, which states, in part: "Receipt of payment by the Contractor from the Owner for the Subcontract Work is a condition precedent to payment by the Contractor to the Subcontractor. The Subcontractor hereby acknowledges that it relies on the credit of the Owner, not the Contractor for payment of Subcontract Work."

[14] *Sasser & Co., supra* note 13.

payment clause set up a fund consisting of money received from the owner, out of which subcontractors were to be paid, and made the fund the only source from which subs were to be paid. This provision was enforced as a paid-when-paid clause, relieving the prime contractor of the obligation to advance monies for progress payments to the subcontractor, because it showed the intent of the parties that the subcontractors' payments were to come only from the fund created by payments from the owner. The subcontractors were not relying upon the prime contractor's credit for payment.[15]

In an effort to avoid making payments to subcontractors even though payment has not been received from the owner, many prime contractors now include a provision in their subcontracts making payment by the owner a "condition precedent" to the prime's obligation to pay its subcontractors.[16] The contract provision must clearly show that the express condition is the mutual intent of the parties and that the parties recognize that payment may not be received from the owner so that the subcontractor assumes this risk as a part of the negotiated contract.[17]

The following should be kept in mind in drafting or reviewing contract language on the terms of payment:

✓ Payment Clause Checklist

(1) *Conditions for Payment:* Which conditions precedent must be met before the subcontractor is entitled to payment? For instance, the prime contract may require: (a) that all work meet the approval of the architect and the owner before payment is considered; and (b) proof that all invoices from subcontractors and suppliers for prior work have been paid. Before there is any entitlement to payment, the contract may also require that bonds or certificates of insurance be submitted and progress schedules and submittals be current.

(2) *Computing the Amount:* The method of determining the amount of progress payments should be clearly described. The contract terms should describe how to determine the basis of payment, such as a percentage of the total estimated value of labor, materials, and equipment incorporated into the work, and a percentage of the value of materials suitably stored, less the aggregate of previous payments.

(3) *Paid-When-Paid:* Is payment to the subcontractor conditioned upon payment by the owner for the same work? If this is the parties' agreement, and it is not against state law or public policy, state that the owner's payment is a "condition precedent;" that the subcontractor expressly accepts the risk that the owner may not pay the contractor; that the subcontractor relies for payment on

---

[15] *Wilson v. Post-Tensioned Structures, Inc.*, 522 So. 2d 79 (Fla. 3d DCA 1988).

[16] *St. Paul Fire & Marine Ins. Co. v. Georgia Interstate Elec. Co.*, 370 S.E.2d 829 (Ga. Ct. App. 1988); *see also* Paragraph 8.2.5 of AGC Document No. 655.

[17] *Galloway Corp. v. S. B. Ballard Constr. Co.*, 464 S.E.2d 349 (Va. 1995); *see also Imagine Constr., Inc. v. Centex Landis Constr. Co.*, 707 So. 2d 500 (La. Ct. App. 1998); *Sheldon Pollack Corp. v. Falcon Indus., Inc.*, 794 S.W.2d 380 (Tex. Ct. App. 1990).

the credit and ability of the owner to pay; and that the contractor's payment bond surety will be obligated only to the same extent as the prime contractor.

(4) *Final Payment Terms:* After the subcontract is fully completed, when will the subcontractor receive its final payment, and what are the conditions to be met before final payment will occur? These conditions may include:

(a) the owner and architect accept the work in writing;

(b) the contractor is fully paid by the owner; and

(c) a release (including a release of lien rights) is executed by the subcontractor for the contractor.

8.17   *Changes to the Payment Terms Must Also Account for the Surety*

After the contract is signed, there remains a potential for problems in the implementation of the agreement. The obvious problems are caused by a delay in payment or a dispute over the amounts earned for progress payments or for extra work. Careful draftsmanship and thoughtful consideration in advance will provide the parties with contract terms to measure and guide their performance. However, the subcontractor and prime contractor may find that unexpected circumstances during performance may require a change in their expected payment procedures. Unexpected results may follow if the parties' actions to accommodate the new circumstances are not carefully considered. For example, the prepayment of a subcontractor may discharge the subcontractor's performance bond surety from liability. If a subcontractor falls behind schedule and is financially unable to increase its workforce to regain the lost time, the prime contractor may consider prepaying the subcontractor to finance the additional crews needed to regain the schedule, while expecting to deduct the amounts advanced from later progress payments.

In one case, a prime contractor agreed to this arrangement but failed to obtain the approval of the subcontractor's payment and performance bond surety.[18] When it sued the surety for the amounts prepaid to the subcontractor, the surety defended on the basis that the prepayments materially altered the subcontract and operated to discharge the surety from its obligations.[19] The prime contractor's payment bond surety may take the same position if the prime contractor is in default of its payment obligations after agreeing to alter the payment terms of its contract without obtaining prior consent of the surety.

However, some courts require that a surety show injury or prejudice in addition to a material alteration of the contract in order to be discharged from bond obligations.[20] The lesson for all parties is that payment terms must carefully be considered

---

[18] *Southwood Builders, Inc. v. Peerless Ins. Co.*, 366 S.E.2d 104 (Va. 1988).

[19] *See also United States v. Freel*, 186 U.S. 309, 316 (1902); *Chas. H. Tompkins Co. v. Lumbermens Mut. Cas. Co.*, 732 F. Supp. 1368, 1377–1378 (E.D. Va. 1990); *Brunswick Nursing & Convalescent Ctr., Inc. v. Great Am. Ins. Co.*, 308 F. Supp. 297 (S.D. Ga. 1970); *In re Liquidation of Union Indem. Ins. Co.*, 632 N.Y.S.2d 788 (N.Y. App. Div. 1995).

[20] *United States v. Reliance Ins. Co.*, 799 F.2d 1382 (9th Cir. 1986); *Reliance Ins. Co. v. Colbert*, 365 F.2d 530 (D.C. Cir. 1966); *Mergentime Corp. v. Washington Metro. Area Transit Auth.*, 775 F. Supp. 14 (D.D.C. 1991).

when initially entering into the contract, and any change in those terms must be reviewed for its impact on the present obligations between the parties and the rights and obligations of sureties and other payment guarantors that may be affected.

8.18   Subcontractor Default Clause

8.19   The Right to Terminate

8.20   Express Termination Rights   Virtually all construction contracts expressly recognize the right to terminate the contract upon the default of either party under certain circumstances. These provisions also recognize the right of the innocent party to recover damages flowing from the default and resulting termination. For example, Subparagraph 10.1.2 of AGC Document No. 650 sets forth the basic steps regarding the termination process as follows:

> If the Subcontractor fails to commence and satisfactorily continue correction of a default within three (3) days after written notification issued under Subparagraph 10.1.1, then the Contractor may, in lieu of or in addition to Subparagraph 10.1.1, issue a second written notification to the Subcontractor and its surety, if any. Such notice shall state that if the Subcontractor fails to commence and continue correction of a default within seven (7) days of the written notification, the Agreement will be deemed terminated . . .

Similarly, Section 7.2.1 of AIA Document A401 (1997 ed.) provides that the contractor may terminate the subcontractor upon seven days notice if the subcontractor "persistently or repeatedly fails or neglects to carry out the work in accordance with the Subcontract Documents or otherwise to perform in accordance with this Agreement." Both AGC Document No. 650 and AIA Document A401 also expressly set forth the grounds for nonpayment, which entitle the subcontractor to terminate the contract with the prime contractor.

8.21   Implied Termination Rights   Even in the absence of an express termination provision, there generally exists an implied right to terminate a contract and sue for damages if the other party has materially breached the contract. It is nonetheless important that the prime contractor have the right to terminate a subcontract (and that a subcontractor be able to terminate a sub-subcontractor's right to proceed) under certain circumstances, and this right must be spelled out in detail, with notice requirements and cure rights specifically delineated. Although the discussion below focuses on the prime contractor/subcontractor relationship, the principles stated are equally applicable to a subcontractor/sub-subcontractor agreement.

8.22   Alternatives to Termination   The subcontract termination clause should provide flexibility to the prime contractor, so that the extreme act of termination is not the contractor's only option in dealing with a subcontractor's default. The subcontract must expressly reserve the prime's right to pursue alternatives in lieu of termination, such as paying the subcontractor's suppliers and subcontractors or supplementing the subcontractor's workforce. A termination for default is the construction industry equivalent of capital punishment. It is an option not to be invoked lightly, and only after careful consideration of other options. Some of the options to termination are discussed in the Default Clause Checklist, which follows.

8.23 *Termination for Convenience*

8.24 *Consequences of Improper Termination* Whether the subcontractor was actually in default at the time of termination is usually a fact question. The facts will determine whether the termination was proper or improper. If the termination was proper, then the prime contractor will be entitled to damages, including the cost of completion; if improper, then the subcontractor may recover as damages the profit it would have received if allowed to complete the work. If there would be no profit pursuant to the contract, the subcontractor may recover damages on a *quantum meruit* basis. If the subcontract contains only a "termination for default" option, the prime contractor may be exposed to significant subcontractor claims if the termination is later deemed improper, even if the prime contractor acted with a good-faith belief that the termination was justified.

8.25 *Termination for Convenience Clauses* To protect the prime contractor in such circumstances, the inclusion of a provision for the "termination for convenience" of the sub is recommended. This provision allows the prime to terminate the sub with or without cause. If one party terminates another for convenience, the terminated party has the right to an equitable adjustment that will return that party to its precontract condition.

8.26 *Limits to Termination for Convenience Rights* While a typical termination for convenience clause appears to give one party the absolute right to terminate another for whatever reason, there is a conflict as to whether the termination must be made "in good faith." At least one court has held that there are circumstances in which a termination, even under a seemingly unrestricted termination clause, may not be allowed where done in bad faith.[21] Other courts have been hesitant to hold that there is a good-faith requirement for the exercise of a termination for convenience right.[22] The question of whether there is a good-faith requirement for termination without cause remains unresolved in many jurisdictions.[23] It is therefore a point that may be argued by any contractor that may have been terminated "in bad faith." In federal contracting, it is clear that the government's right to terminate a contract for its convenience and limit the contractor's recovery in accordance with the Termination Clause is very broad. To avoid the limitations on recovery under that clause, the contractor must prove "bad faith" or "abuse of discretion." Either standard is very difficult to establish.[24]

[21] *Randolph v. New England Mut. Life Ins. Co.*, 526 F.2d 1383 (6th Cir. 1975).

[22] *Niagara Mohawk Power Corp. v. Graver Tank & Mfg. Co.*, 470 F. Supp. 1308 (N.D.N.Y. 1979).

[23] *Id.*

[24] *C.F.S. Air Cargo, Inc.*, ASBCA No. 36, 113, 91-1 BCA ¶ 23,583, *aff'd without opin.*, 944 F.2d 913 (Fed. Cir. 1991).

8.27   Considerations in Drafting Subcontract Default Clause   Some of
the considerations that should be addressed when drafting or reviewing a subcontract
default clause are set out below. Use this checklist to determine if and how the
subcontract addresses major issues in a default situation:

✓ Default Clause Checklist

(1) *Obligation to Proceed:* In the event of a dispute, can the subcontractor be
required to carry out its work as directed by the prime contractor? Even so, if
the subcontractor's refusal to proceed under protest is "reasonable" (e.g.,
where paving in cold weather might subject the subcontractor to later liability
on its express warranty), it is possible that the subcontractor may successfully
argue that its refusal to follow the prime's direction was justified. Accordingly,
any resulting default termination was improper.[25]

(2) *Notice:* Does the subcontract specifically outline requirements for notice to
the subcontractor if the subcontractor fails to comply with the contractor's
instructions or the terms of the subcontract? In the absence of an express notice
provision, some courts may find an implied duty to notify the subcontractor prior
to termination and to give the subcontractor an opportunity to cure the default.[26]

(3) *Cure Right:* The length of time within which the subcontractor will be
given the chance to cure a default should be specified. Some definition of an
effective cure (e.g., a complete correction of the default, or an approved, written program for curing the default and reasonable progress in implementing
such a program) is also warranted. Subcontractors should review the clause to
verify that the contract does expressly provide a right to cure a default.

(4) *Contractor Options:* A well-drafted default clause will give a contractor
several different options in dealing with a potential subcontractor default. If
there is no cure within the specified time period, these options might include:

   (a) Supplementing the subcontractor's workforce;

   (b) Having a second subcontractor take over a portion of the subcontrac-
       tor's work;

   (c) Making direct payments to subcontractor's suppliers, subcontractors,
       and laborers;

   (d) Accelerating the work; or

   (e) Subcontract termination (i.e., taking possession of the subcontractor's
       materials, tools, and so on, and completing the subcontractor's work
       with another subcontractor).

The subcontract should clarify that the decision to first pursue one or more of
these options does not prejudice the prime's right to later terminate or to claim
damages against the subcontractor or its surety.

---

[25] *Wilson v. Kapetan, Inc.*, 595 A.2d 369 (Conn. App. Ct. 1991).

[26] *McClain v. Kimbrough Constr. Co.*, 806 S.W.2d 194 (Tenn. Ct. App. 1990).

(5) *Payment Rights:* What effect will a default have on payment to the subcontractor? This clause might include provisions giving the contractor the right to deduct all monies expended and costs incurred, direct and indirect (including attorneys' fees), as a result of the subcontractor's default, from all amounts otherwise owed to the subcontractor. Also, if the amounts owed to the subcontractor are not enough to cover such expenses, the termination clause would obligate the subcontractor to promptly pay upon demand the full amount of the difference.

(6) *Good-Faith Defense to Wrongful Termination:* If the prime contractor is mistaken about the subcontractor's default or failure to cure such default, but acts on a good-faith belief, will the contractor be liable for additional subcontractor damages (e.g., anticipated profits)? To minimize this risk, the termination clause might convert the "wrongful" termination to a "termination for convenience" and limit the contractor's exposure to the value or cost of the work in place, plus a reasonable profit and overhead markup on that work. The clause could expressly exclude the subcontractor's right to recovery unearned profit, unexpended overhead, attorneys' fees, and other damages. For example, see Subparagraph 10.7 of AGC Document No. 650.

(7) *Proof of Termination Costs:* What information from the contractor will be sufficient to demonstrate the amount of money owed the contractor as a result of the default?

(8) *Default-Triggering Events:* How does the subcontract define those subcontractor acts and omissions that will justify prime contractor action under the termination clause? Careful drafting is required to anticipate the potential problems that might give rise to a contractor's need to invoke the termination clause. In the absence of an express provision justifying a subcontract termination, a contractor must prove that the subcontractor "materially breached" the subcontract.

(9) *Faulty Workmanship Proof:* The current version of the AIA subcontract requires that, when faulty workmanship, materials, or equipment is asserted as the basis for a subcontractor default, the project architect must first determine that the subcontractor's work is not in accordance with the prime contract requirements. From the contractor's perspective, this requirement is unduly restrictive, as the architect may wish to avoid involvement in a prime-sub dispute. For the subcontractor's viewpoint, this provision may offer a layer of protection against an improper termination.

(10) *Use of Subcontractor Resources:* Does the termination clause effectively preserve the contractor's right to take over the subcontractor's materials, tools, and equipment in order to complete the subcontract work? Does the clause preserve the contractor's right of access to subcontractor information (e.g., as-built information) and the option to accept an assignment of subcontractor's contracts with suppliers, equipment dealers, and sub-subcontractors?

(11) *Flow-Down Limitations:* Does the subcontract anticipate that the termination of the subcontract may result from a termination of the prime contract

by the owner? In a properly drafted flow-down clause, a prime contractor may attempt to limit its exposure to termination damages and expenses to whatever damages or costs the contractor is able to collect on the subcontractor's behalf from the owner. In federal government contracting, the government obligates the prime contractor to make a good-faith effort to negotiate the inclusion of a termination for convenience flow-down clause in all subcontracts.

8.28   No Damages for Delay, Except as Paid by the Owner

A contractor may be able to limit delay claim exposure to its subcontractors in proportion to the owner's liability and actual payment to the prime. In *Dyser Plumbing Co. v. Ross Plumbing & Heating, Inc.,*[27] a Florida appellate court upheld a contract clause that limited a subcontractor's delay damages to a percentage of an amount paid by the owner. The court ruled that the subcontract's terms clearly and unambiguously established the extent of any recovery by the subcontractor for delay damages.

If a general contractor hopes to limit a subcontractor's claim for delays to those amounts actually paid by the owner, the subcontract should expressly set out this limitation. Many of the considerations outlined earlier in this chapter at **Sections 8.15** and **8.16** are applicable to the determination of the subcontractor's rights when confronted with such a subcontract provision.

Obviously, these same considerations apply when a subcontractor is drafting its sub-subcontracts and purchase orders.

8.29   Changes

One of the sources of frequent disputes in construction is the contract's changes clause. For the owner and contractor, it is important that the subcontract specify a procedure for allowing changes to the contract. The subcontractor's primary concern is that it be guaranteed the right to be paid for "extra" work. In addition, the subcontractor is frequently concerned that it not be required to finance, for an extended period of time, a significant amount of "extra" work while waiting for (1) a determination of whether the work is "extra" and, if so, (2) a determination of the work's reasonable value. The parties' competing interests lead to frequent disputes.

In judging the completeness and fairness of the subcontract changes clause, contractors and subcontractors should consider the following:

✓ Subcontract Changes Clause Checklist

(1) *The Right to Order Changes:* The contractor should verify that the subcontract clearly states the contractor's right at any time, on written order, without notice to the surety and without invalidating the subcontract, to make changes in the work contracted for and the subcontractor's duty to proceed with the work as directed by the contractor's written order. There is no implied right to order contract changes.

---

[27] 515 So. 2d 250 (Fla. Dist. Ct. App. 1987).

(2) *Notice Requirements:* In the event the subcontractor is faced with an "informal" direction to perform additional work, the subcontract should set out express notice requirements and stated consequences for the failure to observe those notice requirements.

(3) *Specific Timetable for Change Order Resolution:* The contractor and subcontractor both should be concerned that the subcontract specify a timetable and specific steps for the resolution of the adjustment of the subcontract price and schedule. The contractor does not want to surprise the owner with subcontractor claims that remain unknown or unquantified until the end of the job. The subcontractor does not want to finance extra work for a prolonged period. The duties and rights of the parties in the event the work is performed prior to an agreement on price must be detailed.

(4) *Pricing Limitations:* The parties should be aware of any limitations on the allowable adjustment to the subcontract price—for example, the amount allowed by the owner; the amount of the subcontractor's initial estimate; the amount determined by the project architect or some other "final decision" maker; overhead and profit limitation clauses; or other conditions precedent to a price adjustment.

(5) *Pricing Proof:* The subcontract should identify the subcontractor's duty to provide cost data, certifications, and any other information necessary to support its proposal. The subcontract form should require the subcontractor to submit claims for additional costs in a manner and time sufficient to allow the general contractor to submit this information, if need be, to the owner under the terms of the prime contract. A simple flow-down clause may not be sufficient to provide for the timing requirements between the two contracts.

(6) *Binding Effect of the Change Order:* Frequently, the subcontract will grant audit rights to either the owner or the general contractor, so as to hold open the possibility of reopening a change order in the event of defective or inadequate pricing by the subcontractor.

(7) *Emergency Changes:* The subcontract should provide alternate change order procedures, rights, and duties in the event of the need to implement a change during an emergency that endangers life or property.

(8) *Oral Change Orders:* What is the effect of oral orders or directives that are believed to be changes, and what are the parties' duties and obligations under such circumstances? Does the subcontract require that the subcontractor obtain a written work order prior to performing extra work? Such requirements are common and can be enforceable.

(9) *Working under Protest:* From the contractor's perspective, it is important that the subcontractor be obligated to proceed with the directed work, even if the subcontractor disputes the value of the work or if the contractor denies that the work is "extra." Such a subcontract clause appears to be enforceable. For example, in *Keyway Contractors, Inc. v. Leek Corp.*,[28] a Georgia court enforced

---

[28] 376 S.E.2d 212 (Ga. Ct. App. 1988).

a contract provision requiring that the work continue despite pending disputes. Following a dispute over payment, the subcontractor abandoned the work site. The court found that the subcontractor's action constituted a material contract breach. The subcontractor confronted with such a clause must look for some express or implied limit to the obligation to perform work for which it may not be paid. In addition, the subcontractor must be certain that it has the right to proceed "under protest," and that it understands the procedural requirements for preserving that right.

(10) *Change Order Authority:* Does the subcontract contain limitations on the authority of the contractor's representatives to direct changes? Limitations as to who has the authority to direct changes and limits on the amount of change order authority entrusted to a contractor representative are common.

(11) *Alternative Methods for Fixing Change Order Amounts:* Does the subcontract provide unit prices for change order work, or pricing limitations in connection with "force account" work? Since it is likely that many change order amounts will not be agreed upon in advance, the subcontract should provide alternate routes to fixing the change order amount.

(12) *Time Extensions:* The changes clause should require that the subcontractor quantify the time impact, as well as the cost impact, of changes to the work. Subcontractors must make themselves aware of subcontract clauses that would deprive them of time extensions made necessary by changes unless the time extension request is presented in a specified format, with specified support, or in a certain time frame.

8.30   Subcontractor's Indemnification of the Contractor

Traditionally, subcontracts have imposed very broad hold-harmless obligations on subcontractors. Some courts have been reluctant to enforce overly broad indemnification clauses as a matter of public policy. Some state legislatures have also taken steps to limit the effects of indemnity agreements.[29] For example, § 13-8-2 of the Official Code of Georgia (1990) invalidates any attempt to require a contracting party to hold another party harmless from liability arising solely from the latter's own acts. Accordingly, while a broad, general indemnification clause is important, it should be drafted after consideration of the applicable state laws and decisions. Similarly, a clause that is enforceable in one state may be void in a neighboring state. Therefore, prime contractors should be cautious when doing work outside of their home state. Subcontractors should look for provisions that provide that the contract is to be governed by the laws of a particular state.

Subcontract indemnity clauses come in many shapes and sizes. The clauses are typically long and cumbersome to read and understand. Consider the following potential problem areas in drafting or reviewing a subcontract:

---

[29] *See, e.g.,* 770 ILCS 60/21 (2003).

✓ Subcontract Indemnity Clause Checklist

(1) *Scope of Indemnity:* What types of claims and damages are covered? Is the indemnity clause limited to damages arising out of any injury to any person, or any death at any time resulting from such injury, or any damage to any property, which may arise (or which may be alleged to have arisen) out of or in connection with the work covered by the subcontract? Do the damages covered go beyond those connected with property damage or personal injury? Do the damages covered include attorneys' fees and consequential damages? Care in defining the scope of the damages covered is critical for the contractor and subcontractor alike.

(2) *Persons Protected:* Is the indemnity obligation owed only to the contractor, or does it include other named parties or groups? How broad is the definition of the protected class?

(3) *Conduct Creating the Indemnity Obligation:* Is the indemnity obligation limited to damages that flow solely from the conduct of the subcontractor? Does the indemnity obligation arise if the subcontractor is only partially responsible for the damage? Does the subcontract attempt to place the indemnity obligation on the subcontractor even if the damages do not result in any part from the subcontractor's negligence?

(4) *Insurance Availability:* Some types of risks that are assigned to subcontractors through indemnity clauses may be transferred to insurance policies. However, contractors and subcontractors frequently fail to assess and compare the risks presented by indemnity clauses with their insurance coverage.

(5) *Public Policy Limits:* As previously mentioned, several states have taken the position that broad-form indemnity agreements (i.e., those obligating one party to indemnify another for all loss, even if caused solely by the indemnitee's own negligence) are void as against public policy. Illinois, Georgia, New York, Minnesota, California, Michigan, and many other states have such "anti-indemnity" statutes.[30] Depending upon the jurisdiction involved, these

---

[30] Alaska Stat. § 45.45.900; Ariz. Rev. Stat. Ann. § 34-226; Cal. Civ. Code §§ 2782; Conn. Gen. Stat. § 52-572k; Fla. Stat. Ann. § 725.06; Ga. Code Ann. § 13-8-2; Hawaii Rev. Stat. § 431: 10-222; Idaho Code § 29-114; Ill. Ann. Stat. ch. 740, Act 35, § 1; Ind. Code Ann. § 26-2-5-1; La. Rev. Stat. Ann. § 38-2216(D); Md. Cts. & Jud. Proc. Code Ann. § 5-401; Mass. Gen. Laws Ann. ch. 149 § 29C; Mich. Stat. Ann. § 691.991; Minn. Stat. § 337.01-05; Miss. Code Ann. § 31-5-41; Neb. Rev. Stat. § 25-21-187; N.M. Stat. Ann. §§ 56-7-1; N.Y. Gen. Oblig. Law § 5-322.1; N.C. Gen. Stat. § 22B-1; N.D. Cent. Code § 9-08-02.1; Ohio Rev. Code Ann. § 2305.31; Or. Rev. Stat. § 140; R.I. Gen. Laws § 6-34-1; S.C. Code Ann. § 32-2-10; S.D. Comp. Laws Ann. §§ 56-3-18; Tenn. Code Ann. § 62-6-123; Utah Code Ann. § 13-8-1; Va. Code § 11 4.1; Wash. Rev. Code Ann. § 4.24.115; W. Va. Code § 55-8-14. Several states have taken the position that broad-form indemnity agreements cannot be used to protect architects, engineers, and other design professionals. *See, e.g.,* Del. Code Ann. tit. 6, § 2704 (statute is designed to limit indemnity clauses in contracts of preconstruction designers and planners); N.H. Rev. Stat. Ann. § 338-A:1 (prohibiting indemnification agreements by architects, engineers, and surveyors); Pa. Stat. Ann. tit. 68, § 491 (prohibiting indemnification agreements by architects, engineers, and surveyors); Tex. Civ. Proc. & Rem. Code §§ 130.001-005 (architects and engineers are not protected against injuries or damages caused by defects in their plans, designs, or specifications prepared for a construction project); Utah Code Ann. § 13-8-2 (subcontract cannot limit design professional's liability to subcontractor).

anti-indemnity statutes may not preclude the contractor from requiring that the subcontractor obtain insurance to cover the negligent acts of the contractor.[31] Specifically, a court may view as acceptable the long-standing practice in the construction industry whereby parties to a subcontract agree that one party is to purchase insurance that protects "others" involved in the performance of the construction project. Depending on the jurisdiction, a subcontract provision requiring such insurance coverage may or may not be viewed as an unenforceable anti-indemnity agreement. A party contemplating the use of such a provision should check to determine if the protection afforded by the broad subcontract indemnity clause is not taken away by applicable laws and the court's interpretation of such laws.

(6) *Clarity of the Parties' Intent:* Since indemnity provisions tend to reverse the generally preferred rule that wrongdoers should pay for their own mistakes, courts often construe strictly the indemnity language. Loose language used in defining the indemnity obligation may result in a restrictive reading of the scope of the parties' indemnity agreement. Therefore, it is essential to understand the scope of the risk that is intended to be the subject of the indemnity clause and to define it clearly.

(7) *Collection Rights:* Typically, the subcontract may give the contractor the right to withhold from any payment otherwise due the subcontractor such amounts as may be "reasonably necessary" to protect it against damages covered by the indemnity clause. From the subcontractor's perspective, it is desirable to place some safeguards on the process and timetable for determining indemnity losses, and some limits (e.g., indemnity payments will be limited to the amount of available insurance) on the exposure assumed under the subcontract.

8.31   Labor Affiliation

It is important that the prime contractor have the right to determine whether a project will be open shop or union, and to require, insofar as permitted by applicable law, its subcontractors to abide by this policy. The prime should retain the right to require a subcontractor to perform, or be terminated, even if the subcontractor's workers refuse to work as a result of a dispute that involves the general contractor and its employees (not the subcontractor's). The following are some of the points that should be addressed in any subcontract:

(1) *Advice Regarding Labor Practices:* The subcontractor's obligation to keep itself and the prime contractor fully advised of all pertinent local and regional labor agreements and practices, including any local labor union contract negotiations occurring during the term of the subcontract.

---

[31] *See Jokich v. Union Oil Co. of Calif.*, 574 N.E.2d 214 (Ill. App. Ct. 1991); *Holmes v. Watson-Forsberg Co.*, 488 N.W.2d 473 (Minn. 1992) (holding that a subcontract provision obligating the subcontractor to maintain general liability insurance coverage was not an unenforceable indemnification agreement under Minnesota statutes, but rather was a valid agreement to provide specific insurance coverage as allowed by statute).

(2) *Collective Bargaining Agreements:* In the event the subcontractor has a collective bargaining agreement either locally or nationally with a labor union engaged in local negotiations, or if the subcontractor will be affected, either directly or indirectly, by the outcome of local negotiations, is the subcontractor obligated to join such negotiations, if legally permissible, and participate or associate itself with the local contractor or contractors involved in the negotiations in an endeavor to resolve the labor dispute?

(3) *Labor Harmony:* The obligation that all labor used throughout the work shall be acceptable to the owner and the contractor and of a standing or affiliation that will permit the work to be carried on harmoniously and without delay to the project and that will in no case or under any circumstances cause any disturbance, interference, or delay to the progress of the building, structures, or facilities, or any other work being carried on by the owner or the contractor in any other town or city in the United States.

(4) *Labor Agreements:* The subcontractor's obligation to recognize and comply with all agreements of the contractor with local building trade councils and/or separate unions concerning labor and working conditions and otherwise applicable to the work insofar as these agreements do not conflict with or violate any local, state, or federal laws or properly constituted orders or regulations.

(5) *Termination Rights:* The contractor's right to terminate the subcontract and proceed in accordance with the provisions of the subcontract if the subcontractor's work or the contractor's work is stopped or delayed or interfered with by strikes, slowdowns, or work interruptions resulting from the acts or failure to act of the employees of the subcontractor in concert, or if the subcontractor breaches other applicable labor provisions in the subcontract.

(6) *Work Stoppages:* The contractor's remedies when the subcontractor's employees engage in a work stoppage solely as a result of a labor dispute involving the contractor or others and not in any manner involving the subcontractor.

8.32 Disputes Procedures

8.33 Arbitration Considerations The determination to accept or include an arbitration provision in a contract or subcontract involves both practical and legal considerations. This decision must be made before the subcontract is executed. If the subcontract does not contain an arbitration provision, disputes arising thereafter will be arbitrated only if both parties so agree. Such an agreement may not be easy to obtain after the dispute has arisen.

On the other hand, if an arbitration agreement is contained in the subcontract, it will probably be enforceable under federal and, perhaps, state laws. The contractor cannot avoid arbitration at that point over the subcontractor's objection.

Some contracts contain provisions requiring arbitration at the sole election of the contractor. Such unilateral provisions have been enforced by some courts.[32]

---

[32] *TechnoSteel LLC v. Beers Constr. Co.*, 271 F.3d 151 (4th Cir. 2001).

It is generally desirable that the prime contractor tie the subcontractor to the same remedies and disputes process as binds the prime contractor to the owner. Whether in court, arbitration, an administrative disputes process (board hearing), or an alternative disputes resolution procedure (e.g., mediation), the subcontractor should be required to pursue diligently and exhaust those remedies and to be bound by the determination of its claims or rights under the specified disputes procedure.

✓ Disputes Clause Checklist

In drafting or reviewing subcontract provisions governing the resolution of disputes, the following matters should be addressed:

(1) *Flow-Down Effect of Dispute Resolution:* To what extent is the determination of any issue under the terms of the contract between the owner and the contractor binding on the rights of the subcontractor? From the contractor's perspective, the ability to "flow down" the impact of a binding decision under the owner/contractor agreement is critical.

(2) *Subcontractor Participation in Owner/Contractor Disputes Procedures:* Is the subcontractor obligated to assist the contractor in the prosecution or defense of a proceeding under the terms of the general contract? Is the subcontractor obligated to reimburse the prime contractor for any portion of the costs and legal fees incurred? Even if the subcontractor is not a named party to the dispute proceedings, if the subcontractor's rights will be affected by the outcome, it will want the right to participate in the proceedings.

(3) *Decision-Making Authority:* Does the subcontractor have any control over the prosecution and defense of any proceeding under the terms of the general contract that involves or relates to the subcontract? Does the subcontractor have any protection against an unreasonable compromise of its dispute position?

(4) *Obligation to Continue Working:* Is the subcontractor obligated to proceed with the work as directed by the contractor pending resolution of any dispute under the terms of the general contract or any dispute between the contractor and its subcontractor?

(5) *Disputes Not Involving the Owner:* Does the subcontract contain provisions, such as an arbitration clause controlling the resolution of disputes between the contractor and the subcontractor, that are not related to the owner or controlled by the terms of the general contract?

(6) *Third-Party Claims:* Does the subcontract contain provisions addressing the subcontractor's right or duty to proceed against third parties to recover claims for damages? Such clauses are increasingly popular, not only in subcontracts, but in owner/contractor agreements as well.

(7) *Mandatory Pursuit of Administrative Remedies:* Does the subcontract contain provisions requiring the subcontractor to exhaust any contractual disputes process prior to instituting or prosecuting any statutory remedy or action against the contractor or the contractor's surety?

(8) *Mandatory Alternative Dispute Resolution (ADR) Procedures:* In recognition of the high cost and uncertainty of litigation and other "formal" disputes procedures, many in the construction industry are searching for less costly, less divisive, and quicker means for resolving disputes, such as mediation. The ability to control, at least to some extent, the dispute process is also a consideration. Any ADR procedure should be detailed in the subcontract. For example, Subparagraph 11.1 of AGC Document No. 650 provides that the parties shall first seek to resolve a dispute by direct discussions. If those do not resolve the matter, the subcontract requires the parties to participate in mediation under the Construction Industry Mediation Rules of the American Arbitration Association before resorting to any other form of binding dispute resolution.

(9) *The Appointment of Final Decision Makers:* Contracts and subcontracts often attempt to designate some individual as having the authority to make "final and binding" decisions with respect to certain types of disputes. These contracts may also attempt to place short time limits for appeal or protest of a decision, before it becomes "final and binding." Identify such attempts prior to contracting and be aware of their impact.

8.34 Federal Government Projects

If the prime contract is with an agency of the federal government, certain provisions in the contract become more important, and there are other provisions—perhaps unnecessary in private work—that need to be included in the subcontract form. The same may be true with respect to state governments and their agencies. Any contractor who works with a particular governmental agency or agencies would be well advised to consult an attorney concerning what, if any, additional provisions should be included in its standard subcontract form due to the particular way in which that agency conducts its construction contracting business.

The following examples of contract provisions may be useful additions to subcontracts on federal government projects:

(1) *Termination for Convenience:* The government's exercise of its rights under this clause has a significant substantive and procedural effect on the contractor's rights and remedies, including express directions to the contractor concerning its subcontractors and suppliers. The federal government's duty to reimburse the contractor for certain subcontractor/supplier claims may depend on the negotiations between the contractor and subcontractor/supplier concerning the effect of a termination for convenience.[33]

(2) *Cost and Pricing Data:* The subcontract/purchase order should address the subcontractor's/supplier's obligation to provide "cost or pricing" data or other cost and claim certifications required by or necessary under the terms of the prime contract. To the extent that the contractor relies upon and/or is liable to the federal government due to data, information, or certificates provided by the subcontractor or supplier, the subcontract or purchase order should address the issues of indemnity,

---

[33] FAR § 49.108-5(a).

costs of defense, and so on, related to any government claim. In addition, the clause should address the extent and duration of audit rights by any party and any other needed flow-down requirement.

(3) *Flow-Down Consistency:* Particular care must be given to flow-down clauses needed to promote the consistency of the prime contract and the subcontracts for proper administration of a subcontract or purchase order under a government contract. In addition, numerous social and economic clauses must be incorporated into specific subcontracts and purchase orders and further flowed down to lower tiers. Satisfaction of these requirements dictates the careful drafting of appropriate flow-down provisions and a review of the terms of the government contract.

8.35   SHOULD SUBCONTRACTORS BE BONDED?

A performance bond is a guaranty (based on the terms of the bond) that the subcontractor will perform the contract. It is usually intended to mean that if the subcontractor defaults or fails to complete the project, the surety will complete performance or pay damages up to the limit of the penal sum of the bond. (*See* **Chapters 14** and **15** for a more complete discussion of performance and payment bonds.)

A labor and material payment bond helps assure that labor and materials used in the course of the subcontractor's work will be paid for by the surety if not by the subcontractor. A payment bond creates alternatives to the filing of liens on the project property and helps protect the prime contractor from liability to the various tiers of sub-subcontractors and suppliers.

In the past, it was not unusual for prime contractors to require bonds of subcontractors, and for subcontractors to require bonds of sub-subcontractors. The general contractor may decide at the outset that the subcontracted work will be bonded, no matter which subcontractor is chosen to do the work. However, in recent years, these bonds have become more expensive, and sometimes more difficult to obtain. As a result, the question of whether subcontractors should provide bonds has become somewhat more complicated. Consequently, the decision to require bonds may need to be made on a case-by-case basis. Other alternatives may provide some assurance of the subcontractor's performance without involving the expense of a bond. For example, the subcontractor may be willing to post a letter of credit in lieu of a bond; another entity, perhaps a parent company, may be willing to provide a guarantee of performance; or the subcontractor may allow the prime to hold an increased level of retainage.

The prime contractor that decides to have its subcontractors bonded must be aware of the exact language of the bonds. No statutory requirements exist for subcontractors' bonds. They are considered to be common-law bonds, and their wording controls the obligations of the surety.

Subcontractor performance bonds can be worded so that they protect or benefit only the prime contractor and do not provide a direct right of action by third-party subcontractors and suppliers. Alternatively, the bond may expressly state that subcontractors and suppliers can maintain a direct action against the surety. Otherwise, a court may well find that the bond does not create such a right of action in third parties.

If bonds are to be provided, separate payment and performance bonds should be required. The contractor obtains greater protection by requiring two separate bonds. If the bonds are not separate, the penal sum provides the maximum liability of the surety for both the payment and performance bonds. For example, if a payment and performance bond is in the total penal amount of $1 million, the surety is generally liable for no more than $1 million, even though the cost to complete the subcontractor's performance together with the claims of materialmen and suppliers totals more than $1 million. However, if a performance bond is obtained in the amount of $1 million and a payment bond is obtained in the same amount, the general contractor obtains potential protection of $2 million, with $1 million for performance and $1 million for payment.

It is essential that the surety providing the bonds be financially viable and responsible, since bonds from a deficient surety offer little or no protection. Consequently, the subcontract form should contain the limitation that the bonds will be provided by an "acceptable surety."

8.36 DISPUTE AVOIDANCE BY DILIGENT PROJECT ADMINISTRATION

Disputes often can be avoided or minimized by effective project management, by both the prime contractor and the subcontractors. An understanding of some important obligations and rights is critical to dispute avoidance or resolution.

8.37 General Contractor's Duty to Coordinate the Work

Subcontractors are normally engaged by the general contractor to perform various "trade" portions of the work. For the project to proceed smoothly and without unreasonable interference, the activities of the general contractor and of each subcontractor must be sequenced and coordinated so that all can perform their portion in a prompt and efficient manner.

The general contractor usually assumes this responsibility for coordination, which is similar to the responsibility of the owner in the coordination of parallel prime contractors. Since the general contractor is customarily the only party in direct privity with all of the subcontractors, that contractor generally has the duty to coordinate.

8.38 Implied Duty to Cooperate

The duty to cooperate with subcontractors and coordinate their work is implied, even though the subcontract may not expressly provide that the prime or general contractor must respond in damages for any delay or extra cost incurred by a subcontractor as a result of a breach of this duty. Subcontract provisions such as a "no damages" clause may, however, modify, limit, or shift this implied responsibility or the damages for breach of this duty.[34]

---

[34] *See Crawford Painting & Drywall Co. v. J. W. Bateson Co.*, 857 F.2d 981 (5th Cir.1988).

The implied duties to cooperate and coordinate require the general contractor to take reasonable measures to protect a subcontractor from delays or interference by the general contractor or other subcontractors. For example, in *Johnson v. Fenestra, Inc.*,[35] a subcontractor contracted to install panels on the exterior of a building under construction, and the prime agreed to furnish these panels. However, the prime contractor delivered defective panels. Several months elapsed before the correct panels were provided, and the delay prevented the subcontractor from completing work before winter weather set in. The court held that the subcontractor was entitled to damages for being forced into winter work and that the subcontract necessarily implied that the prime would supply panels in time and in quantities that were consistent with the parties' understanding that there would be a "prompt beginning and an early completion" of the job.

The obligation to reimburse for delay and extra cost may arise from provisions that require the prime to perform some act preparatory to the subcontractor's work. In *Manhattan Fire Proofing Co. v. John Thatcher & Son*,[36] the prime agreed that the building under construction would be made available to the concrete subcontractor so that the concrete work could be done "in one operation" and completed by a stated date. However, because the prime delayed the job and was late in turning over the building, the subcontractor was required to divide its work into several phases. The court, in awarding the subcontractor delay damages, held that the provision that the work could be "done in one operation" required the prime contractor to protect the subcontractor from the type of disruption delay experienced on the job.

8.39 Implied Duty to Coordinate

It is not enough for the general contractor to ensure that its own forces do not interfere with the subcontractors. The duty to coordinate includes an additional requirement that the general contractor take reasonable steps to avoid interference between subcontractors. This requires the contractor to (1) schedule the work of all subcontractors so that the work of different trades can be sequenced as contemplated at the time of bidding, and (2) take reasonable steps during performance to maintain the schedule.

A general contractor's responsibility for coordination of all subcontractors is illustrated in *J. J. Brown Co. v. J. L. Simmons*.[37] There, the plastering subcontractor claimed damages for the prime's failure to provide heat in buildings where the plastering work was to be performed. The prime contended that other subcontractors were responsible for the failure to provide heat. The court held that the prime had a duty "to keep the work in such state of forwardness as to enable the subcontractor to perform within a limited time" and that the delays of other subcontractors were the

---

[35] 305 F.2d 179 (3rd Cir. 1962).

[36] 38 F. Supp. 749 (W.D.N.Y. 1941).

[37] 118 N.E.2d 781 (Ill. App. Ct. 1954). *See also Ragan Enters. v. L & B Constr. Co.*, 492 S.E.2d 671 (Ga. Ct. App. 1997).

prime's responsibility and would serve as no defense to the plastering subcontractor's suit.[38]

8.40   Limitation of Liability

A prime contractor may be able to limit liability by disclaiming the responsibility of coordination to subcontractors, as illustrated by *Crawford Painting & Drywall Co. v. J. W. Bateson Co., Inc.*[39] Bateson was the prime contractor on a hospital building project for the Army Corps of Engineers. Bateson's subcontract with Crawford included a clause in which Bateson disclaimed liability for any delay or disruption to Crawford's work.

After excessive change orders were issued, the work was significantly delayed. Crawford sued Bateson, and at trial introduced evidence that Bateson withheld from its subcontractors the actual project schedule and extensions to that schedule which Bateson had negotiated with the Corps. Crawford alleged that Bateson took advantage of the subcontractors in administering the project and in negotiating claim settlements. The jury awarded Crawford $7 million, but a federal court of appeals reversed the jury award and dismissed the lawsuit. The court held that Bateson's actions amounted to nothing more than a failure to coordinate the subcontractors, and Bateson had disclaimed this responsibility in its subcontract. Crawford could not recover.

Although the general contractor can be held answerable for its interference with or failure to coordinate subcontractors, the general may not be liable for delays or interference over which it has no control and that were unforeseeable at the time of contracting. In *Southern Fireproofing Co. v. R. F. Ball Construction Co., Inc.*,[40] the court held that a contractor was not liable for damages caused to a subcontractor by delays attributable to subsurface conditions that were unknown to the parties at the time of subcontracting. A similar result was reached when a prime contractor was held not liable for damages caused by delays that were due to inclement weather.[41]

Success in coordination depends largely upon open and accurate communication between the general contractor and all subcontractors. The general must establish some method to both discover what is going on at the job site (e.g., what problems the subcontractors are having and the problems they anticipate) and to relay suggestions, recommendations, and requirements to the subcontractors to avoid or solve the problems. Efforts to develop these communications must begin at the preconstruction conference and continue throughout the contract period.

---

[38] *Id.* at 785. *See also United States ex. rel. Wallace v. Flintco, Inc.*, 143 F.3d 955 (5th Cir. 1998); *Allied Fire & Safety Equip. Co. v. Dick Enter., Inc.*, 886 F. Supp. 491 (E.D. Pa. 1995); *Cleveland Wrecking Co. v. Central Nat'l Bank of Chicago*, 576 N.E.2d 1055 (Ill. App. Ct. 1991); *Unis v. JTS Constructors/Managers, Inc.*, 541 So. 2d 278 (La. Ct. App. 1989).

[39] 857 F.2d 981 (5th Cir. 1988).

[40] 334 F.2d 122 (8th Cir. 1964).

[41] *Ben Agree Co. v. Sorensen-Gross Constr. Co.*, 111 N.W.2d 878 (Mich. 1961).

8.41   Pay Applications and Partial Lien Waivers

When a general contractor receives a pay application from a subcontractor, it should generally require a partial waiver of liens covering work for which payment is requested. At the end of a project, total lien waivers should be required. Subcontractors should obtain similar partial and total lien waivers from their lower-tier subcontractors and suppliers. Lien laws vary greatly from state to state, so advice of counsel familiar with the applicable lien law should always be obtained. Generally, waivers of lien are strictly construed, must be in writing, and must clearly express the potential lien claimant's unambiguous intent to waive lien rights.

Contractors must not confuse a lien waiver with a release of claims. A lien waiver, unlike a release, generally benefits only the property owner by protecting it from the claim of lien. It does not absolve the contractor from its obligations to the lien claimant.[42] The general contractor should consider using a form that both waives lien rights and releases the contractor from subcontractor's claims, at least to the extent of payment actually received.

8.42   Prime Contractor Financing of Subcontractors

The question of whether a prime should provide financial aid to an ailing subcontractor and, if so, to what extent usually arises when an unbonded subcontractor is on the verge of default.

A prime contractor has several obvious reasons for wanting to help a faltering subcontractor. First, the prime is obligated to complete the project by a specified time. A work slowdown prior to default and delay while obtaining a completion subcontractor may extend the project beyond the completion date. Second, the prime has the obligation to keep the work in a state of readiness so that other subcontractors can proceed efficiently. A failure to coordinate the work may subject the general to delay damage claims by these subcontractors. Third, the defaulting subcontractor may be unable to answer in damages to the prime for the effect of its default.

Other advantages may be gained by working out some form of financial assistance for a troubled subcontractor. The value of maintaining continuity on the job may justify the cost of financial assistance. The subcontractor's personnel have a basic familiarity with the project, and work experience would eliminate the need for another learning curve for replacement workers. The defaulting subcontractor may have executed fixed-price purchase orders that could be lost if the sub is terminated, causing the completing subcontractor's cost (and, correspondingly, the cost to the general contractor) to increase. Also, there may be a shortage of available subcontractors in particular trades and geographic areas at any given time, making it difficult or even impossible for the prime to find a suitable replacement subcontractor.

All these considerations suggest that it may be prudent for a prime contractor to consider providing financial assistance to an unbonded subcontractor faltering on the verge of default. This assistance may come in the form of advanced payments, reduced retainage, guarantees of payment to sub-subcontractors or suppliers, and the like. While

---

[42] *See, e.g., David Shapiro & Co., Inc. v. Timber Specialties*, 233 S.E.2d 439 (Ga. Ct. App. 1977).

these techniques may help the subcontractor complete the job, they also create potential risks by reducing the contractor's financial security in the subcontractor's performance or creating an obligation for the prime contractor that is larger than anticipated.

Different considerations are involved when the faltering subcontractor is bonded, and these problems are reviewed elsewhere. (*See* **Chapters 14** and **15**.) As a general matter, any payments the surety makes to a distressed subcontractor do not result in a credit to the surety against the penal sum of the performance bond.[43] But the prime contractor that lends financial assistance runs a risk of having the surety later claim to be discharged by reason of a material increase in the bonded risk.

8.43   Remedies for Defective Performance

Contract law generally provides that where the performance of a builder is defective, the agreed contract price is subject to a deduction for the costs to remedy the defects. The same rule applies between prime contractors and subcontractors.[44]

If a subcontractor fails to perform its work, the prime contractor may perform the work, backcharge the subcontractor, and deduct the backcharge from the subcontractor's progress payments.

The measure of the prime contractor's damages generally is the reasonable cost of remedying the defects—that is, the cost of making the subcontractor's work conform to the contract.[45] Where the prime contractor retains a portion of the subcontract price, the measure of damages is the reasonable cost of completing the contract and repairing the subcontractor's defective performance less the part of the contract price still unpaid.[46]

A prime contractor's decision to perform the subcontractor's work assumes that the subcontractor is in default. That assumption carries with it some risk. The contractor runs the risk of guessing incorrectly as to whether or not the subcontractor has substantially performed in the first instance and whether the backcharge is valid in the second. In making such an error, the contractor may, itself, be committing a material breach of the subcontract.[47]

8.44   Remedies for Delayed Performance

When a subcontractor fails to complete the work covered by its subcontract within the time specified, and the delay in completion is not excusable, the prime contractor is entitled to recover any resulting, foreseeable damages. A delay is excusable if it results from an event or omission for which the subcontractor is not responsible. Under certain circumstances, the subcontractor's unexcused delay may warrant termination of the subcontract.

---

[43] *See Caron v. Andrew*, 284 P.2d 544 (Cal. Ct. App. 1955).

[44] "The builder . . . may be entitled to a deduction or setoff against such compensation [as is owed the subcontractor] for expenses incurred or damages sustained by reason of the subcontractor's failure to comply with his contract." 17A C.J.S., *Contracts*, § 368 at p. 390.

[45] *Sorensen v. Robert N. Ewing*, 448 P.2d 110 (Ariz. Ct. App. 1968).

[46] *Id.* at 114.

[47] *Howard S. Lease Constr. Co. v. Holly*, 725 P.2d 712 (Alaska 1986).

Termination of a sub for late performance is proper only if the delay is not excusable. When a subcontractor is delayed because of the prime contractor's failure to schedule or coordinate other trades on the project, the delay is excusable and does not warrant a default termination.

In *Tribble & Stephens Co. v. Consolidated Services*,[48] the court held that a subcontractor was wrongfully terminated since the delay in prosecuting its work was excusable. In *Tribble*, the court relied upon evidence showing that the contractor had ordered the subcontractor to relocate electrical junction boxes as a result of another subcontractor's work. In addition, a delay in completing the soffits, which was not in the subcontractor's scope of work, prevented the subcontractor from installing the light fixtures. Finally, certain owner-furnished material arrived late and impeded the subcontractor's wiring in certain areas of the project.

Typically, the liquidated damages assessed by the owner against the prime contractor constitute the owner's measure of damages for delays, although the owner may be able to recover actual damages. A prime contractor may be able to protect itself from liquidated damages when the delay is caused by a subcontractor and the subcontract contains an appropriately worded subcontract provision. For example, in *Taos Construction Co. v. Penzel Construction Co.*,[49] the court ruled that a subcontract's "pass on" of liquidated damages from the prime to its subcontractor was valid.

Krauss v. Greenberg[50] also illustrates the prime contractor's rights to recover damages caused by a subcontractor's delay. Krauss, the subcontractor, sued Greenberg for the value of material furnished in connection with work under a government contract that contained a liquidated damages clause. The prime contractor had been charged liquidated damages by the owner for delays that were attributable to the subcontractor. Therefore, the prime counterclaimed against the subcontractor, raising the question of whether consequential damages could be recovered for breach of a subcontract.

The damages were allowed because the court found that assessment of liquidated damages by the owner in the event of late completion was within the contemplation of the subcontracting parties. However, unless the subcontract language controlling the subcontractor's liability for delay damages is carefully written, a prime contractor's recovery for delays caused by the subcontractor may be limited to the liquidated damages paid to the owner.[51]

8.45   Relationship between Subcontractor and the Owner: May the Prime Contractor Assert the Subcontractor's Rights against the Owner?

There is normally no "privity of contract" between the owner and any subcontractor. As a result, the owner and subcontractor generally cannot sue each other for breach of contract. In addition, the owner's only payment obligation is to the prime

[48] 744 S.W.2d 945 (Tex. App. 1988).

[49] 750 S.W.2d 522 (Mo. App. 1988).

[50] 137 F.2d 569 (3rd Cir. 1943).

[51] *Industrial Indem. Co. v. Wick Constr. Co.*, 680 P.2d 1100 (Alaska 1984).

contractor under the terms of their contract. The prime contractor in turn, however, has a corresponding contractual obligation to make payments to its subcontractors.[52]

In connection with federal government contracts, it is permissible for a prime contractor to bring an action against the government on behalf of a subcontractor that has been injured by government action or inaction. This "sponsorship" rule applies to appeals before the various agency boards of contract appeals as well as before the United States Court of Federal Claims. This right was confirmed in *United States v. Blair*,[53] where the United States Supreme Court stated that Blair (the prime contractor) "was the only person legally bound to perform his contract with the Government and he had the undoubted right to recover from the Government the contract price for the tile, terrazzo, marble and soapstone work whether that work was performed personally or through another."[54]

This same theory may also be available as a basis for an action by a prime contractor on behalf of its subcontractor against a nonfederal government owner, where the prime, in effect, acts as a conduit for the cause of action.[55]

The subcontractor may be entitled to recover from both the prime and the owner when both are found to be responsible for damages. In *Rome Housing Authority v. Allied Building Materials, Inc.*,[56] the court held that the trial court was correct in awarding delay damages to a subcontractor apportioned equally between the contractor and the owner as a result of their failure to resolve disputes in a timely manner. In *Mobile Chemical Co. v. Blount Bros. Corp.*,[57] a general contractor, acting as construction manager, and an owner were found equally liable for damages to subcontractors resulting from their joint decision to accelerate. The court admonished the general contractor because its "first construction schedule was prepared by an employee innocent of the ability to prepare such a schedule for a complex project."[58] The message is clear: the prime contractor's right to insist that subcontractors perform in accordance with the project schedule carries with it a corresponding obligation to ensure that the schedule is accurate, realistic, and consistent with the parties' agreement.

In *Wexler Construction Co. v. Housing Authority of Norwich*,[59] the general contractor was not allowed to sue on behalf of a subcontractor. In that case the court implied, however, that the Blair Doctrine was inapplicable only because there existed an implied contract between the subcontractor and the owner, and thus there was no reason why the subcontractor could not bring the action directly.

---

[52] *Marion Mach. Foundry & Supply Co. v. Colcord*, 294 S.W. 361 (Ark. 1927); *Utschig v. McClone*, 114 N.W.2d 854 (Wis. 1962).

[53] 321 U.S. 730 (1944).

[54] *Id.* at 737.

[55] *See Robert E. McKee v. City of Atlanta*, 414 F. Supp. 957 (N.D. Ga. 1976); *St. Paul Dredging Co. v. State*, 107 N.W.2d 717 (Minn. 1961).

[56] 355 S.E.2d 747 (Ga. Ct. App. 1987).

[57] 809 F.2d 1175 (5th Cir. 1987).

[58] *Id.* at 1177.

[59] 183 A.2d 262 (Conn. 1962).

8.46 The Prime Must Be Liable to the Subcontractor for the Pass-Through Claim: The Severin Doctrine

Many courts have held that a prime contractor can maintain a suit on behalf of one of its subcontractors only if it has reimbursed its subcontractor for the latter's damages, or remains liable for such reimbursement in the future. Courts typically refer to this as the "Severin Doctrine," which was first articulated in *Severin v. United States*.[60] In *Severin*, the contract between the prime contractor and the subcontractor contained an exculpatory clause holding the prime contractor harmless from any claim caused by the actions of the government/owner. The court, therefore, held that it had no jurisdiction to hear any claim based upon damages to the subcontractor.

Exceptions to the Severin Doctrine have been made since the decision was first rendered. In 1965, the Court of Claims held that the doctrine does not apply when subcontractors' claims are asserted as an equitable adjustment under the provisions of a prime contract with the federal government.[61]

8.47 States Have Adopted the Severin Doctrine

Some state courts have adopted the Severin Doctrine as their own. For instance, the Georgia Supreme Court held that a general contractor may not recover on behalf of its subcontractors absent proof of liability to those subcontractors.[62] Thus, if a subcontract absolves a general contractor of liability to its subcontractor for delay damages, the general contractor is precluded from bringing an action to recover for delays on behalf of the subcontractor.

In *Warren Bros. Co. v. North Carolina Department of Transportation*, the North Carolina Court of Appeals created an absolute bar to subcontractor claims against the North Carolina Department of Transportation (DOT) even if the claim is brought by the general contractor and regardless of whether the general contractor is or will ultimately be liable to the subcontractor for the damages in question.[63] In reaching

---

[60] *Severin v. United States*, 99 Ct. Cl. 435 (1943), *cert. denied*, 322 U.S. 733 (1944); *see also J. L. Simmons Co. v. United States*, 304 F.2d 886 (Ct. Cl. 1962).

[61] *Blount Bros. Constr. Co. v. United States*, 348 F.2d 471 (Ct. Cl. 1965). *See also Metric Constructors, Inc. v. United States*, 314 F.3d 578 (Fed.Cir. 2002) (government did not meet its burden of establishing that subcontractor executed iron-clad release sufficient to trigger application of the Severin Doctrine). Boards and courts have limited the Severin Doctrine out of reluctance to leave subcontractors with valid claims out in the cold. Numerous cases have recognized these limitations. *See Ball, Ball & Brosamer, Inc.*, IBCA No. 2841, 97-1 BCA ¶ 28,897; *E.R. Mitchell Constr. Co. v. Danzig*, 175 F.3d 1369 (Fed. Cir. 1999); *Roof-Techs Intern., Inc. v. State*, 57 P.3d 538 (Kan. App. 2002); *Morrison Knudsen Corp. v. Fireman's Fund Ins. Co.*, 175 F.3d 1221 (10th Cir. 1999).

[62] *Dep't of Transp. v. Claussen Paving*, 273 S.E.2d 161 (Ga. 1980). *See also Univ. of Alaska v. Modern Constr., Inc.*, 522 P.2d 1132 (Alaska 1974); *D.A. Parrish & Sons v. County Sanitation Dist. No. 4*, 344 P.2d 883 (Cal. 1959); *Kinsington Court v. Dep't of State Hwys.*, 253 N.W.2d 781 (Mich. Ct. App. 1977); *Buckley & Co. v. State*, 356 A.2d 56 (N.J. 1975); *Tully & DiNapoli, Inc. v. State*, 272 N.Y.S. 667 (N.Y. Ct. Cl. 1966).

[63] 307 S.E.2d 836 (N.C. Ct. App. 1983).

this decision, the court specifically disregarded considerations of the Severin Doctrine. Rather, the court based its decision upon the language contained in § 108-6 of the Standard Specifications for Roads and Structures issued by the North Carolina DOT, providing that a subcontractor will not have any claim against the DOT by reason of the approval of the subcontract by the DOT, interpreting this section to preclude even claims by general contractors on behalf of a subcontractor. However, exceptions to the Warren Doctrine have been recognized where the prime contractor included the subcontractor's damages as a subset of its own damages. Otherwise, the courts reason, there would be no means of recovering the subcontractor's damages.[64]

8.48 Conclusion

Avoidance of subcontract disputes demands diligent subcontract administration and constant vigilance on the part of both the prime contractor and subcontractor.

Dispute avoidance begins at the bidding or negotiations stage of the project. Prime contractors should investigate their potential subcontractors in light of the subcontractor's ability to contribute to the overall success of the project. Subcontractors should be equally diligent in checking out the prime contractor and owner.

The subcontract document should accurately express the parties' agreement. Whether a form subcontract or a specially drafted document is used, the subcontract should be consistent with the requirements of the general contract and address problems that may affect the progress and performance of the work.

Finally, diligent project administration should achieve early detection of problems, which will help avoid disputes or, at least, minimize their consequences.

➤ POINTS TO REMEMBER

Subcontract Default Clause

- Prior to contracting, utilize a Default Clause Checklist to identify the terms and verify the adequacy of a subcontract termination for default clause. The terms of the subcontract should be consistent with the performance and payment provisions of the prime contract.
- Notice of default and the right to cure may be implied by some courts, even in the absence of express language in the default clause.
- The right to terminate a subcontract for the contractor's convenience may be restricted in some courts by a "good faith" requirement in the exercise of the termination right.

---

[64] *Metric Constructors, Inc. v. HSPE*, 468 S.E.2d 435 (N.C. Ct. App. 1996); *Bolton Corp. v. T.A. Loving Co.*, 380 S.E.2d 796 (N.C. Ct. App. 1989).

No Damages for Delay, Except as Paid by the Owner

- A subcontract flow-down provision may limit a subcontractor's right to recover delay damages.
- Subcontractors should carefully review the owner/general contractor contract documents to determine, prior to contracting, the risk assumed by the subcontractor through broad-form subcontract flow-down clauses.
- Subcontractors must be aware that their right to recover may depend upon compliance with documentation and notice requirements in the prime contract.

Changes

- Prior to contracting, utilize a Changes Clause Checklist to verify the adequacy and fairness of the subcontract changes clause.
- Clauses that attempt to limit the type and amount of additional costs (e.g., overhead, profit, indirect losses) recoverable as a result of contract changes are increasingly popular and potentially dangerous.
- Take the sample checklists outlined in this chapter, expand and tailor them to suit your particular practices and industry needs, and require their use in prescreening each potential contract.
- At the beginning of each job, outline for your project management the contract procedures (e.g., notice requirements, time limits, cost support and record requirements, etc.) that will govern and limit your change order rights.

Subcontract Indemnification

- In some states, clauses requiring one party to hold another party harmless from liability arising solely from the latter party's own acts are void, as against public policy.
- Use a Subcontract Indemnity Clause Checklist to determine, in advance of contracting, the exact scope of any indemnity obligation created in the subcontract.

Labor Affiliation

- Ensuring labor harmony on the project should be one of the goals of a properly drafted subcontract.
- Use the labor affiliation checklist in this chapter to help identify the manner in which labor issues are treated in your subcontract.

Subcontract Disputes Procedures

- The contractor should be careful that its subcontract disputes procedure is consistent with any disputes procedure required in the owner/contractor agreement.
- If the subcontractor is to be bound by determinations made as a result of owner/contractor disputes, the subcontract should spell out the subcontractor's rights or duties of participation in that disputes procedure.

- Alternative dispute-resolution procedures can be less expensive and less time-consuming; consider such alternative dispute procedures prior to contracting, in lieu of or as a preliminary step before resorting to litigation or arbitration.

Federal and State Government Projects

- Standard subcontract forms utilized in private work are often inadequate for problems and requirements inherent to public contracting.
- Before doing public contract work, have your subcontract reviewed for any necessary inclusion of contract clauses (e.g., cost or pricing data requirements, notice, scope of work, claims and certification requirements) peculiar to government contracting.

9

CONTRACT CHANGES

9.1 WHAT IS A CHANGES CLAUSE?

Changes are inevitable on any significant construction project. Projects are rarely built exactly as they were originally designed. A multitude of variables can generate the need for a modification.

The "changes" clause in a construction contract allows one party to implement changes in the work while the project is being constructed. A changes clause may also come into play when issues arise involving defective specifications, differing site conditions, impossibility of performance, acceleration, or inspection, acceptance, and warranties. In short, a changes clause is often an umbrella provision, involving numerous aspects of performance under the contract. No other clause more clearly illustrates the uniqueness and complexity of a construction contract.

A changes clause in a construction contract departs from the established principle of contract law that a contract requires the mutual agreement of the contracting parties. Under the common law, a contract is created when two parties reach an agreement on an identified undertaking. Each party agrees to perform specific contract duties in exchange for some performance by the other party. Once the agreement is reached, the terms of the contract define and limit the obligations of each party, and no one party can unilaterally change or modify the contract. Generally, if changes or modifications are necessary, both parties have to reach a separate agreement incorporating any negotiated changes.[1]

---

[1] On occasion, a construction contract will be entered into without having a changes clause. In that event, the common-law rule applies and a contractor cannot be required to perform changes unless the changes are separately agreed to. In one case, a general contractor entered into a subcontract for the removal, storage, and replacement of existing equipment on a renovation job. The subcontract did not contain a changes clause. When the owner decided to pay to have all new equipment, the general contractor deleted the requirement that the subcontractor reinstall the existing equipment. The general contractor took a credit for this deleted work. The sub sued, arguing that the agreement could not be changed unless there was mutual agreement. The court agreed with the subcontractor and held the general contractor liable for this deleted work. *Werner v. Ashcraft Bloomquist, Inc.*, 10 S.W.3d 575 (Mo. App. 2000).

Rigid application of this common-law rule would create practical problems in construction. Requirements and needs often change during the course of a long construction project. Small details left out of the work scope can affect the practical use of the entire project and must be timely addressed. Problems would be caused by the common-law rule due to the dynamic nature of construction, the ever-changing needs of the owner, or frequent encounters with unexpected developments. The changes clause grew out of the practical need for a contract tool to address changes required after contract formation.

While a changes clause is more often found in construction contracts than in other types of contracts, it is not correct to presume that the clause violates principles of contract law. Through a changes clause, the contracting parties agree in advance that one of the parties has the right to revise the work in some way under defined terms. The requirement for legal consideration to support contract promises is satisfied by the provision requiring that the contract sum and/or time be adjusted if the change requires extra work or an extended period of performance.

While there are many variations of changes clauses, the clause used by the federal government illustrates many of the typical elements of a construction contract changes clause. That clause is found in the Federal Acquisition Regulation (FAR) at FAR § 52.243-4 and provides as follows:

CHANGES (AUG 1987)

(a) The Contracting Officer may, at any time, without notice to the sureties, if any, by written order designated or indicated to be a change order, make changes in the work within the general scope of the contract, including changes-

   (1) In the specifications (including drawings and designs);

   (2) In the method or manner of performance of the work;

   (3) In the Government-furnished facilities, equipment, materials, services, or site; or

   (4) Directing acceleration in the performance of the work.

(b) Any other written or oral order (which as used in this paragraph (b), includes direction, instruction, interpretation, or determination) from the Contracting Officer that causes a change shall be treated as a change order under this clause, *provided*, that the Contractor gives the Contracting Officer written notice stating (1) the date, circumstances, and source of the order and (2) that the Contractor regards the order as a change order.

(c) Except as provided in this clause, no order, statement, or conduct of the Contracting Officer shall be treated as a change under this clause or entitle the Contractor to an equitable adjustment.

(d) If any change under this clause causes an increase or decrease in the Contractor's cost of, or the time required for, the performance of any part of the work under this contract, whether or not changed by any such order, the Contracting Officer shall make an equitable adjustment and modify the contract in writing. However, except for an adjustment based on defective specification, no adjustment for any change under paragraph (b) of this clause shall be made for any costs incurred more than 20 days before the Contractor gives written notice as required. In the case of defective specifications for which the Government is responsible, the equitable adjustment shall include any increased cost reasonably incurred by the Contractor in attempting to comply with the defective specifications.

(e) The Contractor must assert its right to an adjustment under this clause within 30 days after (1) receipt of a written change order under paragraph (a) of this clause or (2) the furnishing of a written notice under paragraph (b) of this clause, by submitting to the Contracting Officer a written statement describing the general nature and amount of proposal, unless this period is extended by the Government. The statement of proposal for adjustment may be included in the notice under paragraph (b) above.

(f) No proposal by the Contractor for an equitable adjustment shall be allowed if asserted after final payment under this contract.

A typical changes clause (in a general construction contract) allows an owner to order extra work, delete work, or make changes to the quantity, timing, sequence, or methods of any contract work activity, with commensurate adjustments in the contract price and performance time. Subcontract forms contain similar provisions allowing for the adjustment of contract obligations at the subcontract level.

A "change order" provision, as the changes clause is sometimes called, gives the owner the contractual power to adapt actual conditions to the end product sought—for example, to correct errors in the plans and specifications or to take advantage of newly developed construction techniques and materials. A "changes" clause gives the owner contractual power to "order" the contractor to make changes, so long as the owner follows the terms of the clause and compensates the contractor consistent with the terms of that clause.

Changes clauses often specify the method for determining the amount of additional compensation or performance time that is due the contractor for changed or extra work. Payment for changed work is often accomplished based on an agreed or negotiated lump sum, unit prices, or time-and-materials (cost-plus) basis.

Although owners often prefer to negotiate the extra compensation the contractor is to receive before the changes are implemented, it is common for changes clauses to provide that the contractor may be required to proceed with the work without first reaching agreement on the added (or reduced) compensation and time due. Having the power to direct the contractor to proceed without reaching agreement on compensation first protects the owner against possible work stoppages or delays that might otherwise result while negotiations are under way. For example, the Standard Form of Agreement and General Conditions Between Owner and Contractor, AGC Document No. 200, published by The Associated General Contractors of America (2000 ed.) provides for an "Interim Directed Change," which is signed by the owner and requires the contractor to proceed with changed work.[2] An Interim Directed Change becomes the subject of a "change order" when (if) the owner and contractor agree upon an adjustment to the contract price or contract time or both.

---

[2] AGC Document No. 200 ¶ 8.2.1 (2000 ed.) ("The *Owner* may issue a written Interim Directed Change directing a change in the Work prior to reaching agreement with the *Contractor* on the adjustment, if any, in the Contract Price and/or the Contract Time consisting of additions, deletions or other revisions, the Contract Sum and Contract Time being adjusted accordingly."). (Emphasis added.)

This type of provision requiring changed work to proceed pending an agreement on the compensation can be just as important for the general contractor to assure that subcontractors do not stop if questions arise about changes. Thus, a provision requiring subcontractors to continue work during change order negotiations should be included in all subcontracts.

When a contractor has to proceed with changed work before the price is negotiated, it should protect its interests by keeping complete documentation, including records of all expenditures and impacts caused by the change. Costs incurred for the changed work should be documented using separate cost codes if possible. The ultimate cost generally includes an allowance for the contractor's profit and extended or unabsorbed overhead. Profit and overhead markups will either be defined by the changes clause, or a reasonable markup will be negotiated. Change order costs may need to be certified or approved by the project architect or engineer, making record keeping even more critical.

The contractor may be entitled to an appropriate extension of the contract time if the contract sets out a specific completion date and the changed work impacts the completion of the work. Regardless of whether the contract provides for liquidated damages, the contractor is well served to consider if an appropriate adjustment in the time of performance is due. Time issues generated by a change are normally negotiated at the same time that money issues are resolved and agreements documented in the final written change order form. It is also critical for the contractor to document the extension of performance time required by the change if no agreement can be reached.

The changes clause is also the contract mechanism that courts often will employ when the parties have a dispute over the scope of work or interpretation of the contract documents or if there is an allegation of defective specifications. For whatever reason, a contractor may find that it has to perform work it did not originally envision. In such circumstances, the contractor believes it is being required to perform a change and therefore is entitled to be paid for this "extra." The owner, on the other hand, believes that the work is part of the original scope of the contract, so requiring the contractor to perform it would not be a change and would not give rise to revising the contract price.

While these types of disputes will always be decided by their individual facts, the changes clause is the proper mechanism to employ in the event that the contractor's position is correct. Thus, the changes clause will come into play in circumstances where the parties disagree over whether there has been a change at all. These types of situations are commonly referred to as "constructive changes" and will be covered in more detail later in this chapter.

9.2   RECOVERY UNDER THE CHANGES CLAUSE

There are four primary factors to consider in assessing the contractor's rights to recover under the changes clause:

(1) Is there a change to the contract work?

(2) Who is authorized to order changes?

(3) When are written change orders required?

(4) When is written notice of a claim for additional compensation arising from extra work required?

Each factor is discussed in detail below.

9.3   Is There a Change to the Contract Work?

As mentioned above, the contracting parties may be able to agree whether certain orders from the owner constitute "changes" under the changes clause. Determining the answer to this question depends upon the plans, specifications, and contract provisions for each individual job. As a general rule, a contractor only is required to perform in accordance with its original agreement. If the owner orders work that is beyond what was required in the original agreement, the changes clause will entitle the contractor to additional compensation.[3]

It is important to remember that a changes clause would also apply to changes that decrease the cost of or time required for performance. For example, if the owner deducts certain work activities from the contract, the changes clause will entitle the owner to a decrease in the contract price or time.[4] Deductive changes often are not specifically addressed in changes clauses, and these can generate unique questions over the contract adjustment or credit due. An owner may want to use the numbers in a bid schedule or schedule of values in valuing deleted work. The contractor, on the other hand, may have reasons why such pricing is not appropriate. Moreover, different questions arise when dealing with deductive changes. Does one value deleted work based on the cost savings to the contractor or the value of the deleted work to the owner? How should overhead and profit be addressed in a deductive change? How should discounts be considered? The issues related to the pricing of credits can present some difficult questions of contract interpretation.[5]

---

[3] *See, e.g., E. C. Ernst, Inc. v. Koppers Co., Inc.*, 476 F. Supp. 729 (W.D. Pa. 1979), *modified,* 626 F.2d 324 (3rd Cir. 1980); *Jones v. Pollock*, 208 P.2d 1031 (Cal. Ct. App. 1949), *opinion vacated,* 34 Cal. 2d 863, 215 P.2d 733 (Cal. 1950); *W. R. Ferguson, Inc. v. William A. Berbusse, Inc.*, 216 A.2d 876 (Del. 1966); *see also Town of Palm Beach v. Ryan Inc. Eastern*, 786 So. 2d 665 (Fla. Dist. Ct. App. 2001) (affirming judgment in favor of contractor where additional work was necessary to bring the project into conformity with the overall intent of the contract).

[4] *Ragnar Benson, Inc. v. Bechtel Power Corp.*, 651 F. Supp. 962 (M.D. Pa. 1986) (subcontractor required to give credit for savings realized by the use of a more economical cleaning method).

[5] Deductive change cases often address unusual questions that can arise when parties disagree on how to value deleted work. For example, in *M. P. Paquet, Inc. v. New Jersey Department of Transportation*, 761 A. 2d 122 (NJ Superior Ct. App. Div. 2000), the contractor submitted a lump-sum bid on a bid schedule that required a breakdown of the price into work components. The contractor included the price of a pre-bid quote in the breakdown for painting work. Immediately prior to bid, the contractor got a lower paint quote and reduced its lump-sum bid accordingly, but did not adjust the breakout (contractor used a single line item to make cut/adds in the minutes before bid). When the owner decided to delete the painting, it wanted to use the breakout price rather than what the contractor actually had in its bid. The court had to decide how to value this deductive change, and ultimately ruled that the value should be based on the breakout number listed; otherwise, the breakout would be meaningless.

The rules of contract interpretation discussed in **Chapter 5** often play an important role in a court's resolution of a dispute over whether certain work ordered by the owner is changed or extra work. The contract scope of work is defined by the contract documents. The interpretation of those documents will often decide whether a specific item of work is or is not included in the scope of the project. One of the more important rules of contract interpretation is that the written contract will be construed most strongly against the party who drafted it.[6] In other words, when a contract can have two or more reasonable interpretations (i.e., the contract is ambiguous), it will be construed against the author since it had the discretion or control in describing the requirement. Typically, the owner or its agent (the project architect/engineer) drafts the construction contract. Thus, in order for a contractor to recover for extra work, it is not generally necessary that its interpretation of the contract be the only reasonable interpretation or even the most reasonable interpretation. Rather, if the contractor's interpretation is reasonable, if the contractor can show that it relied on its reasonable interpretation, and if the ambiguity was not "patent" (i.e., obvious), then the contractor's interpretation should prevail over an equally reasonable interpretation advanced by the party who drafted the ambiguous contract documents.[7]

9.4 Who Is Authorized to Order Changes?

The changes clause in most construction contracts identifies who can order changes to the work. Typically, the owner reserves to itself the right to order changes to the work, especially if the change requires a price adjustment. Many contracts will allow the architect/engineer to order minor changes that do not affect price. In federal government contracts, the contracting officer is the only person authorized to order changes on behalf of the government.

The individuals having authority to order changes should be specified in the contract. However, contract documents do not always clearly establish who can order changes. This can be a significant problem if it is not feasible for a contractor to wait for a final change order to be processed before beginning additional work. As a result, the contractor must rely on assurances by the design professional or other owner representatives that additional costs will be paid. These persons may or may not be found to have the legal authority to alter the plans and specifications or impose additional obligations. Risks are created when a contractor proceeds with extras without a fully executed change or without a contractually authorized change directive.[8]

---

[6] *Lytle v. Freedom Int'l Carrier, S.A.*, 519 F.2d 129, 134 (6th Cir. 1975); *Cincinnati Bengals, Inc. v. Bergey*, 453 F. Supp. 129, 149 (S.D. Ohio 1974).

[7] *See Bennett v. United States*, 371 F.2d 859 (Ct. Cl. 1967).

[8] *See, e.g., Smith v. Board of Education of Parkersburg Dist.*, 85 S.E. 513 (W. Va. 1915) (where the contractor was subsequently held responsible for the installation of an item that was specified in the contract and that had been omitted pursuant to the instructions of the architect); *County of Brevard v. Miorelli Engr., Inc.*, 703 So.2d 1049 (Fla. 1997) (sovereign immunity based recovery for extra work); *C.O.B.A.D./Constr. Corp. v. School Board of Broward County*, 765 So. 2d 844 (Fla. 4th DCA 2000) (no recovery for extra work not authorized by a change order).

If the contract is not clear as to who has authority to direct changes, an understanding should be reached as early as the preconstruction conference as to the individuals authorized to order changes and the extent of their authority. These understandings should be confirmed in writing. If there are any questions regarding who may bind the other party, these need to be resolved at the inception of the project.

A lack of clear direction in the contract as to who is authorized to direct compensable changes can cause harsh results if the person directing the change is found to lack the necessary authority. This is particularly true when dealing with public bodies. For example, in *Nether Providence Township School Authority v. Thomas M. Durkin & Sons, Inc.,*[9] the contract required changes be approved in writing by the school board. During performance, a disagreement arose as to whether certain work was required under the contract. Two members of the school board signed a letter to the contractor ordering the contractor to proceed with the disputed work and stating that the disagreement would be resolved at a later time. The court ruled that the letter was neither valid authorization under the terms of the contract nor a waiver of those terms. The court concluded that the contractor was not entitled to additional compensation because it had never been given instructions by the school board, the only party with such authority under the contract.

The *Durkin & Sons* decision is an unfortunate example of what can happen when a contractor does not follow the requirements of the changes clause. That case involved a public body spending tax dollars, and the court felt compelled to strictly follow the contract requirements. Although there are several ways (discussed below) the contractor in *Durkin & Sons* might have recovered, the case is a good example of the substantial risk a contractor accepts when it does not strictly follow the requirements of the changes clause or does not understand the limits of those acting on behalf of another party, particularly a public entity.

A contractor performing extra work at the direction of someone other than the person designated in the contract has two primary legal theories for recovering under the changes clause. The lack of express authority may be overcome by: (1) the implied or apparent authority of the person who requested the extra (i.e., the architect/engineer), or (2) the ratification by the owner of the actions of the person (architect/engineer) who requested the extra. These two theories are discussed below.

9.5 Implied Authority   In preparing plans and specifications for a traditional design-bid-build project, the architect/engineer generally acts as an independent contractor to the owner. However, when providing supervisory functions on a project, including processing change orders for extra work, the architect/engineer typically functions as an agent of the owner. (*See* **Chapter 7** for a general discussion of the architect/engineer's authority.) In an extra work situation, the question often becomes whether the architect/engineer has the "implied" authority to order extra work on the owner's behalf, even though the contract does not give the architect/engineer the "express" authority.

[9] 476 A.2d 904 (Pa. 1984).

"Implied authority" is the authority of an agent to do whatever acts are incidental to, or necessary, usual, or proper for, the exercise of the express authority delegated to that agent by the principal. For example, does an engineer who has the express authority to direct changes in the grade of a railroad also have the implied authority to enter into a supplemental contract to accomplish a grade change? In *Lafayette Railway Co. v. Tucker*,[10] it was held that the engineer did have such implied authority.[11] In federal government contracts, a contractor may not rely upon implied or apparent authority; the person ordering the changed work must have "actual" authority or the contractor proceeds at its peril.[12]

9.6 Apparent Authority In contrast to implied authority, the term "apparent authority" refers to the situation where the owner's representative (i.e., the architect/engineer or some other person) acts in a way that leads the contractor to reasonably believe that the representative has authority beyond that actually possessed. For example, if a prudent contractor forms a reasonable belief from actions or statements made by the owner that the architect has a certain authority, then the owner may be bound by the architect's acts if the architect takes action within this "apparent" authority. For a more complete discussion of these agency principles, *see* **Chapter 7,** and *Wells Fargo Business Credit v. Kozloff, Inc.*,[13] and *AAA Tire & Export, Inc. v. Big Chief Truck Lines, Inc.*[14]

It is often difficult for a court to determine the scope of an agent's authority. Nonetheless, an error in this determination can prove disastrous. Such was the case in *Missouri Portland Cement Co. v. J. A. Jones Construction Co.*,[15] which involved a contract to erect three steel cement storage silos. The plans and specifications contained notations that each silo was to be welded to six supporting columns by a continuous field weld. The connecting points temporarily were secured by high-tensile steel bolts. The owner's representative on the site was not a registered professional engineer, and his main function was to act as liaison between the owner and the contractor. When work had progressed to the point of welding the connections between the silos and columns, the general contractor's superintendent asked the owner's job-site representative whether the connections should be welded or caulked to keep water out and prevent rust. The representative instructed the contractor to caulk the connections; as a result, the welds were never made. Subsequently, at the time of initial loading, one silo collapsed, causing extensive damage to the other two silos.

The general contractor was held liable for breach of contract because the court determined that the owner's representative was not authorized to exercise control

[10] 27 So. 447 (Ala. 1900).

[11] *But see Albert Steinfield & Co. v. Broxholme*, 211 P. 473 (Cal. Ct. App. 1922) (a different result was reached on similar facts).

[12] *Federal Crop Ins. Corp. v. Merrill*, 332 U.S. 380 (1997); *Mil-Spec Contractors, Inc. v. United States*, 835 F.2d 865 (Fed. Cir. 1987).

[13] 695 F.2d 940 (5th Cir.), *rehearing denied*, 699 F.2d 1163 (5th Cir.), *cert. denied*, 464 U.S. 818 (1983).

[14] 385 So. 2d 426 (La. Ct. App. 1980).

[15] 323 F. Supp. 242 (M.D. Tenn. 1970), *aff'd* 438 F.2d 3 (6th Cir. 1971).

over the structural requirements of the job, and had no actual, implied, or apparent authority to interpret the plans or to authorize any deviation from the plans. The general contractor was, however, entitled to indemnification by the steel erection subcontractor who was the party actually responsible for the failure to follow the plans.

9.7 Ratification by the Owner   Although the architect/engineer (or other owner representative) may not have express authority to order extra work, it may nevertheless be possible to establish that the actions of the architect/engineer directing extra work were "ratified" or approved by the owner after the fact. As emphasized in the case of *Kirk Reid Co. v. Fine*,[16] however, it is critical that the owner have actual knowledge of the change that is claimed to have been ratified.[17]

9.8 Summary   The best and safest course of action for any contractor is to not perform extra or changed work without a valid order from a person authorized by the contract to order such work. Failure to obtain proper authorization under the contract changes clause can jeopardize the contractor's claim for extra compensation.

9.9 When Are Written Directives Required for Extra Work?

Problems can arise when oral orders are given for extra work where the contract specifically requires that they be in writing. Most construction contracts today provide that the contractor shall not proceed with any extra or changed work until a written change order has been issued. For example, AGC Document No. 200 requires either a written change order signed by both parties, or a written Interim Directed Change issued by the owner before the contractor may proceed with extra work. Such provisions should be considered valid and binding on the parties, and, if not satisfied, may prevent the contractor from recovering compensation for changed or extra work.[18] For this reason, the contractor should always demand a written change order, or a written work directive, before performing changed or extra work. An instructive example is found in *Environmental Utilities Corp. v. Lancaster Area Sewer Authority*,[19] where the contractor was not allowed to recover for extra work performed because it did not have written orders for the work. Similarly, in *County of Brevard v. Miorelli Engineering*,[20] the Florida Supreme Court denied recovery for changed work without a written change order, rejecting the contractor's argument that the county-owner had waived the written change order requirement by issuing

[16] 139 S.E.2d 829 (Va. 1965).

[17] *Id.* at 834–835.

[18] *See, e.g., Plumley v. United States*, 226 U.S. 545 (1913); *see also County of Brevard, supra* note 8 (rejecting contractor's argument that the county waived the written change order requirement by directing changes in the work without following the formalities contained in the contract). *See generally,* 13 Am. Jur. 2d, *Building and Construction Contracts*, § 22 (1964).

[19] 453 F. Supp. 1260 (E.D. Penn. 1978).

[20] *See supra* note 8.

oral directives to proceed with extras. The court based its decision on sovereign immunity, stating that the sovereign could be left with potentially unlimited liability if the doctrines of waiver and estoppel could be used to defeat the express terms of the contract.[21]

Obtaining a written change order before executing any changed work is always desirable, since it protects both owner and contractor. However, this is frequently ignored in practice. The contractor often cannot stop work, sometimes for weeks, while a formal change order is processed. Realities make it necessary for the contractor to rely on the assurances of the owner's representative or the architect/ engineer that a change order will be forthcoming. In recognition of this reality, AGC Document No. 200 provides that the contractor may proceed with changes directed by the owner in an Interim Directed Change before there is an agreement on the pricing and time associated with the change.[22]

A contractor can sometimes obtain relief when it proceeds with extras without an appropriate written directive or executed change order. A court will sometimes look for a way to avoid enforcing the written work order requirement when it leads to a particularly inequitable result. Various methods and theories have been used for this purpose.

Some courts will make a distinction between an "extra," or work that is not required at all under the contract, and "additional work," which itself is not precisely required, but is a necessary extension of other work that is specified. Where the contractual written change order requirement covers only "extra" work, a court might characterize the work as "additional" work for which the contractor could recover despite not having a written order.[23]

A contractor can also sometimes avoid the harsh results of the written change order requirement by showing that the owner waived, modified, or abandoned the written change order requirement. Courts (focusing on the ultimate question of recovery) have often used these theories interchangeably. The decisions are not altogether consistent as to what particular acts or conduct are sufficient to waive or modify the requirement for a written change order. The general principle is that the written change order requirement can be waived or modified not only by express words, but also by acts or conduct that by implication waive or otherwise derogate the writing requirement.[24] A waiver or modification of the written order requirement

---

[21] *Id.* at 1051. *But see City of Mound Bayou v. Roy Collins Construction Co., Inc.*, 499 So. 2d 1354 (Miss. 1986) (city waived right to have change orders in writing because of prior payments for verbally directed changes and the engineer's bad faith); *Huang Int'l, Inc. v. Foose Constr. Co.*, 734 P.2d 975 (Wyo. 1987).

[22] AGC Document No. 200 ¶ 8.2.1 (2000 ed.). *See also* § 12.1 (2000 ed.) (providing that the contractor "shall continue the Work and maintain the Schedule of the Work during any dispute resolution proceedings."). AIA Document A201 contains similar provisions addressing "Construction Change Directives." *See* A201 §§ 4.3.3 and 7.3 (1997 ed.).

[23] *See Roff v. Southern Constr. Corp.*, 163 So. 2d 112 (La. Ct. App. 1964); *DeMartini v. Elade Realty Corp.*, 52 N.Y.S.2d 487 (1943).

[24] *See* Annotation, "Effect of Stipulation, in Private Building or Construction Contract, That Alterations or Extras Must Be Ordered in Writing," 2 A.L.R.3d 620 (1965 & Supp. 1995).

is most easily established where the owner has made progress payments for some of the extra work without having a written order in place.[25]

Similarly, repeated verbal directives from the owner to perform extra work can create a modification or waiver of the written change order requirement. For example, in *Consolidated Federal Corp. v. Cain*,[26] an owner who verbally ordered several changes could not contend that the contractor breached the contract by requesting additional compensation for those changes. The court recognized that the contract required written change orders but found that the owner had waived that requirement by repeatedly ordering changes verbally.[27]

A waiver or modification also has been found where the owner made verbal statements promising to pay for extra work and the contractor proceeded based on those promises.[28] In *Udevco, Inc. v. Wagner*,[29] a contractor was allowed to recover where the owner had made an express oral waiver of the writing requirement and the contractor relied on the statement in doing the work. Yet, in a Texas case, a subcontractor lost a claim against its prime contractor because of the absence of a written change order, even though the prime's representative promised "they would take care of it down the line."[30] These cases clearly establish that while a contractor may have arguments why it should recover, there is always risk when either party departs from the terms of the contract.

The owner's knowledge that extra work is being performed, without objection, may be an excuse to the written change order requirement.[31] However, mere knowledge on the part of the owner often will not be enough to convince a court that the writing requirement has been waived. In many instances, the owner will not know whether or not certain work is an extra. The owner may argue that it had a right to assume the work was covered by the contract unless there was notice and a change order was worked out.

Generally, a contractor will have an argument that extra work is compensable without a written change order where:

(1) The work was orally ordered or authorized by the owner (as opposed to the design professional or construction representative); or

---

[25] *See Union Bldg. Corp. v. J & J Bldg. & Maintenance Contractors, Inc.*, 578 S.W.2d 519 (Tex. Ct. App. 1979). *See also Safer v. Perper*, 569 F.2d 87 (D.C. Cir. 1977); *Custom Builders, Inc. v. Clemons*, 367 N.E.2d 537 (Ill. App. Ct. 1977) (where the owner only refused to pay for some selected extras without a written order); *W.E. Garrison Grading Co. v. Piracci Construction Co., Inc.*, 221 S.E.2d 512 (N.C. App. 1975).

[26] 394 S.E.2d 605 (Ga. Ct. App. 1990).

[27] *See also Allen & O'Hara, Inc. v. Barrett Wrecking, Inc.*, 898 F.2d 512 (7th Cir. 1990); *Eastline Corp. v. Marion Apartments, Ltd.*, 524 So. 2d 582 (Miss. 1988).

[28] *See, e.g., Meadows v. Kinser*, 603 S.W.2d 624 (Mo. Ct. App. 1980); *Udevco, Inc. v. Wagner*, 678 P.2d 679 (Nev. 1984); *Carolina Mechanical Contractors, Inc. v. Yeargin Constr. Co., Inc.*, 198 S.E.2d 224 (S.C. 1973).

[29] 678 P.2d 679 (Nev. 1984).

[30] *Austin Elcon Corp. v. Avco Corp.*, 590 F. Supp. 507, 513 (W.D. Tex. 1984).

[31] Annotation, *supra* note 24, at 658.

(2) The owner has orally agreed or promised to pay additional compensation for the work in question; or

(3) The parties to the contract, throughout its performance, have entirely or repeatedly disregarded the writing requirement.

While the legal theories of waiver, modification, and estoppel may, in many instances, provide relief where the contractor has not obtained a written change order, these theories present significant proof problems. There are always two sides to a story when parties argue over significant sums of money and where adequate documentation does not exist. The safer course always is to insist on written authorization (if not a formal change order) before proceeding with the work, rather than relying on the oral assurances of the architect/engineer or the owner that the contractor will be compensated for its effort.

A contractor can get some protection by confirming, in writing to the owner, that the work being performed is in addition to that required under the contract and that the contractor anticipates additional compensation in money and time for the extra work.

9.10   When Is Written Notice of a Claim for Additional Compensation Resulting from Extra Work Required?

Owners typically include provisions in their construction contracts requiring written notification within a certain time if the contractor intends to file a claim for work considered to be beyond contract requirements. For example, AGC Document No. 200 requires written notice given to the owner of a claim within 14 days after the "occurrence" giving rise to the claim or within 14 days after the contractor first recognizes the condition giving rise to the claim, whichever is later.[32] Additionally, AGC Document No. 200 also requires written notice to be provided before commencing the work (except in emergency situations).[33] AIA Document A201 (1997 ed.) requires written notice to the architect within 21 days after the occurrence of the event giving rise to the claim or within 21 days after the condition giving rise to the claim is first recognized, whichever is later. Additionally, AIA Document A201

---

[32] See AGC Document No. 200, Standard Form of Agreement and General Conditions Between Owner and Contractor, ¶ 8.2.1.

[33] AGC Document No. 200 ¶ 8.4 provides: "[F]or any claim for an increase in the Contract Price and/or the Contract Time, the *Contractor* shall give the *Owner* written notice of the claim within fourteen (14) days after the occurrence giving rise to the claim or within fourteen (14) days after the *Contractor* first recognizes the condition giving rise to the claim, whichever is later." (Emphasis added.) Paragraphs 12.2, 12.3, and 12.4 require that the parties attempt to settle any dispute arising out of or relating to the contract by, in sequential order, discussions between the parties' representatives, a meeting of the senior executives of the parties, mediation, and if the dispute is not resolved by mediation, then the parties are to submit the dispute to any dispute resolution procedure agreed to by the parties in the contract.

(1997 ed.) requires written notice to be provided before commencing the work (except in emergency situations).[34]

Provisions requiring written notice of claims protect the owner by allowing the owner an opportunity to evaluate the situation before the work is performed and the costs are incurred. Such provisions in subcontracts provide similar protection to the general contractor.

The contractor's failure to give the required notice of a claim for additional compensation may bar the recovery of additional compensation, especially where the owner can show some prejudice for not being notified.[35] However, provisions requiring advanced notification of a claim for extra work may be waived or modified in much the same fashion as the written change order requirement. For example, in *Transpower Constructors v. Grand River Dam Authority*,[36] the contractor on a transmission line project submitted a claim for additional compensation for changes made in the work. The owner denied the claim on the grounds that the contractor had failed to comply with contractual provisions regarding notice and documentation of claims. The court found that in every other instance where the contractor had requested additional compensation, the owner and its engineer had approved payment, notwithstanding that those claims had not been presented in compliance with the provisions relied upon by the owner in this case. Accordingly, the court held that the owner had waived the provisions regarding notice and documentation and upheld the contractor's claim.

In *Macri v. United States*,[37] a general contractor was to construct the foundation upon which a subcontractor was to erect certain tanks. The subcontractor complained that defects in the foundation would delay the subcontractor's performance and increase its costs. After unsuccessfully attempting to repair the foundation, the

---

[34] A201 § 4.3.2 (1997 ed.) provides: "Claims by either party must be initiated within 21 days after occurrence of the event giving rise to such Claim or within 21 days after the claimant first recognizes the condition giving rise to the Claim, whichever is later. Claims must be initiated by written notice to the Architect and the other party." A201 § 4.4.1 (1997 ed.) requires that these claims, excluding those arising under paragraphs 10.3 through 10.5, be initially decided by the architect. The architect's initial decision is a condition precedent to mediation, arbitration, or litigation of all claims between the contractor and owner. A201 § 4.3.5 (1997 ed.) provides: "If the Contractor wishes to make Claim for an increase in the Contract Sum, written notice . . . shall be given before proceeding to execute the Work. Prior notice is not required for Claims relating to an emergency endangering life or property arising under Paragraph 10.6."

[35] *See, e.g., Linneman Construction, Inc. v. Montana-Dakota Utilities Co., Inc.*, 504 F.2d 1365 (8th Cir. 1974); *Associated Mechanical Contractors, Inc. v. Martin K. Eby Construction Co., Inc.*, 983 F. Supp. 1121 (M.D. Ga. 1997), *aff'd in part and rev'd in part*, 271 F.3d 1309 (11th Cir. 2001); *A.H.A. General Construction, Inc. v. New York City Housing Auth.*, 699 N.E.2d 368 (N.Y. 1998). *But see Ronald Adams Contractor, Inc. v. Mississippi Transportation Commission*, 777 So. 2d 649, 653-54 (Miss. 2000) (contractor's failure to provide notice pursuant to the contract of a differing site condition was "irrelevant" and the contractor could recover damages where the state Transportation Commission had actual notice of the differing site condition); *New Pueblo Constructors, Inc. v. State*, 696 P. 2d 185 (Ariz. 1985) (strict enforcement of a contractual notice provision was not required where the state Department of Transportation was aware of the changed conditions for which the contractor was seeking additional compensation and was not prejudiced by the lack of formal notice of such claims).

[36] 905 F.2d 1413 (10th Cir. 1990).

[37] 353 F.2d 804 (9th Cir. 1965).

general contractor ordered the subcontractor to proceed. The court allowed the subcontractor to assert a claim for extras, even though the sub had not clearly placed the general contractor on notice after being ordered to proceed. The court found that the general contractor had knowledge of the subcontractor's claim from the earlier communications and could not claim surprise or prejudice due to the subcontractor's failure to comply strictly with the written notice provision.[38]

In summary, a failure to give prompt written notice may prevent a contractor from recovering compensation to which it otherwise would be entitled. Prompt written notice should be given to the owner or to its authorized representative when any action (or inaction) on the part of the owner (or its representatives) would increase cost or time. Following this simple procedure can minimize disputes later.

9.11 "CONSTRUCTIVE CHANGES"

Under the "constructive change" doctrine, informal actions or inactions by the owner that are not initially acknowledged by the owner to be a change in the scope of work—but that *require* extra work by the contractor—may nonetheless constitute a change in the scope of the work. One author has described the "constructive change" concept as "[owner] conduct which is not a formal change order, but which has the effect of requiring the contractor to perform work different from that prescribed by the original contract, but in theory, which could have been ordered under the changes clause."[39]

Although the term "constructive change" first arose in the context of federal government contracts,[40] the general concept is now well known in connection with private construction contracts. Courts simply use different terminology and legal theories to achieve the same result. Three such legal theories are typically employed in the private owner context:

(1) Directed work (which is most analogous to pure "constructive change" analysis),

(2) Breach of contract, and

(3) Implied contract.[41]

---

[38] *Id; see also General Specialties Co. v. Nello L. Teer Co.*, 254 S.E.2d 658 (N.C. Ct. App. 1979) (court characterized the owner's oral agreement to an extra as a waiver of the formal notice requirement); *Nat Harrison Assocs., Inc. v. Gulf States Utilities Co.*, 491 F.2d 578, *rehearing denied*, 493 F.2d 1405 (5th Cir. 1974) (party to whom written notice was to be given waived the written notice requirement because it had knowledge of the extra work and did not object to it).

[39] C. Gusman, "'Constructive Change'—A Theory Labeled Wrongly," 6 Pub. Cont. L. J., 229 (January, 1974). As Gusman explains:

The "constructive change" doctrine . . . is a recognition that an informal requirement for performance of additional work is substantially equivalent to a formal requirement and must, therefore, be governed by similar principles.

[40] *See Industrial Research Associates, Inc.*, DCAB WB-5, 68-1 BCA ¶ 7069 at 32,685-86.

[41] For cases illustrating these theories, respectively, *see Denton Constr. Co. v. Missouri State Highway Comm'n*, 454 S.W.2d 44 (Mo. 1970); *Udevco, Inc. v. Rocky Wagner*, 678 P.2d 679 (Nev. 1984); *V. L. Nicholson Co. v. Transcon Inv. & Fin. Ltd.*, 595 S.W.2d 474 (Tenn. 1980).

The underlying concept is essentially the same whether the owner is a public or private entity, and similar rules apply in both spheres.

"Constructive changes" typically fall into one of four general categories:

(1) An informal extra work directive or order;

(2) The drawings or specifications are defective and, as a result, the contractor is required to perform extra work;

(3) The owner or its representative misinterprets the contract—for example, where work that actually satisfies contract requirements is erroneously rejected or where an unreasonably high standard of performance is required; or

(4) The owner denies the contractor a justified time extension, requiring compliance with the original completion schedule, and thereby forces the contractor to accelerate performance.[42]

Each of these four categories is discussed below.

9.12 Informal Extra Work Directives

An informal work directive occurs any time an authorized representative of the owner directs the contractor—either orally or in writing, but without a formal change order—to perform work beyond the original scope of the contract. Such conduct constitutes a "constructive change" entitling the contractor, under certain circumstances, to reimbursement of any additional costs incurred in performing the changed work and, possibly, an extension of the contract time. These informal orders or directives differ from advice, comments, or suggestions, which may be offered by technical representatives of the owner.[43] The specific underlying circumstances must be examined on a case-by-case basis, but generally include proper notice that the directive is considered to be a change and documentation of costs.

9.13 Defective Plans and Specifications

A "constructive change" arising in connection with defective plans and specifications has its basis in what is referred to as the Spearin Doctrine (*see* **Chapter 5**). This doctrine provides that, when an owner supplies the plans and specifications for a construction project, the contractor cannot be held liable for an unsatisfactory final result attributable solely to defects or insufficiencies in those plans and specifications. This doctrine assumes the absence of any negligence on the contractor's part and that the contractor made no express warranty with regard to the suitability of the plans and specifications. Under this principle, an implied warranty exists for owner-furnished plans and specifications that if the contractor complies with them, a satisfactory product will result.[44] The delivery of defective plans and specifications is

---

[42] *Gusman, supra* note 39 at 232.

[43] *Industrial Research, supra* note 40.

[44] *R. M. Hollingshead Corp. v. United States*, 111 F. Supp. 285 (Ct. Cl. 1953).

therefore a breach of the implied warranty, absolving the contractor from liability for unsatisfactory results or delays in completion.

The second aspect of the Spearin Doctrine, the right of a contractor to recover its additional costs when defective plans and specifications necessitate extra or remedial work, has found similar acceptance. The general principle has been stated as follows:

> Where defects in the plans and specifications, the sufficiency of which is not warranted by the contractor, necessitate extra work or materials to complete the contract, the contractor may recover therefor from the owner.[45]

For example, in *Fairbanks North Star Borough v. Kandick Construction, Inc.*,[46] the plans and specifications on a roadway project understated the amount of excavation of material to be removed and disposed of away from the project site. The court found that the owner had breached its implied warranty of the adequacy of the plans and specifications, and allowed the contractor to recover its extra costs since the contractor had reasonably relied upon the defective plans and specifications. In *Keller Construction Corp. v. George W. McCoy & Co.*,[47] the court held that the owner warranted the sufficiency of the plans and specifications to the general contractor, and this warranty carried over to a subcontractor, entitling the subcontractor to recover from the general contractor for defects in specifications that required repairing breaks in a sewer line. The court further held that the owner had to indemnify the general contractor for any amounts so paid to the subcontractor. In *Adams v. Tri-City Amusement Co.*,[48] the walls of a building collapsed because the plans and specifications did not make allowances for wet soil conditions. The court held that the contractor was entitled to recover the reasonable value of the work to reconstruct the wall.

9.14   Misinterpretation of Plans and Specifications by the Owner

The third category under the "constructive change" concept relates to misinterpretation of the plans and specifications by the owner or its representatives. This type of constructive change arises from the owner's implied duty not to hinder or delay the contractor in the performance of its work, which is an implied obligation contained in every contract.[49]

This type of "constructive change" arises where, for example, the contract specifies a particular method of performance or allows the contractor to select the method, but the architect or engineer requires a different, more expensive method than that contemplated by the contractor at the time it prepared its bid. For example, in *H. I. Homa Co.*,[50] a constructive change was found where the contracting officer

---

[45] 13 Am. Jur. 2d, *Building and Construction Contracts*, § 19 (1964).

[46] 795 P.2d 793 (Alaska 1990).

[47] 119 So. 2d 450 (La. 1960).

[48] 98 S.E. 647 (Va. 1919).

[49] *See George A. Fuller Co. v. United States*, 69 F. Supp. 409 (Ct. Cl. 1947).

[50] ENG BCA Nos. PCC-41, PCC-42, 82-1 BCA ¶ 15,651.

rejected a bar-type progress chart that satisfied the contract's progress of work clause, and instead required the contractor to provide a CPM schedule.

In *Charles Meads & Co. v. City of New York*,[51] a contract to build a public library gave the contractor the option of performing the work in a certain manner. When the architect required the contractor to use a more complicated and expensive method to attain the same result, the court held the city liable for the contractor's extra costs. A similar principle was applied in *S. Hanson Lumber Co. v. Moss*,[52] where the contractor was entitled to additional compensation when the owner wrongfully refused to allow the use of the material specified in the contract, and instead required a more expensive type of material.

This type of constructive change can also arise from the owner's interpretation of a contract ambiguity in its favor. For example, in *American Asphalt, Inc.*,[53] a contractor was found to be entitled to additional costs of removing excavated soil where the government-prepared plans were ambiguous as to whether the excavated materials were to remain on-site. The government's plans appeared to indicate the material would remain on-site as fill material, but the government intended to show finish grade of paving, not the level for additional fill. The contractor had made no allowance in the bid for the removal of this soil.

Interpretations of contract specification requirements are a repetitive source of "constructive change" claims and disputes. Typically, the contractor must establish that its interpretation fell within the scope of reasonableness and that it relied upon that interpretation during the bid/proposal phase. Failure to prove the latter element can defeat an otherwise valid claim for additional compensation.[54]

9.15   Acceleration

The fourth category of "constructive change" involves acceleration of the work. Constructive acceleration occurs in the absence of an owner-directed acceleration, such as where the owner has refused a valid request for time extensions or threatened other action that requires the contractor to accelerate its work to avoid liquidated damages or other loss or risk of loss. The classic case is when a request for a time extension for excusable delay is denied and the contract provides liquidated damages for late completion. The law construes this as an order by the owner to complete performance within the originally specified completion date, a shorter period of time, and at higher cost than provided for in the contract. The constructive acceleration doctrine allows recovery for the additional expenses the contractor can establish (where the owner refuses to give the contractor a time extension to which the contractor is contractually entitled, thereby forcing the contractor to "accelerate" its work efforts in an attempt to maintain the

---

[51] 181 N.Y.S. 704 (1920).

[52] 111 N.W.2d 681 (Iowa 1961).

[53] ASBCA No. 37349, 91-2 BCA ¶ 23,722.

[54] *Blueridge Gen., Inc.*, ASBCA No. 53663, 03-2 BCA ¶ 32,339.

original work schedule, the contractor is entitled to recover the costs related to the acceleration).[55]

Court decisions have identified five elements normally required to establish a claim for constructive acceleration.[56] Those elements are as follows:

(1) An excusable delay must exist;

(2) Timely notice of the delay and a proper request for a time extension should have been given;

(3) The time extension must have been postponed or refused;

(4) The owner must have ordered (either by coercion, direction, or some other manner) the project completed within its original performance period; and

(5) The contractor must actually accelerate its performance, thereby incurring additional costs.

The contractor should give the appropriate notice of the delay and request an extension of time in order to recover any additional costs of acceleration.[57] It is important, especially when the contractor believes acceleration is occurring without a specific order to accelerate its performance so that it is clear that the acceleration is not being undertaken voluntarily, and further, that the contractor will demand and expect the owner to pay the additional costs incurred. This notice to the owner of "forced" acceleration will assist the contractor greatly in recovering damages. This notice is not absolutely necessary if (a) the acceleration has been expressly directed; (b) the owner has indicated no time extensions will be permitted; or (c) the owner has waived the need for notice. Moreover, if the owner has specific knowledge of excusable delays and unequivocally orders the contractor to complete on the contract completion date without regard to excusable delays, the notice requirement is satisfied. Additionally, it is important that the contractor give detailed information on the delay to the owner, so that the owner can determine the reasonableness of the time extension.

It is imperative that the contractor carefully and fully document all delays and other factors that will aid in proving its entitlement to damages. Courts and boards are willing to find for the contractor on constructive acceleration claims, but if not carefully documented, the damages may not be recovered.

The refusal to grant a time extension can be expressed either by a clear rejection of a time extension or *by the postponement of a decision concerning the request*. The owner owes a duty to the contractor to timely respond and grant or deny the request.[58] By failing to respond to the request, or even putting off the decision until

---

[55] See *Howard J. White, Inc. v. Varian Assoc.*, 2 Cal. Rptr. 871 (Cal. Ct. App. 1960); *Siefford v. Housing Auth. of City of Humboldt*, 223 N.W.2d 816, 820 (Neb. 1974).

[56] *Nat Harrison Associates, Inc. v. Gulf States Utilities Co.*, 491 F.2d 578 (5th Cir. 1974); *Natkin & Co. v. George A. Fuller Co.*, 347 F. Supp. 17 (W.D. Mo. 1972).

[57] *Commercial Contractors Equipment, Inc.*, ASBCA Nos. 59230 et al, 03-2 BCA ¶ 32,381.

[58] *William Lagnion*, ENGBCA No 3778, 78-2 BCA ¶ 13,260.

the completion of the contract, the owner puts the contractor in a precarious position. If the contractor acts as if the time extension will be granted and continues at a pace that will complete the work after the completion date, and the time extension is not granted, liquidated damages may be incurred. If the contractor acts as if the time extension will not be granted and accelerates in order to complete the work at the completion date, the contractor incurs additional expenses that might not be recovered. The contractor's updated schedule showing the contractor's reasonable expectations at the time of the request becomes especially important to support the decision to accelerate. Damages are recoverable even if acceleration is to avoid risk of liquidated damages. If placed on appropriate notice, it is possible that the owner eventually will pay the cost created by postponing its decision on time extension.

The case of *Constructors-Pamco*[59] is a good example of a situation where constructive acceleration had occurred. The board found that the government had made it abundantly clear that work had to be completed without any extension of time by: (1) the use of language in the contract to the effect that the contract date would be strictly enforced; (2) the use of language in the contract to the effect that liquidated damages would be imposed on late-completed work; (3) the refusal to grant a time extension for a blizzard, which was an obviously excusable delay; (4) the refusal to respond to the contractor's request for instructions on how to proceed after it had complained about delays and extra costs; and (5) the daily communications with contractor personnel that no time extensions would be permitted. The board found that the contractor was required to accelerate performance of the work and to work under adverse conditions by direction of the government. A constructive change occurred entitling the contractor to an equitable contract price adjustment.

In *Norair Engineering Corp. v. United States*,[60] the United States Court of Claims set forth three elements that must be proven to recover for the increased costs of acceleration under a changes clause:

(1) That any delays giving rise to the order were excusable (thus entitling the contractor to a time extension);

(2) That the contractor was ordered or required to accelerate; and

(3) That the contractor in fact accelerated performance and incurred extra costs.

The *Norair* court held that the contractor could recover its acceleration costs even though the project was over 500 days "late" because the contractor was entitled to approximately 700 days of time extension and had to accelerate to finish "only" 500 days behind schedule.[61]

This type of constructive change can also arise when an owner's incorrect interpretation of the contract requires the contractor to accelerate. For example, in *Rogers Excavating*,[62] an earthwork contract required the contractor to start work within four

[59] ENGBCA No. 3468, 76-2 BCA ¶ 11, 950 (1976).

[60] 666 F.2d 546 (Ct. Cl. 1981).

[61] *See also Continental Heller Corp.*, GSBCA No. 7140, 84-2 BCA ¶ 17,275.

[62] AGBCA No. 79-180, 83-2 BCA ¶ 16,701.

days after receipt of the Notice to Proceed and finish all work in 90 days. The contractor submitted a proposed schedule showing mobilization to start within four days but actual excavation not starting until 40 days after Notice to Proceed. The owner refused to accept this schedule and required the contractor to start excavation work within the four-day period. The court found this to be an acceleration justifying additional compensation because mobilization was found to be "work" as it was defined in the contract. (However, the contractor ultimately lost the case because it had failed to give the required notice that it considered the owner's action to create a claim situation.)

The term "acceleration" is best known in federal government contracts.[63] However, the same result is achieved, usually under a breach of contract theory, where the private owner fails to grant an extension of time promptly or properly. As the court stated in *Wallace Process Piping Co. v. Martin-Marietta Corp.*:[64]

> The order to complete additional work without an extension of time, which made necessary a workweek in excess of 50 hours, was a change within the meaning of Paragraph 4, the Changes Clause of the contract. The refusal of Martin upon demand timely made by Wallace for an equitable adjustment constituted a breach of contract.

9.16 "CARDINAL CHANGES"

The changes clause of a construction contract does not give the owner an unrestricted right to order extra work. Changed work or extra work must be within the general scope of the original contract.

As a simple example, an owner that contracts for the construction of a house cannot require the contractor, by change order, to build a second house. Such extra work is totally beyond the scope of the original agreement. This would be an example of a "cardinal change." However, a change order requiring the addition of a room or the finishing of the basement probably would be valid under the changes clause. The difficult questions, of course, involve those cases that fall somewhere between the two extremes.

The term "cardinal change" refers to a change or changes ordered by the owner that are beyond the scope of the contract and therefore constitute a material breach of contract.[65] If a change is a cardinal change, the owner is in breach of its contract and the contractor can either refuse to perform or can perform and be paid the reasonable value for the work. However, if a contractor refuses to perform a proper change, incorrectly thinking it to be a cardinal change, it will be in breach for refusing to perform.

If the contractor is confronted with an undertaking *substantially different* from that originally contemplated due to the extensive changes ordered by the owner or

---

[63] *See, e.g., Ensign-Bickford Co.*, ASBCA No. 6214, 60-2 BCA ¶ 2817.

[64] 251 F. Supp. 411, 418–19 (E.D. Va. 1965).

[65] *Keco Indus., Inc. v. United States*, 364 F.2d 838 (Ct. Cl. 1966).

dictated by the owner's actions, then a cardinal change may exist. The contractor has the right to disregard the contract agreement in a cardinal change situation and seek compensation for the reasonable value of all services and materials provided.

In *County of Cook v. Harms*,[66] the court discussed the concept of cardinal change in great detail:

> Obviously, under a contract to construct a framed building at stipulated prices, a party could not be required to construct a stone or brick building, at prices to be fixed by the architect of the other party, by the use of these words in the contract. Nor could a party, by virtue thereof, contracting to build a small and inferior brick or stone building, be required to construct a large and superior stone or brick building. The mere combination of proportions and quantities, even of materials of the same class or grade, may be so different in different buildings of the same dimensions, that a party would not make the same bid, or be able, without financial loss, to construct them all for the same price.
>
> The terms stated in the writing were, we think, the controlling inducement to the contract, and the "changes, additions and alterations" therein provided for must have been contemplated and intended to be but such as were incidental to the complete execution of the work as described in the plans and specifications, and therefore of only minor and trifling importance, for otherwise some definite mode of determining what prices should be paid for them would also have been prescribed by the writing. We think any material departure from the plans and specifications with reference to which the contract was made, which resulted in a new and substantially different undertaking, cannot be regarded as within the meaning of this language
>
> We cannot admit that a party entering into a contract to do a given work at stipulated prices, can, by the use of these words in the written contract, be made to do a different and more expensive work at prices to be named altogether, or in large part, by the architect of the other party.[67]

In *C. Norman Peterson Co. v. Container Corp. of America*,[68] a contractor brought an action for breach of contract and for the reasonable value of the labor and materials used after experiencing significant cost overruns at a paper mill modernization project. The court found that the owner, by imposing hundreds of changes upon the contractor, so altered the scope of the work under the original contract that the owner had abandoned the contract. Accordingly, the guaranteed maximum cost provision of the contract was inapplicable and the contractor was entitled to recover the reasonable cost of its work. The court justified basing the contractor's damages on the total cost method because the owner was to blame for preventing the contractor from making a detailed showing as to how the damages claimed were caused by the breach.

A cardinal change may also result from physical conditions encountered by the contractor that were not expected and that fundamentally change the scope of the work. For example, in *Universal Contracting & Brick Painting Co. v. United States*,[69] a

---

[66] 108 Ill. 151 (1883).

[67] *Id.* at 159–60.

[68] 218 Cal. Rptr. 592 (Cal. Ct. App. 1985).

[69] 19 Cl. Ct. 785 (1990).

contractor entered into an agreement with the federal government calling for paint removal. After contract award, the contractor discovered that the paint contained asbestos. The contractor claimed that this constituted a "cardinal change," entitling the contractor to damages for breach of contract. (This would also constitute a differing site condition entitling the contractor to additional compensation, but the notice provision is more strictly construed than under a changes clause.) The government moved for summary judgment, contending that the presence of asbestos in the paint was not a substantial enough circumstance to constitute a "cardinal change." The court denied the government's motion, ruling that the contractor's claim presented a legitimate claim of "cardinal change" that could be decided only by a trial.

The question of whether a particular change (or group of changes) is sufficient to constitute a cardinal change is a matter of degree—and often is very subjective. The basic tests for a cardinal change are:

(1) Whether the type of work was within the contemplation of the parties when they entered into the contract, and

(2) Whether the job as modified is still the same basic job.

9.17   The Impact of Numerous Changes on Unchanged Work

Contractors occasionally may encounter a project where the owner makes multiple changes to a construction job, and no single change could be considered a cardinal change. However, after agreeing to many of these changes, the contractor realizes that the agreed prices for the changes are not adequate to compensate the contractor for the disruption and inefficiency created by the large volume of changes. This situation can occur when the contractor prices an individual change based on the direct costs to perform the work associated with that one change and does not account for the adverse impact the change could have on performing unchanged work.

Generally, a contractor is bound by the terms of its signed change orders. Thus, if the signed change orders have broad release language or state that they include all the compensation the contractor is entitled to receive for the changed work—covering both direct and indirect costs—the contractor may have little legal recourse.

For example, in *Vanlar Construction, Inc. v. County of Los Angeles*,[70] a contractor brought an action against the county to recover impact costs arising out of the cumulative effect of numerous change orders. The court held that Vanlar was not entitled to impact costs, emphasizing that all of the change orders and supplemental agreements the contractor had entered included direct and indirect costs. The court further pointed out that if Vanlar contemplated a future claim for impact costs, it should have requested that a reservation clause be inserted in each change order and supplemental agreement.

A contractor concerned about possible indirect impacts numerous changes may have on a job should consider adding a clause to proposed change orders stating

---

[70] 217 Cal. Rptr. 53 (Cal. Ct. App. 1985) (unpublished opinion).

that the change order covers only the direct costs of the changed work and that the contractor reserves the right to claim impact costs later.

9.18   IMPOSSIBILITY/IMPRACTICABILITY

The legal theory of "impossibility" can provide relief in appropriate situations from the usual common-law principle that a party must either perform its contract or respond in damages, even though performance proves to be more onerous or expensive than anticipated. The impossibility doctrine permits a contractor to walk away from a contract without penalty if performance is impossible or is so impracticable as to be virtually impossible. The rationale frequently used for excusing a contracting party on the basis of impossibility is that the contract contains an implied condition that the performance contemplated by the parties will in fact be possible at the time performance is due.[71]

The theory of commercial impracticability is related to the doctrine of impossibility. In the leading case of *Mineral Park Land Co. v. Howard*,[72] the court described the concept as follows:

> *A thing is impossible in legal contemplation when it is not practicable; and a thing is impracticable when it can only be done at an excessive and unreasonable cost. . . .* We do not mean to intimate that the defendants could excuse themselves by showing the existence of conditions which would make the performance of their obligations more expensive than they had anticipated, or which would entail a loss by them. But where the difference in cost is so great as here, and has the effect, as found, of making performance impracticable, the situation is not different from that of a total absence of earth and gravel. (Emphasis added.)

In *Mineral Park Land*, the contractor was excused from performing a gravel excavation contract when the cost of performance proved to be 12 times that originally anticipated.

Under traditional legal contract analysis, an unexpected rise in the price of materials is not an excuse for nonperformance. Courts and federal contract appeals boards consistently rule that a contractor signing a lump-sum contract accepts the cost risks associated with performance, including abnormal risks. Therefore, in all but the rarest of cases, the unexpected increase in the cost of goods or construction materials is a risk borne by the contractor.

It is generally stated that the doctrine of impracticability requires objective impracticability. Objective impracticability refers to the contemplated performance being impractical no matter who attempts performance. Subjective impracticability, or impracticability tied to the particular circumstances of the contractor in question, is not sufficient.[73] Thus, a contractor must show that performance would be impractical

---

[71] *Fraught v. Platte Valley Pub. Power & Irrigation Dist.*, 51 N.W.2d 253 (Neb. 1952).

[72] 156 P. 458 (Cal. 1916).

[73] *See, e.g., Pauley Petroleum, Inc. v. United States*, 591 F.2d 1308 (Ct. Cl. 1979).

for the "reasonable contractor"[74] rather than merely impractical for it because of its particular abilities or circumstances.[75] For example, in *Piasecki Aircraft Corp. v. United States*,[76] the court refused to apply the doctrine, cautioning that the doctrine of impracticable performance may be invoked "only when the [contractor] has exhausted all its alternatives" and when all methods of performance are "commercially senseless."

While the concept of impossibility can serve as a defense to excuse a contractor's entire contract performance, it may also prompt revisions or alterations in performance that bring the changes clause into play. For example, when the plans and specifications require the use of certain materials that subsequently prove impossible or impracticable to obtain, the contractor is necessarily forced to find a substitute. This substitution will be a compensable change if it increases the contractor's cost of performance. In *McIntyre v. United States*,[77] the contract required approved Colorado marble; but marble satisfying the specifications was unavailable in Colorado. The court held that the contractor was entitled to the extra costs incurred in obtaining marble from Tennessee, even though government permission to obtain it from the alternate source was subject to the condition that there would be no additional cost chargeable to the government.

A similar rule may apply with regard to methods of performance.[78] However, the federal government contract appeals boards and the U.S. Court of Federal Claims[79] have held that a method of performance dictated by the contract must be followed, even though performance may be more difficult (though short of impossible) or less efficient than anticipated. For example, *Natus Corp. v. United States*[80] involved an $8.5 million contract to produce a portable steel airplane landing mat. The contractor argued that production in accordance with government specifications was commercially "impracticable" and that, as a result, it was entitled to an equitable adjustment. Despite the problems that the plaintiff encountered in developing a suitable production process, the court found that an alternative process, though less economical, appeared to be workable. In the words of the court:

> The law excuses performance (or, in the case of Government contracts, grants relief through a change order) where the attendant costs of performance bespeak commercial senselessness; it does not grant relief merely because performance cannot be achieved under the most economical means.[81]

---

[74] *Guy F. Atkinson Co.*, ENGBCA No. 4771, 88-2 BCA ¶ 20,714 (impossible to achieve required moisture content); *Blount Bros. Corp. v. United States*, 872 F.2d 1003 (Fed. Cir. 1989) (specified material not available).

[75] *Koppers Co. v. United States*, 405 F.2d 554 (Ct. Cl. 1968).

[76] 667 F.2d 50 (Ct. Cl. 1981), *cert. denied*, 444 U.S. 898 (1981).

[77] 52 Ct. Cl. 503 (1917).

[78] *See, e.g.*, *Hol-Gar Mfg. Corp. v. United States*, 360 F.2d 634 (Ct. Cl. 1966); *Hobbs Constr. & Dev., Inc.*, ASBCA No. 34890, 91-2 BCA ¶ 23,755.

[79] Previously the United States Court of Claims and the United States Claims Court.

[80] 371 F.2d 450 (Ct. Cl. 1967).

[81] *Id.* at 457.

➤ POINTS TO REMEMBER

The following key points should be noted:

- *Change order disputes* arise when the contracting parties disagree about:
  - The original scope of the work, or
  - Compliance with notice requirements, or
  - Who has authority to order changes, or
  - Pricing issues
- *Authority issues* arise when a person who has no actual express authority orders a change for which the owner must pay because:
  - The person had implied authority, or
  - The person had apparent authority, or
  - The owner ratifies the change order.
- *The lack of the written notice/written change order* often required by a contract does not necessarily defeat a claim for extra compensation if the requirement for a writing has been waived by agreement or conduct of the parties.
- *Constructive changes* occur when the owner, without issuing a written order, directs the contractor to perform additional work to complete or remedy defective plans and specifications, to meet a higher standard of performance, to change or accelerate its schedule, or to alter the sequence of work from that which the contractor had otherwise planned.
- *Cardinal changes* are those changes or accumulations of changes that so greatly exceed the scope of the contract as to create a material breach of contract.
- *Impact costs* refer to the cumulative or "ripple" cost effect of numerous changes, and can be recovered in addition to the cost of the underlying changes if the contractor has appropriately reserved its right, in each signed change order, to recover later-incurred impact costs.
- *Impossible or commercially impracticable* conditions can excuse a contractor from performance; contractors generally must show that performance by a reasonable contractor was impracticable in order to prove that it was impossible or commercially impracticable to perform.

10

DIFFERING SITE CONDITIONS

A common source of disputes between owners and contractors is the cost to remedy site conditions that are materially different from those contemplated at the time the contract was bid. Unanticipated site conditions often generate extra costs, and they can also substantially delay and disrupt the project. These delays usually occur at the front end of a job, which can have a greater overall impact on the project.

10.1 DIFFERING SITE CONDITION DEFINED

A "differing site condition"—or "changed condition," as it is sometimes called—is a physical condition encountered in performing the work that was not visible and not known to exist at the time of bidding and that is materially different from the condition believed to exist at the time of bidding. Often, this condition could not have been discovered by a reasonable site investigation. Examples of changed conditions or differing site condition problems include soil with inadequate bearing capacity to support the building being constructed; soil that cannot be reused as structural fill; unanticipated groundwater (static or percolating); quicksand; muck; rock formations (or excessive or insufficient quantities of rock); and artificial (man-made) subsurface obstructions.

10.2 RESPONSIBILITY FOR DIFFERING SITE CONDITIONS

Under a traditional contract risk allocation analysis, a prudent contractor would be expected to protect itself against unforeseen conditions by including a contingency factor in its bid. The basic flaw in this approach is that a contractor cannot accurately value a true unknown. Even if included, the bid contingency may end up being totally inadequate, or, alternatively, grossly conservative. The one constant is that including any contingency increases bid prices and thus works to the detriment of the owner if adverse conditions are not encountered. In other situations, the contingency may prove wholly inadequate to cover the contractor's actual increased costs.

To alleviate some of the problems associated with unexpected subsurface conditions, differing site condition clauses have become a common feature in many construction contracts. The underlying reason for the presence of this widely used provision has been explained by many courts, including the United States Court of Claims (now the United States Court of Federal Claims) in *Foster Construction C.A. & Williams Bros. Co. v. United States*:[1]

> The purpose of the changed conditions clause is thus to take at least some of the gamble on subsurface conditions out of bidding.
>
> Bidders need not weigh the cost and ease of making their own borings against the risk of encountering an adverse subsurface condition, and they need not consider how large a contingency should be added to the bid to cover the risk. *There will be no windfalls and no disasters*. The Government benefits from more accurate bidding, without inflation for risks which may not eventuate. It pays for difficult subsurface work only when it is encountered and was not indicated in the logs. (Emphasis added.)

Despite this logic, both private and public owners often choose not to include a changed conditions clause in their contracts. Some owners, in fact, go the opposite direction by including clauses that purport to place all possible risks of a "bad" site on the contractor. These "exculpatory" clauses, or disclaimers, would seem to invite bidders to include contingencies in their bids.

The absence of a differing site conditions provision in the contract, however, does not necessarily mean that a contractor will be denied relief if adverse site problems arise. Several theories of recovery have been advanced in such cases. The most prominent of these theories are: (1) breach of warranty, (2) breach of a duty to disclose available information, (3) mutual mistake, (4) innocent misrepresentation, and (5) fraud. These theories are discussed briefly below, following a more detailed review of the principles involved in changed condition problems.

10.3 STANDARD DIFFERING SITE CONDITIONS CLAUSES

Virtually all of the "standard" form contracts between owners and contractors contain some type of differing site conditions clause. The first such standard clause appeared in 1927 in the federal government's standard fixed-price construction contract. Its purpose was, and is today, to place the risk of reasonably unexpected site

---

[1] 435 F.2d 873, 887 (Ct. Cl. 1970).

conditions on the federal government—granting a price increase and time extension to contractors required to deal with such conditions.[2]

10.4 The Associated General Contractors of America

The Associated General Contractors of America (AGC) has issued AGC Document No. 200, entitled Standard Form of Agreement and General Conditions Between Owner and Contractor (Where the Contract Price Is a Lump Sum) (2000 ed.). Paragraph 3.16, entitled Worksite Conditions, contains a differing site conditions clause, which states as follows:

3.16.1 WORKSITE VISIT The Contractor acknowledges that it has visited, or has had the opportunity to visit, the Worksite to visually inspect the general and local conditions which could affect the Work.

3.16.2 CONCEALED OR UNKNOWN SITE CONDITIONS If the conditions at the Worksite are (a) subsurface or other physical conditions which are materially different from those indicated in the Contract Documents, or (b) unusual or unknown physical conditions which are materially different from conditions ordinarily encountered and generally recognized as inherent in Work provided for in the Contract Documents, the Contractor shall stop Work and give immediate written notice of the condition to the Owner and the Architect/Engineer. The Contractor shall not be required to perform any work relating to the unknown condition without the written mutual agreement of the parties. Any change in the Contract Price and/or the Contract Time as a result of the unknown condition shall be determined as provided in this Article. The Contractor shall provide the Owner with written notice of any claim as a result of unknown conditions within the time period set forth in Paragraph 8.4.

This AGC Agreement also contains another clause under Article 4 Owner's Responsibilities which discusses worksite information which states:

4.3 WORKSITE INFORMATION Except to the extent that the Contractor knows of any inaccuracy, the Contractor is entitled to rely on Worksite information furnished by the Owner pursuant to this Paragraph 4.3. To the extent the Owner has obtained, or is required elsewhere in the Contract Documents to obtain, the following Worksite information, the Owner shall provide at the Owner's expense and with reasonable promptness:

1 information describing the physical characteristics of the site, including surveys, site evaluations, legal descriptions, data or drawings depicting existing conditions, subsurface conditions and environmental studies, reports and investigations. . . .

10.5 Federal Government

The text of the differing site conditions clause used in federal government contracts is set forth in the Federal Acquisition Regulation at FAR § 52.236-2, which states:

---

[2] *See generally* Abernathy and Shull, *Construction Business Handbook*, Chapter 15. Differing Site (Changed) Conditions, Aspen Publishers, Inc. (2004); Currie, Abernathy, and Chambers, *Changed Conditions*, Construction Briefings No. 84-12, Federal Publications, Inc.

DIFFERING SITE CONDITIONS(APR 1984)

(a) The Contractor shall promptly, and before the conditions are disturbed, give a written notice to the Contracting Officer of (1) subsurface or latent physical conditions at the site which differ materially from those indicated in this contract, or (2) unknown physical conditions at the site, of an unusual nature, which differ materially from those ordinarily encountered and generally recognized as inhering in work of the character provided for in the contract.

(b) The Contracting Officer shall investigate the site conditions promptly after receiving the notice. If the conditions do materially so differ and cause an increase or decrease in the Contractor's cost of, or the time required for, performing any part of the work under this contract, whether or not changed as a result of the conditions, an equitable adjustment shall be made under this clause and the contract modified in writing accordingly.

(c) No request by the Contractor for an equitable adjustment to the contract under this clause shall be allowed, unless the Contractor has given the written notice required; *provided*, that the time prescribed in (a) above for giving written notice may be extended by the Contracting Officer.

(d) No request by the Contractor for an equitable adjustment to the contract for differing site conditions shall be allowed if made after final payment under this contract.

10.6   Other Standard Forms

The American Institute of Architects (AIA) and Engineers Joint Contract Documents Committee (EJCDC) [consisting of: ACEC (American Consulting Engineers Council); ASCE (American Society of Civil Engineers); CSI (Construction Standards Institute); and NSPE (National Society of Professional Engineers)] standard contract forms also contain differing site condition provisions:

The AIA A201 (1997 ed.) Contract Clause:

4.3.4 *Claims for Concealed or Unknown Conditions.* If conditions are encountered at the site which are (1) subsurface or otherwise concealed physical conditions which differ materially from those indicated in the Contract Documents or (2) unknown physical conditions of an unusual nature, which differ materially from those ordinarily found to exist and generally recognized as inherent in construction activities of the character provided for in the Contract Documents, then notice by the observing party shall be given to the other party promptly before conditions are disturbed and in no event later than twenty-one (21) days after first observance of the conditions. The Architect will promptly investigate such conditions and, if they differ materially and cause an increase or decrease in the Contractor's cost of, or time required for, performance of any part of the Work, will recommend an equitable adjustment in the Contract Sum or Contract Time, or both. If the Architect determines that the conditions at the site are not materially different from those indicated in the Contract Documents and that no change in the terms of the Contract is justified, the Architect shall so notify the Owner and the Contractor in writing, stating the reasons. Claims by either party in opposition to such determination must be made within twenty-one (21) days after the Architect has given notice of the decision. If the conditions encountered are materially different, the Contract Sum and

Contract Time shall be equitably adjusted, but if the Owner and the Contractor cannot agree on an adjustment in the Contract Sum or the Contract Time, the adjustment shall be referred to the Architect for initial determination, subject to further proceedings pursuant to Paragraph 4.4.

The EJCDC Contract Clause (EJCDC Product No. C-700, 2002 ed.):

4.02   Subsurface and Physical Conditions

A. Reports and Drawings: The Supplementary Conditions identify:

   1. those reports of explorations and tests of subsurface conditions at or contiguous to the Site that Engineer has used in preparing the Contract Documents; and

   2   those drawings of physical conditions in or relating to existing surface or subsurface structures at or contiguous to the Site (except Underground Facilities) that Engineer has used in preparing the Contract Documents.

B. Limited Reliance by Contractor on Technical Data Authorized: Contractor may rely upon the general accuracy of the "technical data" contained in such reports and drawings, but such reports and drawings are not Contract Documents. Such "technical data" is identified in the Supplementary Conditions. Except for such reliance on such "technical data," Contractor may not rely upon or make any claim against Owner or Engineer, or any of their Related Entities with respect to:

   1. the completeness of such reports and drawings for Contractor's purposes, including, but not limited to, any aspects of the means, methods, techniques, sequences, and procedures of construction to be employed by Contractor, and safety precautions and programs incident thereto; or

   2. other data, interpretations, opinions, and information contained in such reports or shown or indicated in such drawings; or

   3. any Contractor interpretation of or conclusion drawn from any "technical data" or any such other data, interpretations, opinions, or information.

4.03   Differing Subsurface or Physical Conditions

C. *Notice.* If Contractor believes that any subsurface or physical condition at or contiguous to the Site that is uncovered or revealed either:

   1. is of such a nature as to establish that any "technical data" on which Contractor is entitled to rely as provided in Paragraph 4.02 is materially inaccurate; or

   2. is of such a nature as to require a change in the Contract Documents; or

   3. differs materially from that shown or indicated in the Contract Documents; or

   4. is of an unusual nature, and differs materially from conditions ordinarily encountered and generally recognized as inherent in work of the character provided for in the Contract Documents; then Contractor shall, promptly after becoming aware thereof and before further disturbing the subsurface or physical conditions or performing any Work in connection therewith (except in an emergency as required by Paragraph 6.16.A), notify Owner and Engineer in writing about such condition. Contractor shall not further disturb such condition or perform any Work in connection therewith (except as aforesaid) until receipt of written order to do so.

D. *Engineer's Review*: After receipt of written notice as required by Paragraph 4.03.A, Engineer will promptly review the pertinent condition, determine the necessity of Owner's obtaining additional exploration or tests with respect thereto, and advise Owner in writing (with a copy to Contractor) of Engineer's findings and conclusions.

E. *Possible Price and Times Adjustments*

1. The Contract Price or the Contract Times, or both, will be equitably adjusted to the extent that the existence of such differing subsurface or physical condition causes an increase or decrease in Contractor's cost of, or time required for, performance of the Work; subject, however, to the following:

   a. such condition must meet any one or more of the categories described in Paragraph 4.03A; and

   b. with respect to Work that is paid for on a Unit Price Basis, any adjustment in Contract Price will be subject to the provisions of Paragraphs 9.07 and 11.03.

2. Contractor shall not be entitled to any adjustment in the Contract Price or Contract Times if:

   a. Contractor knew of the existence of such conditions at the time Contractor made a final commitment to Owner with respect to Contract Price or Contract Times by the submission of a Bid or becoming bound under a negotiated contract; or

   b. the existence of such condition could reasonably have been discovered or revealed as a result of any examination, investigation, exploration, test, or study of the Site and contiguous areas required by the Bidding Requirements or Contract Documents to be conducted by or for Contractor prior to Contractor's making such final commitment; or

   c. Contractor failed to give the written notice as required by Paragraph 4.03.A.

3. If Owner and Contractor are unable to agree on entitlement to or on the amount or extent, if any, of any adjustment in the Contract Price or Contract Times, or both, a Claim may be made therefor as provided in Paragraph 10.05. However, Owner and Engineer, and any of their Related Entitled shall not be liable to Contractor for any claims, costs, losses, or damages (including but not limited to all fees and charges of engineers, architects, attorneys, and other professionals and all court or arbitration or other dispute resolution costs) sustained by Contractor on or in connection with any other project or anticipated project.

An examination of these clauses reveals a basic similarity with minor but important differences.

10.7   TYPES OF CONDITIONS COVERED

Whereas the AGC, FAR, and EJCDC clauses define differing site conditions as "subsurface" or "subsurface or latent physical conditions," the AIA clause uses the phrase "concealed conditions . . . below the surface of the ground or . . . concealed or unknown conditions in an existing structure."

Generally these clauses cover the same types of situations, although it is possible to imagine a few conditions where the wording would make a difference. A review of some of these situations stresses the importance of *reviewing the exact language* of the differing site conditions clause to determine which situations are covered. For example, where actual grade elevations turn out to be lower than those shown on the contract drawings (requiring additional fill to meet the grade requirements), a contractor should be able to recover under the FAR clause's "latent physical conditions" language.[3] But recovery under the AIA clause's "concealed conditions . . . below the surface of the ground or . . . in an existing structure" language might be more difficult.

10.8 Type I and Type II Changed Conditions

The AGC, AIA, EJCDC, and the FAR provisions identify two distinct types of unanticipated conditions that are compensable. These are usually designated as Type I and Type II changed conditions.

A Type I changed condition is, in the language of AGC Document 200, a condition that is "materially different from those *indicated* in the Contract Documents . . . ." The FAR speaks of such conditions as "differing materially from those indicated in the contract."

The FAR and AGC clauses describe a Type II changed condition as unknown physical conditions at the site, of an *unusual* nature, which differ materially from those ordinarily encountered and generally recognized as inhering in work of the character provided for in the contract. The language in the AIA and EJCDC provisions is quite similar.

10.9 Notice Requirements

Differences also exist among these standard clauses with respect to notice requirements. The AGC and FAR clauses require that the contractor stop work and give written notice upon encountering an unexpected condition, and *before* disturbing it, so that the owner's representative will have an opportunity to inspect and evaluate the condition. The EJCDC clause, with its "promptly after becoming aware thereof and before further disturbing" language, appears to be closer in intent to the FAR than it is to AIA Document A201, which only requires that notice of a claim for equitable adjustment be given to the owner within 21 days *after* "first observation of the condition." Regardless of the exact language, it is always preferable that the owner (or its agent, such as the project architect or engineer) be *notified immediately* when materially different conditions are encountered. By giving the owner the option of investigating the condition and, if appropriate, determining how best to proceed, the contractor greatly increases the likelihood of resolving any resulting claim in an expedient and mutually acceptable manner.

---

[3] *See Anthony P. Miller, Inc. v. United States*, 422 F.2d 1344 (Ct. Cl. 1970).

10.10 OPERATION OF THE DIFFERING SITE CONDITIONS CLAUSE

A differing site conditions clause provides a mechanism for dealing with an adverse, changed condition situation. However, a contract adjustment is not automatic. To obtain an adjustment under the clause, one must first establish that the situation falls within the coverage of the clause. Before examining what typically must be proven, it is important to remember what one is *not* required to prove.

If you are a contractor, notification of a suspected differing site condition does not mean that you are attempting to prove fault, bad faith, or defective design by the owner or its representative. There are simply some situations where differing, unanticipated conditions are encountered. This is especially true when dealing with subsurface work or with older structures where only sketchy construction history is available.

An example of this situation is found in the terms of many agreements between soils engineers and owners. For example, standard language recommended by the ASFE (formerly known as the Association of Soil and Foundation Engineers) in its suggested form contract between a geotechnical consultant and an owner (Client) reads:

> *CLIENT recognizes that subsurface conditions may vary from those observed at locations where borings, surveys, or explorations are made, and that site conditions may change with time.* Data, interpretations, and recommendations by GEOTECHNICAL ENGINEER will be based solely on information available to GEOTECHNICAL ENGINEER. GEOTECHNICAL ENGINEER is responsible for those data, interpretations, and recommendations, but will not be responsible for other parties' interpretations or use of the information developed. (Emphasis added.)

The presence of a differing site conditions clause allows the contractor to be reimbursed for its reasonable additional costs, regardless of the owner's knowledge or ignorance of actual conditions. By including a differing site condition provision, the owner has assumed a portion of the risk of such conditions in exchange for the contractor not being forced to include a contingency in its bid.

The converse is also true: The owner is entitled to a cost reduction if conditions prove less onerous than expected. Although such downward adjustments are not common, they do occur. Such credits are consistent with the clauses' central purpose, which is to base the owner's cost and the contractor's compensation on the reasonable value of the work actually performed, thereby eliminating unnecessary risks to each party.

10.11 Recovery for a Type I Changed Condition

In order to recover for a Type I changed condition—one where actual conditions are at variance with the conditions "indicated" by the contract documents—the contractor must show the following: (1) that certain conditions are *indicated* by the plans, specifications, and other contract documents; (2) its *reliance* on the physical conditions *indicated in the contract*; (3) the nature of the *actual* conditions; (4) the existence of a *material variation* between the conditions indicated and the conditions actually encountered; (5) that *notice*, as required by the contract, was given; and (6) that the change resulted in additional performance costs and/or time, as demonstrated by satisfactory *documentation* or proof.

The initial emphasis in Type I changed condition situations is on which conditions were "indicated" in the contract. Some statement or representation must be contained in the contract as to which conditions could be expected, and the actual conditions must differ from that statement or representation.

What is meant by "indicated in the contract" has been defined by numerous case decisions. It is not required that the indications (upon which the contractor is entitled to reasonably rely) be affirmatively expressed on the plans or in specific contract provisions. Instead, such indications may be a reasonable inference based upon reading the contract as a whole. Thus, the contractor may be able to compare actual conditions, not only with the express representations in the contract documents, but also with all reasonable inferences and implications that can be drawn from those documents. As was pointed out in *Metropolitan Sewerage Commission v. R. W. Construction, Inc.,*[4] it is not required that the contract indications be "explicit or specific, but only enough to impress or lull a reasonable bidder not to expect the adverse conditions actually encountered."

In certain situations, a contract indication may be found from documents that are not a part of the contract. For example, one federal court of appeals held that soil borings were a "contract indication" *even though* the borings were not a part of the contract documents. This court held:

> The test boring logs do not have to be strictly considered "a part of the contract documents" (which the Appendix states they are not) to be binding on the [owner] to the extent of their own accuracy. We can accept the [owner's] argument that the Appendix is not an item listed in the Table of Contents (but is in addition to the Table of Contents) and therefore the Appendix is not a part of the contract. However, the differing site conditions clause need not be interpreted to limit reimbursements to situations where the logs themselves are necessarily a part of the contract. The clause entitles the contractor to reimbursement when there are "conditions at the site differing materially from those indicated in this contract." Even though the logs may not be included in the contract, they are "indicated" in the contract. . . .[5]

Examples of situations where *express* representations of conditions in the contract documents were found to have differed materially from the actual conditions encountered include:

(1) *Muddy vs. Dry Conditions:* The contract documents stated that when "test holes were drilled in the area, no water was noted in any of the test holes." During construction, the contractor encountered "subsurface mud covered by a cracked and deceptively dry looking surface. . . ." The Supreme Court of Idaho found the subsurface mud to be materially different from the dry conditions indicated by

---

[4] 241 N.W.2d 371 (Wis. 1976).

[5] *City of Columbia v. Paul N. Howard Co.*, 707 F.2d 338, 340 (8th Cir. 1983).

the contract documents and affirmed the contractor's recovery for a Type I differing site condition.[6]

(2) *Variance from Anticipated Blow Counts:* Soil conditions with actual blow counts that were one-third to one-half the strengths indicated by the contract borings constituted a changed condition. The contractor that encountered this condition during the construction of two underground garages was entitled to additional compensation.[7]

(3) *Limitations on Access:* A playground construction contract called for the contractor to furnish a certain brand of playground equipment, and included a drawing showing the placement and orientation of the equipment. The contractor, in reliance on the drawing, believed that it would be possible to use a dump truck and backhoe to bring in and spread sand after the equipment was in place. However, this proved impossible, and the sand had to be spread by hand. Since the contractor used the specified brand-name equipment, it was justified in relying on the government's drawing and was entitled to an equitable adjustment for a Type I changed condition.[8]

(4) *Hard Clay versus Soft Mud:* The contract specifications required the contractor to remove soft mud, silt, and sand in a river-dredging project. When the contractor encountered hard, undisturbed clay instead of the soft materials specified, the contractor was entitled to an equitable adjustment for a Type I differing site condition.[9]

(5) *Excavated Materials Not Suitable as Fill:* Where the contract specifications required that soil materials located on-site be excavated and reused as fill, but the specified excavation and recompaction was prevented by the physical properties of the soil, which differed materially from the contract indications (which problem was also further impacted by an abnormal amount of rainfall), the contractor was entitled to an equitable adjustment for a Type I changed condition.[10]

Some examples of nonexpress, or *implied*, contract indications are the following:

(1) *Hidden Roof System Not Disclosed:* A system in addition to the roof indicated in the contract specifications and drawings was determined to be a valid Type I differing site condition claim. Nothing contained in the contract specifications or drawings indicated the existence of the additional roof system. Further, an inspection of the roof revealed no evidence that any additional roofing work had been performed after the as-built drawings had been prepared.[11]

(2) *Suitable Equipment for Work:* The Armed Services Board of Contract Appeals upheld a differing site condition claim, holding that the "compaction, and clearing and grubbing" requirements were sufficient contract indications. The board held that, while the contract documents made no express representation regarding

---

[6] *Beco Corp. v. Roberts & Sons Constr. Co.*, 760 P.2d 1120 (Idaho 1988).

[7] *Baltimore Contractors, Inc. v. United States*, 12 Cl. Ct. 328 (1987). *See also Granite-Groves v. Washington Metro. Area Transit Auth.*, 845 F.2d 330 (D.C. Cir. 1988).

[8] *Torres Constr. Co.*, ASBCA No. 25697, 84-2 BCA ¶ 17,397.

[9] *C. J. Langenfelder & Son, Inc.*, Maryland Department of Transportation 1000 (Aug. 15, 1980).

[10] *Southern Paving Corp.*, AGBCA No. 74-103, 77-2 BCA ¶ 12,813; *see also W.R. Henderson Const., Inc.*, ASBCA No. 52938 (2002), 02-1 BCA ¶ 31,741.

[11] *Southern California Roofing Co.*, PSBCA No. 1737 et al., 88-2 BCA ¶ 20,803.

subsurface conditions, the compaction and clearing and grubbing requirements led the contractor to reasonably believe it could utilize heavy equipment to perform its work. The board stated that "where, as here, design requirements cannot be met and procedures and equipment reasonably anticipated cannot be used, the situation represents a classic example of a Type I differing site condition."[12]   Similarly, courts have found an implied representation by requirements in the plans for a specific dredging technique,[13] where a grouting specification stated that groundwater could be controlled to a certain level during construction,[14] and where the contract documents indicated that "trench footings" could be used when in fact the soils on-site would not support them.[15]

(3) *Unanticipated Sloughing of Soils:* A tunneling contractor that encountered "running" ground conditions that were not disclosed by the contract soils information was granted relief under the differing site conditions clause for encountering a Type I condition. The contractor was required to grout in order to stop the sloughing.[16]

(4) *Dry Conditions Implied by Specified Construction Procedures:* When the construction procedures and design requirements set forth in the contract documents, read as a whole, indicated subsurface conditions permitting excavation "in the dry," but actual conditions made it impossible or impracticable to excavate in this manner, a changed condition was held to have been encountered.[17]

(5) *Implied Thickness of Concrete Floor:* The comparison of a 6-inch drain connection shown on the drawings with a cross section of concrete floors on the same drawings indicated the concrete floors were about 6 inches thick. When 12-inch concrete floors were encountered, a changed condition claim was allowed.[18]

10.12   Recovery for a Type II Changed Condition

Type II changed conditions differ significantly from those discussed above. Under a Type II situation, it is possible to recover even where the contract is *silent* about the nature of the condition. To establish a Type II changed condition, one must show that the conditions encountered were *unusual* and *differed materially* from those reasonably anticipated, given the nature of the work and the locale.

To qualify as sufficiently "unknown and unusual," the condition encountered by the contractor does not have to be in the nature of a geological freak—for example,

---

[12] *Kinetic Builders, Inc.,* ASBCA No. 32627, 88-2 BCA ¶ 20,657.

[13] *Midwest Dredging Co. v. McAninch Corp.,* 424 N.W.2d 216 (Iowa 1988).

[14] *S.A. Healy Co. v. Milwaukee Metropolitan Sewerage Dist.,* 50 F.3d 476 (7th Cir. 1995).

[15] *Sherman R. Smoot Co. v. Ohio Dept. of Adm. Serv.,* 736 N.E.2d 69 (Ohio App. 10th Dist., Franklin).

[16] *Shank-Artukovich v. United States,* 13 Cl. Ct. 346 (1987).

[17] *See Foster Constr., C.A. v. United States,* 193 Ct. Cl. 587 (1970). *But see Tricon-Triangle Contractors,* ENG BCA No. 5113, 88-1 BCA ¶ 20,317 (denying a Type I differing site condition claim where the presence of groundwater could be implied from the contract provision requiring the contractor to maintain a dewatering system).

[18] *J.E. Robertson Co. v. United States,* 437 F.2d 1360 (Ct. Cl. 1971).

permafrost in the tropics.[19] Instead, all that is generally required is that the unknown physical condition be one that was reasonably unanticipated, based upon an examination of the contract documents and the site.

The key to recovery for a Type II changed condition is the comparison of actual conditions with what was reasonably expected at the time of bidding. This inquiry into reasonable expectations will raise questions of the contractor's *actual and constructive* knowledge of working conditions in the particular area. For example, awareness of a condition at the site that is common knowledge to other contractors working in the area, and thus reasonably ascertainable by inquiry, may be attributed to the contractor. Moreover, a contractor's failure to visit the work site, particularly when alerted to potential problems by the plans and specifications, and the resulting failure to discover obvious physical conditions, may indicate that the bidder's judgment was simply a "guess . . . premised in error," which forms no basis for recovery as a Type II changed condition.[20]

The following are examples of Type II changed conditions:

(1) *Subsurface Water:* A water table found to be much higher than reasonably could have been anticipated has been held to be a changed condition, where dry and stable subsurface conditions were reasonably anticipated (but not indicated).[21]

(2) *Buried Timber/Rubble:* In leveling land, which had been cleared, a contractor was held to have had no notice of buried timbers, although the contract required the disposal of surface stumps, roots, and other trash encountered. The buried trees thus constituted a Type II changed condition.[22] Similarly, submerged piling in a dredge-filled land area warranted changed conditions relief.[23] Another case that reached the opposite result held that the presence of buried stumps should have been anticipated because the site was in a fill area that contained some protruding stumps, new sprouts, and new branches—indicating growth from buried stumps.[24]

(3) *Undersized Floor Joists:* A contractor entered into an agreement with the federal government to renovate certain family housing units. Rather than encountering 2-by-8 floor joists as would normally be encountered, the contractor found that over 80 percent of the joists were much closer to 7 inches in height. This required substantial shimming and other modifications, which resulted in extra costs. The contractor did not have a Type I differing site condition claim, as the contract plans did not give an exact representation as to the size of the floor joists. However, since the actual dimensions of the joists differed significantly from the conditions an experienced contractor would reasonably expect to encounter on a project of this type, the undersized joists did constitute a compensable Type II differing site condition.[25]

---

[19] *See Ruff v. United States*, 96 Ct. Cl. 148 (1942); *Western Well Drilling Co. v. United States*, 96 F. Supp. 377 (D. Cal. 1951).

[20] *See L.B. Samford, Inc.*, GSBCA No. 1233, 1964 BCA ¶ 4309.

[21] *Loftis v. United States*, 110 Ct. Cl. 551 (1948).

[22] *Morgan Constr. Co.*, IBCA No. 299, 1963 BCA ¶ 3855.

[23] *Caribbean Constr. Corp.*, IBCA No. 90, 57-1 BCA ¶ 1315.

[24] *Gilloz Constr. Co.*, W.D. BCA ¶ 826 (1944).

[25] *Kos Kam, Inc.*, ASBCA No. 24684, 88-1 BCA ¶ 20,246.

(4) *Oversized Walls:* In performing a contract to renovate an existing hospital, the contractor encountered a four-course-thick brick and masonry wall on the interior of the hospital. Such a massive wall was unusual for an interior partition; therefore, the contractor recovered the extra costs associated with the removal of the wall as a Type II differing site condition.[26]

(5) *Utilities:* When a contractor discovered that a third party had performed previous wiring in such a way that the phasing and wiring required by its contract could not be accomplished without extra work, this unknown condition warranted payment.[27] An undisclosed sewage line encountered in attempting to dig a manhole has been judged a changed condition.[28] Similarly, a differing site condition was found to exist when a contractor installing conduit pipe under an airfield perimeter road encountered a sewer line that was not indicated on the contract documents and was not a condition that would generally be expected.[29] However, in a different case where a contractor encountered sewers, gas lines, water lines, and coaxial cables that were not shown on the plans, a changed conditions claim was denied because the site was in a heavily built-up area and manholes were shown on the plans.[30]

(6) *Peculiar Structural Conditions:* A dock-painting contractor was entitled to an equitable adjustment for extra work due to unusual conditions that reasonably could not have been anticipated at the time of contracting. The additional work was caused by peculiar structural features of the dock to be painted that, in combination with the air pressure from incoming tides, caused a continuous water seepage or mist over the dock. Neither the contract documents, nor the contractor's prebid site inspection, nor the contractor's experience as a painting contractor was sufficient to provide notice of this unusual condition.[31]

(7) *Thick Paint:* Where an existing paint layer was much thicker than anticipated, a Type II changed condition was found.[32]

(8) *"Double-Poured" Roof:* Where an existing roof system was found to be "double-poured," and therefore much thicker and expensive to replace, a court found that a Type II changed condition may be found.[33]

(9) *Toxic Substances:* Where a contractor encountered creosote and other tarlike substances in an environment in which they were not anticipated, a Type II changed condition was found.[34]

(10) *Miscellaneous Items:* Where the contractor encountered beer cans, live ammunition, and ladies' underwear in cleaning a duct system in a military barracks, the contractor was granted relief for a Type II changed condition.[35]

[26] *Hercules Constr. Co.*, VABCA No. 2508, 88-2 BCA ¶ 20,527.

[27] *Dodson Elec. Co.*, ASBCA No. 5280, 59-2 BCA ¶ 2342.

[28] *Neale Constr. Co.*, ASBCA No. 2753, 58-1 BCA ¶ 1710.

[29] *Unitec, Inc.*, ASBCA No. 22025, 79-2 BCA ¶ 13,923.

[30] *H. Walter Schweigert*, ASBCA No. 4059, 57-2 BCA ¶ 1433.

[31] *Warren Painting Co.*, ASBCA No. 18456, 74-2 BCA ¶ 10,834.

[32] *R.J. Wilder Contracting Co. v. Ohio Turnpike Comm.*, 913 F. Supp. 1031 (N.D. Ohio 1996).

[33] *Lathan Co., Inc. v. U.S.*, 20 Cl. Ct. 122 (1990).

[34] *Reliance Ins. Co. v. County of Monroe*, 604 N.Y.S.2d 439 (N.Y.S. 4 1993).

[35] *Community Power Suction Furnace Cleaning Co.*, ASBCA No. 13803, 69-2 BCA ¶ 7963.

A Type II differing site condition may result not only from a variance in the type or quantity of a material encountered, but also from the unusual performance of an expected material. Thus, even though clay was expected to be encountered, when, as a result of percolating water, the clay behaved in an unusual, erratic fashion, with an unexpected tendency to slide, there was a changed condition.[36] In the same vein, the unexpected shrinkage of soil, which materially increased the number of cubic yards of earth in a dam, was an unexpected property of the soil that constituted a changed condition.[37] Similarly, a contractor was allowed to recover for the additional cost of handling a subsurface water condition, although subsurface water was to be expected, when the place where it was encountered and the rate of its flow were unusual and unforeseeable.[38]

10.13   STUMBLING BLOCKS TO RECOVERY

While many owners will agree on the insertion of a differing site conditions clause in their contracts, they often seek to include other clauses that attempt to minimize or reduce claims under them. These include clauses relating to site inspection, notice, and various other clauses that seek to limit the ability of contractors to rely on information provided to them during the bidding process. Whether or not these additional contract clauses will bar or foreclose recovery under a differing site conditions clause usually depends on a variety of other factors.

10.14   Site Investigations

Bid invitations commonly require contractors to visit the site prior to submitting their bids. Construction contracts routinely require the contractor to warrant that it has made a site inspection. One example of this type of clause reads as follows:

> The Contractor shall be fully aware of all conditions that might affect successful completion of the work. Before submitting his proposal he shall examine the site and compare the actual conditions on site with those shown or represented by the plans and specifications, and shall determine the existence of all physical features, obstructions above or below the ground, ground elevations, etc., on or adjacent to the site, that might affect the work. No allowance will be made for the Contractor's failure to adequately familiarize himself with all conditions and no claim will be permitted for relief due to unforeseen conditions.

Such a requirement does not automatically nullify the effect of a differing site conditions clause if one is present, and does not necessarily obligate the contractor to discover hidden conditions at its peril.[39] A contractual requirement that the

---

[36] *Paccon, Inc.*, ASBCA No. 7643, 1962 BCA ¶ 3546.

[37] *Guy F. Atkinson*, IBCA No. 385, 65-1 BCA ¶ 4642.

[38] *Norair Eng'g Corp.*, ENG BCA No. 3568, 77-1 BCA ¶ 12,225.

[39] *Farnsworth & Chambers Co. v. United States*, 171 Ct. Cl. 30 (1965).

contractor make a site investigation does not obligate bidders to discover hidden subsurface conditions that would not be revealed by a reasonable preaward inspection.[40] The adequacy of the site investigation is measured by what a reasonable, intelligent contractor, experienced in the particular field of work involved, could be expected to discover—not what a highly trained expert might have found.[41]

The term "site investigation" is generally interpreted to mean, essentially, "sight investigation," and to not extend to making independent subsurface investigations.[42] However, this is not always the case. The contractor will be responsible for being aware of all information reasonably made available to it, as well as all information that could be gained by a "reasonable" site inspection under the circumstances. For example, in *Cook v. Oklahoma Board of Public Affairs*,[43] the Oklahoma Supreme Court overturned a contractor's recovery on a differing site conditions claim where the contractor had neglected to attend *prebid conferences* where site conditions were discussed and only made a cursory drive-through of the site.

Likewise, the Armed Services Board of Contract Appeals held in *Tri-Ad Constructors*[44] that a contractor was not entitled to an equitable adjustment for installing more electrical cable than anticipated because the contractor failed to conduct a prebid site inspection as required by the contract. From its reading of an electrical wiring diagram, the contractor believed that seven electrical substations were located immediately above the main bank of underground ducts running between two switching stations. Had the contractor made an inspection of the site, it immediately would have seen that the electrical substations, each the size of an automobile, were offset some 300 feet from the main line, requiring loops between this duct bank and each substation. The contractor was charged with the knowledge obtainable from a reasonable site inspection, as the ASBCA concluded that even the most cursory inspection would have revealed the need for additional cable between each substation and the main ductline.[45]

In addition to requiring that a contractor conduct a reasonable site investigation, some bid solicitations also require a contractor to review documents concerning the site conditions that are made available for inspection prior to bidding but are not provided to the contractor in the bid package. If the contractor fails to review the available documents before submitting its bid, it may later be precluded from recovering for conditions that are different than expected, but that could have been determined

---

[40] *Warren Painting Co., Inc.*, ASBCA No. 18456, 74-2 BCA ¶ 10,834; *Maintenance Eng'rs*, ASBCA No. 17474, 74-2 BCA ¶ 10,760; *John G. Vann v. United States*, 190 Ct. Cl. 546, 573 (1970). *See also Warren Bros. Co. v. NYS Thruway Auth.*, 309 N.Y.S.2d (1970), *aff'd*, 314 N.E.2d 878 (1974); *L.J. McNulty, Inc. v. Village of Newport*, 187 N.W.2d 616 (1971).

[41] *Stock & Grove, Inc. v. United States*, 493 F.2d 629 (Ct. Cl. 1974); *Commercial Mechanical Contractors, Inc.*, ASBCA No. 25695, 83-2 BCA ¶ 16,768.

[42] *See, e.g., Condon-Cunningham, Inc. v. Day*, 258 N.E.2d 264 (Ohio Misc. 1969).

[43] 736 P.2d 140 (Okla. 1987). *See also Mega Const. Co., Inc. v. United States*, 29 Fed. Cl. 396 (1993).

[44] ASBCA No. 34732, 89-1 BCA ¶ 21,250.

[45] *See also McCormick Constr. Co. v. United States*, 18 Cl. Ct. 259 (1989) (denying a contractor's differing site condition claim because a reasonable site investigation would have revealed the possible subsurface condition).

from a review of the documents made available.[46] For example, a contractor's differing site conditions claim was denied on the ground that the contractor had failed to review records of previous dredgings that contained information regarding the nature of the materials to be dredged and that were available to the contractor prior to bidding.[47]

10.15   Exculpatory Clauses

Contracts frequently contain broad exculpatory clauses that disclaim any liability for the accuracy of plans, specifications, borings, and other subsurface data. An example of such a clause reads as follows:

> Boring logs and results of other subsurface investigations and tests are available for inspection. Such subsurface information, whether included in the plans, specifications, or otherwise made available to the bidder, was obtained and is intended solely for the owner's design and estimating purposes. This information has been made available only for the convenience of all bidders. Each bidder is solely responsible for all assumptions, deductions, or conclusions which he may make from his examination of this information.

Many courts have held that these clauses do not have the sweeping effect the drafter of the clause may have desired. Courts normally will not allow such clauses to eliminate the relief provided to the contractor by the differing site conditions clause.[48] For example, in *Woodcrest Construction Co. v. United States*,[49] the United States Court of Claims allowed a contractor to recover under the changed conditions clause despite the extremely broad exculpatory provisions in the contract. The court stated:

> The effect of an actual representation is to make the statements of the Government binding upon it, despite exculpatory clauses which do not guarantee the accuracy of a description. . . . Here, although there is no (express) statement which can be made binding upon the Government, there was in effect a description of the site, upon which plaintiff had a right to rely, and by which it was misled. Nor does the exculpatory clause in the instant case absolve the Government, since broad exculpatory clauses . . . cannot be given their full literal reach, and, "do not relieve the defendant of liability for changed conditions as the broad language thereof would seem to indicate."[50] [G]eneral portions of the specifications should not lightly be read to override the Changed Conditions Clause. . . .[51]

---

[46] *Id. See also Stuyvesant Dredging Co. v. United States*, 834 F.2d 1576 (Fed. Cir. 1987); *G&P Constr. Co., Inc.*, ASBCA No. 49524, 98-2 BCA ¶ 29,457.

[47] *Stuyvesant Dredging Co.*, 834 F.2d at 1581.

[48] *See Roy Strom Excavating & Grading Co., Inc. v. Miller-Davis Co.*, 501 N.E.2d 717 (Ill. App. Ct. 1986), *opin. superseded* by 509 N.E.2d 105 (Ill. App. Ct. 1986); *Metropolitan Sewerage Comm'n v. R.W. Constr., Inc.*, 241 N.W.2d 371 (Wis. 1976); *contra Cruz Constr. Co. v. Lancaster Area Sewer Auth.*, 439 F. Supp. 1202 (E.D. Pa. 1977).

[49] 408 F.2d 406 (Ct. Cl. 1969).

[50] *Fehlhaber Corp. v. United States*, 151 F. Supp. 817, 825 (Ct. Cl.), *cert. denied*, 355 U.S. 877 (1957).

[51] *United Contractors v. United States*, 368 F.2d 585, 598 (Ct. Cl. 1966).

Even when a contract lacks a differing site conditions clause *and* contains extensive exculpatory language, it may still be possible for the contractor to recover *if* it can show, for example, that an independent subsurface investigation was not feasible, and that it was thus forced to rely on information provided by the owner.[52] For example, in *Raymond International, Inc. v. Baltimore County, Maryland*,[53] the county solicited bids for repairs to the piers of a bridge. Even though the contract documents required the contractor to verify all dimensions in the contract documents, the court held that to require the contractor to make tests to verify the information supplied by the county placed an undue burden on the contractor. The court allowed the contractor to recover the increased costs incurred due to misrepresented conditions in the contract documents.

However, in some states, courts have taken a more literal approach in upholding such disclaimers. In Virginia, for example, one court held that a disclaimer concerning subsurface conditions was to be strictly enforced.[54] Other jurisdictions have come to similar conclusions.[55]

10.16   Notice Requirements

The purpose of the notice requirement for changed conditions is to alert the owner to the existence of the condition and provide the owner an opportunity to evaluate its potential impact on the project. Such an evaluation may cause the owner to make changes in the design or alter the contractor's method of performance.

While it is always advisable for a contractor to comply fully with the notice provisions of the contract, the lack of strict compliance may be excused by the courts. The underlying purposes of the contract requirements may be satisfied by *substantial compliance* with the terms of the notice requirement, or by *actual knowledge* of the condition by the owner or its agent, or if the owner has suffered *no prejudice* from the contractor's failure to give written notice.[56]

Examples of cases where contractors were allowed to recover for a differing site condition despite the lack of strict compliance with the notice requirements include the following:

(1) In *Brinderson Corp. v. Hampton Road Sanitation District*,[57] the contractor encountered extremely wet subsurface conditions that it contended differed from the soil conditions presented in the contract documents. However, the contractor failed to give written notice in accordance with the contract until after the wet soils had been disturbed and at least partially removed. An owner's representative was

---

[52] *See e.g., Robert E. McKee v. City of Atlanta*, 414 F. Supp. 957 (N.D. Ga. 1976).

[53] 412 A.2d 1296 (Md. Ct. Spec. App. 1980).

[54] *McDevitt & St. Co. v. Marriott Corp.*, 713 F. Supp. 906 (E.D. Va. 1989).

[55] *Stabler Constr., Inc. v. Comm., Dept. of Transp.*, 692 A.2d 1150 (Pa. Cmwlth 1997); *Brown Bros. v. Metrop. Gov. of Nashville and Davidson Co.*, 877 S.W.2d 745 (Tenn. Ct. App. 1993).

[56] *Shumate Constructors*, VABCA 2772, 90-3 BCA ¶ 22,946.

[57] 825 F.2d 41 (4th Cir. 1987).

present on-site at the time the unusual conditions were first encountered and inspected the conditions. The court stated that the owner had *actual knowledge* of the conditions and, therefore, the purpose of the notice requirement was satisfied. The court held that the contractor should be allowed to proceed to the merits of its differing site conditions claim, despite the lack of timely written notice.

(2) In *Pat Wagner*,[58] the contract called for the installation of water meters and additional service lines to an existing water system. After the contractor began work, it realized that the existing lines were copper rather than galvanized steel, as indicated by the contract documents. The contractor was forced to tie into the existing system with more expensive copper pipe. Although the contractor failed to provide written notice, the federal government's inspectors were fully aware of the discovery of copper pipe in the existing system. Therefore, the federal government was *not prejudiced* by lack of written notice, and recovery was allowed.

(3) In *Leiden Corp.*,[59] the board allowed recovery under the differing site conditions clause where the contracting officer had constructive notice of the conditions at the site because *actual knowledge* of the changed conditions was imputed to the contracting officer's construction representative on-site and thereby to the contracting officer.

10.17   Record-Keeping Requirements: Proving Damages

Even when a differing site conditions clause is present in the contract, the contractor still must prove how much the unanticipated condition cost in order to be compensated. The importance of good record keeping and the level of detail that may be required by a court are illustrated by the decision in *Ray D. Lowder, Inc. v. North Carolina State Highway Commission*.[60]

In *Lowder*, the contractor's first job superintendent had kept daily reports showing the progress of the work, the number of men, and the equipment on the job. The second superintendent did not show this information on his daily reports. When the contractor was preparing a differing site conditions claim, it rehired the first superintendent to go over the daily reports and prepare a cost summary.

The court held that this cost summary was inadmissible, and would not let the contractor use it to prove damages. Further, the court held that the daily reports themselves were incomplete and unreliable because even the ones that the first superintendent had filled out did not show how many hours each machine was in operation, whether any machines were broken down for part of the day, or even if any had been used that day at all.

The *Lowder* case emphatically demonstrates the need for (1) complete, (2) detailed, and (3) accurate cost records. It is almost certain that, because of the differing site conditions it encountered, the contractor in *Lowder* spent a great deal more money than it was able to prove with reasonable certainty under the criteria set down by that

---

[58] IBCA No. 1612-A-82, 85-2 BCA ¶ 18,103.

[59] ASBCA No. 26136, 83-2 BCA ¶ 16,612.

[60] 217 S.E.2d 682 (N.C. Ct. App. 1975).

particular court. A complete and detailed record-keeping system would have provided the very proof that the court found lacking. Remember that the law does not grant recovery for "possible" losses; it requires "reasonable certainty" as to amount.

10.18   RELIEF IN THE ABSENCE OF A CONTRACT PROVISION

The lack of a differing site conditions clause does not necessarily preclude recovery by the contractor. Instead, a contractor may base a claim on legal theories such as misrepresentation, breach of warranty, or mutual mistake. These theories are sometimes used even when the contract contains a differing site conditions clause. For example, if the clause has been rendered inoperative by the contractor's failure to give notice or to adhere to the clause's express requirements, these legal theories may provide an alternative avenue for recovery.

10.19   Misrepresentation

Misrepresentation or fraud (i.e., intentional misrepresentation) on the part of the owner may afford a contractor a basis for recovering the extra costs incurred because the actual conditions encountered were not as they were represented. A contractor may also be able to recover, even when the owner has made no affirmative misrepresentation, on the basis that the owner has breached its duty to disclose available information: (1) if the owner makes an accurate representation but does not disclose facts that materially qualify the facts disclosed; (2) if the facts are known or accessible only to the owner, and the owner knows they are not known to or reasonably discoverable by the contractor; or (3) if the owner actively conceals information from the contractor.[61]

Some courts have shown a willingness to allow the standard site investigation and disclaimer clauses to undercut a contractor's action for misrepresentation. Other courts are not nearly as harsh, and allow the contractor to utilize the owner's misrepresentations as a basis of liability in spite of site investigation and disclaimer clauses.[62]

In construction, misrepresentations relating to the amount or character of the work to be performed under the contract, or the cost of its performance, may give the contractor grounds to rescind the contract or to sue for damages under a fraud theory.[63] Usually, however, statements of this nature are ruled to be mere estimates or approximations that would not support a fraud action. Each of these cases is controlled by the specific facts and circumstances.

---

[61] *Warner Constr. Corp. v. City of Los Angeles*, 466 P.2d 996, 1001 (Cal. 1970). *See also Davis v. Commissioners of Sewerage*, 13 F. Supp. 672 (W.D. Ky. 1936); *L.I. Waldman & Co. v. State*, 41 N.Y.S.2d 704 (Ct. Cl. 1943).

[62] *See, e.g., Fattore Co. v. Metropolitan Sewerage Comm'n*, 454 F.2d 537 (7th Cir. 1971); *Metropolitan Sewerage Comm'n v. R.W. Constr., Inc.*, 241 N.W.2d 371 (Wis. 1976).

[63] *Busch v. Wilcok*, 46 N.W. 940 (Mich. 1890).

In *Robert E. McKee Inc. v. City of Atlanta*,[64] the United States District Court for the Northern District of Georgia discussed the application of the theory of misrepresentation to changed conditions situations. The city had supplied the contractor with inaccurate information concerning the quantity of rock excavation required by the project. The court noted that a mere showing by the contractor of subsoil conditions not expected by either party would not automatically release the contractor from its obligations under the contract (and therefore the financial risk of the extra rock excavation). The court also recognized that the contract placed the burden of uncertainty on the contractor. Nevertheless, the court held that the city could be held liable if the contractor could show (1) that it was not reasonably able to discover the true facts through investigation and (2) that the misrepresentation was material. Thus, the theory of misrepresentation may be available to a contractor even if it has "assumed" the risk of changed conditions in the contract.[65]

Misrepresentation may also be found notwithstanding generalized statements regarding subsurface data. In some cases, where the owner supplies specific information such as sieve analysis or liquid-limit information, yet also provides general statements about boring logs in conflict with such information, misrepresentation is still found.[66]

10.20   Duty to Disclose

A theory of recovery closely related to the theory of misrepresentation is a theory of recovery based upon the failure of an owner (most often a public owner) to satisfy the duty to disclose all available information.[67] For example, when the public owner had an engineering report in its possession that noted the presence of saturated soil conditions not otherwise known to exist or otherwise represented by the contract, the failure to make this information available to bidders supported recovery against the owner.[68]

In *Pinkerton & Laws Co. v. Roadway Express, Inc.*,[69] the court recognized the legal validity of a contractor's claim based upon the owner's failure to disclose information concerning soil moisture and compaction criteria that the court found important to a contractor's ability to prepare a responsive bid. Interestingly, the *Pinkerton* case involved a private owner, not a public owner or governmental authority, unlike most cases where an owner has been held liable under a duty to disclose theory.

10.21   Breach of Implied Warranty

A contractor's right to recover for differing site conditions is sometimes premised upon the owner's implied warranty of the adequacy of the plans and specifications.

---

[64] 414 F. Supp. 957 (N.D. Ga. 1976).

[65] *See also Raymond Int'l, Inc. v. Baltimore County, Maryland*, 412 A.2d 1296 (Md. Ct. Spec. App. 1980).

[66] *T. Brown Constructors, Inc. v. Pena*, 132 F.3d 724 (Fed. Cir. 1997).

[67] *Jacksonville Port Authority v. Parkhill-Goodloe Co., Inc.*, 362 So.2d 1009 (Fla. App. 1978); *Welch v. State*, 188 Cal. Rptr. 726 (Cal. App. 1983).

[68] *P. T. & L. Constr. Co. v. New Jersey Dep't of Transp.*, 531 A.2d 1330 (N.J. 1987). *See also Alpert v. Commonwealth*, 258 N.E.2d 755 (Mass. 1970).

[69] 650 F. Supp. 1138 (N.D. Ga. 1986).

This warranty stems directly from the 1918 United States Supreme Court decision in *United States v. Spearin*.[70] In essence, this decision holds that the contractor should be able to construct the project in accordance with the plans and specifications, and if so performed, the project should be acceptable. Thus, when the owner has furnished inadequate plans and specifications to the contractor, the owner has breached an implied duty.[71] This principle has become so widely associated with this case that the owner's implied warranty of the adequacy of the plans and specifications is sometimes referred to by courts as the Spearin Doctrine.[72]

10.22   Mutual Mistake

"Mutual mistake" is another legal doctrine under which a contractor may obtain relief from a changed condition. Under the mutual mistake theory, a contractor may be successful in having the contract rescinded and in having the actual cost paid on a *quantum meruit* (literally, "as much as he deserves"; in practice, the "reasonable value" of the materials and services furnished) basis if the contractor can show the existence of a factual condition of which *both* the contractor and owner were unaware and that goes to the "very essence" of the contract. In *Long v. Inhabitants of Athol*,[73] the amount of work to be done under a sewer contract was stated "approximately" by the owner, and the contractor's bid was based on this "approximation." When it became apparent that the construction of the project would require much greater quantities of work than estimated, the court found that a mutual material mistake existed, warranting a rescission of the contract.

➤ POINTS TO REMEMBER

The following key points should be noted:
- *Differing site conditions* or *changed conditions* are a common source of construction disputes.
- A differing site condition or changed condition may be *defined* as a physical condition encountered in performing the work that was not visible and known to exist at the time of bidding and that is materially different from the conditions believed to exist at the time of bidding.
- Under *traditional contract law*, the contractor *generally* assumes the risk of differing site conditions of which neither party is aware.
- *When the contractor assumes the risk* of differing site conditions, the contractor should, in theory, include a *contingency* in its bid to cover the risk.

[70] *Cent. Ohio Joint Voc. School Dist. Bd. of Edn. v. Peterson Constr. Co.*, 716 N.E.2d 1210 (Ohio App. 1998); *Western States Mechanical Contractors, Inc. v. Sandia Corp.*, 798 P.2d 1062 (N.M. App. 1990); *but see Willamette Crushing Co. v. State*, 932 P.2d 1350 (Ariz. App. Div. 1 1997).

[71] *Green Const. Co. v. Kansas Power & Light Co.*, 1 F.3d 1005 (10th Cir. 1993); *Ruby-Collins, Inc. v. City of Charlotte*, 740 F. Supp. 1159 (W.D.N.C. 1990); *Frank Briscoe Co., Inc. v. Clark County*, 857 P.2d 606 (9th Cir. 1988); *Midwest Dredging Co. v. McAninch Corp.*, 424 N.W.2d 216 (Iowa 1988).

[72] 248 U.S. 132 (1918).

[73] 82 N.E. 665 (Mass. 1907).

The inclusion of this contingency means that the contractor will receive a *windfall* if no differing site condition is encountered, but could suffer a *disaster* if the contingency is not sufficient to cover the cost of a significant differing site condition that is encountered.

- In recognition of this fact, the federal government and many public and private owners elect to use a *differing site conditions clause* in their construction contracts, which place the risk of differing site conditions on the owner.

- Some of the *standard differing site conditions clauses* encountered in the construction industry are quoted and discussed above. These include the differing site conditions clause contained in The Associated General Contractors of America contract, the standard federal government construction contract, the clause contained in the American Institute of Architects' Standard Form AIA 201 (1997 ed.), and the clause contained in the EJCDC Standard Form.

- Many differing site conditions clauses recognize two distinct types of differing site conditions: a *Type I changed condition*, which is a condition that is at variance with the conditions indicated in the contract documents; and a *Type II changed condition*, which is a condition unusual in nature that differs materially from the conditions ordinarily encountered in performing the type of work called for by the contract in the geographic area where the project is located.

- Most differing site conditions clauses contain *notice requirements*, requiring the contractor to stop work and provide the owner prompt notice upon encountering a differing site condition, before disturbing it, so that the owner will have an opportunity to inspect and evaluate the condition. Failure to give the required notice may jeopardize a contractor's ability to receive fair compensation for the additional costs incurred as a result of the differing site condition.

- A contractor that encounters a differing site condition should be careful to *follow the procedures* outlined in the contract's differing site conditions clause in order to ensure that proper compensation is received.

- *Good record keeping* is critical to a contractor's ability to recover the costs resulting from a differing site condition.

- To *recover for a Type I changed condition*, a contractor must generally show: (1) certain conditions are indicated by the contract documents; (2) the contractor relied on the physical conditions indicated in the contract documents; (3) the actual conditions encountered materially vary from those indicated; (4) proper notice was given; and (5) the change in condition resulted in additional performance costs and/or time, as demonstrated by appropriate documentation.

- To *recover for a Type II changed condition*, a contractor must generally show that: (1) conditions were encountered which were unusual and differed materially from those reasonably anticipated, given the nature of the work and the locale; (2) proper notice was given; and (3) the change resulted in additional performance costs and/or time, as demonstrated by appropriate documentation.

- *Examples* of some of the kinds of Type I and Type II changed conditions that have been recognized as a basis for additional compensation to a contractor by various courts and administrative boards are provided in this chapter.

- Some construction bid documents contain a *site investigation clause,* which requires the contractor to perform a thorough site investigation and examination of existing conditions prior to submitting its bid.

- Where a set of contract and bid documents contains both a site investigation clause and a differing site conditions clause, the contractor's ability to recover costs resulting from unanticipated conditions will depend upon whether the condition was one that a reasonable, intelligent contractor, experienced in the particular field of work involved, could be expected to discover based upon a *reasonable site investigation.*

- In interpreting site investigation clauses, the term "site" is often interpreted to mean, essentially, "sight," and to not extend to requiring an independent subsurface investigation; however, this is not always the case.

- While many public and private owners utilize differing site conditions clauses to assume the risk of differing site conditions, thereby eliminating the need for the contractor to include a contingency in its bid, other *exculpatory clauses* purport to place the risk of differing site conditions squarely on the contractor.

- An *example of an exculpatory clause* is a clause providing that even subsurface information provided by the owner to the contractor may not be relied upon by the contractor and will not provide a basis for a claim for additional compensation should the information prove incorrect.

- *Courts have held* that such explanatory clauses are generally enforceable but have very narrowly construed them and limited their effect. Some courts have even said that such clauses will not be enforced if it was not feasible for a bidder to perform an independent subsurface investigation.

- *Even in the absence of a differing site conditions clause*, a contractor *may* be able to recover additional costs resulting from a differing site condition if the contractor can establish the facts necessary to support the legal theories of misrepresentation, breach of warranty, or mutual mistake, or can establish superior knowledge and a duty to disclose on the part of the owner.

- A contractor should *never assume* that it either will or will not be compensated for differing site conditions clauses without a careful review of the contract, the specific conditions involved, and all surrounding circumstances.

11

SCHEDULES, DELAYS, AND ACCELERATION

Delays and suspensions, as well as work accelerations required to overcome delays and suspensions, are primary contributors to the cost overruns that affect many projects. Some delays are caused by occurrences beyond any party's (contractor, subcontractor, or owner) control. Many delays, however, result from the failure of one party or another to fulfill its contractual obligations. Any entity involved in the construction process must understand its rights and responsibilities in each type of delay situation.

This chapter discusses (1) the nature of delay claims, (2) the different types of delay, (3) the typical causes of delay, (4) the damages associated with delay, and (5) the claims process.

11.1 CONTRACT TIME

The legal rights and obligations of the parties associated with performance delays arise from either an express contract obligation to perform by a given date or within a specified time frame, or the implied obligation in every contract that each party will not delay, hinder, or interfere with the performance of the other party. A party that hinders or prevents performance by the other party, or that renders performance impossible, may not benefit from its wrong.[1] This rule of law prevents a party from taking advantage of its own contract breach. The same rule also provides a basis for the recovery of costs generated by delays that are the fault or responsibility of one of the contracting parties.

---

[1] *See United States v. Killough*, 848 F.2d 1523, 1531 (11th Cir. 1988) (discussing within the context of quantification of damages the principle that a wrongdoer shall not profit by his wrongdoing at the expense of its victim).

11.2 Time Is of the Essence Clause

Most contract documents provide that "time is of the essence." This clause makes time a material requirement of the contractor's performance obligation and ensures that the owner can recover delay damages for missed milestone or completion dates. In the absence of such a clause, or an expression by the contract as a whole that time is a material element of performance, delay damages may not be recoverable.[2]

A contractor is generally entitled to extra time for any excusable delay that occurs during the execution of the work. The contractor should be aware of clauses that purport to preclude recovery of monetary damages for delays, and limit, to time extensions, the contractor's remedy for delays. Such exculpatory contract clauses include "no-damages-for-delay" clauses.

11.3 Contract Commencement and Completion Dates

The first factors to be analyzed in assessing a delay claim are the contract commencement and completion dates. Construction contracts usually specify performance periods either by setting forth commencement and completion dates or by establishing that the work shall be completed within a specified number of days after the notice to proceed or commencement of work.

Many contracts also include interim milestone dates, specifying the dates upon which certain portions of the work are to be completed. The inability to meet milestone dates may provide the basis for claims that seek to recover actual or liquidated delay damages, termination of the contract, or an acceleration directive.

Where a contract specifies the date for the commencement of work, the owner may be deemed to have warranted the readiness of the work site as of the specified date. If the work site is not in a sufficient state of readiness to permit the contractor to begin work on that date, the owner may be liable for delay damages.[3] In an attempt to avoid liability for such delays, owners often include a statement in the contract that the specified commencement date is only a projection or an estimate. To avoid misunderstandings and disputes, all parties should take great care to clearly define contract commencement dates, interim completion milestones, and contract completion dates.

11.4 Substantial Completion and Final Completion

Most contract documents define "substantial completion" of the work as "the stage in the progress of the work when the work or a designated portion thereof is sufficiently complete . . . so the owner can occupy or utilize the work for its intended use."[4] Generally, an owner may not assess, and a contractor is not liable for, delay or

---

[2] *See, e.g., Oklahoma State Fair Exposition v. Lippert Bros., Inc.*, 243 F.2d 290 (10th Cir. 1957); *MaceRich Real Estate Co. VI v. Holland Properties Co.*, 454 F. Supp. 891 (D. Colo. 1978).

[3] *See, e.g., Howard Contracting, Inc. v. G.A. MacDonald Constr. Co. Inc.*, 83 Cal. Rptr. 2d 590 (Cal. Ct. App. 1998) (modified January 20, 1999).

[4] *See, e.g.*, Section 9.8 of AIA Document A201-1997.

liquidated damages after substantial completion.[5] In achieving substantial completion of the work, the contractor has substantially performed its contract obligation. Thus, even when a contractor has not fully completed the work specified by its contract, or has performed work in a defective manner, the owner may be prevented from collecting actual delay damages or liquidated damages if the contractor has advanced work sufficiently to have achieved substantial completion.

However, it is not unusual for some contracts to contain separate liquidated damage provisions related to the specified date for substantial completion and to the date for final completion. The latter provision might provide a separate specified amount of liquidated damages if final completion of all punchlist work is not accomplished within a stipulated number of days following the date of substantial completion.

11.5 USE OF SCHEDULES IN PROJECT MANAGEMENT

11.6 Types of Project Schedules

Scheduling techniques have made tremendous advances in the past 30 years, in large part due to the availability of personal computers. While bar (Gantt) charts are still used on some projects or as short-term schedules, it is common to find computer-generated critical path method (CPM) schedules used to plan and monitor construction activities. These practices allow the construction team to plan activities and determine those activities that are essential to the timely completion of the project.

The "critical path" in a schedule is the longest continuing duration of activities through a project that establishes the completion date for the project. If one of the critical activities is delayed, then the project completion date will be delayed unless the contractor is able to overcome the delay by resequencing or accelerating its work. The most effective schedules are those that are realistic, contain well-thought-out sequencing plans, have achievable resource requirements, and do not have an unmanageable number of activities in the schedule.

11.7 Use of Schedules to Establish Cause of Delay

The CPM schedules are not only useful in project planning, but they are also helpful in monitoring events that occur during the course of the project. Events that may impact the project's completion can be plugged into the schedule to determine if they will affect critical path activities in the project.

Due to the complexity of construction procedures, rarely are critical tasks—activities along the critical path—the only activities being performed at a given time. Rather, there are numerous activities being pursued on noncritical portions of the project. By definition, these noncritical activities include work activities for which

---

[5] *See William Klingensmith v. United States*, 731 F.2d 805 (Fed. Cir. 1984); *Vogt Bros. Mfg., Co. v. United States*, 160 Ct. Cl. (1963); *Fred Howland, Inc. v. Gore*, 13 So.2d 303 (Fla. 1943).

the contractor's schedule allows for more time for performance than is required. It is this additional time, above and beyond the planned activity performance duration, which is called "float." A one-, two-, or three-day delay in an activity for which there is allowed three days float time will not result in a delay to the construction project as a whole. Rather, the delay uses up the float time available for the performance of that activity. When all float time is gone, the critical path may change to include the previously noncritical activity. Any subsequent delay to that new critical activity will cause a delay to the project completion date.[6]

With this background, it should be easier to understand how courts can, through use of CPM techniques, segregate concurrent delays. If, for example, a government-caused delay occurs along the critical path, and contractor delay used up only float, the impact of the respective concurrent delays can be isolated and the contractor may be able to recover.

Schedules are not perfect. The agency or contractor that drafts the schedule may overestimate the amount of time required for a particular task, or it may deliberately build into a schedule extra time to allow greater flexibility to ensure avoidance of liquidated damages. Other factors that tend to enhance performance time are unusually good weather, a particularly efficient workforce, or especially productive subcontractors and prompt suppliers. Whatever the reason, contractors sometimes finish ahead of schedule. As a result, the contractor is in a position to save considerable sums of money in overhead and variable expenses when it finishes the project ahead of schedule.

Certainly, no contract or court would penalize the contractor for its superior efforts in finishing early—unless, of course, it violates some implied duty of cooperation with other subcontractors still on the job. Nevertheless, a "constructive penalty" could be imposed on the contractor that is in a position to finish early, but is prevented from doing so by the government or owner. If the delay does not extend performance beyond the originally scheduled completion date, the government or owner could argue that because the contractor finished "on time," either the contractor was not delayed or it suffered no damage as a result of the delay. Network Analysis (CPM) techniques make it possible to overcome the first argument, and there is case law that suggests that a contractor is damaged when it is precluded from finishing early.[7]

Several decisions involving recovery of compensation for owner-caused delays to early completion have occurred in the context of federal government construction projects. These cases have articulated several elements, which must be established

---

[6] See *Weaver-Bailey Contractors, Inc. v. United States*, 19 Ct. Cl. 474 (1990) (contractor concentrated manpower in areas which it thought needed earliest attention, leaving "unclassified excavation," a non-critical path activity, for later, properly using up float time; when the government's estimate as to the amount to be excavated was revealed to be 40 percent inaccurate, the resulting additional work caused a delay to the overall project because all float time had been used; contractor was entitled to an equitable adjustment for the delay).

[7] See *Grow Construction Co. v. State*, 391 N.Y.S.2d 726 (App. Div. 1977); *Metropolitan Paving Co. v. United States*, 325 F.2d 241 (Ct. Cl. 1963).

for a contractor to recover for delays that prevented early completion. In general, the contractor must show that:

it intended to complete the contract early;
it had the capability to do so; and
it actually would have completed early, but for the government's actions.[8]

In applying this test, the court or board looks for direct and concrete evidence of the contractor's actual intent to complete early and its actual anticipated work schedule prior to the delay. For example, in *Interstate General Government Contractors v. West*, the contractor had finished 13 days early despite a 136-day delay in the issuance of the notice to proceed. The contractor argued that the actual early completion date in and of itself proved that all along it had the intention and capability to finish at least six months ahead of schedule (the length of the delay) and would have done so, but for the delay.[9] The court disagreed, holding that there was no evidence of an intention to finish early. In fact, there was testimony that the contractor had accelerated the work after the delay by adding personnel not anticipated when the job was first estimated. In the court's view, the need for acceleration belied the contractor's argument that it intended and had planned early completion all along. Similarly, the contractor failed to present any work plan or schedule developed prior to the delay that would have feasibly resulted in early completion. Finally, the court held that the contractor's "post-facto, conclusory, self-serving assertion" that it would have completed earlier but for the delay was insufficient to satisfy the third prong of the test.[10] In applying the logic set forth in *Interstate*, it appears that only those contractors that can present documents or other direct evidence of an actual intent to finish early, which predate the occurrence of the delay, are likely to recover unabsorbed overhead regardless of any actual early completion. [11]

Delay may not only impact the critical path, but it may independently consume float time as well. Loss of this valuable float time may reduce the contractor's flexibility in sequencing work activities and allocating resources, and may end up costing money in terms of increased costs of performance of certain activities, even if there is no overall project delay. To the extent that the contractor uses its own float time, it cannot complain, but owner-caused delays may consume float and ultimately have an impact on the critical path. When all of the float time is thus used, any further contractor-caused delays are critical; that is, they impact directly on the critical

---

[8] *See Interstate General Government Contractors v. West*, 12 F.3d 1053 (Fed. Cir. 1993) (*citing Elrich Contracting, Inc.*, GSBCA No. 10,936, 93-1 BCA ¶ 25,316; *Frazier-Fleming Co.*, ASBCA No. 34537, 91-1 BCA ¶ 23,378.)

[9] *Id.* at 1059.

[10] *Id.* at 1060.

[11] *Cf. RobGlo, Inc.*, VABCA 2879, 91-1 BCA ¶ 23,357 (holding that the contractor finishing early despite the delay must prove that (1) the contractor intended to finish early, (2) the government was aware of the accelerated schedule and agreed to it or acquiesced in it, and (3) delays occurred during the time period in issue for which the government was solely responsible).

path and end up costing the contractor money. Thus, there can be a difference between owners and contractors as to who "owns" float.[12]

Two solutions to this issue have been suggested. One position is that the contractor owns float. In that context, the owner may use float without cost unless the contractor has need of it. To the extent the owner has used float time needed by the contractor, the owner must compensate the contractor. The other position is that the float belongs to the party that uses it first. Thus, once float is gone for one, it is gone for all. Some government agencies and private owners have begun to use clauses specifically dealing with ownership of float. The following clause was contained in a recent U.S. Postal Service facility specification.

> Float or slack is not time for the exclusive use or benefit of either the Government or the contractor. Extensions of time for performance will be granted only to the extent that equitable time adjustments for the activity or activities affected exceed the total float or slack along the channels involved.

Those types of clauses are becoming the rule rather than the exception, so contractors must be aware of the impact they can have on the project.

11.8 TYPES OF DELAYS

11.9 Excusable Delays versus Nonexcusable Delays

The occurrence of a construction delay raises the issue of which party should bear both the responsibility for, and the cost of, the delay. In deciding this question, courts, boards of contract appeals, and arbitration panels look both to the causes of the delay and to the express and implied obligations imposed by the parties' contract. Determining the legal consequences that flow from a given delay, and identifying the party that will bear the legal consequences of the delay, depends upon correctly identifying the type of delay that has occurred.

Construction delays fall into two major categories: excusable delays and nonexcusable delays. An *excusable delay* provides a basis under the contract for an extension of performance time. Excusable delays are also either *compensable*, permitting the recovery of both time and money, or *noncompensable*, permitting solely the recovery of time.

If the cause of delay stems from the conduct of the owner, then the contractor's delay will be excused.[13] Accordingly, the owner is precluded from claiming liquidated damages for its delays.[14] In addition, the contractor may recover delay damages due to owner-caused delays to the project.[15]

---

[12] One of the more comprehensive treatments of float ownership issues is the paper "Who Owns the Float?" Federal Publications, Inc., Construction Briefing No. 91-7 (May 1991) by John C. Person.

[13] *See Hill v. City of Duluth*, 57 Minn 231, 58 N.W. 992 (1894).

[14] *See Higgins v. City of Filmore*, 639 P2d 192 (Utah 1981).

[15] *Id.*

In contrast to an excusable delay, a *nonexcusable delay* provides no basis for recovery of either the time or the monetary impact of the delay. Moreover, the party responsible for that delay may be liable for resulting delay damages or may be subject to other breach of contract claims.

11.10 Excusable Delays

Generally, the parties' contract dictates whether a delay is excusable. Typical examples of excusable delays to a contractor's work are differing site conditions, design problems, changes to the work, inclement weather, strikes, and acts of God.

Most contracts specifically enumerate the types of excusable delays for which a time extension is due.[16] These terms vary from contract to contract. Because contracts differently allocate the risk of both nonperformance and unanticipated occurrences beyond the control of the parties, the precise terms of the contract are critical.

Some contracts exhaustively list each type of excusable delay and seek to limit the granting of time extensions to the listed delays. For example, Section 52.249-10 of the Federal Acquisition Regulation sets forth the standard default termination clause for all federal government fixed price contracts. Subparagraph (b) of that clause defines excusable delays as follows:

> (b) The Contractor's right to proceed shall not be terminated nor the Contractor charged with damages under this clause, if –
>
>   (1) The delay in completing the work arises from unforeseeable causes beyond the control and without the fault or negligence of the Contractor. Examples of such causes include—
>
>   (i)   Acts of God or of the public enemy,
>   (ii) Acts of the Government in either its sovereign or contractual capacity,
>   (iii) Acts of another Contractor in the performance of a contract with the Government,
>   (iv) Fires,
>   (v)   Floods,
>   (vi) Epidemics,
>   (vii) Quarantine restrictions,
>   (viii) Strikes,
>   (ix) Freight embargoes,
>   (x)   Unusually severe weather, or
>   (xi) Delays of subcontractors or suppliers at any tier arising from unforeseeable causes beyond the control and without the fault or negligence of both the Contractor and the subcontractors or suppliers; and
>
>   (2) The Contractor, within 10 days from the beginning of any delay (unless extended by the Contracting Officer), notifies the Contracting Officer in writing of the causes of delay. The Contracting Officer, shall ascertain the facts and the extent of delay. If, in the judgment of the Contracting Officer, the findings of fact warrant such action, the time for completing the work shall be extended. The findings of the Contracting officer shall be final and conclusive on the parties, but subject to appeal under the Disputes clause.[17]

---

[16] *See* Section 8.3 (Delays and Extensions of Time), AIA Document A201-1997; 48 C.F.R. § 52.249-14.
[17] 48 C.F.R. § 52.249-10.

Other contracts may contain somewhat less extensive lists, but may conclude the enumeration of excusable delays with a catchall phrase such as "causes beyond the control, and without the fault or negligence, of the contractor." Each party to a construction contract must have a clear understanding of the intended scope and operation of such a clause when requesting time extensions or analyzing time extension requests.

11.11   Compensable Excusable Delays

Compensable excusable delays are delays for which the innocent party is entitled to both a time extension and additional compensation for the resulting costs. For example, where an owner causes a delay, if the contract does not include a provision exonerating the owner from liability for such delays—which is discussed later in this chapter—the contractor may be entitled to both additional compensation and time.

Building contracts do not usually require the contractor to utilize all of the performance time allotted by the contract. Recognizing this, courts have held owners liable for delaying contractors where, even though the project was finished within the contractually allotted time, the contractor was prevented from achieving an early finish.[18] Thus, timely completion does not necessarily preclude the recovery of delay damages, where a reasonable as-planned schedule would otherwise have yielded early completion.

11.12   Nonexcusable Delays

Nonexcusable delays are those for which the contractor is responsible. The reasons for the delays vary and can include lack of adequate manpower, slow progress due to unqualified workers, poor planning, defective work, failure to forward submittals timely, and so on. In such cases, the contractor is not going to receive additional compensation or time to complete the work and may be liable for damages caused by the delay.

11.13   TYPICAL CAUSES OF DELAY

11.14   Compensable Delays

In most cases, faulty or negligent acts or omissions or other conduct by an owner in contravention of the contractor's rights will not only result in excusable delay, but may also entitle the contractor to recover its increased costs. Similarly, under certain circumstances the contractor may be able to recover damages for breach of contract. Some examples of acts or failures to act resulting in excusable delay are discussed below.

11.15   Defective Drawings or Specifications   Federal courts, as well as most states, have also adopted the Spearin Doctrine, under the terms of which an

---

[18] *See, e.g., Metropolitan Painting Co. v. United States*, 325 F.2d 241 (Ct. Cl. 1963).

owner is generally held to impliedly warrant the plans and specifications it provides to the contractor.[19] If such plans are erroneous or are insufficient to allow the contractor to perform the work in accordance with the intended design, and the defects within the plans and specifications cause delay to the work, the owner may be liable for time extensions and delay damages. But defects and omissions in the plans and specifications will not entitle the contractor to an extension of time if the defects and omissions are not related to the delay.[20]

11.16 Failure to Provide Access The owner is generally required to provide the contractor/subcontractor access to the work site in a timely and properly sequenced fashion.[21] However, in order to limit its exposure, the owner or general contractor may insert an exculpatory clause into the construction contract or request that the contractor waive its rights or expressly assume the risk of restricted access.[22] By inserting an exculpatory clause into the contract, such as a no-damages-for-delay clause, the owner may shift the risk of site-access delays, as well as the risk of many other types of owner-caused delays, to the contractor.

11.17 Improper Site Preparation Closely related to the owner's duty to provide the contractor with access to the work site is the owner's duty to prepare the work site properly.[23] In regard to this duty, an owner may require the contractor to inspect the work site prior to beginning work. Should the contractor fail to discover site preparation problems that a reasonable inspection would have revealed, or should it fail to raise any objections in a timely manner, the contractor may be precluded from recovering delay damages.[24]

11.18 Failure to Supply Materials or Labor Many construction contracts make the owner responsible for supplying certain materials or equipment to the contractor. Should the owner breach this duty by failing to provide the materials or equipment in a timely manner, the owner may be liable for delay damages.[25]

---

[19] *See United States v. Spearin*, 248 U.S. 132 (1918).

[20] *Blinderman Constr. Co., Inc.*, ASBCA 21966, 79-1 BCA ¶ 13,875.

[21] *See, e.g., Blinderman Constr. Co. v. United States*, 695 F.2d 552 (Fed. Cir. 1983).

[22] *A. Kaplen & Son, Ltd. v. Housing Auth.*, 126 A.2d 13 (N.J. Super. Ct. App. Div. 1956); *see also Burgess Constr. Co. v. M. Morrin & Son*, 526 F.2d 108 (10th Cir. 1975); *Broome Constr., Inc. v. United States*, 492 F.2d 829 (Ct. Cl. 1974); *Weber Constr. Co. v. State*, 323 N.Y.S.2d 492 (N.Y. App. Div. 1971), aff'd, 282 N.E.2d 331 (N.Y. 1972).

[23] *Jennings v. Reale Constr. Co.*, 392 A.2d 962 (Conn. 1978) (deciding a suit brought by a subcontractor against a contractor); *E.C. Nolan Co. v. State*, 227 N.W.2d 323 (Mich. Ct. App. 1975); *Columbia Asphalt Corp. v. State*, 420 N.Y.S.2d 36 (N.Y. App. Div. 1979); *Fehlhaber Corp. v. State*, 419 N.Y.S.2d 773 (N.Y. App. Div. 1979); *Commonwealth State Highway & Bridge Auth. v. General Asphalt Paving Co.*, 405 A.2d 1138 (Pa. Commw. Ct. 1979).

[24] *See Morrison-Knudson Co. v. United States*, 84 F. Supp. 282 (Ct. Cl. 1949); *Public Constructors, Inc. v. State*, 390 N.Y.S.2d 481 (N.Y. App. Div. 1977); *Camarco Contractors v. State*, 253 N.Y.S.2d 827 (N.Y. App. Div. 1964); *A.E. Ottaviano, Inc. v. State*, 110 N.Y.S.2d 99 (N.Y. Ct. Cl. 1952).

[25] *See, e.g., GYMCO Constr. Co. v. Architectural Glass & Windows, Inc.*, 884 F.2d 1362 (11th Cir. 1989).

11.19   Failure to Provide Plans/Approve Shop Drawings   The submittal of shop drawings, product technical data brochures, or "cut sheets" for owner review is an important part of the construction process. For contractors, the submittal and review process creates a potential source of delay because the contractor is unable to proceed with the work until the owner or its agent has approved the submittal.[26] With the exception of design-build projects, the owner is typically responsible for providing plans and specifications to the contractor. Should the owner fail to provide plans and specifications in a timely manner, or to timely approve a contractor's shop drawings, the owner may be liable for the resulting delays to the project.[27] Where, however, approval of plans is withheld because the contractor's submission is incomplete, no time extension may be due.[28]

11.20   Failure to Coordinate Prime Contractors   When an owner elects to execute a project with multiple prime contractors, many jurisdictions recognize a duty on the part of the owner to coordinate the work of the separate prime contractors.[29] Thus, the owner may be responsible to one prime contractor for delays caused by another. Even where the owner attempts to shift this duty to one of the prime contractors, the owner still may be liable for delays if that contractor is not also given the power to enforce its responsibilities.[30]

11.21   Failure to Give Timely Orders for Work   If the owner fails to issue the notice to proceed within the time frame set forth in the contract, or within a reasonable time if the contract does not specify a time, the owner will generally be liable for delay. This rule also applies to delays in authorizing extra work, delays in responding to requests for information, and any unreasonable failure to approve materials.[31]

It has been held that, where the contract is silent as to time of issuance of the Notice to Proceed (NTP), the NTP must be issued within a reasonable period of time after award of the contract. An unreasonable delay in issuing the NTP may amount to a breach of contract or a constructive suspension of work.[32]

In determining what is a reasonable period of time within which to issue the NTP, the boards and the United States Court of Federal Claims will consider the time

---

[26] *See* Bruce Jervis, ed., Delay in Shop Drawing Review, 25 *Construction Claims Monthly* 1 & 7 (July 2003).

[27] *See, e.g., Pathman Constr. Co.*, ASBCA No. 23392, 85-2 BCA ¶ 18,096; *see also Sydney Construction Co., Inc.*, ASBCA 21377, 77-2 BCA ¶ 12,719.

[28] *See, e.g., Construction Services, Inc.*, GSBCA 2423, 68-2 BCA ¶ 7154; *Department of Transportation v. Brayman Constr. Corp.-Bracken Constr. Co.*, 513 A.2d 562 (Pa. Cmwlth. 1986) (finding that 10 to 12 weeks was normal for a highway project and any time beyond that constitutes a compensable delay).

[29] *See, e.g., North Harris County Junior College Dist. v. Fleetwood Constr. Co.*, 604 S.W.2d 247 (Tex. Ct. App. 1988).

[30] *Shoffner Indus. v. W.B. Lloyd Constr. Co.*, 257 S.E.2d 50 (N.C. Ct. App.), *rev. denied*, 259 S.E.2d 301 (N.C. 1979).

[31] *See, e.g., Rome Hous. Auth. v. Allied Bldg. Materials, Inc.*, 355 S.E.2d 747 (Ga. Ct. App. 1987).

[32] *Freeman Electric Constr. Co.*, DOTCAB 74-23A, 77-1 BCA ¶ 12,258.

required to resolve any pending bid protest.[33] If the contractor wants the NTP to be issued expeditiously, it should make a specific request.[34]

11.22   Failure to Make Timely Payments to Contractors   Should the owner fail to make timely payment, the contractor may elect to terminate the contract as specified by the contract terms, or may elect to continue with the contract work and seek damages. The contractor can generally recover interest on the late payments, and in some jurisdictions, may also recover consequential damages suffered due to late payment.[35]

11.23   Failure to Inspect   Under the typical contract, an owner may have the right or duty to inspect the contractor's work as it progresses. The owner may be liable to the contractor for inspections that are unreasonably intensive or repetitious, or for failure to timely and promptly inspect.[36]

11.24   Suspensions   A suspension is a form of delay that results from the owner's purposeful interruption of the work. The term is primarily encountered in federal government contracts; the standard suspension of work (SOW)[37] clause provides, in part:

SUSPENSION OF WORK (APR 1984)

(a)   The Contracting Officer may order the Contractor in writing, to suspend, delay, or interrupt all or any part of the work of this contract for the period of time that the Contracting Officer determines appropriate for the convenience of the Government.

This type of clause provides the owner the right to halt construction temporarily, if, for example, the owner experiences funding problems. The clause also provides equitable compensation for the resulting additional costs and extended performance time. Recovery is also allowed in federal government contracts where no formal suspension order is issued, but the effect of the owner's action or inaction is to suspend the work.[38]

Some contract clauses recognize the concept of a constructive suspension of work. The "Suspension of Work" clause used in federal government contracting is an example of a contractual remedy for such delays or interruptions of the work. The clause becomes operative wherever there is an act or omission by the contracting officer resulting in delay to the contractor. It provides, in part, as follows:

---

[33] *DeMatteo Constr. Co. v. United States,* 600 F.2d 1384 (Ct. Cl. 1979).

[34] *See Freeman Electric Constr. Co., supra* note 32.

[35] *See, e.g., Anthony P. Miller, Inc. v. Willington Hous. Auth.,* 165 F. Supp. 275 (D. Del. 1958).

[36] Thomas E. Abernathy, IV, & Thomas J. Kelleher, Jr., *Inspection Under Fixed-Price Construction Contracts,* Briefing Papers, Federal Publications, Inc., Dec. 1976 at 6-8.

[37] 48 C.F.R. § 52.242-14.

[38] *See, e.g., Blinderman Constr. Co. v. United States,* 695 F.2d 552 (Fed. Cir. 1983).

* * * * *

(b) If the performance of all or any part of the work is, for an unreasonable period of time, suspended, delayed, or interrupted (1) by an act of the Contracting Officer in the administration of this contract, or (2) by the Contracting Officer's failure to act within the time specified in this contract (or within a reasonable time if not specified), an adjustment shall be made for any increase in the cost of performance of this contract (excluding profit), necessarily caused by the unreasonable suspension, delay, or interruption, and the contract modified in writing accordingly. However, no adjustment shall be made under this clause for any suspension, delay, or interruption to the extent that performance would have been so suspended, delayed, or interrupted by any other cause, including the fault or negligence of the Contractor, or for which an equitable adjustment is provided for or excluded under any other term or condition of this contract.[39]

Contractors performing on federal government contracts have been allowed to recover under either the express or constructive suspension provisions for costs generated by: (1) delays in making the site available; (2) delays in issuing change orders; and (3) delays caused by defective plans and specifications.

11.25 Excessive Change Orders   When the owner orders an excessive or unreasonable amount of changed or extra work, the contractor may be allowed to recover its resulting delay damages.[40] These damages are commonly referred to as "impact costs."

11.26 Failure to Accept Completed Work   Should the owner unreasonably refuse to make final acceptance of the contractor's work, the owner may be liable for the contractor's delay damages.

11.27 CONCURRENT DELAY

Concurrent delay, in addition to excusable delay and nonexcusable delay, is an analytical framework for identifying and evaluating construction delays. Concurrent delays are delays that occur, at least to some degree, during the same period of time and that impact the critical path of a planned sequence of events. The term "concurrent delay" is one of art that refers to the situation in which an excusable compensable delay and an unexcusable delay occur at the same time or during overlapping time periods. For example, a concurrent delay occurs when a contractor cannot commence work on the second phase of a project because the owner has failed to obtain a necessary right-of-way, and simultaneously, the contractor is prevented from commencing the second phase by its own failure to timely complete antecedent first-phase work.

---

[39] 48 C.F.R. § 52.242-14.

[40] *See Air-A-Plane Corp. v. United States*, 408 F.2d 1030 (Ct. Cl. 1969); *Coley Properties Corp.*, PSBCA No. 291, 75-2 BCA ¶ 11,514; *see generally* Reginald M. Jones, Lost Productivity: Claims for the Cumulative Impact of Multiple Change Orders, 31 Pub. Contr. L. J. 1 (Fall 2001).

Concurrent delay creates complex legal issues regarding assessing responsibility for overall project delay. The analysis of concurrent delays may be further complicated if: (1) the delay periods are different lengths; (2) the delay periods are not totally concurrent; or (3) the delay periods have different impacts on the number and types of work activities they affect, and the severity of the impact upon the affected work activities is different for each of the delays.

11.28   Traditional View: No Recovery by Either Party

Until recently, when project performance was concurrently delayed, neither party was allowed an affirmative recovery from the other. The courts took the view that when a party proximately contributed to the delay, the law would not provide for the apportionment of damages to each party.[41] In *J.A. Jones Construction Co. v. Greenbriar Shopping Ctr.*, the prime contractor caused delay through the failure of its subcontractors and materialmen to timely perform, and the owner caused delay by changes to the design and late issuance of drawings. The court held that neither party was entitled to any affirmative recovery, meaning the owner and contractor each bore its own costs even though one may have been responsible for more delay than the other.

11.29   Modern Trend: Apportionment of Delay Damages

In contrast to the analysis of concurrent delays found in *J.A. Jones Construction Co.*, the current trend in concurrent delay analysis is toward apportionment of the delay between the perpetrating parties. This shift is due in part to the use of the critical path method (CPM) techniques for evaluating delay claims. These techniques make it possible to more accurately segregate and quantify the impact of concurrent delays.

Logically, if the impact of one delay exceeds that of the other, the party responsible for the lesser impact should be allowed to recover damages for the excess impact. Apportionment analysis, at least on its face, would seem to allow for more equitable results than nonapportionment analysis. In apportioning delays, if the effects of concurrent delay cannot be accurately segregated and quantified, the court will likely revert to nonapportionment type review and no damages will be awarded.[42]

In *Essex Electro Engineers, Inc. v. Danzig*, the United States Court of Appeals for the Federal Circuit reversed an Armed Services Board of Contract Appeals (ASBCA) decision denying a contractor's claim for delay damages. The court of appeals determined that each party's delay was apportionable and, thus, should have been allocated to each responsible party.[43]

---

[41] *Malta Constr. Co. v. Henninston, Durham & Richardson, Inc.*, 694 F. Supp. 902 (N.D. Ga. 1988); *J.A. Jones Constr. Co. v. Greenbriar Shopping Ctr.*, 332 F. Supp. 1336 (N.D. Ga. 1971), *aff'd*, 461 F.2d 1269 (5th Cir. 1972).

[42] *See, e.g., SIPCO Services & Marine, Inc. v. United States*, 41 Fed. Cl. 196, 225-226 (1998); *Blinderman Constr. Co., Inc. v. United States*, 39 Fed. Cl. 529, 543-44 (1997).

[43] *Essex Electro Engineers, Inc. v. Danzig*, 224 F.3d 1283 (Fed. Cir. 2000).

The Federal Circuit noted that:

[T]he contractor generally cannot recover for concurrent delays for the simple reason that no causal link can be shown: a Government act that delays part of the contract performance does not delay "the general progress of the work" when the "prosecution of the work as a whole" would have been delayed regardless of the Government's act.[44]

Further, the court held that "in recent cases, the principle has been characterized as requiring the Government's act to have affected activities on the critical path."[45] Thus, the court held that "if 'there is in the proof a clear apportionment of the delay and the expense attributable to each party,' then the government will be liable for its delays."[46]

11.30 NONCOMPENSABLE EXCUSABLE DELAYS

11.31 Weather

Under most contracts, unusually severe weather conditions can give rise to an excusable, but not compensable, delay.[47] Unusually severe weather is weather that is unusual for the time of year and the place it occurred. This may be shown by comparing previous years' weather with the weather experienced by the contractor. The mere fact that the weather is harsh or destructive is not sufficient if the contractor reasonably should have anticipated that type of weather at the time and place it occurred. Some bad weather is always to be expected. If the contract period is 600 days, the contractor obviously does not have the right to expect 600 dry, sunny days with all of its subcontractors working at full force.

11.32 Acts of God

By definition, acts of God are beyond the control and without the fault or negligence of the contractor. The Comptroller General of the United States has defined an act of God as "some inevitable accident which cannot be prevented by human care, skill, or foresight, but results from natural causes such as lightning, tempest, floods and inundations."[48] Examples of acts of God are tornadoes, floods, earthquakes, and other natural disasters.

Unless the contract specifically provides otherwise, acts of natural forces entitle the contractor to an extension of contract performance time but not to a contract

---

[44] *Id.* (*citing Coath & Goss, Inc. v. U.S.*, 101 Ct. Cl. 701, 714-15 (1944)).

[45] *Id.* (*citing Mega Construction Company v. United States*, 29 Fed. Cl. 396, 424 (1993)).

[46] *Id.* (*citing Coath, supra* note 44 at 714; *see also United States v. Killough*, 848 F.2d 1523, 1531 (11th Cir. 1988)).

[47] *See Fru-Con Constr. Corp. v. United States*, 43 Fed. Cl. 306, 328 (1999) (citing *Turnkey Enters., Inc. v. United States*, 597 F2d 750, 754 (Ct. Cl. 1979)).

[48] Comp. Gen. Dec. B-169473 (April 24, 1970).

price adjustment. On this basis, a highway contractor was granted a time extension but denied a contract price increase for delays encountered when the government reasonably refused to alleviate flooding on the work site caused by heavy rains.[49]

11.33 Labor Problems

Similarly, delays resulting from most, but not all, strikes and labor disturbances generally constitute noncompensable excusable delays.[50] If a strike is in effect or anticipated at the time of contracting, it may be determined that because the labor problems were foreseeable, the contractor should have made a provision for them in the contract. Likewise, when a strike is provoked by an unfair labor practice on the part of the contractor, the delay might not be considered to be due to a "cause beyond the contractor's control."

With some exceptions, delays resulting from labor shortages, not caused by labor disputes, will not be excused. Similarly, a time extension generally will not be granted for delays caused by the performance or nonperformance of subcontractors or suppliers. Responsibility for the performance of subcontractors and suppliers is generally assumed by and attributed to the contractor.

11.34 ACCELERATION

When the owner requires its contractor to complete the work by a date earlier than the contract completion date, an "acceleration" occurs. For the purpose of determining whether the contractor's work has been accelerated, the contract completion date should reflect time extensions due the contractor for excusable delays to its work.

An acceleration of the contractor's work occurs under two different circumstances: (1) actual (or directed) acceleration or (2) constructive acceleration. *Actual acceleration* occurs when the owner consciously directs its contractor to complete the project earlier than the contract completion date. *Constructive acceleration* occurs when the owner fails to grant its contractor time extensions to which it is entitled, and the contractor is required to achieve, or strive for, a completion date that is earlier than the properly extended contract completion date. Thus, acceleration may be a by-product of delay or other factors that justify a time extension, which is not formally granted by the owner.

Acceleration damages usually include premium time pay in the form of overtime or shift work, the cost of added crews or increased crew sizes, the cost of additional tools and equipment required for added crews, the cost of additional supervision and job-site overhead, and the cost of labor inefficiency that may occur due to longer hours or increased crew sizes.

---

[49] *Security National Bank of Kansas City v. United States*, 397 F.2d 984 (Ct. Cl. 1968).
[50] *See McNamara Constr. of Manitoba, Ltd. v. United States*, 509 F.2d 1166 (Ct. Cl. 1975).

11.35 Directed Acceleration

In federal government contracts, the changes clause for fixed-priced contracts found at FAR § 52.234-4 specifically allows the contracting officer to direct an acceleration in the performance of the work:

CHANGES (AUG 1987)

The Contracting Officer may, at any time, without notice to the sureties, if any, by written order designated or indicated to be a change order, make changes in the work within the general scope of the contract, including changes:

(1) In the specifications (including drawings and designs);

(2) In the method or manner of performance of the work;

(3) In the Government-furnished facilities, equipment, materials, services or site; or

(4) Directing acceleration in the performance of the work.[51]

Thus, the government's order to a contractor to accelerate modification to an air-conditioning system in a medical facility, to speed completion of operating rooms, was a compensable change because the government was aware that excess costs for overtime would be incurred.[52]

11.36 Constructive Acceleration

In the seminal case *Fermont Division, Dynamic Corporation of America*,[53] the five basic elements of a constructive acceleration claim based upon a government failure to grant a time extension for excusable delay were summarized as follows:

(1) Existence of a given period of excusable delay; and

(2) Contractor notice to the government of the excusable delay, and request for extension of time together with supporting information sufficient to allow the Government to make a reasonable determination;

   Exceptions:

   (a) such notice, request, and information are not necessary if the government's order directs compliance with a given schedule expressly without regard to the existence of any excusable delay,

   (b) the supporting information is unnecessary if it is already reasonably available to the government; and

(3) Failure or refusal to grant the requested extension within a reasonable time; and

(4) A government order, either express or implied from the circumstances, to (a) take steps to overcome the excusable delay, or (b) complete the work at the

---

[51] 48 C.F.R. § 52.243-4.

[52] *E.C. Morris and Son, Inc.*, ASBCA No 20697, 77-2 BCA ¶ 12,622; *see also Gibbs Shipyard, Inc.*, ASBCA No. 9809, 67-2 BCA ¶ 6499.

[53] *Fermont Division, Dynamic Corporation of America*, ASBCA No. 15006, 75-1 BCA ¶ 11,138.

earliest possible date, or (c) complete the work by a given date earlier than that to which the contractor is entitled by reason of the excusable delay. Circumstances from which such an order may be implied include expressions of urgency by the government especially when coupled with (i) a threat of default or liquidated damages for not meeting a given accelerated schedule, or (ii) actual assessment of liquidated damages for not meeting a given accelerated schedule; and

(5) Reasonable efforts by the contractor to accelerate the work, resulting in added costs, even if the efforts are not actually successful.[54]

If these elements are proven, the contractor is entitled to recover the costs incurred in accelerating its performance.[55]

11.37 DELAY DAMAGES

Having once established the legal basis of liability, a contractor, or alternatively, an owner, must establish with reasonable certainty the amount of damages it has incurred. Quantifying damages (i.e., establishing quantum) can be an arduous task and frequently is the stumbling block that stands between the claimant and adequate recovery.

11.38 Contractor Damages

Whenever a delay on a construction project occurs, inevitably costs increase. This is true of direct labor and material costs on the project, as well as indirect costs such as home office overhead. A contractor's damages for delay may include the following elements:

Inefficient or idle labor,

Inefficient or idle equipment,

Acceleration and overtime,

Extended field office overhead,

Unabsorbed or underabsorbed home office overhead,

Escalated material and labor costs,

Legal fees,

Interest,

Loss of profits, and

Loss of bonding capacity.

---

[54] *Id.* at 52,999.

[55] *See Department of Transportation v. Anjo Constr. Co.,* 666 A.2d 753 (Pa. Cmwlth. 1995); *Norair Eng'g. Corp. v. United States,* 229 Ct. Cl. 160, 666 F.2d 546 (Ct. Cl. 1981).

11.39 Overhead

Overhead "refers to indirect costs that a contractor must expend for the benefit of the business as a whole, as opposed to direct costs which are costs specifically identified with a final cost object such as a contract."[56] There are two specific types of overhead costs that are allocated to every project that a construction or government contractor performs.

Home office overhead costs, which include such expenditures as administrative staff salaries, accounting and payroll services, general insurance, office supplies, telephone charges, depreciation, taxes, and utility costs. These costs are "expended for the benefit of the whole business, which by their nature cannot be attributed to any particular contract."[57]

Field office overhead, which is also commonly referred to as extended general conditions, represents the other type of overhead.[58] Extended field office overhead consists of "[c]osts incurred at the job site incident to performing the work, such as the cost of superintendence, timekeeping and clerical work, engineering, utility costs, supplies, material handling, restoration and cleanup, etc."[59]

Contractors typically recognize that recovery of these overhead costs is essential to overall company viability. Similarly, field overhead costs spent for job-site expenses are included in each contract as a part of the contractor's bid. In fact, as Section 31.105(d)(3) of the Federal Acquisition Regulation provides, these are "allowable as direct or indirect costs, provided the accounting practice used is in accordance with the contractor's established and consistently followed cost accounting practices for all work."[60]

Owners expect that both field office overhead and home office overhead will be included in the contractor's bid. When delays or changes occur on a project and these costs are increased, these overhead costs are typically included in the request for compensation for the delay or the pricing of the change order.

The various boards of contract appeals, the government, and most courts recognize that a contractor is entitled to recover field overhead costs on changes that extend the time of contract performance. These changes include both change orders that add to the scope of the contractor's work, as well as changes or events that impact contract performance and that cause a compensable delay on the project. Such costs are attributable to the increase in costs for continuing to run and staff a project for a time period not contemplated at the time of contracting.[61] As with any other type of delay or disruption damage, these costs are recoverable "in order to

---

[56] *See MCI Constructors, Inc.,* DCCAB No. D-924 (June 4, 1996).

[57] *Id.*

[58] *See generally Clark Concrete Contractors, Inc.,* GSBCA No. 14340, 99-1 BCA ¶ 30,280, at pp. 49,755-756.

[59] 48 C.F.R. § 31.105(d)(3).

[60] *Id.*

[61] *M. A. Mortenson,* ASBCA Nos. 40,750, 40,751, & 40,752, 98-1 BCA ¶ 29,658, *affi'g on recon. on different grounds,* 97-1 BCA ¶ 28,623.

make the contractor whole."[62] There is little dispute that such costs may be recovered in such situations, generally on a *per diem* basis.[63]

A contractor may allocate these costs as direct costs or indirect costs, depending upon the contractor's generally used accounting method. For example, if project supervision and administration are stated as direct costs, then "an equitable adjustment for extended field supervision and administration is calculated as a direct cost item."[64] If field overhead is charged to a general expense pool as an indirect cost, it should not be commingled in a direct cost calculation and should be claimed as a separate item in a claim or change order.[65] One recognized means of calculating direct costs for extended field overhead is "to compute a daily rate by dividing total labor supervision and administration costs on the project by the total days of contract performance and then multiplying the result by the number of days of compensable delay."[66] This same accounting method may also be used during the project by dividing expected field overhead costs by expected total days of contract performance to obtain the per-day rate, then multiplying that number by the number of days performance is extended.

As with other claims, it is necessary that a contractor show first that it is entitled to damages for delay. Once this is done, the contractor can recover costs for field overhead, even those not included in the original bid. A relatively recent illustrative case on this comes from the District of Columbia Contract Appeals Board in *MCI Constructors.*[67] In *MCI*, a default termination was converted to a termination for convenience by a prior decision of the board. The board determined MCI's proper amount of resulting compensation, including a claim for extended field overhead costs. The District of Columbia argued that MCI significantly underbid its supervisory costs, failing to include bid items for project engineering, clerical work, main office engineering, and main office expediting—items MCI had intended for the project manager and superintendent to handle at the outset of the project.

In awarding costs for all these items as field overhead, the board stated that it could find "no reason to deny MCI a pro rata share of such costs actually incurred during a compensable delay period . . . [e]ven though MCI commenced charging directly to the job some supervision and administrative costs it had not bid."[68] Such a decision was reached despite the alleged underbidding, because the board was not giving "MCI any undue recovery[,] because this computation applies only the delay period and covers labor supervision and administration that MCI would not have incurred but for the District's constructive changes."[69] Due to the inability to identify what portion of the amount the equation provided had already been recovered

[62] *See MCI Contractors, supra* note 56.

[63] *See M.A. Mortenson, supra* note 61.

[64] *See MCI Contractors, supra* note 56.

[65] *Id.*

[66] *Id.*

[67] *Id.*

[68] *Id.*

[69] *Id.*

through change orders signed during the project and what portion had been allocated to a claim item for pending change orders, the board then awarded an amount based in part upon a jury verdict finding.[70]

The lesson of *MCI Contractors* is apparent: even if a contractor incurs field overhead costs that were not bid originally, it is important to segregate all these costs and apply them to change orders and delay claims. To add additional specificity to the claim, further record keeping should identify the costs allocated to each change order item.

Contractors typically rely on project revenue to support their home office operations, and accordingly, contractors include a markup in their bids for new work. Allocated over the project's planned duration, this markup provides monthly revenue that is used to pay or "absorb" rent, administrative staff salaries, accounting and payroll services, general insurance, office supplies, telephone charges, depreciation, taxes, and utility costs. If the project time is extended without increasing the amount of the markup, the dollars available to absorb monthly overhead are reduced.

Several recent U.S. Court of Appeals for the Federal Circuit decisions appear to make it more difficult for a government contractor to recover unabsorbed home office overhead using the *Eichleay* formula for government caused delays.[71] This section examines those cases, reflects on the evolution of the formula, and summarizes the current state of the law.

11.40 The Original *Eichleay* Decision

The Eichleay formula originated with *Eichleay* Corp., an Armed Services Board of Contract Appeals (ASBCA) case, in which the ASBCA specifically approved the contractor's three-step formula for determining the amount of recoverable home office overhead.[72] Since the original decision, this formula has become the mandatory method for calculating claims for unabsorbed home office overhead on federal government construction contracts.[73]

First, the overhead allocable to the contract was determined by multiplying the total overhead by a ratio of the contract's billings to the total billings of the contractor for the contract period. Second, a daily overhead rate for the contract was computed by dividing the overhead allocable to the contract by the number of days of contract performance. Third, the total overhead recoverable was determined by multiplying the daily overhead rate for the contract by the number of days of delay. This formula may be schematically summarized as follows:

[70] *Id.*

[71] *See P.J. Dick, Inc. v. Principi*, 324 F.3d 1364 (Fed. Cir. 2003); *Nicon, Inc. v. U.S.*, 331 F.3d 878 (Fed. Cir. 2003); *Charles G. Williams Constr., Inc. v. White*, 326 F.3d 1376 (Fed. Cir. 2003).

[72] *See Eichleay Corp.*, ASBCA No. 5183, 60-2 BCA ¶ 2688, *reheard and reaffirmed*, 61-1 BCA ¶ 2894.

[73] *See E.R. Mitchell Construction Co. v. Danzig*, 175 F.3d 1369, 1372 (Fed. Cir. 1999).

STEP ONE:

Contract Billings	$\times$	Total Overhead	$=$	Overhead
Total Billings		for Performance		Allocable
for Company		Period		to Contract

STEP TWO:

$$\frac{\text{Overhead Allocable To Contract}}{\text{Actual Days of Contract Performance}} = \text{Daily Contract Overhead Rate}$$

STEP THREE:

| Daily Contract | $\times$ | No. of Days | $=$ | Amount |
| Overhead Rate | | of Delay | | Recoverable |

Establishing Entitlement: The Standby and Replacement Work Requirements

Since *Eichleay* was first decided, the courts have imposed two major requirements as a prerequisite to the recovery of Eichleay damages:

Standby Requirement: The government required the contractor to stand by during a government-caused delay of indefinite duration; and

Replacement Work Requirement: While and as a result of standing by, the contractor was unable to take on other work.[74]

In *P.J. Dick, Inc. v. Principi*, the Federal Circuit reversed a decision by the Veterans Affairs Board of Contract Appeals (VABCA) denying the contractor's claim for unabsorbed home office overhead.[75] In rendering its decision, the Federal Circuit summarized its view of the standby requirement in great detail and may have made the requirement more difficult to prove in federal government contracting.

In *P.J. Dick*, the VA awarded a contract to the contractor to construct a clinical addition to a medical center in Ann Arbor, Michigan.[76] During contract performance, the VA issued more than 400 change orders, increasing the contract price by more than 5 percent and granting time extensions totaling 107 days. The contractor signed each of the changes and reserved its right to seek delay damages under the Suspension of Work clause. Ultimately, the contractor completed the contract 260 days after the original contract completion date and 153 days after the revised date. The VA and the contractor agreed to a stipulation that to the extent the contractor could prove entitlement of delay under the suspension of work clause, the contractor's recovery for field and home office overhead would be calculated at stated daily rates "without the need for future proof of costs or damages."[77]

---

[74] *See, e.g., Interstate General Government Contractors v. West*, 12 F.3d 1053 (Fed. Cir. 1993).

[75] *P.J. Dick, Inc. v. Principi*, 324 F.3d 1364 (Fed. Cir. 2003).

[76] *Id.* at 1368.

[77] *Id.* at 1374.

The VABCA held that the contractor was not entitled to recover unabsorbed home office overhead under the Eichleay formula because it had been able to continue work on other unaffected portions of the project and had never been placed in a standby position.[78]

On appeal, the Federal Circuit rejected the contractor's argument that a contractor is automatically on standby any time there is a government-caused delay of uncertain duration extending the performance of the contract, at the end of which the contractor can be required to immediately resume work. The court began its analysis by reviewing its earlier decisions discussing the standby requirement.[79]

The Federal Circuit stated that in the absence of a written order suspending work for an indefinite duration and requiring the contractor to remain ready to resume work immediately or on short notice, the contractor must prove standby through indirect evidence.[80] Accordingly, in order to satisfy the standby requirement, a contractor must show that:

(1) The government-caused delay was *not* only substantial but was of indefinite duration;

(2) During the delay, the contractor was required to be ready to resume work on the contract at full speed, as well as immediately; and

(3) Work on much, if not all, of the contract was suspended due to the delay.

In this case, although the contractor characterized its direct billings as "minor," it billed 47 percent of the monthly amounts billed before the delay, and the court concluded that the contractor was able to perform substantial amounts of work during the suspension periods.

The Federal Circuit went on to summarize the current status of recovery for unabsorbed home office overhead in the following words:

A court evaluating a contractor's claim for Eichleay damages should ask the following questions:

(1) Was there a government-caused delay that was not concurrent with another delay caused by some other source;

(2) Did the contractor demonstrate that it incurred additional overhead (i.e., was the original time frame for completion extended);

(3) Did the government contracting officer issue a suspension or other order expressly putting the contractor on standby;

(4) If not, can the contractor prove there was a delay of indefinite duration during which it could not bill substantial amounts of work on the contract and at the end of which it was required to be able to return to work on the contract at full speed and immediately;

---

[78] *See P.J. Dick, Inc.*, VABCA Nos. 5597 *et al.*, 01-2 BCA ¶ 31,647.

[79] *P.J. Dick, Inc. v. Principi, supra* note 75, at 1373.

[80] *Id.* at 1371.

(5) Can the government satisfy its burden of production showing that it was not impractical for the contractor to take on replacement work (*i.e.*, a new contract) and thereby mitigate its damages; and

(6) If the government meets its burden of production, can the contractor satisfy its burden of persuasion that it was impractical for it to obtain sufficient replacement work?[81]

The Federal Circuit elaborated that entitlement under the SOW clause "requires proof entirely different, and less demanding, than that required to show entitlement to Eichleay damages."[82] Accordingly, the court set forth a four-part test to recover under the suspension of work clause:

(1) There must be a delay of unreasonable length extending the contract completion time;

(2) The delay must have been proximately caused by the [government's] action or inaction;

(3) The delay resulted in some injury; and

(4) There is no delay concurrent with the suspension that is the fault of the contractor.[83]

11.41   Delayed Notice to Proceed

In *Nicon, Inc. v. United States*, the Federal Circuit vacated and remanded a U.S. Court of Federal Claims' decision that granted the government summary judgment against a contractor's claim for unabsorbed home office overhead.[84] The court reconfirmed that the Eichleay formula is an "extraordinary remedy" available only where certain facts exist, and determined that only delays that *extend* contract performance give rise to Eichleay damages.

In *Nicon*, the contractor was awarded a contract to repair a dormitory at a military installation. Due in part to a bid protest, the government never issued a notice to proceed. When the government subsequently terminated the contract for convenience, the contractor sought to recover $387,513 in unabsorbed home office overhead for the 288 days between award of the contract and the government's termination.

The Federal Circuit stated that *Eichleay* damages are awarded for the number of days by which a government-caused delay causes the overall contract performance to be *extended*—not the number of days that it causes work to be *suspended*. The court held that if performance has not yet begun, there is no way to determine how long the delay would have extended contract performance. The court further refused to assume that the contractor would have been paid its full contract price.

---

[81] *Id.* at 1373.

[82] *Id.* at 1374.

[83] *Id.* at 1375.

[84] *Nicon, Inc. v. United States*, 331 F.3d 878 (Fed. Cir. 2003).

The U.S. Court of Federal Claims initially denied the contractor's unabsorbed overhead claim, stating that the Eichleay formula could not be modified to fit a situation where the contractor had not yet started work. The contractor had no actual "contract billings" or "days of performance" to plug into the formula. For purposes of the Eichleay formula, the contractor argued that it would have completed the project at the contract price and within the contract time but for the termination. Thus, the contractor computed its "daily contract overhead" by plugging the contract price for "contract billings" and the time the contract allowed for performance for actual "days of performance" into the Eichleay formula. The Federal Circuit ultimately rejected these assumptions and stated that "constructive figures may not be substituted into the Eichleay formula."[85]

After rejecting the contractor's Eichleay claim, the Federal Circuit noted that the terminated contractor nevertheless might be able to recover unabsorbed overhead through "some other method of allocation." The Federal Circuit has, however, consistently held that the Eichleay formula is the *only* acceptable method for computing unabsorbed overhead. The court reasoned that in a termination for convenience setting, where fairness to the contractor is a central concern, it would be inappropriate to rigidly apply the Eichleay formula to deny the contractor fair compensation.[86]

The court cautioned that a contractor seeking unabsorbed overhead as part of its termination for convenience must still prove entitlement to unabsorbed overhead. Thus, the contractor must show that: (1) before the government terminated the contract there was a period of government-caused delay of uncertain duration, (2) the contractor itself played no role in the delay and the delay was not the fault of someone or something beyond the government's control, and (3) the contractor was on standby and unable to take on other work.

11.42 OWNER DAMAGES

The damages that the government or a private owner may recover for delayed completion are often fixed by a liquidated damages clause. Typically, such a provision relieves the contractor of liability for actual damages flowing from a breach and fixes the contractor's liability to an established amount for each day that project completion is inexcusably delayed.

A liquidated damages provision is valid if, at the time the contract was executed (1) the amount liquidated is a reasonable approximation of the actual damages or anticipated loss that will result from a delay, and (2) the actual damages are otherwise difficult to ascertain or prove.[87] If a liquidated damages provision does not reasonably approximate foreseeable actual damages, but appears to act as a penalty, the provision will likely be unenforceable.[88] Under such circumstances, the owner will have to prove its actual damages resulting from delayed completion.

---

[85] *Id.* at 883-884.

[86] *Id.* at 885.

[87] *See, e.g., Space Master Int'l, Inc. v. City of Worcester*, 940 F.2d 16 (1st Cir. 1991).

[88] *See, e.g., Southeastern Land Fund, Inc. v. Real Estate World*, Inc., 227 S.E.2d 340 (Ga. 1976).

Despite their threatening, and sometimes harsh terms, under certain circumstances, a liquidated damages provision may operate to the benefit of the contractor. For example, in the case of *Georgia Port Authority v. Norair Engineering*,[89] the owner, as a result of a contractor-caused delay, incurred actual damages in the amount of approximately $140,000, plus the value of the lost use of the project for the delay period of 177 days. Nevertheless, the court held that the owner could not recover its actual damages, but was limited to recovery under the contract's liquidated damage provision for 177 days at $500 per day, or a total of $88,500.

Similarly, in *Industrial Indemnity Co. v. Wick Construction Co.*,[90] the Alaska Supreme Court held that a standard pass-through liquidated damages clause in a subcontract agreement limited the prime contractor's recovery for delay damages against the subcontractor to the amount for which the general contractor was liable to the owner for liquidated damages. As a result, the trial court's award of damages to the general contractor was substantially reduced.

Liquidated damages provisions should be considered carefully by all parties to a construction contract. Often the stipulated *per diem* amount is substantially less than the actual delay damages an owner may sustain. In such cases, the liquidated damages clause may provide a contractor a welcome safety net for late completion due to inexcusable delay.

The types of actual damages that an owner may be able to recover in the absence of a liquidated damages clause include:

(1) Lost revenues due to delayed occupancy,

(2) Increased engineering and inspection costs,

(3) Increased financing costs and interest, and

(4) Legal fees.

11.43 REQUIREMENT OF NOTICE

Most construction contracts require the contractor to submit written notice to the owner or architect, within a definite period of time after the delay-causing event, prior to submitting any claim for additional compensation or for an extension of time. Such notice requirements are imposed to protect the interest of the owner, who may be unaware of the causes of a particular delay and thereby precluded from taking immediate measures to rectify the situation and mitigate its cost. Failure to give prompt notice may result in a waiver of the contractor's rights, or result in a time-consuming litigation effort, which may ultimately prove unsuccessful.[91]

[89] 195 S.E.2d 199 (Ga. Ct. App. 1973).

[90] 680 P.2d 1100 (Alaska 1984).

[91] *See, e.g., Allgood Elec. Co., Inc. v. Martin K. Eby Constr. Co., Inc.*, 959 F. Supp. 1573 (M.D. Ga. 1997), *aff'd*, 137 F.3d 1356 (11th Cir. 1998).

Formal notice may be unnecessary when the owner has actual or constructive knowledge of the problem, or when the lack of notice does not prejudice a legitimate owner interest. The contractor, however, should never knowingly forgo written notice on the assumption that one of those conditions is present. Some courts view notice as a condition precedent to recovery.[92] The contractor that gives the owner prompt written notice of delays and disruptions that are the owner's responsibility increases its opportunity to recover the costs generated by those problems.

11.44   NO-DAMAGES-FOR-DELAY CLAUSES

Despite the widely recognized right of a contractor to recover damages stemming from delayed or out-of-sequence work caused by the owner, the owner (or the general contractor if the claimant is a subcontractor) may succeed in asserting one of several possible defenses to a delay claim. The most notable potential defense is the no-damages-for-delay clause.

A no-damages-for-delay clause typically provides that the owner will not be liable for monetary damages resulting from any delays or resulting from certain specified delays. Most clauses of this kind provide that a contractor's only relief for delays covered by the clause is a time extension. As a general rule, where the language of the clause is clear and unambiguous, a no-damages-for-delay clause is legally valid and enforceable. No-damages-for-delay provisions do not, however, always constitute an absolute bar to recovery. Though different from state to state, several exceptions to the enforcement of such clauses are recognized.

Traditionally, most jurisdictions have handled exceptions to the enforceability of no-damage-for-delay clauses through their state's common law. The majority view is clearly summarized by the court's opinion in *Corinno Civetta Construction Corp. v. City of New York*:

> A clause which exculpates a contractee from liability to a contractor for damages resulting from delay in the performance in the latter's work is valid and enforceable and is not contrary to public policy if the clause and the contract of which it is a part satisfy the requirements for the validity of contracts generally. The rule is not without its exceptions, however, and even exculpatory language which purports to preclude damages from all delays resulting from any cause whatsoever are not read literally. Generally, even with such a clause, damages may be recovered for:
> (1) Delays caused by the contractee's bad faith or its willful, malicious or grossly negligent conduct,
> (2) Uncontemplated delays,
> (3) Delays so unreasonable that they constitute an intentional abandonment of the contract by the contractee, and
> (4) Delays resulting from the contractee's breach of a fundamental obligation of the contract.[93]

---

[92] *A.H.A. General Constr., Inc. v. New York City Hous. Auth.*, 699 N.E.2d 368 (N.Y. 1998).

[93] *Corinno Civetta Construction Corp. v. City of New York*, 493 N.E.2d 905, 909-10 (N.Y. 1986).

Other courts recognize a slightly different set of exceptions to no-damages-for-delay clauses. Under these exceptions, a contractor may recover delay damages despite the presence of such a clause, provided the delay:

(1) Was of a kind not contemplated by the parties in the contract clause,

(2) Was such as to amount to an abandonment of the contract,

(3) Was the result of fraud, bad faith, or arbitrary action,

(4) Was the result of active interference with the contractor's work on the part of the owner, or

(5) Was unreasonable.[94]

Unlike the courts that follow the analysis set out in *Corrino Civetta*, the courts following the above exceptions hold that a contractor can recover delay damages when the delay is caused by the active interference of the owner. These courts have stated that an owner may become liable for delay where it arbitrarily interferes with the progress of the work by committing some affirmative or willful act intended to interfere with the contractor's efforts to comply with the terms of the contract.[95]

Additionally, in contrast to the exceptions noted above, the courts of at least one state do not recognize delays not within the contemplation of the parties as an exception to the enforcement of a no-damages-for-delay clause.[96] Other courts have also questioned an exception to the no-damages-for-delay clause for delays not within the contemplation of the parties.[97] In *Gregory and Son, Inc. v. Guenther Sons*, the Wisconsin Supreme Court stated:

> Indeed, the adoption of a no-damage-for-delay clause shows that the parties realize that some delays cannot be contemplated at the time of the drafting of the contract . . . . The parties can deal with delays they contemplate by adjusting the start and completion date or by including particular provisions in the contract. "[I]t is the unforeseen events which occasion the broad language of the clause since foreseeable ones could be readily provided for by specific language."[98]

Because no-damages-for-delay clauses are exculpatory, that is, they insulate a party from its otherwise culpable conduct, most courts have adopted a policy of strict construction in determining whether to enforce a particular clause. By strictly construing such clauses, courts often limit application to their literal terms, interpret ambiguity against the exculpated party, and construe the recognized exceptions somewhat liberally.

---

[94] *See, e.g., Peter Kiewit Sons' Co. v. Iowa S. Util. Co.*, 355 F. Supp. 376 (S.D. Iowa 1973); *see also Mississippi Transportation Commission v. Ronald Adams Contractor, Inc.*, 753 So.2d 1077 (Miss. 2000).

[95] *See, e.g., Newberry Square Development Corp. v. Southern Landmark, Inc.*, 578 So.2w 750 (Fla. 1991); *Owen Construction Co. v. Iowa State Dept. of Transp.*, 274 N.W.2d 304 (Iowa 1979).

[96] *United States ex rel. Williams Elec. Co., Inc. v. Metric Contractors, Inc.*, 480 S.E.2d 477 (S.C. 1997).

[97] *See State Highway Admin. v. Greiner*, 577 A.2d 363 (Md. Ct. App. 1990); *Gregory and Son, Inc. v. Guenther Sons*, 432 N.W.2d 584 (Wis. 1988).

[98] *Gregory, supra* note 9, at 587.

An example of the courts' strict construction of no-damages-for-delay clauses is found in how some courts define delay. In order to avoid the harsh consequences of a no-damages-for-delay clause, some courts have recognized a distinction between "delays" and "hindrances." In one case, a court held that a no-damages-for-delay clause that did not include the term "hindrance" only barred the contractor from recovering the cost of an idle (as opposed to inefficient) workforce.[99] Therefore, the contractor could recover damages that resulted when the owner "merely" hindered the contractor's work. The court defined a "hindrance" as conduct that impedes, obstructs, or slows progress. Thus, it can be argued that virtually any act or omission by the owner that impedes, obstructs, or slows the work of the contractor is a hindrance and falls outside the operation of a no-damages-for-delay clause.

An additional distinction is also made between a mere "hindrance" and "active interference." Although a hindrance involves active obstruction by the owner, it is lesser in degree than active interference. A hindrance only requires some degree of impeding the contractor's work. Also, by contrast, in order to constitute active interference, there must be reprehensible conduct on the part of the owner in the form of bad faith, evil motive, or total disregard for the consequences of such conduct.

Thus, where a court finds that the contractor's work was hindered, rather than delayed, the court may find the no-damages-for-delay clause does not apply. By contrast, where a court finds that a delay occurred, the court may refuse to enforce the no-damages-for-delay clause, if it finds that the owner actively interfered with the contractor's work.

In a few states, statutes invalidating the enforcement of certain no-damages-for-delay clauses in public contracts have a relatively long history.[100] But for most states, legislation that bars recovery under no-damages-for-delay clauses for construction contracts has only recently come to the forefront.

Washington was the first state to enact a statute providing that any clause in a construction contract that "purports to waive, release, or extinguish the rights of a contractor, subcontractor or supplier to damages or an equitable adjustment arising out of unreasonable delay in performance which delay is caused by the acts or omissions of the contracted or persons acting for the contracted . . . is void and unenforceable."[101] This language is reflected in the more recent trend of statutory bars to the enforcement of no-damages-for-delay clauses.

For example, in 1998, Ohio enacted a statute that declares any provision of a construction contract or subcontract unenforceable as a matter of public policy where the provision waives liability for delay when the delay is caused by either the owner's or contractor's acts or failure to act.[102] A recent North Carolina statute also provides a blanket prohibition on no-damages-for delay clauses.[103] Some states,

---

[99] *John E. Green Plumbing & Heating Co. v. Turner Constr. Co.*, 742 F.2d 965 (6th Cir. 1983), *cert. denied*, 471 U.S. 1102 (1984).

[100] *See* Cal. Pub. Cont. Code § 7102 (West 1985); Colorado Rev. Stat. § 24-91-103.5 (1990).

[101] Wash. Rev. Code § 4.24.360 (1988).

[102] *See* Ohio Rev. Code Ann. § 4113.62(C)(1) & (2) (Anderson 1999).

[103] *See* N.C. Gen. Stat. § 143-134.3 (1997).

however, have attempted to limit the no-damages-for-delay clause while leaving the clause itself intact by codifying well-recognized exceptions.[104]

11.45 DELAY CLAIMS AND THE USE OF CPM SCHEDULES

To prove or refute delay claims, contractors and owners typically perform a detailed examination of project records and project schedules. Delay claims are typically based upon contemporaneous critical path method (CPM) schedules that were generated during the course of the project or on after-the-fact as-built CPM schedules reconstructed by a scheduling expert. The relative weight to be given to either approach has been vigorously contested over the last three decades. As in other areas of construction law, government contract decisions illustrate some of the key issues related to using CPM schedules to prove delay claims.

For example, the Veterans Affairs Board of Contract Appeals (VABCA) addressed the question of using after-the-fact CPMs in two decisions in 1984 and 1987, both bearing the same name, *Santa Fe, Inc.*[105] The *Santa Fe* decisions indicated that board's clear preference for contemporaneous schedules when assessing delay claims.

In 1984, the VABCA denied a contractor's claim for time extensions because "the delayed activities had not been on the critical path for completion of the project."[106] The VABCA held that the "critical path calculations had been made for each task involved, and these calculations were continuously updated during construction." The board further elaborated that "it is the very existence of the contractually agreed upon CPM procedure which, when properly utilized, allows the contracting officer and subsequent bodies to determine with greater exactitude whether, and to what extent, a particular change order affects critical path and hence delays ultimate performance."

In the 1987 *Santa Fe, Inc.* decision, the VABCA determined that contract extensions "shall be based upon the computer-produced calendar dated schedule for the time period in question and all other relevant information."[107] In this decision, the VABCA held that "submission of proof based on revised activity logic durations and cost is obligatory to any approvals." The board placed reliance on the most current CPM schedule developed when performing an analysis as to whether or not the contractor incurred delay on a VA contract. According to this decision, "There is a rebuttable presumption of correctness attached to CPM schedule upon which the parties have previously mutually agreed." "To put it another way," the board stated, "in the absence of compelling evidence of actual errors in the CPMs, we will let the parties 'live or die' by the CPM applicable to the relevant time frames." The *Santa Fe* decisions illustrate the rationale and preference for contemporaneous schedules when calculating delay claims.

---

[104] *See, e.g.,* Ariz. Rev. Stat. § 41-2617 (1997).

[105] *See Santa Fe, Inc.,* VABCA No. 1943 *et al,* 84-2 BCA ¶ 17,340; *Santa Fe, Inc.,* VABCA No. 2168, 87-3 BCA ¶ 20,104.

[106] *Santa Fe, Inc.,* VABCA No. 1943 *et al,* 84-2 BCA ¶ 17,340.

[107] *Santa Fe, Inc.,* VABCA No. 2168, 87-3 BCA ¶ 20,104.

In *P.J. Dick,*[108] the VABCA reiterated its preference for a contemporaneous schedule as its baseline for delay claims. In this case, the board was faced with a "rather unique situation." The CPMs used during the course of the project were, according to the board:

> properly constituted in its logic and assiduously and properly maintained throughout contract performance. This circumstance is in sharp contrast to the usual problems we encounter in dealing with CPMs where warring as-built schedules are constructed by the parties after the fact because the CPM was either never properly or timely prepared or was not updated in accordance with the contract scheduling requirements.[109]

The VABCA determined that "since there is no dispute concerning the validity of a CPM, these appeals present the circumstance where we have said in the past that we will let the parties 'live or die' by analysis of the CPM to determine the number of days of additional contract performance time."

The *P.J. Dick* decision underscores the recent theme discussed in several boards of contract appeals decisions: the requirement of extensive documentary evidence that demonstrates the alleged claims before awarding the appropriate relief. Boards are becoming more demanding and are requiring more concrete evidence in their analysis of a contractor's delay claim.

These increased demands should have a direct, practical impact on those contractors that rely on government contracts as a source of business. Project schedules should be updated routinely, they should reflect all changes, and they should be approved and shared with all interested parties through the life of the project.

Does the *P.J. Dick* decision end the use of after-the-fact as-built schedules in the analysis of delay claims? Not necessarily. The strong preference expressed by some tribunals for contemporaneous analysis notwithstanding, the quantification of delays may also be developed retrospectively. If contemporaneous schedules are flawed or do not exist, an accurate and realistic after-the-fact schedule can be useful in a delay claim.

✔ DELAY CLAIMS SUPPORTING DOCUMENTATION

CPM analysis is often used to assess or present a delay claim. Basic project documentation is often critical to establishing the validity of the analysis. The following checklist itemizes many of the sources of information to be evaluated when preparing, or attempting to rebut, a delay claim:

(1) Estimates

(2) Original schedules

(3) Schedules used on the project, including look-ahead schedules, CPM logic diagrams, and tabular printouts

---

[108] *P. J. Dick, Inc.*, VABCA Nos. 5597, 5836, 01-2 BCA ¶ 31,647.

[109] Id.

(4) As-built schedules

(5) Daily reports

(6) Diaries

(7) Manpower and manloading reports

(8) Cost accounting records

(9) Scheduling meeting minutes

(10) Material and equipment delivery tickets

(11) Job photographs and videotapes

(12) As-built drawings

(13) Shop drawing logs

(14) Project correspondence

(15) Change orders

(16) Contract documents

(17) Pay applications

(18) Internal memoranda

When evaluating a potential claim for delay, the following checklist is a useful tool for reviewing the pertinent factual information:

(1) *Accuracy*: Are the schedules used for the project accurate? Were they agreed upon and used by the parties, or were they issued for "internal purposes" only? Courts may give more weight to schedules to which the parties have agreed previously.

(2) *Abandonment of Schedule:* Was the selected scheduling technique abandoned during performance? If so, why? A contractor that committed by contract to a particular scheduling technique might be precluded from proving its claim with that technique if it did not meet its scheduling commitments.

(3) *Current Schedule:* Was the schedule updated and kept current on a regular basis? Schedules often change dramatically over the course of a project.

(4) *Changes:* Was the schedule revised to reflect the effect of change orders? The schedule should show whether the change impacted work along the critical path or consumed float. A change order impact analysis is a handy tool for negotiating the price of a change.

(5) *Change Order Compensation:* Was additional overhead included in the change order? Even if the changed work affects only float, it may result in less effective resource utilization or involve unforeseen overhead or job staffing.

(6) *Cross-references:* Are the project records tied into the project schedule by work activity code or designation? Doing so provides data for subsequent updates and for the preparation of an accurate as-built analysis.

(7) *Float Ownership:* Does the contract bar the contractor from seeking compensation, time extensions, or both for delays that consume only float time?

(8) *Coordination Responsibility:* Which party is responsible for coordinating and scheduling?

(9) *Scheduling Experts:* Solicit expert or in-house scheduling assistance early. This may aid in efficient record keeping and assist in minimizing the effect of a delay.

(10) *Choosing an Expert:* An expert should be well versed in:

   (a) The theory and output of all scheduling techniques used;
   (b) The estimating process used and its relation to the contractor's resources;
   (c) The contractual relationships among owner, designers, contractors, subcontractors, and suppliers;
   (d) Good project record keeping and cost accounting; and
   (e) The design and construction of the type of work involved.

➤ POINTS TO REMEMBER

The following key points should be noted:

- Most big-dollar construction disputes are based upon changes—either delay or acceleration—to the construction schedule in the form of delays or acceleration.

- Most construction contracts contain an express obligation that the contractor will complete the work by a given date or within a specified time frame, which is accompanied by an implied obligation that neither party will do anything to delay, hinder, or interfere with the performance of the other.

- Common causes of delays include inclement weather, labor disputes, untimely equipment delivery, defective specifications, changes, and differing site conditions. Which party bears responsibility for each of these types of delays depends upon the language of the contract and the surrounding circumstances.

- The presence of a "time is of the essence" provision in a contract should not be viewed as mere boilerplate. Such a provision makes time a material element of the contract. The provision can be a predicate for the recovery of delay damages and is a signal that timely performance is required.

- An understanding of several key terms is important in determining the party that bears responsibility for construction delays:

   (1) An excusable delay is a delay that entitles the contractor to a time extension under the terms of the contract. Moreover, an excusable delay may be either compensable or noncompensable;

      (a) A compensable excusable delay is a delay that is not only excusable (entitling the contractor to a time extension) but also entitles the contractor to additional compensation for the resulting cost;

      (b) A noncompensable excusable delay is a delay for which the contractor is entitled to a time extension but no additional compensation.

(2) A nonexcusable delay is a delay that does not entitle the contractor to a time extension and may subject the contractor to liability for delay damages arising out of the nonexcusable delay.

- To determine whether a given delay is nonexcusable or excusable and possibly a compensable delay, one must carefully study the contract, the nature of the delay, and all surrounding circumstances.

- Examples of some of the types of delays that may constitute excusable noncompensable delays are weather, acts of God, and labor problems.

- Most construction contracts require the contractor to provide the owner prompt written notice of any excusable delay. A contractor's failure to provide such notice may jeopardize the contractor's right to a time extension and/or additional compensation.

- Examples of some of the causes of delay that may constitute excusable compensable delays include delays due to defective drawings or specifications, the owner's failure to provide access, improper site preparation by the owner or a parallel contractor, the owner's failure to timely supply owner-furnished materials or labor, the owner's failure to timely provide plans and approved shop drawings, the owner's failure to properly coordinate parallel prime contractors, the owner's failure to make timely payments, the owner's failure to perform timely inspections, the owner's suspension of the work, excessive change orders, and the owner's failure to timely accept complete work.

- Acceleration is another common source of construction claims and disputes. Acceleration may take two forms:
  (1) Directed acceleration, and
  (2) Constructive acceleration.

- Directed acceleration describes the situation where the owner explicitly directs the contractor to complete the work earlier than the contractually required completion date.

- Constructive acceleration describes the situation where an owner fails to grant a contractor a time extension to which it is entitled, thereby requiring the contractor to complete, or attempt to complete, the work by a date earlier than contractually required. Thus, constructive acceleration is, in effect, a possible by-product of an excusable delay.

- The essential elements of a claim for constructive acceleration are as follows:
  (1) An excusable delay;
  (2) A timely request for a time extension;
  (3) Failure or refusal by the owner to grant the request for time extension;
  (4) Conduct by the owner that is reasonably construed as requiring the contractor to complete on a schedule that has not been properly extended;
  (5) Effort by the contractor to accelerate performance; and
  (6) Additional costs incurred by the contractor as a result of the acceleration.

- If the contractor can establish each of these six elements of a constructive acceleration claim, the contractor is generally entitled to additional compensation even though the contractor may have been unsuccessful in its attempt to complete the work by the nonextended completion date.

- Examples of acceleration damages include premium time, the cost of added crews or increased crew sizes, the cost of additional tools and equipment required for added or larger crews, the cost of additional supervision and jobsite overhead, and the cost of the labor inefficiency that may occur due to the longer hours or increased crew sizes or numbers.

- "Concurrent delay" is a term of art that refers to the situation where two different delays, caused by different parties, occur simultaneously or in overlapping time periods and one of the delays is a compensable delay, while the other is a nonexcusable delay.

- The early view stated by the courts and administrative boards regarding concurrent delay was that neither party was allowed any affirmative recovery from the other in the case of concurrent delay.

- The modern trend is to apportion responsibility for project delays between the parties whenever it is possible, using modern, sophisticated scheduling techniques such as critical path method (CPM) scheduling to segregate the impact of the concurrent delays.

- Some construction contracts contain a type of exculpatory clause referred to as a no-damages-for-delay clause. A no-damages-for-delay clause typically provides that the owner will not be liable to the contractor for monetary damages resulting from any delays or from certain specified types of delay.

- As a general rule, no-damages-for-delay clauses are legally valid and enforceable; however, in order to avoid harsh results, courts often narrowly construe such provisions and create various judicial exceptions to the general rule of enforceability.

- Some common exceptions to the enforcement of no-damages-for-delay clauses are:

  (1) Delays of a kind not contemplated by the parties;

  (2) Delays that amount to an abandonment of the contract;

  (3) Delays that were the result of fraud, bad faith, or arbitrary action;

  (4) Delays that were the result of active interference; and

  (5) Delays that were unreasonable.

- Some state legislatures have also passed statutes limiting the enforceability of no-damages-for-delay clauses.

- The harsh consequences of a no-damages-for-delay clause can also sometimes be averted by drawing a distinction between a "delay" and a "hindrance," "disruption," "resequencing," "acceleration," and "contract change."

- Some of the types of damages a contractor may be able to recover as delay damages include inefficient or idle labor costs, idle equipment costs, acceleration and overtime costs, extended field office overhead costs, unabsorbed or underabsorbed home office overhead costs, escalated material and labor costs, legal fees, interest, lost profits, and damages resulting from the lost bonding capacity.

• When a contractor fails to complete a project within the contractually specified time, as properly extended for any excusable delays, the owner may recover delay damages from the contractor. These damages may take the form of liquidated damages or, in the absence of a liquidated damages provision, actual damages.

• The types of actual damages an owner may be able to recover in the absence of a liquidated damages provision include lost revenues due to delayed occupancy, increased engineering and inspection costs, increased financing costs and interest, and legal fees.

• A good scheduling analysis and good documentation are critical to the successful presentation of any delay claim.

12

INSPECTION, ACCEPTANCE, COMMISSIONING, AND WARRANTIES

From the owner's perspective, the primary objectives of any construction project generally fall into three categories: cost, schedule, and quality. The owner naturally desires high-quality construction, on schedule, and at a low cost. Unfortunately, these three objectives sometimes conflict with one another, and certain trade-offs are required. The natural give-and-take that occurs between these three project objectives is perhaps best illustrated by the remark often made by contractors to owners in jest: "Cost, schedule, and quality—pick any two; but you can't have all three." As the saying goes, many a truth is sometimes spoken in jest.

Other chapters of this book focus on what happens when construction costs escalate or schedule delays occur. This chapter focuses on the third prong of the cost/schedule/quality triumvirate by discussing three issues that relate directly to construction quality: (1) inspections, (2) acceptance, and (3) warranties.

"Inspections" are the primary vehicle employed by an owner during the course of construction to ensure that appropriate quality standards are being met. Typically, inspections are performed by the owner and/or the owner's authorized representative periodically during the course of construction and again upon project completion. Timely and appropriate inspections afford an informed owner and contractor an opportunity to address quality problems before the work is complete and allow any necessary corrective work to be implemented at a time when it is less costly.

"Acceptance" is a power generally vested by contract in the owner or the owner's representative (e.g., the project architect or engineer). The owner's right to inspect and accept the contractor's work prior to payment can be a valuable tool if used properly. An owner should employ inspection and acceptance procedures that will identify and appropriately address detectable defects in the work and other nonconforming work in a prompt manner and before they are "covered up." Most construction contracts state that the owner's "acceptance" of the work and payment for the work do not preclude the owner from objecting to defective work at a later time. However, an owner that fails to inspect the work in progress and to reject nonconforming work may be doing both itself and the contractor a great disservice.

The word "warranties" has several different meanings in the construction context. One way the word is used is to refer to the various expressed and implied promises contained in every construction contract. Some, but not all, of these promises relate to quality issues. An example is the express warranty contained in most construction contracts whereby the contractor promises to perform its work in a "good and workmanlike manner." Another use of the word "warranties" is to describe the obligations of the contractor or a subcontractor, supplier, or manufacturer to address any quality problems that may be discovered after construction is complete. Typically, a construction contract will provide that the general contractor "warrants" its work for a period of one year (or some other period of time) after substantial completion. Such warranties are often confused with "statutes of limitations," but are actually something much different. It is also common that certain subcontractors, as well as the manufacturers of certain products and systems installed in a project, will provide warranties. One purpose of such warranties is to allocate responsibility for defective work, equipment, and materials or for equipment and materials that cease to function properly after operating for a period of time.

12.1   INSPECTION

12.2   Introduction

The owners of both private and public projects generally employ representatives to inspect the quality of the contractor's work. In private construction, inspections are often performed by an architect/engineer specially retained by the owner. In public construction, however, inspections are often handled by government-employed inspectors.

Inspection is intended for the protection of the owner, not the contractor. Therefore, the owner generally has no duty to inspect outside its contract obligations. Even if the contract allows for owner inspection, that type of provision will generally not obligate the owner to inspect.[1]

However, if the owner assumes a contractual obligation to inspect, the owner can find itself liable for defective inspections or a failure to inspect. In *Continental Insur. Co. v. City of Virginia Beach*,[2] when the contractor filed bankruptcy during construction, the City-owner called on the contractor's surety to complete the project. After discovering that the contractor's work had not been properly performed, the surety sued the City for payments made to the contractor, which the surety contended could have been withheld and available to the surety if the defective work had been discovered through the City's inspection. The court found that the City had assumed the duty of inspecting and testing the contractor's work. The court held that

[1] *Burlington v. Arnold Constr. Co.*, 727 S.W.2d 241 (Tenn. Ct. App. 1987).
[2] 908 F. Supp. 341 (E.D. Va. 1995).

City had breached its inspection obligations, thereby prejudicing the surety when payments were made to the contractor. As a result, the court held that the surety was discharged from its bond obligations to the extent it was prejudiced by the City's conduct.[3]

Owners often place the burden of inspections and quality control on the contractor by requiring the contractor to adhere to stringent quality control specifications, which may include the use of comprehensive quality control procedures during the construction. Failure to inspect effectively, however, may impact the owner's rights under applicable warranties once the project is accepted. Furthermore, the owner cannot, with impunity, perform inspections in such a manner as to delay or disrupt the contractor's work or to alter the requirements of the contract.

12.3   Standard Inspection Clauses

The rights and responsibilities of the owner and contractor in a typical construction project are illustrated by the standard provisions regarding inspections. The standard clause used in federal construction contracting, entitled Inspection of Construction, is set forth in Federal Acquisition Regulation (FAR) § 52.246-12. Standard clauses used in many private construction contracts are contained in AGC Document No. 200 (2000 ed.), Standard Form of Agreement and General Conditions Between Owner and Contractor [AGC 200], Paragraph 3.7, "Tests and Inspections" and AIA Document A201 (1997 ed.) [hereinafter AIA A201], Article 12, "Uncovering and Correction of Work."

The federal clause specifies that the owner has the right to inspect "at all reasonable times before acceptance to ensure strict compliance with the terms of the contract." The clause clearly provides that the inspection is solely for the owner's benefit and does not constitute or imply acceptance of the contractor's work. The contractor, therefore, is not relieved of the responsibility of ensuring compliance with contract requirements merely because the government has conducted inspections.

Other standard federal government contract clauses relate to inspection as well. The "Material and Workmanship" clause, FAR § 52.236-5, provides that materials employed are to be "new and of the most suitable grade for the purposes intended" unless the contract specifically provides otherwise; that references to products by trade name are intended to set a standard of quality and not to limit competition; that anything installed without the required approval may be rejected; and that work must be performed in a "skillful and workmanlike manner."

The "Permits and Responsibilities" clause of the standard federal construction contract, FAR § 52.236-7, requires the contractor to take proper precautions to protect the work, the workers, and the persons and property of others. The clause states that the contractor is responsible for damages to persons or property caused by the contractor's fault or negligence, and places responsibility upon the contractor for all materials delivered and work performed up until completion and acceptance by the government.[4]

[3] *Id.* at 348.
[4] *See* FAR § 36.507.

For private contracts, forms such as the AGC 200 provide that the contractor is to schedule all required tests, approvals, and inspections so as not to delay the project work and to give proper notice to all required parties.[5] The AGC 200 also provides that the owner is responsible for retaining independent testing firms and paying for the inspections; but the contractor is responsible for obtaining the certificates of testing, approval, and inspections.[6] The AGC contract further provides that if the contractor's work fails a test, then the contractor will be responsible for the costs of correction and retesting.[7]

The AGC 200 also provides that the owner can direct the contractor to uncover work that the owner did not require to be inspected so that the work can be inspected.[8] If the work was properly performed, then the owner will pay for the costs of uncovering and inspecting the work and placing it back in its preinspection form. However, if the work does not conform to the contract requirements, then the contractor must pay for the uncovering and correction of the work.[9]

The AGC 200 also provides that the contractor is responsible for safety precautions and programs and that the contractor is to provide the owner with notices required for safety purposes.[10]

In contrast to the AGC 200, the AIA A201 provides that the contractor is responsible during construction for inspection of the work already performed and to determine that the work is in conformance with the contract document so additional work can be performed.[11] The contractor is also required to secure and pay for inspections necessary for the proper execution and completion of the contract work and to obtain any required certificates of testing, inspection, or approval.[12] If there is a defect in the contractor's work, then the contractor bears the costs of correcting the failure.[13]

Article 10 of AIA A201 also makes the contractor responsible for initiating, maintaining, and supervising all safety precautions and programs in connection with the performance of the contract, and requires the contractor to take reasonable precautions for the safety and protection of employees and other persons, the work itself (and materials and equipment incorporated or to be incorporated therein), and other property at or adjacent to the site.[14]

However, the contractor is not an insurer and therefore is not responsible for all job-site injuries. For example, in Georgia, an architect was denied recovery against the contractor when the architect fell off a ladder. The court stated that a contractor must use ordinary care not to cause injuries, but that the architect has the same duty.

---

[5] AGC Document No. 200 ¶ 3.7 (2000 ed.).

[6] *Id.*

[7] *Id.* at § 3.7.3.

[8] *Id.* at § 3.10.

[9] *Id.*

[10] *Id.* at § 3.11.

[11] AIA A201 §§ 3.3.3 and 13.5.1.

[12] *Id.* at §§ 3.7.1 and 13.5.1. (AIA A201 § 4.2.2 limits the architect's responsibility for inspections. That provision states that "[t]he Architect will not be required to make exhaustive or continuous on-site inspections to check the quality or quantity of the Work.").

[13] *Id.* at. § 13.5.3.

[14] AIA A201 §§ 10.1.1 and 10.2.1 (1997 ed.).

The problem with the ladder was obvious and the architect should have known better than to use it. Therefore, the architect recovered nothing.[15]

The standard federal "Use and Possession Prior to Completion" clause, FAR § 52.236-11, provides that the owner may take possession of or use a partially or totally completed part of a project without being deemed to have accepted the work. Prior to such possession or use, the contracting officer must provide the contractor with a list of work remaining to be done on the relevant portion of the project. Even where the owner fails to list a particular defect or item of work, however, the contractor must still comply with the contract terms.[16] Both the AGC 200 and the AIA General Conditions also provide for possession by the owner prior to completion.[17]

12.4   Costs of Inspection

Although the owner may bear its own inspection costs, the contractor generally is required to bear the expense of providing the inspector with the facilities, labor, or material reasonably necessary to perform the test or inspection.[18] However, circumstances may exist that would entitle the contractor to be reimbursed for expenses incurred for inspection or testing. For example, if the owner increases the cost of conducting the inspection or test by changing the location or requiring special inspection devices, the contractor may recover additional costs.[19]

As previously stated, the owner generally may examine completed work and require the contractor to remove or tear out the work. If the work is defective or does not conform to the specifications, the contractor must pay the costs of both the inspection and correction of the work. If, however, the work is satisfactory, the contractor is entitled to a price adjustment for the additional costs and a time extension if completion is delayed.[20]

The cost of reinspection is generally assigned to the party whose action or inaction resulted in the reinspection.[21] If, for example, the contractor's work was not sufficiently complete at the time of the original inspection, the contractor must pay the costs of reinspection. Similarly, if the reinspection is the result of an earlier rejection, the contractor is responsible for the additional costs.[22] Before any reinspection, however, the owner must provide a reasonable notification and a reasonable amount of time for the contractor to correct or complete the work.

---

[15] *Morris v. Barnet*, 381 S.E.2d 597 (Ga. Ct. App. 1989).

[16] *See* FAR § 52.236-11.

[17] *See* AGC 200 ¶ 9.7 (2000 ed.); AIA A201 § 9.9 (1997 ed.).

[18] *See Tecon Corp. v. United States*, 411 F.2d 1262 (Ct. Cl. 1969); *see also,* AGC Document No 200 ¶¶ 3.7 and 9.8.1 (2000 ed.) (owner generally responsible for inspection costs); *but see,* AIA A201 § 13.5.1 (1997 ed.) (contractor is responsible for inspection and test costs, except inspections and tests that do not become requirements until after contract negotiations are concluded).

[19] *See Gordon H. Ball, Inc.*, ASBCA No. 8316, 1963 BCA ¶ 3925; *Corbetta Constr. Co.*, ASBCA No. 5045, 60-1 BCA ¶ 2613.

[20] *See* notes 8 and 9.

[21] *Id.; see Okland Constr. Co.*, GSBCA No. 3557, 72-2 BCA ¶ 9675.

[22] *See* notes 8 and 9; *see also Minnesota Mining & Mfg Co.*, GSBCA No. 4054, 75-1 BCA ¶ 11,065.

The AGC Document No. 200 provides that the owner is responsible for inspection costs.[23] But if the contractor's work fails a test, then the contractor will be responsible for the costs of correction and retesting.[24]

Paragraph 12.2.4 of AIA A201 requires the contractor to "bear the cost of correcting destroyed or damaged construction, whether completed or partially completed, of the Owner or separate contractors caused by the Contractor's correction or removal of work which is not in accordance with the requirements of the Contract Documents." Paragraph 12.3.1 authorizes the owner to accept nonconforming work, instead of having it removed and replaced, and to reduce the contract price to take the defective work into account.

12.5 The Owner's Right to Inspect

12.6 *The Right, Not the Duty* Thorough, but reasonable, contemporaneous inspections can be the contractor's best friend. Such inspections allow the owner or its representative to monitor the work on a daily basis and inspect for deviations from the plans and specifications. If deficiencies do exist, and the owner or its representative reasonably objects, performance can be modified to make the work acceptable with minimal cost. In the event of an ambiguous requirement, the owner's acquiescence to the work, as performed by the contractor, may show that the owner agreed with the contractor's interpretation at the time of performance.[25]

Cognizant of the risks of overlooking defects during inspection, owners have sought to minimize contractors' ability to rely on owners' inspections. Thus, AIA A201 provides in § 9.4.2, with regard to the effect of issuing a Certificate for Payment, that ". . . the issuance of a Certificate for Payment will not be a representation that the Architect has . . . made exhaustive or continuous on-site inspections to check the quality or quantity of the Work. . . ."

The standard federal "Inspection of Construction" clause, as prescribed by FAR § 52.246-12, is more specific: "Government inspections and tests are for the sole benefit of the Government and do not [r]elieve the Contractor of responsibility for providing adequate quality control measures . . . [or] [c]onstitute or imply acceptance. . . ." This provision makes it clear that no inspection duty is imposed upon the government; rather, the government has the right to inspect should it so desire.

The owner would have an affirmative duty to inspect the work when the contract specifically contemplates or requires that the owner perform certain tests during the work.[26] The failure of the owner to inspect or test in accordance with contract terms may cause the owner to lose some of its specific rights and remedies, such as the right to reject items or have defects corrected when a reasonable inspection would have uncovered such defects.

[23] AGC Document No. 200 ¶ 3.7 (2000 ed.).

[24] *Id.* at 3.7.3.

[25] *Milaeger Well Drilling Co. v. Muskego Rendering Co.*, 85 N.W.2d 331 (Wis. 1957).

[26] *See Cone Bros. Contracting Co.*, ASBCA No. 16078, 72-1 BCA ¶ 9444.

12.7 Scope of Inspection The scope of the owner's inspection rights often leads to disputes regarding the interpretation of specifications, quality of workmanship, and other "quality" determinations. The scope of an owner's inspection is usually set forth in the contract; and when no specific inspection requirements are set forth, the inspections must be reasonable in scope. In federal government work, the scope of the inspection requirements depends upon the analysis of the type of work to be delivered.

The standard inspection clause generally controls construction contracts. However, the FAR establishes four categories of contract quality requirements: (1) reliance on the contractor's existing quality assurance systems as a substitute for government inspection and testing for commercial items; (2) government reliance on the contractor to perform all inspections and testing; (3) "standard" inspection requirements contained in the standard clauses, calling for inspections to be performed by both the contractor and the government; and (4) "higher-level quality requirements" prescribing more stringent inspections to be performed by the government.[27]

In most construction projects, the government will perform either the standard inspection or the higher-level quality inspection. The requirements for the standard inspection are set forth in the inspection clause, which provides that: (1) the contractor must establish an inspection system; (2) the government may inspect during performance; and (3) the contractor must maintain inspection records.[28] The higher-level quality inspection requirements are generally set forth in special supplementary contract clauses implementing stricter quality control.[29]

Even if the scope of inspections is set forth in the contract, as a general rule, the federal government contract may impose an unspecified alternative test as a basis for determining contract compliance. The new test must reasonably measure contract compliance. However, if the "specified" test can be viewed as establishing a standard of performance, a different test that increases the level of performance cannot be substituted without a change to the contract price.[30]

Not only does the government have the right to inspect at all places and times, the government also has the right to reinspect the same performance. Generally, the government may conduct reasonable, continuing inspections at any time prior to acceptance.[31] Exceptions exist with regard to the government's right to reinspect. Multiple inspections cannot be wholly inconsistent. Subjecting the contractor to inconsistent inspections amounts to an unreasonable interference with the contractor's work and entitles the contractor to compensation.[32]

[27] FAR § 46.202.

[28] FAR § 46.202-2.

[29] FAR §§ 46.311 and 52.246-11.

[30] *Southwest Welding & Mfg. Co. v. United States*, 413 F.2d 1167 (Ct. Cl. 1969); *Roda Enters., Inc.*, ASBCA No. 22323, 81-2 BCA ¶ 15,419.

[31] *Forsberg & Gregory, Inc.*, ASBCA No. 17598, 75-1 BCA ¶ 11,176.

[32] *WRB Corp. v. United States*, 183 Ct. Cl. 409 (1968).

12.8   Rejection and Correction

After inspection, an owner has the right to accept the performance, reject the performance if it is nonconforming, require correction of nonconforming performance, or, in appropriate circumstances, terminate the contract for default.[33] To enforce its rejection/correction remedy, the federal government must provide the contractor with notice of the alleged discrepancy within a "reasonable time" after discovery of the defects. The notice must include the reasons for the rejection.[34] When the government fails to provide the reasons for the rejection in the initial notice and the contractor is prejudiced by the failure, the rejection can be overturned as ineffective. Furthermore, a failure to reject the performance in a reasonable time can be interpreted as an implied acceptance of the performance.[35]

If the federal government elects to reject the performance, it must ordinarily give the contractor an opportunity to correct the defects if they can be cured within the contract schedule.[36] If the contracting officer orders correction instead of rejecting and requiring replacement of the work, the contractor is entitled to a reasonable time within which to make the correction, without regard to the original schedule.[37]

If the contractor fails to timely replace or correct rejected work, the federal government has three remedies. The government can: (1) terminate the contract for default and reprocure the supplies, services, or construction; (2) replace or correct the defective supplies, services, or construction by contract or by using government resources, at the contractor's expense, under the inspection clause; or (3) retain the nonconforming supplies, services, or construction and reduce the contract price based on the difference in value between the work as delivered and the work contemplated by the contract.[38]

12.9   Limitation on Owner's Inspections

Although the owner has broad rights relating to inspection, improper inspections can give rise to certain rights and remedies on the part of the contractor—if, for example, "constructive changes" to the work or delays and disruptions result from the owner's inspections. Several issues must be addressed to determine whether an inspection creates the basis to assert a "constructive change."

12.10   Authority   Differences in opinion regarding the standards of performance required by the contract or the correct inspection test to be used often cause contractors to claim they are being required to perform extra work. However, even

---

[33] FAR §§ 46.407(a) and 52.246-2(f).

[34] FAR § 46.407(g).

[35] FAR §§ 46.407(g).

[36] FAR § 46.407(b).

[37] *Baifield Indus., Div. A-T-O, Inc.*, ASBCA No. 14582, 72-2 BCA ¶ 9676.

[38] FAR §§ 52.249-8; 52.249-10; 52.246-2(h); 52.246-4(e); 52.246-12(g); 52.246-2(b); 52.246-4(d); 52.246-12(f).

if the contractor's interpretation was correct and the inspector was wrong, the contractor may be confronted with the argument that the inspector lacked the authority to change the contract and bind the owner.

The issue of the inspector's authority can be complicated. Inspectors seldom have authority to change the contract requirements, but they do have authority to reject work. It is usually held, therefore, that an erroneous rejection is within their authority and can form the basis of a contract extra. This assumes, of course, proper notice by the contractor and "performance under protest."[39] To avoid disputes over authority, the best procedure to follow is to routinely provide written notice to an authorized owner-representative whenever the actions of an inspector are causing performance and cost beyond that contemplated by the contract.

The federal government frequently argues that its inspectors lack the authority to make a constructive change. In one case, the specifications for brick were strict and the contractor's chief mason complied with the requirements by rejecting between 20 and 25 percent of the brick. The manufacturer, the government's on-site representative, and the architect agreed that the contractor was being overly critical and told the contractor to stop rejecting brick. Thereafter, the government rejected the brickwork due to an undesirable basket-weave appearance and directed the contractor to remove and replace the brick.

The contractor demanded an equitable adjustment for its costs in removing and replacing the brick. The government argued that its on-site representative did not have the authority to direct the contractor to stop rejecting brick. The board of contract appeals held that the inspector's authority depends on the facts and conduct of each case and that the contracting officer can authorize technical personnel (such as inspectors) to give guidance or instruction about specification problems. Therefore, the government was liable for the constructive change that caused the placement and removal of the defective brick.[40]

12.11 *Higher Standards of Performance* The owner may use any reasonable inspection test. However, it may not require a higher standard of performance through the use of inspection procedures or tests more stringent than those called for by the contract or inconsistent with industry practice.[41] If higher standards or stricter tests are imposed, the contractor is entitled to additional compensation. Similarly, if the contractor is required by the inspector to use materials or construction methods that are not required by the contract and are more expensive than the contractor's chosen materials or methods, a compensable change may result.[42]

Problems may occur in cases in which the contract does not clearly define either the standard of workmanship required of the contractor or the standard of inspection to be employed. In such cases, inspectors will often rely upon industry standards and

---

[39] C. P. Jhong, Annotation, "Effect of Stipulation, in Private Building or Construction Contract, That Alterations or Extras Must Be Ordered in Writing," 2 A.L.R.3d 620 (1965).

[40] *Jordan & Nobles Constr. Co.*, GSBCA No. 8349, 91-1 BCA ¶ 23,659.

[41] *See Warren Painting Co.*, ASBCA No. 6511, 61-2 BCA ¶ 3199.

[42] *See, e.g., Jack Graham Corp.*, ASBCA No. 4585, 58-2 BCA ¶ 1998.

trade customs, or even on subjective standards such as "skillful and workmanlike." Where the use of such criteria actually requires a level of performance in excess of that reasonably contemplated at the time the parties entered into the contract, the contractor may be entitled to extra compensation.

For example, an inspector's use of straightedges and other measuring tools to check stud alignment has been held to amount to a change when no such method was specified in the contract and the normal industry practice was to check alignment by visual inspection.[43]

12.12 *Rejecting Acceptable Work* An inspector's wrongful rejection of acceptable work involves issues similar to the imposition of increased standards of performance. If work that should have been accepted is "corrected" to a higher standard of quality and additional costs are incurred in the process, a compensable change has occurred.[44]

Where specifications are ambiguous, an inspector's silent acquiescence while the contractor performs in accordance with its own reasonable interpretation of the performance standards may establish that the contractor's approach was reasonable and the work acceptable.[45] Also, if the owner submits to the contractor what purports to be a complete list of defects in the work, the owner may later be prevented from rejecting work that had been corrected pursuant to the list on the grounds that its list amounted to a binding interpretation of ambiguous specifications.[46]

Generally, the owner has the right to reject defective work at any time prior to acceptance of the work, and an inspector's observation of nonconforming work does not necessarily preclude later rejection.[47] However, if an owner's delay in rejecting nonconforming work substantially prejudiced the contractor, the owner may be estopped, or prevented, from later rejecting the work.[48] Estoppel will be more likely if the contractor has given clear notice regarding its interpretation of the standards and methods of performance that were used and that later became the subject of the dispute.

12.13 *Delay and Disruption* In each construction contract there is an implied obligation on the part of the owner not to unduly delay or hinder the contractor's work. This duty extends to the owner's exercise of its inspection rights. Thus, the standard federal inspection clause for construction contracts, as prescribed by FAR § 52.246-12(e), states: "[T]he Government shall perform all inspection and tests in a manner that will not unnecessarily delay the work."

---

[43] *See Williams & Dunlap*, ASBCA No. 6145, 63-1 BCA ¶ 3834.

[44] *See Acme Missiles & Constr. Corp.*, ASBCA No. 13671, 69-1 BCA ¶ 7698; *Byson v. City of Los Angeles*, 308 P.2d 765 (Cal. Ct. App. 1957); *Denton Constr. Co. v. Missouri State Highway Comm'n*, 454 S.W.2d 44 (Mo. 1970).

[45] *See Dondlinger & Sons Constr. Co.*, ASBCA No. 13651, 70-2 BCA ¶ 8603.

[46] *See Frederick P. Warrick Co.*, ASBCA No. 9644, 65-2 BCA ¶ 5169.

[47] *Forsberg & Gregory, Inc.*, ASBCA No. 18457, 75-1 BCA ¶ 11,293.

[48] *See Baltimore Contractors, Inc.*, ASBCA No. 15852, 73-2 BCA ¶ 10,281.

This principle is similarly recognized in the AIA A201 § 9.10.1, which requires that the architect, upon receipt of a final payment application and written notice that the work is ready for final inspection and acceptance, "will promptly make such inspection." Paragraph 9.6.1 of AGC Document No. 200 contains a similar requirement for prompt inspections by the owner and its architect/engineer. Thus, where unreasonable delay or interference can be demonstrated on the part of the owner in conducting the final inspection, a contractor may be entitled to a time extension and recovery of additional costs or breach of contract damages.

To determine whether or not a particular delay was unreasonable, reference must be made to the surrounding facts or circumstances. The basic test is whether the inspector's actions were reasonably necessary to protect the owner's interests, or whether the owner's legitimate objectives could have been accomplished by some other, less disruptive, means.[49]

Compensable delays also may be caused by multiple and inconsistent inspections.[50] Likewise, the owner's failure to make a timely inspection after a request by the contractor may result in owner liability.[51]

What may be a timely inspection in one situation can amount to an unreasonable delay in another. For example, in one case, a government inspection three days after the contractor's request was held to be an unreasonable delay, but in another case a 10-day delay was not sufficient to make the inspection untimely.[52]

Unreasonable delays in the review and approval of shop drawings, equipment submittals, material submittals, plans of operations, and the government's determinations as to what corrective action is required when defects are discovered have all been held to entitle the contractor to relief. Likewise, when an inspector interferes with a contractor's employees, disrupts the performance sequence, or otherwise causes the work to be performed less efficiently, the contractor may be entitled to be reimbursed for the cost of resulting extra work. Such actions may also be construed as a breach of contract.[53]

12.14 Inspection by the Architect/Engineer/Inspector

The party performing the actual inspections has the duty and obligation to perform those inspections adequately and without negligence. Architects, engineers, construction managers, and government inspectors may be liable to the owner, contractor, or other third parties as a result of failing to fulfill their inspection duties. For example, in *Dufficy & Sons, Inc. v. BRW, Inc.,*[54] the court found that an inspector

---

[49] *See S. S. Silberblatt, Inc. v. United States*, 433 F.2d 1314 (Ct. Cl. 1970).

[50] *See WRB Corp.*, *supra* note 32; *State Highway Comm'n v. Garton & Garton, Inc.*, 418 P.2d 15 (Wyo. 1966).

[51] *See Larco-Indus. Painting Corp.*, ASBCA No. 14647, 73-2 BCA ¶ 10,073.

[52] *Compare Kingston Bituminous Prod. Co.*, ASBCA No. 9964, 67-2 BCA ¶ 6638 *with Fullerton Constr. Co.*, ASBCA No. 11500, 67-2 BCA ¶ 6394.

[53] *See WRB Corp.*, *supra* note 32.

[54] 74 P.3d 380 (Colo. Ct. App. 2002).

working for the project architect was an agent of the architect. Therefore, the inspector owed the owner *and* the contractor a professional duty to act with the degree of knowledge, skill, and judgment in the manner a reasonably prudent inspector would under the same or similar circumstances. As a result, the inspector's misrepresentations to the owner and the contractor that a subcontractor's work was in conformance with the contract documents rendered the inspector liable to the owner and contractor.

Moreover, the standards for inspection in a contract will be construed to try to reconcile inconsistencies. Where one provision in a contract called for inspections to be performed by sampling supplies by lot while another provision called for all supplies to meet specific standards, the court reconciled the alleged differences in the inspection standards, finding that the inspections of the lots did not override the rights of the owner and contractor to reject individual materials that did not meet the specific standards.[55]

Generally, an architect/engineer is required to visit the site at regular intervals, but is not required to perform exhaustive or continuous on-site inspections to check the quality or quantity of the work.[56] The architect/engineer is also generally required to keep the owner informed of the progress of the work and to guard the owner against defects and deficiencies in the work.

If an inspecting party such as an architect fails to make adequate periodic inspections during the work, an owner may challenge whether that architect is immune from liability by virtue of a contract provision stating that the architect is not responsible for the contractor's acts or omissions. In one case, the court noted that the architect was required to visit the site periodically in order to be familiar with the progress and quality of the work, keep the owner informed about the work's progress and quality, and guard the owner against defects in the work. Furthermore, the architect's obligation to issue certificates of payment required familiarity with both quantity and quality of work. Therefore, the exculpatory provision excusing the architect from responsibility for construction methods and for the acts or omissions of the contractor did not immunize the architect from liability flowing from a breach of its duty to the owner.[57]

In another case, an architectural/engineering firm was held liable to an owner and the contractor's surety for negligently inspecting a roof. Even after repeated warnings by a roofing expert that the roof was not being installed in accordance with the contract specifications, the architect/engineer's resident inspector informed the owner that the roof was fine and that "you don't have to worry about it." In reliance on the inspector's assurances, the owner accepted the building and released all payments to the contractor. A few months later, the roof began to leak and the contractor's attempts to solve the problem were unsuccessful.

---

[55] *Seabury Constr. Corp. v. Jeffrey Chain Corp.*, 289 F.3d 63 (2nd Cir. 2002).

[56] AIA A201 § 4.2.2 (1997 ed.) states that "[t]he Architect will not be required to make exhaustive or continuous on-site inspections to check the quality or quantity of the Work."

[57] *Diocese of Rochester v. R. Monde Contractors, Inc.*, 562 N.Y.S.2d 593 (App. Div. 1989), *aff'd,* 561 N.Y.S.2d 659 (1990).

The court ruled that the architect/engineer had a duty to inspect the roof construction and to protect the owner against poor work by the contractor. An architect/engineer is required to exercise ordinary professional skills and diligence, and this duty is nondelegable. Since the architect/engineer breached its obligation to the owner under the above circumstances, the architect/engineer was liable.[58]

12.15   Inspection by the Contractor

The contractor's inspection duties in the routine performance of a construction contract include not only the inspection of the work in place, but an inspection of job conditions, including job cleanup, potential safety hazards, and monitoring the progress of the work and schedule. In addition to its own work, the contractor must inspect the work of its subcontractors and material suppliers.

Many construction contracts impose specific burdens upon the contractor to perform such inspections.[59] However, even if no specific contract burden is applied, prudence dictates that such inspection be carried out at all levels and in a routine fashion. It should include a regular process for reporting and exchanging information in order for the contractor to promptly, expeditiously, and economically complete the project. Additionally, contractors generally cannot rely on inspection provisions allowing owners to perform inspections to relieve the contractor of its duty to perform its work properly if the owner's inspection fails to detect deficiencies in the contractor's work.[60]

The contractor may also be required to obtain test results on work in place or materials to be used. Normally, these are obtained through designated independent testing laboratories. For example, one usually must make test cylinders of the concrete mix. Sometimes such tests are prescribed by the specifications, and in other cases they are imposed by industry standards incorporated expressly or impliedly in the contract documents. These inspections not only satisfy the contractor's obligations to the owner but also help the contractor monitor its own work. They also establish empirical data and useful evidence in the event disputes later develop or there is a failure.

In federal government construction, the standard federal inspection clause places primary responsibility for contract compliance on the contractor. In addition, most federal agencies have included provisions in construction contracts that place on the contractor the specific duty to conduct inspections and ensure that the work complies with the plans and specifications. For example, one clause provides that "[t]he Contractor shall maintain an adequate inspection system and perform such inspections as will *ensure* that the work performed under the contract conforms to contract requirements. The Contractor shall maintain complete inspection records and make them available to the Government."[61] Similarly, the contract and applicable regulations

---

[58] *URS Co., Inc. v. Gulfport-Biloxi Regional Airport Auth.*, 544 So. 2d 824 (Miss. 1989). *But see Watson, Watson, Rutland/Architects, Inc. v. Montgomery County Bd. of Educ.*, 559 So. 2d 168 (Ala. 1990).

[59] *See* **Section 12.3** and notes 5 to 14.

[60] *See Burlington, supra* note 1.

[61] FAR § 52.246-12(b) (emphasis added).

may also include various contractor record-keeping and/or certification requirements. In one case, the board gave a strict interpretation to such a requirement.[62] The contract required the contractor to designate an individual who would be responsible to specifically test each unit before delivery and to issue a certification. Instead, the contractor relied upon the supplier's testing procedure and certification, which did not comply with the contract's requirements. The contracting officer terminated the contractor for default because of the contractor's failure to provide the required inspection. The default termination was upheld on the grounds that the government was entitled to the specific type of inspection set forth in the contract.

12.16   ACCEPTANCE

12.17   Overview

Acceptance of a project is of great significance. Acceptance generally limits the owner's ability to complain of defects and reject work. Acceptance may also commence the running of warranties. Contractors and owners often dispute when the project is complete, which frequently results in the withholding of formal acceptance by the owner. The theory of constructive acceptance, however, has evolved to help contractors avoid the harsh consequences of the unreasonable withholding of formal acceptance. A theory closely related to constructive acceptance is substantial completion. This theory recognizes the point at which the owner has received the benefit of the bargain—usually in the form of the owner's ability to occupy and use the project for its intended purpose—although every detail may not have been completed or corrected.[63]

It is a well-recognized rule of contract law that a party entitled to performance may waive strict performance.[64] In the context of a construction contract, this means that the owner may acquiesce to the contractor's failure to perform according to the strict terms of the agreement. Such waiver or acquiescence is often established through acceptance. Courts are often reluctant, however, to bar an owner's right to recover for defective construction "merely" because of "acceptance."[65]

The standard Inspection of Construction clause in federal government contracts indicates that ". . . [a]cceptance shall be final and conclusive except as regards latent defects, fraud, gross mistakes amounting to fraud, or the Government's rights under any warranty or guarantee."[66]

In private construction, the AGC 200 provides that final payment constitutes a waiver of claims except those reserved in writing at the time of final payment, and claims relating to liens or similar encumbrances, warranties, defective work, and latent defects.[67]

---

[62] *See Acorn Specialty & Supply Co.*, GSBCA No. 7577, 85-2 BCA ¶ 17,995.

[63] *See J. M. Beeson Co. v. Satori*, 553 So. 2d 180 (Fla. Dist. Ct. App. 1989).

[64] *See Trustees of Ind. Univ. v. Aetna Cas. & Sur. Co.*, 920 F.2d 429 (7th Cir. 1990).

[65] *Davidge v. H. H. Constr. Co.*, 432 So. 2d 393 (La. Ct. App.1988).

[66] FAR § 52.246-12(i).

[67] AGC Document No. 200 ¶ 9.8.6 (2000 ed.).

Under the AIA A201 the owner's making of final payment constitutes a waiver by the owner of all claims except those arising from:

1. liens, Claims [made pursuant to the contract's dispute resolution process], security interests or encumbrances arising out of the Contract and unsettled;
2. failure of the Work to comply with the requirements of the Contract Documents; or
3. terms of special warranties required by the Contract Documents.[68]

12.18 Types of Acceptance: Formal versus Constructive

Acceptance has been found to occur under AIA A201 when there has been final completion and final payment. In federal contracting, execution of the proper form by an authorized government representative may constitute acceptance. Further, where the owner has taken no positive action to accept or reject, a failure to reject noncomplying work within a reasonable time may constitute a "constructive" acceptance.[69]

In *Tranco Industrial Tires, Inc.*,[70] constructive acceptance was found when the government failed to inspect the painting of fuel tanks for three months. The board ruled that the proper standard for timely acceptance or rejection is "a reasonable time for prompt action under the circumstances." In this case, the board held that a three-month delay from paint sample approval to final inspection was unreasonable and that, while a change in contracting officers justified a two-week delay, it did not justify the balance of the government's tardiness.

In contrast, it has long been recognized that mere occupation and use of a structure by the owner does not constitute acceptance or waiver of defects therein.[71] This rule applies as well when the owner has taken possession of the project with the express understanding that defects will be remedied at a later date.[72]

The AGC 200 provides that occupancy or use of a completed or partially completed portion of the project constitutes substantial completion of the portion of the work used or occupied.[73] The contractor is still responsible to complete uncompleted items.[74]

The 1997 edition of AIA A201 General Conditions (like the 1987 edition before it) contains a section regarding partial occupancy or use of the project by the owner, which provides that "[u]nless otherwise agreed upon, partial occupancy or use of a portion or portions of the Work shall not constitute acceptance of Work not complying with the requirements of the Contract Documents."[75]

---

[68] AIA Document A201 § 9.10.4 (1997 ed.).

[69] *See Havens Steel Co. v. Randolph Eng'g Co.*, 613 F. Supp. 514 (W.D. Mo. 1985), *aff'd*, 813 F.2d 186 (8th Cir. 1987).

[70] ASBCA No. 26305, 83-2 BCA ¶ 16,679.

[71] *See Granite Constr. Co.*, ENG BCA No. 4642, 89-3 BCA ¶ 21,946.

[72] *See Brouillette v. Consolidated Constr. Co. of Fla., Inc.*, 422 So. 2d 176 (La. Ct. App. 1982).

[73] AGC Document No. 200 ¶ 9.7 (2000 ed.).

[74] *Id.* at § 9.6.4.

[75] AIA Document A201 § 9.9.3 (1997 ed.).

In federal construction, the concept of constructive acceptance is better developed than in private construction and is recognized in the procurement regulations, which define acceptance as ". . . the act of an authorized representative of the Government by which the Government, for itself or as agent of another, assumes ownership of existing identified supplies tendered or approves specific services rendered as partial or complete performance of the contract."[76]

Similarly, the "Use and Possession Prior to Completion" clause, prescribed by FAR §§ 36.511 and 52.236-11, provides that "the Government shall have the right to take possession of or use of any completed or partially completed part of the work . . . ," but that "such possession or use shall not be deemed an acceptance of any work under the contract." However, in certain cases where that clause was not employed, government use, possession, or control of the project, coupled with a failure to indicate that the work was not complete, has been deemed to amount to an acceptance.[77] In federal procurement, constructive acceptance, as with formal acceptance, commences the warranty period under the contract.[78]

Moreover, one should also realize that individual actions under the contract, standing alone, may not constitute an acceptance. For example, the boards have held that:

- Payment, by itself, does not constitute an implied acceptance;[79]
- Visits by government representatives during fabrication of equipment did not constitute inspection and acceptance;[80]
- The government's failure to inspect is not an implied acceptance waiving strict compliance;[81] and
- Mere acceptance of the delivery of the supplies is not an implied acceptance.[82]

The specific facts and circumstances must be viewed in light of the applicable contract language and the surrounding circumstances to determine if the owner's actions amount to an acceptance.

12.19 Authority as an Element of Constructive Acceptance

The actual authority of the individual whose action or inaction is being relied upon is a factor that may affect the determination of whether there has been a formal or constructive acceptance. This is especially true in federal government work, since the acceptance will be binding only if made by a person authorized to accept on behalf of the government.[83] In private agency law, an employer may be bound by an

---

[76] FAR § 46.101.

[77] *See Bell & Flynn, Inc.*, ASBCA No. 11038, 66-2 BCA ¶ 5855.

[78] *See Paul Tishman Co.*, GSBCA No. 1099, 1964 BCA ¶ 4256.

[79] *See Abney Constr. Co.*, ASBCA No. 26358, 83-1 BCA ¶ 16,246; *G. M. Co. Mfg.*, ASBCA No. 5345, 60-2 BCA ¶ 2759.

[80] *See J. W. Bateson Co.*, GSBCA No. 3157, 71-1 BCA ¶ 8820.

[81] *See Waterbury Co.*, ASBCA No. 6634, 61-2 BCA ¶ 3158.

[82] *See Lox Equip. Co.*, ASBCA No. 8518, 1964 BCA ¶ 4469.

[83] *See Inter-Tribal Council of Nev., Inc.*, IBCA No. 1234-12-78, 83-1 BCA ¶ 16,433.

employee under the legal theory of apparent authority if the employer has permitted the employee to assume authority or has held the employee out as possessing the requisite authority.[84]

Recognizing the importance of effective government control over the conduct of its agents, the boards and courts have generally rejected the apparent authority rule, holding that actual authority is required to bind the government.[85] Even government personnel with official-sounding titles such as contract specialists, negotiators, and administrators, who handle the day-to-day contracting activity of the government, generally do not have authority to order additional work or otherwise obligate the government.[86]

12.20 Limitations on the Finality of Acceptance

In order for the owner to waive strict performance or to acquiesce in the deviation from the contract documents through acceptance, the owner or its authorized representative generally must be aware of the defect or the deviation.[87] However, courts have ruled that an owner waives deviations from the contract where the owner should have been aware of the deviations. Whether particular acts or conduct amount to an acceptance, and thus a waiver of strict performance, is a fact question that depends upon the circumstances of each case.

Defects that are not apparent and that cannot be discovered until a later date (i.e., latent defects) are not deemed to have been accepted. This is especially true on federal construction projects.[88] Also, where a contractor knowingly misrepresents the condition or quality of its work with the intent to deceive, the government is considered to have been induced to accept defective work as a result and may recover the costs of repairing such defects from the contractor.[89]

Similarly, where the contractor makes gross mistakes or misrepresents a material fact without the intent to deceive the government, the contractor may be liable for such defects despite government acceptance of the work. One such case involved contractor changes to a drawing that had been previously approved by the government, and the contractor's subsequent failure to alert government officials to the change before the drawing was used in checking the contractor's production run.[90]

Closely related to waiver by acceptance is the issue of whether progress payments constitute a waiver of defects. The jurisdictions appear evenly divided, as some state courts rule that partial payments constitute a waiver of defects while other states rule

---

[84] Restatement (Second) of Agency § 8.

[85] *See Federal Crop Ins. Corp. v. Merrill*, 332 U.S. 380 (1947).

[86] *See, e.g., General Elec. Co. v. United States*, 412 F.2d 1215 (Ct. Cl.), *mot. for reconsid. denied*, 416 F.2d 1320 (1969).

[87] *See Cantrell v. Woodhill Enters., Inc.*, 160 S.E.2d 476 (N.C. 1968). *See also South Carolina Elec. & Gas Co. v. Combustion Eng'g, Inc.*, 322 S.E.2d 453 (S.C. Ct. App. 1984).

[88] *See Kaminer Constr. Corp. v. United States*, 488 F.2d 980 (Ct. Cl. 1973).

[89] *See Nasatka & Sons, Inc.*, IBCA No. 1157-6-77, 79-2 BCA ¶ 14,064.

[90] *See Catalytic Eng'g & Mfg. Corp.*, ASBCA No. 15257, 72-1 BCA ¶ 9342.

the opposite way.[91] The argument for waiver of defects by partial payment is much more persuasive when the defects were known at the time of payment, when the owner or its representative failed to protest, and when there was no express agreement to remedy them. Generally, however, the contract will provide that the making of a progress payment will not constitute acceptance of any work not in compliance with the contract documents.[92]

Waiver or acceptance of defective performance by the owner may preclude it from refusing to pay the contractor the reasonable value of the work or its price according to the terms of the contract.[93] Similarly, where the owner accepts the work as being in full compliance with the contract, it is generally not possible for the owner to later maintain an action against the contractor to recover for deviations from the contract documents or to recoup such damages in an action brought by the contractor for compensation.[94]

12.21   Contract Provisions Related to the Finality of Acceptance

Contracts often include clauses aimed at qualifying the significance of acceptance. For example, AGC 200 provides that final payment does not constitute a waiver of claims reserved in writing at the time of final payment, and claims relating to liens or similar encumbrances, warranties, defective work, and latent defects.[95] AIA A201 § 9.10.4, quoted above, provides that final acceptance and the making of final payment does not constitute a waiver by the owner of any claims based upon the work's nonconformance with contract requirements.[96]

In the absence of a nonwaiver contract provision, a waiver may be implied if the owner or its representative had an opportunity during the progress of the work to inspect and reject work or materials that obviously did not comply with the contract requirements but failed to do so.[97] In such a case, a failure to object during the progress of the work may amount to a waiver of the defect. However, the mere presence of the owner or the owner's representative at the site does not necessarily constitute a waiver, such as when a defect is not readily discoverable.[98]

Similarly, under the standard "Inspection of Construction" clause in federal government contracts, also quoted above, there are several exceptions to the finality of acceptance, such as latent defects, fraud, and gross mistakes amounting to fraud. In addition, the government has its rights under the warranty or guarantee provisions of the contract.[99]

---

[91] *See* W. R. Habeeb, Annotation, "Partial Payment on Private Building or Construction Contract as Waiver," 66 A.L.R.2d 570 (1959).

[92] *See, e.g.,* AIA Document A201 § 9.6.6 (1997 ed.).

[93] *See Milaeger Well Drilling Co., supra* note 25.

[94] *City of Gering v. Patricia G. Smith Co.,* 337 N.W.2d 747 (Neb. 1983); *John Price Assocs., Inc. v. Davis,* 588 P.2d 713 (Utah 1978).

[95] AGC Document No. 200 ¶ 9.8.6 (2000 ed.).

[96] *See* **Section 12.17** and note 68.

[97] *See Florida Ice Mach. Corp. v. Branton Insulation, Inc.,* 290 So. 2d 415 (La. Ct. App. 1974); *see also Brand S. Roofing,* ASBCA No. 24688, 82-1 BCA ¶ 15,513.

[98] *See J. W. Bateson Co., supra* note 80.

[99] *See* **Section 12.17** and note 66.

12.22 Substantial Completion

Substantial completion has been defined in numerous ways and has been the subject of extensive litigation. Generally, when the owner has the use and benefit of the contractor's work and the project is capable of being used for its intended purpose, substantial completion has occurred.[100]

AIA A201, § 9.8.1, defines substantial completion as "the stage in the progress of the Work when the Work or a designated portion thereof is sufficiently complete in accordance with the Contract Documents so that the Owner can occupy or utilize the Work for its intended use." Similarly, paragraph 2.3.17 of AGC 200 provides that substantial completion occurs on the date when the contractor's work is "sufficiently complete in accordance with the Contract Documents so that the Owner may occupy or utilize the Project, or a designated portion, for the use for which it is intended."

The date of substantial completion is often a crucial date in construction claims and disputes, for several reasons. First, once substantial completion has been attained, the owner has received essentially what was bargained for and the contractor has substantially performed its obligations; thus the contractor is usually entitled to the balance of the contract price less the cost of remedying minor defects. Second, liquidated damages generally stop after this date.[101] Third, substantial completion may trigger the warranty period under the contract.[102]

In many states, substantial completion marks the commencement of a special limitation period, sometimes called a "statute of repose," for actions against persons performing or furnishing design, planning, supervision, observation of construction, or construction of any improvement to real property. Also, upon having substantially completed its contractual obligations, the contractor may also recover on the contract and need not rely upon the equitable theory of *quantum meruit* or some other legal theory in order to recover for work performed and materials supplied.[103]

12.23 Final Completion

Upon final completion (generally defined as when the punchlist work has been completed after substantial completion and the project is ready for final inspection and acceptance[104]), the contractor's work generally should be finally accepted.[105] At final completion, in some states, the contractor will be relieved of liability to third parties with which it did not have a contract.[106] This doctrine, often referred to as the "doctrine

---

[100] *See J. M. Beeson Co.*, *supra* note 63; *Royal Ornamental Iron, Inc. v. Devon Bank*, 336 N.E.2d 105 (Ill. App. Ct. 1975); *Waynick Constr. Inc. v. York*, 319 S.E.2d 304 (N.C. Ct. App. 1984).

[101] *See Hungerford Constr. Co. v. Florida Citrus Exposition*, 410 F.2d 1229 (5th Cir.), *cert. denied*, 396 U.S. 928 (1969); *Phillips v. Ben M. Hogan Co.*, 594 S.W.2d 39 (Ark. Ct. App. 1990).

[102] *See, e.g.*, AGC Document No 200 ¶ 9.6.3 (2000 ed.).

[103] *See Cox v. Fremont County Pub. Bldg. Auth.*, 415 F.2d 882 (10th Cir. 1969); 13 Am. Jur. 2d, Building and Construction Contracts §§ 41 & 110.

[104] *See, e.g.*, AGC Document No. 200 ¶ 9.8 (2000 ed.); AIA A201 § 9.10.1 (1997 ed.).

[105] *Id.*

[106] *See, e.g.*, *First Church of Christ Scientist v. City of Seattle*, 964 P.2d 374 (Wash. Ct. App. 1998); *Fisher v. State Highway Comm'n of Mo.*, 948 S.W.2d 607 (Mo. 1997); *Blake v. Calumet Constr. Co.*, 674 N.E.2d 167 (Ind. 1996).

of completion and acceptance," is based on the concept of avoiding excessive litigation.[107] Even in those states that still accept the doctrine of completion and acceptance, courts have found exceptions to the doctrine, including where the defect is imminently dangerous, the defect is hidden to the extent it cannot be discovered through a reasonable inspection, the contractor knows of the defect but has failed to reveal it, or the contractor's negligence was not part of the contract work.[108]

Other states have rejected the completion and acceptance doctrine, finding that third parties are not barred from suing contractors for injuries after final completion.[109] These courts have generally found that it is unreasonable for an owner's acceptance to prevent third parties from pursuing claims against contractors whose conduct leads to an injury to a third party.

12.24   Revocation of Acceptance

Revocation of acceptance may be available under special circumstances. For federal government contracts, the government may revoke acceptance if it discovers latent defects, fraud, or gross mistakes amounting to fraud.

"Latent defects" are flaws in the contractor's work that existed when the government accepted the work but were not discovered and could not have been discovered by a reasonable inspection.[110] Latent defects must be distinguished from "patent defects," or defects that had been discovered by the time of acceptance or that should have been discovered through a reasonable and competent inspection. Where latent defects give the government the right to revoke acceptance, the government has only warranty rights against the contractor after acceptance of patent defects.

Upon discovery of a latent defect, the government may revoke its previous acceptance and demand the contractor take corrective action. Alternatively, the government may correct the problem and charge the costs against the contractor.

The question therefore typically turns on whether the defect should have been discovered through a reasonable inspection performed with ordinary care. What is "reasonable" varies with the facts and circumstances of each case. For example, welding defects in a heat distribution system that later caused leaks were held to be latent in one case.[111] However, in another contract where the government was responsible for conducting X-ray inspections of structural steel, welding defects were held not to be latent.[112]

Contractor quality control inspection requirements may play a part in the determination of whether a defect is found to be latent. A defect, even if discoverable

---

[107] *See, e.g., First Church of Christ Scientist, supra* note 106.

[108] *See, e.g., Irwin v. Hoover Treated Wood Products, Inc.,* 906 D. Supp. 530 (E.D. Mo. 1995) (accepting the imminently dangerous, hidden defect and superior contractor knowledge exceptions); *First Church of Christ Scientist, supra* note 106 (accepting the exception for negligence in noncontract work).

[109] *See, e.g., Suneson v. Holloway Constr. Co.,* 992 S.W.2d 79 (Ark. 1999); *Pierce v. ALSC Architects, P.S.,* 890 P.2d 1254 (Mont. 1995).

[110] *See Kaminer Construction, supra* note 88; *F. W. Lang Co.,* ASBCA No. 2677, 57-1 BCA ¶ 1334.

[111] *See Cottman Mechanical Contractors, Inc.,* ASBCA No. 11387, 67-2 BCA ¶ 6566.

[112] *See Gordon H. Ball, Inc., supra* note 19.

through a reasonable government inspection, may be found to be latent if the contractor has the primary responsibility to inspect.[113]

The burden of proof is on the government to prove that the defect exists, was latent, and that the defect was unknown at the time of acceptance. Finally, to have a cause of action against the contractor, the government must show injury and a connection between the defect and the injury. The burden of proving each of these elements can be difficult. The passage of time, the departure of witnesses, intervening events, subsequent construction work, improper maintenance or repairs, and natural wear and tear are only some of the problems that the government may have to sort out.

Once the government discovers a latent defect, it must act promptly to demand corrections from the contractor. In one case, a two-year delay between the time the government discovered the defect and the time it demanded corrections from the contractor was found to be a constructive acceptance of the defect.[114]

Fraud may also justify revocation of acceptance. Where a contractor knowingly misrepresents the condition or quality of its work with the intention to deceive, and the government is induced to accept defective work as a result, the government may revoke its acceptance and recover the costs of repairing such defects.[115] (In addition to recovering the costs of repair, the government may also pursue the contractor under both civil and criminal fraud statutes.)

The government may also revoke acceptance of work where the contractor makes "gross mistake amounting to fraud." This type of situation involves a major mistake by the contractor "so serious or uncalled for it was not to be reasonably expected, or justifiable, in the case of a responsible contractor" or a mistake that "cannot be reconciled in good faith."[116]

12.25 PROJECT COMMISSIONING AND POST-ACCEPTANCE FACILITY OPERATIONS

12.26 Performance Risks

One emerging trend with some owners is to combine the traditional quality control procedures with a requirement that the contractor be responsible for the operation and maintenance of the facility for a fixed period of time after the final completion and acceptance. The price for that work is typically fixed as the time of award. The rationale for this added requirement is that this operational responsibility will provide a practical incentive to the contractor to ensure that the equipment, systems, and workmanship meet all of the quality control standards.

For example, the federal government has recently begun to include operation, maintenance, and repair provisions in some contracts, requiring contractors to provide maintenance and inspection services during the course of the project, through

---

[113] *See Tricon-Triangle Contractors*, ENGBCA No. 5553, 92-1 BCA ¶ 24,667.

[114] *See Utley-James, Inc.*, GSBCA No. 6831, 88-1 BCA ¶ 20,518.

[115] *See Henry Angelo & Co.*, ASBCA No. 30502, 87-1 BCA ¶ 19,619.

[116] *See Catalytic Eng'g & Mfg. Corp.*, ASBCA No. 15257, 72-1 BCA ¶ 9342.

commissioning, and postacceptance of the project. In one recent contract for construction of a research facility, the Department of the Navy Facilities Engineering Command included provisions for service calls, preventive maintenance inspections, repair work, and other services that would begin during the construction of the project and last for five years after beneficial occupancy. These services and work activities would be provided at a fixed price established during the bidding or proposal phase for the contract. The specifications stated that the contractor would provide labor, transportation, equipment, materials, tools, supplies, management, and supervision for preventive and corrective maintenance and repairs to maintain building systems, including structural components, exterior and interior finishes, plumbing, HVAC, and electrical systems. The contract obligates the contractor to maintain the facility, including specialty equipment and associated equipment within the facility "to a standard that prevents deterioration and corrects deficiencies in a timely manner to insure full life expectancy of the facility, structures, and associated equipment."

As part of the requirements, the contractor is to develop and implement a preventive maintenance, inspection, and service program (PMIS). The PMIS is to be submitted to the government's designated representative 15 days prior to the beneficial occupancy date. An annual PMIS schedule is to be submitted with the initial program plan and every 12 months thereafter during the contract period. The program plan is to include all inspection checks and maintenance activities called for in the operation and maintenance manuals. Minor deficiencies requiring no more than three hours of labor and a material cost of less than $250 are considered to be part of the contractor's contract price. Deficiencies exceeding those limits are to be corrected as service calls, repair work, or indefinite quantity work; but excessive or repeated system breakdowns or deficiencies are considered as an indication of unsatisfactory performance of the PMIS by the contractor. Changes to correct deficiencies are to be performed at no cost to the government.

While the systems will be initially commissioned effective on the beneficial occupancy date, the contractor is also required to "recommission" the HVAC systems at two years after the beneficial occupancy date and again at the end of the contract maintenance period (five years after the beneficial occupancy date). Recommissioning includes performance tests, the results of which are to be compared with the initial commissioning test results. Any areas showing degraded performance are to be addressed with required maintenance to repair or arrest and correct any reductions in performance identified in the recommissioning process. In effect, the contractor is required to maintain the systems in the project for five years at the level they were performing at beneficial occupancy. This places a very high burden on the contractor because it effectively requires the contractor to ensure that five years after beneficial occupancy the systems operate as effectively as they were required to operate under the contract at beneficial occupancy.

A contractor taking on these responsibilities, in effect, becomes the maintenance contractor and not just a construction contractor. The contractor is assuming the responsibility of providing inspection services and maintenance services at its expense for five years after beneficial occupancy. Construction contractors that are not used to providing maintenance services will probably find it necessary to retain inspection and/or maintenance subcontractors to perform the work. Contractors would need to carefully select the inspection and maintenance subcontractors to be sure that they can perform the work in a cost-effective manner and that they have the financial ability to remain in business for the five-year maintenance period after beneficial occupancy.

12.27   Bonding Considerations

A contractor faced with post-acceptance inspection and maintenance obligations that extend for months or years may be faced with extended bonding requirements, not just the extensive inspection and maintenance obligations. Where a contract requires ongoing inspection and maintenance by the contractor for five years after beneficial occupancy, the contractor's performance bond (and possibly its payment bond) may remain at risk for the entire inspection and maintenance period, plus for some period of time after the maintenance period expires. This may create additional problems for contractors that find their bonding capacity affected for years by the ongoing inspection and maintenance obligations, in addition to extra premiums for bonds at risk for an extended period of time. Contractors facing the extended inspection and maintenance requirements need to clarify during the bidding or proposal stage the extent to which their bonds are to remain in effect if the contract requires extended inspection and maintenance.

12.28   CONTRACTUAL WARRANTIES

It is generally recognized in both commercial law and government contract law that there are two kinds of warranties that accompany virtually any construction contract. These are: (1) express warranties, which are express promises, either oral or written, and (2) implied warranties, which commercial law implies from the nature of the transaction between the parties unless the contract expressly provides that such warranties are inapplicable.

12.29   Express Warranties

Express warranties relating to construction contract performance can be complex and do not have to be labeled as a warranty or guarantee in order to have the effect of an express warranty. An express warranty has been defined as "[a]ny affirmation of fact or any promise by the seller relating to the goods is an express warranty if the natural tendency of such affirmation or promise is to induce the owner to purchase the goods, and if the buyer purchases the goods relying thereon."[117]

In this regard, it is essential that both parties to a construction contract carefully review all the contract plans and documents to determine whether requirements and language that may have the effect of providing an express warranty are intended

[117] S. Williston, *A Treatise on the Law of Contracts* § 970, at 484 (3rd ed. 1964).

and are desirable under all the surrounding facts and circumstances. Without this type of careful review and analysis, the owner may find that it is buying protection that it did not desire. Conversely, the contractor may find that it warranted a certain result or performance and that the risk attending such a warranty was not considered in the preparation of the bid or proposal for the work.

The contractor may "expressly warrant" that the material and workmanship furnished for the project are free from defects for a specified period of time. Liability under these express warranties expands the scope of the contractor's responsibility for defective work beyond the date of final acceptance. Generally, the courts construe these warranties as additions to, not substitutions for, other responsibilities of the contractor.[118]

AGC 200, Paragraph 3.8, provides that the contractor warrants all materials and equipment are new, of good quality, in conformance with the contract documents, and free from defective workmanship. That contract provision also provides that the contractor will provide evidence of the quality and type of materials furnished, and that the contractor's work shall be free from material defects not intrinsic to the design or materials required by the contract. The contractor is also responsible for providing any special or extended warranties required by the contract. AGC 200, Paragraph 3.9, further provides that the contractor will correct any defective work within one year of substantial completion.

Similarly, AIA A201 contains a number of express warranties. One such warranty is a general warranty that guarantees all equipment and materials are new, in conformance with the contract documents, and that all work is of good quality. AIA A201 § 3.5.1 provides:

> The Contractor warrants to the Owner and Architect that materials and equipment furnished under the Contract will be of good quality and new unless otherwise required or permitted by the Contract Documents, that the Work will be free from defects not inherent in the quality required or permitted, and that the Work will conform with the requirements of the Contract Documents.

AIA A201, § 12.2.2.1, also provides that the contractor will correct any defective work within one year of substantial completion.

This express warranty may be limited only by the applicable statute of limitations. Thus the provision could extend the contractor's obligations for a substantial period.[119] Furthermore, this period may be extended even further by the so-called discovery rule. This rule provides that a cause of action does not accrue, and that the statute of limitations period does not even begin to "tick" until the defect is, or should have been, discovered.[120]

---

[118] *See Tassan v. United Dev. Co.*, 410 N.E.2d 902 (Ill. App. Ct. 1980).

[119] *See, e.g., Corp. of Mercer Univ. v. National Gypsum Co.*, 368 S.E.2d 732 (Ga. 1988) (statute of limitations in construction-related cases begins to run upon substantial completion and runs for four years in Georgia) and *Colormatch Exteriors, Inc. v. Hickey*, 569 S.E.2d 495 (Ga. 2002) (reiterating *Mercer University* decision but further holding that applicable statutes of limitation do not begin to run as to claims against a contractor/owner making improvements to its own property for the express purpose of sale of the property until the initial sale of the improved property, regardless of the date of substantial completion).

[120] *See Arst v. Man Barker, Inc.*, 655 S.W.2d 845 (Mo. Ct. App. 1983).

Warranties that expressly state a specific duration, such as 12 months, generally do not limit other avenues of recovery, and do not work to reduce applicable statutes of limitation.[121]

Additional express warranties may be included in a contract in connection with equipment supplied by the contractor. Such specific warranties are usually spelled out under the provisions of the specifications to which they apply, rather than in the general conditions. They often are in the nature of guarantees of performance and an agreement to repair defects for a specified period of time.

A warranty is generally not waived by final payment or completion.[122] The express warranties required by the contract documents generally begin to run from the date of substantial completion.[123] Other special warranties may commence at delivery of the machinery or commencement of operations.

Contractors performing projects with phased completion requirements need to ensure that the warranties from equipment suppliers are consistent with the contractor's warranty to owner. It is not unusual for a contract with phased completion dates to provide that the contractor's warranty to the owner for all systems begins at the date of substantial completion or acceptance of the final phase, even though systems in the earlier phases have been previously put in operation. Equipment suppliers' warranties are often triggered by either delivery or first operation. In this situation, the contractor may face a gap in the warranty coverage. While a supplier may be willing to agree to an extended warranty during the bid or proposal phase at no extra cost, an effort to extend the supplier's warranty at the time of project completion may be very costly.

12.30   Implied Warranties

Both commercial and government contracts have been held to contain warranties that are implied by law for the benefit of one of the parties to the contract. Probably the best-known implied warranty in construction is the implied warranty attached to design information furnished by one of the parties to the contract. *See* **Chapters 5 and 9.**

When there are no express warranties made by the contractor, courts will often imply a warranty of good workmanship. The formulation of this implied warranty differs from jurisdiction to jurisdiction. Courts have stated that contractors warrant that they will perform in a "workmanlike manner and without negligence,"[124] or that the work will be done in a "good and workmanlike manner."[125]

---

[121] *See Mounts v. Parker*, 727 P.2d 594 (Okla. 1986).

[122] *See* AIA Document A201 § 9.10.4 (1997 ed.).

[123] *See, e.g.,* AIA Document A201 § 12.2.2.1 (1997 ed.).

[124] *See Kubby v. Crescent Steel*, 466 P.2d 753 (Ariz. 1970).

[125] *See Moore v. Werner*, 418 S.W.2d 918 (Tex. Civ. App. 1967); *see also Scott v. Strickland*, 69 P.2d 45 (Kan. Ct. App. 1984).

➤ POINTS TO REMEMBER

The following are practical pointers to remember during the construction of a project. These practical pointers relate to the inspection, acceptance, and warranty aspects of a construction project.

Inspection

- Whether you are the owner, architect, contractor, or a subcontractor, quality assurance is a key to avoiding disputes. The principal obligation for assuring quality is on the contractor. The contractor has the responsibility to comply strictly with the plans and specifications. In government contracts, the contractor has an obligation to establish a system to assure quality performance. However, as the case law demonstrates, the owner and architect can also be liable for costs arising from improper inspections.

- The owner and contractor should consider the cost of inspections at the time of bid. Generally, the owner and contractor are each responsible for their cost of inspection. The contractor has the obligation to assist the owner or the government in inspecting completed work. The owner has the right to conduct reasonable inspections. The owner also has the right to reinspect and reject work that was previously inspected. The owner must remember, however, that it cannot conduct unreasonable or wholly inconsistent inspections.

- The owner generally must perform its inspection so as not to unduly delay the contractor's work. The contractor should promptly notify the owner when inspections are required and should also notify the owner or government when the inspections are delaying the contractor's work. As with all construction matters, written documentation regarding delays, hindrances, or interferences is a must to protect your rights.

- If a dispute arises regarding whether certain work was wrongfully rejected, the contractor should investigate the methods used by the inspector. If work is rejected improperly, the contractor may be entitled to an extension of time and added compensation for the extra work. Again, to protect your interests, whether you are the owner or contractor, written documentation regarding the inspections or written notice of the objection to the type of inspection is crucial.

- A constructive change may occur where an inspector improperly interprets the contract specifications. If an inspector is misinterpreting a contract requirement, the contractor should immediately bring this to the attention of the owner or contracting officer. In federal government contracts, if the contractor gets a ruling from the inspector and not the contracting officer, the contractor might not be entitled to additional costs because the government may argue that the inspector did not have authority to make the constructive change.

Acceptance

- Contractors must differentiate between the authority required under a federal government contract versus a private contract. In a federal government contract, acceptance may only occur when the individual with actual authority accepts the work. Generally, only the contracting officer has actual authority to accept the work. However, in private contracts, inspectors and other representatives for the owner may be held to have apparent authority to accept the work.

- Generally, final acceptance requires final completion and final payment. However, under certain circumstances "constructive" acceptance can occur where the owner utilizes an area of the project and acts without objection to any of the contractor's performance. Similarly, where a party delays formal acceptance or rejection for an unreasonable time, constructive acceptance can occur.

- Generally, once the work is accepted, a contractor is relieved of responsibility, except with respect to any remaining warranty obligations. However, a contractor can be liable for latent defects that could not have been discovered at the time of acceptance. In addition, postcompletion operation and maintenance requirements may substantially increase the contractor's responsibilities for the facility.

- An owner can be held to have waived a defect when the owner knew or should have known of the defect at the time of acceptance and accepted the work anyway. However, if the contractor makes a knowing misrepresentation with intent to deceive the owner regarding the completion of the work, the contractor may be liable for the results of the defective performance and for fraud.

- One issue related to acceptance concerns substantial performance. Substantial performance in the construction industry has many legal ramifications. Substantial completion generally occurs when the owner receives what it has bargained for and can occupy and use the project for its intended purpose. Typically the contractor is entitled to recover the contract price minus the cost of remedying minor defects at that time. Furthermore, when substantial completion occurs, the owner is generally not entitled to assess additional liquidated damages.

Warranties

- All parties in the construction realm must be very cautious regarding the creation of express warranties. Most construction contracts contain express warranties; and affirmations of fact or assurances made outside the contract may create an express warranty as well. Generally, the extent of a party's responsibility under an express warranty is limited only by statutes of limitation, in the absence of an express time limitation within the warranty itself.

In some states, the "discovery rule" may even extend the applicable statute of limitation indefinitely.

- Every construction contract carries with it certain implied warranties as well. In the context of project acceptance, the implied warranty of good workmanship may create rights not expressly stated in the contract.

13

MANAGEMENT TECHNIQUES TO LIMIT RISKS AND AVOID DISPUTES

13.1 CONSTRUCTION: A RISK-PRONE BUSINESS

Every business enterprise involves risk identification and management. Construction is especially risky, for nearly every project is unique. Unlike a manufacturing operation in which standard products are assembled in a controlled environment by a relatively stable workforce, construction projects are typically unique structures built on unique sites by a team that has been assembled for that specific purpose. To that extent, each construction project can be viewed as involving the development of a prototype. Even if the actual structure or building is essentially repetitive, the possible variation in the site conditions, the historical low-profit margins, the vagaries of weather, and the changing team of trade contractors and vendors create the potential for significant risks and losses. The allocation of risk and the economic consequences of risk are significant contributors to the fact that construction is a disputes-prone industry. Therefore, prudent participants in the construction process strive to identify and manage risks and seek to avoid disputes by implementing prudent management techniques.

Even successful projects can have claims. Claims are a natural outgrowth of a complex and highly competitive process during which the unexpected often happens. Careful organization and coordination of numerous parties are required, and it may then be outside parties that control many of the circumstances and events that generate claims. The possibility that a claim might develop should not be ignored. The responsible owner, contractor, trade contractor, or designer must recognize the need to anticipate the circumstances that foster claims and develop effective and affirmative strategies for dealing with them.

The best way to handle claims is to anticipate them and avoid them to the extent possible. Despite the uniqueness of each project and its participants, there are certain recurring problems that generate disputes. History repeats itself. Some of those recurring problems can be avoided, or their impact mitigated. At a minimum, some preparation can be made to more effectively address a dispute if one should occur. Of course, too intense a focus on eliminating all risks and anticipating claims and disputes can also create problems or a paralysis, which impairs one's ability to conduct business effectively. A certain element of risk must be recognized and accepted. Risk can only be mitigated, not eliminated.

This chapter focuses on those measures that can be taken at the outset of a project to identify risks, avoid them, or effectively prepare for and successfully deal with disputes when they cannot be avoided. Common sense, planning, skill, and experience can help identify those strategies for avoiding and effectively dealing with disputes.

13.2 QUALIFYING THE PROJECT AND THE PARTICIPANTS

Construction is a cooperative enterprise involving numerous entities and disciplines. These include the design professionals, the owner or developer, the lender, the prime contractor, subcontractors and suppliers, and any sureties. Each has an essential function. A failure by any participant to properly perform its obligations can mean disaster for the entire project and the rest of the participants. Equally important to a successful project is the nature of the work, its location, and any other special requirements or conditions affecting the proposed work. Consequently, it is essential to risk management and dispute avoidance to qualify the project and the key players well before making any commitment to participate in the project.

13.3 Qualifying the Project

Qualifying the project requires that management evaluate all aspects of the work and the probable conditions affecting performance. This evaluation should be done in a systematic manner in order to provide management with an effective tool to qualify the project and to evaluate the company's ability to successfully complete the work. A practical first step in this process is to answer a series of yes/no questions about the potential project, such as those set forth in Table 13.1.

Table 13.1   Qualifying the Project

Topic/Issue	Yes	No
• Does your firm have sufficient relevant experience with this type of work?		
• Does your firm have sufficient relevant experience with projects of this size and complexity?		

Table 13.1   (Continued)

Topic/Issue	Yes	No
• Does your firm have sufficient relevant experience with the performance of similar work in terms of weather conditions and location, and does it have a reliable source of trained workers?		
• Has your prior experience with this type of work included meeting or exceeding the anticipated project margin?		
• Do you have sufficient, relevant experience with the proposed project delivery method?		
• Do you have available a project team and job-site staff with successful experience in managing a project of this type, size, and complexity?		
• Do you have the home office support required for this project?		
• Does the realistic profit potential offset the project risks?		
• Can your company bond the project?		
• Does the bonding requirement substantially impact the company's overall bonding capacity?		
• Does the project involve bonded, postcompletion obligations such as long-term system operation, etc.?		

The term "relevant" is especially important and is intended to ascertain that the experience reflects, in large part, contemporaneous experience of the company's current employees. Depending upon the nature of the question and the response, senior management should carefully review the decision to compete for the work. That review should include an analysis of the risks associated with the project, the actions to mitigate those risks, as well as the potential benefit or profit from performing the work.

Every company should develop an overall business plan, which addresses the company's goals in terms of volume, project size and types, and geographic market. There is no right plan for all companies. One firm might decide to only seek work within a defined geographic area or radius of the home office. Another might focus on particular types of work. The key is to develop a realistic plan and evaluate potential projects against that plan.

13.4   Qualifying the Project Participants

The initial choice of project participants often dictates the destiny of the project, hence is one of the first steps in avoiding claims. Many headaches and actual losses can be avoided simply by investigating the past performance record of the other parties, rather than looking solely at the lowest price or the opportunity to obtain new work. By dealing with reputable companies and individuals with a proven ability to perform, by running credit checks, and by inquiring about the experience of others with that particular company, major risks and big mistakes may be avoided.

Traditionally, the owner is in the best position to control the selection of the project participants, because under many project delivery systems, the owner separately selects the designer and the contractor.[1] The owner can also have a significant impact on subcontractor selection through the use of a subcontract award approval clause. The prime contractor, standing in an analogous position to the owner, has the greater control over the selection of subcontractors, as does the architect or lead designer over the selection of its subconsultants. When the choice of a specific party would create a risk of performance failure, claims, or disputes, to the extent that any reasonable return would be jeopardized, that party should not be used on the project, regardless of price. While the prime contractor cannot select the owner or developer of a project, it can decide on the parties with which it wants to do business, as can subcontractors. Sometimes the risks of a project or of doing business with a particular owner, architect, contractor, or subcontractor are simply too great, and prudence dictates that certain opportunities be forgone.

Higher-volume and backlog figures are meaningless if they engender unnecessary risks and do not translate to profit. Despite the time crunch and euphoria often associated with the beginning of a project, everyone involved should consider certain key factors when evaluating or selecting project participants: the financial condition of the parties, their qualification for bonds, evidence of their technical skills, and their reputation in the industry. Even a cursory investigation of potential project participants may yield clues to future problems.

Similar to the routine use of a checklist to qualify the project, the development of a checklist approach to qualifying the potential participants in a project may help identify situations with an unacceptable level of potential risk or a potential for claims. Table 13.2 contains a series of topics and questions, which are intended to facilitate the qualification of the project participants.

Table 13.2   Qualifying the Participants

The Owner		
Topic/Issue	Yes	No
• Have you previously constructed a project for this owner?		
• If yes, are the key personnel different?		
• Has the owner provided adequate assurance of sufficient financing?		
• Does the owner have experience with the project delivery system selected for the project?		
• Has the owner previously built a project of similar size and complexity to this project?		

---

[1] This process reflects the traditional design-bid-build delivery method. On a design-build project, owners often evaluate the contractor and designer as a team.

Table 13.2   (Continued)

Topic/Issue	Yes	No
• Does the owner have an experienced staff to facilitate the resolution of problems?		
• Does the owner have a history of disputes and litigation?		
• Does the proposed contract allocate risks consistent with customary practices in the industry?		
• If not, is the owner willing to make modifications to the proposed contract documents?		
• Does the proposed contract contain a requirement to exchange documents electronically? Is there a protocol established for that purpose?		
• Will the project use a project Web site or a third-party provider to exchange information electronically?		
• Have the owner and design professional clearly defined those portions of the design, which will be delegated to the contractor?		

The Contractor/Subcontractor

Topic/Issue	Yes	No
• Have you previously worked with this concern?		
• If yes, are the key personnel different?		
• Has your prior experience with this firm been satisfactory?		
• Do you have information on the contractor's/subcontractor's current backlog?		
• Do you have adequate information on the contractor's/subcontractor's finances?		
• Does the contractor/subcontractor have a reputation for promptly paying its subcontractors/vendors?		
• Can the contractor/subcontractor provide bonds?		
• If yes, have you investigated the financial capacity of the proposed surety?		
• Has the contractor/subcontractor identified key project personnel?		
• If so, do they have experience with projects of this type, size, and complexity?		
• Does the contractor/subcontractor have a history of disputes and litigation?		
• Has the contractor/subcontractor been assessed liquidated damages in the past five years?		

Table 13.2   (Continued)

Topic/Issue	Yes	No
• Has the contractor/subcontractor ever failed to complete a project for any reason?		
• Has the contractor/subcontractor ever been terminated for default?		

The Design Team (A/E)

Topic/Issue	Yes	No
• Have you previously built a project with this A/E?		
• If so, are the same people assigned to this project?		
• If so, was the prior experience satisfactory?		
• Is this project similar in size, type, and complexity to prior projects designed by this A/E?		
• Is there any indication that the A/E was not provided adequate fee or time to complete the design?		
• Does the A/E have a good reputation for fairness?		
• Does the A/E have a good reputation for prompt decision making?		
• Do the design documents appear to be complete and coordinated?		
• Are there missing details, incorrect cross-references, dimensions that do not add up, discrepancies between large-scale drawings and details?		
• Do the contract documents contain language purporting to shift the responsibility for the design or the adequacy of the design to the contractor?		
• Do the documents contain unusual requirements for coordination of the various disciplines?		
• Does the design appear to have sufficient space for MEP system installation?		

Depending upon the nature of the answers to these questions, the potential project participants may be able to "qualify" the other participants on the project and to identify circumstances or conditions that are indicative of unusual risks or a potential for disputes. Prudent application of a tailored prequalification checklist should be as essential to risk management as the customary site visit.

Development and consistent use of a standard form to obtain a statement of qualifications on a contractor or subcontractor can facilitate the receipt of information consistent with the goal of qualifying prospective participants in the project. By providing prospective contractors or trade contractors with a document outlining the categories to be addressed, it is possible to increase the possibility of making "apples to applies" comparisons and to elicit more relevant information. Attached to this chapter at **Appendix 13.1** is a copy of a standard form document published by The Associated General Contractors of America (AGC), AGC Document No. 221, Contractor's Statement of Qualifications for a Specific Project. This document is contained in AGC's DocuBuilder® contract document software as part of its 200 Series of documents and provides an excellent tool to solicit prequalification information in its current form or modified for specific trade contractors.

Money, if not "the root of all evil," is the source of many disputes and claims that arise on a construction project. The financial resources of the owner are of paramount concern. An underfinanced owner virtually dooms any project. Although the possibility of lien rights might provide comfort, if the owner goes under, the probability of full and complete payment to the contractor is very low. Considering the preeminent influence of the owner on the success or failure of a project, contractors and architects are wise to subject the owner's background to an informal "prequalification" process, like that used on other project participants, to confirm that the owner has the capacity to meet its commitments. In addition to other independent sources that may be available to obtain information about the owner's finances, many industry standard form contracts expressly obligate the owner to provide evidence of project financing at the inception of the project.

For example, Paragraph 4.2 of the Standard Form of Agreement and General Conditions Between Owner and Contractor, AGC Document No. 200 (2000 ed.), published by The Associated General Contractors of America obligates the owner to provide to the contractor evidence of financing of the project, and states that evidence of financing is a condition precedent to the contractor's obligation to proceed with the work. The standard General Conditions published by the American Institute of Architects, AIA Document A 201 (1997), contains a similar provision.

Both the AGC and the AIA form documents address the owner's obligation to furnish information pertaining to the property title. The AGC document makes mandatory the disclosure by the owner of such information and other relevant information regarding the site.[2] The comparable section of AIA A 201 requires the owner to furnish information regarding title when requested by the contractor.[3] Regardless of the form of the contract, prospective contractors should routinely inquire about and seek from the owner any relevant information regarding the site and its characteristics.[4]

The financial condition of contractors and subcontractors is also extremely important. A subcontractor that has insufficient working capital may bring myriad problems, such as slow deliveries of materials as suppliers grow concerned about the subcontractor's ability to pay. This can have a ripple effect on other work. Similarly, a contractor needing cash flow may front-load its proposal and pay requests. The early overpayment caused by front-loading may result in the contractor's default on the latter part of the project as contract funds run out. Unfortunately, there are few,

---

[2] *See* Paragraph 4.3 of AGC Document 200.

[3] *See* Section 2.1.2 of AIA Document A 201.

[4] Paragraph 4.3 of AGC Document 200 can provide a useful checklist of possible types of information to be requested and reviewed.

if any, effective remedies against an unbonded, insolvent contractor. The typical action to recover completion costs is often pointless when the default resulted directly from the contractor's financial problems.

An obvious source of financial protection for owners is to require payment and performance bonds. Bonding serves two purposes. First, the contractor's competence and financial well-being are endorsed by the surety's underwriting department, which is also trying to avoid bad risks. If a contractor is incapable of obtaining bonding, it means sureties have a grave concern about its ability to complete a project. That warning is probably best heeded. Second, and more directly, the bonds represent a financial guarantee. A performance bond usually means that if the contractor defaults and fails to complete, the surety will complete performance or pay damages up to the limit of the penal sum of the bond. In contrast, a labor and material payment bond helps assure the owner that labor and materials will be paid for and creates alternatives to the filing of liens on the project. (Many general contractors require that subcontractors furnish payment and performance bonds for similar reasons.) (*See* **Chapters 14** and **15** for a specific discussion of payment and performance bonds, respectively.)

Even if provided, payment and performance bonds are not a cure-all. It is also necessary to carefully consider the financial stability of the surety itself. Sureties can suffer bankruptcy. Moreover, even solvent, well-financed sureties are far from an automatic source of relief. Claims under the bond can themselves be the subject of lengthy disputes and litigation. Trade associations such as the AGC can provide useful materials on topics such as bonds and bond claims. For, example, the AGC's Surety Bonding Committee has released an educational publication on bonds and bond claims, which is available from that organization.

Of course, there are concerns about technical qualifications that go beyond money. For example, licensing requirements provide some protection from incompetent and inexperienced contractors, particularly in the skilled areas such as electrical and mechanical work. Licensing should be deemed a bare minimum requirement, however, not an endorsement of qualifications for any type of work authorized by a particular license. Inquiries into the contractor's experience on particular types and sizes of projects should also be pursued. There is a significant difference between installing plumbing in a low-rise apartment building and installing the mechanical systems for a major health care facility. The owner's technical capabilities and qualifications to handle a particular type or size of project are also relevant. However, the owner's shortcoming may be offset by the association of capable consultants.

More subjective reports about other parties should also be considered, but perhaps be given lesser weight. For example, engaging a subcontractor with a reputation for shoddy or defective work may result in the general contractor being required to remedy unsatisfactory work at its own expense. A particularly litigious owner may refuse to negotiate a settlement in the event of a dispute in this type of situation, forcing the contractor into more expensive arbitration or court battles.

Even if an owner, designer, contractor, or subcontractor appears to have good qualifications and an established track record, it is important to consider the personnel it will assign to the particular project. Companies can be too successful, causing them to be stretched too thin, with all their capable and experienced personnel assigned to and consumed by other projects. The company is certainly important, but the individuals representing those companies, executing responsibilities, and working in the field are no less important.

13.5 Qualifying the Site and Locale

Similar to qualifying the type of project and the project participants, experience demonstrates that the site for the project also requires prequalification. This inquiry extends beyond the physical characteristics at the location of the project and includes questions about state and local license requirements, lien laws, taxes, availability of labor, and so on. Table 13.3 contains examples of topics that should be addressed when contemplating the locale of any project and, particularly, a project location that is unfamiliar.

Table 13.3 Qualifying the Project Site/Locale

Project Site Topic/Issue	Yes	No
• Has there been an adequate prebid site and subsurface investigation?		
• Is there a changed conditions (differing site conditions) clause in the contract?		
• Do the design documents indicate that environmental permits have been obtained and environmental restrictions observed?		
• Are existing utilities clearly located on design documents?		
• Are there site access restrictions?		
• Have you requested that the owner furnish all available site, subsurface, and environmental information?		
• Is there any prior history of environmental hazards on or near the site?		
• Have you evaluated the likely impact of conditions affecting the site (e.g., weather, traffic, work restrictions, storage problems, etc.)?		

Project Locale Topic/Issue	Yes	No
• Does your company have sufficient prior experience in the project jurisdiction?		
• Was the prior experience in this jurisdiction profitable?		
• Does your company possess the required licenses to work in this jurisdiction?		
• Are local licenses/permits required?		

Table 13.3   (Continued)

Topic/Issue	Yes	No
• Are the insurance policies/coverages adequate for work in this locale?		
• Does your company understand bond/lien claim rights and requirements in this jurisdiction?		
• Do the laws in this jurisdiction create special risks or require changes to subcontract forms or documentation systems?		
• Is the available local labor force adequate and sufficiently skilled?		
• Is the labor market in site's locale predominantly union or nonunion?		
• Is there a required project/union agreement for this work?		
• Are there state/local taxes to be considered?		
• Are materials and equipment available locally?		
• Has your company identified any local or required labor rates and fringes?		
• Are there project/local Minority Business Enterprise / Women Owned Business Enterprise (MBE/WBE) requirements?		
• Are there unusual business or political circumstances that may affect the project?		

The answers to these questions are critical to qualifying the project and evaluating the risks (potential or actual) in the performance of the work. Many of the questions on each of the tables flag a risk depending upon whether the answer is yes or no. Possibly a greater potential risk is signaled if the answer to any question is "don't know." If the answer is unknown, it is very likely that the evaluation of the potential risk and reward is a guess. That only compounds the inherent risks of working in the construction industry.

Environmental risks and potential issues associated with performance in a different state from a firm's traditional or home base of operations require careful review to avoid unforeseen risks or obligations. Attached to this chapter at **Appendix 13.2** and **Appendix 13.3,** respectively, are checklists addressing Prebid/Proposal Environmental Considerations and Contracts in Foreign States. These checklists reflect examples of questions or concerns that should be addressed prior to submitting a bid or proposal in order that the firm more completely evaluates the risks and obligations associated with the work.

13.6   DEFINING RIGHTS, RESPONSIBILITIES, AND RISKS: THE PARTIES AND THEIR CONTRACTS

A written contract generally provides the foundation for each of the numerous relationships, and binds the disparate project participants into a cohesive force to get the job built. Keeping those participants together requires anticipating issues and events that might generate disputes and detract from the goal of prompt and cost-effective project completion. This is done both by allocating risks among the parties, so it is clear who will have to bear the burden if the risk becomes reality, and providing mechanisms for resolving disputes when the risk allocation is not clear or there is disagreement. A well-drafted contract is another important element in effectively managing a project and avoiding or efficiently dealing with claims.

Clarity, common sense, and precision are essential when drafting contract language. Such efforts will, hopefully, limit later uncertainty and misunderstanding among the parties and the need to refer to some third-party decision maker, court, or arbitration, to determine how the contract will be interpreted. Unreasonable and overly burdensome terms should be avoided, as they can unnecessarily drive up the cost of the work through inflated contingencies and may be difficult to enforce. On the other hand, a contractor or subcontractor should not ignore such terms in an unrealistically optimistic belief that they will not be enforced. The parties must grapple with the tough issues raised by their conflicting interests in the contract-preparation stage or face the prospect of much more serious disagreements and disputes during the performance of the contract.

13.7 CONTRACT FRAMEWORK

Establishing the contract framework for the project is a threshold decision that must be made by the owner. The selection depends on a variety of factors, including the owner's needs and its expertise and capabilities. Construction projects have traditionally been designed, bid, built, and paid for within a framework of strictly defined roles, relationships, and procedures. This has proven satisfactory for many construction projects, but perceived weaknesses in the traditional method have led to consideration and use of new, alternative methods, such as the various forms of construction management, multiprime contracting, and design-build.[5] The new methods have provided many advantages, but their divergence from clearly defined practices and roles requires careful attention in the contract drafting phase to be certain that the advantages are not lost through unanticipated problems and disputes.

13.8 Standard Contract Forms and Critical Contract Provisions

There are a number of available standard contract forms that establish the various relationships on a construction project. The series, or families, of documents published by The Associated General Contractors of America (AGC), the American Institute of Architects (AIA), and the Engineers Joint Contract Documents Committee (EJCDC) are widely used in the construction industry. These common forms permit all parties to focus on critical variables when negotiating construction transactions and obviate the need to start from scratch with each new construction transaction.

---

[5] *See generally* Bynum, "Construction Management and Design-Build/Fast-Track Construction from the Perspective of a General Contractor," 46 Law & Contemp. Probs. 25 (1983).

Reference to or utilization of a family or series of documents can be advantageous, as those documents have been screened by committees composed of industry participants and counsel in an effort to provide a more integrated and comprehensive approach to the contracting process. For example, the AGC's library of forms and documents, which is included as part of its DocuBuilder software package, contains the following five series of documents:

AGC 200 Series (General Contracting Documents)

AGC 400 Series (Design-Build Documents)

AGC 500 Series (Construction Management Documents)

AGC 600 Series (Subcontracting Documents)

AGC 800 Series (Project Management Documents)

Each of these series of documents is a family of documents. For example, the AGC 400 Series, Design-Build series, currently contains 18 separate documents, including teaming agreements for design-build projects, statements of qualifications, subcontract forms, bond forms, and so on, in addition to a basic Owner/Design-Builder Preliminary Agreement (AGC Document No. 400). The AIA documents are also fairly well integrated, with the terms of the various contract forms coordinated with and complementing each other.[6] Consistency potentially enhances usefulness of these documents.

Historically, AIA documents have enjoyed acceptance by owners, particularly in the traditional design-bid-build delivery system, where the owner first engages a designer. However, they may not necessarily meet the needs of each and every project, and some modification may be required for each specific situation. To the extent that documents such as the AIA documents may protect the interests of the design professional, at the expense of the owner and contractor, alternate clauses can be introduced into standard AIA contracts to address any perceived bias.[7] Similarly, the documents in the other families of construction contract forms may warrant review and modification to fit particular needs or requirements. Computer-based families of documents such as the AGC's DocuBuilder facilitate custom tailoring and tracking of modifications.

Whether reliance is placed on a standard form, a custom-drafted contract, or some combination of the two, certain contract provisions are of critical importance in anticipating, avoiding, and resolving claims. They are:

- Payment
- Time for completion and time extensions
- Damages for delay
- Changes in the work
- Termination for default and for convenience

---

[6] *See generally* J. Sweet, *Sweet on Construction Industry Contracts* (John Wiley & Sons, Inc., 3rd ed., 1996).

[7] *See* Glower Jones, *Alternative Clauses to Standard Construction Contracts* (Aspen Law & Business, 2nd ed., 1990).

- Changed conditions
- Dispute resolution (arbitration, litigation, ADR)
- Insurance
- Indemnity

Careful attention should also be paid to the use of liquidated damages or no-damage-for-delay clauses, as well as exculpatory clauses and attorneys' fees provisions, which can weigh heavily in the resolution of claims. It is also worthwhile to consider whether the parties intend for Article 2 of the Uniform Commercial Code, which governs the sale of goods, to apply to the transaction. A detailed discussion of these provisions is beyond the scope of this chapter.[8] Arbitration as a means of resolving construction claims is discussed separately in **Chapter 21**.

13.9   AVOIDING AND PREPARING FOR DISPUTES THROUGH PROPER MANAGEMENT AND DOCUMENTATION

The prudent and realistic contractor designs and utilizes systems and procedures to manage, monitor, and document the work and progress on the project. This serves two important functions. First, these systems and procedures ensure an adequate flow of information to facilitate proper project control and coordination, including adjustments needed to respond to unexpected circumstances. Second, they aid in the compilation of an accurate and complete record of job conditions and problems and their impact on the project. The contractor certainly bears the bulk of responsibility during construction as it installs the work and generally controls the means and methods employed. The architect and owner should not, however, abdicate all responsibility and oversight and totally remove themselves from the construction process in an effort to insulate themselves from liability. They cannot avoid all liability. Moreover, some interaction and monitoring of the construction is always required of the owner and architect, and is in their interests. If the owner and/or the architect becomes too removed from the construction, they can neither anticipate nor promptly address problems requiring their assistance. The level of activity and monitoring will vary depending on the type and terms of the contract involved, but should not be so active or intrusive as to constitute interference and disruption of the contractor's work. Although it may be somewhat unpleasant to begin a project with an eye to possible future claims, a failure to adopt such prudent management procedures almost ensures that disputes will develop.

13.10   PRUDENT AND RESPONSIBLE ESTIMATING

Efforts to effectively manage work on the project and avoid claims should begin for the general contractor or trade contractor before it even mobilizes or reaches the site.

---

[8] *See* **Chapter 6**.

Many risks and claims arise not in the field but in the estimating department. Prudent estimating and bidding can avoid a host of performance problems and claims. A project that starts out "in the hole" because of bad estimating generally cannot climb out. Instead, the hole gets bigger and deeper, expanding the problem and drawing more parties into it.

Failure at any level to accurately perceive and then price the scope of the work or the risks associated with it results in unnecessary losses and difficulties that tend to ripple throughout the project. Estimates and bids should be supported by worksheets and backup documentation of sufficient detail under the circumstances. Such backup, and the entire estimating process, should be subject to standard forms and procedures and management review to ensure their accuracy.

Overly optimistic estimates based on vague or incomplete designs should be avoided or at least clearly identified and qualified as such. Performance specifications often entail more responsibility and cost more than may be initially apparent and are often another soft spot in the estimating effort. The zeal applied to selling the project or submitting an early guaranteed maximum price to satisfy the owner must be balanced with caution against establishing an unrealistic budget or inflated expectations that, regardless of any contractual significance, are bound to cause disappointment, distrust, and disagreement when they are not met.

This scrutiny must be applied to bids received from trade contractors (subcontractors) as well as those generated in-house. It is not always the case that the contractor may have recourse against the subcontractor. More important, the contractor has its own obligations to the owner and other subcontractors and may not evade that responsibility or liability simply by pointing to the trade contractor or subcontractor that is unable to perform because of an estimating error. Owners should likewise beware of a contractor bid that seems too good to be true—it probably is! Success in initially enforcing a mistaken or reckless bid can reap bitter returns later in the project when the contractor's financial problems adversely affect the project.

13.11   ESTABLISHING STANDARD OPERATING PROCEDURES

Construction projects run by the seat of their participants' pants are accidents waiting to happen. Every project should have formalized, standard operating procedures with which all project personnel are completely familiar. The procedures should identify the specific authority and areas of responsibilities for each project staff position. Ideally, these should be standardized within a company and be basically consistent from project to project. Standard job descriptions can then be used to define the roles of the individuals on a particular project. The standard procedures should address the duties and responsibilities for processing change orders and extra work, purchasing and receiving, submittal review, project documentation, and costs and accounting.

As the project team is being assembled and mobilized and the standard procedures are adjusted, defined, and implemented for the particular project, it is a good idea to reassess the project in terms of estimating, scheduling, procurement, cost accounting, and the like before construction begins. This reassessment can serve as an additional safeguard for the early identification and correction of problems that might otherwise have a serious impact on the project at some later date if left undetected.

13.12   ESTABLISHING LINES OF COMMUNICATION

The ability of the parties on the project to establish and maintain constructive lines of communication is essential to the success of any project. Prosecution of the work must be recognized as a cooperative effort that demands a team approach rather than adversarial conflict. The owner, architect, contractor, and the trade contractors (subcontractors) must establish some method to both discover what is going on at the job site (for example, what problems the subcontractors are having, and the problems they anticipate) and relay suggestions, recommendations, and requirements as to how these problems can be avoided or solved. Satisfactory communications can be achieved only if the parties have personnel who can sustain professional and reasonable working relationships with one another. The subcontractor's workers should have sufficient confidence in the prime contractor's on-site personnel so that they will not hesitate to report difficulties and seek the prime contractor's recommendations as to how those difficulties can be avoided or resolved. Efforts to develop this confidence should begin at the preconstruction conference and should continue throughout the contract period.

One activity, which has proven successful on many projects, is partnering. Partnering can be seen as an organized effort at team building. Typically, the process begins contemporaneously with the preconstruction meeting. One of the primary purposes of a partnering program is to assist the project participants to recognize and affirm that they have many interests in common and that a collaborative approach to problem solving is in the general interest. Partnering meetings can be conducted by the project participants, with or without the involvement of a third-party facilitator. Regardless of the label, or the use of a facilitator, the key is to promote a project atmosphere that is not adversarial.

An important procedural aid to establishing and maintaining the required lines of communications is to hold regular job meetings. Weekly, biweekly, or at least monthly meetings should be scheduled and held. The participants and the frequency of the meetings will depend on their purpose and the status or level of activity on the job. Field coordination meetings should involve the project superintendent, subcontractor superintendents, and key foremen. Brief but regular meetings can aid the process of coordinating and scheduling the work. They can also help identify problem areas and information needed for progress before a situation becomes critical.

Regular meetings between the architect's staff and the contractor's personnel are helpful for keeping up on the status of submittals, shop drawings, and areas requiring clarification. Meetings between the contractor, architect, and owner should also take place, but probably on a less frequent basis. These meetings can be used to apprise the owner of important developments and to work out contractual issues such as changes. Further, the parties can discuss problems that are not being worked out on a more operational level and require the owner's intervention. The contractor should be wary of allowing the owner to get too far removed from the construction effort.

13.13 PROJECT DOCUMENTATION

Consistent and complete project documentation is the key to successfully asserting and/or defending against construction claims. The process of project documentation should not be reserved for "problem" jobs. If adequate documentation is not maintained from start to finish, the circumstances giving rise to a dispute will often go unrecorded. Paperwork on a construction project may seem to be overwhelming, but it is essential. The contractor typically generates and maintains the bulk of the documentation on a construction project, but all participants have an interest in it.

Contracts often require that the contractor maintain certain documentation, with copies and/or access available to the owner and others. Project documentation creates an accessible history of the project that serves two roles: (1) planning and managing the project and (2) aiding in resolving claims and disputes. It must be organized and maintained in such a manner that it is a help, not a hindrance, to effective project management and prosecution or defense of claims. Making the documentation both routine and uniform is essential to an effective system of project documentation. The procedures should be standardized not only for the project but for the company as a whole. Only with that level of emphasis and indoctrination can all the fruits and benefits of a system be reaped.

Evaluation of the adequacy of the project's documentation system is an essential preperformance step. Even though an analysis of risk allocation is part of the pre-bid/proposal project evaluation, a company's established project documentation system should be reevaluated in light of the specific requirements of each project. Table 13.4 illustrates the type of questions to be addressed at the inception of a project.

Table 13.4 Qualifying the Project Documentation System

Topic/Issue	Yes	No
• Have we identified and reviewed *every* document that will be part of our contract?		
• Has the contract been reviewed to determine if modifications to our "standard" project documentation system are required?		
• Does the contract impose specific cost accounting requirements?		
• Does the contact define recoverable direct or indirect costs?		
• Does the contract contain special notice requirements?		
• Have we identified notice and claim deadlines?		
• Are special procedures or cost limitations imposed on change order work?		

Table 13.4   (Continued)

Topic/Issue	Yes	No
• Does the contract contain unusual risk-shifting clauses that our project documentation system should take into account?		
• Do we need the input of legal counsel on documentation practices in light of contract risk-shifting provisions?		

The answers to these questions should be reviewed with senior management. Based upon that review, the firm's documentation system can be adapted to the particular project's requirements. Notice checklists and standard form letters should be prepared or modified, as needed, for a particular project. **Appendix 13.4** to this chapter contains examples of notice checklists and various forms and logs, which can be modified for use. In particular, it is essential to identify all notice requirements using a checklist approach and then to develop a specific project checklist addressing the contract provision, subject matter of notice, time requirements, form of notice, and the stated consequences of a lack of notice. Based upon that study, standard forms can be adapted as necessary.

The system and procedures must be written down. The length and level of detail of the written description will vary with the size and complexity of the project. Some description may be obviated by the use of computerized tracking systems, such as for cost accounting, as well as for tracking submittals, modifications, Requests for Information (RFIs), and so on. Regardless of how extensive the procedures are, it is imperative that they be clear and specific. If they are vague and general or allow for personal interpretation and selective application, there will be no system at all. Instead, a hodgepodge of personal record keeping and filing systems will result.

Simply putting procedures on paper is not enough. The procedures must be reviewed with all levels of personnel who will be responsible for implementation so they are understood, used, and enforced. The critical importance of project documentation must be emphasized and that emphasis maintained throughout the project and from project to project.

Certain basic information should be maintained and organized in separate files:

- The contract, including all its components, and all change orders or amendments, including a bid or original set of project plans and specifications
- All documents, worksheets, and forms associated with the original bid estimate and subsequent revisions
- Subcontractor or vendor files, including bids, quotes, subcontracts, or purchase orders, together with changes and correspondence
- Project schedules, including the original schedule and all updates and look-aheads
- Insurance requirements and information for all parties.

The standard procedures relating to documentation should also address the creation, maintenance, and orientation of certain specific types of documentation:

(1) *Correspondence:* Procedures for date-stamping, copying, routing, filing, and indexing incoming and outgoing correspondence should be the responsibility of secretarial or clerical support staff to perform in accordance with standard procedures. A copy of all correspondence should go in a master correspondence file. The party responsible for responding to or acting on incoming correspondence should be identified. Even if there is a decision to utilize a browser or network-based project management system, the disciplined approach must be used. In addition, each project participant should carefully consider the extent to which "hard copies" need to be maintained as backup, and so on.

As a matter of routine, project management personnel should be drilled on the importance of complying with technical notice requirements in the contract. Discussion with other parties should likewise be confirmed in writing with the involved parties, with copies to the file. Such confirmation will help immediately resolve any misunderstanding that might exist and preserve the substance of the discussion if there is a dispute at some later date.

(2) *Meeting Notes:* Regular job-coordination meetings between the various parties on the project, on a cumulative basis, probably cover more issues and can contribute more to the exchange of information necessary to complete the work than all the correspondence on the project. Therefore, what occurs at such meetings is of great importance. Someone should be designated to maintain the minutes or notes for each meeting, preferably the same person at each meeting. That person should record the subjects covered, the nature of the discussion, the future actions to be taken, who has responsibility for the future action, and the applicable deadline for action. The name, title, and affiliation of each participant should be listed. The notes should be concise but accurate and informative. The items discussed should be indexed or designated in a manner so that they can be located for future reference. The notes should then be distributed to all participants and those affected on a regular basis.

A computer can be valuable for updating regular meeting notes, as certain items will likely remain open to discussion through several meetings. At the opening of each regular meeting, the notes from the previous meeting can be reviewed to confirm their accuracy and the mutual understanding of the participants. By identifying those items that remain outstanding, the previous week's minutes can also serve as an agenda for the current meeting.

(3) *Job-Site Logs or Daily Reports:* Job-site logs or daily reports are generally maintained by the project superintendent and can provide the best record of what happens in the field. They help keep management and office personnel informed of progress and problems. In the event of a claim, they are often among the most helpful documents in re-creating the progress on the job and as-built schedules. They can be essential documents in the evaluation of claims for disruption and loss efficiencies.

The daily log or report must be a part of the superintendent's daily routine. If it is too burdensome, it either will be ignored or will detract from the superintendent's primary function of getting the job built. Key information should be elicited, requiring as little narrative as possible to describe the conditions. The information covered at a minimum should include:

- Manpower, preferably broken down by subcontractors
- Equipment used and idle
- Major work activities
- Any delays or problems and the activities affected
- Areas of work not available
- Safety and accidents
- Oral instructions and informal meetings
- Weather summary
- Job-site visitors
- Key inspections

The burden on the superintendent can be eased and the information maintained in a more organized manner by using a standard form. The process can be further expedited simply by allowing the superintendent to dictate entries and having the report typed up by office staff. An electronic mail format can also be used for ease of transmission of the information to the home office.

All key project personnel, such as foremen, project engineers, and project managers, should also be encouraged to maintain personal daily logs and follow the procedures established to facilitate this effort. The information they should record should be similar to that maintained in the job log or daily report, but it need not be as extensive or detailed.

These types of routine, contemporaneous descriptions of work progress, site conditions, labor and equipment usage, and the contractor's ability (or inability) to perform its work can provide valuable information necessary to accurately reconstruct the events of the project in preparation of a claim. In maintaining these reports or logs, project personnel must be consistent in recording the events and activities on the job, particularly those relating to claims or potential claims. Failure to record an event, once the responsibility of a daily report or log is undertaken, carries with it the implication that the event did not occur or was insignificant and threatens the credibility of the entire log.[9]

(4) *Standard Forms and Status Logs:* There is a constant flow of information among the project participants by means of a variety of media. Drawings are revised; shop drawings are submitted, reviewed, and returned; field orders and change orders are issued; questions are asked; and clarifications are provided. Cumulatively and individually, these bits and pieces of information are essential for building the job and for reconstructing the progress of events on paper in the event of a claim. The standard procedures must include the means for providing, eliciting, recording, and tracking this mass of data so that it can be used during the course of the job and efficiently retrieved in an after-the-fact claim setting.

Routine transmittal forms should be customized to address specific, routine types of communications in order to expedite the process, but also to ensure that required information is provided. For example, separate specialized forms can be prepared

[9] *See* Federal Rule of Evidence 803(7).

for transmittal of shop drawings and submittals, requests for clarification, drawing revisions, and, of course, field orders and change orders. When possible, the forms should provide space for responses, including certain standard responses that simply can be checked off or filled in. At a minimum, the forms should identify the individual sender, the date issued, and specific and self-descriptive references to the affected or enclosed drawings, submittal, or specification. If a response is requested by a certain date, that date should be identified on the form. Again, while a computer network- or browser-based system can significantly expedite the prompt exchange of information, the key to good project management is the development of a systematic and consistently followed routine. If a computer network system is employed, it does not mean backups or hard copies can be eliminated.

Ideally, each discrete type of communication or specialized form should be numbered or somehow identified in a chronologically sequential manner based on the date it is initiated. Shop drawings and submittals, however, are best identified by specification section, with a suffix added to indicate resubmittals. This provides a basis for easy reference and orientation. Copies of the completed forms should be maintained in binders in reverse chronological/numerical order. Although various project staff members may require working copies, a complete master file should be maintained as a complete reference source and historical document.

In order to maintain the status of and track these numerous and varied communications, which can number many thousands, logs should be maintained. These logs need only address key information such as number assigned, date, and a self-descriptive reference. Proposed change orders and change order logs should also identify any increase or decrease in contract amount, as well as time extensions. Such logs can be kept on personal computers using inexpensive, commercially available software or even on a word processor to expedite updating. Logs should be maintained for internal record keeping and for distribution to other parties on the project. The logs serve as a reminder of outstanding items and can highlight action required to keep the work progressing.

The contractor should use standard forms and procedures for communications with subcontractors, as well as with the owner and architect. Ideally, subcontractors should be encouraged to standardize their communications so there will be a more integrated approach for the entire project. In that regard, the adoption of a network-based project management system can facilitate the use of standardized approach to project communications.

(5) *Photographs and Videotapes:* Photographs and videotapes are helpful, easy, and inexpensive means to monitor, depict, and preserve conditions of the work as those conditions change and the work progresses. They are particularly helpful in claims situations. One approach, incorporated in many contracts, is to accumulate a periodic pictorial diary of the job through a series of weekly or monthly photographs and pictures of significant milestones in the construction. This encourages personnel to take photographs of site conditions on a routine basis, perhaps concentrating on problem areas and those areas associated with crucial construction procedures and scheduling. Photographs are also the best evidence of defective work or problem conditions that are "cured" or covered up and cannot be viewed later.

Cameras capable of producing quality photographs and negatives should be used. However, it is also a good idea to use as a backup a self-developing camera that allows the party responsible for taking pictures to check the content and clarity of the photos while he or she is still at the site and before conditions are altered. Digital cameras offer an excellent method for taking, storing, and transmitting project images.

Pictures should always be marked with notations as to time, date, location, conditions depicted, personnel present, and the photographer. Some of this information can be imprinted on the negative or stored digital image. This should be done at the time the photograph is taken if a self-developing camera is used. Otherwise, a log should be kept as the photos are taken, the log should be checked immediately when the photos are developed, and the appropriate entries should be made on the back of the prints. Without this information correlated to specific photographs, the utility of the entire effort can be substantially undermined. Negatives should also be retained in an organized, retrievable manner.

In some situations, videotape can be considerably more informative than a still photograph, such as when attempting to depict an activity or the overall status of the project. Static conditions, however, are best photographed. The availability of a contemporaneous narrative as part of the video can give the after-the-fact viewer a much better idea of what is being depicted and why. A monthly videotape is an excellent way of preserving and presenting evidence. Again, properly trained job-site personnel can operate the video recorder and later testify in conjunction with the showing of the tape.

13.14   COST ACCOUNTING RECORDS

The use of effective cost accounting methods and the maintenance of appropriate cost records can minimize many of the proof problems inherently associated with construction claims. Unfortunately, even though a claimant may be able to prove that an event has occurred that entitles it to additional compensation, it will be able to recover only that amount of damages that it can prove with reasonable certainty. Proving the actual dollars lost is crucial to the claim.

Cost accounting systems utilized by contractors vary drastically in their level of sophistication. More often than not, the accounting function suffers from a lack of priority by senior management until a dispute arises and the claim development process begins. The procedures described earlier to effectively capture and document events or occurrences to prove liability are only half the battle. Without effective job cost accounting systems, the development of a clear, concise, and winning claim is haphazard at best. In addition, accounting rules for the construction industry are sometimes subjective, and in many cases different conclusions can be reached on a single set of circumstances by accounting professionals and businesspeople. Hence, it is important that accounting policies and procedures be documented and their application be appropriately monitored for compliance by management. This approach tends to improve the consistency of the manner in which items pertaining to all contracts are accounted for and, therefore, improves the credibility of the way in which matters are treated in developing a claim. Further, and perhaps of primary importance, a good job cost accounting system is invaluable in providing timely information to management for decision-making purposes and for monitoring financial performance.

13.15   MONITORING THE WORK THROUGH SCHEDULING

The general contractor or construction manager should continuously monitor the work of all subcontractors or trade contractors to determine that each is meeting its deadlines so that the work of other trades can proceed as originally scheduled. The owner must perform the same task when multiple prime contractors are involved. Even when the contractor has primary scheduling responsibility, which is most often the case, the owner should nonetheless monitor the progress of the work and the scheduling effort. Most prime contracts require the preparation of a bar (Gantt) chart or progress schedule, which provides the easiest means of monitoring the work. The critical path method (CPM) schedule required by the prime contract on many large projects can be even more valuable as a scheduling tool if properly developed, updated, and utilized.

The input of subcontractors and all project participants in the development and updating of any project schedule is critical to its usefulness. As a practical matter, a schedule that is developed without the input of the parties actually performing the work may result in an unworkable product, hence the schedule as an instrument of coordination will be wasted. By obtaining the participation of all parties in the preparation of the schedule, it becomes a much more meaningful and productive project management device. In addition, through its involvement, each party has in effect admitted or acknowledged what was reasonable and expected of it. If a party later fails to perform or follow the schedule, its ability to dispute the relevance of the project schedule and what was required of that party can be substantially reduced.

A project schedule can be a double-edged sword for the prime contractor, particularly if it is a CPM that shows the interrelationship of all activities and trades. A properly developed schedule can be used to demonstrate how a subcontractor is behind schedule and how its delayed performance is impacting the entire project.[10] Conversely, a subcontractor may also use a project schedule against the prime contractor to show how the subcontractor reasonably expected and planned to proceed with the work and how that plan was disrupted by the prime contractor, another subcontractor, or the owner, for which the affected subcontractor is entitled to additional compensation.[11] If the schedule is not properly maintained, updated, and enforced so that it bears little relationship to the actual progress of the work or the parties' contractual obligations, it may be dismissed by a court or arbitrators as merely

---

[10] *See, e.g., Illinois Structural Steel Corp. v. Pathman Constr. Co.,* 318 N.E.2d 232 (Ill. App. Ct. 1974); *Santa Fe, Inc.,* VABCA No. 2168, 87-3 BCA ¶ 20,104; *Santa Fe Eng'rs, Inc.,* ASBCA No. 24578, 94-2 BCA ¶ 26,872; *Kaco Contracting Co.,* ASBCA NO. 44937, 01-2 BCA ¶ 31,584.

[11] *See United States ex. rel. R.W. Vaughn Co. v. F.D. Rich Co.,* 439 F.2d 895 (8th Cir. 1971).

representing "theoretical aspirations rather than practical contract requirements."[12] The heavy use of scheduling information and analysis in resolving claims underscores the importance of preparing, and maintaining through updates, a realistic schedule that secures subcontractor involvement and agreement.

13.16   CONCLUSION

Effectively dealing with construction disputes begins with the recognition that disputes are best avoided. The identifiable recurring causes of claims permits planning and preparation to try to steer clear of major risks or handle claims responsibly when they cannot be avoided. The same policies and procedures that aid in limiting claims also contribute to comprehensive and effective preparation of claims. The potential for claims cannot be ignored. Skillful and determined management are required both before and during construction to handle the threats and challenges they present.

➤ POINTS TO REMEMBER

- When considering a new project, evaluate it against your firm's business plan, experience, and available resources. Ascertain if the project locale presents unusual risks or requirements.
- Parties can reduce the risk of construction disputes by dealing with reputable companies that have demonstrated their ability to perform. Careful consideration should be given the prospective project participant's financial strength, bonding capacity, licensing, available project management personnel, and experience on similar projects.
- Allocating risks and providing for effective dispute resolution can be accomplished by a well-drafted written contract, particularly when nontraditional construction contract methods are employed.
- Use of generally accepted standard contract forms and an integrated family of documents provides a starting point for parties to negotiate critical variables such as clauses addressing payment terms, time, damages, changes, termination, insurance, and dispute resolution.
- Prudent estimating and bidding, as well as proper project management and documentation, will help reduce the risk that disputes will develop. Moreover, proper project documentation can provide valuable information necessary to accurately reconstruct the events of the project in preparation of a claim.
- Proper project documentation involves procedures to systematically maintain bidding documents, vendor files, correspondence, meeting notes, job-site logs or daily reports, schedules, standard forms and status logs, photographs, and videotapes.

---

[12] *Id.* at 900.

- Company operating procedures should be standardized and consistent from project to project.
- Project participants should establish and maintain open lines of communication by engaging in regular job meetings.
- Because problems of proof are inherently associated with construction claims, maintenance of a good cost accounting system is crucial.
- A realistic project schedule that secures the involvement and agreement of all project participants should be prepared and routinely updated and maintained.

APPENDIX 13.1: AGC DOCUMENT NO. 221— CONTRACTOR'S STATEMENT OF QUALIFICATIONS FOR A SPECIFIC PROJECT

THE ASSOCIATED GENERAL CONTRACTORS OF AMERICA

AGC DOCUMENT NO. 221
CONTRACTOR'S STATEMENT
OF QUALIFICATIONS
FOR A SPECIFIC PROJECT

The **CONTRACTOR** _____ ◆
(Name)

submits this Contractor's Statement of Qualifications dated _____ to ◆

the **OWNER** _____ ◆
(Name and Address)

in connection with the following

PROJECT _____ ◆

The contents of this Contractor's Statement of Qualifications shall be treated as confidential by the Owner.

1   CONTRACTOR'S ORGANIZATION

1.1   General Information

Address: _____ ◆
_____

Telephone and Facsimile: _____ ◆

E-mail address: _____ ◆

Web site: _____ ◆

If address given above is a branch office address, provide principal home office address:
_____ ◆
_____

Attach brochure or promotional information.

AGC DOCUMENT NO. 221 **CONTRACTOR'S STATEMENT OF QUALIFICATIONS** **FOR A SPECIFIC PROJECT**	

1.2   Type of Organization

The Contractor's Organization is a:

☐ **Corporation**   ♦

Date and State of Incorporation: _____   ♦

Executive Officers: *(Names and Addresses)*   ♦

_____
_____
_____

☐ **Partnership**   ♦

Date and State of Organization: _____   ♦

Type of Partnership: ☐ General   ☐ Limited   ☐ Limited Liability   ☐ Other: _____   ♦

Current General Partners: *(Names and Addresses)*   ♦

_____
_____
_____

☐ **Joint Venture**   ♦

Date and State of Organization: _____   ♦

Joint Venturers: *(For each indicate the name, address and form and state of organization, as well as the managing or controlling Joint Venturer if applicable.)*

_____   ♦
_____
_____

☐ **Limited Liability Company**   ♦

Date and State of Organization: _____   ♦

Members: *(Names and Addresses)*

_____   ♦
_____
_____

2

AGC DOCUMENT NO. 221 · CONTRACTOR'S STATEMENT OF QUALIFICATIONS FOR A SPECIFIC PROJECT
© 2002, The Associated General Contractors of America

☐ **Sole Proprietorship** ♦

Date and State of Organization: _____ ♦

Owner or Owners: *(Names and Addresses)* ♦

_____

_____

_____

_____

☐ **Other** ♦

Type of Organization: _____ ♦

State of Organization: _____ ♦

Owners and/or Principals: *(Names and Addresses)*

_____ ♦

_____

_____

_____

In addition to the above categories of business entities, indicate whether Contractor's organization is certified as a:

☐ Disadvantaged Business Enterprise   Certified by: _____ ♦

☐ Minority Business Enterprise   Certified by: _____ ♦

☐ Women's Business Enterprise   Certified by: _____ ♦

☐ Historically Underutilized Business
     Zone Small Business Concern   Certified by: _____ ♦

2   LICENSING AND REGISTRATION

2.1   Jurisdictions in which Contractor is legally qualified to practice: *(Indicate license or registration numbers for each jurisdiction, if applicable, and type of license or registration. Attach separate sheet as necessary.)*

_____ ♦

_____

_____

_____

2.2   In the past five (5) years, has Contractor had any business or professional license suspended or revoked?

☐ Yes   ☐ No ♦

If yes, describe circumstances on separate attachment, including jurisdiction and bases for suspension or revocation.

3

AGC DOCUMENT NO. 221 · CONTRACTOR'S STATEMENT OF QUALIFICATIONS FOR A SPECIFIC PROJECT
© 2002, The Associated General Contractors of America

3   **CONTRACTOR'S PERSONNEL AND APPROACH**

3.1   **Key Construction Personnel**   List on Schedule A, attached, the construction experience of Contractor's Key Construction Personnel who are directly involved in construction operations and the percentage of time that is anticipated to be devoted to the Project.

3.2   List types of work generally performed by Contractor's own work force:

_____ ◆
_____
_____
_____
_____

3.3   **Subcontractors**

a. Indicate criteria used in the selection of subcontractors: *(Indicate if Not Applicable.)*

_____ Price   ◆

_____ Financial strength   ◆

_____ Bonding capacity   ◆

_____ Previous experience with Contractor   ◆

_____ Previous experience in industry   ◆

_____ Subcontractor's reputation in industry   ◆

_____ Availability of sufficient personnel   ◆

_____ Safety record   ◆

_____ Other: _____ ◆

b.   State Contractor's policy on the bonding of its subcontractors:

_____ ◆
_____
_____
_____
_____

3.4   Describe Contractor's proposed technical and management approach to the Project, including approaches to quality, time and cost control: *(Attach additional sheets as necessary.)*

_____ ◆
_____
_____
_____
_____

4

4 CONTRACTOR'S RELEVANT EXPERIENCE

4.1 Past Projects List on Schedule B, attached, at least five construction projects Contractor has worked on in the past five (5) years with project delivery systems similar to the one to be employed for this Project. *(For Joint Ventures, list each joint venturer's projects separately.)* The Owner may contact the owners of the projects listed on Schedule B.

4.2 Current Projects List on Schedule C, attached, all current projects of the Contractor, including projects not yet underway, approximate dollar value of each and the percentage of completion of each project. *(For Joint Ventures, list each joint venturer's projects separately.)*

4.3 Annual Construction Volume Indicate the annual volume of work completed for the past three years:

Year _____ _____ ◆
Year _____ _____ ◆
Year _____ _____ ◆

4.4 In the past five (5) years, has Contractor defaulted, been terminated for cause or failed to complete a construction contract awarded to it?

☐ Yes ☐ No ◆

If yes, describe circumstances on separate attachment, including dates and owner, and if applicable, Contractor's surety.

4.5 In the past five (5) years, has any officer, partner, joint venturer or proprietor of the Contractor ever failed to complete a construction contract awarded to that person or entity in their name or on behalf of another organization?

☐ Yes ☐ No ◆

If yes, describe circumstances on separate attachment, including dates and owner, and if applicable, surety.

4.6 Describe all litigation arising from Contractor's active projects or projects worked on within the last five (5) years. *(Attach additional sheets as necessary.)*

◆

5

5 CONTRACTOR'S SAFETY PROGRAM

5.1 If Contractor has a written safety program, attach a copy.

5.2 Does the Contractor's safety program include instructions on the following: *(If yes, attach.)*

a. Safety work practices	☐ Yes	☐ No	◆
b. Safety supervision	☐ Yes	☐ No	◆
c. Toolbox safety meetings	☐ Yes	☐ No	◆
d. Emergency procedures	☐ Yes	☐ No	◆
e. First aid procedures	☐ Yes	☐ No	◆
f. Accident investigation	☐ Yes	☐ No	◆
g. Fire protection	☐ Yes	☐ No	◆
h. New workers' orientation	☐ Yes	☐ No	◆

5.3 Do you have a safety officer/department in your company?

☐ Yes   ☐ No   ◆

If yes, Name: _____   ◆

Title: _____   ◆

Phone: _____   ◆

5.4 Do you conduct project safety inspections?

☐ Yes   ☐ No   ◆

If yes, how often? _____   ◆

Who conducts this inspection?

Name: _____   ◆

Title: _____   ◆

5.5 Do you hold project safety meetings for field supervisors?

☐ Yes   ☐ No   ◆

If yes, how often? ☐ Weekly   ☐ Bi-weekly   ☐ Monthly   ☐ Less often as needed   ◆

5.6 Do you have in place an instruction program on safety for newly hired or promoted supervisors?

☐ Yes   ☐ No   ◆

If yes, please attached a copy of program format.

6

AGC DOCUMENT NO. 221 · CONTRACTOR'S STATEMENT OF QUALIFICATIONS FOR A SPECIFIC PROJECT
© 2002, The Associated General Contractors of America

5.7 If craft "toolbox" safety meetings are held, what is their frequency?

☐ Weekly ☐ Bi-weekly ☐ Monthly ☐ Less often as needed ◆

5.8 Do you have a drug and alcohol testing policy?

☐ Yes ☐ No ◆

If Yes, attach a copy of the policy.

5.9 Provide Contractor's OSHA No. 200 Log and Summary of Occupational Injuries and Illnesses for the past five (5) years.

5.10 List all OSHA Citations and Notifications of Penalty, monetary or other, received within the last five (5) years: *(Indicate final disposition as applicable. Attach additional sheets as necessary.)* ◆

_____
_____
_____
_____
_____
_____
_____
_____
_____

5.11 List all safety citations of violations under state law received within the last five (5) years: *(Indicate final disposition as applicable. Attach additional sheets as necessary.)* ◆

_____
_____
_____
_____
_____
_____
_____
_____

5.12 List Contractor's Workers Compensation Experience Modification Rate (EMR) for the past five (5) years. *(The EMR may be obtained from your insurance agent. Attach a copy of the insurance agent's EMR verification letter.)*

Year: _____ EMR: _____ ◆

Year: _____ EMR: _____ ◆

Year: _____ EMR: _____ ◆

Year: _____ EMR: _____ ◆

Year: _____ EMR: _____ ◆

7

AGC DOCUMENT NO. 221 • CONTRACTOR'S STATEMENT OF QUALIFICATIONS FOR A SPECIFIC PROJECT
© 2002, The Associated General Contractors of America

5.13   List Contractor's Total Recordable Frequency Rate (TRFR) for the past five (5) years. *(The TRFR may be obtained from your insurance agent. Attach a copy of the insurance agent's TRFR verification letter.)*

Year: _____   TRFR: _____   ◆

Year: _____   TRFR: _____   ◆

Year: _____   TRFR: _____   ◆

Year: _____   TRFR: _____   ◆

Year: _____   TRFR: _____   ◆

5.14   List Contractor's total number of man hours worked for the past five (5) years:

Year: _____   Total Number of Man Hours Worked: _____   ◆

Year: _____   Total Number of Man Hours Worked: _____   ◆

Year: _____   Total Number of Man Hours Worked: _____   ◆

Year: _____   Total Number of Man Hours Worked: _____   ◆

Year: _____   Total Number of Man Hours Worked: _____   ◆

5.15   Comment on any additional areas of your company's safety program and policies that you feel will be appropriate in our evaluation:

_____   ◆

_____

_____

6   **SURETY AND INSURANCE**

6.1   Surety Company: *(Name and Address)* _____   ◆

_____

6.2   Agent: *(Name, Address and Telephone Number)* _____   ◆

_____

_____

6.3   Total bonding capacity: $ _____   ◆

Limit per project: $ _____   ◆

6.4   Available bonding capacity as of this date: $ _____   ◆

6.5   Can Contractor provide a bid bond for this project, if applicable.

☐ Yes   ☐ No   ◆

6.6   Commercial General Liability Carrier and summary of liability coverage:

_____   ◆

_____

8

7   CONTRACTOR FINANCIAL INFORMATION

7.1   List principal banks used, the approximate value of outstanding loans and general repayment history, as well as the Name, Address and Telephone Number of a contact person:

_____   ♦
_____
_____
_____

7.2   Attach audited financial statements for the past three (3) years, including latest balance sheet, containing but not limited to the following information:
    a. Current Assets
    b. Net Fixed Assets
    c. Other Assets
    d. Current Liabilities _(i.e. accounts payable, notes payable, accrued expenses, provision for income taxes, advances, accrued salaries and accrued payroll taxes)_
    e. Other Liabilities _(i.e. capital, capital stock, authorized and outstanding shares par values, earned surplus)_
    f.   Retained Earnings and Net Worth
    g. Date of Statement
    h. Name of firm preparing statement

7.3   State whether Contractor, or any of the individuals identified in Article 1, has/have been the subject of any bankruptcy proceeding within the last five (5) years.

    ☐ Yes   ☐ No   ♦

    If yes, describe circumstances on separate attachment.

8   INDUSTRY AGREEMENTS, AFFILIATIONS, MEMBERSHIPS, AWARDS AND HONORS

8.1   List Trade Unions or Associations with which Contractor has an Agreement:

Trade	National Agreement	Local Agreement	Expires
			♦

8.2   Industry Affiliations and Memberships:

_____   ♦
_____
_____

8.3   Industry Awards and Honors and dates:

_____   ♦
_____
_____

9

9   **STATEMENT OF POTENTIAL CONFLICTS OF INTEREST**   Provide information about any business associations, financial interests or other circumstances that may create a conflict of interest with the Owner or any other party known to be involved in the Project.   ◆

_____

_____

_____

_____

_____

_____

_____

_____

_____

_____

10   **OTHER INFORMATION**

10.1   Within the past five (5) years, has Contractor or any of the individuals identified in Paragraph 1.2 and/or Schedule A been the subject of any criminal indictment or judgment of conviction for any business-related conduct constituting a crime under state or federal law?

    ☐ Yes   ☐ No   ◆

    If yes, describe circumstances on separate attachment.

10.2   Within the past five (5) years, has Contractor or any of the individuals identified in Paragraph 1.2 and/or Schedule A been the subject of any federal or state suspension or disbarment?

    ☐ Yes   ☐ No   ◆

    If yes, describe circumstances on separate attachment.

10.3   Within the past five (5) years, has Contractor or any of the individuals identified in Paragraph 1.2 and/or Schedule A been the subject of any formal proceeding or consent order with a state or federal environmental agency involving a violation of state or federal environmental laws?

    ☐ Yes   ☐ No   ◆

    If yes, describe circumstances. (*Attach additional sheets as necessary.*)   ◆

_____

_____

_____

_____

_____

_____

_____

_____

_____

10

AGC DOCUMENT NO. 221 • CONTRACTOR'S STATEMENT OF QUALIFICATIONS FOR A SPECIFIC PROJECT
© 2002, The Associated General Contractors of America

11   REFERENCES

Provide references for each of the following categories.
(Additional references may be provided on a separate attached sheet.)

Owner

Name: _____ ♦

Address: _____ ♦

Telephone No.: _____ ♦

Contact Person: _____ ♦

Architect/Engineer

Name: _____ ♦

Address: _____ ♦

Telephone No.: _____ ♦

Contact Person: _____ ♦

Subcontractor

Name: _____ ♦

Address: _____ ♦

Telephone No.: _____ ♦

Contact Person: _____ ♦

The Undersigned, on behalf of the Contractor, certifies under oath that the information provided herein, including any schedule or attachment, is true and sufficiently complete so as not to be misleading.

CONTRACTOR

By: _____ ♦

Title: _____ ♦

Date: _____ ♦

5/02

11

AGC DOCUMENT NO. 221 · CONTRACTOR'S STATEMENT OF QUALIFICATIONS FOR A SPECIFIC PROJECT
© 2002, The Associated General Contractors of America

APPENDIX 13.2: CHECKLIST—PREBID/ PROPOSAL ENVIRONMENTAL CONSIDERATIONS

Risk Assessed By:	✓	**
The Contract Documents		
Do the plans or specs include any remediation work, asbestos abatement, or lead-based paint removal?		
Do the plans or specs make reference to the performance by others of remediation work, asbestos abatement, or lead-based paint removal?		
Do the Contract Documents attempt to allocate the risk or responsibility for hazardous materials or asbestos?		
Is there a contract requirement for the indemnification of the Owner or others for losses associated with hazardous materials or asbestos?		
Is the Contractor/Subcontractor indemnified against losses associated with hazardous waste or asbestos encountered on the Project?		
If unanticipated asbestos, lead-based paint, tanks, drums, contaminated soil, PCBs, or other hazardous material or waste are encountered, does the Contract specify the Contractor's rights and duties?		
If the Contract completion is delayed by unexpected environmental problems, does the Contract provide for a time extension, an equitable Contract price adjustment, or termination rights?		
Are any environmental permits necessary?		
Who is contractually responsible for any necessary environmental permits?		
What is the extent of the site investigation required by the Contract Documents?		
The Site Observation		
Did the site visit indicate any distressed vegetation, hydrocarbon or chemical contamination, underground storage tanks, transformers, drums, suspect lead-based paint, or suspect asbestos-containing materials?		
Has any prior cleanup taken place at the site?		
Have tanks been removed or filled?		
Is there any Closure Report?		
Are there structures on the site that must be moved or demolished?		
What is the extent of the required excavation and grading operation?		
Will fill material be brought to the site?		
Will waste material be hauled off to another site?		
Owner-Furnished Information		
Has the Owner been requested to disclose any available information regarding any hazardous materials, asbestos, lead-based paint, waste materials, contaminated soil or water that might affect the Contractor's work?		
Has a request been made for the results of any Environmental Site Assessment?		
Has a request been made for any building surveys or inspection reports on asbestos, lead-based paint, underground storage tanks, soil or water quality, or hazardous waste present at the site?		
Has a request been made for all information regarding any prior clean-up on or near the site?		
Environmental Risk Allocation		
If environmental problems are encountered, is insurance coverage available?		
Are there insurance policy exclusions or limits which that affect potential insurance coverage?		
Are environmental risks shared with appropriate Subcontractors?		
If Subcontractors will be or may be involved in work which that could encounter environmental problems, do the Subcontractors have adequate insurance coverage or proper bond protection?		
Personnel Readiness		
Are responsible project personnel familiar with and able to recognize likely environmental hazards?		
Is there an in-house response plan for dealing with environmental hazards?		
Other Environmental Considerations		

APPENDIX 13.3: CHECKLIST— CONTRACTS IN FOREIGN STATES

Risk Assessed By:	✓	Comments
Foreign Corporation Registration Requirements		
Ascertain Required Fees		
Obtain Certificate of Authority		
Establish Registered Agent/Office		
State Revenue Department Requirements		
Tax Bond Requirements		
Consequences of Violation		
Sales and Use Tax Liability		
Ad Valorem Taxes		
State Licensing Requirements		
Application Process		
Ascertain Testing Requirements		
Obtain Prior to Bid?		
Consequences of Violation		
Environmental Permits/Filings		
Vehicle/Equipment Licenses		
Local Licensing/Permit Requirements		
City/County License		
Permit Requirements		
Building Code Requirements		
Other Requirements		
Special Insurance Requirements		
Nature of Insurance Required		
Additional Rider Required?		
Filing/Reporting Requirements		
Preservation Lien/Bond Rights		
Public or Private Project?		
Verify Existence of Lien Rights		
Property Legal Description/Owner Information		
Verify Payment Bond(s)		
Pre-Contract Filing Requirements		
Preliminary/Early Notice Requirements		
Post-performance Notice Requirements		
Limitations on Lien/Bond Recovery		
Request for Bond/Lien Information		
Mandatory Lien Waiver Forms		
Payment Security Verification		
Verify Adequacy of Financing		
Notice to Lender Requirements		
Lender Approvals Required		
Extra Work Payment Limitations		
Change Order Authority Limitations		
Existence of State Prompt Payment Statute		
Trust Fund/Retainage Requirements		
Existence/Validity of Pay-If-Paid Clause		
Existence/Validity of No-Damages-for-Delay Clause		
Impact of Foreign Jurisdiction's Laws		
Identification of Controlling Law		
Public Policy Limits on Exculpatory Clauses		
Impact on Subcontract/Purchase Order		
Unusual State/Local Requirements		
Labor, Equipment and Material Impacts		
Available Local Labor		
Union/Nonunion Market		
Materials/Equipment Availability		
Applicable Sales Taxes		
Applicable Labor Rates/Fringes		
Project/Union Agreements		
Political Climate Assessment		
MBE/WBE Requirements		
Identify Special Political Ties/Circumstances		
Business Climate Considerations		
Other Special Risks		

APPENDIX 13.4: LOGS AND FORMS

APPENDIX 13.4A: SAMPLE NOTICE CHECKLIST: FEDERAL GOVERNMENT CONSTRUCTION CONTRACTS

Clause Reference	Subject Matter of Notice	Time Requirements For Notice	Writing Required	Stated Consequences Of a Lack of Notice
Changes **FAR** **52.243-4**	Proposal for adjustment.	**30 DAYS** from receipt of a written change order from the Gov't or written notification of a constructive change by the contractor.	Yes	Claim may not be allowed. Notice requirement may be waived until final payment.
Constructive Changes **FAR** **52.243-4**	Date, circumstances and source of the order & that the contractor regards the Government's order as a contract change.	No starting point stated, but notice within **20 DAYS** of incurring any additional costs due to the constructive change fully protects the contractor's rights.	Yes	Costs incurred more than **20 DAYS** prior to giving notice cannot be recovered, except in the case of defective specifications.
Differing Site Conditions **FAR** **52.236-2**	Existence of unknown or materially different conditions affecting the contractor's cost.	From the time such conditions are identified, notice must be furnished **"promptly"** and before such conditions are disturbed.	Yes	Claim not allowed. Lack of notice may be waived until final payment.
Suspension of Work **FAR** **52.212-12**	(1) Of "the act or failure to act involved," . . .	(1) Within **20 DAYS** from the act or failure to act by the C.O. (not including a suspension order.) (2) "As soon as practicable" after termination of the suspension, delay, or interruption.	(1) Yes (2) Yes	(1) Costs incurred more than **20 DAYS** prior to notification cannot be recovered. (2) Claim not allowed, but claim may be considered until final payment.
Termination for Default Damages for Delay Time Extensions **FAR** **52.249-10**	Causes of delay beyond contractor's control.	**10 DAYS** from the beginning of any delay.	Yes	Contractor's right to proceed may be terminated and the Government may sue for damages.
Disputes **FAR** **52.233-1**	Appeal of any final decision by the Contracting Officer (C.O.).	(1) **Boards of Contract Appeals** **90 DAYS** from receipt of C.O.'s final decision. (2) **U.S. Court of Fed. Claims** **1 YEAR** from receipt of C.O.'s final decision.	(1) Yes Notice of Appeal (2) Yes Filing of Complaint	C.O.'s decision becomes final and conclusive. C.O.'s decision becomes final and conclusive.

Sample Notice Checklist AIA A201 General Conditions (1997)

Time Limits on Claims: Articles 4.3.2, 4.3.5 &4.3.7	Claims by either party. Contractor claims for time shall include cost estimate Claims for increase in price due before starting work, except for emergency.	Within **21 DAYS** after claimant first recognizes condition giving rise to claim or **21 DAYS** after occurrence of event giving rise to claim, **whichever is later**.	Yes	??????????
Concealed or Unknown Site Conditions: Article 4.3.4	Materially different, subsurface or otherwise concealed physical site conditions.	Promptly, before disturbing the conditions but no later than **21 DAYS** after observing such conditions. If the Architect does not agree, a claim must be filed within **21 DAYS**.	Yes	??????????
Injury or Damage to Person or Property Article 4.3.8	Claim of injury or damage to property caused by act or omission of other party or agent.	Within a reasonable time not exceeding **21 DAYS** after discovery. Notice must provide enough detail to permit the other party to investigate the matter.	Yes	??????????
Arbitration Notices And Demands Article 4.4	Demand for Arbitration. (Note: Mediation must precede arbitration.)	If the Architect's written decision states that it is **FINAL** but subject to Arbitration, demand for Arbitration of the Claim must be made within **30 DAYS** after the date on which the party making the demand received the Architect's written final decision.	Yes. See 4.6.5 regarding need to assert other Claims when filing the Arbitration demand.	Failure to demand Arbitration within the **30-DAY** period shall result in the Architect's decision becoming final and binding on the Owner and the Contractor.

General Notes on Preparation of a Checklist

The **Tables** above are sample formats for **Notice Checklists**. Regardless of your familiarity with the contract, each contract should be carefully reviewed as **special notice requirements are often in "*standard*" contracts!** The checklist should identify the clause, time requirements for notice, the subject of the notice, whether notice must be in writing and the stated consequences for failing to give notice. **The checklist should not be provided to the project staff.** Rather, those responsible for giving timely notice should prepare the checklist for every contract. The checklist can be contained on a single sheet of paper, threeholepunched, and retained in the project manual.

©2004 Smith, Currie & Hancock LLP

APPENDIX 13.4B: FORMAT FOR NOTICE CHECKLIST

Clause Reference	Subject Matter Of Notice	Time Requirement for Notice	Form of Notice	Stated Consequences of Lack of Notice
Changes Paragraph # __	Proposal for adjustment	(Sent)(Rec'd) in _days Triggering Event:_____ _____ Other Action Required:_ _____	_ Written _ Certified _ Registered Sent to: _____	
Constructive Changes Paragraph # __	Date, circumstances and source of the order and that the contractor regards the order as a contract change	(Sent)(Rec'd) in _days Triggering Event:_____ _____ Other Action Required:_ _____	_ Written _ Certified _ Registered Sent to: _____	
Differing Site Conditions Paragraph # __	Existence of unknown or materially different conditions affecting the contractor's cost	(Sent)(Rec'd) in _days Triggering Event: ____ _____ Other Action Required:_ _____	_ Written _ Certified _ Registered Sent to: _____	
Suspension of Work Paragraph # __	The act or failure to act involved and the amount claimed	(Sent)(Rec'd) in _days Triggering Event:_____ _____ Other Action Required:_ _____	_ Written _ Certified _ Registered Sent to: _____	
Time Extensions Paragraph # __	Causes of delay beyond contractor's control	(Sent)(Rec'd) in _days Triggering Event:_____ _____ Other Action Required:_ _____	_ Written _ Certified _ Registered Sent to: _____	
Claims Paragraph # __	Notice of event or condition giving rise to a claim	(Sent)(Rec'd) in _days Triggering Event:_____ _____ Other Action Required:_ _____	_ Written _ Certified _ Registered Sent to: _____	
Termination for Default Paragraph # __	Notice of intent to terminate for default	(Sent)(Rec'd) in _days Triggering Event:_____ _____ Other Action Required:_ _____	_ Written _ Certified _ Registered Sent to: _____	

Termination for Convenience Paragraph # __	Notice of intent to invoke right to terminate for convenience	(Sent)(Rec'd) in _days Triggering Event:_____ _____ Other Action Required:_ _____	_ Written _ Certified _ Registered Sent to: _____	
Injury or Damage to Person or Property Paragraph # __	Claim of injury or damage to property caused by act or omission of other party or agent	(Sent)(Rec'd) in _days Triggering Event:_____ _____ Other Action Required:_ _____	_ Written _ Certified _ Registered Sent to: _____	
Arbitration Notices and Demands Paragraph # __	Demand for arbitration	(Sent)(Rec'd) in _days Triggering Event:_____ _____ Other Action Required:_ _____	_ Written _ Certified _ Registered Sent to: _____	
Disputes Paragraph # __	Appeal of A/E or C.O. Final Decision	(Sent)(Rec'd) in _days Triggering Event:_____ _____ Other Action Required:_ _____	_ Written _ Certified _ Registered Sent to: _____	
Mechanic's Lien Paragraph # __	Notices to be sent or filed to preserve lien rights	1st Notice Required: ___ Notice Deadline: _____ Other Action Required: _ Foreclosure Deadline: __	_ Written _ Certified _ Registered Sent to: _____	

APPENDIX 13.4C: FORMS

SAMPLE NOTICE LETTER: EXTENSION OF TIME FOR DELAYS
(AND EXTRA COSTS IF APPROPRIATE)

ECC # _____

Addressee:

(To Prime Contractor) or
(Owner and A/E)

Dear:

We are continuing to pursue the completion of our work as rapidly as is reasonably possible under the current circumstances. We have, however, recently encountered certain *delays* to our performance through no fault of our own and which are beyond our control. We have continued to keep your job representatives informed of these delays and of their effect on overall job completion. You may be assured that we will diligently seek to reasonably minimize the effects of these delays on our work.

Specifically, we have been delayed in the following particulars:

Accordingly, we hereby request an extension of [_____ days]* to our contract completion to take into consideration the above delays under Clause _____ of the contract provisions.

**[Such delays have also had a serious effect on costs of performance in that it has created additional time for performance with resultant additional costs for supervision, overhead, rentals, etc., and loss of efficiency for direct labor. Accordingly, this is to place you on notice that we are entitled to additional compensation for all costs flowing from these delays and interference that have been imposed on us through no fault of our own. We will provide you with the specific amount of additional compensation covered by this notice as soon as we research this matter and have computed it.]

Sincerely yours,

Eager Construction Company, Inc.

By _____
            (Title)

*   To be inserted where specific time of delay is known.
** To be used where extra money is claimed for delay.

APPENDIX 13.4C (CONTINUED)

SAMPLE NOTICE LETTER: CLAIM FOR EXTRAS

ECC # _____

Addressee:

(To Prime Contractor) or
(Owner and A/E)

Re: (Describe Extra Work)

Dear:

This is to notify you that (on _____ we will begin) (we are about to begin) this extra work and are expecting to be compensated for it. If you do not want us to perform this work as an extra to the contract, please immediately notify us before we incur additional costs in the preparation for performance of this extra work. If we do not hear from you right away, we will proceed on the basis that you agree with our plan to perform this work.

OR

This work was performed pursuant to your representative's requirement and entitles us to additional compensation. We have proceeded to complete this work so as to minimize the cost of the work and any delay to (our work) (the job). We will be pleased to review this matter with you at your convenience.

We will provide you with a detailed cost breakdown for this added work as soon as we are able to compute it.

Sincerely yours,

Eager Construction Company, Inc.

By _____
(Title)

SAMPLE NOTICE LETTER: CONFIRMING CHANGE DIRECTIVE

ECC # _____

DATE

SUBJECT (Contract Name)

Gentlemen:

We were given instructions by (insert name) on (date) (put in time also if pertinent) to (describe work added or changed).

This change order is for work not within the scope of our present contract, and we therefore request a written modification to cover the added (material, labor, equipment, etc.) required to perform the work as ordered. (Give notice of other factors involved such as delay, acceleration, diversion of men or equipment from contract work, material shortages, etc.)

Our proposal for the added cost resulting from this change order is being prepared and will be submitted for your approval as soon as possible. We cannot determine at this time the effect on contract completion date or other work under the contract, and will advise when a full analysis has been made.

As ordered, we (are proceeding) (have proceeded) at once to (procure materials) (perform the work) in order to complete this change order at the earliest possible time. In the event you do not approve of such action, please advise immediately in order that we may stop this effort and minimize the cost involved.

Your signature at the bottom of this letter will satisfactorily confirm the oral instructions.

Very truly yours,

Eager Construction Company, Inc.

By _____
(Title)

Confirmation:

The above-stated report of our instruction is confirmed.

COMPANY: _____

BY: _____

Title: _____

File No.: _____

SAMPLE NOTICE LETTER: ORAL DIRECTIONS OF EXTRA WORK

ECC # _____

DATE

SUBJECT (Contract Name)

Gentlemen:

On the ____ day of _____, 19____, we received certain oral instruction (or orders, approvals, changes, as the case may be) from (insert name). These instructions were confirmed by our _____, 19____, letter and should have been given to us in writing under the terms of our agreement. Your (insert name) has refused to confirm the oral instructions (or orders, approvals, changes, as the case may be) that we have recited in our referenced letter. Accordingly, we must advise that we will not (proceed with) (continue to follow) these verbal instructions unless we receive your immediate written confirmation. In any event, we will expect reimbursement for all costs reasonably incurred in reliance upon your direction.

We understand that it may take time to go though all the steps necessary to bring about a written authorization for extra work, and that sometimes it is more practical to do the work before that written authorization can be obtained. It has been our past practice to try to recognize your need to follow this method of operation. However, in this case, and in order to avoid any misunderstanding, we think it appropriate that you first provide us with a formal written authorization for changed work.

Very truly yours,

Eager Construction Company, Inc.

By _____
          (Title)

NOTE: Where the work already has been performed, it may be important to establish a prior history of reliance by the parties on oral directives. If the work has been fully performed, then the second paragraph should be deleted and the last sentence of the first paragraph replaced with the following:

As you know, we proceeded immediately as directed to perform this additional work. We did so in order to minimize your extra cost, and in the same manner in which we have handled other verbal directives in the past. Consistent with that past practice, we will provide you with our costs as soon as they are fully known and expect your prompt reimbursement.

SAMPLE NOTICE LETTER: CONFIRMING EXTRA COST DIRECTIVE

ECC # _____

DATE

SUBJECT (Contract Name)

Gentlemen:

We were given direction by (name or letter dated _____) on (date) (put in time also if pertinent) to (describe work and specific location). This directive stipulates and orders that we are to complete this work by (date and time).

This directive necessarily (accelerates, delays, diverts men and equipment from contract work, involves inefficiencies, interrupts contract work, involves excessive working hours, shortages, causes manpower shortage for contract work, inefficient working conditions, involves work under hazardous conditions, etc.) and thereby will result in increased cost to _____ on this contract.

Our proposal for the added costs resulting from this directive is being prepared and will be submitted for your approval as soon as possible. We cannot determine at this time the effect on contract completion date and will advise after a full analysis has been made.

Very truly yours,

Eager Construction Company, Inc.

By _____
                (Title)

File No._____

APPENDIX 13.4D: REQUEST FOR INFORMATION

REQUEST FOR INFORMATION

TO: _____ **DATE:** _____

_____ **PROJECT:** _____

ATTENTION:_____

We are this date requesting the following information, clarification, or direction:

_____
_____
_____
_____
_____
_____
_____
_____

The above information is needed:

* As soon as possible, to avoid *disrupting* the work

* Immediately, to minimize *disruption* and added costs already being incurred

* Not later than _____, or the work may experience *disruptions* and added costs

Thank you for your prompt attention to this matter.

COMPANY: _____

BY: _____
       (Signature and Title)

Response:

_____
_____
_____
_____
_____
_____

COMPANY: _____

BY: _____
       (Signature and Title)

DATE: _____

APPENDIX 13.4E: TELEPHONE CONVERSATION MEMORANDUM

TO: _____

DATE: _____

PROJECT: _____

I talked to _____

at telephone number _____

regarding _____
_____
_____
_____

To: _____

For your files and use, I am providing you with this confirmation of our telephone conversation described above.

_____

_____
Signature

COPIES TO:

* Construction Manager   * Job Superintendent

* Project Manager   * Construction Accounting

* General Superintendent

A CONFIRMATION LETTER:

* Has been sent

* Will be sent

* Need not be sent

APPENDIX 13.4F: SAMPLE DAILY REPORT

DAILY REPORT

Job or Area: _____ Date: _____

Weather Conditions: _____

_____

_____

Temperature: _____

_____

High: _____ Low: _____

Rainfall Amount: _____

Critical Activities Affected Duration of:

By Adverse Weather   By Adverse Weather

_____   _____

_____   _____

_____   _____

Personnel	G. Foreman	Foreman	Journeyman	Apprentice	Labor	New Hires	Laid Off
Carpenters							
Laborers							
Operators							
Finishers							
Teamsters							
Pipe Fitters							
Pipe Laborers							

Work Performed Today: _____

_____

_____

Remarks: *(Such as testing, conflicts, verbal instructions, delays, safety problems, visitors*

_____

_____

Major Equipment and Materials Received:

Item   *Carrier*   *Description*

_____

_____

Subcontractors   *Work Performed and Number of People*

_____

_____

Superintendent:

_____

APPENDIX 13.4G: NOTICE OF BACKCHARGE
WORK TO BE PERFORMED

Location:_____ **Backcharge No.:**_____

Charge To:_____ **Subcontractor No.**_____

Date:_____ **P.O. Reference:**_____

Description:_____

_____

_____

_____

Notes:

* Labor shall be charged at actual costs plus % to cover payroll additives.

* Material shall be charged at actual delivered cost.

* Equipment rental shall be charged at prevailing job site rates of the area.

* _____% shall be added for indirect costs, overhead, supervision, and administration.

APPROVALS

_____
Representative   **Date**   **Supplier/Subcontractor**

Project Name: _____
Project Number: _____
Owner: _____

Page No. _____
Status Date: _____
Contractor: _____

Job No.	Owner's Field Order #	Authorized by	Date of Order	Description of Work	Work Performed by	Date Work Started	Date Work Completed	Comments on Work	Invoice No.	Date of Bill	Amt. of Bill	Amt. Paid
									1.			
									2.			
									1.			
									2.			
									1.			
									2.			
									1.			
									2.			
									1.			
									2.			
									1.			
									2.			
									1.			
									2.			
									1.			
									2.			
									1.			
									2.			
									1.			
									2.			

To: _____: To keep you aware of the status of added work directed in the field, we will submit updates of this status chart as frequently as is practical. With this form you should be able to track our planned start dates for field work and the status of the work. In the absence of a field order number from you, we will assign our own field number to each field directive.

APPENDIX 13.4I: CORRESPONDENCE LOG—INCOMING

Incoming Correspondence from _____

(Contractor/Supplier)

| Ref. No. | Date | Subject | Author | Reply Required | | Reply | |
				Yes	No	Ref. No.	Date

*Page No.*____

APPENDIX 13.4J: CORRESPONDENCE LOG—OUTGOING

Outgoing Correspondence to _____

(Contractor/Supplier)

Ref. No.	Date	Subject	Author	Reply Required		Reply	
				Yes	No	Ref. No.	Date

*Page No.*_____

14

PAYMENT BONDS

Through a payment bond, the surety becomes the guarantor of payment to subcontractors and suppliers but only according to the terms of that bond. The obligation of the surety to payment bond claimants is separate from any performance bond obligation. As such, the surety must respond to payment bond claims even though the surety may have a valid defense to performance bond obligations. In order to assert a payment bond claim, an unpaid supplier or subcontractor should have a copy of the bond and, if the payment bond is a statutory bond, the claimant should also have a working understanding of the statute. In most cases, legal advice is necessary.

14.1 WHEN PAYMENT BONDS ARE REQUIRED BY STATUTE

The most prominent statutory regulation of payment bonds is the federal Miller Act, 40 U.S.C. §§ 3131-3134. On any contract in excess of $100,000, the Miller Act requires the general contractor to furnish a payment bond, in an amount equal to the contract price, unless the contracting officer determines that it is impractical to obtain a bond in that amount and specifies an alternative amount for the bond.[1] The purpose of this bond is to guarantee payment to parties supplying labor and materials to contractors or subcontractors engaged in the construction, alteration, or repair of any public building or public work of the United States. The Miller Act protects subcontractors and suppliers that would otherwise be without a remedy against an insolvent contractor due to the lack of lien rights against the property of the federal government.

---

[1] On projects in excess of $25,000 up to $100,000, the contracting officer is required to obtain either a payment bond or alternative payment protection equal to 100 percent of the contract price. 40 U.S.C. § 3132; 48 CFR § 28.102-2(c).

Many states have enacted statutes requiring bonds for construction of state and local public works. These statutes, known as "little Miller Acts," usually follow the policies and procedures of the federal Miller Act.[2] Where such a state statute is patterned after the Miller Act, state courts look to federal case law interpreting the Miller Act to aid in interpretation of the state statute. Although decisions interpreting the federal act are not binding on a court's interpretation of a state's "little Miller Act," they do provide persuasive authority.[3] Statutory bonds are viewed as remedial statutes, and bonds provided pursuant to those statutes are construed liberally in favor of claimants.

It is important to remember that federal Miller Act cases do not control a state court's decision, and state court decisions can be inconsistent. Furthermore, since statutory terms are incorporated by law into public works bonds, familiarity with a state's specific requirements regarding payment bond recovery is essential to ensure that a claimant does not lose any of its bond rights.[4]

Some states have enacted legislation relating to payment bonds on private work as well. Unlike payment bonds for public work, however, no uniform pattern has emerged in these state requirements for bonding of private work.

In some states, where a statute requiring the furnishing of a payment bond is ignored and no payment bond is procured, a subcontractor or supplier may still obtain some relief. Under Georgia law, for example, a government agency is statutorily liable to the extent of the payment bond, had it been furnished.[5] Absent such a statutory provision, a subcontractor or supplier may still be able to recover from the governmental agency on a theory that the agency was negligent in failing to enforce the statutory requirements, and this proximately caused the subcontractor's inability to recover from the payment bond surety.[6] Other jurisdictions, however, will deny recovery in spite of the public body's failure to require the mandated bond.[7]

In some states, a subcontractor may still be able to recover even if it has waived all of its rights against bonds posted by a prime contractor on a public works contract. *In Coastal Caisson Drill Co. v. American Casualty Co. of Redding Pa.,*[8] a prime contractor on a state bridge project required its subcontractors to sign a subcontract

---

[2] *See, e.g.*, Ala. Code § 39-1-1; Ga. Code Ann. § 36-91-50; Fla. Stat. Ann. § 255.05; Ariz. Rev. Stat. Ann. § 34-222; Cal. Civ. Code §§ 3247,10221; N.C. Gen. Stat. § 44A-25; S.C. Code Ann. §§ 11-25-3020, 11-35-3030.

[3] *See, e.g., General Fed. Constr., Inc. v. D.R. Thomas, Inc.*, 451 A.2d 1250 (Md. 1982); *Syro Steel Co. v. Eagel Constr. Co., Inc.*, 460 S.E.2d 371 (S.C. 1995); *Rish v. Theo Bros. Constr. Co., Inc.*, 237 S.E.2d 61 (S.C. 1977).

[4] *See A.C. Legnetto Constr. Inc. v. Hartfield Fire Ins. Co.*, 702 N.E.2d 830 (N.Y. 1988).

[5] *See* Ga. Code Ann. § 36-82-102; *Hall County Sch. Dist. v. C. Robert Beals & Assocs., Inc.*, 498 S.E.2d 72 (Ga. Ct. App. 1998); *Atlanta Mechanical, Inc. v. DeKalb County*, 434 S.E.2d 494 (Ga. Ct. App. 1993).

[6] *See, e.g., Housing Auth. of Prattville v. Headley*, 360 So. 2d 1025 (Ala. Civ. App. 1978); *but see Warrior Hinkle v. Andalusia City Sch. Bd.*, 469 So. 2d 1285 (Ala. 1985) (government agency protected by sovereign immunity).

[7] *See Haskell Lemon Constr. Co. v. Independent Sch. Dist. No. 12*, 589 P.2d 677 (Okla. 1979).

[8] 523 So. 2d 791 (Fla. Dist. Ct. App. 1988); *Ruyon Enter., Inc. v. S.T. Wicole Constr. Corp. of Florida, Inc.*, 677 So. 2d 909 (Fla. Dist. Ct. App. 1996).

stating that the subcontractor "waived all rights under any bond . . . executed by Contractor and its surety."[9] When the owner failed to pay, the subcontractor sued the prime's surety on the statutory public works payment bond. The court held that the subcontract agreement provision waiving rights against the surety was void as against public policy. The court found that the public works statute, requiring bonds on such projects, expressed a strong public policy, and that such waivers undermine public policy, making subcontractors reluctant to bid on public projects.

14.2 WHO MAY CLAIM UNDER A PAYMENT BOND

Historically, payment bonds listed only the owner as obligee, and early case law held that subcontractors and suppliers had no direct right of action against the surety.[10] Recognizing that most payment bonds are intended for the protection of subcontractors and suppliers, however, courts began to interpret these bonds to allow subcontractors and suppliers to claim directly against the surety as third-party beneficiaries of the bond obligation.

Obviously, many parties contribute to the progress of each project. The language of the Miller Act—"all persons supplying work and materials in the prosecution of the work"—is extremely broad, suggesting that any party with any remote connection to the project could recover under a payment bond. However, to consider all of these contributing parties as beneficiaries of a Miller Act bond would be extremely impractical and impossible to monitor. As a result of the Miller Act's broad language, the courts continually define and redefine the scope of the statute and determine where Miller Act protection stops.

In *Clifford F. MacEvoy Co. v. United States ex rel. Tomkins Co.,*[11] the United States Supreme Court identified two general classes of claimants entitled to protection under the federal Miller Act. The first class is composed of all laborers, materialmen, subcontractors, and suppliers that deal directly with the prime contractor—the first tier. The Court also defined a second class of Miller Act claimants composed of all materialmen, subcontractors, and laborers with a direct contractual relationship with a first-tier subcontractor—the second tier. The effect of *MacEvoy*, therefore, is to limit Miller Act protection to include only those parties that have direct relationships with the prime or a first-tier subcontractor. For example, the suppliers of a second-tier subcontractor are not protected by the Miller Act.[12]

Although the Supreme Court's decision in *MacEvoy* solved one interpretation issue, it did not precisely define the term "subcontractor" for purposes of Miller Act payment bond coverage. Thirty years later, *in F. D. Rich Co. v. United States ex rel.*

---

[9] *Coastal Caisson, supra* note 8.

[10] *See, e.g., Travelers Indem. Co. v. Sasser & Co.,* 226 S.E.2d 121 (Ga. Ct. App. 1976).

[11] 322 U.S. 102 (1944).

[12] *See J. W. Bateson Co., Inc. v. United States ex rel. Board of Trustees,* 434 U.S. 586 (1978). *But see D&L Bldg., Inc. v. State ex. rel. Maltby Tank & Barge, Inc.,* 747 P.2d 517 (Wyo. 1987) (Wyoming little Miller Act coverage not limited to first two tiers).

Industrial Lumber Co.,[13] the Supreme Court reiterated *MacEvoy*'s functional definition of "subcontractor" and emphasized that whether one is a subcontractor relates to "the substantiality and importance of his relationship with the prime contractor."[14]

While federal courts have given the term "subcontractor" a narrow definition under the Miller Act, and this limitation of coverage has generally been applied to little Miller Act statutes as well, public work bonds are usually liberally construed in favor of bond claimants.[15] In general, any person having a direct contractual relationship with the prime contractor or a first-tier subcontractor will fall within the scope of the payment bond.

In determining whether a party qualifies as a subcontractor, courts focus on the contractual relationship between the claimant and the prime contractor.[16] A party that merely supplies materials will probably fail to qualify as a "subcontractor." A party that installs materials would be far more likely to meet the test. In the gap, however, is the specialty subcontractor that supplies "customized materials," designed or fabricated specially for the project, and having little or no commercial value outside the particular project.

In some cases, the provider of such "customized" materials is considered a subcontractor for Miller Act purposes. In *United States ex rel. Parker-Hannifin Corp. v. Lane Construction Corp.,*[17] the court held that a manufacturer of custom-made gates for a dam project was not a supplier. Instead, the court held that the manufacturer was a subcontractor since the sole purpose and usefulness of the gates would be their functioning as an integral portion of the dam.[18]

The distinction between a supplier and subcontractor at the second tier is critical, as it will determine whether the Miller Act protects the claimant. The Act does protect suppliers to prime contractors and subcontractors, but not suppliers to suppliers. For example, in *United States ex rel. Gulf States Enterprises, Inc. v. R. R. Tway, Inc.,*[19] the court found that the provider of a bulldozer and operator was a supplier, not a subcontractor, because the provider was not responsible for doing a definable part of the contract performance. The agreement with the contractor was not to do specific work, but rather to provide a dozer and operator at an agreed-upon hourly rate "as needed." As a supplier instead of a subcontractor, the company that actually owned and leased the dozer to the provider could not recover unpaid lease payments from the prime contractor's surety under the Miller Act.

---

[13] 417 U.S. 116 (1974).

[14] *Id.* at 123.

[15] *See United States ex rel. Gray-Bar Elec. Co. v. J. H. Copeland & Sons Constr., Inc.*, 568 F.2d 1159 (5th Cir. 1978), *cert. denied*, 436 U.S. 957 (1978).

[16] *United States ex rel. Conveyor Rental & Sales Co. v. Aetna Cas. & Sur. Co.*, 981 F.2d 448 (9th Cir. 1992); *Aetna Cas. & Sur. Co. v. United States ex rel. Gibson Steel Co.*, 382 F.2d 615 (5th Cir. 1967).

[17] 477 F. Supp. 400 (M.D. Pa. 1979); *see also United States ex rel. Newport News Shipping & Dry Rock Co. v. Blount Bros. Constr. Co.*, 168 F. Supp. 407 (D. Md. 1958); *but see Eastern Indus. Mktg., Inc. v. Desco Elec. Supply*, 651 F. Supp. 140 (W.D. Pa. 1986).

[18] *Parker-Hannifin, supra* note 17.

[19] 938 F.2d 583 (5th Cir. 1991).

Other factors considered in determining whether a party qualifies as a subcontractor under the Miller Act include: whether a payment or performance bond was required, whether the price included sales tax, whether progress payments and retainage were withheld, and whether shop drawings and certified payrolls were submitted.[20]

Also arising under the general issue of "who is a subcontractor" is the issue of "telescoping" contractual relationships. A prime contractor will not be allowed to insert a dummy subcontractor between itself and actual performing subcontractors simply to avoid Miller Act liability. When subcontractors or suppliers go unpaid by the dummy subcontractor, they may still sue on the bond.[21] Unless courts find evidence of bad faith or fraud, however, they will generally not look beyond formal contractual relationships.

The scope of the term "subcontractor" varies among the little Miller Acts. Coverage under state law is often broader than that under the federal Act.[22] Where there is no statutory definition provided, courts will often apply the definition of "subcontractor" developed under the Miller Act.[23] Other factors that state courts consider include: trade customs; whether the materials are specially fabricated; and the extent to which the claimant has assumed responsibility for the prime contractor's performance.[24]

The payment bond form used frequently on private projects, as well as on many state and local public works, is the American Institute of Architects' (AIA) Document A312 (1984 ed.), which defines a claimant as follows:

> An individual or entity having a direct contract with the Contractor or with a subcontractor of the Contractor to furnish labor, materials or equipment for use in the performance of the contract. The intent of this Bond shall be to include without limitation in the terms "labor, materials or equipment" that part of water, gas, power, light, heat, oil, gasoline, telephone service, or rental equipment used in the Construction Contract, architectural and engineering services required for performance for the work of the Contractor and the Contractor's subcontractors, and all other items for which a mechanic's lien may be asserted in the jurisdiction where labor, materials or equipment were furnished.

This definition is much more specific than that contained in its predecessor, AIA A311. While this newer definition maintains the limitation of claimants down to the second tier, it also relies on local lien laws for a description of the type of work covered by the bond.

---

[20] *Conveyor Rental, supra* note 16; *see also United States ex rel. Consolidated Pipe & Supply Co. v. Morrison-Knudsen Co., Inc.,* 687 F.2d 129 (11th Cir. 1982); *United States ex rel. Pioneer Steel Co. v. Ellis Constr. Co.,* 398 F. Supp. 719 (E.D. Tenn. 1975); *United States ex rel. Potomac Rigging Co. v. Wright Contracting Co.,* 194 F. Supp. 444 (D. Md. 1961).

[21] *See Ragan v. Tri-County Excavating, Inc.,* 62 F.3d 501 (3d Cir. 1995); *Continental Cas. Co. v. United States ex rel. Conroe Creosoting Co.,* 308 F.2d 846 (5th Cir. 1962).

[22] *See Tom Barrow Co. v. St. Paul Fire & Marine Ins. Co.,* 421 S.E.2d 85 (Ga. Ct. App. 1992).

[23] *See, e.g., Lennox Indus. Inc. v. City of Davenport,* 320 N.W.2d 575 (Iowa 1982).

[24] *See Tiffany Constr. Co. v. Hancock & Kelley Constr. Co.,* 589 P.2d 978 (Ariz. 1975).

The standard payment bond form published by The Associated General Contractors of America, AGC Document No. 261 (2000 ed.), defines a claimant as "an individual or entity having a direct contract with the Contractor or having a contract with a subcontractor having a direct contract with the Contractor. . . ." Essentially, the classes of protected parties are the same under either industry standard form.

14.3 WORK QUALIFYING FOR PAYMENT BOND COVERAGE

After determining who is protected by a payment bond, the next step is to determine what qualifies for protection. The Miller Act simply provides payment protection for labor and materials furnished "in the prosecution of the work." Courts have generally interpreted this language liberally, holding that it covers not only work incorporated in the project, but also work done for the benefit of the project.[25]

In *United States ex rel. National U.S. Radiator Corp. v. D. C. Loveys Co.*,[26] a claimant obtained relief from a Miller Act surety for material that was damaged in transit and then delivered to the project. Although the material was not incorporated into the project itself, the court held that the material was nevertheless furnished "in the prosecution of the work," because the subcontractor had assumed the risk of loss or damage during shipment.[27]

Similarly, in another case, a supplier recovered for delivery of equipment to a subcontractor in spite of the subcontractor's subsequent removal of the material from the job site and use on another project.[28] Following this general line of federal cases, state courts have ruled that a supplier need not show that the materials delivered to the site were actually incorporated into the project.[29]

As a general rule, the Miller Act applies if the material is substantially consumed or rendered useless in the prosecution of the work.[30] This includes parts and equipment necessary to and wholly consumed by the project and material used in construction but not incorporated into the project, such as concrete formwork.[31]

---

[25] *See United States ex rel. Sunbelt Pipe Corp. v. United States Fidelity & Guar. Co.*, 785 F.2d 468 (4th Cir. 1986); *United States ex rel. Westinghouse Elec. Supply Co. v. Endebrock-White Co.*, 275 F.2d 57 (4th Cir. 1960); *United States ex rel. Skip Kirchdorfer, Inc. v. Aegis/Bublin Joint Venture*, 860 F. Supp. 387 (E.D. Va. 1994).

[26] 174 F. Supp. 44 (D. Mass. 1959).

[27] *Id.*

[28] *See Glassell-Taylor Co. v. Magnolia Petroleum Co.*, 153 F.2d 527 (5th Cir. 1946); *see also United States ex rel. Carlson v. Continental Cas. Co.*, 414 F.2d 413 (5th Cir. 1969).

[29] *See, e.g., Solite Masonry Units v. Piland Constr. Co., Inc.*, 232 S.E.2d 759 (Va. 1977); *see also Key Constructors, Inc. v. H & M Gas Co.*, 537 So. 2d 1318 (Miss. 1989); *Mid-Continent Cas. Co. v. P&H Supply, Inc.*, 490 P.2d 1358 (Okla. 1971) (evidence that materials were delivered to project site creates rebuttable presumption that materials were actually consumed in construction).

[30] *See Sunbelt Pipe, supra* note 25; *see also United States ex rel. Tom P. McDermott, Inc. v. Woods Constr. Co.*, 224 F. Supp. 406 (N.D. Okla. 1963).

[31] *Sunbelt Pipe, supra* note 25; *Kirchdorfer, supra* note 25; *United States ex rel. Chemetron Corp. v. George A. Fuller Co.*, 250 F. Supp. 649 (Mont. 1966).

Guarantee work or repairs that become necessary and are performed after substantial completion of the project may also be the subject of Miller Act recovery. The cost of incidental repairs necessary to maintain equipment during its use on the project may also be recoverable under a bond.[32] However, substantial "replacement" repairs are not covered, on the theory that they add value to the construction equipment by extending its useful life beyond the project in question.

The cost of the fair rental value of equipment leased for use in the prosecution of the contract work may be covered by a Miller Act bond.[33] Many little Miller Acts, however, expressly include coverage for leased equipment under statutory payment bonds.[34] AIA Document A312 (1984 ed.), quoted above, expressly contemplates coverage for leased equipment.

Miller Act payment bonds have also been construed to cover transportation and delivery costs.[35] Food and lodging have been found to be covered when they are a necessary and integral part of performance.[36]

Typically, coverage will include union contributions, and contributions to employee funds, such as health and welfare.[37] In contrast to these broad definitions of qualifying "labor, materials or equipment," courts usually require some direct involvement with and benefit to the project.[38] For example, in *Wasatch Bank of Pleasant Grove v. Surety Insurance Co. of California*,[39] a bank that made loans to a subcontractor, which the subcontractor used to pay for materials and labor, could not recover on the subcontractor's payment bond. The court held that the bond's protection extended only to contracts for providing labor and materials, and not to lenders that provided funds to purchase them.

---

[32] *See Finch Equip. Corp. v. Frieden*, 901 F.2d 665 (8th Cir. 1990); *Massachusetts Bonding & Ins. Co. v. United States ex rel. Clarksdale Mach. Co.*, 88 F.2d 388 (5th Cir. 1937); *Maryland Cas. Co. v. Ohio River Gravel Co.*, 20 F.2d 514 (4th Cir. 1927), *cert. denied*, 275 U.S. 570 (1927); *but see Transamerica Premier Ins. Co. v. Ober*, 894 F. Supp. 471 (D. Me. 1995).

[33] *See Kirchdorfer, supra* note 25; *see also United States ex rel. Miss. Rd. Supply Co. v. H.R. Morgan, Inc.*, 542 F.2d 262 (5th Cir. 1976), *cert. denied*, 434 U.S. 828 (1977); *Friebel & Hartman, Inc. v. United States ex rel. Codell Constr. Co.*, 238 F.2d 394 (6th Cir. 1956); *United States ex rel. D&P Corp. v. Transamerica Ins. Co.*, 881 Supp. 1505 (D. Kan. 1995) (may recover rental value of owned equipment).

[34] *See, e.g.*, Pa. Stat. Ann. tit. 8 § 193(a)(2); R.I. Gen. Laws § 37-12-1.

[35] *See United States ex rel. Benkurt Co. v. John A. Johnson & Sons, Inc.*, 236 F.2d 864 (3d Cir. 1956); *United States ex rel. Carlisle Constr. Co., Inc. v. Coastal Structures, Inc.*, 689 F. Supp. 1092 (M.D. Fla. 1988).

[36] *Brogran v. National Sur. Co.*, 246 U.S. 257 (1918); *United States ex rel. T.M.S. Mechanical Contractors, Inc. v. Millers Mut. Fire Ins. Co. of Texas*, 942 F.2d 946 (5th Cir. 1991).

[37] *United States ex rel. Sherman v. Carter*, 353 U.S. 210, 218 (1957).

[38] Carlisle, *supra* note 35.

[39] 703 P.2d 298 (Utah 1985).

14.4   RECOVERY UNDER PAYMENT BONDS
FOR EXTRA WORK OR DELAY COSTS

Work done by a qualifying claimant under a change order is generally within the payment bond's protection. Indeed, recovery for such extra work under the Miller Act does not depend on the prime contractor's ability to recover its additional costs from the government.[40]

Traditionally, delay damages have been viewed as outside the scope of Miller Act coverage.[41] (Note: A restriction on a claim for delay damages under a payment bond does not affect the claimant's general right to collect delay damages from the contractor or subcontractor causing the damage.[42])

This traditional prohibition of delay damage claims against payment bonds has begun to erode, and the federal courts are split on whether or not such damages are covered. For example, in *United States ex rel. Mandel Bros. Contracting Corp. v. P. J. Carlin Construction Co.*,[43] a federal district court held that the bond claimant could recover costs of delay on a *quantum meruit* ("value added") theory. In *Mandel Bros.*, the claimant alleged that the general contractor's failure to provide access to the work site restrained the claimant's performance and was such a substantial interference with the claimant's progress that it amounted to an abandonment of the contract. The court rejected the traditional doctrine that breaches of contract predicated on delays were not compensable under the Miller Act, reasoning that a *quantum meruit* claim is one for labor and materials actually furnished in the prosecution of the work, and therefore is within the scope of the payment bond.

In *T.M.S. Mechanical*,[44] the court held that a subcontractor may recover delay costs under a payment bond if the costs are actual out-of-pocket increases. No profit was allowed.[45]

In another case, *United States ex rel. Pertun Construction Co. v. Harvester's Group, Inc.*,[46] although the subcontract contained a "no-damages-for-delay" clause, the court read the clause as conditioned upon the subcontractor being granted reasonable time extensions for delays. The court found that the prime contractor wrongfully and prematurely terminated the subcontractor, and as a result, neither the contractor nor its surety could claim protection under the no-damages-for-delay clause.[47]

---

[40] *See Mai Steel Serv. Inc. v. Blake Constr. Co.*, 981 F.2d 414 (9th Cir. 1992); *United States ex rel. Warren Painting v. J. C. Boespflug Constr. Co.*, 325 F.2d 54 (9th Cir. 1963); *United States ex rel. Kilsby v. George*, 243 F.2d 83 (5th Cir. 1957).

[41] *See McDaniel v. Ashton-Median Co.*, 357 F.2d 511 (9th Cir. 1966); *United States ex rel. Pittsburgh-Des Moines Steel Co. v. MacDonald Constr. Co.*, 281 F. Supp. 1010 (E.D. Mo. 1968).

[42] *See United States Fidelity & Guar. Co. v. Ernest Constr. Co.*, 854 F. Supp. 1545 (M.D. Fla. 1994).

[43] 254 F. Supp. 637 (E.D.N.Y. 1966).

[44] *T.M.S. Mechanical, supra* note 36; *see also Mai Steel, supra* note 40.

[45] *Id.*

[46] 918 F.2d 915 (11th Cir. 1990).

[47] *Id.*

14.5 THE EFFECT OF PAYMENT BONDS ON LIEN RIGHTS

Most jurisdictions hold that a right to claim under a payment bond supplements rather than replaces a subcontractor's lien rights. The existence of a payment bond simply provides a subcontractor or other qualified claimant with a separate right of recovery, in addition to any lien rights.[48] However, in some jurisdictions, the existence of a right to claim under a payment bond abrogates the claimant's lien rights.[49]

14.6 THE SURETY'S DEFENSES TO PAYMENT BOND LIABILITY

In any claim against a payment bond, the surety is entitled to assert any defenses of the principal, including the defense of offset or recoupment. The surety may have additional defenses of its own. Generally, such independent defenses are found in the applicable bond statute and/or the terms of the bond itself. The most common surety defenses are a claimant's failure to comply with notice requirements and time limitations. When asserting technical defenses relating to the timing and sufficiency of the required notice, however, the surety should deal with bond claimants in good faith.[50]

It is imperative that potential claimants review the terms of the payment bond, as well as any applicable statutes and case law, to determine the exact timing, nature, recipient of notice, or any other requirements necessary to secure their rights under the bond. Any deviation may defeat an otherwise valid claim.[51] This careful review is equally important when responding to a payment bond claim.

Pay-when-paid clauses are found in many subcontracts and are the subject of considerable litigation regarding their interpretation and enforcement (*see* **Chapter 8**). If that effective pay-when-paid language is included in the subcontract, a question remains when that defense to the payment obligation also applies to the obligation under the payment bond. Some courts have held that the payment bond is a separate agreement and that the inability to bring an action on the subcontract does not necessarily preclude recovery on the payment bond.[52] Some states have statutes allowing a payment bond surety to include conditional payment language in the

---

[48] 57 C.J.S. *Mechanics Liens* § 258.

[49] *See* Fla. Stat. Ann. § 713.23; *Scheifer v. All-Shores Constr. & Supply Co.*, 260 So. 2d 270 (Fla. Dist. Ct. App. 1972); *Globe Indem. Co. v. West Texas Lumber Co.*, 34 S.W.2d 896 (Tex. Civ. App. 1930).

[50] *See Szarkwoski v. Reliance Ins. Co.*, 404 N.W.2d 502 (N.D. 1987) (Supreme Court of North Dakota recognized a cause of action by an unpaid subcontractor against a surety for its alleged bad-faith refusal to pay on the bond); *United States ex rel, Ehmcke Sheet Metal Works v. Wausau Ins. Co.*, 755 F. Supp. 906, 909 (E.D. Cal. 1991) (state law may provide a cause of action against Miller Act surety for breach of covenant of good faith and fair dealing); *see also K-W Industries v. National Surety Corp.*, 855 F.2d 640 (9th Cir. 1988).

[51] *See United States ex rel. B&R, Inc. v. Donald Lane Constr.*, 19 F. Supp. 2d 217 (D. Del. 1998).

[52] *OBS Co. v. Pace Const. Corp.*, 558 So. 2d 404 (Fla. 1990).

payment bond.[53] Typically, the required language is specified in the statute.[54] Contractors and their sureties need to carefully evaluate such language and its application. For example, in *Everett Painting Co., Inc. v. Padula & Wadsworth Const., Inc.*[55] the court held that the condition-precedent language in the subcontract did not bar an action on the payment bond on a public school project. Moreover, since the payment bond was issued pursuant to Florida Statutes § 255.05, the inclusion of conditional payment language would have been ineffective as that public bond statute does not authorize the use of conditional payment bonds on public projects.

14.7   Time of Notice

Under the Miller Act and most little Miller Act statutes, notice must be received by the prime contractor within a certain number of days from the date the claimant last performed work or supplied materials for which the claim is made. The Miller Act notice period is 90 days for second tier claimants.[56] The notice period for most little Miller Act statutes is 90 days as well.[57]

While notice under the Miller Act must be sent to the prime contractor, the surety does not have to receive notice.[58] The Miller Act requires notice to be sent "by any means which provides written third party verification of delivery."[59] Oral notice by itself, however, will generally be insufficient.[60] Since notice is intended to protect the contractor that provided the payment bond, the written notice must expressly or impliedly inform the contractor that the claimant is looking to it or the surety for payment.[61] Per 40 U.S.C. § 3133(b)(2), the notice must also state with substantial accuracy the amount claimed and the name of the party to which the materials or services were provided. The Miller Act notice requirements, however, do not apply to subcontractors and suppliers in direct privity with the prime contractor.

14.8   Time of Lawsuit

A lawsuit to enforce the provisions of a payment bond under the Miller Act must generally be brought within one year of "the day on which the last of the labor was

---

[53] Florida Statutes § 713.245.

[54] *Id.*

[55] 856 So.2d 1059 (Fla. Dist. Ct. App. 2003)

[56] 40 U.S.C. § 3133 (b)(2); *see also B&R, Inc., supra* note 51.

[57] *See, e.g.*, Ga. Code Ann. § 36-82-104.

[58] *See Continental Cas. Co. v. United States ex rel. Robertson Lumber Co.*, 305 F.2d 794 (8th Cir. 1962), *cert. denied*, 371 U.S. 922 (1962).

[59] 40 U.S.C. § 3133(b)(2)(A).

[60] *See United States ex rel. Brothers Builders Supply Co., v. Old World Artisans, Inc.*, 702 F. Supp. 1561 (N.D. Ala. 1988); *Fleischer Eng'g & Constr. Co. v. United States ex rel. Hallenback*, 311 U.S. 15 (1940).

[61] *See MacCaferri Gabions, Inc. v. Dynateria, Inc.*, 91 F.3d 1431 (11th Cir. 1996), *reh'g denied*, 102 F.3d 557, *cert. denied*, 117 S. Ct. 1430; *Bowden v. United States ex rel. Malloy*, 239 F.2d 592 (9th Cir. 1956), *cert. denied*, 353 U.S. 957 (1957).

performed or material was supplied by [claimant]."[62] Federal courts consider this one-year rule jurisdictional in nature, and, as such, it cannot be waived by the surety.[63]

A substantial body of law has developed defining "the day on which the last of the labor was performed or material was supplied by [claimant]." For example, in *General Insurance Co. of America v. United States ex rel. Audley Moore & Son,*[64] the court refused to regard the act of "inspecting" within the definition of "labor" as used in the Miller Act. However, the correction of prior work has been held to constitute "labor" where the government has refused to accept the project until such work has been completed. The correction of defects or warranty work done after completion of the original subcontract work most likely will not constitute the furnishing of labor or materials for purposes of the Miller Act's time limitation.[65]

These Miller Act cases distinguish "guarantee work" from "punchlist work." In other words, work that the government demands to be finished in accordance with the contract plans and specifications by a punchlist or other similar device is considered to be contract work. Performance of this work will normally toll the provisions of the Miller Act governing when notice must be given and suit must be filed. On the other hand, work performed under a warranty or to repair latent defects is regarded by the courts as being noncontract work, and, as such, outside of the term "labor" as used in the Miller Act.[66]

Despite the profusion of federal case law fixing the date from which the one-year limitation period runs, the interpretation of the same issue under a little Miller Act may differ. Ultimately, the issue is often a fact question for the court to decide. In *Johnson Service Co. v. Transamerica Insurance Co.,*[67] the court observed: "Common to all of these decisions . . . is the notion that each case must be judged on its own facts and that sweeping rules about 'repairs' offer little help in the necessary analysis."[68]

14.9 Misrepresented Status of Payments

Often, a subcontractor may get a materialman to sign lien waivers in order for the subcontractor to receive final payment from the prime contractor. To induce the signing of these lien waivers, the subcontractor promises to pay the materialman as soon

---

[62] 40 U.S.C. § 3133(b)(4).

[63] *See United States ex rel. Celanese Coatings Co. v. Gullard,* 504 F.2d 466 (9th Cir. 1974); *United States ex rel. Soda Montgomery,* 253 F.2d 509 (3d Cir. 1958); *but see United States ex rel. American Bank v. C.I.T. Constr., Inc. of Tex.,* 944 F.2d 253 (5th Cir. 1991).

[64] 406 F.2d 442 (5th Cir. 1969), *cert. denied,* 396 U.S. 902 (1969).

[65] *See United States ex rel. Light & Power Utils. Corp. v. Liles Constr. Co.,* 440 F.2d 474 (5th Cir. 1971); *United States ex rel. Automatic Elevator Co. v. Lori Constr.,* 912 F. Supp. 398 (N.D. Ill. 1996). *See also Southern Steel Co. v. Union Pac. Ins. Co.,* 935 F.2d 1201 (11th Cir. 1991) (involving a private bond but using Miller Act decisions as precedent); *Johnson Serv. Co. v. Transamerican Ins. Co.,* 485 F.2d 164 (5th Cir. 1973) (same).

[66] *See, e.g., United States ex rel. State Elec. Supply Co. v. Hesselden Constr. Co.,* 404 F.2d 774 (10th Cir. 1968); *United States ex rel. Hussman Corp. v. Fidelity & Deposit Co. of Md.,* 999 F. Supp. 734 (D.N.J. 1998).

[67] 485 F.2d 164 (5th Cir. 1973).

[68] *Id.* at 173.

as the subcontractor receives payment from the prime contractor. If a subcontractor does not make good on this promise, because of the intervention of bankruptcy or judgments, the materialman then sues on the payment bond for any outstanding balance. When this occurs, a surety may raise as a defense the materialman's misrepresentation to the contractor of the status of the subcontractor's account and, by so doing, waiver of its right to payment. In denying relief to the materialman, the courts rely on the theory of estoppel to prevent the materialman from claiming under the bond since the prime contractor relied upon the materialman's acts to the prime contractor's and surety's detriment. By signing the waivers, the materialman may discharge the prime contractor and its surety from any obligation on the bond.[69]

14.10   Claim or Lien Waivers

In addition to the defense of estoppel based on misrepresentation by a claimant, a claimant may have simply waived its bond rights. The subcontract agreements used by general contractors sometimes ask a subcontractor to waive its lien rights and bond rights. On private projects, a subcontractor may be asked to waive any lien rights and instead look only to the payment bond. As discussed previously, in most states, payment bonds are mandated for public construction works.

On federal government projects, a waiver of Miller Act rights by a party otherwise protected must be specific. One court has said that to be an effective waiver of Miller Act rights, the Miller Act must be mentioned. Courts do not favor a finding that a subcontractor has contractually waived its rights under the Miller Act.[70]

The Miller Act also addresses the timing of any waiver of the right to sue on the payment bond. 40 U.S.C. § 3133(c) provides:

> (c) A waiver of the right to bring a civil action on a payment bond required under this subchapter is void unless the waiver is –
>
> (1) in writing;
>
> (2) signed by the person whose right is waived; and
>
> (3) executed after the person whose right is waived has furnished labor or material for use in the performance of the contract.

This text reflects the substance of a 1999 amendment to the Miller Act, and any comparable state little Miller Act legislation should be carefully considered when drafting subcontract or purchase order terms and conditions, especially those addressing subcontractor/supplier recovery on claims or the application of the disputes process in the prime contract to the subcontractor or supplier.

---

[69] *See United States ex rel. Krupp Steel Prods. Inc. v. Aetna Ins. Co.*, 923 F.2d 1521 (11th Cir. 1991); *United States ex rel. Gulfport Piping Co. v. Monaco & Son, Inc.*, 336 F.2d 636 (4th Cir. 1964). *See also United States ex rel. Westinghouse Elec. v. James Stewart Co.*, 336 F.2d 777 (9th Cir. 1964).

[70] *See H.W. Caldwell & Son, Inc. v. United States for Use and Benefit of John H. Moon & Sons, Inc.*, 406 F.2d 21, 23 (5th Cir. 1969); *United States for the Use and Benefit of DDC Interiors, Inc. v. Dawson Construction Company, Inc.*, 895 F. Supp. 270 (1995), *aff'd*, 82 F.3d 427 (1996).

Many general contractors typically require waiver forms to be submitted with each pay application. Such waiver forms vary considerably in form and content. Often, the form will include a waiver of lien and/or payment bond rights through a certain date or for work performed up to a certain date. In defending a payment bond suit, a surety will examine the underlying contract, pay applications, and monthly waiver forms to determine if a waiver has occurred.

➤ POINTS TO REMEMBER

- A payment bond provides a financial guarantee of payment from the surety to suppliers and subcontractors, but only subject to the terms of that bond and applicable statutes and case law.
- Payment bonds are most prevalent on public works projects on which they are required by statute to replace the protection provided by lien rights, which generally do not exist on public projects.
- A payment bond required by statute will generally be construed according to the terms of the statute. Private payment bonds (those not required by statute) are essentially private contractual undertakings in which the terms of the bond will be determinative. In any event, potential claimants should review and be familiar with the terms of the payment bond relevant to a particular project.
- The federal Miller Act governs payment bond requirements for federal construction projects. Most states have enacted "little Miller Acts," which govern payment bonds on state and local projects, which are modeled after the federal Miller Act. Regardless of similarities, claimants should make themselves aware of the requirements applicable to the jurisdiction that governs the project.
- In most jurisdictions, payment bond coverage does not extend beyond second-tier subcontractors and suppliers—subcontractors to subcontractors and suppliers to subcontractors. Under the federal Miller Act and many little Miller Acts, coverage does not extend to suppliers to suppliers.
- Payment bonds, whether statutory or private, involve various notice and timing requirements relating to claims and litigation. Such requirements must be identified and complied with. Failure to comply may bar otherwise valid claims.

15

PERFORMANCE BONDS AND TERMINATION

When the contract of a contractor or subcontractor is terminated for default, the contractor's performance bond and performance bond surety become key ingredients in the completion of the construction contract. Performance bonds, or bonds assuring the performance and completion of construction contract responsibilities, have long been a statutory requirement in public contracting and frequently are mandated in private construction contracts.[1] Just as the project owner looks to the performance bond surety for protection from a contractor default on its performance obligations, contractors and subcontractors may require performance bond protection in their contracts and subcontracts with lower-tier contractors. (This chapter discusses performance bonds and terminations in the context of a contract between an owner and the general contractor, but the principles are equally applicable to contracts between general contractors and their subcontractors, etc.)

Essentially, the performance bond is a three-party contract involving a principal (e.g., a contractor), a surety guaranteeing the principal's performance, and the obligee, the owner or contractor for whose benefit the bond is provided. The form of the performance bond reflecting this tri-party relationship may take many different forms. In recent years, surety companies, contractors, and owners have struggled over the definition of the rights and liabilities flowing from performance bonds, and every construction industry participant is well advised to develop some basic understanding of the rights and potential liabilities associated with performance bonds. Although contract terminations and the enforcement of performance bond obligations are encountered less frequently than some of the other problems and issues discussed in this book, the termination of a contract and the resulting demand on a

---

[1] *See* AGC Document 200 (2000 ed.), ¶ 10.

performance bond surety often are accompanied by extraordinary risks for those involved in or affected by the contract termination process.

In addition to being important during a crisis, performance bonds also indirectly serve as a screening device for contractor selection. A surety will not, or should not, underwrite bonds for contractors that may not be able to perform, whether because of a lack of expertise or a lack of adequate finances. If a contractor cannot obtain the required bond, the requesting owner or prime contractor is forewarned of the risk of nonperformance in going forward with that contractor.

In this chapter, claims against performance bonds, as well as the rights and risks for each party to the tri-party bond, are examined. The fundamentals of the law of suretyship are outlined as an introduction to the discussion of cases arising out of performance bond disputes. Following the discussion of performance bonds, issues and options presented by terminations for default and for convenience are addressed.

15.1 PERFORMANCE BONDS

15.2 Fundamentals of Suretyship

A claim on a performance bond involves a default or alleged default on the part of the contractor. Therefore, an understanding of the legal principles related to performance bonds is imperative.

15.3 Performance Bonds Are Not Insurance Policies

To understand the law of suretyship, one must appreciate the distinction between a surety bond and an insurance policy. A surety bond is not an insurance policy, although in some respects they are similar.[2] "Insurance has been defined as a contract whereby one undertakes to [indemnify] another against loss, damage or liability arising from an unknown or contingent event; whereas a contract of suretyship is one to answer for the debt, default or miscarriage of another. . . ."[3]

Two parties enter into an insurance contract: the insurer and the insured. A performance bond, however, involves three parties: the "principal," the party whose faithful performance is being bonded; the "obligee," the party for whose protection the bond is being issued; and the "surety," the party that, together with the principal, jointly binds itself to the obligee for the faithful performance of the principal's obligation.

Under this tripartite arrangement, the principal (the contractor) remains primarily liable to the owner/obligee. The surety's obligation is secondary and arises only upon the failure or default of the principal.[4] Before any surety liability arises, the

---

[2] *See Farmers Ins. Exch. V. Midwest Emery Frgt. Sys., Ins.*, 215 N.W.2d 623 (Minn. 1974).

[3] *Meyer v. Building & Realty Servs. Co.*, 196 N.E. 250, 253–254 (Ind. 1935) (emphasis added); *see United States v. Frisk*, 675 F.2d 1079, 182 n.6 (9th Cir. 1982); *Madison County Farmers Ass'n v. American Employers Ins. Co.*, 209 F.2d 581, 585 (5th Cir. 1954).

[4] *See Meyer, supra* note 3 at 253.

principal must be "in default" of its contract obligations. In order to constitute a default, there must be a clear declaration of default by the obligee, and the default must constitute a material breach of the contract.[5] The surety has no duty to act in the face of "mere obligee complaints" or threats to declare the principal in default. The surety is not liable to the obligee for partial or minor breaches that do not rise to a level of a material contract breach.[6]

15.4   Indemnification—the Bottom Line   Implied within the contract of suretyship is the principal's obligation to reimburse its surety for any cost, loss, or liability the surety may suffer as the result of the surety's bond obligations.[7] A far more common source of the principal's liability, however, is an express indemnification agreement required by the surety to induce it to execute a performance bond for the contractor. Such indemnity agreements will be required of the contractor principal and often are required of contractor corporation shareholders or officers (and oftentimes their spouses). These indemnity arrangements typically require (1) that the principal assign to the surety, in the event of a principal default, all tools, materials, and equipment on the job site and the principal's interest in future contract payments; (2) that the principal indemnify and hold harmless the surety from any loss, expense, or claims; and (3) that the principal deposit funds with the surety in the amount of a reserve established by the surety as additional security for any potential bond claim.

Despite the broad language contained in typical indemnity agreements, an indemnitor of a surety is not without certain defenses. The obligation of the surety only comes into play upon the default of the principal.[8] Thus, if the principal is not in default, and has not confessed default to the surety, the surety has no liability to the owner/obligee under the bond. If a surety responds to the demands of the owner to remedy the contractor's alleged default, and the surety does so over the contractor's objections, the contractor may nonetheless argue that it has discharged any liability under the indemnity agreement with the surety if it is established that the owner's termination of the contractor was improper.[9] On the other hand, where the surety has unreasonably failed to accept a favorable settlement offer that would have reduced the indemnitor's exposure, such unreasonable behavior may discharge the indemnitor to the extent that the actual damages sought exceed the settlement offer.[10]

The above factual circumstances notwithstanding, the standard industry language typically included in indemnity agreements, including the surety's unequivocal right to settle, is generally enforceable.[11] However, the surety has a duty of good faith and fair dealing as to all parties, including the principal(s), the obligee(s), and the

[5] *L&A Contracting Co. v. Southern Concrete Servs.*, 17 F.3d 106 (5th Cir. 1994).

[6] *Id.*

[7] *See, e.g., Kimberly-Clark Corp. v. Alpha Bldg. Co.*, 591 F. Supp. 198 (N.D. Miss. 1984).

[8] *Travelers Indem. Co. v. United States ex rel. W. Steel Co.*, 362 F.2d 896 (9th Cir. 1966).

[9] *See Seaboard Sur. Co. v. Dale Constr. Co.*, 230 F.2d 625 (1st Cir. 1965); *Angle v. Banker's Sur. Co.*, 210 F. 289 (N.D.N.Y. 1913).

[10] *See Briggs v. Travelers Indem. Co.*, 289 So. 2d 762 (Fla. Dist. Ct. App. 1974).

[11] *See, e.g., U. S. Fidelity & Guaranty v. Napier Electric & Construction Co.*, 571 S.W.2d 644 (Ky. App. 1978).

indemnitor(s). Absent a showing of a breach of the surety's good-faith duty, a surety will likely be able to enforce an indemnity agreement.[12] The standard for establishing a breach of the good-faith duty is very high. In circumstances where an indemnitor sought to avoid its obligation to the surety based on the surety's "bad-faith" settlement of the obligee's claims, a Connecticut court recently stated that the indemnitor must "establish something more than mere negligence," but something less than fraud.[13] The court explained that the claimant must show that the surety acted with an "improper motive" or a "dishonest purpose."[14]

15.5 "Common Law" versus "Statutory" Bonds Performance bonds often are statutorily required in connection with public construction projects at the federal, state, and even municipal level. With certain limited exceptions, performance bonds are required on federal government construction projects by the Miller Act.[15]

Because legal rights and responsibilities associated with claims on statutory bonds often differ from those associated with a common-law bond, it is critical to ascertain whether the bond is a common-law or statutory bond. The primary test depends upon an examination of the bond, concentrating on the obligations imposed upon the principal and its surety. The test requires a comparison of the minimal requirements enunciated in the statute and the language contained within the bond.[16] When the surety's obligations have not been extended beyond the statutory minimum requirements, the bond is statutory.[17] It is important to note that, even though a bond is furnished incident to a public works project, it is not necessarily construed as a statutory bond.[18] Furthermore, merely because a bond fails to reference a particular statute does not automatically render it a common-law bond.[19]

15.6 The Surety's Obligations The nature of the surety's obligation is strictly financial, as expressed by the terms of the bond itself. The performance bond surety binds itself jointly and severally with its principal to pay to the obligee, the owner of the project, a sum certain or penal sum, generally equal to the contract amount. Any such payment, however, is due only if the principal wrongfully and without justification defaults on the primary obligation (the contract) and only to the extent of any loss to the obligee (the owner). Generally, the surety's liability is strictly limited by both the terms of the bond and by the terms of the underlying contract, which is typically incorporated into and made a part of the bond.

---

[12] *See, e.g., Artnz Contracting Co. v. St. Paul Fire & Marine Ins. Co.*, 47 Cal. App. 4th 464 (Cal. App. 1996).

[13] *PSE Consulting, Inc. v. Frank Mercede and Sons, Inc.*, 838 A.2d 135 (Conn. 2004).

[14] *Id.*

[15] 40 U.S.C. §§ 3131-3134

[16] *Florida Keys Community College v. Insurance Co. of N. Amer.*, 456 So. 2d 1250 (Fla. Dist. Ct. App. 1984). Statutory bonds are those that meet the minimal requirements of the statute; common-law bonds are those that provide coverage in excess of the minimum statutory requirements.

[17] *Id.*

[18] *Id. See also Martin Paving Co., v. United Pac. Ins. Co.*, 646 So. 2d 268 (Fla. Dist. Ct. App. 1994).

[19] *Florida Keys Community College, supra* note 16.

Since the express purpose of the bond is to secure the performance of the underlying contract, the bond and the contract are read together.[20] In this manner, the surety's obligations are found in the contract, the plans and specifications, and the bond.[21]

Consequently, the surety possesses all nonpersonal defenses, including offset, which would normally be available to the principal.[22] "Since liability of a surety is commensurate with that of the principal, where the principal is not liable on the obligation, neither is the guarantor."[23]

15.7   Extension of Performance Bond Surety's Liability to Third Parties

Although the obligee is the intended beneficiary of a performance bond, sureties increasingly are being held liable to other project participants on a third-party beneficiary theory. In these cases, the claimant asserts that the parties to the performance bond intended to confer rights to the claimant as against the surety. For example, a federal court has held that the Miller Act's dual requirement of performance and payment bonds would allow suppliers frustrated by the exhaustion of the penal sum on the payment bond to claim alternatively against the performance bond.[24] In reaching this result, the court reasoned that performance of the construction contract, guaranteed by the performance bond, included payment for the work that was the basis of the unpaid supplier's claims.[25]

In addition, parallel primes on multiprime projects often assert claims against the performance bond of another parallel prime. The performance bond surety traditionally has attempted to defend claims by other prime contractors on the basis that the performance bond was only for the benefit of the named obligee, the owner, not third parties. This defense has been successful in some cases.[26]

In other instances, the performance bond surety has been held responsible for a multiple-prime contractor under a third-party beneficiary theory. In essence, the surety

---

[20] *Pacific Employers Ins. Co. v. City of Berkeley*, 204 Cal. Rptr. 387 (Cal. Ct. App. 1984).

[21] J. Milana, "The Performance Bond and the Underlying Contract: The Bond Obligations Do Not Include All of the Contract Obligations," 12 Forum 187, 188 (1976); *see American Home Assurance Co. v. Larkin Gen. Hosp. Ltd.*, 593 So. 2d 195 (Fla. 1992); *St. Paul Fire & Marine Ins. Co. v. Woolley/Sweeney Hotel*, 545 So. 2d 958 (Fla. Dist. Ct. App. 1989) (arbitration agreement in contract bound surety); *United States Fidelity & Guar. Co. v. Gulf Fla. Dev. Corp.*, 365 So. 2d 748 (Fla. Dist. Ct. App. 1978).

[22] *See State Athletic Comm'n v. Massachusetts Bonding & Ins. Co.*, 117 P.2d 80 (Cal. Ct. App. 1941).

[23] *U. S. Leasing Corp. v. DuPont*, 70 Cal. Rptr. 393, 403 (Cal. 1968); *see Riley Constr. Co. v. Schillmoeller & Kroff Co.*, 236 N.W.2d 195, 198 (Wis. 1975).

[24] *See United States ex rel. Blount Fabricators, Inc. v. Pitt General Contractors, Inc.*, 769 F. Supp. 1016 (E.D. Tenn. 1991); *United States ex rel. Edward Hines Lumber Co. v. Kalady Constr. Co.*, 227 F. Supp. 1017 (N.D. Ill. 1964).

[25] *See Royal Indem. Co. v. Alexander Indus., Inc.*, 211 A.2d 919 (Del. 1965); *Amelco Window Corp. v. Federal Ins. Co.*, 317 A.2d 398 (N.J. 1974); *Kalady Constr., supra* note 25.

[26] J. *Louis Crum Corp. v. Alfred Lindgren, Inc.*, 564 S.W.2d 544 (Mo. Ct. App. 1978); *M.G.M. Constr. Corp. v. New Jersey Educ. Facilities Auth.*, 532 A.2d 764 (N.J. Super. Ct. Law Div. 1987).

is deemed to guarantee the performance of the principal's obligation to coordinate and cooperate with other parallel prime contractors and protect additional prime contractors from any damages sustained by the principal's failure.[27]

15.8 Increase of the Surety's Liability under a Performance Bond

In addition to claims from third parties, performance bond sureties must be increasingly concerned with additional claims beyond the express terms of the bond and in excess of the penal sum of the bond.

In *Continental Realty Corp. v. Andrew J. Crevolin Co.*,[28] the court extended a surety's performance bond liability on grounds that the surety's failure (1) to complete the project in a timely manner or (2) to pay the cost of completion constituted a breach of the surety's contractual bond obligation independent of the principal's default. Significantly, the obligee recovered damages equal to the actual damages suffered—that is, damages in excess of the penal sum of the bond.

In essence, the surety in the *Crevolin* case became liable for costs that necessarily could have been avoided had the surety performed in a timely fashion. For instance, water damage occurred to the building when the contractor abandoned the project prior to completing the roof. Had the surety undertaken to perform its performance bond obligations within the 15-day period set forth in the agreement, the moisture damage could have been prevented.

In addition to a waiver of the penal sum, insurance regulations applicable to surety companies often specifically provide in certain instances that reasonable attorneys' fees be awarded in addition to the penal sum. In *Boland v. Trans Coastal Roofing*,[29] the Florida Supreme Court allowed attorneys' fees in excess of the penal sum, expressly noting that such an award was proper under Florida statues even though there had been no misconduct on the part of the surety.[30] A surety may also be liable for interest on bond payment awards outside of the penal sum. In *Town of Clarkstown v. North River Ins. Co.*,[31] a federal district court included interest in an award in excess of the penal sum. The court held that under New York's General Obligations law, the purpose of prejudgment interest was to return the claimant to the financial position it would have been in had the surety paid the obligation promptly.[32]

In certain circumstances, performance bond sureties may also be found liable for attorneys' fees expense even absent an express contract provision or a specific statutory right. If the principal's construction contract entitles the obligee to attorneys'

---

[27] *See M. T. Reed Constr. v. Virginia Metal Prods. Corp.*, 213 F.2d 337 (5th Cir. 1954); *see also Aetna Cas. & Sur. Co. v. Doleac Elec. Co.*, 471 So. 2d 325 (Miss. 1985).

[28] 380 F. Supp. 246 (S.D.W. Va. 1974).

[29] 851 So. 2d 724 (Fla. 2003).

[30] *Id.*

[31] 803 F.Supp. 827 (S.D.N.Y. 1992).

[32] *Id.*

fees, and if the performance bond incorporates the construction contract, the surety may be required to pay the obligee's attorneys' fees.[33]

The penal sum notwithstanding, a surety's conduct may be so egregious that punitive damages are awarded. The general rule is that punitive damages cannot be obtained in breach of contract actions except in cases where an independent tort exists.[34] However, insurance regulations applicable to surety companies specifically provide in certain instances that punitive damages or penalties, or both, may be recovered against a defaulting surety.[35] Where the statute provides for such a recovery, claimants under performance bonds have been able to recover such punitive damages or penalties against a defaulting surety.[36] For example, in *Fisher v. Fidelity & Deposit Co. of Maryland*,[37] a vexatious and unreasonable delay in settling a performance bond claim entitled the owner to attorneys' fees and other costs in addition to compensatory damages resulting from the delay.[38]

Questionable conduct on the part of the surety may also give rise to complaints of bad faith, and, consequently, the assertion of tort claims and punitive damages. As previously discussed in **Section 15.4**, the legal basis for a claim that a surety has acted in bad faith is found in the universal requirement in all contracts that the parties exercise good faith and engage in fair dealing. When actual malice, fraud, or willful and wanton disregard for the obligee's rights is proven, punitive damages may be recovered against the surety.[39] For example, a Colorado court found that a performance bond surety breached its duty of good faith and fair dealing when it unreasonably refused to settle a claim.[40] The Colorado court concluded that, if performance bond sureties were not held liable on bad-faith claims for taking unreasonable settlement positions, then sureties would always be motivated to deny claims, earn interest on the payments deferred by the claim denial, and attempt to force compromise claim settlements. As previously described, the burden of proving "bad faith" is significant.[41]

---

[33] *Austin v. Parker*, 672 F.2d 508 (5th Cir. 1982); *HOH Company v. Travelers Indemnity Co.*, 903 F.2d 8 (D. C. Cir. 1989) (postproject change to general contractor/subcontractor contract obligated surety to reimburse attorneys' fees); *see also North American Specialty Ins. Co. v. Chichester School Dist.*, 158 F.Supp.2d 468 (E. D. Penn. 2001) (under Pennsylvania law, conditions of contract allowing attorneys' fees could not extend the surety's obligation beyond that stated in the bond).

[34] *Oliver B. Cannon & Son, Inc. v. Fidelity & Cas. Co. of New York*, 484 F. Supp. 1375 (D.C. Del. 1980).

[35] *See generally* 44 Am. Jur. 2d, Insurance, §§ 1798–1799; A. S. Klein, Annotation, "Insurer's Liability for Consequential or Punitive Damages for Wrongful Delay or Refusal to Make Payments Due under Contracts," 47 A.L.R. 3d 314 (1973 & Supp. 1995).

[36] *See Ray Ross Constr. Co., Inc. v. Raney*, 587 S.W.2d 46 (Ark. 1979).

[37] 466 N.E.2d 332 (Ill. App. Ct. 1984).

[38] *See also* Fla. Stat. Ann. §§ 627.428, 627.756 (1996 ed.) (Florida has enlarged an insurer's liability for attorneys' fees for bad-faith failure to settle to cover sureties issuing payment bonds).

[39] *See, e.g., Hoskins v. Aetna Life Ins. Co.*, 452 N.E.2d 1315 (Ohio 1983); *Riva Ridge Apartments v. Robert G. Fisher Co.*, 745 P.2d 1034 (Colo. Ct. App. 1987).

[40] *Brighton Sch. Dist. 27J v. Transamerica Premier Ins. Co.*, 923 P.2d 328 (Colo. Ct. App. 1996).

[41] *PSE Consulting, Inc. v. Frank Mercede and Sons, Inc.*, 838 A.2d 135 (Conn. 2004).

On the other hand, many states are reluctant to recognize bad-faith claims against performance bond sureties. In these states, courts are likely to focus on the differences between insurance contracts and contracts of suretyship, and to conclude that the regulatory powers of the states are sufficient to deter bad-faith acts by sureties.[42]

15.9 The Surety's Defenses to Performance Bond Liability

As previously stated, a surety's liability is coextensive with that of its principal; the surety's liability for the principal cannot be greater than the principal's liability.[43] Conversely, a defense normally available to the principal, but which the principal is barred from asserting, is likewise unavailable to the surety.[44]

Additionally, the surety may have independent defenses, arising out of the language of the performance bond itself (also known as "technical defenses") or the circumstances that give rise to the claim. For example, a surety generally is not liable for the acts of the principal that occurred prior to the posting of the bond.[45]

The obligee also has an obligation to perform faithfully and comply with any conditions precedent in order to recover under the performance bond.[46] A failure to do so can result in the discharge of any liability the surety may otherwise have under the bond. In determining the extent of any waiver, discharge, or conditions precedent to liability under the bond, the terms of the bond as well as the terms of the principal's construction contract must be reviewed.[47]

A "material alteration" in the bond principal's performance obligation resulting in an "increase in risk" for the surety also may provide the surety with an independent defense.[48] Where the surety does not consent to a material change to the endeavor that it has financially guaranteed, the surety may be discharged, either in whole or to the extent of injury caused by a material alteration. This discharge is based on the theory that the bond only binds the surety to certain risks, and consent of the surety is necessary in order to expand its liability beyond the terms of the bond.[49] In recognition

---

[42] *See, e.g., Tudor Dev. Group, Inc. v. United States Fidelity & Guar. Co.*, 692 F. Supp. 461 (M.D. Pa. 1988).

[43] *See* Stearns, *Law of Suretyship* (5th ed.). *See also* Cal. Civ. Code § 2809; *State Athletic Comm'n v. Massachusetts Bonding & Ins. Co.*, 117 P.2d 80 (Cal. 1941) (the liability of the contractor is the measure of the surety's liability); *Aetna Cas. & Sur. Co. v. Warren Bros. Co.*, 355, So. 2d 785 (Fla. 1978); *Village of Rosemont v. Lentin Lumber Co.*, 494 N.E.2d 592 (Ill. App. Ct. 1986).

[44] *Indemnity Ins. Co. v. United States*, 74 F.2d 22 (5th Cir. 1934). *See also Rhode Island Hosp. Trust Nat'l Bank v. Ohio Cas. Ins. Co.*, 789 F.2d 74 (1st Cir. 1986).

[45] *Morton Regent Enters., Inc. v. Leadtec California, Inc.*, 141 Cal. Rptr. 706, 708 (Cal. Ct. App. 1977); 74 Am. Jur. 2d Suretyship § 29 (Supp. 1985).

[46] *See Easton v. Boston Inv. Co.*, 196 P. 796 (Cal. Ct. App. 1921).

[47] *Pacific Employers Ins. Co. v. City of Berkeley*, 158 Cal. Rptr. 145 (Cal. Ct. App. 1984).

[48] *See, e.g., Ramada Dev. Co. v. United States Fidelity & Guar. Co.*, 626 F.2d 517 (6th Cir. 1980); *Continental Bank & Trust Co. v. American Bonding Co.*, 605 F.2d 1049 (8th Cir. 1979), *aff'd in part, rev'd in part on other grounds*, 630 F.2d 606 (8th Cir. 1980).

[49] *See United States ex rel. Army Athletic Ass'n v. Reliance Ins. Co.*, 799 F.2d 1382 (9th Cir. 1986); *Maryland Cas. Co. v. City of South Norfolk*, 54 F.2d 1032 (4th Cir.), *modified*, 56 F.2d 822, *cert. denied*, 286 U.S. 562 (1932).

of this doctrine, most bond forms permit the owner and the principal to alter the terms of the underlying construction contract by change orders and provide that the surety consents to such modifications in advance.[50] In any event, a surety normally must show some harm caused by the alteration.

The surety also may be released from liability under the performance bond when the owner makes unauthorized or premature payments, or fails to withhold retainage.[51] For example, in *Southwood Builders, Inc. v. Peerless Insurance Co.,*[52] a subcontractor posted payment and performance bonds on a courthouse project. The subcontractor fell behind schedule but refused to add another crew to the project. The prime contractor did not terminate the sub, but agreed to pay for the addition of an extra crew and for all additional materials ordered for the job. Such payments were to be deducted from later subcontractor progress payments. The prime contractor did not notify the subcontractor's surety.[53] When the subcontractor was later unable to continue, the prime contractor completed the subcontractor's work and sued the surety to recover the cost of completing the work. The court held that the prime contractor's advance payment for the subcontractor's men and materials was a "material variation" in the subcontract terms. This material contract change released the surety from its bond obligations.

The rationale for this rule is that the surety relied upon provisions of the contract in executing the bond. Contract terms such as payment according to schedule and a retainage requirement in certain percentages benefit the surety. Overpayment by the owner to the contractor may discharge the surety's obligations because such voluntary action by the owner reduces the contract balance available to the surety for completion of the project after a default. This is clearly true when the architect or owner fraudulently certifies progress payments beyond the defaulting principal's actual progress.

Overpayments made in good faith, however, may not discharge the surety. Moreover, unauthorized prepayments made by an owner may not discharge a compensated surety so long as (1) the funds were used in actual construction of the project and (2) the surety was not prejudiced by the prepayments.[54] However, when an architect has negligently certified progress payments to a contractor, thereby damaging the surety by reducing the contract balance available to the surety upon completion of the work, the surety may have a cause of action against the architect for the resulting damage.[55]

---

[50] *See, e.g., Trinity Universal Ins. Co. v. Gould,* 258 F.2d 883 (10th Cir. 1958); *Massachusetts Bonding & Ins. Co. v. John R. Thompson Co.,* 88 F.2d 825 (8th Cir.), *cert. denied,* 301 U.S. 707 (1937).

[51] *See Prairie State Nat'l Bank v. United States,* 164 U.S. 227 (1896); *Fireman's Fund Ins. Co. v. United States,* 15 Cl. Ct. 225 (1988), *rev'd on other grounds,* 909 F.2d 495 (Fed. Cir. 1990).

[52] 366 S.E.2d 104 (Va. 1988).

[53] *See Balboa Ins. Co. v. Fulton County,* 251 S.E.2d 123 (Ga. Ct. App. 1978) (overpayments made in reliance on progress payment requests certified by architect).

[54] *See Basic Asphalt & Constr. Corp. v. Parliament Ins. Co.,* 531 F.2d 702 (5th Cir. 1976); *Firemen's Fund Ins. Co. v. United States,* 15 Cl. Ct. 225 (1988).

[55] *See Sweeney Co. of Md. v. Engineers-Constructors, Inc.,* 823 F.2d 805 (4th Cir. 1987); *Peerless Ins. Co. v. Cerny & Assocs., Inc.,* 199 F. Supp. 951 (D. Minn. 1961).

If the principal engages in fraud to induce the surety to issue a bond, the surety cannot assert that defense to a claim by the obligee.[56] If the obligee has perpetrated a fraud on the surety or even participated in it, however, the surety will be discharged from any obligation.[57] A problem arises when there is no active fraud on the part of the obligee but there is a question about the extent to which the obligee is affirmatively required to disclose facts that would be relevant to the surety. In *Sumitomo Bank v. Iwasaki*,[58] the court held that the obligee does have such an obligation to disclose under the following circumstances:

- The obligee must have reason to believe that the facts materially increase the risk beyond that which the surety intends to assume;
- The obligee has reason to believe such facts are unknown to the surety; and
- The obligee has a reasonable opportunity to reveal such facts to the surety.[59]

The nature and extent of the dealings between the obligee and surety also may be relevant. For example, if over a course of dealing the obligee knows that the surety relies upon the obligee for certain information, the obligee may have a higher duty to disclose.

15.10   Surety Entitlement to Contract Funds

Upon the failure of the contractor-principal to perform, the surety becomes entitled to the contract funds then due and to all remaining contract funds as they become due. These funds must be applied to reduce or satisfy any loss incurred by the surety in the performance of the defaulted principal's contract obligations.[60]

The surety's right to these funds is strong, and is superior to a claim by a financial institution with a security interest in those funds.[61] The surety even has a superior right to the contract funds over a bankruptcy trustee in the event of the bankruptcy of the contractor-principal, at least to the extent of satisfying any loss incurred by the surety.[62] At the same time, there are limits to a surety's priority with respect to contract proceeds. For example, a federal court of appeals in New York

---

[56] *Chrysler Corp. v. Hanover Ins. Co.*, 350 F.2d 652 (7th Cir. 1965), *cert. denied,* 383 U.S. 906 (1966).

[57] *Filippi v. McMartin*, 188 Cal. App. 2d 135 (1961). *See also St. Paul Fire & Marine Ins. Co. v. Commodity Credit Corp.*, 646 F.2d 1064 (5th Cir. 1981).

[58] 58 447 P.2d 956 (Cal. 1968).

[59] *Id.; see* Restatement of Security §124.

[60] *Aetna Cas. & Sur. Co. v. United States*, 845 F.2d 971 (Fed. Cir. 1988). *But see Aetna Cas. & Sur. Co. v. United States*, 12 Cl. Ct. 271 (1987) (funds advanced or paid out under the payment bond do not give the surety the same right), *rev'd on other grounds*, 845 F.2d 971 (Fed. Cir. 1988).

[61] *See Prairie State Nat'l Bank v. United States*, 164 U.S. 227 (1896); *Kansas City, Mo. v. Tri-City Constr. Co.*, 666 F. Supp. 170 (W.D. Mo. 1987); *Mid-Continent Cas. Co. v. First Nat'l Bank & Trust Co.*, 531 P.2d 1370 (Okla. 1975); *Interfirst Bank Dallas, N.A. v. United States Fidelity & Guar. Co.*, 774 S.W.2d 391 (Tex. App. 1989).

[62] *Pearlman v. Reliance Ins. Co.*, 371 U.S. 132 (1962).

determined that a surety that had tendered a completion contractor for its defaulted principal, and entered into a completion agreement with the owner that guaranteed its priority to contract proceeds, could not defeat the "super priority" claim of the New York Department of Labor for back wages under the state's prevailing wage laws or the Internal Revenue Service claims against the contract balance proceeds.[63]

In some cases, a performance bond surety has been provided with priority to the contract funds before permitting setoffs by the owner.[64] Because of the potential setoff by the owner, a surety, when called to honor the bond, ordinarily requires the owner's agreement to pay any remaining unpaid contract balances to the surety as completion of the project is achieved.

The surety may be limited to the funds from the specific project on which it completed performance. For example, a performance bond surety for a contractor on two federal government contracts, having incurred losses when it took over and completed performance of the second contract, may not recover, under the doctrine of equitable subrogation, funds payable by the government to the contractor as a result of an equitable adjustment on the first contract.[65]

15.11 The Effect on the Surety of Arbitration of Construction Disputes

Arbitration is a common method of dispute resolution in the construction industry, especially in the private sector. Many standard construction contract forms provide that disputes between the owner and contractor will be resolved by arbitration. Typically, no reference is made to the surety in such provisions. As a basic rule, arbitration is enforceable only when there is an agreement between the parties to arbitrate. Unless the surety has agreed to arbitrate disputes, the mere fact that the principal has entered into an arbitration agreement may not be a basis to compel the surety to arbitrate.[66] The obligee may be forced to pursue relief in two separate forums: in court against the surety and in arbitration against the principal. Such a piecemeal dispute-resolution process creates additional expense and the risk of inconsistent results. However, some courts have required that sureties that issue performance bonds arbitrate claims asserted against those bonds.

For example, in *Cianbro Corp. v. Empresa Nacionale de Ingenieria*,[67] a general contractor sought to compel its subcontractor's surety to arbitrate a dispute arising out of a subcontract that contained an arbitration clause. As is typical, the surety's bond specifically incorporated the subcontract by reference. Although the surety signed the bonds, it did not sign the subcontract. Nonetheless, the court held that the surety was bound to arbitrate under the arbitration agreement that was incorporated

---

[63] *Titan Indem. Co. v. Triborough Bridge & Tunnel Auth., Inc.*, 135 F.3d 831 (2d Cir. 1998).

[64] *Trinity Universal Ins. Co. v. United States*, 382 F.2d 317 (5th Cir. 1967), *cert. denied*, 390 U.S. 906 (1968); *Covenant Mut. Ins. Co. v. Able Concrete Pump*, 609 F. Supp. 27 (D.C. Cal. 1984).

[65] *Transamerica Ins. Co. v. United States*, 989 F.2d 1188 (Fed. Cir. 1993).

[66] *Transamerica Ins. Co. v. Yonkers Contracting Co.*, 267 N.Y.S.2d 669 (1966); *Windowmaster Corp. v. B.G. Danis Co.*, 511 F. Supp. 157 (S.D. Ohio 1980).

[67] 697 F. Supp. 15 (D. Me. 1988).

by reference into the bond. As further support for its decision, the court relied upon the strong policy favoring arbitration expressed by Congress in the Federal Arbitration Act.

Even if the surety may not be compelled to arbitrate with the owner and contractor, the surety's obligations may be affected by the outcome of the arbitration. For example, in *Fidelity & Deposit Co. of Maryland v. Parsons & Whitemore Contractors Corp.*,[68] a bonded subcontractor defaulted, and the contractor sought damages for breach of contract from the subcontractor and its performance bond surety. The bond incorporated the subcontract by reference. The subcontract provided that all disputes would be submitted to arbitration. The contractor demanded arbitration, and the surety objected. The court held that the liability of the surety was predicated on the contract obligation to accept binding arbitration as provided in the subcontract documents.[69] In addition, a surety has been held bound to an arbitration award against the contractor (its principal) when the surety knew of the arbitration and had the opportunity to participate.[70]

Thus, the surety may be bound by the arbitration of disputes concerning the liability of the contractor to the owner, although the surety may retain the right to assert any separate defense in a distinct proceeding. Finally, authority exists for the proposition that an arbitration award is admissible as *prima facie* evidence of the liability of the surety. However, the surety has the right to plead any other defenses available to it, including the defense that the arbitration included matters outside of the liability of the surety or matters not covered by the performance bond.[71]

15.12 Alternatives to Bonds: "Subguard" Programs

"Subguard" is a subcontractor default insurance policy developed in the mid-1990s as an alternative method of assuring subcontractor performance other than subcontractor performance bonds. Subcontractor default insurance policies are designed for use by general contractors on projects involving multiple subcontractors. While the product is available to owners, its primary users have been large general contractors.

There are several significant advantages to the use of subcontractor default insurance. First and foremost, it allows the general contractor direct control over evaluating the financial stability of its selected subcontractors. Further, in the event of a subcontractor default, the subcontractor default insurance is much more flexible in allowing the general contractor to fashion an appropriate remedy. The insurance policy allows the general contractor to control insurance and financial concerns of the project with one master policy issued to the general contractor, as opposed to dealing with multiple surety bonds and, most likely, multiple surety companies. Use of the policy allows the general contractor to prequalify the subcontractors and avoid the inconvenience of dealing with a subcontractor, which fails to provide a bond

---

[68] 397 N.E.2d 380 (N.Y. 1979).

[69] *See also Kearsarge Metallurgical Corp. v. Peerless Ins. Co.*, 418 N.E.2d 580 (Mass. 1981).

[70] *Von Eng'g Co. v. R. W. Roberts Constr. Co.*, 457 So. 2d 1080 (Fla. Dist. Ct. App. 1984).

[71] *P. R. Post Corp. v. Maryland Cas. Co.*, 271 N.W.2d 521 (Mich. 1978).

after bid award. Finally, the subcontractor insurance policy allows for a negotiated contract of insurance in which the terms can be modified, added, or deleted to customize the policy for a specific project.

While the subcontractor default insurance is a very useful tool in some circumstances, it is not an appropriate method of insuring a project in all cases. Like surety bonds, the costs of coverage varies with the type of project, the parties involved, and the risks involved. The subcontractor insurance policy typically requires the insured general contractor to fund any default and make a claim only after the covered loss has occurred. Further, unlike the surety bond, the insurance policy includes a significant deductible per event, which ranges from $500,000 to much higher, depending upon the value and type of project, and includes an aggregate deductible often in excess of $2,000,000 before recovery on the policy is realized. Thus, the general contractor takes on a significant risk for reliance upon the subguard insurance policy.

While a surety bond is generally not cancellable, absent fraud or misrepresentation of the obligee, the subcontractor default policy may be cancelled for nonpayment, material change, or postissuance violation of policy terms or applicable qualifications. Thus, the subcontractor insurance policy must be modified to prevent cancellation in order to satisfy the statutory bond requirements in many jurisdictions.

The general contractor considering utilizing this product will be required by the insurer to first qualify itself and the project under the policy requirements. At that point, the insurer will assist the general contractor in establishing a subcontractor control program by which each eligible subcontractor must also qualify for the policy.

15.13   TERMINATIONS

15.14   Overview

Claims against performance bond sureties arise only upon the default or alleged default of the contractor principal. The surety's involvement is generally the result of the owner's (general contractor's) termination of the contract due to the contractor's (subcontractor's) default. Virtually all construction contracts expressly recognize the right to terminate the contract for the default of the other party in certain specific circumstances. Such provisions also recognize the right of the nonbreaching party to recover damages resulting from the default and resulting termination. Even in the absence of an express termination provision, an implied right to terminate a contract generally exists if the other party has materially breached the contract.

In addition, many public contracts and an increasing number of private construction contracts contain "termination for convenience" clauses authorizing the owner (or prime contractor) to terminate the prime contractor (or subcontractors) even in the absence of default. Payments to the terminated contractor are limited usually to actual cost incurred, and ordinarily do not include standard breach of contract damages or lost profits.

15.15 Termination for Default

The right to terminate a construction contract for default generally arises only when a material or substantial provision of the contract has been breached or a party has failed to perform a material obligation. The rights and liabilities of the parties are controlled by the common law and by the terms of the contract, which anticipate and provide the termination of further performance upon default. At common law, a minor deviation in performance or failure to meet an objective that is not material to the subject of the contract was not grounds to terminate for default. While such a deviation or failure in performance may give the nonbreaching party a corresponding right to damages, it does not rise to the level of significance that would merit a complete termination of the contract. Determination of the materiality of a breach depends upon the importance of the event or act to the purpose of the contract as a whole or to the basis of the agreement between the parties.

By the terms of the contract, the parties can expand, limit, or redefine the grounds for termination for default that exist at common law. They also can provide for the payment of damages and for the imposition of other obligations after the contract is terminated for default.

15.16 Standard Industry Forms: Grounds for Default Termination

Federal construction procurement contracts provide an example of the allocation of the rights and duties of the parties upon the occurrence of a default. The standard federal government construction contract affords the government several remedies in addition to the relief generally available at common law. If a contractor fails to perform by the date specified, produces defective or nonconforming work, or refuses or fails to prosecute the work in such a way as to ensure its timely completion, the government may pursue its administrative remedy under the terms of the default clause. That is, the government may terminate the contract and complete the work at the contractor's expense. The contractor also is liable for any liquidated or actual damages caused by unexcused delays in the completion of the work.

At the same time, the commonly used default termination clauses give the contractor the right to contest the default termination. However, under a contract with the federal government, a successfully challenged wrongful termination is automatically converted to a termination for the government's convenience under the "Termination for Convenience" clause of the contract, which provides a more limited recovery than general breach of contract damages.

The default clause used by the federal government in fixed-price construction contracts is set forth at FAR § 52.249-10. The following is a brief analysis of the major provisions of that clause. Paragraph (a) of the clause provides the basic authority for termination by the federal government—that is, where the contractor refuses or fails to prosecute any or all of the contracted work with sufficient diligence to ensure timely completion, or fails to complete the work within the specified time. In such circumstances, the government is given the right to terminate the contract in accordance with the provisions of the clause. The government then may take over the contractor's work and carry it to completion by a variety of means. Paragraph (a) also establishes the government's right to recover breach of contract damages from the contractor and its surety. Paragraph (b) sets forth the criteria for determining "excusable delay," which provides a major exception to the contractor's exposure to default termination and/or damages for delay.

Section 14.2.1 of AIA Document A201 (1997 ed.) likewise describes the instances in which an owner may terminate a contractor. In addition to circumstances relating to the contractor's financial situation, the clause identifies the following bases for termination:

[I]f the Contractor:

1. persistently or repeatedly refuses or fails to supply enough properly skilled workers or proper materials;
2. fails to make payment to Subcontractors for materials or labor in accordance with the respective agreements between the Contractor and the Subcontractors;
3. persistently disregards laws, ordinances, or rules, regulations or orders of a public authority having jurisdiction; or
4. otherwise is guilty of substantial breach of a provision of the Contract Documents.

The AIA form also requires that the architect certify that sufficient cause exists for the termination.[72]

Paragraph 11.2 of AGC Document No. 200, Standard Form of Agreement and General Conditions Between Owner and Contractor (2000 ed.), sets forth similar grounds for default if not remedied by the contractor subsequent to a receipt of a notice to cure. Unlike the AIA form, the AGC document does not require an architect's certification that cause exists to justify the default.

For the most part, the federal FAR termination clause, as well as the AGC and the AIA termination clauses, basically restate what would most likely be deemed material breaches of contract at common law. Specific situations in which sufficient grounds for termination of a construction contract have been found to exist are discussed below. Keep in mind, however, the right of the parties to define in their construction contracts the breaches of contract that will be deemed sufficiently "material" to justify a default termination.

15.17 Refusal or Failure to Prosecute the Work A typical default termination clause might provide: "[I]f the contractor refuses or fails to prosecute the work, or a separable part thereof, with such diligence as will ensure its completion within the time specified in [the] contract," the contract may be terminated for default.[73] However, the terminating party has the burden of proof to show not only a

---

[72] AIA Document A201 (1997 ed.) § 14.1
[73] FAR § 52.249-10(a).

significant lag in performance, but also that the contractor, at the time of the termination, could not have completed performance on time.[74]

The mere fact that the contractor makes little or no progress during one stage of the work may not, alone, support termination. For example, a termination for default has been overturned as premature where sufficient time remained in the contract schedule for the contractor to complete performance.[75] Although the factual determinations vary from situation to situation, many cases have interpreted the standard default clause to require a showing that timely completion was clearly in jeopardy.[76]

15.18 Failure to Complete on Time The contract may be properly terminated if the contractor fails to complete performance on time without excusable delay. As a general rule, time is of the essence, or basic to the terms of a contract that contains fixed or specific performance dates. If timely performance does not occur, the government can immediately terminate without notice and without an opportunity to cure.[77] However, when time is not of the essence, late performance is only one of a number of factors to be considered in determining the adequacy of performance and the justification for a default termination. For example, a substantial delay in final completion may not justify a default termination if the work is sufficiently complete that it can be used for its intended purpose.[78]

15.19 Repudiation by the Contractor A termination based on a contractor's repudiation or anticipatory breach of the contract is closely related to the contractor's refusal or failure to prosecute the work. However, when a contractor repudiates the existence of the contract, it is subject to default termination regardless of the previous rate of progress in performance.[79]

To terminate a contract on the basis of repudiation by the contractor, the owner must have a clear indication from the contractor that it cannot or will not perform the contract. The cases speak in terms of a "positive, definite, unconditional and unequivocal manifestation of intent, by words or conduct, on the part of a contractor" not to perform.[80] In any case, it must be apparent that the contractor is unable to or will not perform the contract. A failure to make progress alone does not constitute anticipatory repudiation absent some objective manifestation of intent not to perform.

The contractor may be considered to have repudiated the contract by refusing to perform during a dispute about contract interpretation.[81] Similarly, where the contract

---

[74] *Litcom Div., Litton Sys.*, ASBCA No. 13413, 78-1 BCA ¶ 13,022.

[75] *Strickland Co.*, ASBCA No. 9840, 67-1 BCA ¶ 6193.

[76] *Discount Co. v. United States*, 554 F.2d 435 (Ct. Cl. 1977), *cert. denied,* 434 U.S. 938 (1977).

[77] *National Farm Equip. Co.*, GSBCA No. 4921, 78-1 BCA ¶ 13,195; *see Dallas–Fort Worth Regional Airport Bd. v. Combustion Equip. Assoc., Inc.*, 623 F.2d 1032 (5th Cir. 1980).

[78] *Franklin E. Penny Co. v. United States*, 524 F.2d 668 (Ct. Cl. 1975).

[79] *See First Nat'l Bank of Aberdeen v. Indian Indus.*, 600 F.2d 702 (8th Cir. 1979).

[80] *Mountain State Constr. Co.*, ENG BCA No. 3549, 76-2 BCA ¶ 12,197.

[81] *Tester Corp.*, ASBCA No. 21312, 78-2 BCA ¶ 13,373.

obligates the contractor to continue the work during a contract dispute, a contractor has been found not entitled to stop work while awaiting issuance of contract modifications or resolution of a request for price escalation for inflation.[82]

In certain circumstances, a contractor's refusal to perform will not be regarded as an anticipatory breach or repudiation of the contract. For example, when the contract specifications are impossible to perform, the contractor has a right to stop work on the basis that no other practical alternative exists.[83] Furthermore, a contractor should not be terminated for default where it is reasonably awaiting clarification from the government of drawings, specifications, or other central requirements. If the contractor is unable to proceed until it obtains guidance from the government, the delay in work is justified.[84]

Most standard changes clauses include only changes "within the general scope of the contract." Changes beyond that scope are termed "cardinal changes." A contractor's refusal to perform a contract because of an actual or constructive cardinal change is not a valid basis for a default termination.[85] However, stopping performance on the grounds of an alleged cardinal change is highly risky. The question of whether the act or failure to act amounted to a cardinal change will be strongly contested in the context of the litigation or arbitration regarding the validity of the termination for default.

When an owner materially breaches the contract, the contractor's subsequent repudiation is justified and may not be the basis for default termination. For example, when the owner withholds payments that are due on a contract, the contractor may stop performance.[86]

15.20 Failure to Comply with Other Provisions of the Contract The failure of the contractor to comply with certain terms of the contract will be a material breach entitling the owner to terminate the contract for default. The owner must first prove that the provision of the contract that has not been performed is material to the contract and also that the failure to perform is a material breach of the contract.

In *Antonio Santisteban & Co., Inc.*,[87] a contractor's failure to furnish a performance bond constituted a material breach. Likewise, some federal boards have held that a contractor's failure to furnish Miller Act bonds pursuant to 40 U.S.C. § 3131 et seq. justifies default termination.[88]

---

[82] *Fraenkische Parkettverlegung R.*, ASBCA No. 18453, 75-2 BCA ¶ 11,388.

[83] *Chugach Elec. Ass'n v. Northern Corp.*, 562 P.2d 1053 (Alaska 1977); *L. J. Casey Co.*, AGBCA No. 75-148, 76-2 BCA ¶ 12,196.

[84] *Electromagnetic Indus., Inc.*, ASBCA No. 11485, 67-2 BCA ¶ 6545.

[85] *Allied Materials & Equip. v. United States*, 569 F.2d 562 (Ct. Cl. 1978); *P. L. Saddler v. United States*, 287 F.2d 411 (Ct. Cl. 1961); *Cray Research Inc. v. Department of Navy*, 556 F. Supp. 201 (D.D.C. 1982).

[86] *United States ex rel. E. C. Ernst, Inc. v. Curtis T. Bedwell & Sons*, Inc., 506 F. Supp. 1324 (E.D. Pa. 1981); *Contract Maintenance, Inc.*, ASBCA No. 19603, 75-1 BCA ¶ 11,097. *See* AIA Document A201 § 14.1.1.3 (1997 ed.).

[87] ASBCA No. 5586, et al., 60-1 BCA ¶ 2497.

[88] *H.L. & S. Contractors, Inc.*, IBCA No. 1085-11-75, 76-1 BCA ¶ 11,878.

15.21 Defenses of the Contractor

15.22 *Excusable Delay* Virtually all construction contracts contain some provision excusing delayed performance when specified criteria are met. As an example, paragraph (b) of the default clause used by the federal government provides that termination for default is improper in cases where a contractor's work is delayed by "unforeseeable causes beyond the control and without the fault or negligence of the contractor." That provision continues with a description and examples of typical causes of excusable delay.[89] In order to take advantage of such excusable delay provisions, contractors generally must satisfy the contract requirements for the granting of time extensions (e.g., timely notice of excusable delay and a time extension request).

15.23 *Waiver by the Owner* Another defense that may be available to a contractor faced with default termination is a claim that the owner has waived strict compliance with the contract completion date, or other contract performance provisions, and thereby forfeited its right to terminate. Even if the terms of the contract are specific and state that they may not be waived, its terms may be waived by the expression of consent to or the disregard of the failure of performance. A waiver can be effective without further consideration or a new contract agreement.[90] There will be no waiver, however, if the owner's forbearance in terminating was based on a misrepresentation by the contractor.[91]

While the right to terminate a contract for default may be waived if not exercised in a timely manner, it can also be expressly reserved. In *Indemnity Insurance Co. of North America v. United States*,[92] the government expressly reserved its right to terminate a takeover surety for default by informing the surety that it was continuing to assess liquidated damages and by providing the surety with a cure notice once the completion date had passed. The failure of the government to terminate the contract immediately after expiration of the completion date did not constitute a waiver under those circumstances.

An owner may not be deemed to have waived a valid basis for a termination for default simply because it relied on a different basis at the time of the termination. In *Joseph Morton v. United States*,[93] the government's decision to terminate for default was upheld on the grounds of the contractor's fraud, even though the government was unaware of the fraud at the time of the termination. In *FJW Optical Systems, Inc.*,[94] the Armed Services Board of Contract Appeals held that a termination for default was valid even though initially there had only been a termination for convenience.

---

[89] *See Crawford Painting & Drywall Co. v. J.W. Bateson Co.*, 857 F.2d 981 (5th Cir.), *cert. denied*, 488 U.S. 1035 (1988).

[90] *See Olson Plumbing & Heating Co.*, ABSCA No. 17965, 75-1 BCA ¶ 11,203.

[91] *W. M. Z. Mfg. Co.*, ASBCA No. 28347, 85-3 BCA ¶ 18,169.

[92] 14 Cl. Ct. 219 (1988).

[93] 757 F.2d 1273 (Fed. Cir. 1985).

[94] ASBCA No. 29780, 85-2 BCA ¶ 18,049.

However, the United States Claims Court has held that, even when a contractor was technically in default, a termination for default may be reversed if the contracting officer's decision was motivated by hostility to the contractor and was not in the best interests of the government.[95]

✔ 15.24   Contractor Response to Termination Notices

For the contractor or subcontractor faced with a termination threat or notice, the following checklist may provide some assistance in formulating a plan of action:

- *Assess and document the factual accuracy of the notice.* If the complaints being made are not accurate, document their inaccuracy—in writing, with photographs or video, or in some other appropriate manner. Rebut, in writing, the inaccuracies in the termination threat.

- *Assess the legal adequacy of the termination threat.* Check your contract documents to determine the substantive and procedural adequacy of the termination notice. Does the contract provide a right of termination for the type of contract breach complained of in the notice? Has the termination threat followed all of the contract's procedural requirements (adequate notice, right to cure, etc.) specified in the contract?

- *Invoke your right to cure.* If there is any legitimacy to the complaints being made, address those complaints in a curative plan of action developed and communicated to the complaining party within the contractual cure period. Even if the contract provides no specific cure period, develop and communicate such a plan immediately.

- *Implement the cure plan.* Take action immediately that will show some effort to implement the plan to cure any legitimate complaints.

- *Treat an improper termination notice as an acceleration order.* If the termination threat is unwarranted, consider your right to treat the termination threat as an order to accelerate under the contract changes clause. Advise the complaining party of your intention to do so.

- *Document the status of the work.* Document (e.g., by marking up plans to show as-built conditions, with photographs or video) the state of your work at the time of the termination threat, as well as any obstacles to your performance of the work.

- *Inventory the material and equipment on-site.* If the contract gives the complaining party the right to take possession of materials and equipment, make certain that you have an adequate record of the materials and equipment on site.

- *Assess subcontractor and supplier termination rights.* Review subcontracts and purchase orders to determine if they contain provisions that address termination rights and liabilities. Consider your notice obligations and subcontractor entitlement to termination costs.

[95] *Quality Env't Sys. v. United States*, 7 Cl. Ct. 428 (1985).

- *Consider the possible loss of project staff members.* A termination of a construction contract frequently is accompanied by the loss of valuable members of a contractor's project staff. Now is the time to memorialize the knowledge of your project staff with respect to the issues likely to be disputed in a contest of the termination decision. Memories will fade and ex-employees will lose their interest in a former employer's job problems.
- *Take steps to ensure the protection of project records.* After termination, the terminating party may request project records to assist in the completion of the contractor's work. Confidential or sensitive information must be protected.
- *Reassure your performance bond surety.* A threat to terminate a contractor's contract is likely to draw the keen interest of the contractor's performance bond surety. Take some steps to assure your surety that you are responding properly to the threat.
- *Anticipate potential subcontractor and supplier claims.* Assess and document the status of work by subcontractors and suppliers, in anticipation of potential termination claims.
- *Seek competent legal advice.* Immediate legal assistance from someone familiar with construction contract termination situations is imperative. Decisions must be made quickly and competently if the contractor's legal position is to be adequately protected.

15.25   Remedies of the Owner

When a contractor is terminated for default, typically the owner may (1) complete the contract work itself, (2) let a contract to another contractor to complete the work, or (3) allow the defaulted contractor's surety to complete construction. Usually an owner will only complete the work with its own employees or forces if the project is substantially complete and little work remains. Otherwise, the owner commonly will enter into another contract or will rely on the surety to complete, assuming the project is bonded and the surety agrees.

Where the owner completes either on its own or through a completion contractor, reasonable steps must be taken to minimize additional costs. This duty to mitigate damages limits the recovery a party can obtain as a result of breach of contract by requiring that reasonable efforts be taken to complete the contract economically and efficiently.[96] The reasonableness of these actions will be determined in light of the facts and circumstances of each case.

Under the standard performance bond, the defaulting contractor's surety is obliged to indemnify the owner up to the amount of the bond. Although the surety is not usually obligated to complete the contract work, at least where the default is not contested by the contractor, most sureties will cooperate with the owner in arranging for completion of the contract. In most cases, the surety will be allowed to

---

[96] *Marley v. United States*, 423 F.2d 324, 333 (Ct. Cl. 1970).

take over the work unless there is reason to believe that the party proposed by the surety to complete the work is incompetent or unqualified to such an extent that the interests of the owner would be substantially prejudiced by their efforts.[97]

Where the surety tenders another contractor to complete the work, the bonds of the surety under the original contract are still effective. In addition, the owner often has the benefit of any additional surety bonds provided by the completion contractor.

Where a surety elects to have the work completed by another firm, without either a valid assignment or a takeover agreement, it may seek to assert the defaulted contractor's claims against the owner. The surety's ability to do this may be subject to other laws. For example, on federal government contracts, a surety cannot prosecute a claim against the federal government under the "disputes" clause in its own name, because it has not become a party to the contract.[98] Under such circumstances, it must assume the name of the defaulted contractor and submit the claim in a representative capacity.[99]

15.26 Reprocurement Costs Under the default clause, the federal government is entitled to recover its "increased costs"—that is, those additional costs in excess of the original contract price that are necessarily incurred in completion of the work. However, the government cannot recover the administrative costs of reprocurement.[100]

When the scope of the newly procured work exceeds the coverage of the terminated contract, the government may recover from the defaulted contractor only those additional costs that are attributable to the work in the original contract.[101] Also, a court or a board of contract appeals generally will reduce an award of excess reprocurement costs where the government has failed to mitigate damages.[102] Finally, if the reprocurement contract contains significant deviations from the original contract, no excess costs may be assessed against the defaulting contractor.[103]

In the absence of a default clause in the contract, and often as a supplement to the rights granted by such a clause, the common-law rights for breach of contract apply. The owner is entitled to the payment of damages that would put it in the same position as if the contract had not been breached.

15.27 Delay Damages The federal government default clause provides that regardless of whether the contractor is terminated for default, the contractor and its sureties will be liable for damages resulting from the contractor's refusal or failure to complete the work within the specified time. Absent a liquidated damages provision, the owner is entitled to actual damages caused by the contractor's delay.

---

[97] FAR § 49.404(c).

[98] *Fireman's Fund Ins. Co.*, ASBCA No. 50657, 00-1 BCA ¶ 30,802.

[99] *Sentry Ins.*, ASBCA No. 21918, 77-2 BCA ¶ 12,721.

[100] *Evans*, ASBCA No. 10951, 66-1 BCA ¶ 5316.

[101] *M.S.I. Corp.*, VACAB No. 599, 67-2 BCA ¶ 6643.

[102] *See, e.g., A & W Gen. Cleaning Contractors*, ASBCA No. 14809, 71-2 BCA ¶ 8994.

[103] *Blake Constr. Co.*, GSBCA No. 4013, *et al.*, 75-2 BCA ¶ 11,487.

Actual damages include, for example, the cost of keeping a government inspector on the job after the specified completion date.[104]

When the contract contains a liquidated damages provision, the owner is entitled to damages based upon the period between the contract completion date and the actual date of completion, whether the contract is completed by the contractor, the surety, or a reprocurement contractor. The default clause provisions attempt to secure for the federal government a common law measure of recovery, putting it in as good a position as it would have enjoyed had the delay not occurred. Liquidated damages may be recovered in addition to the excess costs of reprocurement.

15.28 Termination for Convenience

The parties to a construction contract may wish to include a clause that will allow one party (usually the owner) the right to terminate another party without cause—that is, for convenience. While the federal government's right to terminate a contract for convenience is generally deemed to be implied as a matter of law, in order for one party to a private commercial contract to do so, it must have an express provision in the contract giving it the right. If one party terminates another for convenience, the terminated party has a right to compensation, which may be limited by the contract's terms.

15.29 Standard Industry Forms

The owner's right to terminate for convenience is as unique as the specific convenience provision included in the contract at issue. However, there are several fairly typical convenience termination clauses. For example, AGC Document No. 200, Standard Form Agreement and General Conditions Between Owner and Contractor (2000 ed.), provides in Paragraph 11.4.1 for termination of the contract at the convenience of the owner as follows:

> Upon written notice to the Contractor, the Owner may, without cause, terminate this Agreement. The Contractor shall immediately stop the Work, follow the Owner's instructions regarding shut down and termination procedures, and strive to minimize any further costs.

The AGC contract continues to describe payment for the work performed prior to termination of the contract and identifies the contractor's obligations to the owner upon termination of the contract by either convenience or cause.[105]

Most, if not all, public contracts include provision by which the public owner can terminate the contract for the owner's convenience. These causes are usually very broadly based, allowing the governmental owner complete flexibility as to when a contract may be terminated. The Standard Specification for Roads and Structures of the North Carolina Department of Transportation includes a typical termination

---

[104] *B & E Constructors, Inc.*, IBCA No. 526-11-65, 67-1 BCA ¶ 6239.
[105] AGC Document No. 200, ¶¶ 11.4.2, 11.4.3.

of contract clause. The contractor may apply for a convenience termination based on the impossibility of performance due to factors beyond the contractor's control, or the contract may be terminated simply if the Department of Transportation Board determines that termination of the contract is in the best "public interest."[106] In order to initiate a convenience termination under this provision, the contractor must provide written notice with verification of the circumstances requiring convenience termination or, if initiated by the Department of Transportation, a written notice to the contractor of the board's action. As is typical in a public contract, the North Carolina DOT provision specifically outlines those payments for work performed and costs associated with the convenience, which will be recoverable.[107]

Federal government contracts include a termination for convenience clause at the Federal Acquisition Regulation Subpart 49, simply stating the contracting officer shall issue a termination for convenience when "it is in the Government's interest."[108] The government is required to issue a written notice by certified mail or hand delivery with return acknowledgment. That notice will state that the contract is being terminated for the convenience of the government under the contract clause authorizing the termination. In addition, the notice will provide the effective date of the termination, the extent of the termination if it is a partial termination, and instructions as to what steps the contractor must take with regard to concluding work under the contract.[109]

15.30   "Bad-Faith" Convenience Terminations: Theory and Reality

Although a typical termination for convenience clause appears to give one party the absolute right to terminate another for whatever reason, there is a conflict as to whether the termination must be made in good faith.[110] At least one court has held that there are circumstances in which a termination, even under a seemingly unrestricted termination clause, may not be allowed if done in bad faith.[111]

Other courts have hesitated to hold that there is a good-faith requirement in terminations for convenience. A federal court applying New York law found "on the basis of existing precedents, that such a [good-faith] restriction would probably not be imposed."[112] The court did point out, however, that this conclusion was not critical to its holding in the case because it was probable that the terminating party could show that the termination was not in bad faith.

The question of whether there is a good-faith requirement for termination without cause is unresolved in many jurisdictions. It is, therefore, a viable point that may be argued by any contractor that may have been terminated in bad faith.

---

[106] Standard Specification for Roads and Structures of the North Carolina Department of Transportation, § 108-13.

[107] *Id.*

[108] FAR § 49.101(b).

[109] FAR § 49.102.

[110] *Randolph v. New England Mut. Life Ins. Co.*, 526 F.2d 1383 (6th Cir. 1975).

[111] *Id.* at 1386.

[112] *Niagara Mohawk Power Corp. v. Graver Tank & Mfg.*, 470 F. Supp. 1308 (N.D.N.Y. 1979).

In the federal procurement context, the government's right to terminate for convenience is extremely broad. Termination is permitted "whenever the Contracting Officer shall determine that such termination is in the best interest of the Government."[113] That provision expresses a right that has long been recognized, even in the absence of a termination for convenience clause in the contract.[114]

Nonetheless, the contracting officer's discretion is not absolute and cannot be exercised in bad faith. Thus a terminated contractor that alleges bad faith by the contracting officer in issuing a convenience termination is allowed to present evidence in an effort to demonstrate bad faith.[115] "The termination of a contract for the convenience of the government is only valid in the absence of bad faith or a clear abuse of discretion."[116] However, in order to demonstrate bad faith in a Termination for Convenience, the contractor must prove by clear and convincing evidence that the government acted with malice and the specific intent to harm the contractor.[117]

In *Municipal Leasing Corp. v. United States*,[118] the U.S. Claims Court ruled that a finding of bad faith was not necessary to invalidate a termination for convenience. The court held that:

> The termination for convenience clause can appropriately be invoked only in the event of some kind of change from the circumstances of the bargain or in the expectations of the parties.

> The termination for convenience clause will not act as a constructive shield to protect defendant from the consequences of its decision to follow an option considered but rejected before contracting with plaintiff.[119]

Thus, while the government may have broad discretion to terminate for convenience, there must be no bad faith, and some changed circumstances must exist to warrant the action.

15.31 Convenience Termination Costs

In federal procurement law, the contractor whose contract is wholly or partially terminated for convenience should be made financially whole by compensation for the direct consequences of the government's termination. Negotiated termination settlements are limited only by the requirements of reasonableness of cost and the original contract price. Individual cost items need not be negotiated. Also recoverable are those costs incurred where the contract is terminated for convenience prior to any actual work being performed.[120]

---

[113] FAR § 52.249-2(a).

[114] *United States v. Corliss Steam Engine Co.*, 91 U.S. 321 (1875).

[115] *See National Factors, Inc. v. United States*, 492 F.2d 1383 (Ct. Cl. 1974).

[116] *Id.* at 1385.

[117] *Am-Pro Protective Agency, Inc. v. U.S.*, 281 F.3d 1234 (Fed. Cir. 2002).

[118] 7 Cl. Ct. 43 (1984).

[119] *Id.* at 47. *See Torncello v. United States*, 681 F.2d 756 (1982).

[120] *Nicon v. U.S.*, 329 F.3d 848 (Fed. Cir. 2003).

In addition, the contractor is entitled to a "fair and reasonable" profit on work performed, unless it can be demonstrated that the contractor would have lost money on the contract.[121] Anticipatory profits are not allowed. Profit is allowable only on the work performed. If, however, it can be shown that the completion of the contract would have resulted in a loss for the contractor, the contractor will not be entitled to a profit markup and the termination costs may be reduced by the anticipated loss percentage.

The standard termination for convenience clause entitles the contracting officer to terminate all or part of a contract. Where only a portion of the contract is terminated, the contractor's measure of cost recovery is governed by the same principles applicable to the termination of the entire contract. The contractor may recover costs incurred until the date of the termination, including a fair and reasonable profit, and the cost of settlement with subcontractors, suppliers, and the government. The partial termination settlement proposal must be submitted within 90 days after the effective date of the partial termination.

In addition, the contractor is entitled to an equitable adjustment in the price of the work that has not been terminated if it can be shown that the elimination of a portion of the work caused an increase in the cost of the remaining work.

➤ POINTS TO REMEMBER

- Performance bonds are not insurance. Do not expect sureties to react to claims in the same way that an insurance company can be expected to respond to, for example, a general liability insurance policy claim.
- The language of the bond is critical; read it carefully. It may contain certain claim requirements or refer you to a statute that contains such requirements.
- Determine if the bond is a "statutory" or "common-law" bond—this distinction may affect claim requirements.
- The penal sum of the bond may not always be the surety's limit of liability.
- A surety has all of the defenses of its principal plus any additional "technical" defenses.
- A surety may be bound by arbitration requirements on the principal's contract. Obligees should insist that surety bonds specifically incorporate by reference the principal's contract documents.
- Subcontractor performance insurance is available and should be considered as an alternative to performance bonds for each subcontractor.
- Termination for default is a remedy of last resort. Carefully consider your options.
- Any attempt to terminate usually requires an opportunity to "cure" any of the performance deficiencies, even if the contract does not specifically provide for a cure period.

---

[121] *C. W. McGrath, Inc.*, GSBCA No. 4586, 77-1 BCA ¶ 12,379.

- The primary defenses to termination are excusable delay and failure to pay.
- Converting a termination for default to a termination for convenience generally allows the contractor to recover the costs of performance on the work completed, plus termination costs.
- A contract clause that provides for the automatic conversion of a wrongful termination for default to a termination for convenience will substantially reduce the risks associated with a contract termination decision.

16

PROVING COSTS AND DAMAGES

The issue in construction disputes that generally receives the most attention and focus is liability. Does a differing site condition exist? Who caused the delay and is it compensable? However, the issue of damages or costs flowing from the events that give rise to liability is no less important. Too often, the issue of calculating costs and proving damages is given a backseat, with little precision or scrutiny applied until late in the dispute resolution process. That approach can result in an entirely misguided claim effort, missed opportunities for settlement, and loss at trial or in arbitration. The inability to prove damages with a reasonable degree of certainty may prevent the claimant from recovering the full amount, or even a substantial portion, of the damages to which it may be entitled. An early and realistic analysis of damages can help determine whether a claim really exists and the best means of preparing and positioning the claim for the affirmative recovery sought.

16.1   BASIC DAMAGE PRINCIPLES

16.2   The Compensatory Nature of Damages

Several basic premises underlie the theory of damages. For example, when a claimant seeks to recover additional costs and damages resulting from another party's breach of contract, the court generally will attempt to put the claimant in the same position it would have been in had the contract been performed by all parties according to its terms.[1] This theory of the measure of damages applies to all breach

[1] *United States ex rel. Morgan & Son Earthmoving, Inc. v. Timberland Paving & Constr. Co.*, 745 F.2d 595 (9th Cir. 1984); *Bennett v. Associated Food Stores, Inc.*, 165 S.E.2d 581 (Ga. Ct. App. 1968); *E. B. Ludwig Steel Corp. v. C. J. Waddell Contractors, Inc.*, 534 So. 2d 1364 (La. Ct. App. 1988)

of contract actions—not just those arising from construction contracts.[2] The law of contract damages is compensatory in nature and, as such, is designed to reimburse the complaining party for all "losses caused and gains prevented" by the other party's breach.[3]

In contrast, the goal in a tort (noncontractual wrong) case is to put the injured party in the same position it would have been in had the tort not been committed.[4] In the construction area, tort claims are generally asserted for negligence, misrepresentation, and, in rare cases, on the basis of strict liability.[5] Computation and proof of tort damages are often complex, requiring an evaluation of the foreseeability of the injury and the possible contributory or comparative negligence of other parties, or assumption of risk. While tort damages may be broader in scope than contract damages, many courts have limited tort damages to cases involving either personal injury or property damage, and deny recovery for purely economic loss.[6] For these reasons, and because most construction claims are based primarily on a breach of contract, this section focuses on the computation of contract damages.

16.3   Categories of Damages

Damages resulting from breach of a construction contract are generally of two basic types: *direct* and *consequential*. A third category, *punitive* damages, only rarely comes into play.

While it may be difficult to determine which category a claimant's damages fit within, the increased use of damage waivers within contracts has made this analysis more important than ever. Specifically, both the 1997 version of AIA A-201 General Conditions and the 2000 version of AGC Document No. 200 contain a waiver by both the owner and the contractor of consequential damages. Therefore, before deciding whether to execute a contract containing such a clause, one would obviously need to be familiar with the type of damages included within the waiver.

16.4   *Direct Damages*   Direct damages, sometimes referred to as "general damages," are those that result from the direct, natural, and immediate impact of the breach, and are recoverable in all cases where proven.[7] In a contractor's case these damages may include idle labor and machinery, material and labor escalations, and

---

[2] *Meares v. Nixon Constr. Co.*, 173 S.E.2d 593 (N.C. Ct. App. 1970).

[3] Calamari & Perillo, *The Law of Contracts*, § 327 (West, 1970).

[4] Restatement (2d), Torts, § 901.

[5] For a discussion of the application of strict liability principles in construction litigation, see "Strict Liability and the Building Industry," 33 Emory L.J. 175 (1984).

[6] *See, e.g., AFM Corp. v. Southern Bell Tel. & Tel. Co.*, 515 So. 2d 180 (Fla. 1987); *Florida Power & Light Co. v. Westinghouse Elec. Corp.*, 510 So. 2d 899 (Fla. 1987); *Casa Clara v. Toppino*, 588 So. 2d 631 (Fla. Dist. Ct. App. 1991); *State v. Mitchell Constr. Co.*, 699 P.2d 1349 (Idaho 1984); *Bates & Rogers Constr. Corp. v. North Shore Sanitary Dist.*, 471 N.E.2d 915 (Ill. App. Ct. 1984). *See also* **Chapter 7, Section 7.15**.

[7] *Spang Indus., Inc. v. Aetna Cas. & Sur. Co.*, 512 F.2d 365 (2d Cir. 1975).

extended job-site general conditions and home office overhead. The owner's direct damages are generally those costs incurred in completing or correcting the contractor's work and the cost of delay, which is either its actual cost in terms of lost rent and loss of use or liquidated damages.

16.5 Consequential Damages

16.5 Consequential Damages   The second category of contract damages is consequential damages, sometimes referred to as "special damages." Consequential damages do not flow directly from the alleged breach, but are an indirect source of loss. In order to be included within the claimant's recovery, consequential damages must have been within the contemplation of the parties when they contracted, or flow from special circumstances attending the contract that were known to both parties at the time the contract was executed. These losses, which are only indirectly related to the breach, may include loss of profits or a loss of bonding capacity. These are more difficult to prove, because the causal link between such damages and the act constituting the breach may be tenuous and uncertain.

Recovery of consequential damages for breach of contract requires proof: (1) that the consequence was foreseeable in the normal course of events; (2) that the loss in fact would not have occurred but for the breach; and (3) that the amount of the loss can be reasonably ascertained.[8] The first element is satisfied by showing that the particular type of injury was reasonably foreseeable to the other party at the time of contracting. The "reasonably foreseeable" test was originally enunciated in the English case of *Hadley v. Baxendale*,[9] and has since been widely adopted by American courts.[10]

The second element the claimant must prove is that the damages flowed "naturally" or "proximately" from the breach. In lay terms, this means that the injury must be the result of the breach rather than some other cause.[11]

The third limitation on the recovery of consequential damages is that the damages sought must not be too remote or speculative.[12] This general requirement is frequently codified under state law. Questions and issues of the "remote and speculative" nature of claimed damages frequently arise when a claimant seeks to recover profits that have allegedly been lost as a result of the breach—for example, as a result of tied-up capital or reduced bonding capacity. Although statutes covering consequential damages may require "exact computation," most courts have taken a somewhat less stringent approach. The court in one such case explained:

> The proof of damages because of breach of a contract must be made with a reasonable degree of certainty. The damages, to be recoverable in such a case, must not be remote or speculative. There must be sufficient data produced by the claimant to permit a

---

[8] *Town of North Bonneville, Wash. v. United States*, 11 Cl. Ct. 694 (1987).

[9] 156 Eng. Rep. 145 (1854).

[10] *See Tousley v. Atlantic City Ambassador Hotel Corp.*, 50 A.2d 472 (N.J. 1947); *Bumann v. Maurer*, 203 N.W.2d 434 (N.D. 1972).

[11] *Kline Iron & Steel Co. v. Superior Trucking Co.*, 201 S.E.2d 388 (S.C. 1973).

[12] *Dileo v. Nugent*, 592 A.2d 1126 (Md. Ct. Spec. App. 1991); *Baker v. Riverside Church of God*, 453 S.W.2d 801 (Tenn. Ct. App. 1970).

determination with reasonable certainty of the loss occasioned by the breach relied upon. . . . Restatement, Contracts, § 331, p. 515, states the rule: "Damages are recoverable for losses caused or for profits and other gains prevented by the breach only to the extent that the evidence affords a sufficient basis for estimating their amount in money with reasonable certainty." [13]

In seeking consequential damages, the claimant assumes a much heavier burden of proof as compared to direct damages. Moreover, many contracts, and particularly public construction contracts, by their terms exclude claims for consequential damages. [14]

16.6   *Punitive Damages*   Punitive damages are awarded where there is evidence of oppression, malice, fraud, or wanton and willful conduct on the part of the defendant, and are above what would ordinarily compensate the complaining party for its losses. These damages are not compensatory in nature, but rather are intended to punish the defendant for its wrongful behavior or to make an example in order to deter others from similar conduct. [15] Many jurisdictions refer to punitive damages as "exemplary damages" and define them similarly. California, for example, defines exemplary damages as "damages other than compensatory damages which may be awarded against a person to punish him for outrageous conduct." [16]

Traditionally it has been held that punitive damages are not recoverable in an action for breach of contract, absent proof of fraud or malicious intent. [17] This is so even if the breach is intentional. [18]

In some states, however, the courts may permit the award of punitive damages where there is sufficient evidence of "malice" or utter disregard for the rights of others so as to constitute a willful and wanton course of action, or other tortious conduct amounting to fraud. [19] Additionally, some states allow for recovery of punitive or exemplary damages through their unfair trade practice statutes, many times referring to them as "treble damages." Finally, although the expenses of litigation are not generally allowed as damages in an action for breach of contract, such fees may be awarded if the defendant has acted in bad faith, has been stubbornly litigious, or has caused the plaintiff unnecessary trouble and expense. [20] This rule, which changes the common law of many jurisdictions, has been codified in some states. [21]

---

[13] *Bitlev v. Terri Lee, Inc.*, 81 N.W.2d 318, 330–31 (Neb. 1957).

[14] Subparagraph 10.2 of AGC Document No. 200 (2000 ed.) and Subsection 4.3.10 of AIA Document A201 (1997 ed.) are examples of an express waiver of consequential damages.

[15] *Tibbs v. Nat'l Homes Constr. Corp.*, 369 N.E.2d 1218 (Ohio 1978).

[16] *Wetherbee v. United Insurance Company of America*, 18 Cal. App. 3d 266, 95 Cal. Rptr. 678, 680.

[17] *Roger Lee, Inc. v. Trend Mills, Inc.*, 410 F.2d 928 (5th Cir. 1969); *Otto v. Imperial Cas. & Indem. Co.*, 277 F.2d 889 (8th Cir. 1960); *Smith v. Johnston*, 591 P.2d 1260 (Okla. 1979).

[18] *Pogge v. Fullerton Lumber Co.*, 277 N.W.2d 916 (Iowa 1979).

[19] *Walker v. Signal Cos.*, 149 Cal. Rptr. 119 (Cal. Ct. App. 1978).

[20] *A.W. Easter Constr. Co. v. White*, 224 S.E.2d 112 (Ga. Ct. App. 1976).

[21] *See* O.C.G.A. § 13-6-11. *See also* the Equal Access to Justice Act, 5 U.S.C. § 504, which permits the recovery of limited attorneys' fees for prevailing parties if the position of the government was not "substantially justified."

16.7   Causation

In order to successfully prosecute a claim, a claimant must establish the liability of the other party, the amount of its own damages, and prove that the damages were caused by the acts giving rise to liability. It is essential that the claimant demonstrate causation, meaning that the damages presented flow directly or indirectly from the liability issues presented. Without making this link, even the most thoroughly prepared and well-documented construction claim will not be able to withstand competent attack. It is not essential to establish the extent of the damage with absolute certainty if there is no question as to the fact that damage did occur. While speculative damages are not recoverable, the courts generally recognize that there is a difference in the measure of proof needed to show that the claimant sustained damage and the measure of proof needed to fix those damages.

One reliable method of establishing this link between liability and damages is to first prepare an analysis showing the differences between the construction costs as bid and the costs actually incurred. The focus of this type of analysis would be a demonstration that the overruns being claimed did in fact occur in the areas of work where the liability exists and that the increased costs were incurred because of specific acts of the owner.

16.8   Cost Accounting Records

The availability of proper cost accounting techniques when the claim is identified can substantially reduce the problem of calculating and proving damages. In fact, utilizing such techniques on a consistent basis may even help in the early identification of a potential claim if the actual recorded costs vary from the anticipated costs. Accounting measures can be established to segregate and carefully maintain separate records. If such a procedure is followed, proof of damages can be reduced to little more than the presentation of evidence of separate accounts. Unfortunately, this ideal situation seldom exists; either the problem is not recognized in time to set up separate accounting procedures, the maintenance of separate accounts is simply not possible because of an inability to isolate costs, or no attempt is made to establish the requisite procedures. These circumstances necessitate the development of some formula that is sufficiently reliable to permit the court or arbitrators to allow its use as proof of damage. If settlement is being sought, the claimant must likewise convince the other side of the validity and reliability of its damage calculations.

16.9   Mitigation of Damages

In a breach of contract action, the amount of recovery is generally limited to those losses and damages caused by the breach that are considered unavoidable.[22] The complaining party may not stand idly by and allow the losses to accumulate and increase, when reasonable effort or cost could have reduced the losses. This requirement is

---

[22] 22 Am. Jur. 2d Damages § 33.

known as the "duty to mitigate damages." In construction cases it usually arises where, upon a breach by one of the parties, there is a need for protection of partially completed work, timely reprocurement, assignment of equipment or work crews, or reduction of delay costs. In particular, it has been held that an owner that makes no effort to obtain a reasonable contract price upon reprocurement on a defaulted project cannot expect to recover the full difference between the original contract and the inflated costs to complete.[23]

The duty to mitigate calls for reasonable diligence and ordinary care. The party's actions need only be reasonable under the circumstances.[24] The law does not require that the defaulted party undertake extraordinary expense or effort to avoid losses flowing from a breached contract.[25]

16.10 Betterment

A related concept holds that a party cannot expect compensation for more than the loss arising from a breach of contract. For example, necessary repairs or replacement of a structure may, in fact, provide the owner with a "better" building than that provided for in the plans and specifications.[26] In such instances, where the owner obtains a "betterment" from the efforts of the contractor, any award of damages for breach must be reduced by the value of the betterment that the owner receives.[27]

16.11 METHODS OF PRICING CLAIMS

There are several basic methods for pricing construction claims. The simplest method is the *total cost method*. The oversimplicity of the total cost method causes it to be frowned upon and accepted only in extreme cases. The *modified total cost method* attempts to address those weaknesses. The other, more complicated but more widely accepted method is the discrete or *segregated cost method*. Finally, there is the *quantum meruit* approach to pricing a claim, which ignores costs and focuses instead on the value of the material and services provided.

16.12 The Total Cost Method

A total cost claim is simply what the name implies. It essentially seeks to convert a standard fixed-price construction contract into a cost-reimbursement arrangement. The contractor's total out-of-pocket costs of performance are tallied and marked up for overhead and profit. Payments already made to that contractor are deducted from

---

[23] *Metal Building Prods. Co. v. Fidelity & Deposit Co.*, 144 So. 2d 751 (La. Ct. App. 1962).

[24] *Halliburton Oil Well Cementing Co. v. Millican*, 171 F.2d 426 (5th Cir. 1948).

[25] *T.C. Bateson Constr. Co. v. United States*, 319 F.2d 135 (Ct. Cl. 1963).

[26] *Main St. Corp. v. Eagle Roofing Co.*, 168 A.2d 33 (N.J. 1961).

[27] *Correlli Roofing Co. v. National Instrument Co.*, 214 A.2d 919 (Md. 1965).

that amount, and the difference is the contractor's damages. Of course, this approach can be refined or adjusted to meet particular needs and circumstances, but the basic components and approach remain: costs associated with the basis for the claim are not segregated. The total cost method is often used for impact disruption claims when the segregation of costs may be more difficult.

The total cost approach, although preferred by claimants because of the ease of computation, is generally discouraged by the courts because it assumes that the contractor was virtually fault-free and is fraught with uncertainties. For these reasons, numerous court decisions have established fairly rigorous requirements for the presentation of total cost claims:

1.   Other methods of calculating damages are impossible or impractical;
2.   Recorded costs must be reasonable;
3.   The contractor's bid or estimate must have been accurate (that is, contained no underbidding);
4.   The actions of the plaintiff must not have caused any of the cost overruns.[28]

The second requirement, the reasonableness of recorded costs, is typically not a difficult assumption to prove. The claimant must demonstrate the appropriateness of costs, the reliability of the contractor's accounting methods and systems, and a relationship to industry practices and standards. Ironically, the more detailed and well documented the claimant's costs are, the more vulnerable the claimant is to an argument that it can use another method for calculating damages and, therefore, fails to satisfy the first requirement for use of the total cost method.

The remaining two requirements are the most difficult to meet. Proving that the contractor's bid was strictly accurate can be challenging. That proof might require a comparison of other bids and supplier and subcontractor quotes to bid amounts, as well as the comparison of material quantity estimates to contract drawings. Presenting such an analysis is expensive, often difficult to follow, and easily refutable because most bids rely heavily on assumptions. Due to the nature of the bidding process, many of these assumptions are accumulated in the absence of accurate information.

Establishing that the claimant was blameless for any overruns is perhaps the most difficult aspect of a total cost claim and why the method so rarely succeeds. The claimant essentially attempts to prove causation by showing that the damages were not its own fault and therefore must be due to the acts of the other party. The premise is easily attacked by demonstrating only a single area of potential blame attributable to the contractor, which could erode the credibility of the entire total cost claim. That is why this method has often been defeated in practice, and why parties may instead pursue a "modified" total cost method, as discussed in **Section 16.14**.

Owners probably view contractor total cost claims with even greater suspicion and distrust than do the courts, so much so that the credibility of the entire claim and

---

[28] *Chicago College of Osteopathic Medicine v. George A. Fuller Co.*, 719 F.2d 1335 (7th Cir. 1983); *John F. Harkins Co. v. School Dist. of Phila.*, 460 A.2d 260 (Pa. Super. Ct. 1983).

the claimant can be undermined. The difficulties of establishing the prerequisites for use of a total cost calculation in court, combined with the skepticism it can generate, counsel against use of the total cost method whenever possible.

16.13   Segregated Cost Method

The segregated cost method of pricing claims is more difficult to use than the total cost method, but it is usually a more accurate, reliable, and persuasive way of presenting damages. Under this approach, the additional costs associated with the events or occurrences that gave rise to the claim are segregated from those incurred in the normal course of performance of the contract. For example, on an extra work claim, the pricing would reflect an allocation (actual or estimated) for the additional labor, materials, and equipment used in performing the extra work. If the project was delayed, costs of field overhead and home office overhead would also be calculated.

The use of this cause-and-effect methodology most often yields an accurate, well-defined, and defensible presentation of damages. It may, however, be extremely difficult to accomplish in the absence of detailed job cost record keeping and sophisticated cost-control systems that segregate changed or impacted work. This method tends to have added credibility when the person presenting the damage shows that the sum of all specifically identified damages does not equal the total difference between the bid cost and total cost (that is, the total cost method). The difference remaining represents the costs related to contractor-caused events that have been excluded from the claim.

16.14   Modified Total Cost Method

Another general approach to calculating and presenting damages borrows from the concepts of both the specific identification and total cost methods. The modified total cost method employs the inherent simplicity of the total cost approach but modifies the calculation to demonstrate more direct cause-and-effect relationships that exist between the costs and acts giving rise to liability. The success of the approach often depends upon the extent of the modifications that demonstrate the cause-and-effect dynamics.

The initial step in calculating damages using the modified total cost method involves adjusting the contractor's bid for any weaknesses uncovered during job performance, whether they were judgment or simple calculation errors. A reasonable bid (an as-adjusted bid) is thus established. The recorded project costs are then similarly examined for reasonableness, and reductions are made for costs that cannot be attributed to the owner, such as unanticipated labor material cost escalations that are not tied to the alleged basis for liability.

Focusing on specific areas of work can further refine the modified total cost calculation or cost categories related to the claim issues. For example, if the claim relates to a differing site condition that affected only site work and foundations and not the balance of the project, the claimant should focus only on those areas in the calculation and eliminate extraneous costs and issues that complicate and dilute the credibility of the pricing.

Although the modified total cost approach is often viewed as a method of avoiding the unfavorable scrutiny generally given to a total cost analysis, recent cases imply that courts and boards of contract appeals may apply the same standards of admissibility to modified total cost claims as they have in the past to traditional total cost claims.[29] If the claimant has properly modified the cost calculation and not relied on a simplistic approach, the modified total cost method is far more likely to withstand scrutiny and offer a credible means of quantifying a claim.

16.15   *Quantum Meruit* Claims

A final type of damage theory involves an analysis of the "reasonable value" of the work performed. *Quantum meruit* is an equitable doctrine and means "as much as deserved." This method of recovery typically measures damages under an implied contract and is based upon the concept that no one should unfairly benefit from another's labor or materials. In these circumstances, the law creates a promise to pay a reasonable amount for these services, furnished, even absent a specific contract. For instance, mechanic's liens allow contractors and subcontractors to recover the reasonable value of their labor and materials used in improving property.

Quantum meruit is also often used in damage claims when a subcontractor does not have a direct contractual relationship with an owner but the owner has been "unjustly enriched" by work performed by the subcontractor.

Quantum meruit may also be available if there has been a material breach of the contract and the contractor opts to rescind the contract and seek the reasonable value of the benefits.[30] In most states, the contractor is not limited to the price specified in the initial agreement. The proper preparation and presentation of such a claim can often render proof of damages much easier, avoid the problems inherent in seeking a "total cost" recovery on a pure contract breach theory, and bring about recovery in excess of actual contract prices.[31]

16.16   THE CONTRACTOR'S DAMAGES

The following sections are not intended to provide an all-inclusive listing of categories of potential claims or cost elements, because the cost elements will vary depending upon the circumstances of each case. These elements are examples of the more common types of claim items in construction disputes.

16.17   Contract Changes and Extras

In most instances, a contractor presenting an affirmative claim to the owner will be seeking damages arising from changes in the anticipated quality, quantity, or method

---

[29] *Servidone Constr. Corp. v. United States*, 931 F.2d 860 (Fed. Cir. 1991).

[30] *Schulman Inv. Co. v. Olin Corp.*, 477 F. Supp. 623 (S.D.N.Y. 1979).

[31] *See, e.g., United States ex rel. Susi Contracting Co. v. Zara Contracting Co.*, 146 F.2d 606 (2d Cir. 1944); *Murray v. Marbro Builders, Inc.*, 371 N.E.2d 218 (Ohio 1977).

of work. Obviously, quantity and quality changes are relatively easy to discern. One clear, colorful, and effective way of describing such changes is to say that "the owner had the contractor build a Mercedes rather than the Ford required by the contract."

The owner that requires a contractor to perform an additional quantity of work is susceptible to a claim if the contractor has kept accurate records of the amount of work performed and can prove the difference between actual performance and what a reasonable interpretation of the contract would require.[32] However, the contractor that seeks to recover additional costs associated with changes in the anticipated method or sequence of construction—a category that includes delay, disruption, and acceleration damages—faces potential problems. These damages are more speculative than those mentioned above, hence more difficult to understand and prove with reasonable certainty. In addition, the contractor's records may furnish little support for the total claimed impact of a change in the anticipated method or sequence of work.

In recognition of the frequency of disagreements over pricing, contracts frequently include terms that provide the methodology for determining the price of extra or changed work. For example, the American Institute of Architects (AIA) A201 standard form general conditions provide several methods of determining costs for changes, including: (1) mutual acceptance of a substantiated lump-sum price, (2) contract or subsequently agreed-upon unit prices, (3) cost plus a mutually acceptable percentage or fixed fee, or (4) a method determined by the architect when the contractor fails to respond promptly or disagrees with the chosen method for adjustment in the contract sum. When a method determined by the architect is employed, the contractor must present an itemized accounting with supporting data, and is generally limited to recovery of the costs of labor, materials, supplies, equipment, rentals, bond and insurance premiums, permit fees, taxes, direct supervision, and other related cost items.

Paragraph 8.3, "Determination of Cost," in AGC Document No. 200, Standard Form of Agreement and General Conditions Between Owner and Contractor (2000 ed.), contains the following provisions regarding the pricing of a change in the work:

8.3   DETERMINATION OF COST

8.3.1   An increase or decrease in the Contract Price and/or the Contract Time resulting from a change in the Work shall be determined by one or more of the following methods:

.1   unit prices set forth in this Agreement or as subsequently agreed;

.2   a mutually accepted, itemized lump sum;

.3   costs calculated on a basis agreed upon by the Owner and Contractor plus a Fee (either a lump sum or a Fee based on a percentage of cost) to which they agree; or

.4   if an increase or decrease cannot be agreed to as set forth in Clauses .1 through .3 above, and the Owner issues an Interim Directed Change, the cost of the change in the Work shall be determined by the reasonable actual expense and savings of the performance of the Work resulting from the change. If there is a

---

[32] *Sornsin Constr. Co. v. State*, 590 P.2d 125 (Mont. 1978).

net increase in the Contract Price, the Contractor's Fee shall be adjusted accordingly. In case of a net decrease in the Contract Price, the Contractor's Fee shall not be adjusted unless ten percent (10%) or more of the Project is deleted. The Contractor shall maintain a documented, itemized accounting evidencing the expenses and savings.

8.3.2 If unit prices are set forth in the Contract Documents or are subsequently agreed to by the parties, but the character or quality of such unit items as originally contemplated is so different in a proposed Change Order that the original unit prices will cause substantial inequity to the Owner or the Contractor, such unit prices shall be equitably adjusted.

* * * *

Based either on common sense or a contract clause, the *reasonableness* of any claimed cost will be a critical factor in any pricing dispute. In federal government construction contracting, the controlling guidance on what is a reasonable cost is provided by the following provision of the Federal Acquisition Regulation:

FAR § 31.201-3 Determining Reasonableness.

(a) A cost is reasonable if, in its nature and amount, it does not exceed that which would be incurred by a *prudent person in the conduct of competitive business.* Reasonableness of specific costs must be examined with particular care in connection with the firms or their separate divisions that may not be subject to effective competitive restraints. *No presumption of reasonableness shall be attached to the incurrence of costs by a contractor.* If an initial review of the facts results in a challenge of a specific cost by the contracting officer or the contracting officer's representative, the burden of proof shall be upon the contractor to establish that such cost is reasonable.

(b) What is reasonable depends upon a variety of considerations and circumstances, including

(1) Whether it is the type of cost generally recognized as ordinary and necessary for the conduct of the contractor's business or the contract performance;

(2) Generally accepted sound business practices, arm's length bargaining, and Federal and State laws and regulations;

(3) The contractor's responsibilities to the Government, other customers, the owners of the business, employees, and the public at large; and

(4) Any significant deviations from the contractor's established practices.[33]

The types of direct damages sought by contractors in connection with the quantity, quality, and method variations discussed above include, among others, the extra costs of labor, materials, equipment, and extended job-site and home office overhead. The most frequently sought types of consequential damages are lost profits (stemming from reduced bonding capacity), interest on tied-up capital, and damage to business reputation. These types of consequential damages are most often sought in connection with delay claims.

---

[33] 48 CFR § 31.201-3. (Emphasis added.)

16.18   Wrongful Termination or Abandonment

A contractor may be damaged before beginning work if there is a breach of contract by the owner that prevents the contractor from performing the contract. In such a situation, the contractor is entitled to be placed in as good a position as it would have been in had the contract been performed. This generally means that the contractor can seek lost profits so long as they are not too speculative and can be proven with reasonable certainty.[34] This rule also applies to subcontractors that may be prevented from performing, as in the case of wrongful termination of the subcontract by the general contractor.[35] However, many private and public contracts now contain provisions permitting the owner (or government) to terminate a contract for its own convenience.[36] These provisions typically provide that the terminated contractor is not entitled to recover anticipated lost profits.

Once the contractor begins performance, it may find that the owner (or, if it is a subcontractor, the general contractor) has committed a material breach of some obligation, either express or implied. In these circumstances, and if the breach is a major one, the contractor could treat the breach as terminating its contract, suspend construction activities, and seek to recover damages.

If such an election were made, the contractor could pursue a number of means of establishing damages. First, it might seek to recover out-of-pocket expenses, less the value of any materials on hand, plus lost profits.[37] Alternatively, the contractor might seek recovery based upon the total contract price, less the total cost of performing the contract, plus any expenses incurred in performing until the material breach.

In addition, if there is some reasonable basis for pursuing this method, the contractor might seek the contract price of work performed up until the time of material breach, plus a profit on all unperformed work.[38] Obviously the election made by the contractor will depend upon the applicable rule of damages in the particular jurisdiction, the extent of the contractor's records, whether or not the contractor would have made a profit, and provisions of the construction contract, which may limit the remedies available.

More typically, however, the contractor will continue to perform after the "breach" by the owner (or the general contractor) and will seek to recover damages after completion of the contract.[39]

16.19   Owner-Caused Delay and Disruption

In the "typical" delay-disruption case, one of the contractor's tasks is to establish and isolate the period of delay attributable to the adverse party. Once this is done, proof of damages involves itemizing those fixed (ongoing) costs that were incurred during

---

[34] *Innkeepers Int'l, Inc. v. McCoy Motels, Ltd.*, 324 So. 2d 676 (Fla. Dist. Ct. App. 1975); *Cetrone v. Paul Livoli, Inc.*, 150 N.E.2d 732 (Mass. 1958).

[35] *See* John *Solely & Sons v. Jones*, 95 N.E. 94 (Mass. 1911).

[36] *See, e.g.,* 48 CFR § 52.249-2 (federal government termination for convenience clause).

[37] 5 Corbin on Contracts, §1094. *See also Autrey v. Williams & Dunlop*, 343 F.2d 730 (5th Cir. 1965).

[38] *See M & R Contractors & Builders, Inc. v. Michael*, 138 A.2d 350 (Md. 1958).

[39] *Underground Constr. Co. v. Sanitary Dist. of Chicago*, 11 N.E.2d 361 (Ill. 1937).

that period of delay. If, however, the period of delay itself cannot be isolated in this manner, the ensuing problems can be difficult. For example, generally courts will not make any effort to apportion damages in a situation where both parties are found to have contributed to the delays in completion of the contract.[40] Thus, where each party proximately contributes to the delay, "the law does not provide for the recovery or apportionment of damages occasioned thereby to either party."[41] All courts, however, do not adhere to this general rule.[42]

In addition to costs directly associated with the extended duration of a project, a project of extended duration also generates indirect costs, costs that present difficult proof problems. Among these costs are labor inefficiency that results from demobilization and subsequent remobilization, loss of learning-curve efficiency, and loss of efficiency when laborers work overtime during an acceleration period. Although proving labor inefficiency is a difficult task, excellent studies have been undertaken and the results published on many aspects of this problem. These can often be used as support for a contractor's claim.

One of the more obvious indirect costs attributable to a delay is the home office overhead cost incurred by the contractor. A large number of cases have recognized that home office overhead, like job-site overhead, is an element of damage that is recoverable by the contractor in a delay situation.[43] The method most frequently employed to prove extended home office overhead was set out in *Eichleay Corp.*[44] The formula is:

(1) $\dfrac{\textit{Total contract price}}{\substack{\text{Total billings for}\\\text{Full contract period}}}$ × Total home office overhead = Home office overhead allocable to the contract

(2) $\dfrac{\textit{Allocable overhead}}{\substack{\text{Total days of performance}\\\text{(including the delay period)}}}$ = Daily rate for home office overhead

(3) Daily rate × Number of days of compensable delay = Amount recoverable

[40] *See United States v. United Eng'g Contracting Co.*, 234 U.S. 236 (1914).

[41] *Malta Constr. v. Henningson, Durham & Richardson*, 694 F. Supp. 902 (N.D. Ga. 1988); *J.A. Jones Constr. Co. v. Greenbrier Shopping Ctr.*, 332 F. Supp. 1336 (N.D. Ga. 1971), *aff'd*, 461 F.2d 1269 (5th Cir. 1972).

[42] *See United States ex rel. Heller Elec. Co. v. William F. Klingensmith, Inc.*, 670 F.2d 1227 (1982); *see also Wilner v. United States*, 23 Cl. Ct. 241 (1991); *Inversiones Arunsu S.A.*, ENG BCA No. PCC-77, 91-2 BCA ¶ 24,584; *JEM Dev. Corp.*, VABCA No. 3272, 91-2 BCA ¶ 24,010.

[43] *See State v. Feigel*, 178 N.E. 435 (Ind. 1931); *A.E. Ottaviano v. State*, 110 N.Y.S.2d 99 (1952). For a discussion of a federal government contract case that attempts to limit the amount of overhead and profit a contractor can recover, *see Reliance Insurance Co. v. United States*, 931 F.2d 863 (Fed. Cir. 1991).

[44] ASBCA No. 5183, 60-2 BCA ¶ 2688, *aff'd on reh'g*, 61-1 BCA ¶ 2894 (commonly referred to as the Eichleay formula). For more recent cases discussing the conditions for using the Eichleay formula in federal government contract claims, see *Nicon v. United States*, 331 F.3d 878 (Fed. Cir. 2003); *P. J. Dick, Inc. v. Principi*, 324 F.3d 1364 (Fed. Cir. 2003); *Melka Marine, Inc. v. United States*, 187 F.3d 1370 (Fed. Cir. 1999); *E.R. Mitchell Construction Co. v. Danzig*, 175 F.3d 1369 (Fed. Cir. 1999); *West v. All State Boiler, Inc.*, 147 F.3d 1368 (Fed. Cir. 1998).

Although the use of the Eichleay formula is sometimes questioned, and there are several significant conditions on its use, recent decisions point to a continuing acceptance of this method by courts[45] and boards of contract appeals.[46]

The Eichleay formula is used to compensate a contractor when a delay on a project prevents the contractor from obtaining new business during the delay period. This prevents the infusion of new funds that will absorb the fixed time-related home office overhead costs incurred. Therefore, to recover unabsorbed home office overhead, the contractor generally must show that the delay affected its operations so that it was not practical to undertake other work during the delay period and, as a result, home office costs were not absorbed.[47]

Other delay and disruption types of damages include:

(1) Increased or protracted equipment rentals;[48]

(2) Increased labor costs, including wage or benefit increments, such as when an owner-caused delay forces contract performance into a new labor contract period;[49]

(3) Increased material costs;[50] and

(4) The costs of an idle workforce and equipment.[51]

In certain circumstances, a contractor may also be able to recover future profits lost as a result of owner-caused delays. A delay on one project can cause the contractor's bonding capacity to be reduced, which in turn prevents the contractor from bidding on new projects that would generate future profits. Courts, however, generally view such damages as too speculative to allow recovery.[52]

16.20   Owner-Caused Acceleration

Acceleration arises from the requirement that the contractor complete performance of the contract, or a portion thereof, on a date earlier than that originally contemplated and specified by the contract or required by a properly adjusted schedule. There are two types of acceleration that may entitle the contractor to damages: (1) "directed acceleration" occurs when the owner requires the contractor to complete

---

[45] *Gladwynne Const. Co. v. City of Baltimore*, 807 A.2d 1141 (Md. App. 2002); *Complete Gen. Constr. v. Ohio Dept. of Transportation*, 760 N.E. 2d 364 (Ohio 2002); *Triple R. Paving, Inc. v. Broward County*, 774 So. 2d 50 (Fla. App. 2000); *Broward County v. Russell, Inc.*, 589 So. 2d 983 (Fla. App. 1991).

[46] *Roy McGinnis & Co., Inc.*, ASBCA No. 49867, 02-1 BCA ¶ 31,720.

[47] *See P.J. Dick, supra* note 44; *Gregory Constructors, Inc.*, ASBCA No. 35960, 88-3 BCA ¶ 20,934; *Ricway Inc.*, ASBCA No. 29983, 86-2 BCA ¶ 18,841.

[48] *See Shore Bridge Corp. v. State*, 61 N.Y.S.2d 32 (Ct. Cl. 1946).

[49] *See Weaver Constr. Co.*, ASBCA No. 12577, 69-1 BCA ¶ 7455.

[50] *See Samuel N. Zarpas, Inc.*, ASBCA No. 4722, 59-1 BCA ¶ 2170.

[51] *See State v. Feigel*, 178 N.E. 435 (Ind. 1931).

[52] *See, e.g., H.H.O., Inc. v. United States*, 7 Cl. Ct. 703 (Cl. Ct. 1985); *but see Laas v. Montana State Highway Comm'n*, 483 P.2d 699 (Mont. 1971).

the contract before the scheduled completion date; and (2) "constructive acceleration" occurs when the owner refuses to grant the contractor a time extension in the
event of owner-caused or other excusable delays. When the contractor must accelerate the pace of performance, the contractor's increased costs are generally compensable.[53] These costs may include, among other things, overtime and shift
premiums, supervision costs, extra equipment costs, loss of efficiency, overhead,
and profit.[54] If prolonged overtime is required, the effect may be an overall decrease
in worker productivity for both overtime and regular (straight) time activities.[55]

The contractor must be able to demonstrate that it has incurred extra costs due to
the accelerated efforts. For example, where the owner clearly ordered the contractor
to accelerate its work, but there was no evidence that the contractor did anything different or suffered any damage as a result of the acceleration order, the contractor's
claim for acceleration was denied.[56]

16.21   Defective Drawings or Specifications

Where the owner supplies the plans and specifications to be used in construction, it
is usually held to impliedly warrant that the plans and specifications will be adequate
to achieve the purposes contemplated.[57] If the plans and specifications are defective
or contain omissions, the contractor may incur substantially increased costs of performance. These costs, including the costs of identifying and correcting defects in
the drawings or specifications, along with any delay costs arising therefrom, may be
recovered if the contractor properly relied upon such drawings in attempting to perform its contractual obligations.[58] In addition, where defective specifications create
"wasted effort" and hinder the contractor's performance, the resulting delay may be
excusable, and usually no damages can be recovered by the owner in the event of
delayed completion.[59]

16.22   Inefficiency Claims

The loss of efficiency can be defined as the increased level of effort required to complete an activity above that reasonably estimated and anticipated by the contractor.
If an activity that was reasonably estimated to take 8 hours requires 16 hours due to

---

[53] *J. W. Bateson Co.*, ASBCA No. 6069, 1962 BCA ¶ 3529; *Tyee Constr. Co.*, IBCA No. 692-1-68, 69-1
BCA ¶ 7748.

[54] *See* Nash, *Government Contract Changes* (Federal Publications, Inc. 1975).

[55] *See* Business Roundtable Constr. Indus. Cost Effectiveness Task Force, "Scheduled Overtime Effect on
Construction Projects" (Nov. 1980).

[56] *Utley-James, Inc. v. United States*, 14 Cl. Ct. 804 (1988).

[57] *United States v. Spearin*, 248 U.S. 132 (1918).

[58] *La Crosse Garment Mfg. Co. v. United States*, 432 F.2d 1377 (Ct. Cl. 1970); *Hol-Gar Mfg. Corp. v.
United States*, 360 F.2d 634 (Ct. Cl. 1966); *Celesco Indus., Inc.*, ASBCA No. 18370, 76-1 BCA ¶ 11,766.

[59] *Warner Constr. Corp. v. City of Los Angeles*, 466 P.2d 996 (Cal. 1970); *Souza & McCue Constr. Co. v.
Superior Court of San Benito County*, 20 Cal. Rptr. 634 (Cal. 1962).

factors beyond the contractor's control, the overrun in labor (8 hours) is viewed as the inefficiency loss. This is often expressed in the form of a percentage, which, in this case, would be a 50 percent productivity loss. Although loss of efficiency claims most frequently involve significant labor overruns, dramatic overruns in equipment usage and costs can arise from inefficient operations.

Construction projects are perceived as having some inherent degree of confusion. An inefficiency claim must therefore demonstrate that the disruption experience went beyond that reasonably anticipated. Recovery of additional compensation for loss of efficiency requires that the claimant establish the other party's liability for the events giving rise to the claim and the amount of damages associated with those events. Some of the factors that may adversely affect a contractor's efficiency are:

- Excessive overtime
- Out-of-sequence work
- Restricted access to the working area
- Trade stacking
- Overmanning
- Excess changes that disrupt the planned sequence of the unchanged work
- Differing site conditions
- Adverse weather
- Acceleration

Studies conducted by the Business Roundtable's Construction Industry Cost Effectiveness Task Force indicate that overtime impairs productivity because of physical fatigue, increased absenteeism, increased likelihood of accidents, and overall reduced quality of work installed.[60] As a general rule, courts and boards have accepted the proposition that overtime results in loss of efficiency.[61]

Weather has a significant impact on construction[62] if the work is exposed to the elements. The types of weather impacting productivity include rain, abnormal humidity, frozen ground, subfreezing temperatures, extreme heat, and excessive wind. Relief for weather is usually limited to an extension of contract time for completion without any monetary compensation.[63] If an earlier compensable delay forces the contractor to perform work during a period of inclement weather, then the contractor may be entitled to additional time for the delay as well as compensation for loss of efficiency suffered by its labor force.[64]

---

[60] Business Roundtable Constr. Indus. Cost Effectiveness Task Force, *supra* note 55.

[61] *See Maryland Sanitary Mfg. Corp. v. United States*, 119 Ct. Cl. 100 (1951); *Casson Constr. Co.*, GSBCA No. 4884, 83-1 BCA ¶ 16,523; *Metro Eng'g*, AGBCA No. 77-121-4, 83-1 BCA ¶ 16,143.

[62] National Electrical Contractors Ass'n, "The Effect of Temperature on Productivity" (Feb. 1987).

[63] *Turnkey Enter., Inc. v. United States*, 597 F.2d 750, 754 (Ct. Cl. 1979).

[64] *See Abbett Elec. Corp. v. United States*, 162 F. Supp. 772 (Ct. Cl. 1958); *F.H. McGraw & Co. v. United States*, 82 F. Supp. 338 (Ct. Cl. 1949).

One of the best ways to demonstrate productivity losses is through the use of data specific to the project. However, such records are generally not maintained on the majority of construction projects. There are many ways to collect productivity data for a particular project at the job site. One example is illustrated by the inefficiency claim presentation in *Barrett Co.*[65] In that case, the contractor noted on a daily basis the events that adversely affected efficient performance and the consequences of those events. This contemporaneous record was described by the board as "well described and documented,"[66] and the contractor recovered the amounts claimed.

One effective way to establish the loss of efficiency is a comparison of actual production before and after the problem was encountered, referred to as a "measured mile" analysis.[67] This technique is especially effective for a contractor that routinely performs a particular division of the work with its own forces and has historical, as well as job-specific, records. The availability of this approach depends upon the nature and validity of the project documentation system.

In a loss of efficiency claim, the cause-and-effect relationship may be less capable of exact scientific measurement. This does not mean that a loss of efficiency claim is fiction. The effect of a disruption upon a construction project can be devastating in terms of labor dollars or equipment hours expended. In addition, due to the intricate and subtle dependencies between the various trades and activities (the ripple effect) there may be a need for an expert to offer an opinion as to the cause of a disruption and its effect on the project. In *Luria Bros. & Co. v. United States*,[68] the court stated: "It is a rare case where loss of productivity can be proven by books and records; almost always it has to be proven by the opinion of expert witnesses." Thus, the opinion of an expert witness may be required to quantify the nature, the cause, and the amount of inefficiency experienced on the project.

Good documentation combined with appropriate historical data or measured mile studies provide an objective basis for the opinions of experts. Expert opinions and testimony may be extremely valuable in laying the foundation for an inefficiency claim and proving damages. However, without corroboration, the cases indicate that it is quite possible that the opinion testimony will be discounted if there is no other independent basis to support the opinions.

16.23   THE OWNER'S DAMAGES

Liability and damages can flow both ways in a construction dispute. The owner's costs can be the same type of costs of construction a contractor incurs if the owner is required to complete the project or remedy defective work. The owner's consequential

---

[65] ENG BCA No. 3877, 78-1 BCA ¶ 13,075 at 63,853.

[66] *Id.* at 63,854.

[67] *Goodwin Contractors, Inc.*, AGBCA No. 89-148-1, 92-2 BCA ¶ 24,931.

[68] 369 F.2d 701 (Ct. Cl. 1966).

damages, however, can be very different from that of a contractor, and potentially of a much larger magnitude. Generally speaking, the law provides that the owner is entitled to receive what it contracted for.

16.24 Direct Damages

A contractor can breach a construction contract in a variety of ways: it can fail to commence work at all; it can commence work but fail to complete it as required by the contract (i.e., abandon the project or fail to complete it within the time period specified by the contract); or it can substantially complete the work but have deviated from the plans in some major or minor respect. In each of these cases the owner may be entitled to recover damages for the contractor's breach.

Where the contractor has breached the contract by its failure to commence work at all, no consistent method of computing damages has been recognized and applied by the courts. However, one approach, utilized in *Ross v. Danter Associates, Inc.*,[69] was to compute the difference between the price at which the original contractor agreed to do the construction and the price at which the owner was able to obtain a replacement contractor or the fair market price of erecting the building.[70]

Where a contractor abandons the work prior to completion, the generally recognized measure of direct damages is the amount it costs the owner to complete the structure in accordance with the terms of the original agreement. The contract is the first place one should look to determine what damages it is entitled to seek from the contractor in the event of default. For example, subparagraph 11.3.1 of AGC Document No. 200 provides that, after termination, the owner is entitled to the difference between the contract price and the owner's costs arising out of the contractor's failure to cure, including the cost of completing the work and any reasonable attorneys' fees. In *Schmidt Bros. Construction Co. v. Raymond Y.M.C.A. of Charles City*,[71] the court set out what appears to be the majority rule in this regard:

> The contract contained no provision respecting the completion of the building in case of the failure of the contractor to complete the same. Under these circumstances, [the owner] had the right to complete the building and charge the reasonable cost and expense thereof to [the contractor]. . . . [The contractor] having abandoned the contract, [the owner] was not required to submit the cost of completing the structure to competitive bidders, nor to complete the same at the lowest possible cost, but had the right to expend such sum for labor and material as was fairly and reasonably necessary to complete the structure in accordance with the contract and the plans and specifications of the architect.

---

[69] 242 N.E.2d 330 (Ill. App. Ct. 1968).

[70] *See generally* John P. Ludington, Annotation, "Modern Status of Rule as to Whether Cost of Correction or Difference in Value of Structure Is Proper Measure of Damages for Breach of Construction Contract," 41 A.L.R.4th 131, § 15 (1985).

[71] 163 N.W. 458, 462 (Iowa 1917).

When the contractor fails to complete the contract within the time period specified, the owner may be entitled to damages for delayed completion.[72] The amount of such damages may be stipulated in the contract by a liquidated damages provision. However, where there is no liquidated damages clause, the proper measure of damages for completion delay in construction contracts is generally held to be the loss of reasonable rentals from the property for the period of the contractor's unexcused delay.[73]

Where the contractor has substantially completed work under the contract but has deviated to some extent from the plans and specifications, the measure of direct damages to the owner will generally be based on some variation of one of the following two theories: (1) the "cost" rule or (2) the "value" rule.[74] The cost rule measures either the cost of completing or the cost of repairing the contractor's work. The value rule measures the difference between the actual value of the building as delivered and the value promised.

Under either of these theories of recovery, the owner, like the contractor, must fully document and prove its damages. Where the damage or injury is so slight as to be insignificant, no recovery is allowed.[75] These two methods of computing damages are widely accepted. However, the "cost to complete" measure appears to be the more commonly used, particularly in those cases where the specific defect or omission of which the owner is complaining can be remedied at reasonable cost and without destroying work that has already been done.[76]

When as a practical matter defects and omissions cannot be remedied except at unwarranted expense and with excessive economic waste, the courts usually apply the "value" rule. This "diminution in value" rule measures damages by calculating the difference between the value of the work if it had been performed in accordance with the contract and the value of the work as it was actually done or, alternatively, the difference between the value of the defective structure and the structure if properly completed.[77] However, in some situations, when it is necessary to recover the benefit of the bargain, an owner may be able to recover the costs of repair, even when it would result in economic waste.[78]

Finally, it should also be noted that these two methods of calculating damages can, under some circumstances, be used together to arrive at an acceptable, overall damage figure. Some of the items of damage may properly be calculated under the "cost to complete" approach, while others may be more suited to a "diminution in value" calculation.

---

[72] *Potter v. Anderson*, 178 N.W.2d 743 (S.D. 1970).

[73] *Kaltoft, Inc. v. Nielson*, 106 N.W.2d 597 (Iowa 1960); *Hemenway Co. v. Bartex, Inc.*, 373 So. 2d 1356 (La. Ct. App. 1979).

[74] Dobbs, Remedies § 12.21, at 897 (1973).

[75] *General Refrigeration Co. of Lake Charles, Inc. v. Style Home Builders, Inc.*, 379 So. 2d 1211 (La. Ct. App. 1980).

[76] *R.I. Turnpike & Bridge Auth. v. Bethlehem Steel Corp.*, 379 A.2d 344 (R.I. 1977).

[77] *Robbins v. C.W. Myers Trading Post, Inc.*, 111 S.E.2d 884 (N.C. 1960); *City of Charlotte v. Skidmore, Owings & Merrill*, 407 S.E.2d 571 (N.C. Ct. App. 1991).

[78] *LaPiere v. Samco Bev. Corp.*, 406 S.E.2d 646 (N.C. Ct. App. 1991).

16.25 Consequential Damages

The previous discussion focused on direct damages recoverable by an owner. However, owners, like contractors, can recover consequential damages attributable to a breach under certain circumstances (if not excluded by contract, such as in the 1997 revision to AIA Document A201 or the 2000 version of AGC Document 200) and upon adequate proof. An excellent example of such a situation arose in *Northern Petrochemical Co. v. Thorsen & Thorshov, Inc.*[79] There the owner brought an action against the general contractor, the architect, and the structural engineer for defective construction and design. The presence of numerous major defects in design and construction required reconstruction of a major portion of the facility, with a resulting eight-month delay in its availability for use. In addition to the costs of reconstruction and the overall diminution in value of the building, the owner was also allowed to recover for the eight-month loss of use of the facility because the court determined that the loss was a direct and proximate result of the injury and that the parties could have reasonably contemplated such damages when entering into the contract.

The court also permitted the owner to recover the following damages, as explained by the court:

> *Loss of profits* has been recognized as an appropriate measure of the damages resulting from the loss of use *when the anticipated profits can be proved to a reasonable, although not necessarily absolute, certainty*. In the instant case, the evidence on loss of profits was superbly marshaled and, in part because of the industry-wide inability to produce sufficient extruded plastic film to meet the demand, easily met the burden of reasonable certainty required for recovery of lost profits. . . . [W]e have no trouble finding the proof sufficiently certain to affirm the court's award in the instant case.[80]

The contractor must therefore recognize that the risk of substantial consequential damages may exist, depending on the specific details and circumstances of the particular project and contract.

16.26 Liquidated Damages

Owners often include in the proposal and contract documents a provision that states the contractor will pay the owner a certain stipulated sum of money for each day of delay in contract completion. In theory, the owner and the prospective contractor have agreed at the time of contract formation on the method of calculating the owner's damages in the event of the contractor's breach at a future date. In practice, however, very little negotiation or "agreement" among the parties is experienced. Due to the difficulty inherent in determining actual damages on a construction project, the owner, or its representative, will determine a dollar figure that appears to be sufficient to cover any anticipated excess costs arising out of delayed completion,

---

[79] 211 N.W.2d 159 (Minn. 1973).
[80] *Id*. at 163. (Emphasis added).

and insert that figure into the documents. Often, this figure is stated as a per diem dollar amount of the actual damages an owner will suffer. If a dispute subsequently arises as to the application of the liquidated damages provision, the courts will try to determine the reasonableness of the figure by examining the condition and positions of the parties at the time of contract execution rather than at the time of breach.

A liquidated damages provision is not necessarily invalid merely because it is at variance with the usual legal rules for computing damages or because it allows an innocent party to recover despite the fact that it is unable to prove exactly the amount of its actual damages. The crucial factors to be considered are:

(1) Whether the liquidated damage amount bears some reasonable relationship to actual or anticipated damages contemplated by the parties when the contract was made so that it does not constitute a penalty;[81]

(2) Whether actual damages were difficult to compute at the time the contract was signed;[82] and

(3) Whether the breach in question is one covered by the liquidated damage provision.[83]

Many states now presume that liquidated damage clauses are valid, and place the burden on the party challenging the provision to prove that the clause amounts to a penalty.[84] The rationale behind upholding a valid liquidated damages provision has been explained as follows:

The modern trend is to look with candor, if not with favor, upon a contract provision for liquidated damages when entered into deliberately between parties who have equality of opportunity for understanding and insisting upon their rights, since an amicable adjustment in advance of difficult issues saves the time of courts, juries, parties, and witnesses and reduces the delay, uncertainty, and expense of litigation.[85]

The requirement that liquidated damages be reasonably proportionate to actual damages stems from the fact that courts have traditionally refused to enforce what amounts to a penalty for breach of contract.[86] One primary objection to penalties is

---

[81] *Georgia Income Property Corp. v. Murphy*, 354 S.E.2d 859 (Ga. Ct. App. 1987); *Mattingly Bridge Co. v. Holloway & Son Constr.*, 694 S.W.2d 702 (Ky. 1985); *Psaty & Fuhrman Inc. v. Housing Auth. of Providence*, 68 A.2d 32 (R.I. 1949); *Ray v. Electrical Prods. Consol.*, 390 P.2d 607 (Wyo. 1964).

[82] *Osceola County v. Bumble Bee Constr., Inc.*, 479 So.2d 310 (Fla. Dist. Ct. App. 1985); *Mosler Safe Co. v. Maiden Lane Safe Deposit Co.*, 93 N.E. (N.Y. 1910).

[83] *Grant Constr. Co. v. Burns*, 443 P.2d 1005 (Idaho 1968).

[84] *Farmers Export Co. v. M/V Georgis Prois, Etc.*, 799 F.2d 159 (5th Cir. 1986); *Hubbard Business Plaza v. Lincoln Liberty Life Ins Co.*, 649 F. Supp. 1310 (D. Nev. 1986); *Coe v. Thermasol Ltd.*, 615 F. Supp. 316 (W.D.N.C. 1985), *aff'd*, 785 F.2d 511 (4th Cir. 1986).

[85] *Gorco Constr. Co. v. Stein*, 99 N.W.2d 69 (Minn. 1959).

[86] *See, e.g., Dahlstrom Corp. v. State Highway Comm'n of State of Miss.*, 590 F.2d 614 (5th Cir. 1979); *Precon, Inc. v. JRS Realty Trust*, 47 B.R. 432 (D.C. Me. 1985); *Unis v. JTS Constructors/Managers, Inc.*, 541 So. 2d 278 (La. Ct. App. 1989).

that while the law favors reimbursement for loss, it does not approve of granting windfalls or unearned profits, even to an innocent party. To allow an injured party to recover an amount in excess of the actual damages it has suffered would, in effect, put that party in a better position than it would have been in had the contract been performed. This result would be inconsistent with the basic theory of contract damages, as discussed above.

For these reasons, if the liquidated damage amount set by the parties is found to be a penalty, the party seeking to enforce the provision will not be allowed to rely on it but instead will be required to prove actual damages caused by the breach of contract. Whether a stipulated sum should be upheld as allowable liquidated damages or struck down as a penalty is a question of law that the court must decide.[87]

Another condition that most courts impose in connection with liquidated damages is that the actual damages resulting from the breach must be difficult or impossible to prove. Substitution of damages agreed upon in advance would not be justified if actual damages could be readily measured. For this reason, a liquidated damages provision will not generally be upheld where actual damages are readily ascertainable by some adequate and approved legal standard. However, the reasonableness of the liquidated damages must be viewed at the time of contracting, not at the time of the breach.

The rules governing liquidated damages have wide application in construction contracts, particularly in those situations involving late completion of the contract. The typical liquidated damages provision provides that the contractor will be assessed a certain dollar amount for each day the project remains uncompleted beyond the specified completion date. Such a provision avoids the difficulties of calculating lost revenues that the owner would otherwise be receiving. Where a contractor has been granted time extensions for whatever reason, liquidated damages do not begin to accrue until the period of the extensions has passed.

Three specific factors should be noted in connection with the assessment of liquidated damages. First, liquidated damages cannot be imposed where the owner is the sole cause of a delay suffered by the contractor.[88] Second, because of the difficulties inherent in apportioning responsibility for delays caused by the owner and the contractor, many courts will not assess liquidated damages where a concurrent delay has occurred.[89] Numerous cases have recognized and applied the principle that the owner-caused portion of the delays so confuses the issue of responsibility for time overruns that liquidated damages cannot fairly be assessed against the contractor.

The third factor is that an owner generally has no right to assess liquidated damages for delay after the contractor has achieved substantial completion of the project. The justification for this rule is that the owner has received essentially what was contracted for, and therefore the assessment of liquidated damages would constitute a penalty.[90]

---

[87] *Farmers Export Co.*, supra, note 84; *United States v. Swanson*, 618 F. Supp. 1231 (E.D. Mich. 1985); *Florence Wagon Works v. Salmon*, 68 S.E. 866 (Ga. Ct. App. 1910).

[88] *Department of Transp. v. W. P. Dickerson & Son, Inc.*, 400 A.2d 930 (Pa. Commw. Ct. 1979).

[89] *Gillioz v. State Highway Comm'n*, 153 S.W.2d 18 (Mo. 1941); *cf. Southwest Eng'g Co. v. United States*, 341 F.2d 988 (8th Cir. 1965).

[90] *See Continental Ill. Nat'l Bank v. United States*, 101 F. Supp. 755 (Ct. Cl. 1952); *Powers Contracting Co.*, ASBCA No. 1430 (1953).

Similarly, final payment from the owner to the contractor may waive the owner's right to later seek payment of liquidated damages for the contractor's late completion. In *Centerre Trust Co. v. Continental Insurance Co.*,[91] the owner was found to have waived its right to liquidated damages by making final payment, rather than retaining funds to offset accruing liquidated damages. The owner would have been within its rights to withhold all remaining contract balances to recover the accruing liquidated damages if it had not made final payment to the contractor.

Additionally, an owner may waive its right to recover liquidated damages from a contractor by failing to place the contractor in default. In *Sun-Cal, Inc. v. United States*,[92] the General Services Administration ("owner") terminated the contractor for default. The contractor disputed the termination, claiming that the default was not authorized because the original contract completion date had been waived and a new completion date had never been established. The contract between the parties contained a liquidated damages clause that assessed $1,000 per day as damages against the contractor for each calendar day completion was delayed beyond the contract completion date.

Due to owner delay, the parties had agreed to delay the contract completion date for one month. Although the contractor did not complete the construction by the newly established contract completion date, the owner encouraged the contractor to continue with its work on the project. A new and final contract completion date was never established by the owner.

The court in *Sun-Cal* determined that the owner had surrendered its right to terminate the contractor by failing to enforce the newly established contract completion date within a reasonable time period. The court also determined that the parties failed to agree on a new contract completion date. Consequently, since the owner chose not to place the contractor in default when it did not meet the original contract completion date or the newly established contract completion date, and since a new contract completion date was never reached, the owner could not assess liquidated damages against the contractor.

A liquidated damages provision may occasionally operate to the contractor's benefit. If such a provision is held enforceable, the clause cannot be attacked by the owner merely because the fixed amount turns out to be less than the owner's actual damages. In *Brower Co. v. Garrison*,[93] a liquidated damages provision fixed damages at $50 per day and was upheld despite the fact that the owner's actual damages were $230 per day. Thus, a liquidated damages provision, if upheld, will preclude the owner's right to bring an action for actual damages in most situations.

Contractors may include liquidated damages in their subcontracts. Depending upon the wording of the subcontract clause, collection by the prime contractor of liquidated damages from a subcontractor may be limited to the amount the prime contractor has paid the owner.[94]

---

[91] 521 N.E.2d 219 (Ill. App. Ct. 1988).

[92] 21 Cl. Ct. 31 (1990).

[93] 468 P.2d 469 (Wash. Ct. App. 1979).

[94] *See Industrial Indem. Co. v. Wick Constr. Co.*, 680 P.2d 1100 (Alaska 1984); *Mattingly Bridge Co. v. Holloway & Son Constr. Co.*, 694 S.W.2d 702 (Ky. 1985); *see also Hall Constr. Co. v. Beynon*, 507 So. 2d 1225 (Fla. Dist. Ct. App. 1987) (holding that where a purchase order to a supplier contained a pass-through of liquidated damages clause, the contractor's recovery of delay damages was limited to that amount).

Finally, there is no apparent reason why a liquidated damages provision cannot be inserted in a contract to cover anticipated damages incurred by the contractor, as a result of owner-caused delay, disruption, and so on. Such clauses are being discussed and utilized more frequently, under the proper circumstances.

➤ POINTS TO REMEMBER

- The general nature of damage principles is to compensate the injured party for its losses, and not to create a windfall.
- Direct damages are those costs flowing directly from the wrongful acts of the other party, such as increased costs of project completion.
- Consequential damages are the reasonably foreseeable, but indirect, injury incurred from the contract breaches, such as lost profits on other projects due to lost bonding capacity.
- Punitive damages are not compensatory. Their purpose is to punish the wrongdoer. Punitive damages are generally not recoverable in contract actions or construction disputes.
- Liquidated damages are stipulated amounts that the parties agree will be assessed for a failure of performance, typically late completion. Liquidated damages are generally in lieu of and not in addition to actual (direct and consequential) damages.
- In order to recover for a claim, the claimant must establish liability, the amount of the additional costs incurred, and that there is a causal relationship between the facts giving rise to liability and the damages claimed.
- Every party has an affirmative obligation to mitigate or minimize their damages, even if the damages are the result of another's wrongful conduct. A claimant cannot unreasonably incur extra costs.
- Construction claims are ideally priced using the discrete cost method, in which specific costs are tied to specific acts of the other party. When it is not practical to do so, other less desirable methods such as the modified total cost method and total cost method are available.
- The total cost method is frowned upon by the courts and should be used only if absolutely necessary.
- Good cost accounting is necessary to credibly price and pursue a claim.
- Even with good documentation, the assistance of experts is necessary to calculate and prove damages, particularly when the claim is based on inefficiency costs rather than pure extra work or delay.

17

CONSTRUCTION INDUSTRY ENVIRONMENTAL AND SAFETY CONCERNS

Construction projects must be approached with the knowledge that both environmental and safety laws and regulations will impact many aspects of the work and may, at times, completely disrupt and dictate the pace of job progress. While the risk of encountering hazardous environmental wastes and its associated risk of potentially limitless liability may be small on many projects, the risk of encountering other environmental problems always exists. For example, the improper discharge of storm water runoff could result in civil and criminal liabilities. Similarly, every project carries with it the risk of workplace injury, with complications such as lost worker time, and resulting investigations.

Unfortunately, there is a maze of federal, state, and local environmental and safety laws and regulations that could affect a construction project. It is important to appreciate and generally understand the scope of these statues, and how the courts are interpreting them, in order to better plan for your project. The time to address safety and environmental considerations on construction projects begins at the proposal stage. Contractors must be able to satisfy any particular licensing, insurance, or qualifications requirements before even considering submitting a bid or proposal. Contingency plans and management policies must be in place and ready for execution. Contract terms and insurance coverage must be scrutinized in light of the possibility, regardless of how remote, that environmental wastes will be encountered or created or that a worker will be injured on the job. The purpose of this chapter is to further sensitize, educate, and alert the reader to the urgent need to be prepared and to expect the unexpected when it comes to liability for environmental or safety issues.

17.1   SOURCES OF ENVIRONMENTAL REGULATION AND LIABILITY

The federal government's regulation and imposition of liability for hazardous wastes is far-reaching and grabs the most media attention. The Comprehensive Environmental Response, Compensation and Liability Act of 1980,[1] commonly known as CERCLA or "Superfund," is the flagship of environmental liability laws, but it is certainly not the only statute that may apply to the construction owner, contractor, or subcontractor. In addition to the federal laws, the states have enacted their own statutory schemes to regulate and assess liability for hazardous waste problems. Regardless of the existence of any specific statutes, liability may also be imposed under traditional civil law theories of tort, nuisance, and trespass. The consequence of running afoul of this web of environmental liability is not limited to job delays and civil liability payable by a company, but can involve fines and criminal penalties assessed against individuals. This chapter focuses on the civil liability aspects of CERCLA and other key federal statutes, which, despite their importance, are by no means the only legal requirements that may apply to a situation.

17.2   CERCLA Liability

CERCLA is generally aimed at addressing liability for cleanup costs for past contamination of sites by hazardous wastes. Other federal statutes, such as the Resource Conservation and Recovery Act of 1976 (RCRA),[2] deal with the current handling, storage, treatment, and disposal of hazardous wastes. Because contamination may occur in the process of handling, storing, treating, or disposing hazardous wastes, there can be some considerable overlap between CERCLA and RCRA.

   CERCLA is intended to impose liability for cleanup costs on those parties responsible for the contamination. The parties on whom CERCLA may impose liability are referred to as "potentially responsible parties," or "PRPs." The manner in which "responsible party" under CERCLA has been interpreted by the courts is far broader than the conventional understanding of that term. It is the breadth of CERCLA liability and the extraordinarily low level of involvement at which this liability is triggered that makes it such a major threat to many construction projects. In addition, CERCLA enforcement is not left to the federal government. Private individuals who are forced to incur cleanup costs are authorized to pursue responsible parties to recover those costs.

17.3   *Strict Liability*   Under CERCLA, if you are within the statutory definition of "responsible party," you are liable. Even if you took all reasonable precautions and operated in a legally and generally acceptable manner, liability attaches. CERCLA imposes "strict liability," which means automatic liability

---

[1] 42 U.S.C. §§ 9601–9657 (1995), as amended.

[2] 42 U.S.C. §§ 6901–6992k (1995), as amended.

without regard to fault or negligence. Only a few and very limited defenses are allowed under CERCLA. CERCLA was specifically created to deal with the serious need to address environmental damage from hazardous wastes. The tough measures were deemed necessary to fulfill the statute's important remedial purpose.

There is an exception to strict liability under CERCLA for the contractor specifically engaged to clean up hazardous wastes—called a "response action contractor," or "RAC"— that enjoys the privilege of immunity from strict liability. This somewhat anomalous response is due to the recognition that without some insulation from strict liability, it would be impossible to get any responsible contractor to perform cleanup work. The RAC is not totally relieved from liability under CERCLA; it remains liable under CERCLA for negligence, gross negligence, and intentional wrongdoing in connection with the cleanup. The CERCLA exception to strict liability for RACs applies only to federal statutes and does not in any way limit the RAC's potential liability, including strict liability, that may be imposed under state law.

17.4 Responsible Parties CERCLA lists four categories of responsible parties. If a party falls into one of the categories, that party is liable:

(1) The current owner or operator of the facility;

(2) The owner or operator of the facility at the time the hazardous substance was released;

(3) Any party that, by contract or otherwise, arranged for the disposal of the hazardous substance owned by them or by another party; and

(4) Any person that accepted any hazardous substance for transport or disposal that results in a release of hazardous substances.

On their face, the categories are broad. Over time, they have been interpreted even more broadly by the courts. These categories would appear inapplicable in the context of the contractor who encounters an unexpected hazardous waste, as the hazardous waste is not something for which the contractor assumed responsibility. However, liability is imposed without regard to fault or negligence. That is the basic concept of strict liability. In theory, that means that the contractor who unwittingly stumbles upon and innocently transports hazardous wastes that result in contamination of a site is just as liable for cleanup costs under CERCLA as the party who knowingly handles and purposely disposes of hazardous wastes in an illegal fashion. That may sound like a theoretical worst-case scenario that has no relevance in the real world, but it is not. Consider the contractor's treatment in *Kaiser Aluminum & Chemical Corp. v. Catellus Development Corp.*[3]

In the *Kaiser* case, the court held that a site-work contractor could be liable under CERCLA simply by cutting and filling soil on a site that, unknown to the contractor, had been contaminated by hazardous waste decades earlier. The contractor was hired by the property owner of the site to grade and prepare the site for a housing

---

[3] 976 F.2d 1338 (9th Cir. 1992).

development. This required certain "excavation" and "dispersal" of some of the material on-site. No material was removed from the site and no material was imported to the site. After the contractor's work was under way, it was discovered that the site and some of the material handled by the contractor were contaminated by hazardous chemicals decades earlier, in the 1940s.

Once the contamination was discovered, the owner had to clean up and restore the site per CERCLA and the United State Environmental Protection Agency's (EPA) requirements. The owner then sued the developer, who had sold the site to recover the costs of the cleanup and restoration of the site. CERCLA allows a responsible party to seek contribution from other responsible parties for cleanup costs. The developer responded by also suing the contractor under CERCLA. In its claim, the developer claimed that the contractor had made the situation worse by excavating contaminated soil and then spreading it on uncontaminated areas at the site. The claim against the contractor was initially dismissed, but that decision was reversed on appeal. The court of appeals found that, under the facts alleged, the contractor could be an "operator" of the property and also a "transporter" of hazardous substances and therefore liable for the cleanup costs under CERCLA.

17.5 Liability as an Operator   The court of appeals ruled that the "yardstick" for determining whether a party was an "operator" of a facility was the degree of control the party is able to exert over the activity causing the contamination at the time the contamination occurs. In *Kaiser*, the court found that the activity that produced the contamination was the excavation and grading of the site, which occurred during construction and while the site was under the contractor's control. Therefore, the contractor had sufficient control over this phase of the development to be an "operator" under CERCLA.

The fact that the original contamination of the site took place in the 1940s, decades before the contractor ever moved so much as a shovel of dirt, made no difference to the court. Regrading, or simply moving contaminated soils to uncontaminated areas of the same site, was sufficient to constitute disposal under CERCLA. In reaching this conclusion, the court relied on the broad definition of "disposal" under CERCLA, which includes "the discharge, deposit, injection, dumping, spilling, or placing of any . . . hazardous waste into or on the land. . . ." The court further reasoned that the term "disposal" should not be limited solely to the initial contamination of the site. Instead, consistent with the remedial purpose of CERCLA, the term "disposal" should be read broadly to include subsequent movement, dispersal, or release of hazardous substances during landfill excavations and fillings. In the court's view, to limit liability for "disposal" to the initial contamination would result in "a crabbed interpretation [which] would subvert Congress' goal that parties who are responsible for contaminating property be held accountable for the costs of cleaning it up."

17.6 Liability as a Transporter   The court went on to find the contractor potentially liable as a "transporter" of hazardous substances as well. CERCLA defines "transportation" simply as "the movement of a hazardous substance by any mode." In the court's view, the contractor's movement of contaminated soil in the excavation and grading was well within the definition. The court did note the reference in the statute to transportation "to . . . sites selected by" the contractor, but ruled that transporting hazardous substances to an uncontaminated area of the same site was no different from transporting them to another site.

17.7 Joint and Several Liability In addition to strict liability, CERCLA imposes joint and several liability. It is a relatively simple concept with a very significant impact. Joint and several liability means that if you are a responsible party liable for any part of the contamination (e.g., 20 percent of the contamination is your fault), you are liable for 100 percent of the cleanup costs. Thus the party seeking to recoup the costs of cleanup, whether the federal government or a private party, can pursue any responsible party for the entire cost, regardless of the relative contributions of the various responsible parties to the contamination. Not surprisingly, this joint and several liability provision makes solvent companies with deep pockets even bigger targets for prosecution by the government and private litigants.

17.8 Contribution The impact of joint and several liability on a responsible party can be diluted by the ability of one responsible party to seek contribution from other responsible parties for the cleanup costs. The contribution provision was added to CERCLA by the CERCLA Amendments and Reauthorization Act of 1986, known as SARA.

As previously mentioned, contribution means that if just one responsible party is sued, it can bring a separate action against another responsible party that it contends is partially or completely responsible for cleanup costs actually assessed. Frequently, the initial PRPs will claim against a number of additional potentially responsible parties, and those responsible parties are then able to directly assert contribution claims against each other in the same lawsuit. If the claimant has not named all the responsible parties, the responsible party named may be able to bring additional responsible parties into the original lawsuit. Otherwise, a separate contribution action may be initiated by one responsible party against another. It is important to note that if a responsible party has previously resolved its liability for cleanup costs with the federal or state government (formal settlement agreement), it is protected from contribution claims by other responsible parties.

The costs and burdens of CERCLA litigation are so great that they provide considerable financial incentives for a named responsible party to contribute to a settlement with the federal or state government, regardless of the strength of its defense. Consequently, once a CERCLA action is initiated, it is generally in the interest of the claimant and each individual potentially responsible party to have most, if not all, responsible parties involved in the litigation as soon as possible. However, even if a right of contribution from other responsible parties exists, it does not diminish the basic liability to the party prosecuting the underlying claim for cleanup costs. Consequently, if the other responsible parties are no longer around or lack the financial resources to meaningfully contribute to a settlement or judgment, the deep-pocket responsible party can be left to pay the complete tab, regardless of its relative fault.

These are some of the dynamics that have caused many to call for the revamping of CERCLA so that there is less focus on protracted litigation and attorneys' fees and more dollars actually expended on the cleanup of hazardous wastes.

17.9   Storm Water Runoff

The Clean Water Act[4] makes it unlawful for any person to discharge any pollutant unless a permit for such a discharge is issued under the Clean Water Act. This now applies to discharge of storm water from construction sites larger than one (1) acre beginning in 1999.[5] Previously (under Phase I of the phase-in of this Act), EPA had required permits only for sites greater than five (5) acres. The permitting process is expedited by EPA's adoption of a general permit for storm water discharges from construction sites. EPA's general permit does not apply in states that have opted to administer the permit process on their own, but the federal requirements constitute the minimum requirements of such state-administered programs. Contractors must consult with state agencies and local EPA offices to confirm the applicable standards and permitting procedures.

In order to come under EPA's general construction permit, the "operator" of the site must establish a site-specific storm water pollution control plan and then file a "Notice of Intent" with EPA. In most cases, the general contractor will be the operator, along with the owner and developer and sometimes a grading subcontractor. The site-specific control plan must meet requirements established by EPA or the state, and include storm water control measures, maintenance of those control measures, and the identity of the contractors or subcontractors that will implement the plan.[6] The key to proper job-site management and the reduction of potential liability is the continual implementation of best management practices.

When storm water discharges associated with construction are eliminated, the operator may file a "Notice of Termination" of the permit. With the notice, the operator must execute a certificate stating that storm water discharges have ended or that it is no longer the operator of the site. Violators of the Clean Water Act are subject to civil penalties of up to $25,000 per day and criminal penalties of up to $25,000 per day and prison up to one year.

17.10   Air Quality, Asbestos, and Lead

The Clean Air Act[7] requires the EPA to establish outdoor air-quality standards. The EPA has set standards for the concentrations of a number of air pollutants, including sulfur oxides, hydrocarbons, carbon monoxide, nitrogen oxides, lead, ozone, and total suspended particulate matter.

---

[4] 33 U.S.C.A. §§ 1251–1376 (2001), as amended.

[5] NPDES Storm Water Phase II Final Rule, 64 Fed. Reg. 68,721-68,770 (1999).

[6] *See* EPA's "Storm Water Management for Construction Activities—Developing Pollution Prevention Plans and Best Management Practices" (1998).

[7] 42 U.S.C.A. §§ 7401–7642 (2003), as amended.

Although construction generates relatively few air pollution concerns, certain types of projects, such as renovation and demolition, present grave risks of exposure to airborne asbestos and lead, and special risks to workers. These risks are so common and serious that the Occupational Safety and Health Administration has promulgated regulations specifically outlining the safety and health measures to be followed on construction projects involving these substances.[8] The majority of the procedures and requirements are similar for both these substances, but there are important differences that cannot be overlooked. There may also be state and local regulations in some cases.

The regulations covering asbestos and lead apply to all construction work, including demolition or salvage, renovation, remodeling, repair, installation of products containing these materials, transportation, disposal, and emergency cleanup situations. Each regulation contains an action level that represents the maximum concentration of the substance allowable before the contractor must comply with most aspects of the regulation, and a permissible exposure level (PEL), which is the maximum level of exposure to the substance that the contractor's employees can endure without the use of respirators.

Each contractor must initially determine if any employee may be exposed to one of the substances at or above the action level on the job site. This initial determination can be waived, however, when the contractor is able to prove through objective data that its employees cannot be exposed to concentrations of the substance above the action level even in worst-case scenarios, or when the contractor has monitored for substance exposures within the last 12 months during work operations conducted under workplace conditions closely resembling the current operation.

When the initial determination shows the possibility of substance exposure at or above the action level, the contractor must conduct monitoring that is representative of the exposure for each employee in the workplace who is exposed to the substance at least every six months and must notify affected employees of the monitoring results. If exposure is above the PEL, periodic monitoring must be performed every three months. If the initial monitoring shows no possibility of substance exposure above the action level, no further monitoring is necessary. Regardless of previous measurements, however, the contractor must repeat the initial monitoring process whenever there has been a change in process, control equipment, personnel, or work practices that may result in new or additional exposures above the action level limit.

The contractor must employ engineering controls and work practices to reduce and maintain employee exposure to the substances below the PEL to the extent such controls are feasible. Wherever the feasible engineering controls and work practices are not sufficient to reduce the substance concentration below the PEL, the contractor must supplement the controls with respiratory protective devices, protective clothing, changing and shower facilities, special signage, and training programs, among other measures. The contractor is also required to institute a rigorous medical surveillance program of exposed employees, including blood tests and examinations.

---

[8] *See* 29 C.F.R. § 1926.58 (2003) (asbestos); 29 C.F.R. § 1926.62 (2003) (lead).

17.11 MINIMIZING ENVIRONMENTAL RISKS

Before entering into the bidding process or negotiations for a contract on a construction project, the contractor should assess the environmental aspects of the work in an effort to minimize the potential risks. This is a detailed process involving much more than a routine site investigation.

17.12 Conduct a Prebid Environmental Review of the Contract Documents

The prudent contractor will adopt and implement procedures that ensure a prebid environmental review of each proposed contract. Although reviewing the plans and specifications for specifically delineated hazardous substance work is essential, it is not enough. One common trap that has snared more than its share of contractors is a set of plans and specifications that does not identify any particular work involving hazardous substances but has generic provisions that address asbestos, lead-based paint, and/or hazardous waste. In this contractual context, owners, including public owners, have argued successfully that the parties to the contract obviously contemplated the contractor performing the hazardous-substance work because the contract contained the generic clauses. The contractor is put into the position of having to subcontract out the work and hope that no claims arise.

17.13 Exclude Hazardous Substances from the Scope of Work If the contractor wants to minimize its exposure on a private job that, according to the contract documents, involves no work with or relating to hazardous substances, the generic hazardous substances specification sections and related clauses should be stricken and the contractor's bid submission should take exception to the performance of any work involving hazardous substances. On a similar public project, a similar qualification exception may render the bid nonresponsive. Accordingly, the contractor must decide whether it wants to take the risk of possibly being directed to perform work that involves hazardous substances.

17.14 Determine What Materials Will Be Encountered Any renovation or demolition contract, or portion of a contract, requires the contractor to deal with building materials in place. It is incumbent upon the contractor to know what materials it is dealing with, or run the very significant risk of environmental violations and lawsuits by workers and others exposed to the hazardous substances in the workplace. Therefore, the contractor should be able to answer the following questions prior to submitting a bid or proposal for the work:

(1) Do the plans and specifications include any remediation work, asbestos abatement, or removal of lead-based paint?
(2) Do the specifications make any reference to standards for performing remediation work, abatement work, or removal of lead-based paint?

(3) Is any part of the work affected by hazardous materials, asbestos, lead-based paint, underground storage tanks, wetlands, or protected natural resources?

(4) If the specifications describe environmental work, do you have insurance coverage for environmental risks?

(5) Is there any allocation of risk or responsibility for hazardous materials or asbestos? Is the contractor required to indemnify the owner for losses associated with hazardous materials or asbestos?

(6) Is the owner aware of any hazardous materials, asbestos, lead-based paint, waste materials, or contaminated soil or water that might affect the contractor's scope of work?

(7) Have any environmental site assessments been conducted? Are there any building surveys or inspection reports on asbestos, lead-based paint, underground storage tanks, soil or water quality, or hazardous waste on the site?

(8) Did the site visit and inspection indicate any distressed vegetation, hydrocarbon or chemical contamination, underground storage tanks, transformers, drums, suspect lead-based paint, or suspect asbestos-containing materials?

(9) Has any cleanup taken place? Have tanks been removed or filled? Is there any closure report? Is the owner aware of any residual soil or water contamination?

(10) If unanticipated asbestos, lead-based paint, tanks, drums, contaminated soil, PCBs, or other hazardous materials or waste are encountered, what are the contractor's obligations?

17.15 Make an Environmental Prebid Inquiry on Every Renovation and Demolition Project Obviously, there is no way for the contractor to answer many of its questions without the owner's input. Therefore, the contractor should continue making a written environmental prebid inquiry in order to obtain information from the owner. This inquiry should seek answers to the following questions:

(1) Is the owner aware of any lead-based paint, asbestos, PCBs, hazardous materials or waste, contaminated soil or water, or underground storage tanks that are included in any portion of the proposed scope of work or that might affect the proposed scope of work?

(2) If unanticipated lead-based paint, asbestos, PCBs, hazardous materials or waste, tanks, drums, contaminated soil or water, or other physical conditions that constitute toxic contamination or potential environmental impairment of portions of the work are encountered, what are the contractor's obligations?

(3) Have any environmental site assessments been conducted or are there any building surveys or inspection reports on asbestos, lead-based paint, underground storage tanks, soil or water quality, or hazardous waste on the site? If so, are the reports available to the bidders for inspection?

In addition, given the prevailing regulatory scheme, a comprehensive site visit should be conducted prior to the submission of a bid or proposal. Make a good record of what was observed and observable with photographs, videotapes, and trip reports. Look for distressed vegetation, unusual depressions, storage tanks, drums, suspect lead-based paint, and suspect asbestos-containing materials. Review any as-builts that might exist in order to obtain additional information as to building components and materials. Follow up the site visit with written questions to the owner asking about specific questionable areas or conditions and building materials that are suspected to contain asbestos or be layered with lead-based paint. Make a request for copies of any bulk sample results and paint analyses.

This approach shifts at least some of the initial burden of identifying hazardous substances onto the owner and forces disclosure by the owner of what it knows or should know about the building or property. Although this is a good start, contractors need to be aware that the courts are assuming that contractors are fully knowledgeable about building materials. As such, courts will not allow a contractor to escape liability for violations of environmental laws based on its blind reliance on plans and specifications. Each phase of the proposed project should be thoroughly reviewed with an eye toward possible environmental risks and concerns. Only when the contractor has satisfied those concerns, or has fully appreciated and priced the environmental risks, should the proposal or bid be submitted.

17.16   Contract Provisions and Indemnification

The risks of unanticipated hazardous wastes are so great that the risks should be the subject of specific contract terms and conditions that allocate the risks among the parties in an appropriate and equitable manner. The need for specific contract clauses is underscored by the extent to which routine contract clauses that impose considerable risks on the contractor for the unknown can be applied to unanticipated hazardous wastes. Consider a standard site investigation clause that requires the contractor to examine the site and attempts to shift responsibility for concealed or unexpected conditions. What if the unexpected condition is a concealed hazardous waste contamination rather than some additional rock or muck removal? Likewise, broad indemnity clauses that benefit the owner are generally considered burdensome under routine circumstances. If applied to a hazardous wastes situation, they can be devastating. On the other hand, a standard differing site conditions clause may afford the contractor some protection from the costs associated with unanticipated hazardous wastes, but far greater specificity is preferred to ensure protection.

The need for specific contract provisions to address the unfortunate possibility of contamination by hazardous waste has been recognized, but is by no means fully addressed nor universally applied. The American Institute of Architects' Document A201, The General Conditions of the Contract for Construction (1997 ed.), includes provisions that address the discovery of unanticipated hazardous substances. The General Conditions also provide indemnity for the contractor from the owner "if, without negligence on the part of the Contractor, the Contractor is held liable for the cost of remediation of hazardous material or substance solely by reason of performing Work as required by the Contract Documents," and indemnity for the owner if the contractor brings the substances to the site. Under AIA A201, contractors must stop work in the affected area and notify the owner when any material present at the site cannot be managed safely using reasonable precautions. Work cannot resume until the owner and contractor enter into a written agreement.

The 1996 Standard General Conditions of the Construction Contract published by the Engineers Joint Contract Documents Committee (EJCDC) affords protection by expressly placing the responsibility for virtually all unanticipated hazardous wastes, not just asbestos and PCBs, on the owner. The EJCDC General Conditions set forth specific procedures for notice by the contractor to the owner about the contamination encountered, and the required response by the owner that must be implemented before the contractor can be directed or required to resume the work in the affected area.

Whether the project is the traditional design-bid-build with a competitive bid lump sum or a design-build project, the potential issues and risks related to hazardous materials warrant consideration and treatment in the contract documents. One example of the treatment of hazardous materials in the context of a design-build project is found in paragraph 3.6 in the Standard Form of Design-Build Agreement and General Conditions Between Owner and Design-Builder, AGC Document 410 (1999 ed.), issued by The Associated General Contractors of America. That provision reads as follows:

3.6   HAZARDOUS MATERIALS

3.6.1   A Hazardous Material is any substance or material identified now or in the future as hazardous under any federal, state or local law or regulation, or any other substance or material that may be considered hazardous or otherwise subject to statutory or regulatory requirement governing handling, disposal and/or cleanup. The Design-Builder shall not be obligated to commence or continue work until any Hazardous Material discovered at the Worksite has been removed, rendered or determined to be harmless by the Owner as certified by an independent testing laboratory and approved by the appropriate government agency.

3.6.2   If after the commencement of the Work Hazardous Material is discovered at the Project, the Design-Builder shall be entitled to immediately stop Work in the affected area. The Design-Builder shall report the condition to the Owner, and, if required, the government agency with jurisdiction.

3.6.3   The Design-Builder shall not be required to perform any Work relating to or in the area of Hazardous Material without written mutual agreement.

3.6.4   The Owner shall be responsible for retaining an independent testing laboratory to determine the nature of the material encountered and whether it is a hazardous material requiring corrective measures and/or remedial action. Such measures shall be the sole responsibility of the Owner, and shall be performed in a manner minimizing any adverse effects upon the Work of the Design-Builder. The Design-Builder shall resume Work in the area affected by any Hazardous Material only upon written agreement between the parties after the Hazardous Material has been removed or rendered harmless and only after approval, if necessary, of the governmental agency or agencies with jurisdiction.

3.6.5 If the Design-Builder incurs additional costs and/or is delayed due to the presence or remediation of Hazardous Material, the Design-Builder shall be entitled to an equitable adjustment in the GMP, compensation for Design Phase Services, the Design-Builder's Fee and/or the Date of Substantial Completion and/or the Date of Final Completion.

3.6.6 Provided the Design-Builder, its Subcontractors, Material Suppliers and Subsubcontractors and the agents, officers, directors and employees of each of them, have not, acting under their own authority, knowingly entered upon any portion of the Work containing Hazardous Materials, and to the extent not caused by the negligent acts or omissions of the Design-Builder, its Subcontractors, Material Suppliers and Subsubcontractors, and the agents, officers, directors and employees of each of them, the Owner shall defend, indemnify and hold harmless the Design-Builder, its Subcontractors and Subsubcontractors, and the agents, officers, directors and employees of each of them, from and against any and all direct claims, damages, losses, costs and expenses, including but not limited to attorney's fees, costs and expenses incurred in connection with any dispute resolution process, arising out of or relating to the performance of the Work in any area affected by Hazardous Material. To the fullest extent permitted by law, such indemnification shall apply regardless of the fault, negligence, breach of warranty or contract, or strict liability of the Owner.

3.6.7 Material Safety Data (MSD) sheets as required by law and pertaining to materials or substances used or consumed in the performance of the Work, whether obtained by Design-Builder, Subcontractors, the Owner or Others, shall be maintained at the Project by the Design-Builder and made available to the Owner and Subcontractors.

3.6.8 During the Design-Builder's performance of the Work, the Design-Builder shall be responsible for the proper handling of all materials brought to the Worksite by the Design-Builder. Upon the issuance of the Certificate of Substantial Completion, the Owner shall be responsible under this Paragraph for materials and substances brought to the site by the Design-Builder if such materials or substances are required by the Contract Documents.

3.6.9 The terms of this Paragraph 3.6 shall survive the completion of the Work and/or any termination of this Agreement.[9]

This is a thorough, comprehensive, and balanced contract provision dealing with the possibility of unexpected hazardous wastes and the associated risks and liabilities.

Regardless of whether a standard contract form, modified form, or custom-drafted contract is utilized, it is imperative that the risk of unexpected hazardous waste be specifically allocated. In addition, definitive procedures need to be set forth so that the parties know precisely how they are to respond and react to the situation if encountered.

Obtaining indemnification for the consequences of hazardous wastes is of critical importance, but is by no means foolproof. Many states have statutes or decisions that

[9] A similar provision is found at paragraph 3.13 of AGC Document No. 200, Standard Form of Agreement and General Conditions Between Owner and Contractor (Where the Contract Price Is a Lump Sum) (2000).

limit the scope of enforceability of indemnity clauses. These laws and cases reflect a public policy against allowing anyone to obtain indemnification for their own negligent acts. As liability under CERCLA is strict and without regard to negligence, this limitation may not be applicable in many situations. Nonetheless, it is prudent for the contractor to consider the law applicable to its contract and the extent of the enforceability of any indemnity associated with hazardous wastes.

Many contractors assume tremendous potential liability by naively believing that they can subcontract the environmental risk away. Although it is true that specialty environmental (e.g., asbestos) abatement subcontractors are available, it is also true that a contractor is still exposed to regulatory enforcement actions and personal injury actions despite the best subcontract language and indemnification clauses. Given that potential liability, it is recommended that the contractor subcontract its environmental abatement work to only the most experienced, financially healthy environmental abatement subcontractors.

From the contractor's perspective, the better course, if it is possible, is to delete the environmental abatement work from the proposed contract and have the owner enter into a direct contract with the environmental abatement contractor. This way the owner is responsible for the adequacy, the timing, and the waste stream associated with the environmental abatement work. This significantly reduces the environmental risk for the contractor.

If the job is commenced with no knowledge of the environmental hazards and then hazards are encountered during the project performance, many owners will attempt to get the contractor to simply subcontract out the environmental abatement portion of the work. This is extremely risky for the contractor. In addition, it likely places the contractor into an uninsured position while possibly compromising any potential claim it might have for suspension of its work due to the undisclosed hazards.

17.17   Insurance

Once the size of the threat of environmental liability was recognized, insurance coverage rapidly receded. Now new forms of coverage are becoming available as the insurance market readjusts. Still, coverage is far from complete and often comes at substantial cost. As a general matter, however, standard forms of insurance, such as commercial general liability insurance, will not afford protection for liability associated with hazardous waste. Therefore, specific pollution coverage must be procured.

Complete insurance protection for unanticipated hazardous waste is either impossible or financially impractical to obtain. Evaluating some specific environmental coverage is nonetheless an appropriate step. Insurance planning for construction projects, particularly as it relates to insuring environmental risks, is too complex and specialized to be left to the inexperienced layperson. Even those contractors that are able to employ full-time insurance specialists or risk managers must rely on professional insurance brokers to assist in the procurement of proper coverage at a competitive price. This is particularly true in the environmental insurance market, which continues to experience rapid change and evolution as new environmental hazards continue to surface, such as mold exposure.

Before the contractor makes a decision to assume responsibility—for example, for asbestos abatement—it is important to scrutinize the contractor's own insurance in order to verify that there will be coverage and/or a defense if any claims are made against the contractor. The standard Comprehensive General Liability (CGL) policy contains a pollution exclusion that affords the contractor no coverage under the CGL policy for any of the risks inherent in dealing with asbestos. Unless a specialized policy is purchased, there is no insurance coverage available, and yet the potential liability is virtually unlimited even where the work has been subcontracted.

17.18   PROPER MANAGEMENT TECHNIQUES

The increasing use and intensity of environmental site assessment by owners and lenders will hopefully reduce the likelihood of encountering unexpected contamination, but the risk will always exist. Constant recognition and review of the risk must be maintained on the management level, and vigilance and preparedness enforced on the job site, in order to guard against the risks of unanticipated hazardous wastes.

17.19   Management Review of Environmental Risks

It is in the interest of each contractor to designate a senior company officer as having overall responsibility for environmental matters. That individual can serve as a resource to the entire company to aid in the evaluation of and protection against unanticipated hazardous wastes on all projects. In order to serve effectively in this capacity, the individual must become thoroughly familiar with the federal and state laws and regulations affecting the work. This manager must be able to evaluate the environmental risks not only in light of the existing laws, but also in the specific context of the applicable contract provisions, the nature of the construction, the peculiarities of the site, and the ability to procure insurance. The official responsible for environmental matters must also have the authority to respond to unacceptable environmental risks directly or through direct reporting to other company officials. Environmental risk management is far too important to the future of the company to delegate it to an individual who lacks the authority to enforce it. The company should also have a specific and mandatory written procedure to be implemented immediately upon encountering unexpected hazardous wastes. The contents of the procedure and the nature of the response are discussed in greater detail below.

One individual, however, cannot possibly stay on top of all risks of unanticipated wastes a contractor may encounter in its ongoing operations. Therefore, all personnel, especially project management, must be educated and sensitized to the risks. If they do not know how to respond immediately to a situation involving hazardous waste, they will at least appreciate the severity of the situation and recognize the need to seek advice and direction from someone who does know how to respond.

All the planning, evaluation, and efforts to deal with environmental risks on a management level will be wasted if the planning and ability to execute the plan does not extend to each job site and the individuals actually performing work in the field.

17.20   Have a Response Plan

The response of project personnel should not be left to chance. The appropriate response should be set forth in a written and mandatory procedure that has been the subject of in-house training and indoctrination. At the outset of each project and before construction starts, the standard procedure should be reviewed and supplemented with the areas of responsibility for specific individuals. The names and telephone numbers should be listed for any federal, state, or local agencies requiring notification or from which an emergency response may be required. The procedure should also be coordinated with representatives of the owner, design professional, and construction manager, as well as subcontractors. Although the response will be the primary responsibility of project management personnel, the response cannot be triggered or properly implemented without the aid of all project personnel, including subcontractors and their employees. Once the response plan is developed, it should be reviewed in project meetings, subcontractor coordination meetings, and toolbox safety meetings at the level of detail appropriate for the gathering to ensure that it has been reviewed and understood.

17.21   Immediately Stop Work in the Affected Area

In very broad terms, unanticipated hazardous wastes are typically not the contractor's responsibility. If they are exposed or discovered but not disturbed or released, the hazardous wastes certainly present a problem, but, from the contractor's perspective, a problem of limited scope. If, however, the contractor goes beyond merely exposing the hazardous wastes and disturbs them in any manner, the contractor may well have unwittingly thrown itself into one or more of the categories of "potentially responsible parties" under CERCLA, as the contractor did in the *Kaiser* case discussed earlier. That is why the first response to encountering hazardous waste or any unknown substance or material that might be a hazardous waste is to STOP! As previously mentioned, this is a requirement in the AGC Document 410 and the AIA A201 Document. Do no further work in the affected area or any other areas where the same condition might exist. It should be a reflexive response to encountering anything suspicious, whether it is an unusual color in the soil, a faint but unfamiliar odor, or anything out of the ordinary.

17.22   Inadvertent Asbestos Abatement   The general construction contract may quickly be transformed into an asbestos abatement project if the contractor unknowingly demolishes or disturbs asbestos-containing building materials. Under the National Emission Standards for Hazardous Air Pollutants, demolition and renovation work become an asbestos-abatement project whenever the regulated asbestos-containing materials are greater than 260 linear feet of linear systems, such as pipe insulation, or 160 square feet of surface areas, or if the total waste product generated exceeds 35 cubic feet. If a contractor performs renovation or demolition of asbestos-containing materials exceeding these thresholds without notification, it is conducting an illegal asbestos abatement operation and is subject to penalties for each subsection of the asbestos regulations that it is violating.

In terms of possible violations, consider that it is generally necessary to notify the regulators 10 working days before beginning any asbestos-abatement project, and the notice must be updated if the quantity of asbestos-containing materials changes by 20 percent or more. The only exceptions to this notification requirement would be for emergency operations and unsafe buildings. Further, a new notification is required if the commencement date of the asbestos abatement changes.

If the contractor inadvertently renovates or demolishes building materials exceeding the regulatory thresholds, then, in addition to being subject to citation for violation of the notification requirement, it also may be fined for failing to properly control the asbestos emissions. Obviously, if the contractor is not aware that it is dealing with asbestos, it will commit the following violations:

- Failure to set up proper containment
- Failure to provide its workers with proper respiratory protection and protective clothing
- Failure to set up containment with negative pressure machines
- Failure to provide hygiene facilities for its workers
- Failure to train its workers properly
- Failure to properly employ the necessary medical surveillance
- Failure to wet the building materials adequately during the demolition
- Failure to maintain a properly certified project supervisor on the project
- Failure to properly seal its asbestos waste
- Failure to label the waste properly
- Failure to dispose of or transport the waste properly
- Failure to maintain proper records of the asbestos-abatement project

In addition, the contractor may be subject to an additional penalty based on an economic benefit multiplier that is calculated according to the amount of work performed. Recently, contractors that have failed to conduct asbestos-abatement activities properly have been fined up to $20 per square foot or linear foot of illegal demolition activities.

Given these sanctions and the fact that the contractor that has conducted an illegal asbestos-abatement project is also exposed to litigation from its workers, tenants, and others, it is clear that a prudent contractor should always determine whether the materials that are to be demolished or disturbed during construction operations contain asbestos.

17.23 Inadvertent Lead Abatement   Similarly, if lead is present, and the contractor accidentally disturbs it or does not perform the initial exposure assessment, the contractor must assume exposure at a level of 10 times the maximum permissible exposure level. With that assumption, the contractor must provide its workers with respiratory protection and protective clothing, provide hygiene facilities, conduct medical surveillance, conduct employee training, maintain extensive records, and post warning signs at all entrances and exits to the work areas. Failure to comply with this standard makes the contractor liable for citation for violation of each subsection of the standard.

The standard informs the contractor in no uncertain terms that, if lead is present, it must presume that the construction activities will cause airborne emissions of lead in excess of permissible exposure limits. The contractor cannot assume that its activities will not violate this standard. Therefore, the contractor should obtain all sampling and test data from the owner prior to commencing its demolition and renovation activities. Further, the contractor should request the owner to perform appropriate testing in all areas that will be affected by the construction activities and must not commence its operations until it receives the requested test results.

17.24   Provide Immediate Notice

The contractor should provide immediate notice to the owner, the design professional, and construction manager that a suspected hazardous waste has been uncovered, even if the contractor cannot identify the substance. The initial notice should be verbal, with written confirmation provided as soon as practical thereafter. The notice should make it clear that the unanticipated hazardous wastes are the responsibility of the owner and that the contractor is awaiting direction from the owner as to how to proceed. The contractor should also consider expressly reserving its rights to seek indemnity for any claims arising from the hazardous wastes, as well as adjustments in contract time and price based on the work stoppage and any additional response required to deal with the situation.

The owner or its agents should be responsible for reporting the release or spill of a hazardous waste to the appropriate government officials. However, the contractor may also be deemed a "person in charge" of the site and therefore be required to make a prompt report. It is best for the contractor to err in favor of caution and also make a report if there is any uncertainty as to who is required to do so or whether the owner will make the report.

17.25   Do Not Resume Work without Proper Authorization

The contractor should not resume work in the affected areas without written authorization from the owner and the government agency with authority over the situation. Such authorization should be explicit and in writing.

If the owner's response is to direct the contractor to clean up the hazardous waste, the contractor should insist on specific written instructions on how to accomplish the cleanup, as well as confirmation that the response has been approved by the responsible government agency. The contractor should also require that the owner specifically indemnify the contractor for undertaking the cleanup. Even if the owner obliges on these points, the contractor should consider whether it wants to undertake the additional risks of cleanup work. Remember, the owner's indemnification is only as good as its ability to pay and does not insulate the contractor from claims by third parties. Undertaking the cleanup of hazardous wastes may also cause some problems with the contractor's insurance carrier and surety if cleanup work is not within the contractor's typical line of work on which its insurance and bonding was based.

17.26   Mold: Developing a Program to Limit Liability

The term "toxic mold" has become another in the modern lexicon of environmental construction terms. Many have predicted that mold may surpass asbestos as a source of construction claims and disputes and multimillion dollar lawsuits. The frequent occurrence of mold during or as a result of the construction process, combined with the potential health risks and a heightened public awareness of the risk, has created a breeding ground for litigation and the risks, costs, and uncertainty that litigation entails.

To prevent the rampant growth and spread of mold requires controlling humidity and the presence of moisture in the construction environment. To prevent, limit, and control the presence of moisture requires a cooperative and coordinated effort by owners, design professionals, and construction professionals, which includes: (1) a good design, (2) consideration of mold risks in the selection and specification of building materials as well as the means and methods of construction, (3) a thorough construction quality control program (including, but not limited to documented inspections), and (4) proper project documentation.

One of the first questions an owner or a contractor should ask in assessing and addressing the risk of mold is: "Do I have insurance for this?" As is often the case in the legal arena, the answer may be unclear. The standard CGL policy carried by most contractors contains a number of exclusions that may allow the contractor's insurance carrier to assert that the risk of mold is not covered. These include certain "business risk" exclusions and the "pollution exclusion." The courts that have addressed the issue have reached conflicting conclusions as to whether mold-related claims are covered by a contractor's CGL policy or whether the insurance carrier is relieved of responsibility for such claims under the standard pollution exclusion.

The primary legal theory under which mold contamination litigation arises is the common-law doctrine of negligence.[10] In these cases, the engineer, architect, contractor, subcontractor, or developer owes a duty of care to the plaintiff. To determine whether a party has breached its duty of care, the plaintiff must determine the "duty" by examining relevant construction standards. By demonstrating a specialist's failure to abide by the practices of other similarly situated specialists, claims of negligence involving an engineer or an architect are often accompanied by a claim for professional malpractice.

Claims for fraud and misrepresentation arise from a false statement that is made by a defendant if the defendant knew the statement was false when the statement was made, it intended the plaintiff rely upon the statement, and if the plaintiff did rely upon it to its detriment. An owner may be liable for fraud and misrepresentation if the owner makes a representation that the structure was inspected and found to be "clean" when such an inspection was never conducted and mold was found to be present. If such a

---

[10] *Sabella v. Wisler*, 377 P.2d. 889 (Cal.1963).

fraudulent statement or false impression causes another party to enter into a contract in reliance on such a statement or impression, the innocent individual may have a right to have the contract rescinded due to the fraudulent inducement to enter into the contract.

17.27 CONSTRUCTION SAFETY

Despite ever-increasing safety standards and improving safety records, construction remains a dangerous business. Accidents still happen. When one does, everyone is a source for blame, but most responsibility usually rests with the injured worker's employer and those in direct contract with that employer—that is, general contractors and subcontractors.

17.28 Sources of Safety Requirements: OSHA-Specific Project Procedures

The predominant safety regulatory scheme on construction projects has been established by the federal Occupational Safety & Health Act (OSHA)[11] and the regulations promulgated thereunder.[12] Violation of these regulations may lead to substantial civil and criminal penalties. Violations can also be used as evidence of negligence or even to establish negligence as a matter of law, known as "negligence per se."[13]

Some states have also enacted safety statutes and other regulations such as training and licensing requirements that can affect your liability. This is often the case in areas where accidents are still frequent, such as underground construction and environmental remediation. Violations of state regulations also give rise to civil and criminal penalties and can constitute evidence of negligence or establish negligence as a matter of law.[14] Violations of state regulations can even give rise to private causes of action against the violator.[15]

17.29 Successfully Working with OSHA

The best way to avoid liability for personal injuries on the job is to try to prevent accidents from ever happening. Preventing accidents will: (1) reduce exposure to fines and liability under federal and state safety statutes and regulations, like OSHA; (2) reduce premiums for workers compensation and liability insurance; and (3) reduce the odds that the company may be liable for injuries that are not covered by indemnification or insurance. There are some basic steps you can take to prevent accidents from ever happening.

---

[11] 29 U.S.C. §§ 651-678 (1999), as amended.

[12] 29 C.F.R. Parts 70-71, 1900-1906, 1908, 1910-1913, 1915, 1917-1922, 1924-1928, 1949, 1952-1956, 1977-1979, 2200-2205, 2400 (2003).

[13] *See, e.g., Kelley v. Howard S. Wright Constr. Co.*, 582 P.2d 500 (Wash. 1978).

[14] *See, e.g., Larabee v. Triangle Steel, Inc.*, 451 N.Y.S.2d 258 (1982).

[15] *See, e.g., Bortz v. Rammel*, 376 A.2d 1261 (N.J. Super. Ct. App. Div. 1977).

First and foremost, every company on the job site should develop a safety program and put it down in writing in a safety manual. Second, you should make sure that management and employees are committed to safety and your written safety program. Third, you should appoint a person trained or qualified in safety to coordinate the program by conducting inspections and employee training, establishing minimum safety standards, and keeping records. Fourth, job foremen should continuously perform safety inspections on projects and conduct necessary safety training or toolbox safety meetings.

17.30   Who Is Responsible for Project Safety: Owners, General Contractors, Construction Managers, or Subcontractors?

Because of the numerous different entities involved in virtually every construction project, finding the complete answer to this question can be extremely difficult. Statutes and regulations such as the federal OSHA regulations often impose part of the answer. The contractual relationships between owners, general contractors, subcontractors, suppliers, construction managers, architects, engineers, and other design professionals can also shuffle, shift, and ultimately allocate primary responsibility for many recurring issues, and therefore help answer the question. Common-law principles, like tort negligence, also help resolve the issue.

17.31 Contractors   A contractor, just like anyone else, is liable for any act that directly causes an injury. A contractor can also be liable, however, even though it does not directly cause an injury. Although one contractor is generally not responsible for acts of an independent contractor,[16] there are many exceptions to this traditional rule of nonliability. For example, under certain circumstances, a general contractor can be held liable for the injuries to a subcontractor's employee even though the employee's injuries were directly caused by the negligence of the subcontractor.

Some jurisdictions impose responsibilities upon contractors to prevent subcontractor employees from being exposed to hazards not ordinarily found on a construction project. Liability can even be imposed for "ordinary" hazards if the contractor knows, or should know, that the subcontractor employee is failing to protect itself against a known hazard.[17] Other jurisdictions impose liability upon contractors for injuries to subcontractor employees where the contractor retains "control" over common work areas or the subcontractor's means and methods.[18] This is especially common when a contractor assumes some type of safety supervisory duty such as providing a safety supervisor, initiating a safety program, or ensuring compliance with safety rules and regulations.[19]

---

[16] *See, e.g., Shannon v. Howard S. Wright Constr. Co.*, 593 P.2d 438 (Mont. 1979).

[17] *See Silvas v. Speros Constr. Co.*, 594 P.2d 1029 (Ariz. 1979); *Tect Constr. Co. v. Frymyer*, 246 S.E.2d 334 (Ga. Ct. App. 1978).

[18] *See Shannon, supra* note 16; *Kelley, supra* note 13.

[19] *See Kelley, supra* note 13.

Other courts have predicated liability upon the general contractor's safety responsibilities in its contract with the owner.[20] This is troublesome for general contractors, since many owner contracts impose extensive safety obligations on the general contractor. For example, AIA A201 Document, General Conditions of the Contract for Construction Subsections 10.1.1, 10.2.1, 10.2.3 and 10.2.6 (1997 ed.) address the contractor's obligations. Similarly, AGC Document No. 200, Standard Form of Agreement and General Conditions Between Owner and Contractor (2000 ed.), provides a comprehensive safety provision as follows:

3.11   SAFETY OF PERSONS AND PROPERTY

3.11.1   SAFETY PRECAUTIONS AND PROGRAMS. The Contractor shall have overall responsibility for safety precautions and programs in the performance of the Work. While this Paragraph 3.11 establishes the responsibility for safety between the Owner and Contractor, it does not relieve subcontractors of their responsibility for the safety of persons or property in the performance of their work, nor for compliance with the provisions of applicable laws and regulations.

3.11.2   The Contractor shall seek to avoid injury, loss or damage to persons or property by taking reasonable steps to protect:

1. its employees and other persons at the Worksite;

2. materials and equipment stored at on-site or off-site locations for use in the Work; and

3. property located at the site ad adjacent to Work areas, whether or not the property is part of the Work.

3.11.3   CONTRACTORS SAFETY REPRESENTATIVE. The Contractor's Worksite Safety Representative is _____, who shall act as the Contractor's authorized safety representative with a duty to prevent accidents in accordance with Subparagraph 3.11.2. If no individual is identified in this paragraph 3.11, the authorized safety representative shall be the Contractor's Representative. The Contractor shall report immediately in writing to the Owner all recordable accidents and injuries occurring at the Worksite. When the Contractor is required to file an accident report with a public authority the Contractor shall furnish a copy of this report to the Owner.

3.11.4   The Contractor shall provide the Owner with copies of all notices required of the Contractor by law or regulation. The Contractor's safety program shall comply with the requirements of governmental and quasi-governmental authorities having jurisdiction.

3.11.5   Damage or loss not insured under property insurance which may arise from the Work, to the extent of the negligence attributed to acts or omissions of the Contractor, or anyone for whose acts the Contractor may be liable, shall be promptly remedied by the Contractor.

3.11.6   If the Owner deems any part of the Work or Worksite unsafe, the Owner, without assuming responsibility for the Contractor's safety program, may require the Contractor to stop performance of the work or take corrective measures satisfactory to the Owner, or both. If the Contractor does not adopt corrective

---

[20] *See Farris v. General Growth Dev. Corp.*, 354 N.W.2d 251 (Iowa 1984); *Kelley, supra* note 13; *Smith v. United States*, 497 F.2d 500 (5th Cir. 1974).

measures, the Owner may perform them and deduct their cost from the Contract Price. The Contractor agrees to make no claim for damages, for an increase in the Contract Price or for a change in the Contract Time based on the Contractor's compliance with the Owner's reasonable request.

17.32   Architects and Engineers   An architect/engineer can also be liable for the injuries of someone else's employee even though the architect/engineer is not directly responsible for the employee's injuries. Such liability can be based upon either the contractual, or voluntary assumption of, certain responsibilities.[21]

While most construction contracts place the primary responsibility for project safety upon the general contractor, they also name the architect/engineer as the owner's representative during construction and require the architect/engineer to inspect or observe the work to ensure compliance with plans and specifications. Often an injured worker will try to establish that the architect/engineer failed to adequately fulfill these duties, resulting in an unsafe work condition that caused the resultant injury.

Most courts, however, hold that architects and engineers have no safety duties unless such duties are clearly written into their contracts. These courts have found that the architect/engineer's supervisory duties on a project only run to the owner and are just to ensure that work is completed in accordance with the construction documents.[22] Other courts have found a duty to provide safety supervision even though a general contractor may have contractually assumed the primary responsibility for project safety. These courts hold that the architect/engineer has a duty to ensure that the contractor complies with its contractual duties.[23] In response to these decisions, architects/engineers often place provisions in their contracts clarifying their safety obligations on a project. An example of such a provision is AIA A201 Subsection 4.2.3 (1997 ed.).

Even though an architect/engineer may not be contractually responsible for safety, the architect/engineer can be liable for personal injuries on the job by voluntarily assuming extra-contractual responsibilities given the following factors: (1) The scope of the architect/engineer's actual supervision or control over the work; (2) The extent of the architect/engineer's participation in the project; and (3) Whether the architect/engineer assumed responsibility for safety precautions.[24] An architect/engineer can also be held liable for failing to take appropriate action where it actually knows of a safety violation even though it has not contractually or voluntarily assumed safety responsibilities.[25]

---

[21] *See, e.g., Bartak v. Bell-Galyardt & Wells, Inc.*, 629 F.2d 523 (8th Cir. 1980).

[22] *See Young v. Eastern Eng'g & Elevator Co.*, 554 A.2d 77 (Pa. Super. Ct. 1989); *Hanna v. Huer, Johns, Neel, Rivers & Webb*, 662 P.2d 243 (Kan. 1983); *Waggoner v. W & W Steel Co.*, 657 P.2d 147 (Okla. 1982); *Krieger v. J.E. Greiner Co.*, 382 A.2d 1069 (Md. 1978); *Wheeler & Lewis v. Slifer*, 577 P.2d 1092 (Colo. 1978); *Baker v. Pidgeon Thomas Co.*, 422 F.2d 744 (6th Cir. 1970). *See also* 59 A.L.R.3d 869 (1974).

[23] *See Heath v. Huth Eng'rs, Inc.*, 420 A.2d 758 (Pa. 1980); *Swarthout v. Beard*, 190 N.W.2d 373 (Mich. 1971), *rev'd on other grounds, Smith v. City of Detroit*, 202 N.W.2d 300 (Mich. 1972).

[24] *See Hanna, supra* note 22; *Heath, supra* note 23; Restatement (Second) of Torts § 324A (1965).

[25] *See Wenzel v. Boyles Galvanizing Co.*, 920 F.2d 778 (11th Cir. 1991); *Hanna, supra* note 22; *Balagna v. Shawnee County*, 668 P.2d 157 (Kan. 1983).

17.33   Construction Managers   Although there is relatively little case law on the liability of the construction manager, courts will no doubt look to the construction manager's contractual duties to determine whether the construction manager is responsible for the safety of others. Generally, a construction manager is responsible for reviewing safety programs developed by each contractor and coordinating a safety program for the entire project. A construction manager with such responsibilities may be responsible for personal injuries on the job even though the construction manager did not directly cause the injuries.

17.34   Owners   An owner usually delegates responsibility for project safety to an independent contractor, such as a general contractor, architect, or construction manager. As a general rule, one is not responsible for the acts of an independent contractor.[26] Under certain circumstances, however, an owner can be liable for personal injuries caused by others on the job.

For example, sometimes owners retain certain responsibilities for safety. This can lead to liability.[27] An owner can also be held liable for retaining control over the independent contractor's work.[28] For this exception to apply, the owner generally must retain some degree of control over the manner in which the independent contractor performs its work. It is usually not enough to merely retain the right to stop the work, to inspect its progress, or to make suggestions or recommendations that need not be followed. There must be a retention of supervision such that the independent contractor is not entirely free to do its work in the way it sees fit.[29]

17.35   Indemnification

An advisable way to insulate yourself from exposure is to seek contractual indemnification for any losses. While it may not always be possible to obtain favorable contract language, at the very least, never sign a contract that does not specifically state what your responsibilities will be for project safety. You will always be responsible for the safety of your own employees. What you want to make clear is your absence of responsibility for the safety of others on the project. State this clearly in your contract.

If you agree to be contractually responsible for project safety, you may be responsible to nonemployees injured on the project even though you did not directly cause their injuries. In the event you have to assume such responsibilities, it may be possible to demand some sort of indemnification agreement from other companies on the project.

---

[26] *See, e.g., Shannon, supra* note 16.

[27] *Phillips v. United States*, 956 F.2d 1071 (11th Cir. 1992).

[28] *See* Restatement (Second) of Torts § 414 (1965).

[29] *See* Restatement (Second) of Torts § 414 cmt. (1965).

17.36   Worker's Compensation Statutes and Workplace Safety Liabilities

The most typical claim a construction company is likely to encounter will be from a worker injured during construction. The applicable state worker's compensation statute will in large part determine liability for such a claim.

Every state has some type of worker's compensation statute that requires employers to obtain insurance usually covering medical expenses, disability income, and death benefits. Standard worker's compensation insurance policies usually cover third-party claims against the employer as well. For example, an employee may sue a jackhammer supplier for his or her injuries, claiming that the injury was caused by a defect in the jackhammer. The jackhammer supplier may then try to bring the employer into the lawsuit, alleging that the employee's injuries were not caused by a defect in the jackhammer, but by the employer's failure to properly maintain the jackhammer. Such a third-party claim is usually covered by the worker's compensation policy.

Under the applicable worker's compensation statute, the employer will be liable for its employee's injuries regardless of fault. In return, the compensation benefits the employer is liable for to the employee are limited by the terms of the applicable statute. The recovery of the statutorily mandated benefits is the employee's exclusive remedy against the employer. This statutory immunity from civil suit can be lost under certain circumstances. First, the employer's immunity may be stripped if the employer fails to procure the required worker's compensation insurance.[30] Second, an employer generally will not have any immunity for "willful" or "intentional" conduct. What constitutes willful or intentional conduct varies from state to state. Courts in many states have interpreted this exception as applying only if the employer specifically intended to cause the employee's injuries.[31] Some courts and legislatures, however, have required less than intentional harm, and apply this exception to situations where an employer is aware of a high degree of risk created by the violation of a safety statute.[32]

➤ POINTS TO REMEMBER

- Many overlapping federal and state laws create a complex web of rules relating to hazardous wastes, environmental issues, and workplace safety that affect construction. These laws impose legal liability as well as regulatory and reporting requirements.
- Conduct a prebid environmental review of the contract documents. Assess potential safety or environmental risks for each particular project prior to entering into a contract.

---

[30] *See, e.g., Pryse Monument Co. v. District Court*, 595 P.2d 435 (Okla. 1979).

[31] *See, e.g., Love v. Flour Mills of Am.*, 647 F.2d 1058 (10th Cir. 1981); *Courtney v. BASF Wyandotte Corp.*, 385 So.2d 391 (La. Ct. App. 1980). *See also* 96 A.L.R. 3d 1064 (1979).

[32] *See, e.g.,* W. Va. Code § 23-4-2 (2004).

- Make an environmental prebid inquiry on every project.
- During contract negotiations, be wary of standardized contract clauses that may impose responsibility and liability for workplace safety or environmental risks upon you. Make sure that the risk of encountering unexpected hazardous substances is allocated within the contract through specifically drafted clauses.
- Appoint a senior manager, or risk assessment team, to become thoroughly familiar with federal, state, and local environmental and safety statutes and regulations and to oversee compliance with these statutes and regulations.
- Educate your workforce regarding these statutes and regulations and what must be done to comply with them. Make everyone part of the environmental and safety risk-management team.
- Develop a comprehensive safety plan and environmental response plan. Educate your employees to be safety conscious and sensitive to environmental risks.
- Know whether your insurance covers environmental risks and liabilities.
- Carefully review and understand the scope of your rights, obligations, and risks under any indemnity provision.

18

CONSTRUCTION
INSURANCE

18.1 THE IMPORTANCE OF INSURANCE PLANNING

Insurance is a crucial consideration in construction project planning as a means of covering losses and minimizing disputes among the parties on a project. No party involved in any aspect of the construction industry can afford to neglect or overlook the substantial impact and effects that insurance considerations may have on potential costs, fees, rights, and damages. Such neglect is a mistake that can leave a party exposed to liability for which it was never prepared.

Construction insurance is a highly specialized and complex field, which is often confusing and mysterious to the uninitiated. In addition, in an effort to control and predict insurers' relative liabilities, the insurance industry is constantly changing and revising policy language in reaction to changes in the industry as well as to court decisions interpreting and applying the language of insurance policies to determine the rights and obligations of both the insurers and insured. There is no all-encompassing policy or coverage for any construction project or party to such a project. Instead, a web of policies, coverages, exclusions, deductibles, policy limits, and excess and umbrella coverages are stitched together among the parties to cover those relatively limited number of risks that are insurable on a construction project. Insurance policies generally begin by purporting to give broad coverage for a variety of risks and potential damages. However, upon more careful review, most policies dramatically scale back that purported coverage through exclusions, deductibles, policy limits, and other tools to limit the insurers' liability.

Insurance planning for construction projects is extremely complex and specialized; therefore, it would be ill-advised to leave such planning to an inexperienced layperson. Even those companies that are able to employ full-time insurance specialists or risk managers must further rely on professional insurance brokers to assist in the procurement of the proper coverage at a competitive price.

This chapter presents an overview of: (1) the types of insurance that are available and frequently at issue on construction projects; (2) the basic scope and framework of different insurance coverages and exclusions; (3) practical considerations in responding to potential insurance claims; and (4) some recurring coverage issues. It is important to note that the unique terms of individual policies and the peculiarities of individual state laws limit generalizations that can be made about insurance issues. The broad principles described in this chapter, therefore, cannot substitute for specific reference to the contracts and the insurance policies actually at issue and the applicable state law.

18.2 TYPES OF INSURANCE

The types of insurance policies that are typically purchased for construction projects, and are therefore discussed in this chapter, are commercial general liability, builder's risk, and errors and omissions. There are many other forms of insurance that may also come into play on a construction project, which can range from everyday reliance on worker's compensation insurance to a more unusual claim against a corporate officers' and directors' liability policy. Although some of the general principles described may apply to those other forms of insurance, this chapter will focus on the aforementioned three most common forms of insurance relied upon in resolving construction-related claims.

18.3 Commercial General Liability

Commercial general liability (CGL) insurance protects the insured party from injuries it may cause to *other parties or property*. A CGL policy, however, will not cover the insured's additional costs arising out of the insured's own defective material or workmanship.[1] Accordingly, a CGL policy is "third-party insurance" in that it protects the insured from claims of loss by third parties, but does not protect the insured from losses it directly incurs. The insurance industry's rationale for this limited coverage is that business risks that are in the control of the contractor (e.g., additional costs incurred because of inefficient or substandard work), for which the contractor seeks a profit, should not be the subject of insurance.

18.4 CGL Insurance: "Occurrence" versus "Claims-Made" A CGL policy can be either an "occurrence policy" or a "claims-made policy"; the difference between the two relates to the timing of coverage. An occurrence policy

---

[1] *Indiana Ins. Co. v. Brown*, 2003 WL 23008788 (Ky. App. 2003).

provides coverage regardless of when the claim is actually made, provided the insured occurrence took place during the policy period. A claims-made policy is basically the opposite, extending coverage to claims made during the policy period, regardless of when the insured risk occurred.[2]

18.5 CGL Insurance: Costs of Defense and Deductibles Another important distinction between types of CGL policies is whether the cost of defense is excluded from the policy coverage limits. If the cost of defense is excluded or is in addition to the policy limits, the cost the insurance company incurs in defending a claim does not reduce the value of the coverage. For example, if there is a $100,000 claim on which the insurance company expends $25,000 to defend, the insured's coverage is still the full $100,000 policy limit. If, however, the cost of defense is included in the policy limits, the liability protection afforded is considerably reduced. In the prior example, the $25,000 in defense costs would reduce the insured's liability coverage to $75,000.

Policy limits define the ceiling of financial protection afforded by insurance, but there is also a floor to that protection, the deductible, which is the loss or expense the insured must absorb before the insurance company has any obligation to pay. The combined effects of a high deductible, policy limits, and included costs of defense can dramatically limit the real financial protection afforded by a CGL policy on many claims.

18.6 CGL Insurance: Layers of Insurance CGL coverage is often purchased in multiple layers. The basic coverage is the "primary" policy, with the additional increments of coverage being "excess" or "umbrella" policies. The excess carrier typically will have no duty to defend or indemnify until the primary or other lower coverage is collected, reduced, or exhausted, similar to the deductible requirement. The specific language used in an excess policy to determine where the excess coverage will begin, the so-called attachment point, will control the events that will trigger that excess coverage; therefore, an insured must pay careful attention to the specific terms of those policies.[3] Regardless of when the excess coverage attaches, however, prompt notice is required to all carriers.

18.7 CGL Insurance: Additional Insured The overall impact of CGL coverage on a construction project can be substantially expanded by the inclusion under a policy of other parties as "additional insureds," which then also enjoy coverage.[4] It is not uncommon for owners to require the general contractor and subcontractors to include the owner as an additional insured on their CGL policies.[5] General contractors,

---

[2] *National American Ins. Co. v. American Re-Insurance Co.*, 358 F.3d 736, 741 (10th 2004); *Marshall v. Kansas Medical Mut. Ins. Co.*, 73 P.3d 120, 125 (Kan., 2003).

[3] *Louisiana Ins. v. Interstate*, 630 So.2d 759, 761-62 (La. 1994); *Kelly v. Weil*, 563 So.2d 221, 222 (La. 1990).

[4] Richmond & Black, "Expanding Liability Coverage: Insured Contracts and Additional Insureds," 44 Drake L. Rev. 781, 790 (1996).

[5] Standard Form of Agreement and General Conditions Between Owner and Contractor, AGC Document No. 200 (2000 ed.) ¶ 10.31.

likewise, typically require subcontractors to name the general contractor as an additional insured. Inclusion as an additional insured not only provides protection to the named party against claims by third parties, it also protects the additional insured from subrogation claims by the insurance carrier. Subrogation is the theory by which the insurance company, after paying on a covered claim, can pursue the rights of the covered party against the party actually responsible for the damages.[6]

Whenever an owner or contractor requires that it be named as an "additional insured," it should confirm that coverage by obtaining a copy of each policy, rather than by accepting a broker's binder or even a certificate. The terms of that policy should be reviewed to determine which policy is primary in the event of a claim and to understand the coverage exclusions in that policy.

18.8 CGL Insurance: Environmental Liability The potentially far-reaching liability for environmental hazards is an ever-increasing concern in construction. Unfortunately, the protection afforded under a typical CGL policy is significantly limited when compared to the risk. Most CGL policies exclude coverage for all pollution damages except for that which is "sudden and accidental." Policies are available to separately address broader environmental risks, but such coverage is costly and far from all-inclusive. For a broader discussion of the issue, especially in the context of mold claims, see **Sections 18.35–18.40** of this chapter.

18.9 Builder's Risk Insurance

Builder's risk insurance provides coverage for damages to the project during construction. Accordingly, it protects against the *insured's* loss, as distinguished from compensating the losses of others as with a CGL policy.[7] Builder's risk insurance is typically purchased for large private projects by the owner, but often includes coverage extending to the general contractor and subcontractors. The general contractor and subcontractors also have an insurable interest and can procure coverage on their own.

18.10 Builder's Risk: "All-Risk" versus "Specified" Builder's risk coverage comes in two similar, but different, types of policies: all-risk insurance and specified perils. All-risk insurance purports to broadly cover all risks and damage, but is usually severely limited by equally broad exclusions.[8] A specified perils policy, in contrast, provides coverage only for listed risks and damage. In reality, although these two types of policies approach coverage from two extremes, the scope of coverage actually afforded typically is not that different.

18.11 Builder's Risk: "Occurrence" Coverage Trigger As to the timing of an "occurrence" under a builder's risk policy, which has the same effect as with a CGL policy of establishing which insurers will be liable in the event of multiple

---

[6] *Peerless Ins. Co. v. Progressive Ins. Co.*, 822 A.2d 1125 (Me. 2003).

[7] Coverage Under Builder's Risk Insurance Policy, 97 A.L.R.3d 1270.

[8] *Dawson Farms v. Millers Mutual*, 794 So.2d 949, 951 (La. App. 2001).

policies between the time of the initial exposure to injury and the eventual manifestation of the same, courts have looked to the same "occurrence trigger" options as they have with CGL policies. See **Section 18.25** for a more detailed description of the possible "occurrence trigger" tests used in various jurisdictions.

18.12 Errors and Omissions Insurance

Errors and omissions (E&O) insurance is professional liability or malpractice insurance that covers the professional negligence of design professionals.[9] The cost of such coverage is substantial, and, like most insurance, ever-increasing. Moreover, many design professionals believe that investing in E&O coverage actually encourages claims rather than protects against them.

Owners are increasingly requiring construction managers to carry professional liability coverage similar to that maintained by design professionals. Similarly, design-build contracts often require contractors to obtain the coverage of an E&O policy or to require the design member of the team to carry such insurance.

18.13 Alternatives to Traditional Insurance Programs

Although notoriously cyclical, the insurance industry, like any business, is dynamic and adaptive. Policies evolve as underwriters adjust the premiums, terms, and conditions consistent with the perceived risk. Further, underwriting is susceptible to competitive pressures. In addition, new insurance products are "rolled out" in a regular fashion, especially at the upper ranges of premium risk. Insurance is available for contractor and subcontractor default. An owner can procure an insurance policy that will pay liquidated damages. Loss mitigation policies are available in the extreme situation when a risk must be completely transferred from a company's balance sheet. Owner-Controlled Insurance Programs (OCIPs) are constantly evolving in their comprehensive nature of coverage for a particular construction project.

Even when an owner is providing builder's risk coverage, whether through its regular property insurance or through a separate policy purchased just for that specific project, most contractors also have a master builder's risk policy. Many contractors, especially those doing design-build work, also have a professional liability policy, which can cover errors and omissions on the part of the design professional.

The evolution of insurance has recently been most apparent in the "reinsurance" market, which provides a secondary layer of coverage for primary insurers. Recent catastrophic losses, consolidation, and bankruptcies in the primary insurance market have resulted in significantly tightened underwriting standards in the reinsurance market.

As the commercial insurance market in general has grown more restrictive in its underwriting, so-called insurance captives are being utilized to provide direct insurance and/or reinsurance. These captives allow more direct management of the risk, as well as potential savings and rebates. Captives can also provide more expansive underwriting.

---

[9] *Brown Daltas v. General Acc. Ins.*, 48 F.3d 30 (1st Cir. 1995).

18.14 CONTRACT REQUIREMENTS FOR INSURANCE

Insurance must be planned for each individual project. Although there are certain industry standards regarding which party provides what kind of coverage, insurance is too important and too specialized to assume anything. It is essential that each party review the individual contracts on each project to confirm how insurance requirements are addressed. This review is necessary to confirm compliance with the contract and to verify that others are providing the protection, which is required by the terms of the contract. It is important to confirm that those contractually defined requirements are satisfied by all involved. Unexpected gaps in coverage are unpleasant surprises.

18.15 Standard Contract Clause

The typical insurance arrangement is reflected in the AIA Document A201 (1997 ed.) as well as the AGC Document No. 200 (2000 ed.) The contractor procures CGL coverage.[10] The owner can also obtain liability coverage, but is not required to do so.[11] The owner is, however, required to obtain all risk builder's insurance,[12] and this builder's risk protection extends to subcontractors on the project.

The AIA Document A201 provides that the owner may require the contractor to provide Project Management Protective Liability Insurance to cover the owner's, contractor's, and architect's vicarious liability for construction operations.[13] To the extent that damages are covered by Project Management Protective Liability Insurance, the owner, contractor, and architect are required to waive subrogation rights against each other.[14]

Both the AGC Document No. 200, Standard Form of Agreement Between Owner and Contractor (2000 ed.), and AIA A201, General Conditions of the Contract for Construction (1997 ed.), leave blanks or use exhibits to specify the types of coverage and policy limits required.[15] Ideally, the general contractor would like the subcontractor's insurance to mirror what the general contractor is required to procure.[16] Such broad coverage for subcontractors, however, is often not practical, necessary, or cost-effective.

---

[10] General Conditions of the Contract for Construction, AIA Document A201-1997, § 11.1.1; Standard Form of Agreement and General Conditions Between Owner and Contractor, AGC Document No. 200 (2000 ed.), ¶ 10.3.1.

[11] General Conditions of the Contract for Construction, AIA Document A201-1997, § 11.2.1.

[12] General Conditions of the Contract for Construction, AIA Document A201-1997, ¶ 11.3.1; Standard Form of Agreement and General Conditions Between Owner and Contractor, AGC Document No. 200 (2000 ed.), ¶ 10.4.1.

[13] General Conditions of the Contract for Construction, AIA Document A201-1997, § 11.3.1.

[14] General Conditions of the Contract for Construction, AIA Document A201-1997, § 11.3.2.

[15] Standard Form of Agreement and General Conditions Between Owner and Contractor, AGC Document No. 200 (2000 ed.), ¶ 10.3; General Conditions of the Contract for Construction, AIA Document A201-1997, § 11.3.1.

[16] *See* Standard Form Construction Subcontract AGC Document No. 650 (1999 ed.).

After certain minimums are applied, the specific nature and scope of a subcontractor's work should bear upon the extent of the coverage required. If particularly hazardous work is required, even greater levels of insurance may be necessary.

18.16   Waiver of Subrogation

Waiver of subrogation rights is an important component in planning insurance coverage on a project. As noted earlier, subrogation is the theory by which the insurance company, after paying on a claim, can pursue the rights of the insured against the party responsible for the damages. By including a waiver of subrogation clause in a contract, however, the parties can insulate themselves from such subrogation claims and have any potential claims primarily resolved through insurance. Because the waiver of subrogation can substantially affect the insurance company's risk by cutting off its potential rights to recoup losses on claims, the insurance company should be notified of the inclusion of such waiver in a contract to avoid any jeopardizing of coverage.[17]

Both the AGC Document No. 200 (2000 ed.) and the AIA Document A201 (1997 ed.) require the owner and contractor to waive their subrogation rights and require them to obtain similar waivers with other contracts, hopefully protecting all parties on the project from subrogation claims.[18] This waiver of subrogation is also often incorporated into standard subcontracts.[19]

18.17   Proof of Insurance

It is not sufficient to merely identify what each party is required to do with respect to insurance. The greatest insurance planning is wasted if there is no execution and follow-through in accordance with the plan and contract requirements. Compliance with insurance requirements should be confirmed by written certificates of insurance describing the coverage and identifying the insurance company. Copies of the actual policies should be obtained, whenever possible. Proof of insurance by all parties should be a contract requirement and, further, should be confirmed as soon as possible prior to starting work.[20] If a loss occurs prior to procuring the insurance, the ability to get coverage for that event is extremely limited.

Failing to promptly require proof of insurance may not only leave gaps in coverage. If work has commenced without proof of coverage, there may be a question of whether it is possible to terminate a contractor or subcontractor that cannot obtain

---

[17] *Liberty Mut. Ins. Co. v. Altfillisch Constr. Co.*, 139 Cal. Rptr. 91 (Cal. Ct. App. 1977).

[18] Standard Form of Agreement and General Conditions Between Owner and Contractor, AGC Document No. 200 (2000 ed.), ¶ 10.4.3; General Conditions of the Contract for Construction, AIA Document A201-1997, § 11.4.7.

[19] AGC Document No. 650 (1998 ed.), ¶ 9.2.8.

[20] Standard Form of Agreement and General Conditions Between Owner and Contractor, AGC Document No. 200 (2000 ed.), ¶ 10.3.1; *see* General Conditions of the Contract for Construction, AIA Document A201-1997, § 11.1.3.

insurance. In addition to the practical risks and difficulties associated with terminating a contractor or subcontractor, it is very likely that an argument that failure to procure insurance is not a material breach justifying termination for default or that the insurance requirement was waived by allowing work to proceed without insurance will be advanced. The better course is to obtain satisfactory proof of coverage prior to allowing the contractor or subcontractor to start work.

18.18   PROMPT ACTION TO PROTECT POTENTIAL COVERAGE

18.19   Sensitivity to Insurance Issues

Effective insurance planning not only involves the acquisition of coverage, it must also involve sensitizing project personnel to the potential for coverage of losses and claims as well as the need to react and preserve such potential relief. Project management personnel should be sufficiently trained and experienced to affirmatively deal with insurance notice requirements. At a minimum, project management personnel must know when to alert others with expertise or responsibility for insurance matters when potential coverage issues arise on a project. Ideally, there should be at least one resource person in every construction organization who, through special training and experience, can deal with specific situations and coverage questions beyond the broad concepts introduced in this chapter.

A starting point for effectively dealing with potential coverage issues is obtaining familiarity with all the insurance policies that may apply to the organization as well as the specific project. Reading the policies is essential, but, unfortunately, not necessarily enough. Without some background in insurance, much of the policy language affirmatively describing coverage and the litany of exclusions may not make any sense.

18.20   Prompt Action to Protect Potential Coverage: Immediate Notice

When confronted with a potential loss or claim, the possibility of insurance coverage must be considered *first*, not last, after all other possible avenues of relief or defense have been exhausted. Prompt notice to the insurance company of a potential claim is of critical importance to satisfy policy requirements and protect coverage. Early consideration of coverage in dealing with claims or losses is also important in developing the documentation or posture that will enhance an argument in favor of coverage on those claims in which coverage may be disputed.

If a claim is asserted, the defense of that claim should be affirmatively and immediately tendered to the insurer. Even if the defense is tendered to the insurer, the insured should take all immediate actions necessary to preserve any defense or rights available to either the insured or the insurer.

Lack of timely notice to the insurer can be the basis for loss of coverage in some states, even if the insurer experienced no actual prejudice as a result of the timing of the notice.[21] In other states, late tender of the defense will bar recovery of attorneys' fees and cost of defense incurred prior to the tender.

The tender should be as complete and as informative as possible. The insured party should provide copies of demand letters or pleadings, as well as other documents that describe the nature and circumstances of the claim. If the basis for coverage is not entirely clear, it is also a good idea to provide documents or an explanation that highlights or depicts the circumstances that may establish coverage. For example, in tendering a claim under a CGL policy, the property damage or bodily injury of the claimant should be pointed out if it is not obvious.

In preparing any explanation or description that is provided to the insurer, the insured should bear in mind that the coverage may be disputed or that communication may be subject to discovery in subsequent litigation with the claimant. This concern should not preclude an insured party from taking appropriate action or keeping the insurer informed, but it should be a consideration.

18.21   THE INSURANCE COMPANY'S RESPONSE TO CLAIMS

An insurance company has three basic choices in responding to a tender of the defense of a claim: (1) the tender can be accepted without reservation; (2) the tender can be accepted with a reservation of rights disputing coverage; and (3) the tender of defense can be flatly refused.

Acceptance of the defense without reservation by the insurer is obviously the best result. With the exception of deductibles and policy limits, the claim becomes the financial responsibility of the insurance company.[22] However, the insured still has a duty to cooperate with the insurer in defense of the claim, and this can have its own financial and administrative burdens in protracted litigation.

18.22   The Insurance Company's Reservation of Rights

If coverage of a claim is subject to some dispute, the insurance company will frequently err in favor of caution by accepting the defense with a "reservation of rights." In making this reservation of rights, the insurer describes why the claim may not be covered and confirms its right to subsequently refuse coverage if the facts or policy language demonstrate no coverage exists. In the meantime, the insurer provides the defense.[23]

---

[21] *See* Windt, *Insurance Claims and Disputes: Representation of Insured and Insurers 1–23* (Shepards-McGraw, 1982).

[22] 44 Am. Jur. 2d Insurance § 1413 (2003); *Henning v. Continental Cas. Co.*, 254 F.3d 1291 (11th Cir. 2001).

[23] *W.E. O'Neil Const. Co. v. General Cas. Co. of Illinois*, 748 N.E.2d 667 (Ill. App. 2001).

Unfortunately, the insurer's reservation of rights can create a conflict of interest with the insured. In defending the claim under a reservation of rights, an insurance company could seek to protect its interest by defeating or settling the claim on the merits or try to push the claim or pursue the defense so that the outcome supports the insurance company's position that there is no coverage; the insured could end up with liability, but without coverage.[24] Fortunately, it is generally recognized that counsel for an insured, even though appointed and paid by an insurance company, cannot put that insurance company's interests ahead of the insured's interests. Nevertheless, if the insured is not able to pay the cost for legal counsel, it is a good idea to have the insurance company pay counsel, which the insured selects.

18.23   Litigation with the Insurance Company

Disputes over coverage can themselves be the subject of separate litigation while the underlying claim is also in dispute. Either the insured or the insurance company may initiate an action for declaratory relief against the other to resolve the issue of whether or not the underlying claim is covered under the policy.[25] The lawsuit asks the court to declare the rights of the parties under the policy so they know how to deal with the defense of the underlying claim.

The declaratory relief action may be brought while the insurance company is defending the claim under a reservation of rights. If so, the insurance company may seek to stay any litigation of the underlying claim until the declaratory relief action is concluded and the coverage issue is resolved. The insured will typically want the litigation of the underlying claim to proceed first. As a practical matter, the further the insurance company gets into the defense, the harder it is to get out, or the more likely the insurance company will participate in some settlement of the underlying claim, which will also invariably include a settlement of the coverage dispute.

Usually it is the insured that has the upper hand on the question of which litigation should go first. In construction cases, there typically are similar or identical factual issues in the declaratory relief action and the litigation of the underlying claim. As the resolution of the underlying claim will be more likely to resolve those issues, the insured is in a better position to succeed in getting the declaratory relief action stayed. Of course, if the insurance company has not accepted the defense and the insured faces substantial costs of defending the underlying claim, the insured may want the litigation of the underlying claim stayed while coverage is resolved.

18.24   ROUTINE COVERAGE ISSUES

The language of specific policies, changes to the standard policy language over time, and the divergent views of courts around the country make it difficult and dangerous

---

[24] *See also All America Ins. Co. v. Broeren Russo Const., Inc.*, 112 F.Supp.2d 723 (C.D. Ill. 2000); *Cassey v. Stewart*, 727 So.2d 655 (La. App. 1999).

[25] *See generally State Farm Lloyds v. Borum*, 2001 WL 931136 (Tex. App. 2001); *Gallant Ins. Co. v. Wilkerson*, 720 N.E.2d 1223 (Ind. App. 1999).

to presume anything regarding insurance coverage. The application of general principles to specific situations is risky. There are, however, a number of issues that routinely arise, the results of which can be somewhat predicted. These routine issues generally involve the type of occurrences and damages that do not enjoy coverage.

For example, construction defects generally are not covered under either CGL or builder's risk policies. In addition to the specific exclusions that operate to bar coverage for construction defects, there is a public policy in favor of barring protection for one's own defective work. The contractor is provided the incentive to exercise care in performing its work, and limiting coverage in this manner keeps the costs of insurance down.[26]

18.25   CGL Coverage Issues: Continuing Damages

Construction-related claims often involve a continuing problem rather than one catastrophic instance, such as a leak or other defect that becomes worse or creates more damage over time. Because several policies may have been in effect over the extended duration of the problem and the resulting damages, the question arises of which or how many policies may afford coverage. On claims-made policies, the coverage will be limited to the policy in effect when the first claim was made against the insured, regardless of whether the damages incurred continue to increase after that policy's period. If, however, occurrence policies are involved, the coverage is less clear.

In a CGL "occurrence policy," there still remains the question of when the "occurrence" actually occurs for purposes of triggering coverage. This question generally arises when an insured has several CGL policies spanning over a period of time and certain damages began to be incurred during one policy period, but were not actually discovered until a later and different policy period. In cases with injuries that evolve over time, there are generally five separate theories for the "trigger" of coverage that courts in different jurisdictions, with differing results, will use to determine which insurers will be liable for the loss: (1) the exposure theory, (2) the manifestation theory, (3) the continuous-trigger theory, (4) injury-in-fact approach, and (5) the double-trigger theory.[27]

The "exposure theory" establishes the occurrence and, thereby, assesses insurer liability at the time the insured's property is first contacted by or exposed to the injury-producing agent or event.[28] In contrast, the "manifestation theory" establishes the occurrence at the time the injury actually manifests itself or is discovered, regardless of when the injury actually began.[29] The "continuous-trigger theory" is a broad test that establishes occurrence as continuous from the time of the first exposure until the injury manifests or is discovered, holding liability under all policies in existence during that period.[30] The "injury-in-fact approach," which assumes that

[26] *See Western Employers Ins. Co. v. Arciero & Sons, Inc.,* 194 Cal. Rptr. 688 (Cal. Ct. App. 1983).

[27] *Atchison, Topeka & Santa Fe Ry. Co. v. Stonewall Ins. Co.,* 71 P.3d 1097, 1126 (Kan. 2003); *Owens-Illinois, Inc. v. United Ins. Co.,* 650 A.2d 974 (N.J. 1994).

[28] *Auto Owners Ins. Co. v. Travelers Cas. & Surety Co.,* 227 F.Supp.2d 1248, 1266 (M.D. Fla. 2002).

[29] *James Pest Control, Inc. v. Scottsdale Ins. Co.,* 765 So.2d 485, 491 (La. App. 2000).

[30] *American Family Mut. Ins. Co. v. American Girl, Inc.,* 673 N.W.2d 65, 85 (Wis. 2004).

several determinable and separate "occurrences" resulted in the eventually mani-
fested injury, holds that each of the individual "occurrences" triggered coverage
under the specific policy in place at that time, but not necessarily all policies in
place between the first exposure and the subsequent manifestation.[31] The "double-
trigger theory" establishes the occurrence both at the time of exposure and at the
time of manifestation, triggering coverage under the policies in place at those two
specific times, but not triggering coverage for intervening policies in place between
those two times.[32]

A further theory provides for "stacking," or multiple, coverage by all policies
in effect from the time the injury began until it was discovered, similar to the
"continuous-trigger theory." Stacking provides the insured the protection of multiple
policy limits.[33] This is an area of frequent dispute and can be addressed only by reference to the terms of the policies and the applicable court decisions.[34]

18.26   CGL Coverage Issues: Diminution in Value

Under most CGL policies, physical damage, destruction, or loss of use of tangible
property is required for coverage. A recurring issue in construction disputes is
whether installation of defective or substandard work or materials constitutes "physical damage," which is covered, or merely "diminution in value," which is not covered. This is an issue on which apparently very similar facts and operative policy
language have resulted in divergent treatment by the courts in different jurisdictions.[35]

In one case, coverage was found for the diminished value of a building caused by
defective plaster, even though the policy required "injury to or destruction of property."[36] But in another case, in which the policy required "physical injury to or
destruction of tangible property," there was no coverage for the costs of replacing
defective studs.[37]

18.27   CGL Coverage Issues: Completed Operations

"Completed operations" coverage, defined as liability arising for damage or injury
incurred after the contractor has completed or abandoned its work, is an important

---

[31] *In re Silicone Implant Ins. Coverage Litigation*, 667 N.W.2d 405, 420 (Minn. 2003).

[32] *Zurich Ins. Co. v. Raymark Indus., Inc.*, 514 N.E.2d 150, 161 (Ill. 1987).

[33] *Cole v. Celotex Corp.*, 599 So.2d 1058 (La. 1992).

[34] *See generally* Bunshoft & Seabolt, "The Contractor's Insurance Coverage Under Its Liability and
Builder's Risk Policies," *Construction Litigation; Representing the Owner,* 196–97 (Wiley 1986).

[35] *Mutual Ben. Group v. Wise M. Bolt Co., Inc.*, 227 F.Supp.2d 469 (D. Md. 2002); *Structural Building
Products Corp. v. Business Ins. Agency, Inc.*, 722 N.Y.S.2d 559 (N.Y. App. 2001).

[36] *Hauenstein v. St. Paul-Mercury Indem. Co.*, 65 N.W.2d 122 (Minn. 1954); *but see Minneapolis Soc. of
Fine Arts v. Parker-Klein Assocs. Architects, Inc.*, 354 N.W.2d 816 (Minn. 1984).

[37] *Wyoming Saw Mills v. Transportation Ins. Co.*, 578 P.2d 1253 (Or. 1978); *but see Isspro Inc. v. Globe
Indem. Co.*, 106 F.3d 407 (9th Cir. 1997).

provision that is too often overlooked by the contractor or subcontractor.[38] Failing to obtain or confirm this coverage can prove to be expensive by barring all such coverage for damage occurring after the contractor has completed or abandoned its work.[39]

18.28 CGL Coverage Issues: "Care, Custody, and Control"

Most CGL policies exclude coverage for damages to the property in the "care, custody, and control" of the insured. Policies vary, however, on whether this exclusion applies to both real and personal property or simply personal property.[40] Regardless of the precise scope of the exclusion, its purpose is to coordinate coverage between CGL policies, which address liability to third parties, and builder's risk policies, which address the insured's own loss.[41] Because the general contractor will generally be deemed to maintain "care, custody, and control" of the entire project, this exclusion is usually broadly effective against general contractors. Subcontractors, on the other hand, are typically performing a discrete scope of work rather than the entire project, so this exclusion may only narrowly apply to subcontractors.

18.29 CGL Coverage Issues: The "Work Product"

Most CGL policies also include what are referred to as "work product" exclusions. These exclusions bar coverage for property damage to or arising from the insured's products or its work, and generally preclude coverage for a contractor or subcontractor's cost to repair or replace its own defective work.[42] These exclusions are described as "the heart and soul" of the insurance industry's efforts to avoid assuming the contractor's business risk through the CGL policy.[43] As with the "care, custody, and control" exclusion, the work product exclusion is generally an effective bar to claims by the general contractor, as the entire project will typically be the general contractor's "work product." Some courts, however, have held that site preparation and/or construction of the building itself constitute a "service," not a "product" and, therefore, this exclusion would not apply.[44] Further, if the defective work of Subcontractor A damages the work of Subcontractor B, Subcontractor A may enjoy

---

[38] *American Family Mut. Ins. Co. v. American Girl, Inc.*, 673 N.W.2d 65 (Wis. 2004); Standard Form of Agreement and General Conditions Between Owner and Contractor, AGC Document No. 200 (2000 ed.), ¶ 10.3.3.

[39] *American States Ins. Co. v. Powers*, 2003 WL 21138957 (D. Kan. 2003).

[40] Scope of Clause Excluding from Contractor's or Similar Liability Policy Damage to Property in Care, Custody, or Control of Insureds, 8 A.L.R.4th 563.

[41] *See Estrin Constr. Co. v. Aetna Cas. & Sur. Co.*, 612 S.W.2d 413 (Mo. Ct. App. 1981). *But see Peters v. Employers Mut. Cas. Co.*, 853 S.W.2d 300 (Mo. 1993).

[42] *Kvaerner Metals v. Commercial*, 825 A.2d 641 (Pa. Super. 2003).

[43] *See* note 34; *Vintage Contracting, L.L.C. v. Dixie Bldg.*, 858 So.2d 22, 28 (La. App. 2003).

[44] *McKellar Development v. Northern*, 837 P.2d 858 (Nev. 1992); *Maryland Casualty Co. v. Reeder*, 270 Cal. Rptr. 719, 727 (1990).

coverage for Subcontractor B's claim because it does not involve Subcontractor A's work product.[45] Again, the way the contractor addresses this lack of coverage under the CGL policy is through property or builder's risk insurance.

18.30   CGL Coverage Issues: Contractual Liability Exclusion

Virtually all CGL policies contain an exclusion against contractually assumed liability. This exclusion is intended to avoid coverage for the insured's contractual obligations, including indemnity agreements between the insured and a third party, and thereby limit the insurer's coverage to the insured's direct liability.[46]

18.31   Builder's Risk Coverage Issues: Policy Periods

Builder's risk coverage generally covers damage to the project during construction. The precise time period of coverage, however, is often the subject of dispute. Some builder's risk policies describe the policy period in terms of fixed calendar dates.[47] This level of precision, however, can create problems due to the uncertainties of the construction process and the possibility of delays. For example, if the policy expires on a date certain that is geared to the original contract completion date, delays to the project can result in lack of coverage. This problem can be avoided by extending the policy period before it runs out.

On the other hand, many builder's risk policies simply describe the policy period as "during construction."[48] In that case, it is well settled that for coverage to commence, some actual, physical construction must have started. Defining completion of "construction," however, is frequently a more difficult task if it has not been defined in the policy or the construction contract. Completion will frequently be found if the project is sufficiently complete to permit the owner to utilize the structure for its intended purpose. Many policies expressly provide for termination of coverage when the building becomes occupied.

The AIA's General Conditions of the Contract for Construction, AIA Document A201-1997, addresses the potential impact of owner occupancy on coverage by precluding the owner's use of the structure without advising and obtaining the consent of the builder's risk insurer.[49]

18.32   Builder's Risk Coverage Issues: Fortuitous Loss

A fundamental aspect of builder's risk coverage is that it protects only against "fortuitous" losses. This means the loss must be a matter of chance and not something

---

[45] *See, e.g., Todd Shipyards Corp. v. Turbine Serv., Inc.*, 674 F.2d 401 (5th Cir. 1982), *aff'd in part, rev'd in part sub nom, Todd Shipyards Corp. v. Auto Transp., S.A.*, 763 F.2d 745 (5th Cir. 1985).

[46] *Thermo Terratech v. GDC Enviro-Solutions, Inc.*, 265 F.3d 329, 336 (5th 2001).

[47] Coverage Under Builder's Risk Policy, 97 A.L.R.3d 1270, § 4.

[48] *Id.*

[49] General Conditions of the Contract for Construction, AIA Document A201-1997, § 11.4.1.5.

that is certain to occur, such as depreciation or ordinary wear and tear.[50] The losses arising from the insured's deliberate conduct are likewise excluded.[51] Losses from the negligence of the insured or its employees or subcontractors, however, are considered fortuitous, as they are not intended by the insured.[52]

Some builder's risk policies require that losses result from an external cause in order to establish coverage.[53] In general, the so-called external cause requirement excludes damages arising from an inherent defect in the property. This limitation can be viewed as another version of the requirement for a fortuitous loss.[54]

18.33   Builder's Risk Coverage Issues: Exclusions

In addition to the coverage issues addressed, many builder's risk policies also contain express exclusions that bar claims for defective design, faulty workmanship and material, inherent defects, equipment breakdown, and earth movement.[55]

18.34   CONCURRENT CAUSES

Losses on construction projects often arise from a combination of forces. Some policies specifically exclude coverage in cases of multiple causation.[56] If the issue of multiple causes is not addressed in the policies, the courts are divided on how to resolve the question of coverage. Some courts have held that if at least one cause is not excluded, coverage exists.[57] In other cases, however, courts have gone through the intricate process of identifying the cause that set the other causes in motion and then evaluating the coverage issue from the standpoint of whether or not that "efficient proximate cause" is subject to an exclusion.[58] If such courts find that the original or "efficient proximate cause" was covered, the resulting damage will also be deemed covered, regardless of any intervening cause that was excluded.

---

[50] *City of Burlington v. Indemnity Ins. Co. of North America*, 2003 WL 21310376 (2nd Cir. 2003); *Johnson Press of America, Inc. v. Northern Ins. Co. of New York*, 791 N.E.2d 1291 (Ill. App. 2003).

[51] Cal. Ins. Code § 533.

[52] *J. Aron & Co. v. Chown*, 647 N.Y.S.2d 8 (N.Y. App. 1996). *See also C.H. Leavell & Co. v. Fireman's Fund Ins. Co.*, 372 F.2d 784 (9th Cir. 1967), *but see Trinity Indus., Inc. v. Insurance Co. of N. Am.*, 916 F.2d 267 (5th Cir. 1990).

[53] *Wolstein v. Yorkshire Ins. Co., Ltd.*, 985 P.2d 400 (Wash. App. 1999).

[54] *See Standard Structural Steel v. Bethlehem Steel Corp.*, 597 F. Supp. 164, 191–93 (D. Conn. 1984).

[55] *Swire Pacific Holdings, Inc. v. Zurich Ins. Co.*, 845 So.2d 161 (Fla. 2003).

[56] *See* 43 Am. Jur. 2d Insurance § 480 (2003).

[57] *Phillips Home Builders, Inc. v. Travelers Ins. Co.*, 700 A.2d 127 (Del. 1997).

[58] *Western Nat. Mut. Ins. Co. v. University of North Dakota*, 643 N.W.2d 4 (N.D. 2002).

18.35   CONSTRUCTION INSURANCE AND MOLD CLAIMS

Over the past 20 years, the construction industry has seen a dramatic and substantial rise in both the volume of and costs associated with litigation relating to the presence of what is commonly and collectively referred to as "mold." Consequently, construction insurers, both CGL (third-party) insurers and Builder's Risk (first-party) insurers, have sought interpretation of certain policy exclusions in a manner that would insulate them from liability for the vast potential damages associated with mold, encountering varying results depending on the specific language of the policy and the jurisdiction interpreting the same.

Prior to the mid-1980s, most pollution exclusionary language contained in construction insurance policies further provided an exception to the exclusion for "sudden and accidental" releases of pollutants. Many courts at that time accepted the insurance industry's arguments that, since environmental injury had to be both "sudden" and "accidental" in order to be covered, gradual release or development of mold causing damage was not covered. However, as many courts began to hold the language of "sudden" to be ambiguous and, thereby, broadened coverage for environmental injury in favor of the insureds, the insurance industry responded with a new and, presumably, stronger exclusion for such liability.

In the mid-1980s, the so-called absolute pollution exclusion, containing no exception for "sudden and accidental" injury, was introduced and quickly became standard policy language throughout the insurance industry.[59] Generally, such provisions purported to broadly exclude coverage for injury related to the "discharge, dispersal, seepage, migration, release, or escape" of a "pollutant." Since that time, jurisdictions have split as to whether this exclusionary language will be broadly or narrowly interpreted and, thus, whether it will or will not exclude damages arising out of the presence environmental agents, including mold. According to a recent court, "[t]he scope of the [absolute] pollution exclusion is an evolving area of law, subject to differing interpretations. The [absolute] pollution exclusion is one of the most frequently litigated exceptions found in a staple insurance industry product. . . . Cases may be found for and against every issue any litigant has ever raised, and often the cases reaching the same conclusion as to a particular issue do so on the basis of differing, and sometimes inconsistent, rationales."[60]

18.36   Mold Claims: "Pollutant"

The first general question in considering coverage for mold under a policy containing an absolute pollution exclusion is whether or not mold is considered a "pollutant"

---

[59] William H. Howard, *Asbestos, Environmental and Mold Claims*, Litigation and Administrative Practice Course Handbook Series: Insurance Coverage "2003 Claim Trends & Litigation" 166 (Practicing Law Institute 2003).

[60] *Porterfield v. Audubon*, 856 So.2d 789, 800 (Ala. 2003), *quoting Kemper v. Heaven Hill*, 82 S.W.3d 869 (Ky. 2002).

as provided in such exclusions. Generally, this question is resolved by considering whether the injurious agent at issue is an irritant or a contaminant, or is toxic, and/or poses a health hazard due to exposure.[61] Courts have been fairly consistent in finding that mold is a "pollutant" in this context.

18.37   Mold Claims: "Discharge, Dispersal, Seepage, Migration, Release, or Escape"

The second general question in considering coverage for mold under a policy containing an absolute pollution exclusion is whether or not the environmental injury at issue would qualify as a "discharge, dispersal, seepage, migration, release, or escape" as provided in such exclusions. Some courts have held that this language requires "movement" and/or an "active and clearly perceived physical event."[62] In such instances, courts have found certain environmental injuries that are "continual, imperceptible, and inevitable" as covered.[63] Further, some courts will find in favor of an insured if the court deems such language in an absolute exclusion to be "ambiguous" as to what damage is excluded.[64]

In other jurisdictions, however, courts have found the "transmission of . . . mold spores" constitutes a "release" or other action provided in the absolute pollution exclusion and, therefore, is not covered under the policy.[65]

18.38   Mold Claims: "Efficient Proximate Cause"

Some jurisdictions have applied the so-called efficient proximate cause rule to conclude that coverage exists when an insured can "identify an insured peril as the proximate cause of the loss even if subsequent or concurrent events are specifically excluded from coverage."[66] Therefore, in such jurisdictions, if mold is caused by water leakage that, in turn, was originally caused by a covered injury, the resulting mold will be deemed covered, regardless of an excluded intervening injury.

Other jurisdictions have ignored the "efficient proximate cause" rule and held "there is no coverage for losses caused by mold, even though a covered water event may have [caused] the loss."[67]

---

[61] *Porterfield v. Audubon*, 856 So.2d 789, 801 (Ala. 2003); *Anderson v. Highland*, 757 N.E.2d 329, 332 (Ohio 2001).

[62] *Sphere Drake v. Y.L. Realty*, 990 F. Supp. 240, 243 (S.D.N.Y. 1997); *Byrd v. Blumenreich*, 722 A.2d 598 (N.J. Super. 1999).

[63] *Lititz Mutual v. Steely*, 785 A.2d 975, 981-82 (Pa. 2001).

[64] *Cincinnati v. Becker*, 635 N.W.2d 112, 118-19 (Neb. 2001).

[65] *Lexington v. Unity/Waterford*, 2002 WL 356756 (N.D. Tex. 2002); *West Am. v. Desenberg*, 925 F. Supp. 758, 761 (M.D. Fla. 1996).

[66] *Bowers v. Farmers*, 991 P.2d 734, 738 (Wash. App. 2000).

[67] *Cooper v. American Family*, 184 F. Supp. 2d 960, 962 (D. Ariz. 2002).

18.39   Mold Claims: "Reasonable Expectations"

Some jurisdictions, in reading any ambiguity in liability exclusions *against* the insurer and *in favor* of the insured, look to the "reasonable expectations" of the insured, instead of the technical definitions of the language contained in the policy. If, based on the purpose of the policy and the language at issue, the insured could have "reasonably expected" that its policy would cover mold damages, such courts will find coverage.[68]

Other jurisdictions, however, have found the absolute pollution exclusion is not ambiguous and, therefore, the insured is not entitled to such a favorable interpretation.[69] Such jurisdictions have held that the absolute pollution exclusion "exclude[s] coverage for all claims alleging damage cause[d] by pollutants."[70] Further, some courts will narrowly evaluate whether the insured's expectations were "reasonable," and "a subjective belief developed after the loss [will be deemed] insufficient to create coverage where none exists under the policy."[71]

18.40   Mold Claims: Specific Mold Exclusions

As mentioned earlier, the insurance industry takes notice of varying courts' interpretations of policy language and responds to protect its interests. Accordingly, due to the rise in volume and cost of mold claims, many insurers have begun to include additional policy exclusions that expressly and specifically address mold and mold-related damage. Although an insured can obtain additional coverage in such circumstances that would provide mold coverage, such additional coverage is often cost-prohibitive.

As with all insurance-related issues, it is important to read and know the specific language of the applicable insurance policy as well as the law in the relevant jurisdiction. Slight variations in either of these circumstances can have drastic and costly repercussions when determining who must pay for damage.

> ➤ **POINTS TO REMEMBER**

Insurance Planning

- Planning is crucial for avoiding loss and limiting disputes.
- It requires special training and experience.
- The assistance of an insurance professional who is familiar with construction is necessary.

---

[68] *Anderson v. Highland*, 757 N.E.2d 329, 332 (Ohio 2001); *Regional Bank v. St. Paul*, 35 F.3d 494, 498 (10th Cir. 1994).

[69] *Cincinnati v. Becker*, 635 N.W.2d 112, 118-19 (Neb. 2001).

[70] *Id.*

[71] *Darner Motor v. Universal*, 682 P.2d 388, 395 (Ariz. 1984).

Types of Insurance

Commercial General Liability (CGL) Insurance

- CGL provides protection against claims by third parties and not the insured's own losses.
- A CGL policy can be a "claims-made" or "occurrence" policy; which type it is determines the timing of coverage.
- If costs of defense are not excluded from the policy limit, the financial protection afforded can be greatly reduced.
- Liability insurance can be purchased in multiple layers. Prompt notice is required to all layers.
- Inclusion of others on CGL policy as additional insureds extends protection and eliminates subrogation claims.
- CGL coverage affords extremely limited protection against environmental liability.

Builder's Risk Insurance

- Builder's risk coverage is first-party insurance; it protects against the insured's loss rather than against the claim of third parties.
- Builder's risk coverage is typically procured by the owner, with protection extended to the contractor and subcontractors.

Errors and Omissions (E&O) Insurance

- E&O insurance is professional liability insurance for design professionals.
- Similar insurance is increasingly required for professional construction managers.
- E&O coverage by the design professional is not always a contract requirement.

Contract Requirements for Insurance

- Never assume insurance coverage; always consult the contracts on the project to confirm how it is set up.
- Typically, the contractor procures CGL coverage; the owner procures builder's risk insurance.
- Most construction contracts include "waiver of subrogation" clauses that preclude the insurance company from trying to recoup its losses from others on the project.
- It is imperative to require proof of insurance and to confirm that the parties have complied with the contract requirements before they start work.

Prompt Action to Protect Potential Coverage

- Project management personnel should be educated to deal with potential insurance issues and refer them to an appropriate individual with special training in insurance.

- Prompt notice of potential claims should be made to the insurance company to avoid the risk of losing coverage.
- The notice or tender of defense should be as complete and informative as possible.

The Insurance Company's Response to Claims

- The insurance company will often accept the defense of a claim with a reservation of rights to later deny coverage.
- In that situation, a potential conflict of interest may exist that requires the insured to retain independent counsel, hopefully at the insurance company's expense.
- Disputes over coverage may have to be resolved through separate litigation, a declaratory judgment action, between the insured and the insurance company.

Routine Coverage Issues

- Construction defects are generally not covered by CGL or builder's risk insurance.
- CGL coverage issues:
  - A claim resulting in continuing damages can raise the question of which of several policies apply.
  - CGL policies generally require physical damage or destruction or loss of use of tangible property for coverage so that diminished value is not covered; however, the cases conflict as to what constitutes diminished value.
  - Completed operations cover liability for claims arising after the contractor completes its work; it is often, but not always, part of a CGL policy.
  - The exclusion for property under the "care, custody, and control" of the insured in effect extends to the entire project for the general contractor, but may be more limited for subcontractors.
  - The "work product" exclusion precludes coverage for the costs of repairing or replacing one's own defective work, and its scope is similar to the "care, custody, and control" exclusion.
  - CGL policies exclude contractually assumed liability that does not involve the insured's negligence.
- Builder's risk coverage issues:
  - The policy period extends to a specific date or to when the project is completed, which is often the subject of dispute.
  - Builder's risk coverage extends only to "fortuitous" losses, not that which can be expected, such as ordinary wear and tear.
  - The loss must also be the result of some external cause, not an inherent defect in the property.
- The existence of concurrent causes contributing to a loss may impact coverage.

Mold-Related Issues

- Courts have widely split as to whether certain exclusionary language in construction insurance policies will or will not exclude damages arising out of the presence environmental agents, including mold.
- Courts have been fairly consistent in finding that mold is a "pollutant" in the context of the absolute pollution exclusion.
- Courts have split as to whether mold constitutes the type of "discharge, dispersal, seepage, migration, release, or escape" that will be excluded under the absolute pollution exclusion.
- Courts have split as to whether the "efficient proximate cause" rule will establish that if a covered damage eventually leads to mold, the resulting damage will be covered, regardless of an excluded intervening injury.
- Courts have split as to whether ambiguity exists in the absolute pollution exclusion and, therefore, the court can look to the parties "reasonable expectations" as to coverage of mold instead of the technical definitions of the language contained in the policy.
- Many insurers have begun to include additional policy exclusions that expressly and specifically address mold and mold-related damage.

19

SUCCESSFULLY MANAGING WORKERS IN THE CONSTRUCTION INDUSTRY

In dealing with today's labor market, employers are constantly confronted with the possibility that their employees may institute legal proceedings to address perceived concerns about their working conditions. There are workplace laws and regulations that govern all aspects of the employment relationship, from the initial hiring decision to the decision to terminate employment. Accordingly, employees have myriad federal, state, and local laws to rely upon when seeking redress to concerns about employment decisions or their working environments. To protect themselves from the risks associated with defending against the variety of claims that employees can pursue, employers must be aware of the duties imposed upon them by employment laws, and implement workplace policies that satisfy these obligations.

This chapter will provide an overview of and discuss the most common issues facing construction employers. Due to the variety of state and local laws that construction employers may face as a result of the location of a specific project, this chapter focuses primarily on the applicable federal statutes and regulations. Keep in mind, however, that many states have enacted legislation that may provide coverage similar to the federal laws described below. Moreover, in some instances, state laws provide employees with greater protection than that afforded by the federal statutes.

19.1 UNION ACTIVITY

The National Labor Relations Act (NLRA) governs protected concerted activity in the workplace of covered employers. The NLRA provides employees of covered employers with the right to discuss wages, hours, and work conditions, and to organize a union and collectively negotiate the terms and conditions of their employment, or to refrain from such conduct. The NLRA also prohibits certain conduct on the part of employers, including threats, interrogations, promises of benefits to avoid unionization, or spying that is intended to interfere with the employees' rights. The National Labor Relations Board (NLRB) has the authority to administer and enforce the NLRA.

After a period of decline during the 1980s and early 1990s, unions have again assumed an offensive stance in organizing employees and adding to their membership rolls. Unions have adopted aggressive strategies to (in the words of AFL-CIO President John Sweeney) "organize every working woman and man who needs a better deal and a new voice."[1] This enthusiasm seems to have rejuvenated union activists. Many unions have scaled back traditional organization drives and moved toward a new culture of innovation. This section will provide insight into the innovative tactics adopted by union organizers and discuss strategies for employers to use in order to reduce the likelihood of a successful union campaign.

19.2 Union-Organizing Tactics

19.3 Salting One familiar tactic that continues to be popular is "salting,"[2] the practice of sending a union member or sympathizer to apply for a job at a nonunionized workplace. These individuals, who are either volunteers or paid by the union, are known as "salts." The NLRA expressly protects union organizers from discharge based on union affiliation, and the United States Supreme Court has extended the same protection to job applicants.[3] In that case, a union filed a complaint with the NLRB after the company refused to interview 10 of 11 job applicants when it learned that they were union members. Despite the fact that these 10 individuals were paid union organizers, the Court held that they fell within the NLRA's definition of "employee" and could not be discriminated against because of their union affiliation. As a result, salts often openly disclose their union membership or advocacy when applying for work, which has the effect of putting the employer on notice that the salts fall within the legal protection of the NLRA.

19.4 Intermittent/Partial Strikes In an intermittent strike, workers halt production or work as part of a plan to force the company to accede to certain worker demands. They generally occur when a union salt has found his or her way into an

---

[1] 44 Daily Labor Report (BNA) (March 6, 1996).

[2] *See Tualatin Elec., Inc. v. Int'l Bhd. of Elec. Workers, Local No. 48*, 1993 WL 361183 (1993) (explaining the origin of the term as derived from the use of the term "salt" as in "salting a mine," which is the artificial introduction of metal or ore into a mine by subterfuge to create the false impression that the material was naturally occurring).

[3] *NLRB v. Town & Country Elec., Inc.*, 516 U.S. 85 (1995).

operation. As a rule, however, intermittent strikes by union employees aimed at forcing an employer to bow to their contract requests are unlawful. This principle extends to employees' refusal to work mandatory overtime. The courts and the NLRB grant a small amount of leeway to intermittent strikes, though, and usually do not find unlawful behavior where the intermittent strike is a one-time incident or occurs several times for unrelated reasons. More latitude is granted to intermittent strikers by the courts when the strikers are nonunionized.

A related tactic is the partial strike, in which employees refuse to perform a certain aspect of their jobs. It too is illegal, but courts generally hold that a partial strike exists only when employees blatantly refuse to perform some essential duty while remaining on the job.

One final strike-type approach is dubbed "work-to-rule," in which employees perform only those tasks absolutely required by their employment, while refusing to do things they previously did out of goodwill or because the employer requested it. The NLRB has not ruled on the legality of this tactic, meaning it will recur until and unless it is found illegal in a future ruling.

19.5   Nontraditional Picketing   John J. Sweeney won the presidency of the AFL-CIO based on a promise of new aggressive organizational strategies. Because of this emphasis, the AFL-CIO and its affiliated unions have spent millions of dollars to develop a more focused, strategic approach and new nontraditional methods of organizing unions.

Picketing and passing out handbills at job sites have been favorite traditional union activities for decades. However, more recently, unions have attempted nontraditional picketing methods to facilitate union organization. Nontraditional picketing is nontraditional in location rather than style. It moves the picketing from the work site to corporate headquarters or a corporate executive's home. Although nontraditional picketing lessens the union's chance for contact at the picket line with workers whom the union seeks to organize, the union may receive heightened media attention due to its chosen location. If the media attention is sympathetic in nature, it may aid the union in organizing workers.

Another new nontraditional method of organizing is high-tech in nature, via the Internet. Through the Internet, unions may be able to reach people in their homes with electronic handbills. Additionally, the Internet can be used to organize boycotts and protests.

19.6   Appropriate Employer Responses to Union Activism

Employers may legally ban nonemployee union organizers and sympathizers from company property, unless there is no other reasonable means for the union to reach employees. In light of the fact that in most situations there are other reasonable ways to get the union's message to employees, a nonsolicitation/distribution policy prohibiting access to employees (including work areas, cafeteria, and parking lots), if strictly enforced, will generally suffice to keep out nonemployee union advocates. However, in order to be effective, any nonsolicitation/distribution policy must be applied in a nondiscriminatory fashion—that is, it must be invoked to prohibit any acts that violate it, not just those that arouse management concern. For example, in *Lucile Salter Packard Hospital v. NLRB*,[4] the defendant hospital had a nonsolicitation policy that prohibited nonemployees from distributing literature or soliciting on hospital property. Despite this rule, the hospital allowed several outside groups (including an insurance company and credit union) access to the hospital to solicit employees. When a union representative attempted to distribute union literature on hospital grounds, she was denied access pursuant to the hospital's nonsolicitation policy. Her union filed an unfair labor practice against the hospital, insisting that the policy was discriminatorily applied to keep out union activists. The union prevailed.

As the foregoing case makes clear, a company that permits employee solicitations by certain organizations, including charities, on work time cannot legally hide behind its nonsolicitation policy to bar union solicitations during the same hours. As a result, a nonsolicitation policy is only as good as the supervisors who enforce it. Therefore, it is important that contractors ensure that their supervisors understand the importance of consistent application to all employment policies.

In addition to the policy against solicitation and distribution, uniform application of the following policies will also assist employers in combating union organization: (1) no loitering—a policy that requires nonworking employees and nonemployees to leave the premises unless conducting business with the company; (2) restrictions on access to employee names and addresses—access to employee information should be restricted to upper-level management of the company, so as to avoid requests for employee information by the union prior to the establishment of the bargaining unit; and (3) limited use of company bulletin boards—bulletin boards should be limited to company use only, so as to avoid sharing bulletin board space with union activists. Again, keep in mind that the foregoing policies must be strictly and uniformly enforced.

Additionally, one of the simplest tactics to avoid unionization, and salting in particular, is to explain in some detail during the interviewing process the terms and conditions of employment. Wages or fringe benefits that fall below what the union is accustomed to may discourage the casual or underfunded salt from completing the application process. Moreover, a thorough application procedure, requiring references and other information, can reveal salts who, despite the legal protections, attempt to evade being discovered during the hiring process. As with all employment policies, contractors need to ensure that all individuals involved in the hiring process, including nonmanagement personnel, strictly follow any and all prerequisites to the letter to avoid a union claim that nonunion applicants were not asked for references or otherwise faced less of a hurdle to employment. It is important to note that even employees who are not members of management can significantly damage the company's chances of prevailing in a union campaign. For example, statements made by a receptionist regarding the company's position on hiring union members when taking applications from salts could result in an unfair labor practice charge

---

[4] 97 F.3d 583 (D.C. Cir. 1996).

regarding the company's hiring practices. Only people who fully understand company policies and the legal consequences should comment on them to prospective employees.

19.7   UTILIZING EMPLOYEE BACKGROUND INVESTIGATIONS

One of the most important tools used in making a hiring decision is the background investigation. Employers generally rely upon factors such as credit history, prior employment history, criminal background, and driving record in considering whether a particular applicant is qualified to fill a vacant position. To obtain pertinent background information, some employers have traditionally relied upon consumer reporting agencies. However, in 1996, Congress amended the Fair Credit Reporting Act of 1970 with the Consumer Credit Reporting Act of 1996[5] (CCRA, or Act), which places significant restrictions on an employer's use of certain personal information about prospective or current employees obtained through consumer reporting agencies. The requirements outlined in the CCRA specifically apply to circumstances in which an employer seeks to rely upon such information to make employment decisions (e.g., hiring, promotion, reassignment, and retention).[6] The Act applies only if the employer relies upon information obtained from a consumer reporting agency, and does not apply to information employers obtain through their own background investigations.[7] The amendments are designed to ensure: (1) that individuals are aware that consumer reports may be used for employment purposes, and agree to such use; and (2) that individuals are notified promptly if information in a consumer report may result in a negative employment decision.[8]

Employers face a variety of penalties if they violate the Act, including criminal prosecution (if false pretenses are used to obtain a consumer report); employee's or applicant's actual damages or $1,000, whichever is greater; injunctive relief; litigation filed on behalf of the employee or applicant; punitive damages; suits by state or federal regulatory agencies (including the Federal Trade Commission); and attorneys' fees and costs.[9] Generally, actions to enforce rights under the CCRA must commence within two years of the alleged violation, or the aggrieved party is statutorily barred from pursuing a claim under the Act.[10]

[5] 15 U.S.C. § 1681, *et seq.*

[6] 15 U.S.C. § 1681b.

[7] Simply obtaining such firsthand information is not sufficient to bring an employer that is otherwise not engaged in the business of providing "consumer reports" within the definition of a "consumer reporting agency" under the Act. *See* 15 U.S.C. § 1681b.

[8] 15 U.S.C. § 1681b.

[9] 15 U.S.C. §§ 1681n, 1681o, and 1681q.

[10] 15 U.S.C. § 1681p.

Under the CCRA, a "consumer reporting agency" is defined as follows:

Any person or entity which, for monetary fees, dues, or on a cooperative nonprofit basis, regularly engages in whole or in part in the practice of assembling or evaluating consumer credit information for the purpose of furnishing consumer reports to third parties, and which uses any means or facility of interstate commerce for the purpose of preparing or furnishing consumer reports.[11]

A "consumer report" is "any written, oral, or other communication of any information . . . bearing on a consumer's creditworthiness, credit standing, credit capacity, character, general reputation, personal characteristics, or mode of living."[12]

If an employer seeks to rely upon a consumer report obtained from a consumer reporting agency to assist it in making an employment decision, it must also do the following:

(1) Certify to the consumer reporting agency that the employer has or will comply with the specific requirements of the Act, including the disclosure requirements, and that the employer will not use the report in violation of any applicable federal or state equal opportunity law.

(2) Inform the employee or applicant that the employer may request a consumer report in a clear and conspicuous manner before obtaining the report, and in a separate document (i.e., the disclosure cannot be a statement in a handbook or on the employment application). The employer must also obtain the employee's or applicant's written permission to obtain the report.

(3) If the employer plans to take an adverse employment action based, in whole or in part, on information contained in the consumer report, the employer must provide the employee or applicant with a copy of the report and a written statement of his or her rights before taking the adverse action. At least five days is an appropriate waiting time, but individual circumstances should be considered. The definition of an adverse employment action is broad, and can include hiring an applicant with a better credit history. If the consumer report has any bearing whatsoever on the employer's decision, disclosure is required under the Act.

(4) After the employer takes an adverse employment action based upon the consumer report, it is required to provide the employee or applicant with notice of the adverse action, which must include information about the consumer reporting agency and the employee's or applicant's rights.[13]

The Act imposes additional responsibilities on employers that seek to rely upon consumer reports obtained through personal interviews with neighbors, friends, or associates of the individual reported on or with others with whom the individual

---

[11] 15 U.S.C. § 1681b.

[12] 15 U.S.C. § 1681b.

[13] 15 U.S.C. § 1681b.

being reported is acquainted or who may have knowledge concerning any such items of information. Such detailed reports are described as "investigative consumer reports" under the Act.[14] In addition to the responsibilities required for employers that rely upon consumer reports, employers must do the following when seeking to rely upon investigative consumer reports:

(1) Inform the employee or applicant in writing, within three days of the request, if the employer actually orders such a report.

(2) Inform the employee or applicant that he or she can request a disclosure of the nature and scope of the investigation upon written request. This must be done before the employer actually gets the report. If the employee or applicant makes a written request regarding the investigative consumer report, the employer must promptly provide a complete disclosure of the nature and scope of the requested investigation.[15]

The principal step in avoiding liability under the CCRA is to determine whether the information being obtained reveals factors that are appropriate for consideration with regard to a current employee or applicant. For example, an employer may wish to use consumer reports only after determining whether an employee or applicant is otherwise qualified, instead of using consumer reports as a preliminary screening device to narrow the field of candidates. However, an employer exposes itself to considerable liability under the Act if the information obtained is not kept confidential. Furthermore, in order to obtain a consumer report, an employer may require an applicant to reveal otherwise unknown information pertaining to a protected classification, such as the applicant's date of birth. Accordingly, if the consumer report does not reveal information pertinent to the position sought, the employer could face liability based upon the fact that the information obtained has the effect of excluding certain protected classifications from the position in question.

If, after considering the appropriateness of utilizing a consumer report, the employer determines that it is a useful tool to assist it in making difficult employment decisions, care must be given to ensure detailed compliance with the requirements of the Act. Employers should also include a disclaimer when requesting protected information, as well as take other measures that are appropriate, to ensure that the information is not used for impermissible purposes.

19.8 EMPLOYEE SAFETY AND HEALTH

The Occupational Safety and Health Act[16] (OSHA or Act) was enacted in 1970 with the intention to "regulate commerce among the several States and with foreign nations and to provide for the general welfare, to assure so far as possible every

[14] 15 U.S.C. § 1681b.
[15] 15 U.S.C. § 1681d.
[16] 29 U.S.C. § 651, *et seq.*

working man and woman in the Nation safe and healthful working conditions and to preserve our human resources. . . ."[17] In light of the potential hazards that are often present on construction sites, OSHA has particular significance to the construction industry. Accordingly, in order to avoid civil and criminal liability, construction industry employers must be cognizant of their responsibilities under the applicable provisions of the Act.

OSHA requires employers to comply with certain safety standards and furnish a work environment for employees that is "free from recognized hazards that are causing or are likely to cause death or serious physical harm to his employees." Employer liability for violations of OSHA could potentially include injunctions, as well as civil and criminal penalties ranging from $5,000 to $70,000 per violation, depending upon the severity of each violation, and imprisonment.[18]

Employers have dual responsibilities under OSHA. Principally, employers are required to follow codified regulations regarding unique aspects of their respective work environments.[19] In addition to the regulatory guidelines, however, the Act also imposes a "general duty" upon employers to maintain a safe and healthful work environment by eliminating otherwise unregulated working conditions that may be hazardous to the health or safety of employees.[20] OSHA's coverage extends to all persons engaged in a business affecting commerce who have employees, but excludes the United States or any state or political subdivision.[21] The definition of a business affecting commerce is extremely broad, and employers engaged in the construction industry fall under the Act's coverage.

OSHA empowers the Secretary of Labor with the responsibility of implementing safety standards through rule-making proceedings.[22] The Secretary of Labor is also responsible for conducting on-site inspections to ensure employer compliance with the requirements of OSHA.[23] Compliance checks can be initiated as a result of routine inspections or employee complaints. The Secretary has the authority to obtain a warrant for inspection if the employer refuses to allow inspectors access to the facility. If the employer receives a citation for alleged workplace hazards, it can challenge the citation by seeking review before the Occupational Safety and Health Review Commission.[24] If the employer is unsuccessful in its challenge before the Occupation Safety and Health Review Commission, it can seek redress in the federal court system.[25]

[17] 29 U.S.C. § 651(b).
[18] 29 U.S.C. § 666.
[19] 29 U.S.C. § 654(2).
[20] 29 U.S.C. § 654(1).
[21] 29 U.S.C. § 652(5).
[22] 29 U.S.C. § 655.
[23] 29 U.S.C. § 657.
[24] 29 U.S.C. § 661.
[25] 29 U.S.C. § 660.

19.9   WAGE AND HOUR REQUIREMENTS

The Fair Labor Standards Act (FLSA) is a federal law that requires certain employers covered by the Act to pay their employees a minimum wage. This Act also imposes requirements on overtime rates of pay and regulates the occupational job duties and hours of child labor under the age of 18. In addition to the provisions contained in the FLSA, several other federal and state laws affect the employer's wage scheme. Many states have their own wage and hour laws that apply to individual employers. Because penalties for noncompliance with federal and state wage and hour laws can be significant, it is particularly important to be aware of these laws and how they affect each particular enterprise.

The wage and hour provisions of the FLSA apply to all employers who are engaged in "[interstate] commerce or in the production of goods for [interstate] commerce." Employers are engaged in interstate commerce if their work involves any movement of goods, people, or communications across state lines. Construction work that has a close tie with interstate production (producing or receiving goods shipped across state lines) is also covered.[26] For example, even if an employer's enterprise consists only of unloading goods that came from another state, the provisions of the FLSA apply. Coverage applies to all employers who expect or have reason to believe that any goods used or moved by their employees will cross or have crossed state lines, even if the goods are sold locally.

The activities of the employee, not the activities of the employer, determine whether the FLSA covers the employees in question. For example, most construction trade workers perform duties covered by the minimum wage and overtime provisions of the FLSA. However, work performed by executive, administrative, or professional employees as defined in the FLSA are exempt from the minimum wage and overtime requirements of the Act even if performed in conjunction with the work of other employees on a construction site. At times, an employee may be subject to coverage for some work and not covered for other work performed during the same week. In that case, the employee is entitled to coverage for the entire week, as long as the covered work was not isolated and sporadic.[27]

Any work (including maintenance, repair, reconstruction, redesigning, improvement, replacement, enlargement, or extension) performed on a covered facility is subject to the FLSA. If the project is covered, then everyone who works on the project is covered. Even on FLSA-exempt projects, some employees may still be subject to federal wage provisions if their individual activities involve interstate activity. For example, employees who regularly order or procure materials and equipment from outside the state, or receive, unload, check, or watch such goods while they are still in transit, are covered by the FLSA.

Coverage also depends on the existence of an employer-employee relationship. While individual "employees" are covered by the FLSA, independent contractors

---

[26] 29 CFR Chap. V § 776.24(b).
[27] 29 CFR Chap. V § 776.24(c).

hired to perform a service for the employer are not covered. This distinction is misleading, however, because of the broad definition of the employer-employee relationship in the FLSA. An employee is defined by the FLSA as "any individual employed by an employer."[28] An employer is defined as "any person acting directly or indirectly in the interest of an employer in relation to an employee."[29]

19.10 Basic Calculation

The regular rate of pay is based on the number of hours worked during a standard workweek. The workweek is defined as seven consecutive days, or 168 hours. The employer must calculate the wage by considering each workweek separately and may not average weeks in which less than the statutory minimum wage was earned. The employee is entitled to straight-time pay for the first 40 hours worked during a workweek and one and a half times the regular rate of pay for each hour worked in excess of 40 hours.

The FLSA does not require that employees be paid by the hour. Compensation systems involving weekly, monthly, or yearly salaries or piecework rates are perfectly acceptable as long as the total straight-time compensation divided by the straight-time hours worked equals the minimum wage. Dividing straight-time compensation by the number of straight-time hours results in the "regular rate of pay." The regular rate of pay determines the amount of overtime due to a particular employee.

Currently, the federal minimum wage for nonexempt employees is $5.15 per hour for the first 40 hours worked.[30] In most cases, employees must receive payment free and clear in cash or negotiable instrument. The only exception occurs in certain situations when employers may credit against the minimum wage the reasonable costs incurred in paying for the employee's room, board, or other facilities customarily provided to employees.[31]

Other expenses incurred may not be credited against the minimum wage. For example, although the FLSA does not prevent employers from requiring employees to wear uniforms, it does prevent employers from forcing employees to pay for the uniforms or the cleaning of the uniforms if doing so would push the standard rate of pay below the required minimum wage. Additionally, employers may not deduct expenses for tools of the trade, breakage, or suspected theft if the deduction will send the weekly wage below the statutory minimum. Deductions for theft resulting in a weekly wage below the minimum standard may be applied only after the guilt of an employee has been determined in a criminal proceeding.

---

[28] FLSA § 3(e)(1), 29 U.S.C.A. § 203(e)(1).

[29] FLSA § 3(d), 29 U.S.C.A. § 203(d).

[30] 29 U.S.C.A. § 206(a)(1).

[31] 29 U.S.C.A. § 203(m).

19.11   Overtime Calculation

In most instances, calculating overtime is not a difficult task. The employer simply multiplies the employee's regular rate of pay by 1.5 for each hour worked in excess of 40 hours. There are, however, certain situations where it is difficult for the employer to discern whether time spent by the employee constitutes compensable or noncompensable work time. Any time considered "work time" will affect the regular rate of pay, as well as the overtime calculation for each employee. Determining what constitutes compensable work time is vitally important to complying with the provisions of the FLSA.

19.12   Preliminary and Postliminary Time   One problem occurs when the employer must determine whether time spent by the employee preparing for the day's work should be compensated. Courts have recognized that small amounts of time beyond scheduled work hours may be disregarded when determining compensation. However, time spent in excess of an extremely small time span is usually considered compensable. The key question is whether the time spent by the employee outside of scheduled work time predominantly benefits the employer. If so, then the employee should be compensated.

The Portal-to-Portal Act[32] was enacted by Congress to clarify this particular situation. The Act allows employers to exclude activities that occur either prior to the time on any given workday at which an employee begins working ("preliminary time") or after the time on any given workday at which he or she stops working ("postliminary time").[33] The Portal-to-Portal Act eliminates from compensable time activities such as travel and walking time before and after work. Preliminary and postliminary time is compensable, however, if it is considered an integral part of the principal job. If considered integral, then the activity is characterized as "preparatory" and is compensable work time. For example, while time spent washing hands and changing clothes at the end of a workday is usually not compensable, time spent filling up the fuel tanks of delivery vehicles is most likely compensable.

The distinction between preparatory and preliminary is difficult to determine in many situations. As in most instances of wage and hour law, the key inquiry is to determine who is the main beneficiary of the time in question. If the questioned activity primarily benefits the employee, then the time is most likely not considered work time. If, however, the employer is the prime beneficiary, then wages for the time spent during the activity must be paid.

19.13   Waiting and On-Call Time   Employers must pay employees for all time spent "on duty." In many situations, it is fairly simple to determine when a particular employee is on or off duty. Problems develop, however, when employers attempt to determine whether to compensate employees who are "on-call," or waiting to be called to work. When considering whether to compensate such

---

[32] 61 Stat. 84, 29 U.S.C. § 251.

[33] 29 U.S.C. § 254(a).

employees, employers must pay close attention to all of the factors in order to ensure compliance with the FLSA.

Employees who are waiting for materials to arrive or waiting to work while on duty must generally be compensated.[34] It is particularly important to compensate employees for all time in which they are under the control of the employer and are unable to use the time for their own benefit. For example, time spent waiting because of machinery breakdown and delivery delays is usually compensable. Although there are no specific guidelines for each individual circumstance, it is fairly clear that if the employee is completely under the control of the employer and is unable to pursue his or her own interests, then compensation is appropriate.

Employees who are completely relieved of duty are not entitled to compensation for idle hours. An employee is considered completely relieved of duties if told "in advance that he may leave the job and that he will not have to commence work until a definitely specified hour has arrived."[35] In short, employees are off duty if they are able to spend the idle time pursuing their own interests.

Employees who are required to remain "on-call" or who must remain so close to the employer's business that they cannot use their off-duty time to their own benefit are often considered to be "working while 'on-call.'"[36] Employees who are working while on call are entitled to compensation under the provisions of the FLSA. However, simply because an employee is on-call does not necessarily entitle that person to compensation. The determination of whether payment is owed depends on a fact-specific examination of the control exerted on the employee by the employer during the period in question.

On-call employees who are permitted to use the bulk of their on-call time to perform activities for their own benefit are generally not entitled to compensation. The greater the ability of the employee to use on-call time to pursue personal interests and to travel at free will, the less likely it is that this on-call time will be considered compensable work time. Courts generally take into consideration the frequency of callbacks and the effect of the callback on the employees' time. For example, where callbacks occur throughout the on-call period, making it nearly impossible for the employee to pursue personal interests, courts generally determine that the time is compensable.[37]

Compensation for time spent on-call must be included in the regular rate of pay calculation in addition to all hours worked.[38] On-call compensation must equal or exceed minimum wage. If the employee's duties while on-call are significantly different from the employee's duties during regular working hours, then compensation may be paid at a different rate, as long as statutory minimums are met.[39]

---

[34] *Donovan v. 75 Truck Stop, Inc.*, 1981 WL 2333 (M.D. Fla. 1981).

[35] 29 CFR Chap. V, § 785.16(a).

[36] *Id.*

[37] *See Renfro v. City of Emporia*, 948 F.2d 1529 (10th Cir. 1991); *Cross v. Arkansas Forestry Comm'n*, 938 F.2d 9112 (8th Cir. 1991).

[38] 29 CFR § 778.223.

[39] *See Townsend v. Mercy Hosp.*, 689 F. Supp. 503 (W.D. Pa. 1988).

19.14   Government Contracts

In addition to the FLSA, other state and federal laws affect the administration of wages in the construction industry. State laws vary, and each company should be aware of the relevant law in its jurisdiction. On the federal level, there are several labor law[40] statutes that can affect public construction work and those performing such work. These include:

(1) Contract Work Hours and Safety Standards Act (CWHSSA).[41] The CWHSSA covers laborers and mechanics on contracts exceeding $100,000 for public works of the United States or the District of Columbia. This law requires overtime wages beyond a 40-hour week and specifies health and safety requirements.[42]

(2) Copeland (Anti-Kickback) Act.[43] The Anti-Kickback Act is intended to protect the wages of any person engaged in the construction or repair of a public building or public work (including projects financed at least in part by federal grants or loans). This act prohibits employers from exacting "kickbacks" from employees as a condition of employment and requires contractors and sub-contractors to submit weekly payroll reports and statements of compliance.

(3) Service Contract Act of 1965 (SCA).[44] Contractors performing any "service contract"[45] shall pay their employees not less than the FLSA minimum wage. Contracts in excess of $2,500 are subject to wage and fringe-benefit determinations. These wage determinations are either set by the Department of Labor (DOL)[46] or as established by a predecessor contractor's collective bargaining agreement.[47]

---

[40] While not normally considered to be a labor law, the Miller Act, 40 U.S.C. §§ 3131-3134, provides for a statutory payment bond that provides a payment guarantee to certain individuals or parties furnishing labor for the construction, alteration, or repair of public buildings or work of the United States. *See* **Chapter 14** for a more detailed discussion of the application of the Miller Act to those furnishing labor.

[41] 40 U.S.C. §§ 3701-3708.

[42] It is the policy of the United States that overtime not be utilized, whenever practicable. *See* FAR § 22.103-2.

[43] 18 U.S.C. § 874; 40 U.S.C. § 3145. Both statutes invoke potential criminal sanctions. Violation of the anti-kickback statute (18 U.S.C. § 874) carries a potential fine of up to $5,000 or five years imprisonment, or both. 40 U.S.C. § 3145 contains an express cross-reference to § 1001 of Title 18—The False Statements Act.

[44] 41 U.S.C. §§ 351–358. Violations of the SCA provide for the debarment of the contractor absent unusual circumstances (41 U.S.C. § 354(a)) and contract cancellation (41 U.S.C. § 352 (c)). *Universities Research Assocs., Inc. v. Couter*, 450 U.S. 754 (1981).

[45] The definition of a "service contract" does not encompass construction, alteration, or repair of public works of the United States, including painting or decorating. *See* FAR § 22.1003-3. However, the SCA does cover support services such as grounds maintenance and landscaping, as well as the operation, maintenance, or logistical support of a federal facility. *See* FAR § 22.1003-5 and 29 C.F.R. § 4.130. (These types of contracts may include activities normally considered to be "construction.")

[46] This is termed as the "prevailing wage" determination by DOL. *See* FAR § 22.1002-2; 29 C.F.R. § 4.143. This wage determination typically includes multiple classifications of workers and varying rates. A major area of risk for the contractor involves the classification of certain activities and wage rates.

[47] FAR 22.1008-3(b); 29 C.F.R. § 4.163; *Klate Holt Co. v. International Brotherhood of Elec. Workers*, 868 F.2d 671 (4th Cir. 1989); *Professional Servs. Unified, Inc.*, ASBCA No. 45799, 94-1 BCA ¶ 26,580.

(4) Davis-Bacon Act (DBA).[48] This act requires contractors to pay mechanics and laborers a "prevailing wage"[49] on federal construction projects performed in the United States that exceed $2,000. Violation of the DBA may result in a debarment of the contractor if the Comptroller General of the United States finds that the contractor "disregarded their obligations to employees and subcontractors."[50]

Of these four federal statutes, the Davis-Bacon Act has traditionally been the most frequent basis or source of DOL or agency actions involving contractors or their subcontractors on covered construction projects. The DBA applies to construction activity performed on "the site of the work." Generally, construction activity does not encompass manufacturing, supplying materials, or performing service/maintenance work.[51] The "site of the work" is usually limited to the geographical confines of the construction job site.[52] Transportation of materials to and from the project site is not considered to be construction for the purposes of the DBA.[53] The DBA may also apply to construction work performed under a nonconstruction contract—for example, an installation support contract. If the contract requires a substantial and segregable amount of construction, the DBA applies.[54]

The prevailing wage is the key to Davis-Bacon labor standards. "Wages" include both basic hourly rates for various classifications of labor needed for the project plus fringe benefits. DOL wage determinations are not subject to review by the Government Accountability Office, the agency boards of contract appeals, or the United States Court of Federal Claims.[55] Laborers and mechanics employed by a contractor or subcontractor at any tier are covered. Working foremen who devote more than 20 percent of their time during a workweek to performing duties as a laborer or mechanic are also covered.[56]

Many DBA disputes involve issues regarding the proper classification of work to a particular craft (wage rate) and accurate record keeping. Employees who "work with the tools" part of the time and also perform work as laborers can lead to alleged violations and enforcement questions.

[48] 40 U.S.C. §§ 3141-3148; FAR Subpart 22.4; 29 C.F.R. Part 5.

[49] 40 U.S.C. § 3142(b). DOL "prevailing wage" determinations for the area in which the project is being performed are seen by many as reflective of the local union wage agreements and job classifications.

[50] 40 U.S.C. § 3144(b)(1). This standard is more liberal to the contractor than the equivalent debarment provision of the SCA. Private causes of action also exist under the DBA. *Hartt v. United Constr. Co.*, 655 F. Supp. 937 (W.D. Mo. 1987), *aff'd without opin.*, 909 F.2d 508 (8th Cir. 1990).

[51] FAR § 22.402.

[52] *Ball, Ball and Brosamer, Inc. v. Reich*, 24 F.3d 1447 (D.C. Cir. 1994).

[53] *See Building & Constr. Trades Dep't, AFL-CIO v. Dept. of Labor Wage Appeals Bd.*, 932 F.2d 985 (D.C. Cir. 1991). *Cf.* 29 C.F.R. § 3.2(b); 29 C.F.R. § 5.2(j).

[54] DFARS § 222.402-70. These DOD regulations contain specific tests to assist in the determination of whether the DBA (repair) or SCA (maintenance) applies.

[55] *American Fed'n of Labor—Congress of Indus. Org., Bldg, and Constr. Trades Dep't*, 211189, Apr. 12, 1983, 83-1 CPD ¶ 386 The Government Accountability Office was formerly the General Accounting Office; *Woodington Corp.*, ASBCA No. 34053, 87-3 BCA ¶ 19,957. *But see Page Constr. Co.*, ASBCA No. 39685, 90-3 BCA ¶ 23,012.

[56] FAR § 22,401; 29 C.F.R. § 5.2(m).

Enforcement of the Davis-Bacon Act may begin with either the DOL or the contracting agency. The contracting officer must withhold contract payments if the contracting officer believes that a violation of the DBA exists or if requested to do so by the DOL. If an alleged violation of the DBA is not resolved at the local level, the DOL resolves the dispute. Disputes related to the interpretation and enforcement of the Davis-Bacon Act are not subject to the disputes clause of the government contract, even though the contracting officer makes the initial withholding of funds.[57] However, if the dispute is based on contractual rights and obligations of the parties, there exists a basis to submit the claim or dispute to the board or U.S. Court of Federal Claims.[58]

19.15   Independent Contractor Status Considerations

One of the most common disputes in wage and hour law arises from situations in which the status of an employee is in dispute. When determining whether an employee is a true "employee" or an independent contractor, courts examine several different factors. These factors include (1) the degree of control exercised by the alleged employer; (2) the extent of the relative investments in equipment and material; (3) the worker's opportunity for profit and loss through managerial skill; (4) the skill and initiative required by the work; (5) the permanence of the relationship; and (6) the extent to which the service rendered is an integral part of the alleged employer's business. Courts examine the entirety of the circumstances when examining these factors. When the status of an employee is in doubt, employers should err on the side of caution and make certain that they are in compliance with state and federal wage laws.

19.16   Illegal Immigrants

Congress passed the Immigration Reform and Control Act of 1986 (IRCA) in an effort to curb the flow of illegal immigrants into the United States.[59] The IRCA imposes a dual burden on employers: (1) employers must ensure the lawful right to work of all applicants; and (2) that in confirming the lawful right to work, employers do not discriminate on the basis of the applicant's race or national origin.[60] Violations of the IRCA can result in fines against employers and even jail time for the violators.[61] In order to verify an applicant's right to work, employers must check documents specified by the Immigration and Naturalization Service (INS) and the Employment Eligibility Verification Form (I-9). The I-9 requires employers to check both the identity of the applicant and the right to work. Generally, identity may be proven by presenting a government-issued photo identification, and the right to work may be

---

[57] *Emerald Maint., Inc. v. United States*, 925 F.2d 1425 (Fed. Cir. 1991). Federal district courts can entertain appeals from DOL decisions. *See, e.g., Building and Constr. Trades Dept. AFL-CIO v. Sec'y of Labor*, 747 F. Supp. 26 (D.D.C. 1990).

[58] *See, e.g., Central Paving, Inc.*, ASBCA No. 38658, 90-1 BCA ¶ 22,305.

[59] 8 U.S.C. §§ 1324a-1324b.

[60] *Id.*

[61] 8 U.S.C. § 1324b.

proven by presenting documents such as a Social Security card and a birth certificate. Some documents, such as a passport, establish both identity and eligibility.[62] When employers comply with the I-9 verification requirements, they may assert the defense of not knowing that the applicant was not in fact eligible for employment.[63]

19.17 EMPLOYMENT DISCRIMINATION

There are numerous laws that are applicable to construction industry employers that prohibit discrimination against certain protected classifications. The key federal antidiscrimination statutes that pertain to the operations of construction employers are described below. Employers must be familiar with these provisions in order to comply with the law and avoid potential liability. As mentioned previously, many state and local governments have enacted laws that are similar in scope to the following federal statutes. In fact, some of the state and local legislation may protect additional classifications that are not protected on the federal level (e.g., sexual orientation and marital status). Accordingly, construction industry employers should survey the employment-related laws in each location where they have employees or anticipate competing for work.

19.18 Equal Employment Opportunity Commission

The Equal Employment Opportunity Commission (EEOC) is the agency responsible for enforcement of various federal laws that prohibit employment discrimination, including Title VII of the Civil Rights Act of 1964,[64] the Age Discrimination in Employment Act, the Americans with Disabilities Act, and the Equal Pay Act. The EEOC's responsibilities entail acceptance and investigation of complaints, known as charges of discrimination, filed by employees and other affected persons. The EEOC also has the authority to file lawsuits in cases where it determines that there is cause to believe discrimination has occurred. Congress has also provided for private rights of action for the individuals who claim to be aggrieved by discriminatory conduct. Prior to filing a lawsuit, however, many state and federal civil rights laws require individuals to file a Charge of Discrimination with the EEOC or state agency, and to observe other technical requirements prior to initiating litigation.

19.19 Title VII of the Civil Rights Act of 1964

Title VII of the Civil Rights Act of 1964,[65] as amended by the Civil Rights Act of 1991,[66] prohibits employers from discriminating against employees or applicants on

---

[62] 8 U.S.C. § 1324a(b)(1)(B).
[63] 8 U.S.C. § 1324a(a)(3).
[64] 42 U.S.C. § 2000e, *et seq.*
[65] *Id.*
[66] 42 U.S.C. § 1981a.

the basis of race, color, religion, sex, or national origin, unless the employer can establish that discrimination based on one of the foregoing factors is permitted as a bona fide occupational qualification. Title VII also prohibits employers from retaliating against an employee based upon activity that is protected under the Act, such as making complaints regarding discrimination or participating in an investigation involving allegations of discrimination. Employees who claim that they have been intentionally discriminated against in violation of Title VII are entitled to a jury trial, and may be awarded relief, including compensatory and punitive damages.

One of the most widely utilized areas of Title VII jurisprudence involves claims of sexual harassment in the workplace. The term "sexual harassment" contemplates conduct on the part of a coworker, supervisor, or patron that is based upon sex and is sufficiently severe or pervasive to alter the terms, conditions, or privileges of the victim's work environment. Sexual harassment continues to be an ever-developing area of law, and can expose employers to significant liability. Moreover, in light of the historical male dominance of positions in the construction industry, prevention of sexual harassment should be a top priority for construction employers. To avoid complaints of sexual harassment, employers are encouraged to implement and disseminate workplace rules and policies prohibiting harassment, and to act promptly to investigate and correct any harassing conduct.

19.20   The Americans with Disabilities Act

The Americans with Disabilities Act[67] (ADA) was enacted by Congress in order to ensure that qualified individuals with disabilities are given the same employment opportunities as those provided for individuals without disabilities. Accordingly, the ADA prohibits employers from discriminating against a qualified employee or applicant based upon a disability. Nonetheless, employers are not required to employ or retain disabled individuals if they are incapable of performing the essential functions of their jobs. In such circumstances, the individual is not considered to be qualified for the position in question. Under the ADA, the term "disability" has three alternate meanings: (1) a physical or mental impairment that substantially limits one or more of the major life activities of an individual; (2) a record of such an impairment; or (3) being regarded as having such an impairment.[68] Homosexuality, bisexuality, temporary disabilities, and current use of illegal drugs are examples of conditions that are excluded from the coverage of the ADA. Where mitigating measures (such as medicine, eyeglasses, or prosthetic devices) would remove or reduce the impact of an individual's impairment, the ADA may not recognize the impairment as a disability within the meaning of the Act.

---

[67] The ADA has three titles that prohibit varying forms of discrimination by both public and private entities. Title I prohibits discrimination by private-sector employers. *See* 42 U.S.C. § 12111, *et seq.*

[68] It is important to note that under the three-part definition above, an employer can be held liable for a violation of the Act if it acts in a manner that indicates that it regards an employee as having a disability, even if the employee, in fact, does not suffer from a disability within the meaning of the Act (i.e., an impairment that substantially limits a major life activity). *See* 42 U.S.C. § 12102(2).

In order to be protected under the provisions of the ADA, an employee must be an individual with a disability, and qualified to perform the responsibilities of the job he or she holds or desires, with or without reasonable accommodation.[69] Covered employers are required to provide reasonable accommodations to qualified employees (including applicants) with disabilities absent undue hardship to the employer. In determining whether an employer has an undue hardship, the ADA allows consideration of the nature and cost of the accommodation in relation to the size, financial resources, nature, and structure of the employer's operation, as well as the impact of the accommodation on the specific facility providing it.

In addition to the defense of undue hardship, employers can utilize qualification standards and tests to screen out individuals who are incapable of performing the requirements of a particular position, if such qualification standards are job-related or reveal conditions that would pose a direct threat to the health and safety of the employee in question or his or her coworkers. The ADA provides:

> It may be a defense to a charge of discrimination . . . that an alleged application of qualification standards, tests, or selection criteria that screen out or tend to screen out or otherwise deny a job or benefit to an individual with a disability has shown to be job-related and consistent with the business necessity, and such performance cannot be accomplished by reasonable accommodation. . . .[70]

Moreover, to rely upon the direct threat defense, employers must demonstrate the applicability of the following factors: (1) a significant risk of substantial harm; (2) a specific risk that is identifiable; (3) a current risk rather than a speculative or remote risk; (4) an objective medical assessment of the risk; and (5) whether the risk could reasonably result in an undue hardship.

The ADA covers employers, including state and local governments, with 15 or more employees who are engaged in an industry affecting commerce. The definition of an employer also includes individuals who are agents of the employer, such as managers, supervisors, foremen, or others who act on behalf of the employer, including agencies used to conduct background checks on prospective employees. Employers can be held responsible for their agents' violations of the ADA. Under the ADA, employees are entitled to the same remedies afforded under Title VII of the Civil Rights Act of 1964.

---

[69] The ADA does not provide a comprehensive definition of the term "reasonable accommodation" under varying circumstances; however, the Act provides that "reasonable accommodations" may include any of the following: (1) making existing facilities used by employees readily accessible to and usable by an individual with a disability; (2) job restructuring; (3) modifying work schedules; (4) reassigning employees to other vacant positions; (5) acquiring or modifying equipment or devices; (6) adjusting or modifying examinations, training, materials, or policies; and (4) providing qualified readers or interpreters to disabled employees. *See* 42 U.S.C. § 12111(9).

[70] 42 U.S.C. § 12113(a).

19.21   Age Discrimination in Employment Act

The Age Discrimination in Employment Act[71] (ADEA) protects employees and applicants who are over age 40 from discrimination on the basis of age. In 1990, Congress amended the ADEA by enacting the Older Workers Benefit Protection Act of 1990 (OWBPA), providing guidelines for settlement or waiver of ADEA claims. The OWBPA also provides guidelines for employers to implement a layoff as a result of a reduction in force, and requires employers to justify any decrease in benefits offered to employees within the protected age classification in comparison with employees who are not protected by the Act. Employers can defend allegations of age discrimination if the discrimination is the result of a bona fide occupational qualification. In such circumstances, the employer must demonstrate that the individual's age is simply incidental to other factors that are reasonably necessary to the normal operation of the particular business.[72] The ADEA provides for back pay, liquidated or double damages, and other relief, including trial by jury.

19.22   Equal Pay Act

The Equal Pay Act[73] (EPA) prohibits employers from differentiating between employees on the basis of sex by paying wages to employees in such establishment at a rate less than the rate at which the employer pays wages to employees of the opposite sex in such establishment for equal work on jobs the performance of which requires equal skill, effort, and responsibility, and which are performed under similar working conditions. The EPA provides for limiting exceptions under circumstances where such disparate payments are made pursuant to (1) a seniority system; (2) a merit system; (3) a system that measures earnings by quantity or quality of production; or (4) a differential based on any factor other than sex. However, an employer who is paying a wage rate differential in violation of the EPA shall not, in order to comply with its provisions, reduce the wage rate of any employee. The EPA generally has the same remedial scheme as the ADEA, except that no charge or government agency involvement is required before litigation.

19.23   FEDERAL CONTRACTOR AFFIRMATIVE ACTION

In addition to the above-mentioned laws that prohibit certain covered employers from discriminating against employees based upon protected classifications, there are also federal statutes and executive orders that further regulate the workplace of employers who perform services under contracts with the federal government. In particular, Executive Order 11246, the Rehabilitation Act of 1973, and the Vietnam

---

[71] 29 U.S.C. § 621, *et seq.*

[72] 29 U.S.C. § 623(f)(1).

[73] 29 U.S.C. § 206, *et seq.*

Era Veterans Readjustment Assistance Act of 1974 all have detailed record-keeping and affirmative action requirements that federal contractors must satisfy. Penalties for failure to follow the foregoing laws and regulations could lead to revocation of federal contracts and debarment from participation in future federal contracts.

19.24   Office of Federal Contract Compliance Programs

The Office of Federal Contract Compliance Programs (OFCCP) has been delegated the responsibility of ensuring that federal contractors do not discriminate against individuals based upon certain classifications, and that federal contractors abide by affirmative action requirements of creating, maintaining, and implementing affirmative action plans. The OFCCP also has authority to initiate compliance evaluations to ensure that covered entities are in compliance with their nondiscrimination and affirmative action obligations. The OFCCP can conduct compliance evaluations by any one or combination of the following methods: (1) desk audit of the contractor's written affirmative action plan; (2) on-site review to investigate unresolved problem areas identified in the contractor's written affirmative action plan (including examination of personnel and employment policies); (3) off-site review of records; (4) compliance check (visit to the facility to determine whether information submitted is complete and accurate); and (5) on-site "focused review" (restricted to analysis of one or more components of the contractor's organization or employment practices).

The OFCCP has the authority to implement enforcement proceedings and regulations for Executive Order 11246 and the Vietnam Era Veterans Readjustment Assistance Act (VEVRAA) of 1974.[74] Moreover, although the Department of Labor has enforcement authority with regard to the Rehabilitation Act of 1973, it has adopted regulations that parallel those implemented under Executive Order 11246 and the VEVRAA.

19.25   Executive Order 11246

Executive Order 11246 prohibits employment discrimination based on race, color, religion, sex, or national origin by contractors and subcontractors operating under federal service, supply, use, and construction contracts, and contractors and subcontractors performing under federally assisted construction contracts. Additionally, all contracts and subcontracts covered under Executive Order 11246 must include a clause pledging not to discriminate because of race, color, religion, sex, or national origin, and to take affirmative action to ensure that applicants are employed and that employees are treated during employment without regard to those protected classifications. These dual obligations are contained within an Equal Employment Opportunity clause that all contracting federal agencies are required to include with their contracts with private employers. The Executive Order applies to companies doing business with the federal government under contracts or subcontracts that

---

[74] 38 U.S.C. § 2012.

exceed $10,000. Moreover, employers with 50 or more employees, and who have federal contracts worth at least $50,000, are required to prepare and maintain written affirmative action plans.

19.26   Vietnam Era Veterans Readjustment Assistance Act of 1974

The Vietnam Era Veterans Readjustment Assistance Act of 1974 (VEVRAA) requires government contractors and subcontractors to take affirmative action to employ and advance in employment qualified disabled veterans and veterans of the Vietnam era. The Act's coverage is triggered where a contractor or subcontractor has contracts of $10,000 or greater with the federal government. Additionally, employers with 50 or more employees, and contracts of $50,000 or greater, must also prepare written affirmative action plans, as well as comply with the other provisions of the VEVRAA. Coverage, however, is not triggered by federally assisted contracts or employment agreements.

Part of a covered employer's affirmative action obligation is to include in each covered contract and subcontract—and in any contractual modifications, renewals, or extensions—a clause declaring that it will not discriminate against an employee or applicant because he or she is a disabled veteran or veteran of the Vietnam era, with regard to any position for which the employee or applicant is qualified. The VEVRAA requires that all covered employers list job openings with the local employment service office (also referred to as the "mandatory listing" requirement).

19.27   Rehabilitation Act of 1973

The Rehabilitation Act of 1973[75] requires certain federal contractors and subcontractors that enter into contracts in excess of $10,000 with a federal department or agency to take affirmative action to employ and advance in employment individuals with disabilities and to treat qualified individuals with disabilities without discrimination. Under the Act, all covered employers must include an equal employment opportunity clause in all federal contracts. Additionally, all covered employers with at least 50 employees, and a federal contract of at least $50,000, must prepare and maintain an affirmative action plan at each establishment that must be updated annually.

19.28   FAMILY AND MEDICAL LEAVE ACT

The Family and Medical Leave Act[76] (FMLA) requires employers to provide unpaid leave (up to 12 weeks per year) for an eligible employee with a serious health condition, or for the birth or adoption of a child, and for the care of a child, spouse, or parent who has a serious health condition. The FMLA prohibits employers from discriminating against an employee as a result of a request for leave and requires

---

[75] 29 U.S.C. § 791.
[76] 29 U.S.C. § 2601, *et seq.*

reinstatement to the employee's original position upon expiration of leave. Employers are also required to provide access to continued health insurance, at the employee's expense, during the term of the employee's leave period. The Department of Labor has enforcement and regulatory authority of the FMLA.

The FMLA allows eligible employees of a covered employer to take job-protected, unpaid leave, or to substitute appropriate paid leave if the employee has earned or accrued it, for up to a total of 12 workweeks in any 12-month period. The FMLA also provides for employees in certain circumstances to work a part-time schedule or take leave on an intermittent basis rather than all at one time, if such a schedule is medically necessary.

The FMLA defines an "eligible employee" as an employee of a covered employer who: (1) has been employed by the employer for at least 12 months; (2) has been employed for at least 1,250 hours of service during the preceding 12-month period prior to the commencement of the requested leave; and (3) is employed at a work site where 50 or more employees are employed by the employer within a 75-mile radius. The Act defines an employer as "any person engaged in commerce or in any industry or activity affecting commerce who employs 50 or more employees for each working day during each of 20 or more calendar workweeks in the current or preceding calendar year."[77] Employers covered by the FMLA also include any person acting, directly or indirectly, in the interest of a covered employer to any of the employees of the employer, any successor in interest of a covered employer, and any public agency.

An eligible employee can take FMLA leave only as a result of a birth or adoption, or an employee's serious health condition or a serious health condition affecting a close family member of the employee. The FMLA defines a serious health condition as an illness, injury, impairment, or physical or mental condition that involves either inpatient care or continuing treatment by a health care provider.

Due to the fact that both the ADA and FMLA regulate circumstances in which an employee's health condition has an impact on his or her work performance, there is a substantial amount of overlap and interplay between the two statutes. However, the leave-of-absence provisions outlined in the FMLA are wholly distinct from an employer's responsibility to provide a reasonable accommodation pursuant to the ADA.[78] For example, under the ADA, if an employee is a qualified individual with a disability within the meaning of the ADA, the employer must make reasonable accommodations barring undue hardship to the employer. However, a covered employer under the FMLA must also afford an eligible employee his or her FMLA rights for a serious health condition. Although the ADA's notion of a "disability" and the FMLA's notion of a "serious health condition" are distinct concepts, both could apply to protect an employee in the same circumstance.[79] For example, a reasonable accommodation under the ADA may be accomplished by providing an employee

---

[77] 29 U.S.C. § 2611(4)(A).

[78] 29 C.F.R. § 825.702(a).

[79] 29 C.F.R. § 825.702(b).

with a reduced work schedule or an alternative part-time position with no health benefits for an undetermined amount of time. However, under the FMLA, the employee would be protected to work only on a reduced leave schedule (or in a part-time position) until the equivalent of 12 workweeks of leave was utilized, with group health benefits maintained during this period at cost to the employee. Under the ADA, in determining whether an employee's leave entitlement that would exceed 12 workweeks would amount to an "undue hardship," the regulations permit an employer to consider the amount of FMLA leave already taken. Nonetheless, employers are required to apply the ADA's undue-hardship analysis to each individual case to determine whether leave in excess of 12 workweeks would pose an undue hardship.

It is important to remember that an employee can select both the FMLA and ADA to redress concerns regarding entitlement to disability leave. The employee can recover under either or both statutes, but double relief may not be awarded for the same loss. Accordingly, if an employer has any question regarding the amount of benefits available under either statute, it should act cautiously and provide benefits under the statute that offers the most protection for the particular factual scenario.

➤ POINTS TO REMEMBER

- Never threaten an employee or discipline or discharge for union activity.
- Never promise that the company will reward those who oppose the union.
- Never seek or ask employees to seek information about union meetings or who is for or against the union.
- Always remember to disclose to applicants and employees that background checks will be relied upon, and obtain permission prior to seeking background investigation materials from a credit reporting agency.
- Prepare and maintain a safety manual outlining employee responsibilities and workplace safety requirements under the Occupational Safety and Health Act.
- Never discharge or discipline an employee for raising legitimate safety concerns regarding the work environment.
- Ensure that employees are being compensated at a rate not less than minimum wage or rates established by your contract with a public agency.
- Ensure that employees are compensated at a rate not less than one and one-half times minimum wage for all hours worked in excess of 40 during the workweek.
- Ensure that all employees are treated equally with regard to the terms, conditions, and privileges of employment.
- Never ask applicants questions related to previous worker's compensation injuries or medical history.

- Always ask applicants whether they can perform the essential functions of the position sought, with or without reasonable accommodation.
- Ensure that any employer obligations to provide an employee with a leave of absence satisfy the requirements of both the Americans with Disabilities Act and the Family and Medical Leave Act, to the extent that these statutes are applicable.
- Always ensure that all employment policies are strictly and uniformly applied.

20

BANKRUPTCY IN THE CONSTRUCTION SETTING

20.1 INTRODUCTION

When bankruptcy strikes a construction project, all parties involved, from the party filing for bankruptcy (the "debtor"), to the owner, other contractors, subcontractors, and suppliers, may be affected. As the bankruptcy proceeds, the debtor will be processed through the bankruptcy system and will either be liquidated or reorganized with a discharge of prior debts. In the interim, the bankruptcy may cause a major adverse impact to other parties on the project.

This chapter examines the impact of bankruptcy on three key areas of a construction project: (1) the status of contracts with the debtor, (2) the status of materials in the debtor's possession at the time of bankruptcy, and (3) the status of contract funds and alternate sources of funds. This chapter also suggests approaches to minimize the impact of a bankruptcy on a construction project.

20.2 THE BANKRUPTCY CODE

Bankruptcy laws are contained in the United States Bankruptcy Code (the Code), which is codified in Title 11 of the United States Code. The Code provides for two types of bankruptcy, both of which may be encountered on a construction project. A debtor may file under Chapter 11 to "reorganize" or under Chapter 7 to "liquidate."

Under Chapter 11, the debtor remains in control of its business and property as a "debtor in possession" unless there is a good reason for a trustee to be appointed by the court to control the debtor's property. A debtor in possession has considerable discretion and authority to continue operating its business. However, the debtor must develop and obtain court approval of a plan of reorganization that includes payments to creditors. Once the plan is approved, the debtor emerges from bankruptcy with a fresh start.

The other form of bankruptcy often encountered on a construction project is a Chapter 7 liquidation. Under Chapter 7, the debtor's assets are liquidated, creditors are paid a pro rata share of the proceeds of the liquidation, and the debtor corporation then ceases to operate. In a Chapter 7 liquidation, the bankruptcy court appoints a trustee to handle the liquidation and winding up of the business.

Whether a Chapter 11 reorganization or a Chapter 7 liquidation, the basic goal of the bankruptcy process is to give the debtor relief from debts that no longer can be paid in the ordinary course of business. Under Chapter 11, the debtor is discharged from, and does not have to pay, otherwise lawful debts. Under Chapter 7, a corporate debtor is not discharged from its debts, but all assets obtained from the liquidation are distributed, and the corporate debtor ceases to exist.

From a creditor's standpoint, a basic premise of bankruptcy law is that creditors in the same class should be treated equally. In most bankruptcies, there are several different classes of creditors, including secured creditors, which hold a security interest in the debtor's property, and general unsecured creditors, which have no security interest in property. Within each class, creditors should receive equal treatment so that no one creditor receives more than its fair share of money or other assets from the debtor. Assets of the debtor are protected in various ways to facilitate an orderly gathering and distribution of funds to all creditors.

20.3   The Automatic Stay

A fundamental element of the bankruptcy system is the automatic stay, a rigidly enforced prohibition against taking any steps that are hostile to the debtor or that affect the debtor's property. Once a debtor has filed for bankruptcy, all actions against the debtor by its creditors are automatically brought to a standstill. The stay allows the debtor in possession or trustee the necessary breathing space to determine what steps to take in order to reorganize or liquidate the company. The automatic stay also prevents any one creditor from obtaining more money or property than other creditors.[1]

The automatic stay prohibits almost all creditor attempts to collect debts or property from the debtor. The stay prohibits such actions as:

(1) Filing a lawsuit or demanding arbitration against the debtor;

(2) Continuing a lawsuit or arbitration against the debtor;

(3) Terminating a contract with the debtor due to its insolvency;

(4) Seizing the debtor's materials, tools, equipment, or supplies;

(5) Filing or foreclosing a lien against the debtor (in some states); and

(6) Collecting a judgment against the debtor.

---

[1] 11 U.S.C. § 362.

The stay is "automatic" because no court order is necessary to implement the stay. Instead, the stay is legally in effect from the moment the bankruptcy petition is filed.

20.4 Sanctions for Violation of Automatic Stay

The automatic stay is enforced by the bankruptcy court, which may impose sanctions against a creditor for violating the automatic stay. Such sanctions may include imposition of administrative penalties and attorneys' fees. Any individual injured by reason of the violation may recover actual damages, costs, attorneys' fees, and in some instances, punitive damages against the violator. Violation of the stay in connection with a contract, such as terminating the contract for default, may be treated as a breach of contract by the party terminating the contract. Because the consequences of violating the automatic stay can be severe, before a creditor takes any action against a debtor, the creditor must determine whether the planned action is a violation of the stay.

20.5 Relief from the Automatic Stay

A creditor is not, however, without an avenue for relief from the impact of the automatic stay, particularly with regard to efforts to obtain secured property held by the debtor, or to determine amounts owed by the debtor in a litigation or arbitration forum. The United States Bankruptcy Code provides that a creditor may petition the bankruptcy court for relief from the automatic stay to allow the creditor to proceed against the debtor or the debtor's property.[2] A court may grant relief from the automatic stay when the property against which the creditor seeks to take action is of no value to the estate because the debtor does not have any equity in the property. Relief from the stay may also be obtained "for cause."[3]

A debtor lacks equity in certain property when the value of the property is less than the security interest in the property. For example, a debtor may have, prebankruptcy, pledged a piece of earthmoving equipment as security for a bank loan. If the amount of the bank's security interest exceeds the value of the equipment, the bank could move for relief from the automatic stay on the ground that the debtor has no equity in the property. Because the debtor has no equity, the property would have no value to the estate nor to other creditors, and therefore the bank should be permitted to foreclose its interest.

Other circumstances may justify relief from the automatic stay "for cause." For example, a common problem in a construction setting is the failure of the debtor to maintain insurance on equipment. A creditor with a security interest in the equipment could move for relief from the automatic stay to allow foreclosure if the debtor is not adequately protecting the security interest by maintaining insurance. Relief from the automatic stay may be justified if the debtor fails to maintain or secure materials or equipment.

---

[2] 11 U.S.C. § 362(d).
[3] 11 U.S.C. § 362(d)(1).

A creditor may also seek relief from the automatic stay to allow arbitration or litigation to proceed to determine the amount of a debt owed by the debtor. In this instance, the creditor would not be allowed to proceed to judgment and collection; however, the alternate forum (which presumably would be more familiar with construction cases) would be permitted to determine the amount of the debt. The creditor's pro rata share of the proceeds of the bankruptcy liquidation or reorganization would then be calculated according to the amount of the debt established by the arbitration or litigation proceeding.

In order to obtain relief from the automatic stay, a creditor must file a motion with the bankruptcy court having jurisdiction over the debtor's case. The court must take some action on the motion within 30 days after the motion is filed or the stay is automatically terminated as to the moving party.[4] Although the court may simply set the motion for a hearing within that 30-day time limit, the time limitation allows a creditor to shorten what could otherwise be a lengthy process.

20.6 Preferential Transfers

The Code allows a trustee, and in some cases a debtor in possession, to void a prebankruptcy transfer of property or money from the debtor to a creditor. If a transfer is voided, the creditor is required to return the money or property to the debtor's estate. A transfer is voidable if it is a transfer of an interest in the debtor's property:

(1) To or for the benefit of a creditor;

(2) For an antecedent debt of the debtor;

(3) Made while the debtor was insolvent;

(4) Made within 90 days before the date of bankruptcy or one year before the date of bankruptcy if the creditor was an "insider"; and

(5) The transfer allows a creditor to receive more than the creditor would receive under a Chapter 7 liquidation.[5]

A transfer that satisfies all of the above is voidable even if the payment to the creditor was a lawfully made payment of a preexisting debt. Such transfers are termed "preferential" transfers, even though no intent to defraud other creditors is necessary. Simply stated, a preferential transfer is voidable to prevent one creditor from receiving more than its fair share of property from the debtor, even if the creditor's increased share was obtained prior to the debtor filing for bankruptcy.

Transfers that may qualify as preferential transfers include voluntary payments by the debtor,[6] involuntary collections by creditors,[7] signing of a release of claims by

---

[4] 11 U.S.C. § 362(e).

[5] 11 U.S.C. § 547(b).

[6] *Johns v. United Bank & Trust Co. of California*, 15 F.2d 300 (9th Cir. 1926), *cert. denied*, 273 U.S. 753, 47 S. Ct. 457, 71 L. Ed. 874 (1927).

[7] *Wheeler v. Johnson*, 26 F.2d 455 (8th Cir. 1928).

the debtor,[8] and garnishments of contract funds owed to the debtor.[9] A mechanic's lien that becomes effective prior to the debtor's insolvency or bankruptcy filing is generally not considered a preferential transfer because the Code provides an exclusion for statutory liens.[10]

20.7   Exceptions to the Preferential Transfer Rule

The Code provides exceptions to the preferential transfer rule.[11] Exceptions include:

(1) transfers made for new value contemporaneously given to the debtor;

(2) payments made in the ordinary course of business;

(3) loans made to the debtor for the purchase of property secured through a purchase money security interest;

(4) valid statutory liens;

(5) consumer-type debt payments;

(6) payments made on a running or open account in the regular course of business, even if made within 90 days of the bankruptcy filing; and

(7) claims of a perfected security interest holder in inventory or receivables.

Of these, perhaps the most important exception is the contemporaneous exchange of property for new value.[12] For example, a release of lien or bond rights in exchange for a payment of past-due amounts may be considered as an exchange for new value so that the payment is not a voidable preference.[13]

Although a waiver and release of lien or bond rights is not universally held to be an exchange for new value,[14] a contractor or supplier receiving a payment from an owner or another contractor in shaky financial condition can improve its chances of

---

[8] *In re Energy Co-op, Inc.*, 832 F.2d 997 (7th Cir. 1987) (release of contractual obligations is not considered new value).

[9] *See In re Riddervold*, 647 F.2d 342 (2d Cir. 1981) (payments made within 90 days prior to the filing of bankruptcy pursuant to a garnishment writ executed prior to the 90-day preference period did not constitute a "transfer of property to the debtor" and was not a voidable preference); *In re Conner*, 733 F.2d 1560 (11th Cir. 1984) ("transfer" that could be voided occurred when employer was served with summons of garnishment rather than when payments were made); *but see Matter of Freedom Group, Inc.*, 50 F.3d 408 (7th Cir. 1995) (garnishment or attachment does not transfer money or other property to a creditor, for purposes of determining whether the transfer is an avoidable preference, until a final order of garnishment or attachment is issued).

[10] 11 U.S.C. § 547(c)(6).

[11] 11 U.S.C. § 547(c).

[12] 11 U.S.C. § 547(c)(1).

[13] *In re E.R. Fegert, Inc.*, 88 B.R. 258 (B.A.P. 9th Cir. 1988) (release of payment bond right was new value); *see Matter of Fuel Oil Supply Terminaling, Inc.*, 837 F.2d 224, 228 (5th Cir. 1988) (release of letter of credit and collateral was new value).

[14] *In re Hatfield Elec. Co.*, 91 B.R. 782 (Bankr. N.D. Ohio 1988) (subcontractor's waiver of lien rights as to owner's land was not "new value" given in exchange for payment from debtor-contractor); *In re Nucorp Energy, Inc.*, 80 B.R. 517 (Bankr. S.D. Cal. 1987) (forbearance to file lien not "new value").

keeping the payment even if the payor files for bankruptcy within 90 days of the payment. The contractor or supplier receiving the payment should document that any lien or bond rights that are waived or released as a result of the payment are being given up expressly in exchange for the funds received. The waiver or release language should also be worded carefully to state that the waiver or release is contingent upon actual receipt of the funds.

In jurisdictions where a waiver and release are not treated as new value, the contractor or supplier may still be able to preserve lien or bond rights by entering into an agreement with the debtor that the waiver and release are contingent upon the paying party not filing for bankruptcy within ninety days after the payment is made. Although the payment still could be treated as a voidable preferential transfer, the contractor or supplier would at least retain its lien or bond rights. Depending upon the notice and filing requirements in the jurisdiction, however, it may be necessary to proceed with perfecting lien or bond rights during the 90-day preference period to avoid losing such rights for failure to comply with applicable time limits.

A second exception to the voidable preference rule relevant to the construction industry concerns payments made in the ordinary course of business.[15] The rationale for this exception is that payments in the ordinary course of business neither drain funds from the debtor's estate nor treat other creditors unfairly because the debtor has received something of value, that is, short-term credit.

Courts will look to the parties' past dealings to determine whether the payment at issue is consistent with those past dealings.[16] The ordinary course of business exception should apply to a progress payment made to a contractor or subcontractor in accordance with the contract payment terms or other terms established by the course of dealings between the parties. When a contractor has made irregular payments to a subcontractor or supplier over the course of the contract at issue or over the course of other contracts between the same parties, those irregular payments may constitute the "ordinary" course of business between the parties and therefore be within the exception to the voidable preference rule.[17] Courts will consider such payments on a case-by-case basis. The closer that a payment is to the ordinary business dealings between the parties, the more likely it is that the court will treat it as an exception to the preferential transfer rule.

20.8 Discharge

At the conclusion of a bankruptcy case, the debtor is discharged. The discharge is accomplished by a court order that bars the debtor's liability on most claims.[18] On discharge, the automatic stay is replaced by a permanent injunction against all judicial

---

[15] 11 U.S.C. § 547(c)(2).

[16] *In re Ewald Bros. Inc.*, 45 B.R. 52, 57 (Bankr. D. Minn. 1984) (late payments were not in ordinary course of business because payments never had been made late before).

[17] *See In re White*, 58 B.R. 266 (Bankr. E.D. Tenn. 1986) (mechanical contractor's irregular payments to a supplier were its ordinary course of business).

[18] 11 U.S.C. § 524(a).

proceedings and nonjudicial collection efforts against the debtor for debts that have been discharged. In a Chapter 7 liquidation, an individual is discharged from liability for prepetition debts. Corporations cease to exist under a Chapter 7 liquidation rather than being discharged. Pursuant to Chapter 11, a corporation is discharged by the order confirming a plan of reorganization, which generally provides for payments to creditors over an extended period of time.[19]

20.9   Nondischargeable Debts

Certain debts of an individual are not dischargeable. Such nondischargeable debts include debts for money, property, or services obtained through false statements or fraud, debts obtained through false financial statements upon which the creditor relied and which the debtor provided with the intent to deceive, and debts arising from fraud while the debtor was acting in a fiduciary capacity.[20]

In the construction setting, a construction trust fund statute usually treats all parties having possession of the funds as "trustees." Courts have reached conflicting results when deciding whether a construction trust fund statute creates a fiduciary duty on the "trustee" so that the breach of the fiduciary duty renders a debt nondischargeable.[21] Whether a debtor's violation of a construction trust fund statute results in a nondischargeable debt depends upon the state construction trust fund statute and the particular bankruptcy court's prior decisions interpreting the statute.

If the bankruptcy court determines that a debt is nondischargeable, the debtor is still exposed to liability for suit and collection. Any debt owed by a debtor on a construction project should be investigated carefully to determine whether there is a basis for claiming fraud or a breach of a fiduciary duty. Whether a transaction will fall within the nondischargeable debt exception depends upon the facts of the case and applicable state law.

20.10   STATUS OF THE DEBTOR'S CONTRACTS

20.11   Executory Contracts

When a party files for bankruptcy, all "executory" contracts remain in full force and effect. Under the United States Bankruptcy Code, an executory contract is one in which there are material obligations remaining to be performed by both parties.[22] In determining whether a contract is executory, courts typically conclude that if the failure to complete performance by either party would constitute a material breach

---

[19] 11 U.S.C. § 1141(d)(1)(A).

[20] 11 U.S.C. § 523.

[21] *Matter of Angelle*, 610 F.2d 1335 (5th Cir. 1980) (Louisiana statute making it a crime to misappropriate construction funds did not make debtor-contractor a fiduciary); *In re Johnson*, 691 F.2d 249 (6th Cir. 1982) (Michigan Building Contract Fund Act created trust fiduciary obligation).

[22] 11 U.S.C. §365; *In re Lewis*, 185 B.R. 66 (Bankr. N.D. Cal.1995).

of contract, the contract is executory.[23] Generally, a construction contract is considered executory prior to substantial completion. However, considerable punchlist work remaining after substantial completion may constitute a substantial obligation on the part of the contractor. Likewise, payment of retainage may be considered a substantial obligation. Therefore, under certain circumstances, even if substantial completion has occurred on a construction project, the construction contract may still be treated as an executory contract.

The Code provides a number of protections for the debtor in possession or trustee to address executory contracts of the debtor. For example, the Code prohibits termination of a contract solely because of the insolvency or bankruptcy of the debtor. A contract clause that gives the right of termination for insolvency or bankruptcy is void and unenforceable.[24]

20.12 Affirmance or Rejection

Under the Code a debtor in possession or trustee may affirm or reject an executory contract.[25] In a Chapter 7 bankruptcy, the trustee has 60 days to affirm or reject an executory contract.[26] Under Chapter 11, the debtor in possession can affirm or reject a contract at any time up until the plan of reorganization is approved by the court.

The debtor in possession or trustee may affirm or reject an executory contract only in accordance with relevant bankruptcy procedures, which involve petitioning the court for permission to act.[27] If the debtor in possession or trustee fails to obtain court approval for rejection, the contract continues in effect automatically.[28] In the case of a trustee under Chapter 7, the contract continues in effect only until the expiration of the 60-day period for the trustee to affirm or reject.

If the debtor in possession or trustee decides to affirm a contract that is in default, any default must first be cured and the other party must be given adequate compensation for damages incurred as a result of the default. In addition, adequate assurance of future performance must be given.[29] As a practical matter, curing existing defaults and giving adequate assurance of future performance can be insurmountable obstacles if the debtor's estate is in a condition sufficient to warrant filing for bankruptcy.

If an executory contract is affirmed, performance of contract obligations by both parties can continue in the normal course of business. An affirmed contract creates additional obligations on the part of the debtor in possession or trustee and gives substantial rights to the other party to the contract. All debts and expenses incurred

---

[23] *In re Alexander*, 670 F.2d 885 (9th Cir. 1982); *In re Ridgewood Sacramento, Inc.*, 20 B.R. 443 (Bankr. E.D. Cal. 1982).

[24] 11 U.S.C. § 365(e); *In re Computer Communications, Inc.*, 824 F.2d 725 (9th Cir. 1987).

[25] 11 U.S.C. § 365(d)(2).

[26] 11 U.S.C. § 365(d)(1).

[27] *In re W. T. Grant Co.*, 474 F. Supp. 788, 793 (S.D.N.Y. 1979).

[28] *Id.* at 793.

[29] 11 U.S.C. § 365(b).

by the debtor's estate for an affirmed contract are considered as "administrative expenses" of the estate. "Administrative expense" is a term of art applied to expenses and debts incurred by the debtor during the administration of the bankruptcy estate. Typically, an expense or debt must be shown to benefit the debtor's estate in order to be treated as an administrative expense. For example, ordinary expenses and debts incurred in the course of operating the debtor's business or liquidating the estate will be treated as administrative expenses.[30] Administrative expenses are entitled to high priority in the distribution of funds from the estate. For this reason, a party to an affirmed contract does have some assurances that the debts and expenses associated with the affirmed contract will be given high priority in any ultimate distribution in the bankruptcy.

If, on the other hand, an executory contract is rejected rather than affirmed, the rejection constitutes a breach of contract.[31] This breach of contract is treated as having occurred prior to the filing of the petition in bankruptcy.[32] Thus, damages for breach of contract by virtue of the rejection are treated as general unsecured debts that are entitled to no special treatment or priority.

20.13   Assignment

Although the debtor in possession or trustee may assign an executory contract,[33] adequate assurance of performance by the assignee must be given.[34] An executory contract may be affirmed and then assigned even if the contract contains a nonassignment clause.[35] However, if applicable state law or nonbankruptcy federal law provides that the other party would have to consent to an assignment of the contract, an executory contract cannot be assigned without such consent.[36]

20.14   Minimizing the Impact on Executory Contracts

Between the automatic stay prohibiting termination of a contract in default and the right of the debtor in possession or trustee to affirm or reject a contract, the other party to a contract with a debtor is effectively denied the freedom to take immediate action regarding a contract with a party that has filed for bankruptcy. Most construction projects require quick decisions and aggressive actions to continue the progress on the work. If a party in bankruptcy continues to perform without difficulty, the

---

[30] 11 U.S.C. § 503(b); *In re Ridgewood Sacramento, Inc.*, 20 B.R. 443 (Bankr. E.D. Cal. 1982).

[31] 11 U.S.C. § 365(g).

[32] 11 U.S.C. § 365(g).

[33] 11 U.S.C. § 365(f).

[34] 11 U.S.C. § 365(f)(2)(B).

[35] 11 U.S.C. § 365(f)(1).

[36] 11 U.S.C. § 365(c)(1); *See Matter of West Electronics, Inc.*, 852 F.2d 79 (3d Cir. 1988) (government contract not assignable unless the government consents (41 U.S.C. § 15)); *In re Pioneer Ford Sales, Inc.*, 729 F.2d 27 (1st Cir. 1984) (franchise agreement not assignable under state law without consent); *In re Braniff Airways, Inc.*, 700 F.2d 935 (5th Cir. 1983) (airport landing slots not assignable under local law).

bankruptcy may not have any impact. However, if the debtor in possession or trustee ceases performance but fails to take prompt action to reject the contract, the impact on the progress of construction can be immediate and severe. Fortunately, certain measures can be taken to minimize the impact of a debtor's executory contract on a construction project.

20.15   *Terminate before Bankruptcy*   In many cases, there are advance signs that a party on a construction project is about to file for bankruptcy. The problems inherent in having an executory contract with a debtor can be avoided by terminating the contract prior to the bankruptcy filing. However, the termination must be based on a default for some reason other than insolvency or impending bankruptcy, or the contract must contain a termination for convenience clause. In order for a termination to be effective, all applicable contract termination procedures must be followed. Any required notice and cure period must run in full before the bankruptcy filing. Otherwise, the termination cannot be made final because of the automatic stay.

The right to affirm or reject a contract does not apply if the contract has been terminated before the bankruptcy petition is filed. After termination, there is no legally existing contract to be affirmed or rejected.

20.16   *Exercise Contract Rights*   A typical construction contract includes a clause allowing an owner or general contractor (or a subcontractor in the case of a sub-subcontractor in bankruptcy) to supply the necessary labor, materials, and equipment to complete the other party's work in the event of a failure of performance. If a contractor or subcontractor files for bankruptcy and ceases performance, the other party to the contract could use such a clause to supplement the debtor's forces without violating the automatic stay and without violating the right of the debtor in possession or trustee to affirm or reject the contract. Typically, such a contractual clause would permit the costs incurred for supplementing the debtor's forces to be backcharged to the debtor in possession or trustee. Costs not recovered through backcharges become general, unsecured claims against the estate when a contract has been rejected, and administrative expenses of the estate when a contract has been affirmed.

20.17   *Seek Relief from the Automatic Stay*   If the debtor is in default of its contract, the other party may petition for relief from the automatic stay to allow termination of the contract. Such a request limits the period of uncertainty as to whether the debtor will affirm or reject the contract. The motion forces the debtor in possession or trustee to take a position on the contract, and the other party to the contract is assured that the bankruptcy judge will act within a reasonable time on the motion. A party that can demonstrate that the contract is seriously in default and has few hopes for a cure would likely establish good cause for lifting the stay. As a practical matter, if the debtor's situation is hopeless, the debtor in possession or trustee may not oppose lifting the stay to allow termination, thereby agreeing to the requested relief.

20.18   Seek a Time Limit on Affirming or Rejecting the Contract   If the debtor continues performing the contract, and is not in default, there are no grounds for terminating the contract. As previously discussed, neither insolvency nor bankruptcy standing alone is a ground for termination. The Chapter 11 debtor that continues performance, therefore, has a prolonged period of time during which it may decide to affirm or reject the contract. However, even if a contract is not in default, the Code allows the nonbankrupt party to petition the bankruptcy court to set a "reasonable" time limit on the debtor in possession's or trustee's choice to affirm or reject the contract. While the question of what is a "reasonable" time depends on the circumstances of each case, where the contract is not in default, this request for a time limit to affirm or reject the contract is the only way to shorten the process.

20.19   STATUS OF MATERIALS AND EQUIPMENT

On a construction project, materials and equipment incorporated into the work can easily amount to half the value of the project. At any given moment during construction, materials and equipment needed for the project will be in the possession of suppliers, subcontractors, the contractor, or the owner. In addition, materials and equipment may or may not be paid for, depending upon whether the materials are installed, stored, stored at site, in transit, or still in the possession of a supplier. When any party on a construction contract files for bankruptcy, the question of ownership of materials and equipment inevitably arises.

20.20   Property of the Debtor's Estate

In the event of a bankruptcy, unless the debtor in possession or trustee continues performance, construction materials and equipment intended for the project may be seized by the debtor in possession or trustee and used for reorganization of the estate in the case of a Chapter 11 or in a liquidation of assets in a Chapter 7. Problems with materials and equipment arise primarily when the debtor in possession or trustee attempts to make materials and equipment part of the estate rather than allowing materials and equipment to be incorporated into the project.

The debtor's bankruptcy estate consists of all of the debtor's legal and equitable interests in property as of the date of filing the bankruptcy petition.[37] The extent and validity of the debtor's interest in such property, however, is a question of state law rather than bankruptcy law.[38]

The ultimate use of materials and equipment intended for incorporation into the project depends upon who has possession of materials, whether the materials are paid for, the terms and conditions of the contract, and the intentions of the debtor in possession or trustee regarding affirming or rejecting the contract. If as of the bankruptcy filing the debtor has not yet been paid for the materials in a progress payment, the materials will be considered property of the debtor's estate. If the debtor rejects

[37] 11 U.S.C. § 541(a)(1).
[38] *In re Livingston*, 804 F.2d 1219 (11th Cir. 1986).

the construction contract, the materials may be used for a Chapter 11 reorganization or a Chapter 7 liquidation. If the debtor in possession or trustee affirms the contract, the materials and equipment can be installed and paid for in a progress payment in the ordinary course of business.

20.21 Supplier's Right to Recover Goods

A supplier must exercise caution in recovering materials from a debtor in possession or trustee. However, if the debtor has not paid for the materials or equipment, the supplier of the materials or equipment can repossess them in certain circumstances. Under the Code, a supplier of goods can regain possession of materials delivered to an insolvent debtor if the supplier demands their return within 10 days after the debtor's receipt of the goods.[39] Although the automatic stay does not apply to the supplier's reclaiming of the goods in such a circumstance, suppliers must be extremely diligent in exercising the right to recover goods. The 10-day demand period is obviously very short, and the right to recover goods cannot be exercised if the debtor was solvent at the time of delivery.

An owner, contractor, or subcontractor must be alert to the possibility that stored materials or equipment for which payment has been made may be seized by the supplier for nonpayment. The safe course is to make sure that the goods were delivered more than 10 days prior to making payment. After the 10-day recovery period has run, with certain narrow exceptions, the automatic stay prohibits seizure. Even if the materials or equipment are covered by a security agreement giving the supplier a security interest in the goods, the supplier cannot repossess them without obtaining relief from the automatic stay from the bankruptcy court.[40]

The supplier may recover materials and equipment only where the goods are still in the debtor's possession.[41] Materials and equipment that have been incorporated into the work are not subject to seizure. On the other hand, stored materials and materials stored at the project site could be at risk, depending on the contract terms governing possession, risk of loss, and title to the goods.

20.22 Stored Materials

Special problems arise when materials have been paid for but have not been permanently incorporated into the work. The debtor in possession or trustee could claim that stored materials are property of the bankruptcy estate because the debtor has some legal or equitable interest, even though the materials have already been paid for in a progress payment.[42] The contrary argument is that the debtor's estate no longer has any legal or equitable interest in the materials or equipment because the debtor received full value upon payment.

[39] 11 U.S.C. § 546(c).

[40] 11 U.S.C. § 362(d).

[41] *In re Rawson Food Serv., Inc.*, 846 F.2d 1343 (11th Cir. 1988).

[42] *See In re A-1 Hydro Mechanics Corp.*, 92 B.R. 451, 457 (Bankr. D. Haw. 1988).

The owner, contractor, or subcontractor can obtain some protection against claims of a debtor in possession or trustee to stored materials by including appropriate terms in the contract. One alternative is to include a contract clause that treats stored materials as a bailment arrangement. As a "bailee," the debtor does not have any property interest in the materials or equipment. Lacking a property interest, the debtor in possession or trustee would have no right to use the property in a Chapter 11 reorganization or a Chapter 7 liquidation.[43] Another option is to include a clause that passes title to stored materials to the owner or general contractor upon payment. In light of such a clause, it would be unlikely that the debtor in possession or trustee would prevail in claiming that the debtor's estate has a property interest in the goods.[44] Clauses affecting title and possession of materials and equipment must be coordinated carefully with clauses on insurance and risk of loss.

20.23 Voiding Unperfected Security Interests

The Code gives a debtor in possession or trustee the authority to void unperfected security interests in property.[45] Under the Code, a debtor in possession or trustee obtains a secured interest in property in which the debtor has any legal or equitable interest other than mere possession. If the debtor in possession or trustee voids an unperfected security interest in property, the security interest given to the debtor in possession or trustee takes priority and allows seizure of the goods. This provision of the Code is known as the "strong-arm" provision.

The strong-arm provision has been applied to construction materials to allow a trustee to seize materials provided by a general contractor to a debtor-subcontractor for installation on the project. Even though the general contractor retained title to the materials, the general contractor's interest was treated as a mere security interest. The trustee was permitted to void the general contractor's security interest because a Uniform Commercial Code (UCC) financing statement had not been recorded, a requirement for perfecting the general contractor's security interest. Thus, the trustee was entitled to possession of the materials.[46]

The lesson to be learned from the above example should be obvious. If there is any indication that the jurisdiction in which the project is being constructed would treat the owner's or contractor's interest in stored materials as a security interest, the safest course of action is to file a UCC financing statement to protect the security interest from being voided under the strong-arm provision of the Code.

---

[43] *Matter of Ray Slattery, Inc.*, 54 B.R. 642 (Bankr. D. N.J. 1985).

[44] *In re American Boiler Works*, 220 F.2d 319 (3d Cir. 1955) (ships and shipbuilding materials became property of the government under a contract clause passing title, and therefore, stored materials were not part of the debtor's estate).

[45] 11 U.S.C. § 544.

[46] *In re A-1 Hydro Mechanics Corp.*, 92 B.R. 451 (Bankr. D. Haw. 1988).

20.24 STATUS OF CONTRACT FUNDS

At any given moment on a project, construction funds will be flowing through the system for payment to the contractor, subcontractors, laborers, and suppliers. If one of the parties in the payment process files for bankruptcy, any funds in the system could be claimed by the debtor in possession or trustee as property of the estate. It is possible, though unlikely, that payment will be made downstream in the ordinary course of business. On the other hand, the debtor in possession or trustee may hold or seize funds intended to be paid to those downstream in the payment process. Unless those entities downstream gain control of the construction funds in the payment system at the time of bankruptcy, the funds may be absorbed into the debtor's estate and used in a Chapter 11 reorganization or a Chapter 7 liquidation.

From the point of view of the nonbankrupt participants in the construction project, the best result is for payments to be made downstream in the ordinary course of business. The filing of a bankruptcy petition, however, can set off an intense competition among the debtor in possession or trustee, those downstream seeking payment for labor and materials already provided, those upstream asserting backcharges, and banks, guarantors, and sureties that have put money into the project to make up for the debtor's financial shortcomings.

In an ideal world, all of the claimants are entitled to be made whole. The reality, however, is that only claimants with valid claims under the Code and applicable state law will be successful. Numerous Code provisions and state laws apply in the process of sorting out the competing rights and interests in contract funds.

20.25 Unearned Contract Funds

Problems arise only for funds earned for work performed. The debtor in possession or trustee cannot claim portions of the contract price for work that has not been performed any more than a contractor, subcontractor, or supplier not in bankruptcy is entitled to payment for work not performed or for materials not supplied.

20.26 Earned but Unpaid Contract Funds

A number of theories have been advanced to claim funds flowing through the payment pipeline at the time one of the parties on the project files a petition in bankruptcy. Most of these theories involve the principle that it is more equitable for the parties downstream that have spent time and money on the project to be paid the funds than for the debtor to keep the funds for use in a reorganization or a liquidation.

20.27 Constructive Trust One of the most important theories used in capturing contract funds is the constructive or "construction" trust doctrine. The constructive trust doctrine holds that construction funds are held in trust for the benefit of contractors, subcontractors, materialmen, and laborers. If contract funds are treated as being held in trust, a debtor does not have any property interest in the funds.[47] Whether or not a constructive trust exists depends upon state law.

A constructive trust may be created by a builder's trust fund statute[48] or by terms of the owner/general contractor contract that create a retainage fund for the payment of subcontractors and suppliers.[49] At least one court has held that owner/general contractor contract terms obligating the general contractor to pay for labor and materials in performing the work create a constructive trust for payment of subcontractors and suppliers.[50]

20.28   *Equitable Lien*   Rather than treating the contract funds as being held in trust, certain courts have given claimants an equitable lien on the funds.[51] Third-party beneficiary entitlement to funds is another theory that may be applied. The debtor's contract may contain terms that expressly make downstream claimants third-party beneficiaries of the payment terms of the contract. In that event, the claimants could claim funds as beneficiaries of rights created under the contract.[52]

20.29   Joint Check Agreements

Joint check agreements are entered into routinely by some owners and general contractors, but completely avoided by others. If joint check agreements are used, the wording of the agreement will have an impact on whether joint check funds can be seized by a debtor that is a joint payee on the check. A joint check agreement that expressly states that joint check funds are the property of the ultimate recipient of the funds and not the property of the other joint payee (the debtor) will make it very difficult for the debtor or trustee to claim that the funds are property of the debtor's estate rather than the property of the other joint payee.[53]

20.30   Setoff

Cases involving constructive trust or other equitable theories focus on the rights of claimants downstream in the payment process. However, equally valid and often superior rights to funds exist in relation to parties upstream of a debtor. These rights include setoffs and backcharges for claims against the debtor. In addition, parties

---

[47] *Georgia Pacific Corp. v. Sigma Serv. Corp.*, 712 F.2d 962 (5th Cir. 1983).

[48] *Selby v. Ford Motor Co.*, 590 F.2d 642 (6th Cir. 1979); *In re D & B Elec. Inc.*, 4 B.R. 263 (Bankr. W.D. Ky. 1980).

[49] *In re La Follette Sheet Metal, Inc.*, 35 B.R. 634 (Bankr. E.D. Tenn. 1983).

[50] *Crocker v. Braid Elec. Co.* (*In re Arnold*), 908 F.2d 52 (6th Cir. 1990).

[51] *Matter of Gebco Inv. Corp.*, 641 F. 2d 143 (3d Cir. 1981).

[52] *Id.* at 147.

[53] *See Mid-Atlantic Supply, Inc. of Virginia. v. Three Rivers Aluminum Co.*, 790 F.2d 1121 (4th Cir. 1986); *T & B Scottdale Contractors, Inc. v. United States*, 866 F.2d 1372 (11th Cir. 1989) (joint check agreement specified that funds in construction account were to pay sub-subs and suppliers); *but see Georgia Pac. Corp. supra* note 47 (joint check funds held to be part of the debtor's estate).

upstream often have the right to insist that contract funds be paid to downstream claimants rather than be seized by a debtor in midstream as property of the debtor's estate.

The Code provides parties upstream of the debtor a valuable right to set off certain claims against the debtor's right to payment of contract funds.[54] The right of setoff is available for mutual prepetition debts.[55] Setoff is available even though the mutual debts arise out of different transactions or contracts.[56] The right of setoff is recognized by the Code but not created by the Code. Such setoff is only available if allowed under applicable state law.

Setoff is most important for a party upstream of the debtor when the upstream party wants to pay contract funds to claimants downstream of the debtor and bypass the debtor in possession or the trustee. A general contractor may pay off claimants with claims against a debtor-subcontractor and set them off against the debtor's claim for contract payments arising out of the subcontract.[57] A project owner may set off amounts paid to a debtor/general contractor's subcontractors and suppliers against balances due to the debtor/general contractor.[58] Setoff is limited, however, to cases where the party paying off the claims has an independent obligation, such as under a payment bond or mechanic's lien statute, to make such payments. Setoff is allowed even though the claims of subcontractors and suppliers are not liquidated at the time of the petition of bankruptcy. It is sufficient that the claimants have claims that may be liquidated at some later point in settling up with the owner or general contractor.[59]

Although setoff is permitted in certain contexts, it is an action against the debtor that is prohibited by the automatic stay.[60] Therefore, a party seeking to pay claims and set them off against amounts owed to the debtor must obtain relief from the automatic stay before asserting a right of setoff.[61] Prior to making any payments to claimants, the safe course is first to develop a list of all outstanding claims and then to petition the court to allow the payment of those claims, and to set off the amount of the payments against the debtor's claims against contract funds.

---

[54] 11 U.S.C. § 553.

[55] *In re Fulghum Const. Co.*, 23 B.R. 147 (Bankr. M.D. Tenn. 1982).

[56] *In re Mohawk Indus., Inc.*, 82 B.R. 174 (Bankr. D. Mass. 1987).

[57] *In re Flanagan Bros., Inc.*, 47 BR 299 (Bankr. D. N.J. 1985). In *Flanagan*, a general contractor paid off claimants of an electrical subcontractor for work performed prior to the petition of bankruptcy. Because the general contractor had provided a payment bond and was obligated to pay off the subcontractor's debts, the general contractor was allowed to pay the debts and then set off the amounts of the payments against the debtor-subcontractor's claim for payments due from the general contractor. The rationale for allowing setoff is the debtor would have its liability extinguished by the general contractor's direct payments to suppliers under the payment bond and would achieve a windfall if allowed to collect those amounts from the general contractor for the benefit of the debtor's estate.

[58] *In re Fulghum Const. Corp.*, *supra* note 55, at 152. In *Fulghum*, the project owner had an independent obligation to pay claimants under the state mechanic's lien law.

[59] *Id.* at 151–152.

[60] 11 U.S.C. § 362.

[61] *In re A-1 Hydro Mechanics Corp.*, *supra* note 42, at 453.

20.31   Recoupment

Another valuable right that can be asserted by parties upstream from the debtor in the payment process is known as "recoupment." Recoupment is available for claims arising out of the same transaction or contract, and is not subject to the Code requirements governing setoff. Recoupment allows an owner or a general contractor or subcontractor to reduce the debtor's claims to contract funds by deducting backcharges or other claims against the debtor arising out of the same contract.[62] Recoupment is available for prepetition and postpetition obligations. Mutuality of debt is not required.[63] An owner or general contractor can assert recoupment as a matter of right to reimburse itself for costs incurred in supplementing the debtor's forces. The right of recoupment also applies to completion costs in the event the debtor stops work and the owner or general contractor is forced to complete the work.[64]

20.32   Surety Claims to Funds

A bond surety often will be obligated to step in and pay off claimants on a payment bond provided by a contractor or subcontractor that petitions for bankruptcy. The surety then is held to have stepped into the shoes of those claimants. This entitles the surety to assert all of the constructive trust and equitable lien rights that the claimants would have had to recover contract funds.[65] Because the surety's rights "relate back" to the date of the surety bond, the surety's rights often are held to be superior to other claimants, such as construction lenders, that may seek to use construction funds to pay off other obligations of the debtor.[66]

20.33   OTHER SOURCES OF FUNDS

Because of the difficulties and costs inherent in battling over construction project funds, parties on a construction project will generally seek to recover from any other available source of funds. An added advantage to recovering from alternate sources of funds is that the assertion of claims against parties other than the debtor generally does not require obtaining relief from the automatic stay. Alternate sources of funds and theories of recovery against those sources are reviewed in the following sections.

20.34   Payment Bond Claims

A claim may be asserted against a payment bond surety even though the principal on the bond is in bankruptcy.[67] Because the automatic stay does not extend to actions

---

[62] *In re Clowards, Inc.*, 42 B.R. 627 (Bankr. D. Id. 1984).

[63] *In re Mohawk Indus., Inc.*, *supra* note 56, at 174.

[64] *In re Clowards, Inc.*, *supra* note 62, at 627.

[65] *In re Massart Co.*, 105 B.R. 610 (Bankr. W.D. Wash. 1989).

[66] *Framingham Trust Co. v. Gould-Nat'l Batteries, Inc.*, 427 F.2d 856 (1st Cir. 1970).

[67] *In re Kora & Williams Corp.*, 97 B.R. 258 (Bankr. D. Md. 1988) (stay did not extend to little Miller Act surety).

against parties other than the debtor, relief from the automatic stay is not needed to pursue a payment bond claim.[68]

Sureties, however, sometimes seek an injunction against a payment bond claim under the court's equitable powers. A court may issue an injunction preventing a payment bond claim against a surety when the debtor's officers and employees are necessary and essential to assist the surety in defense of the claim.[69] The rationale is that the involvement of the officers and employees in the surety lawsuit would unnecessarily distract them from participation in reorganization or liquidation of the debtor's estate. The injunction prevents such an adverse impact on the debtor's estate. Once the plan of reorganization is approved or liquidation is completed, however, the injunction should be lifted to allow the suit to proceed against the surety. (*See* **Chapter 14.**)

20.35 Mechanic's Liens

On private projects, contractors, subcontractors, laborers, and materialmen ordinarily have the right to file a mechanic's lien under applicable state law to collect unpaid sums due on a construction project. The impact of bankruptcy on mechanic's lien rights depends upon which party files the petition in bankruptcy and the nature of the mechanic's lien right under underlying state law.

In the case of an owner bankruptcy, the automatic stay may prohibit filing a mechanic's lien against the owner's property, depending upon the nature of the lien under the applicable state law. In many states, filing a notice of a mechanic's lien is retroactive to the date on which the services and materials were first supplied. In these states, filing a notice of mechanic's lien does not violate the automatic stay, because the filing is said to "relate back" to a date prior to the filing of the petition.[70] If state law does not provide that filing the notice relates back to the date services were first provided, then filing a lien violates the automatic stay.[71] In states where the filing does not relate back, a motion for relief from the stay should be filed immediately to seek permission to file the lien prior to the expiration of the period allowed under state law.

If a mechanic's lien already was filed prior to the owner's bankruptcy, the automatic stay prohibits filing an action against the owner to foreclose the lien.[72] While actually filing in state court to foreclose the lien is prohibited, the Code does allow the filing of a notice to temporarily satisfy a state law requirement for filing suit to perfect the lien.[73] The Code also tolls the running of the period for filing suit to perfect the lien until 30 days after relief from the stay is granted or the underlying

---

[68] *United States ex rel Central Bldg Supply, Inc. v. William F. Wilke, Inc.*, 685 F. Supp. 936 (D. Md. 1988).

[69] *Id*. at 938–39.

[70] *Matter of Peek Const. Co.*, 80 B.R. 226 (Bankr. N.D. Ala. 1986) (mechanic's lien relates back under Alabama law).

[71] *Matter of Gotta*, 47 B.R. 198 (Bankr. W.D. Wis. 1985).

[72] *In re Bain*, 64 B.R. 581, 583 (Bankr. W.D. Va. 1986).

[73] 11 U.S.C. § 546(b).

bankruptcy case is discharged.[74] Some states allow perfection of a mechanic's lien by filing a proof of claim in the bankruptcy court. In these states, no other action is necessary to perfect the lien after the proof of claim is filed.

In the case of a general contractor bankruptcy, claimants downstream may file a lien against the owner's property without violating the automatic stay because the automatic stay extends only to the debtor and the debtor's property. Whether the claimants can file suit to foreclose on the lien depends upon underlying state law. In states where the general contractor is treated as a necessary party to the foreclosure action, filing suit to foreclose a mechanic's lien violates the automatic stay, and the claimant must obtain relief from the automatic stay in order to foreclose on the lien.[75] In states treating the general contractor as a necessary party to a foreclosure action, the claimant should act immediately to obtain relief from the automatic stay to allow the foreclosure proceeding to go forward against the owner's property.

20.36 Guarantors

The parties on a construction project sometimes obtain guarantees of performance from the other parties with which they contract. This may take the form of a personal guarantee by a corporate shareholder or a guarantee by a parent company of a subsidiary. A debtor's guarantor is not treated as being the same entity as the debtor and therefore is not protected by the automatic stay.[76] As with bond sureties, some courts will issue an injunction precluding an action against a guarantor where the guarantor is a principal of the debtor and its full attention is needed for a reorganization or liquidation of the estate.[77]

➤ POINTS TO REMEMBER

The Bankruptcy Code

- There are two types of bankruptcy: Chapter 11 reorganization and Chapter 7 liquidation. A Chapter 11 debtor is discharged from its debt and can continue to run its business with a court-approved plan of reorganization. A Chapter 7 debtor has its business liquidated by a court-appointed trustee.

The Automatic Stay

- The automatic stay prevents any creditor from taking a step that is hostile toward the debtor, including filing a lawsuit, terminating a contract, filing a lien, and so on.

---

[74] 11 U.S.C. § 108.

[75] *In re Nash Phillips/Copus, Inc.*, 78 B.R. 798 (Bankr. W.D. Tx. 1987).

[76] *Browning Seed, Inc. v. Bayles*, 812 F.2d 999 (5th Cir. 1987).

[77] *In re Otero Mills, Inc.*, 25 B.R. 1018 (Bankr. D. N.M. 1982) (debtor's shareholder); *In re Johns-Manville Corp.*, 26 B.R. 420 (Bankr. S.D.N.Y. 1983) (debtor's key employees); *In re Comark*, 53 B.R. 945 (Bankr. C.D. Cal. 1985) (general partners of debtor).

- The stay does not require a court order, and persons violating it are subject to sanctions.
- Relief from the automatic stay can be obtained "for cause," such as when the creditor has no equity in the property, fails to maintain insurance on the property, fails to maintain or secure the property, or when proceedings are necessary to determine the debt owed by the debtor.

Preferential Transfers

- Under certain conditions, a debtor can have a "prebankruptcy" transfer of property to the creditor voided.
- A contemporaneous exchange of property for new value is not a voidable preference.
- When the debtor receives valuable property in exchange for a transfer made in the ordinary course of business, the transfer cannot be voided.

Discharge

- After bankruptcy, the debtor is discharged of all its remaining debts, and a permanent injunction is placed against all creditors. Debts arising from fraud or false statement tend to be nondischargeable, leaving the debtor liable to them after bankruptcy.

Status of the Debtor's Contracts

- All construction contracts remain in effect after bankruptcy until substantial completion.
- The debtor has the right to affirm or reject any executory contract.
- To affirm a contract in default, the default must be cured and adequate assurances of future performance must be given by the debtor.
- Debts and expenses incurred by the debtor for an affirmed contract are treated as administrative expenses of the estate.
- Debtors can assign executory contracts if allowed under state law.

Minimizing the Impact on Executory Contracts

- The following methods can minimize the impact of contracting with a debtor: (1) terminate the contract before bankruptcy if nonfinancial reasons for default exist, (2) exercise protection rights under the contract, (3) seek relief from the automatic stay, and (4) seek a time limit on affirming or rejecting the executory contract.

Status of Materials and Equipment

- Materials and equipment slated for installation into the project may be used by the debtor for the reorganization or liquidation of its estate.
- A party can recover goods in the debtor's possession that have not been paid for and have not been incorporated into the project.
- Precautions must be taken to prevent a debtor from claiming property in its possession that another party has already paid for.

Voiding Unperfected Security Interests

- This strong-arm provision of the Bankruptcy Code allows a trustee to void an unperfected security loan in construction materials.

Status of Contract Funds

- A party can use several methods to recover contract funds from a debtor.
- The debtor cannot seize contract funds that are held in constructive trust for the benefit of the nonbankrupt parties.
- Pursuant to specific contract provisions, parties may have an equitable lien on contract funds held by the debtor.
- The use of joint check procedures can prevent the ultimate seizure by the debtor of contract funds slated for a lower-tier subcontractor or supplier.
- Owners and general contractors can set off monies paid to lower-tier subcontractors and suppliers against contract funds owed to the debtor/subcontractor when the owner or general contractor has an independent obligation to pay the claims of lower-tier parties. The party can then recoup contract funds it owes to the debtor in an amount representing backcharges or other claims it has against the debtor.
- The surety of the debtor that has made payments to the debtor's claimants has the same rights against the debtor as those bond claimants.

Other Sources of Funds

- Parties can seek relief from a debtor's surety unless the surety secures an injunction preventing the claim.
- Depending upon state law, the filing of a mechanic's lien against a bankrupt owner may violate the automatic stay.
- The automatic stay prevents filing an action against a bankrupt owner to foreclose a valid lien.
- State law determines whether an action to foreclose a lien for monies owed by a bankrupt contractor violates the automatic stay.
- An action on the guarantee of an entity or person other than the debtor does not violate the automatic stay.

21

RESOLUTION OF CONSTRUCTION DISPUTES

On a construction project of any complexity, disputes are often the rule, not the exception. Avoidance or quick resolution of disputes is often crucial to the economic success of the project. In this regard, one point must be stressed at the outset: the key to quick resolution of disputes is the use of systems designed to collect, preserve, and organize information, including documents, throughout the project. Project documentation helps all parties avoid disputes and facilitates prompt resolution through negotiation. This chapter addresses presentation of claims and dispute resolution through alternative dispute-resolution measures and litigation.[1]

It is always advisable to try to settle construction disputes before resorting to more formal dispute procedures. Anyone who has been involved in a typically costly and time-consuming legal battle will affirm the old adage: "A poor settlement beats a good lawsuit."

21.1 EARLY CLAIM RECOGNITION AND PREPARATION

Before there can be any preparation or prosecution of a claim, the claim must be recognized. Early recognition is required to ensure that notice requirements are met and that evidence needed to support the claim is preserved. Familiarity with the contract requirements is needed to recognize claims and to avoid unknowingly providing or accepting a nonconforming quantity, quality, or method of performance. Consequently, all job-site personnel should be familiar with the contract terms, including the plans and specifications, the general conditions, schedules, and special provisions, so they

---

[1] The basic discussion in this chapter on claim preparation and documentation also applies to claims on federal government construction projects. The specific procedures and statutes governing the submission and resolution of a claim on a federal government project are addressed in **Chapter 22** of this book.

can evaluate the performance actually rendered or demanded, as compared to the performance specified in the contract. In-house educational programs to enhance this ability and better equip job personnel to identify and handle possible claim situations should also be considered.

Of course, asserting a claim for every minor incident or disagreement would be counterproductive. Filing claims with little merit or significance merely wastes resources, strains project relationships, and squanders credibility. Conversely, never filing a claim on the assumption that every dispute can be amicably resolved at the end of the project without "ruffling feathers" is naïve. Part of an effective program for identifying claims requires targeting those incidents that are sufficiently meritorious and substantial to justify the cost of preparing and prosecuting a claim.

Once a determination is made that a claim merits prosecution, comprehensive preparation and organization should be promptly undertaken. The facts, evidence, and documents bearing on the claim should be assembled, organized, and reviewed when they are fresh and before they are lost or forgotten. This preparation should be undertaken with an eye toward resolving the claim in the formal setting of arbitration, litigation, or another dispute-resolution process, while still seeking early resolution through informal and less onerous means. If early resolution is not achieved, complete preparation at an early stage provides important insight for developing a claim strategy and a factual foundation that can be relied upon, subject to revision, as prosecuting the claim continues.

The first step in claim preparation should be an exhaustive investigation of the claimant's own records and sources of information about the project and the claim. Project records are generally voluminous. Although the review of the records must be sufficient in scope to cover the documents relevant to the claim and anticipated defenses, it must also be sufficiently focused and specific enough to avoid inundating the claim-preparation process with unnecessary and irrelevant documents. There are certain categories of documents that almost always merit some consideration, such as the contract documents, change orders, RFIs, pay applications, daily logs or reports, bonds and insurance policies, and certain key correspondence. Some further organization of the documents may be required beyond that used during construction in order to make individual documents relating to the claim more readily accessible.

Although documentation is certainly critical in any construction claim, it is not everything. At arbitration or trial, the witnesses will bring life to the documentary evidence with their words, perceptions, and recollections. Those individual resources should not be overlooked in the claim-preparation process, but they often are. The more remote claim preparation is from the people actively involved in the field, the more likely there will be unpleasant surprises and inconsistencies as the claim is subjected to greater scrutiny in discovery or at trial. Consequently, the field personnel involved should be interviewed to confirm that management's secondhand understanding about the facts and circumstances of the claim is accurate and complete. To the extent possible, project personnel should be utilized to staff and assist in the claim-preparation effort. At a minimum, field personnel should be given the opportunity to review the claim at various stages of preparation, and certainly before it is submitted, to confirm that they can vouch for its accuracy.

21.2 EARLY INVOLVEMENT OF EXPERTS AND ATTORNEYS

Construction claims often require the assistance of experts to help solve problems and to assemble and analyze the facts. Part of a program of prompt and cost-effective claim preparation requires considering the involvement of attorneys experienced with construction claims and other technical experts at an early stage. Of course, the use of outside assistance will depend on the size and complexity of the claim, but in most claims such early involvement will facilitate prompt resolution or better preparation for arbitration or trial and will be worth the investment. Scrimping on experienced and qualified legal and technical support for a claim can prove very costly in the long run.

The advice and guidance of an attorney experienced in construction claims and litigation is often desirable at the earliest stages of claim preparation. The construction attorney who would ultimately be charged with presenting the claim to judge, jury, or arbitrator should be consulted to ensure that the claim and supporting documentation and evidence are being assembled and preserved in a manner consistent with favorable resolution of the claim in a formal proceeding. The construction attorney need not take over the claim effort, but should be consulted to ensure that the claim effort will not be wasted or undercut the claimant's position in any proceeding that may ensue. An experienced construction attorney can also suggest competent technical consultants in specialized areas such as accounting and scheduling, and thereby help avoid the expense and frustration of relying on an individual who does not have the proper qualifications to ultimately testify in the case. Early involvement of an attorney does not presuppose a resort to litigation or arbitration. On the contrary, it should facilitate comprehensive claim preparation, which hopefully contributes to the early resolution of disputes.

Early involvement of technical and accounting expertise can likewise enhance claim-preparation efforts, and hopefully the claimant's leverage in negotiation or persuasiveness at trial. Construction is a complex process, involving a broad spectrum of scientific and technical disciplines. The immediate concern with technical qualifications must be balanced with the need to have a witness who is capable of persuasive testimony in the forum selected for resolution of claims. A technical expert respected in a particular field may be understood by a technically oriented arbitration panel but be incomprehensible to a lay jury.

Delay is a frequent subject of construction claims. Hence, scheduling analysis and scheduling experts are often involved in claims resolution. Beyond their scheduling expertise, scheduling consultants must have a detailed, working knowledge of the construction process so their analysis reflects the practical problems and difficulties experienced on the construction site, not merely a computer-generated abstraction. Likewise, it is essential that the scheduling expert involved in a claim be provided access to contemporaneous project documentation, which accurately reflects the manner in which the work proceeded. Costly and complex "as-built" scheduling analyses presented in support of claims can be severely undermined if the dates and data used in the analysis conflict with those contained in project documentation, such as daily reports or monthly schedule updates.

Certified public accountants who are familiar with the construction industry and its financial and accounting practices can also contribute significantly to quantifying and proving the financial consequence of the technical problems that generated the claim.

If it is possible, and cost-effective, to involve an expert during the actual construction phase, when a claim is merely a probability, that option should be considered. At such an early stage, the expert may be able to suggest alternative construction methods or ways of reducing the impact of an injurious condition. The expert can also assist in identifying, compiling, and preserving evidence and creating demonstrative evidence for use during negotiation, mediation, arbitration, or trial. Further, testimony based on firsthand observation of the construction can be more credible and persuasive than testimony based solely on secondhand input. There are, however, some significant disadvantages to relying solely upon the dual fact witness/expert witness to present expert opinion testimony at arbitration or trial. The expert's involvement in the project may rise to such a level that the expert develops a "personal stake" in the facts in dispute, compromising that person's credibility as the expert shifts from neutral observer to active and adversarial participant. The dual role of such an expert as both fact witness and expert witness also raises some difficulties for the attorney in discovery and at trial under the Federal Rules of Evidence. These concerns include the potential loss of the attorney-client privilege and work-product protections over communications and information shared between the attorney and the expert. These risks can be weighed only on a case-by-case basis.

21.3   THE USE OF DEMONSTRATIVE EVIDENCE

Demonstrative evidence has the special advantage of presenting in pictorial form abstract, complicated, and extensive facts. It can clarify or explain oral testimony or documentary narrative in concrete terms. In addition, demonstrative evidence adds interest and avoids the tedium of a relentless one-dimensional recitation of facts. The simplicity and clarity demonstrative evidence can provide is particularly effective in large, highly technical, and complex construction claims. But the utility of demonstrative evidence should not be overlooked in smaller, more straightforward disputes.

Demonstrative evidence can range from photographs and videos to charts summarizing facts or making comparisons, such as a chart comparing as-planned manpower to as-built manpower in order to graphically depict an overrun. Charts and graphs are often used in connection with scheduling presentations, again usually comparing the as-planned schedule to the as-built schedule, with a focus on those problems that created delays. By displaying this information in an attractive visual way, in combination with other written and oral presentations, the claim can be advanced in a more compelling and persuasive manner. The goal of the demonstrative presentation is lost if it is not clear, understandable, and firmly supported by the facts.

Discussions of the importance and usefulness of demonstrative evidence as a means of persuasion generally are found in trial advocacy materials. But there is no need to hold such a powerful and effective tool in reserve until trial. Demonstrative evidence should be developed and used to simplify the claim and persuade the other side as soon as possible.

21.4   IMPORTANCE OF CONTEMPORANEOUS RECORDS

The importance of creating and maintaining contemporaneous project records cannot be overemphasized. The success of any claims presentation, whether formal or informal, is largely dependent upon the quality of the documentary and visual evidence that can be relied upon. Contemporaneous records engender integrity and trustworthiness essential to persuasion. Federal and state rules of evidence require contemporaneity in order to admit certain types of documents at trial. The "business records" exception to the hearsay rule is often the only avenue by which certain project records are admissible. Under the Federal Rules of Evidence, a project document qualifies as a "business record" when it: (1) contemporaneously records events or conditions; (2) is authored by a person with knowledge; and (3) is routinely kept in the regular course of the business.[2]

All projects need documentation systems in place at the start of the project that are maintained through completion. Documentation programs must be designed and implemented in a manner that accurately and comprehensively records job progress and problems in "real time." Documentation programs can take many forms and can be in paper or electronic format, or both. Common types of project records include requests for information, meeting minutes, daily reports, correspondence and e-mail, job-site diaries, progress schedules, progress and defective work photographs and videotapes, as-built drawings, and cost documentation. The documentation system should be designed to record project progress and events on a continual basis. Compliance with contractual notice provisions, the circumstances giving rise to requests for time extensions, extra work, changes, differing site conditions, and the grounds for or against termination should all be thoroughly documented at the time they occur. The properly implemented documentation program, faithfully followed, greatly enhances the likelihood of resolving disputes without arbitration or litigation and winning disputes that cannot be amicably resolved.

21.5   THE COMPONENTS OF A WELL-PREPARED CLAIM DOCUMENT

Simplicity to promote prompt understanding, while making the claim interesting and appear to be well supported, is the key to effective claim preparation and presentation. One means by which to synthesize the claim is to use a claim document—that is, a written synopsis of the claim that can be presented to the opposition at the early stages of the dispute. As with essentially every other aspect of claim preparation, the claim document serves two alternate purposes. First, its immediate and primary goal

---

[2] *See* Fed. R. Evid. 803(6).

is to bring about a prompt and satisfactory resolution of the claim. Failing that, the second purpose of the claim document is to provide a blueprint or plan for further prosecution of the claim.

The claim document provides an opportunity for the claimant to explain its grievance in a complete and comprehensive fashion. The process of preparing the claim document is an important step in developing a claim strategy, because it requires the claimant to refine and synthesize the claim from beginning to end. The claim document should be viewed as telling a story. It should have a clear and definite theme that can be readily communicated, understood, and remembered. The theme should be the strongest argument supporting the claimant's theory of recovery. There will certainly be a considerable quantity of facts gathered in support of the claim, but trying to present and argue each and every one of these facts will simply overwhelm and confuse the reader. As a result, the claim document as a tool of persuasion will be a failure. When multiple and unrelated claims are presented in one document, the document must be structured to emphasize the strongest claim.

The primary communicative component of the claim document is the factual narrative. Although this narrative will certainly focus on the claimant's point of view, it should not be expressed in overly argumentative or combative terms. Instead, to the extent possible, the facts presented should be permitted to speak for themselves. The writing style should be clear and precise, but should not read like technical specifications. It is, after all, a story, not simply a recital of a string of facts. The narrative should be comprehensive and logically organized, so it can be used as a resource throughout negotiations and further prosecution of the claim. If the complexity of the matter is such that the narrative is exceedingly long, an executive summary should be prepared.

The factual narrative is often followed by a written discussion of the applicable legal principles that support and illustrate the theories on which the claim is based. Assistance from an experienced attorney in construction claims is generally required to fashion the legal arguments and otherwise to ensure that the factual narrative is presented in a manner consistent with the applicable legal principles. The need for or extent of a legal discussion is generally geared to the expertise or experience of the ultimate decision maker for the opposition. For example, in federal construction contracts, certain theories of entitlement are so firmly established and recognized on all levels that no or only a limited legal discussion is required. In other situations, the legal discussion may be a crucial element in causing the other side to recognize its liability and exposure. A one-time owner may have no idea of what a differing site condition is or why the contractor should be paid for it. On the other hand, claims against local governmental entities that contract regularly may be ruled upon by elected officials who also require an education about construction law before they can be expected to recognize the need to settle a claim.

Pricing the claim and supporting such calculations is every bit as important as establishing liability for the claim. The claim document must recognize the importance of damages and include a specific dollar figure and fairly detailed cost analysis and breakdown. Supporting information and sources should be identified and appended if they are not too voluminous.

Finally, the claim document should be used to showcase and highlight the most persuasive documentary and demonstrative evidence. The most potent documents should be quoted or even reproduced in their entirety in the body of the narrative. Those documents that do not merit incorporation into the text, but which are referenced and support the claim, can be included in an indexed appendix that is cross-referenced with and organized like the factual narrative. In this manner, the narrative can be reviewed without having to sift through every bit of paper, but that backup is readily available should further review be desired.

In addition to documents, charts, graphs, drawings, and photographs, other demonstrative and visual evidence should be incorporated into the claim document to the extent practical. Similarly, consideration should be given to including relevant reports by experts as attachments to the claim document as exhibits, with appropriate references to and quotes from the reports in the narrative.

In certain situations, the nature of the claim or the character or capacity of the opposition may counsel against submitting an extensive claim document. The opposition may not have the financial resources or genuine interest in resolving the claim by negotiation, which is a primary goal of the claim document. Instead, the opposition may seek a one-way flow of information, it being willing to receive a detailed presentation of the claim but unwilling to explain or document any response, defense, or counterclaim until trial. The claimant must evaluate whether pursuing the "race for disclosure" by providing a claim document will ultimately eliminate the roadblocks to negotiation and settlement, or simply better equip the opposition to defend the claim, without a commensurate benefit to the claimant. Generally, but not always, a sound, well-documented and prepared claim should be able to withstand and be improved through feedback from the opposition's scrutiny. Moreover, even if the judgment is made that an extensive claim document should not be submitted, that conclusion does not necessarily mean a claim document should not be prepared for internal use to better synthesize the claim and prepare for whatever proceeding may follow. Of course, if formal claim submission is mandated by the contract, such a requirement should be followed, although the extent of the submission may vary.

21.6 IMPORTANCE OF CALCULATING AND PROVING DAMAGES

The issue in construction disputes that generally receives the most attention and focus is liability. Does a differing site condition exist? Who caused the delay and is it compensable? However, the issue of damages or costs flowing from the events that give rise to liability is no less important. Too often, the issue of calculating and proving damages is given a backseat, with little precision or scrutiny applied until the eve of the trial. That approach can result in an entirely misguided claim effort, missed opportunities for settlement, and loss at trial or in other dispute forums. An early analysis of damages can help determine whether a claim really exists and the best means of preparing and positioning the claim for the affirmative recovery sought.

The problem of calculating and proving damages can be substantially reduced by initiating proper cost accounting at the inception of the project. This may help provide an early indication of the unanticipated early work, delay, or disruption. Once a claim is identified, these cost accounting procedures can be used to "capture" the extra or unanticipated costs—for example, by cost-coding extra work. Accounting measures can be established to segregate and carefully maintain separate records. If such a procedure is followed, proof of damages can be reduced to little more than the presentation of evidence of separate accounts. Unfortunately, this ideal situation seldom exists; either the problem is not recognized in time to set up separate accounting procedures, the maintenance of separate accounts is simply not possible because of an inability to isolate costs, or no attempt is made to establish the requisite procedures. These circumstances necessitate the development of some sufficiently reliable formula that permits the court or arbitrators to allow its use as proof of damages. If settlement is being sought, the claimant must likewise convince the other side of the validity and reliability of its damage calculations.

The sections that follow present specific approaches and alternatives for pricing and proving claims of the types frequently encountered. Many of the principles and possible approaches are common to all construction claims.

21.7 PURSUING NEGOTIATION AND SETTLEMENT

Although claims and disputes are a part of the construction process, they need not and should not dominate the process. When claims and disputes cannot be avoided, efforts should be redoubled to resolve them as quickly as possible. The complexity, time, and cost of arbitration, litigation, and other forms of alternative dispute resolution naturally cause the parties to favor negotiation and settlement. An approach favoring prompt resolution should be part of a claims policy, and project personnel and management should be indoctrinated and trained along those lines. Although contract provisions regarding notice of claims and other technical requirements should be complied with, other lines of communication on the project should not be overlooked as a means of bringing a claim to quick settlement and avoiding the need to have the disputes process run its full course. It is far easier and less expensive to resolve problems in the field, where they arose, than in the courtroom. Even if early settlement is not achieved, the negotiations force the claimant to seriously examine the merits of its claim and also reveal the strengths and weaknesses of the claim at an early stage.

Comprehensive and careful preparation of a claim greatly enhances the likelihood of early resolution and settlement. A party attempting to settle a claim should know its own case intimately and should anticipate as many of the opposing party's points as possible without the benefit of discovery. Use of a well-prepared claim document, as discussed above, is helpful both as a starting point and as a reference during settlement discussions. People with firsthand, detailed knowledge of the underlying facts and with the authority to negotiate are also an essential part of any negotiating effort. There is simply no substitute for the person who lived with the project's problems on a daily basis. And, most important, negotiating a claim most often means compromise, even if you believe you are in the right.

21.8 ALTERNATIVES TO LITIGATION: ADR

Alternative dispute resolution (ADR) is now well known in the construction industry as a means of resolving disputes when negotiations break down. ADR includes
mediation, Med-Arb, mini-trials, dispute review boards, and several other methods
of conflict resolution.

21.9 Dispute Review Boards

In disputes involving state and local public projects, many state and local government authorities are requiring disputes between the government authority and the
contractor to be first heard by a dispute review board (DRB) before litigation is initiated. The goal is to create a mechanism whereby disputes that occur throughout the
project are addressed without waiting until the end of the project and without inter-
rupting the progress of work. The process is somewhat similar to presenting claims
before the various boards of contract appeals on federal government projects, with
the exception that the parties have more control over the process and selection of the
panel members who will decide the case.

Typically, the DRB is composed of three panel members, one selected by the government authority and one selected by the contractor; these panel members in turn
select a third member. The parties present their case to the panel in a manner similar to the way in which they would present their case in arbitration, and the panel
then renders a decision. The difference between the DRB and arbitration is that the
DRB's decision is subject to a full appeal, unlike an arbitration decision that may be
overturned only under very limited circumstances.

21.10 Mini-trials/Summary Jury Trials

The mini-trial and summary jury trial are hybrids of the more formal arbitration and
litigation procedures. In the mini-trial, each of the parties presents its case to a mediator and to senior representatives from each party, who are generally unfamiliar with
the dispute—usually corporate executives. After hearing the presentation, the corporate representatives attempt to negotiate the dispute with the assistance of the mediator. The benefit of this process is that representatives from the disputing parties
themselves are serving as the judge, jury, and negotiators. The goal is for the representatives to hear the evidence and, with the help of the mediator, reach a settlement
based on the evidence presented, weighing the strengths and weaknesses of each
side's case.

In a summary jury trial, the parties engage in an abbreviated trial before a judge and
a mock jury. The entire trial generally lasts no more than a day. The jury then renders
an advisory opinion, which is nonbinding on the parties. Again, the purpose of the procedure is to allow the parties to see the strengths and weaknesses of their respective
cases and reach a resolution without the protracted trial and trial preparation.

21.11   Mediation

Mediation has become a popular method for attempting to resolve construction disputes. Many standard-form contracts require mediation as part of the formal process for dispute resolution. Although not a panacea for all project ills, mediation can provide a unique opportunity to resolve disputes without the costs of arbitration and litigation.

Mediation, unlike arbitration, is nonbinding. Rather, it relies on the parties' true desire to end the dispute and their willingness to compromise their respective positions to reach this goal. The mediator, therefore, does not "decide" who is right or wrong, but facilitates the process of bringing about a mutually acceptable (or in many cases distasteful) solution to the problem. Also, mediation is much less costly than arbitration or litigation and is a relatively quick process.

Because mediation is nonbinding, the timing of the mediation is a critical component in reaching a successful resolution of the claim. To have a successful mediation, the parties must agree that a compromise is in their respective best interests. This typically means that they must appreciate the strengths and weaknesses of their cases and their opponents, the legal costs of prosecuting and defending against the claim, and the costs in committing personnel to move forward with arbitration or litigation. In some cases, the parties may understand these factors early in the dispute. In other cases, however, it may require one or both of the parties to proceed with a more formal claims procedure (e.g., arbitration or litigation) until they appreciate the factors more fully. It is important to realize that forcing mediation when the parties are not ready may be a waste of time and money.

21.12   Arbitration

Arbitration is initiated when the parties are unable to amicably resolve the claim between themselves. The availability of arbitration—or, for that matter, any ADR procedure—as a means of resolving construction claims and disputes, however, must be planned and provided for at the outset of the project, preferably in the contract itself. Although the parties are free to agree to arbitrate after a dispute has arisen, without mutual agreement, the parties must look to the courts. Generally, no particular form or special words are necessary to establish an agreement to arbitrate a dispute between the parties. There must, however, be a clear indication from the contract language that the parties intended the disputed issue to be subject to arbitration.

To avoid any dispute about the scope of the agreement to arbitrate, it is best to expressly state that all disputes arising from the contract will be arbitrated. For example, a widely used arbitration clause, contained in AIA Document A201 (1997 ed.), provides a simple and clear directive for the use of arbitration:

> Any controversy or claim arising out of or related to the contract, or the breach thereof, shall be settled by arbitration in accordance with the Construction Industry Arbitration Rules of the American Arbitration Association.

Arbitration is not new to the construction industry. Contract clauses providing for arbitration of disputes have been commonplace in the construction industry for many years. Although arbitration is generally perceived as a way to avoid the delays and problems associated with litigation, time has demonstrated the drawbacks as well as the advantages of relying on arbitration as a means of resolving construction claims. It is noteworthy that many of the issues discussed below with respect to arbitration may also be equally applicable to other forms of ADR.

21.13   TIME AND COSTS OF ARBITRATION

On balance, and particularly for smaller claims, arbitration does provide a faster resolution. Given the right set of circumstances, however, arbitration can be as excruciatingly time-consuming and expensive as litigation. A dispute over the existence, scope, or validity of an arbitration agreement itself can engender a protracted court proceeding and appeal before there is a determination of whether and to what extent the parties should proceed with arbitration. In addition, arbitration of larger claims involving multiple parties can match the delays and complexity of the most arcane court proceeding.

Although ultimately dependent on the parties involved and the scope and complexity of the issues, the cost of arbitration may be less than that of a comparable court proceeding. Generally, a shortened period for resolution will keep costs down, but there are certain costs that may be incurred in arbitration, just as in litigation. These costs include the examination and analysis of documents, legal research, the use of experts, the development of demonstrative evidence, and limited discovery.

The costs that can be avoided in arbitration usually involve certain trade-offs. For example, unless provided for by agreement or statute, discovery may be either unavailable or significantly limited.[3] The costs of discovery, which can be substantial, can thus be avoided, or at least diminished. The lack of discovery, however, means less preparation for and knowledge of the opposition's case. It can also possibly lead to a less focused hearing, which may then require more time and increased costs. In addition, there are costs that are unique to arbitration, such as arbitrators' fees as well as administrative fees and the cost of meeting rooms, all of which can be substantial.

21.14   Selection of Arbitrators

The qualifications and fairness of each arbitrator are essential to the viability of arbitration as a means of resolving disputes. The selection of arbitrators, like the selection of jurors, can be a major factor in the success or failure of a claim. Some considerations must be addressed well in advance of any dispute at the contract

---

[3] *See* Tupman, "Discovery and Evidence in U.S. Arbitration: The Prevailing Views," *The Arb. J.* (Mar. 1980).

drafting phase of the project, when the terms of the arbitration clause are determined. Some basic but strategic considerations are the number of arbitrators and the manner in which they are selected.

The fact that arbitrators generally have more expertise in the construction industry than a judge or jury is generally cited as one of the major advantages of arbitration. Of course, as with a juror, an arbitrator's experience and background can predispose the arbitrator for or against a particular argument or party. For example, an owner in a dispute with an architect might fear placing an architect or engineer on the panel. On the other hand, an owner with a strong claim against an architect might actually benefit from the heightened scrutiny another architect might apply to a fellow professional. Another scenario might bring an arbitrator to the panel who is considered by many, including him- or herself, to be a preeminent authority in a particular field applicable to the dispute. If the arbitrator rejects the testimony of your expert, it is likely he or she will also prevail in convincing his or her fellow arbitrators to do the same. As with the selection of a jury, many factors go into the selection of an arbitration panel.

In terms of numbers, the basic choice is between a single arbitrator and a three-member panel. A single arbitrator costs less and will probably simplify scheduling hearings. On the other hand, a three-member panel would probably be more balanced. The three-member panel generally decides by majority vote—that is, two of the three panel members can render a decision over the objection or dissent of the third member.

Parties in an arbitration are free to agree to their own procedures for arbitrator selection. The procedure is often set forth in the arbitration clause of the contract. Provided both sides agree, the procedures can also be established or changed at the time the claim is submitted to arbitration. The method for selecting arbitrators set forth in the American Arbitration Association (AAA) Construction Industry Arbitration Rules is most widely employed. The AAA procedures provide for selection of one or three neutral arbitrators, either by mutual agreement of the parties or by administrative appointment if no agreement can be reached. An alternative procedure that is sometimes used to select a three-member panel allows each party to appoint one arbitrator, with the two party-appointed arbitrators jointly selecting a third "neutral" arbitrator. As a practical matter, this process often makes the neutral arbitrator the "swing vote" that decides the arbitration. Many arbitrators decline the invitation to serve as neutrals on these panels. The prospect of having the respective positions of the parties reargued by one's fellow arbitrators during deliberations does not appeal to everyone.

21.15   Informality and Limited Appeals in Arbitration

The emphasis on the technical expertise of arbitrators usually involves a substantial deemphasis of legal principles, evidentiary rules, and procedures, including the right of appeal. This aspect of arbitration is often cited as a positive, but the contrary can be argued as well.

In arbitration proceedings, strict rules of evidence do not apply and arbitrators are generally liberal in their acceptance of evidence. This permits an easier and faster presentation of records, correspondence, documents, photographs, and live testimony. In fact, the AAA Rules encourage arbitrators to accept any and all evidence that may shed light on the dispute. In the more relaxed environment of arbitration, substantive legal defenses such as statute of limitations, no-damage-for-delay clauses, and notice requirements may be given little weight.

In addition to the arbitrators being granted considerable latitude in their conduct of hearings and rendering of awards, the right of appeal by means of a challenge of an award is extremely limited in scope. This limited scope of judicial review of arbitration awards is yet another trade-off. Although it certainly curtails a party's rights as compared to the scope of an appeal of a jury verdict, the limited scope tends to reduce the number and length of appeals from arbitration awards. This is, of course, in contrast to the court system with its lengthy and expensive appellate procedures.

21.16   Enforceability of Agreements to Arbitrate

In addition to the arbitration clause in the contract, a party's right to arbitration depends upon its ability to go to court and enforce the agreement to arbitrate. At common law, the courts were historically jealous of their jurisdiction and very protective of a person's right of access to the courts. Today, however, the overburdened court system has made alternative methods of dispute resolution a necessity, and most states have attempted to broaden the right to arbitration either by statute or by court decision.

In addition to state laws, construction arbitration agreements are often enforceable under the Federal Arbitration Act (FAA),[4] which is an expression of a strong federal policy favoring arbitration.[5] The FAA applies only if the arbitration clause is in a contract "evidencing a transaction involving commerce," meaning interstate commerce. Transactions of the type generally involved in a large construction project often satisfy this interstate commerce requirement and come within the scope of the FAA.[6] If the interstate commerce requirement is met, the FAA must be enforced, even in state court, and it preempts and supersedes all contrary and inconsistent state law.[7] State law, however, incorporated into the contract by a choice of law provision, may still affect the manner in which the arbitration proceeds, even if the Federal Arbitration Act were applicable.[8]

---

[4] 9 U.S.C. §§ 1–16 (1999).

[5] *J.S.&H. Constr. Co. v. Richmond County Hosp. Auth.*, 473 F.2d 212 (4th Cir. 1973).

[6] *See, e.g., Electronic & Missile Facilities, Inc. v. United States*, 306 F.2d 554 (5th Cir. 1962), *rev'd on other grounds*, 374 U.S. 167 (1963); *Metro Indus. Painting Corp. v. Terminal Constr. Co.*, 287 F.2d 382 (2d Cir. 1961); *Pennsylvania Eng'g Corp. v. Islip Resource Recovery Agency*, 710 F. Supp 456 (E.D.N.Y. 1986).

[7] *Perry v. Thomas*, 482 U.S. 483 (1987); *Southland Corp. v. Keating*, 465 U.S. 1 (1984); *Moses H. Cone Memorial Hosp. v. Mercury Constr. Corp.*, 460 U.S. 1 (1983).

[8] *Volt Info. Sciences Co. v. Board of Trustees of Leland Stanford Junior Univ.*, 489 U.S. 468 (1989).

21.17   Special Problems Involving Multiple Parties

A recurring issue in the administration of construction arbitrations is the consolidation of a number of separate arbitrations and multiple parties on the same project into one proceeding. The potential for problems and the desirability of consolidation need to be considered at the time the arbitration clause is being drafted and the contract signed, long before any claim develops. Although the consolidation of court proceedings involving numerous parties is common, few construction contracts presently provide for such consolidated proceedings in arbitration. Even without contractual authorization, however, some courts have required consolidation as an expeditious means to resolve construction disputes.[9] The traditional and majority rule, however, appears to be that, without express contractual consent to multiparty arbitrations, courts will not require consolidation.[10] In *Stop & Shop Co. v. Gilbane Building Co.*,[11] the court insisted that "if multi-party arbitration is to become a standard procedure, arbitration clauses and the rules and procedures of the AAA and other concerned organizations should be redrawn to provide for it." The AAA Rules currently provide a mechanism for consolidation or joinder of related arbitrations if the parties' agreement or law permits consolidation or joinder.

Reflecting the perspective of design professional organizations, which drafted the document, the arbitration clause contained in AIA Document A201, Article 4.5.5 (1997 ed.), imposes strict limits on consolidation and prohibits consolidation of the owner's claim against the architect in any arbitration between the owner and the contractor. The AIA arbitration clause does, however, allow for consolidated proceedings involving parallel contractors. The prohibition against joining the architect can put the owner in the unenviable position of having to defend in arbitration the contractor's claim for the architect's defective design, without being able to compel the architect to join the same arbitration as a party. This places the burden of defending the architect's design or conduct on the owner. The prohibition against consolidation also causes the owner to run the risk of inconsistent results as well as extra expenses from duplicative arbitration proceedings. For example, an owner could lose on a contractor's claim of defective design in one arbitration, only to fail to convince a separate arbitration panel that the design was defective and that the architect should therefore reimburse the owner for its loss to the contractor. If the owner wants to avoid this situation, it must be addressed in advance in the arbitration clauses of its contracts with the contractor and the architect.

---

[9] *See Episcopal Hous. Corp. v. Federal Ins. Co.*, 255 S.E.2d 451 (S.C. 1979); *Exber, Inc. v. Sletten Constr. Co.*, 558 P.2d 517 (Nev. 1976); *James Stuart Polshek & Assoc. v. Bergen County Iron Works*, 362 A.2d 63 (N.J. Super. Ct. Ch. Div. 1970); *Grover-Diamond Assoc. v. American Arbitration Ass'n*, 211 N.W.2d 787 (Minn. 1973).

[10] *Consolidated Pac. Eng'g v. Greater Anchorage Area Borough*, 563 P.2d 252 (Alaska 1979); *Cumberland Perry Vocational Technical Sch. Auth. v. Boyor & Bink*, 396 A.2d 433 (Pa. Super. 1978).

[11] 304 N.E.2d 429, 432 (Mass. 1973).

21.18 Med-Arb

Med-Arb is a term of art meaning "mediation followed by arbitration," if the mediation is unsuccessful. In Med-Arb, the parties may elect to have the same person serve as both the mediator and arbitrator. Such an arrangement has its advantages in that the mediator becomes familiar with the parties, the project, and the dispute, thus, ideally, leading to a more efficient process and a more thorough understanding of the issues. The disadvantage in the mediator serving as the arbitrator is that any biases or preconceptions that the mediator acquires during mediation will likely carry over to the arbitration. Consequently, Med-Arb may be most useful in cases where the stakes are not that high and the parties want a quick resolution of the dispute.

21.19 Arbitration Agreements and Procedures

American courts recognize the rights of parties to contractually bind themselves to an arbitration process in order to resolve their disputes. The parties are free to select the method and manner of arbitration, and may agree to arbitrate before or after a dispute arises. A number of organizations provide for the administration of formal arbitration proceedings that parties may choose to reference in their project contracts or in subsequent arbitration agreements. The suitability of one organization over another depends largely upon the nature of the parties, the underlying transaction, and personal preference.

21.20 American Arbitration Association (AAA) Rules and Procedures

The AAA is probably the most widely used organization in the United States for the resolution of construction disputes. The AAA is a public service, not-for-profit organization that offers a broad range of dispute resolution procedures, including arbitration. The AAA publishes arbitration rules and procedures that provide a framework for the resolution of construction disputes of any size or complexity, whether national or international in scope. The applicable rules and procedures vary depending upon the size and complexity of the dispute, with larger and more complex construction disputes being subject to a higher degree of subject-matter discovery and procedural management. Administrative fees are determined on a sliding scale in relation to the size of the claims in dispute. Arbitrators are selected from a large panel of industry professionals and construction lawyers and are paid based on individual hourly or daily rates. The AAA rules and procedures can be found at www.adr.org.

21.21 Center for Public Resources (CPR) Rules and Procedures

The CPR serves as a vehicle and resource for self-administered arbitration of private and public business disputes in the United States and abroad. The rules and procedures of the CPR emphasize flexibility in permitting sophisticated business entities to craft dispute resolution procedures appropriate for their particular dispute without the traditional assistance of outside organizations. Members of the CPR include multinational corporations, law firms, legal academics, and public institutions. As with the AAA, the CPR suggests contract language that parties may include in their arbitration clauses and provides a framework of rules and procedures the parties may employ in arbitrating a dispute.

21.22 International Chamber of Commerce (ICC) Rules and Procedures

Established in 1923, the International Court of Arbitration ("the Court") organizes and supervises arbitrations held throughout the world under the Rules of Arbitration of the ICC. The primary function of the Court is to provide for the resolution by arbitration of business disputes of an international character, although parties are free to invoke the ICC Rules in noninternational cases. The ICC Rules have a particularly international flavor and are designed to provide a mutually acceptable arbitration framework for adversaries that may not share common customs, culture, or language. The rules and procedures of the ICC vary considerably from those of the AAA and the CPR. One significant difference is that the arbitrator's fees under the ICC Rules are generally calculated on a sliding scale in relation to the amount in dispute. Before agreeing to an arbitration clause that binds one to an ICC arbitration, the importance of gaining an understanding of the rules and procedures that will apply cannot be overemphasized.

21.23 Party-Drafted Arbitration Agreements: Federal and State Law Considerations

The Federal Arbitration Act (FAA) was enacted in 1925, then reenacted and codified in 1947 as Title 9 of the United States Code. Its "purpose was to reverse the long-standing judicial hostility to arbitration agreements that had existed at English common law and had been adopted by American courts, and to place arbitration agreements upon the same footing as other contracts."[12] "It was enacted to promote the enforcement of arbitration agreements and to make arbitration a more viable option to parties weary of the ever-increasing cost and delays of litigation."[13]

The U.S. Supreme Court has held that the FAA applies whenever the parties' transaction, as evidenced by their contract, "affects" interstate commerce.[14] If the parties' underlying transaction affects interstate commerce, then the FAA applies to any agreement made between them to arbitrate their disputes. Today it is difficult to find a large construction project that does not "affect" interstate commerce so as to trigger coverage of an arbitration clause under the FAA.

---

[12] *Gilmer v. Interstate/Johnson Lane Corp.*, 500 U.S. 20, 24 (1991).

[13] *Dean Witter Reynolds, Inc. v. Byrd*, 470 U.S. 213 (1985).

[14] *Allied-Bruce Terminix Companies, Inc. v. Dobson*, 513 U.S. 265, 273 (1995).

The U.S. Supreme Court has subsequently ruled that the FAA was intended by Congress to create not merely federal *procedural* law, but also a federal *substantive* law of arbitration.[15] Consequently, arbitration clauses subject to the FAA are to be liberally construed in favor of arbitration, notwithstanding any state substantive or procedural policies to the contrary.[16] This is true in both federal and state court proceedings.[17]

State arbitration statutes have been tailored closely to the Uniform Arbitration Act (UAA) as drafted by the National Conference of Commissioners on Uniform State Laws in 1955. The UAA was substantially revised in 2000 in the form of the Revised Uniform Arbitration Act.

21.24   LITIGATION

When there is no arbitration provision, the traditional avenue for obtaining relief is litigation. The rules governing court proceedings are quite complex and vary among federal, state, and local courts from jurisdiction to jurisdiction. For this reason, the following discussion presents only a thumbnail sketch of what is involved in "going to court."

21.25   Profile of the Construction Trial

The trial of a construction contract dispute offers a unique challenge to both sides of the case. Complex antitrust cases are perhaps the closest parallel, since both involve numerous parties and virtual mountains of documentation. Certain problems, however, are unique to construction controversies.

In contrast to the typical civil dispute or crime where the wrong occurred at a single point in time, construction claims generally grow out of an accumulation of events developing over many months or years. To further complicate matters, a single activity constituting a breach of contract may have a "ripple" effect on the remainder of the project, expanding the effect of the breach and entitling the injured party to recover "impact" costs as an additional element of damages. The category of impact damages includes the cost of inefficiency and lost productivity resulting from out-of-sequence or accelerated work. Although at times difficult to prove, such damages can often be substantial.

An added difficulty in a construction case is the large cast of characters, which can include one or more prime contractors, subcontractors, suppliers, the owner, one or more sureties, design professionals, construction managers, lenders, and others. As soon as litigation becomes inevitable, the contractor and its counsel must carefully analyze the list of possible parties from the standpoint of liability, financial

---

[15] *Moses H. Cone Memorial Hosp. v. Mercury Const. Corp.*, 460 U.S. 1 (1983).

[16] *Id.* at 24-25.

[17] *See Southland Corp. v. Keating*, 465 U.S. 1, 104 S.Ct. 852, 79 L.Ed.2d 1 (1984).

responsibility, jurisdiction, venue, access to facts, and the other factual and legal viewpoints.

In a contract action, the most obvious parties are those that have direct contract relations, or "privity," with one another—owner and prime contractor, or prime contractor and subcontractor. However, other parties may become involved. For example, assume that an owner-plaintiff sues a bonded prime contractor for defective work. The owner would also likely join the contractor's surety as a defendant. Assume that the prime contractor believes the defects are not its fault but the responsibility of one of its subcontractors. Since there was no "privity of contract" between the owner and the subcontractor, the owner could not sue the subcontractor directly. The prime contractor, by virtue of the subcontract, has a direct contractual relationship with the subcontractor and therefore may "join" the subcontractor as a "third-party defendant." This mechanism is referred to as "third-party practice."

This scenario often results in counterclaims by the prime contractor against the owner for delays, defective plans, or the like. Every party considering whether to file suit should take into account the defendant's likely counterclaim, which may make it impossible to withdraw from litigation once suit has been filed.

The subcontractor may repeat the process. It may believe one of its subcontractors or suppliers is actually responsible for the defect and may, in turn, join that party as a "fourth-party defendant." What was once a simple, two-party lawsuit can quickly mushroom into one involving numerous parties and their counsel, with the attendant increase in complexity, delay, and expense.

21.26 The Court System   A decision that must be made concurrently with the selection of parties is the choice of the most desirable court or, in legal terminology, the "forum." From the standpoint of strategy and convenience, it is generally a distinct advantage to be the plaintiff and to select the forum. The plaintiff tells its story first to the judge or jury. The plaintiff also has some latitude in determining where to initiate the lawsuit. Frequently, this allows a convenient or "hometown" location to be selected.

In order to evaluate the factors that bear on the selection of a particular court, it is helpful to have a basic understanding of the various court systems. Essentially, there are two court systems within the United States: one federal and a variety of state court systems. The federal judicial system is composed of the United States District Courts (approximately 90 in number), the United States Courts of Appeals (12 in number), and the United States Supreme Court. This chapter will look only at the federal system.

The federal courts are courts of "limited jurisdiction." In contrast, state courts are courts of "general jurisdiction." The term "limited jurisdiction" refers to the fact that some specific statutory basis must be established before a party can have its case heard in federal court. In other words, jurisdiction is "limited" to those special instances prescribed by law. In contrast, a presumption exists that a state court has jurisdiction over a particular controversy, unless a showing is made to the contrary.

"Subject matter" jurisdiction refers to the power of a court to hear a particular type of case. The subject matter jurisdiction of the federal courts in construction cases typically has a "federal question" or "diversity of citizenship" basis. "Federal question" jurisdiction encompasses disputes arising "under the Constitution, laws or treaties of the United States." The second basis for subject matter jurisdiction in the federal courts—and by far the more common in construction disputes—is the "diversity of citizenship" basis.[18] Diversity in this sense refers to controversies between citizens of different states or between citizens of a state and an alien. To satisfy the jurisdictional requirement, diversity of citizenship must be complete—that is, all defendants must be from states different from all plaintiffs.[19]

"Diversity" cases are also subject to a $75,000 threshold limit on the amount in controversy, exclusive of interest and costs. This means that suits where the realistic recovery is less than $75,000 are barred from federal courts even if they are between citizens of different states.

The second facet of jurisdiction—"personal" jurisdiction—focuses on whether the defendant has sufficient contact with the forum state to give the court the right to resolve the dispute. The most common bases for personal jurisdiction include the defendant's physical presence within the jurisdiction, or, in the case of a corporation, transacting business within the area of the court's control—such as performing work on a construction project in the forum state.

Venue also presents a preliminary problem in any lawsuit. The term "venue" refers to the proper geographic location for bringing suit, rather than which court system has appropriate jurisdiction to hear and decide the case.[20] Venue considerations apply in both federal and state courts, although they tend to be more complex under state law due to the characteristic focus of state statutes on the county of residence of the defendant.

21.27 The Federal Rules of Civil Procedure The Federal Rules of Civil Procedure, which govern all procedural aspects of federal trials from initial pleadings to judgment, are the product of years of study, analysis, and recommendations by attorneys and scholars. They represent an effort to provide a workable procedural system. Many states have adopted the Federal Rules in whole or in part for use in their own court systems or have developed minor variations. Substantial variations in the rules of civil procedure do exist from state to state. This is in contrast to the standardization of the Federal Rules of Civil Procedure in all federal courts across the country. Although local federal district court rules may vary in some particulars, the attorney familiar with the Federal Rules of Civil Procedure will ordinarily not feel handicapped in a district court outside of that attorney's usual geographic area of practice.

21.28 Discovery Discovery under the Federal Rules of Civil Procedure and its counterparts at the state level is designed to eliminate courtroom surprise and foster

---

[18] *See* 28 U.S.C. § 1332 (a).

[19] *Owen Equipment & Erection Co. v. Kroger*, 437 U.S. 365 (1978); *Strawbridge v. Curtiss,* 2 L. Ed. 435 (1806).

[20] *See* 28 U.S.C. § 1391.

settlement. Discovery is particularly important in construction litigation because most complicated cases are predicated on vast amounts of files, plans, specifications, engineering data, and other volumes of paper. Discovery is the statutory means by which a party is able to elicit facts from the opposing party, and thereby narrow issues, pin down the opposition's contentions, and generally prepare for trial. The most important discovery devices for construction cases are described below:

(1) *Interrogatories* (Fed. R. Civ. P. 33(a)): Interrogatories are written questions prepared by one party to the lawsuit and directed to another party. Answers are generally prepared with the assistance of the party's counsel. This involvement of counsel in the preparation of written answers often restricts the information provided in response to the interrogatories. Nonetheless, interrogatories are a useful tool for initially obtaining information upon which subsequent discovery can be based.

(2) *Depositions* (Fed. R. Civ. P. 30, 31, and 32): A deposition is the oral examination of any person, whether or not a party to the action, whose knowledge and perspective are important to the case. The deposition allows the questioner a more effective method of obtaining information, since questions can be tailored to prior responses of the deponent, and the questioner has an opportunity to follow up spontaneously on new avenues of inquiry.

Depositions play a crucial part in the development of trial strategy because the testimony is taken under oath and recorded by a stenographer. Since there is an opportunity for cross-examination during the course of a deposition, a deposition transcript may be used at trial when a witness dies in the interim or is otherwise unavailable. The deposition may also be used for the purpose of contradicting, or "impeaching," the courtroom testimony of the witness whose testimony contradicts prior deposition statements.

(3) *Requests for Admission* (Fed. R. Civ. P. 36): One party can require another party to the lawsuit to admit, in writing, the truth of certain facts, by means of a formal request for admission. This saves both time and money, and allows the parties to direct their energies toward those issues that are truly disputed.

(4) *Motion for Entry upon Land* (Fed. R. Civ. P. 34(a)): This rule provides a means for one party to request permission to enter a premises for the purpose of inspecting, surveying, photographing, testing, or sampling the property or any designated object or operation. The value of this procedure is readily apparent if the contractor has relinquished control over the site and subsequently needs to photograph site conditions or sample the soil in connection with a differing site condition claim.

(5) *Production of Documents and Things* (Fed. R. Civ. P. 34(a)): This rule allows a party to compel another party to furnish designated documents (including writings, drawings, graphs, charts, photographs, and other data compilations) or tangible objects having a bearing on the case and that are in the possession of the other party. A request for production under this rule frequently accompanies a set of interrogatories, with the requested documents or objects to be produced or made available for inspection, copying, testing, or sampling at the same time that the answers are filed. Production of documents and objects at a deposition can also be required by means of a subpoena *duces tecum.*

21.29   Judge or Jury?   An important decision associated with a trial is the choice between presenting the case to a judge or a jury. This choice lies with the parties.[21]

A number of factors enter into the decision. For example, a judge sitting alone may be more likely to admit disputed evidence, which would normally be excluded from consideration by a jury, on the rationale that it is better to let in doubtful evidence than to face reversal on appeal because relevant evidence was not admitted. In such a case, the judge is relying on experience and training to give the evidence only the weight it deserves. On the other hand, a judge is less likely to be swayed by sympathy factors and equities that frequently work in a party's favor before a jury.

The type of construction project may also have a bearing on this decision. A local jury may prove disastrous if the case involves construction of a public facility such as a school or hospital—particularly one funded by local property taxes or levies, or one that is highly controversial. A similar result may occur if the party being sued is a local business concern—for example, a subcontractor or supplier—and the plaintiff is an outsider.

Ultimately, the determining factor may be that many construction cases are simply too complex for the average jury—although some trial attorneys will argue that most judges are likewise not familiar, through experience or background, with construction principles. In any event, the complexity of the matter and the relative advantage that may be gained by simplification (or, on the other hand, by confusion) are factors to be weighed in deciding whether to proceed before a judge or jury.

21.30   The Trial   The final focal point of the litigation process is the presentation of evidence calculated to persuade the trier of fact of entitlement to relief. Evidence is presented through: (1) live testimony or by deposition if a witness is not available at the time of trial; (2) documentary evidence; and (3) demonstrative evidence. The trial attorney weaves the case by combining the facts with legal theories supporting the client's entitlement.

21.31   Live Testimony   Live testimony is, in most instances, the most persuasive type of proof. It is crucial, however, that witnesses be prepared well in advance of trial to ensure their knowledge of important facts as well as to bolster confidence. Live testimony is needed to explain and authenticate documentary and demonstrative evidence used in the trial. See **Sections 21.3 and 21.4.**

The client must assist counsel in selecting the most effective witnesses. In most cases, effectiveness can be equated with personal knowledge of the facts. Often it is not the president of the company who has this firsthand knowledge, but superintendents or inspectors, who are "in the trenches" on a daily basis, fighting the battle, who ultimately wind up in the courtroom. Another important point to consider is that these individuals—who use the unique language of the construction industry in expressing themselves—frequently make excellent witnesses. They have the capacity to translate complicated construction problems into simple, everyday language that is frequently both colorful and persuasive.

---

[21] *See* Fed. R. Civ. P. 38.

Members of management are usually most effective in establishing broad overview points, such as assumptions about labor productivity that ultimately were translated into the bid and how those assumptions and expectations were frustrated. Management, including operation and finance personnel, are also frequently needed to prove damages claimed by a party.

In addition to field and office personnel, "expert" witnesses are often used. The use of experts is commonplace in construction litigation, especially in the ever-increasing number of complex "delay damages–interference–impact" cases. It is common practice in such cases for an expert to be used to analyze the validity of the CPM or similar schedule originally relied upon by the contractor in submitting its bid, as well as in the preparation of an as-built schedule if needed to depict where and how the job went wrong. Testimony from such an expert is important to quantify the impact of breaches and delays and the assessment of damages.

One pitfall of using expert witnesses in construction cases is the failure to provide the expert with reliable source material, of the kind usually relied upon, to use in forming opinions and conclusions. It is appropriate for the opposing party to inquire into the foundation, facts, and data upon which an expert's opinion is based. If it is found that the facts and data are untrustworthy or not of the type an expert would normally rely upon, then the testimony of the expert witness is subject to attack. As a part of its ruling on the admissibility of expert opinion testimony, the trial court will review the reasonableness of the witness's reliance on facts or data to determine if the expert has deviated from the recognized area of expertise by basing an opinion on untrustworthy material. It is then the responsibility of the court to rule whether the testimony can be received or should be excluded.[22]

Live witnesses—lay and expert alike—are subject to "direct" examination by counsel representing their side of the dispute and "cross-examination" by opposing counsel. The primary function of direct examination is to place all pertinent facts into evidence for consideration by the trier of fact. To assure that this is properly done, counsel will generally discuss with the witness the types of questions that will be asked, although the answers should be those of the witness.

On cross-examination, opposing counsel has a different goal and will take a different approach in an effort to discredit the witness or the testimony, by, for example, pointing out inconsistencies in the testimony or showing bias. A cardinal rule generally followed by attorneys during cross-examination is "never ask a question you don't know the answer to." Given this, it is frequently possible for the construction attorney and the client to anticipate and prepare for most of the questions that will come up during cross-examination.

The litigation process can be long, drawn out, and expensive. Consequently, it is no wonder that other forms of dispute resolution are finding their way to the forefront among parties attempting to resolve claims. This does not mean that litigation should never be used: it is often an effective means for addressing claims. This is not, however, typically the case, and other means of reaching a resolution of the claim should always be investigated and considered before turning to the courts.

---

[22] *See generally Kumho Tire Co. v. Carmichael,* 526 U.S. 137 (1999).

➤ POINTS TO REMEMBER

- Early claim recognition and preparation with the assistance of "experts" is important to ensure that the claim and supporting documentation and evidence are assembled and prepared in a manner likely to result in a favorable resolution.

- Preparation and use of demonstrative evidence can be an effective tool in simplifying and advancing a claim in a persuasive manner.

- A well-drafted claim should be an exercise in storytelling that will educate, inform, and hopefully persuade its reader.

- Early analysis of actual damages is essential in determining if a claim really exists and the best means for either advancing the claim or encouraging an early resolution and settlement.

- The advantages as well as the drawbacks of the various methods of dispute resolution should be considered at the time of contracting. If a particular form of dispute resolution is desired, it should be provided for in advance.

- Procedures for selecting neutrals, as well as the consolidation of multiple parties, should be considered when drafting the construction contract's dispute-resolution clause.

- Generally, arbitrators are granted considerable latitude in conducting hearings and rendering awards, and the right of appeal is extremely limited.

- Enforceability of agreements to arbitrate may be governed by both state and federal laws.

- In the absence of an alternative dispute-resolution provision, the traditional avenue for obtaining relief is litigation. Construction claims are inherently complex. They often involve multiple parties, and the governing laws vary widely among federal, state, and local jurisdictions.

- Selection of the court that will hear the claim depends on several factors, including the total dollar amount in controversy and the state citizenship of all the parties.

- The Federal Rules of Civil Procedure provide numerous important discovery devices that are designed to elicit facts and narrow the issues in preparation for trial.

- Parties to a complex construction claim must carefully consider whether to present evidence of the claim to a judge or to demand a jury trial.

- Whether witnesses were actual participants in the project giving rise to a claim or are hired "experts," it is crucial that all witnesses be prepared well in advance of a trial to ensure their effectiveness.

22

FEDERAL GOVERNMENT CONSTRUCTION CONTRACT DISPUTES

22.1 THE SCOPE AND IMPORTANCE OF FEDERAL CONSTRUCTION CONTRACTING

Since the 1940s, the federal government (hereinafter "government") has been the largest single buyer of construction services in the world. The procurement and administration of construction contracts, as well as the resolution of disputes on federal construction projects, are governed by multiple statutes and extensive regulations that are rigorously enforced. An array of administrative boards of contract appeals (hereinafter "boards") and special courts have operated for decades for the sole purpose of resolving disputes on federal contracts.[1] These tribunals have generated a tremendous number of decisions that collectively provide the single largest body of law in the area of construction disputes. Many of the decisions noted in this book, which address substantive principles of construction law, involve the resolution of disputes and claims on federal government construction contracts. Numerous fundamental principles of construction law have their genesis in federal government construction contracts. It is impractical to speak of modern American construction law without the consideration of federal procurement law, and the discussion of that law is interlaced in each of the substantive chapters of this book. Considering the volume of federal construction contracts, it is also appropriate to provide this general outline of the legal framework applicable to the resolution of claims and disputes on federal construction contracts.

Federal government construction contracts reflect policies contained in statutes and in Federal Acquisition Regulation (FAR). In addition to containing numerous

---

[1] Similar to the extensive body of law, which developed around the resolution of disputes on government contracts, the resolution of award issues and disputes ("bid protests") has resulted in the growth of an extensive body of legal principles and regulations. *See* **Chapter 4**.

standard contract clauses, the FAR also contains extensive guidance to the federal agencies and their personnel regarding the award and administration of federal construction contracts.[2]

Disputes arising out of or related to the performance of a government construction contract are governed by the Contract Disputes Act (hereinafter CDA or Act).[3] The CDA and its implementing regulations set forth a comprehensive approach to the resolution of contract claims by contractors and the government.

The citations in this chapter are to the appropriate provisions of the CDA, other relevant statutes, and the applicable regulations, particularly the FAR, as well as to the cases. The CDA and the other cited statutes are found in West Publishing Company's United States Code Annotated. FAR citations are from Title 48 of the Code of Federal Regulations (CFR).

Government contract case law is found in a variety of sources. Since 1921, selected bid protest decisions issued by the United States Government Accountability Office (GAO) have been published in the Decisions of the Comptroller General of the United States.[4] Beginning in 1974, Federal Publications, Inc., now part of the West Group, has published the *Comptroller General's Procurement Decisions* (CPD) service containing the full text of all of the GAO's bid protest decisions.[5] Court decisions regarding bid protests have been issued by the federal district courts,[6] the various federal circuit courts of appeals, the United States Claims Court (now the United States Court of Federal Claims),[7] and the United States Court of Appeals for the Federal Circuit. The case law involving claims and disputes arising out of or related to the performance of a contract basically consists of the decisions of the various boards, United States Court of Claims, United States Claims Court, United States Court of Federal Claims (hereinafter "Court of Federal Claims"), and the United States Court of Appeals for the Federal Circuit (hereinafter "Federal Circuit").[8]

---

[2] In addition to the FAR, many of the major federal departments have supplements to the FAR, for example, the DFARS published by the Department of Defense, as well as regulations specific to a particular agency such as the U.S. Army Corps of Engineers. These supplements can substantially alter a contractor's rights, obligations, and remedies on a government contract.

[3] 41 U.S.C. §§ 601–613.

[4] Formerly, the General Accounting Office. Each year the GAO selects decisions for publication that it believes would be of widespread interest. Typically, 10 percent of all of the GAO's decisions in a given year are included in this publication.

[5] Until 1974, the vast majority of the GAO's decisions on bid protests were not published and were not readily available.

[6] The U.S. Federal District Courts' jurisdiction over bid protests ended as of January 2001.

[7] 28 U.S.C. § 1491 (1992).

[8] These forums dispose of the vast majority of all contract-related issues. However, Congress has also granted the Executive Branch extraordinary powers to be used in the course of procurements related to the national defense. One of these laws, 50 U.S.C. §§ 1431–435, permits certain procuring activities to grant relief to contractors who may have no legal right to such relief—for example, an amendment without consideration. This avenue for relief is not a substitute for relief under the CDA and will be considered only after it is determined that the CDA does not provide an adequate remedy. The procedures related to extraordinary contractual actions are found in 48 CFR Part 50.

The Court of Claims, which was abolished in 1982, had jurisdiction to entertain suits involving government contract claims, including claims under the CDA. When Congress abolished the Court of Claims, it created the Claims Court, now the Court of Federal Claims,[9] and granted to it all of the original jurisdiction of the Court of Claims.[10] At the same time, Congress also created a new United States Court of Appeals for the Federal Circuit.[11] The Federal Circuit reviews appeals of decisions from the boards and the Court of Federal Claims.[12] The Court of Federal Claims and the Federal Circuit view decisions of the old Court of Claims as binding precedent.[13]

22.2   SCOPE OF THE CONTRACT DISPUTES ACT

Prior to the enactment of the CDA, the government contract disputes process was a mixture of statutes, regulations, and interpretive case law. Government contracts contained a disputes clause,[14] and every federal agency utilized a board of contract appeals. Reflecting a series of United States Supreme Court decisions,[15] the boards became the principal forum for the resolution of contractor claims, while the United States Court of Claims assumed the more limited role of an appellate court under the Wunderlich Act.[16] Except for the relatively unusual circumstance that could be characterized as a claim for breach of contract, nearly all claims arising under a contract had to be brought to the boards. However, the boards' jurisdiction was limited to "contract" claims and any suit alleging breach of contract had to be filed in the United States Court of Claims.

Each board had its own rules and procedures, which had varying degrees of formality. In some agencies, board members or judges served only on a part-time basis. In those cases, the board judge often had other duties within the same agency that had awarded and administered the contract. In addition, due to the decision of the

---

[9] 28 U.S.C. § 171.

[10] 28 U.S.C. § 1491. The United States Court of Federal Claims has the same basic jurisdiction, but broadened to include nonmonetary claims. See **Section 22.24** *infra*.

[11] 28 U.S.C. § 41.

[12] 41 U.S.C. § 607(g)(1); 28 U.S.C. § 1295(a)(10), (a)(3).

[13] *South Corp. v. United States*, 690 F.2d 1368, 1369 (Fed. Cir. 1982) (en banc); United States Court of Federal Claims Gen. Order No. 33, 27 Fed. Cl. xyv (1992).

[14] *See* Shedd, *Disputes and Appeals: The Armed Services Board of Contract Appeals*, 29 Law & Contemp. Probs. 39 (1964).

[15] *United States v. Wunderlich*, 342 U.S. 98 (1951); *United States v. Moorman*, 338 U.S. 457 (1950); *United States v. Holpuch*, 328 U.S. 234 (1946).

[16] The reaction to the *Moorman* and *Wunderlich* decisions resulted in the passage of the Wunderlich Act, which limited the finality of board decisions. 41 U.S.C. §§ 321–22. This act was subsequently interpreted by the U.S. Supreme Court in *United States v. Bianchi*, 373 U.S. 709 (1963); *United States v. Grace & Sons, Inc.*, 384 U.S. 424 (1966). *Grace* and *Bianchi* establish that a court reviewing a board decision was confined to the record created during the board proceeding and could not conduct an independent evidentiary hearing into issues not addressed by the board. Thus the boards became the primary fact-finding bodies, with significant emphasis placed on the development of a record that would support the board's findings with substantial evidence.

United States Supreme Court in *S&E Contractors, Inc. v. United States*,[17] the government had no right of appeal from an adverse decision by a board. The *S&E* decision also precluded a review of board decisions by the GAO, which review had the potential effect of negating a decision that was adverse to the agency's interests.

Attempting to improve the overall disputes process, the CDA created a comprehensive statutory basis for the disposition of contract disputes. The Act applies to any express or implied contract that is entered into by an "executive agency" of the federal government for the "procurement of [the] construction, alteration, repair, or maintenance of real property."[18] The Act also applies to "the executive agency contracts for the procurement of property, other than real property, for the procurement of services and for the disposal of personal property, as well as for supplies."[19]

The term "executive agency" is defined in 41 U.S.C. § 601(2). It encompasses those entities that are commonly thought of as government agencies, such as the Department of Defense (DOD), the General Services Administration (GSA), the Department of Energy (DOE), the Department of Transportation (DOT), and the Department of Veterans Affairs (VA). It also encompasses the U.S. Postal Service, the Postal Rate Commission, and various independent bodies and government corporations.[20] The comprehensive statutory basis in the Contract Disputes Act for the resolution of disputes made significant changes in the old process. It made the boards and their members more professional by requiring that all board members be full-time positions. In other words, it was no longer possible for a board judge to function as an attorney for the agency on a part-time basis. Secondly, it gave the contractor a choice of forums with respect to the appeal of a final decision by the contracting officer. The contractor could elect either to appeal to a board or to file a suit on the final decision in the United States Court of Federal Claims (formerly the U.S. Claims Court). This concept became known as "contractor's right of direct access." Furthermore, the Act's provisions applied "notwithstanding any contract provision, regulation, or rules of law to the contrary."[21] Accordingly, it is not possible to agree by contract to limit the right of appeal to a particular forum.[22] In addition, the Act effectively reversed the *S&E* decision by giving the government the right to appeal an adverse board decision to the Federal Circuit.

The CDA seeks to address the processing of claims from their initiation to final disposition and payment. It describes the manner in which claims are asserted and seeks to provide time frames for decisions on such claims by the contracting officer. The Act also provides for a contractor's right to appeal the contracting officer's final

---

[17] 406 U.S. 1 (1972).

[18] 41 U.S.C. § 602(a).

[19] It is well established that the Act applies to leases for real property. *See George Ungar*, PSBCA No. 935, 82 1 BCA ¶ 15,549; *Goodfellow Bros. Inc.*, AGBCA No. 80-189-3, 81-1 BCA ¶ 14,917; *Robert J. DiDomenico*, GSBCA No. 5539, 80-1 BCA ¶ 14,412. However, jurisdiction over a dispute outside of the terms of the lease, such as a decision to expand the area subject to the lease, has been rejected by a board. *See John Barrar & Marilyn Hunkler*, ENG BCA No. 5918, 92-3 BCA ¶ 25,074.

[20] The Act also contains provisions covering the Tennessee Valley Authority. *See* 41 U.S.C. § 602(b).

[21] 41 U.S.C. § 609(b).

[22] *OSHCO-PAE-SOMC v. United States*, 16 Cl. Ct. 614 (1989).

decision or the lack of a final decision, as well as the time frames for appeals to each of the alternate forums (boards or Court of Federal Claims) and any appellate review of those decisions. Since the primary focus of the Act is the disposition of a claim, this chapter begins with a discussion of an assertion of a claim and follows the processing of that claim through a decision and any appeal. It will also review provisions of the CDA and related laws dealing with fraudulent or inflated claims,[23] small claims,[24] interest on amounts found due the contractor,[25] payment of claims,[26] and recovery of attorneys' fees by certain contractors pursuant to the Equal Access to Justice Act.[27]

Under the contract provisions utilized prior to the CDA, the typical disputes clause extended only to disputes "arising under" the contract. Typically, this meant that breach-of-contract claims were not subject to the disputes clause and were outside the jurisdiction of the boards.[28] The Act extends to all disputes arising under or related to a contract. This broader formulation of the scope of the disputes process clearly includes claims for breach of contract. However, by its terms, and as its name implies, the Act is applicable only to contract disputes; tort claims or claims seeking specific performance are not subject to the Act.[29] While the Act is specifically applicable to any "express or implied contract," the Federal Circuit has held that the CDA did not give jurisdiction to the boards to hear claims based upon an implied contract by the government to treat bids fairly and honestly,[30] which is the basis for bid protest and bid preparation cost actions. The Federal Circuit held that the implied contract to treat bids fairly and honestly is not a contract for the procurement of "goods or services"; thus it did not fall within the definition contained in § 3(a) of the Act. Similarly, efforts by contractors to obtain board or court review of unfavorable past performance evaluations by a federal agency have been unsuccessful. The boards and the Court of Federal Claims have consistently ruled that a disagreement regarding a past performance evaluation is not a "claim" under the CDA.[31]

While § 605(a) of the Act provides that all claims related to a contract shall be submitted to the contracting officer for a decision, the Act also states that the authority of that subsection did not extend to "a claim or dispute for penalties or forfeitures prescribed by statute or regulation which another federal agency is specifically authorized to administer, settle, or determine." Therefore, disputes arising under the

---

[23] 41 U.S.C. § 604.

[24] 41 U.S.C. § 608.

[25] 41 U.S.C. § 611.

[26] 41 U.S.C. § 612.

[27] 5 U.S.C. § 504.

[28] *United States v. Utah Constr. & Mining Co.*, 384 U.S. 394 (1966).

[29] 41 U.S.C. § 602(a); *Malnak Assoc. v. United States*, 223 Ct. Cl. 783 (1980); *Siska Constr. Co.*, VABCA No. 3524, 92-2 ¶ 24,825; *Maritime Equipment & Sales, Inc. v. General Services Administration*, ASBCA No. 15266, 00-2 BCA ¶ 30,987; *Midwest Properties, LLC v. General Services Administration*, GSBCA Nos. 15822, 15844, 03-2 BCA ¶ 32,344.

[30] *Coastal Corp. v. United States*, 713 F.2d 728 (Fed. Cir. 1983); *but see LaBarge Prods., Inc. v. West*, 46 F.3d 1547 (Fed. Cir. 1995) (contractor entitled to assert a claim for reformation of contract based on government's allegedly improper preaward actions).

[31] *TLT Construction Corp.*, ASBCA No. 53769, 02-2 BCA ¶ 31,969.

Walsh-Healey Act,[32] the Davis-Bacon Act,[33] and the Service Contract Act of 1965[34] are not subject to the CDA. These Acts involve labor laws that are administered by the Secretary of Labor, and disputes related to the enforcement of these statutes are generally beyond the jurisdiction of the boards or Court of Federal Claims.[35]

22.3 THE FREEDOM OF INFORMATION ACT:
A CLAIM PREPARATION AND PROSECUTION TOOL

Often, agency files contain documents that may provide support for a contractor's request for a contract adjustment, for the contractor's understanding of its contract obligations, or the agency's responsibilities under the contract. Typically, these materials are available during discovery. However, this is after a claim has been submitted, a final decision has been issued, and an appeal or suit has been initiated. The Freedom of Information Act (FOIA)[36] often provides a means for a contractor to obtain access to the records maintained by the government prior to the submission of a claim. Contractors and their counsel should consider using FOIA requests as a means of obtaining additional information pertaining to the contract. Agencies subject to the FOIA include: (1) any department or agency of the Executive Branch; (2) government corporations; (3) government-controlled corporations; or (4) any independent regulatory branch.[37] The FOIA does not apply to the federal courts or to the Congress.

Basically, information is made available to the public in three ways: (1) publication in the Federal Register;[38] (2) by sale to the public or availability for examination in public reading rooms;[39] or (3) upon request for documents that are reasonably described.[40] This third category of records is generally the best source of information pertaining to contract performance issues. To obtain these documents in the third category, it is necessary to submit a written FOIA request. Each agency's procedures governing the submission should be carefully reviewed and followed when making a FOIA request.[41] The regulations are generally contained in the Code of Federal Regulations (CFR) and usually identify the FOIA official to whom a request should be sent and provide the appropriate address. In addition, these procedures set forth time limits for agency responses and appeal procedures if the request is denied.

---

[32] 41 U.S.C. § 35, *et seq.*

[33] 40 U.S.C. § 276(a).

[34] 41 U.S.C. § 351, *et seq.*

[35] *Emerald Maintenance, Inc. v. United States*, 925 F.2d 1425 (Fed. Cir. 1991); *Tele-Sentry Sec., Inc.*, GSBCA No. 10945, 91-2 BCA ¶ 23,880.

[36] 5 U.S.C. § 552.

[37] 5 U.S.C. § 552 (f).

[38] 5 U.S.C. § 552(a)(1); 1 CFR Part 5.

[39] 5 U.S.C. § 552(a)(2).

[40] 5 U.S.C. § 552(a)(3)(A).

[41] 5 U.S.C. § 552(a)(3)(B).

Following these procedures will usually save time in processing the request. In addition, it will avoid having a court decline jurisdiction over a suit to compel disclosure due to a failure to follow these rules.[42]

Generally, a request for agency documents will usually be processed more quickly if it clearly states that it is an FOIA request and acknowledges that the government may be entitled to be paid certain fees and costs for responding to the request.[43] In addition, it is necessary to provide a "reasonable description" of the desired records.[44] A "reasonable description" is one that enables a professional employee of the agency who is familiar with the subject area of the request to locate the record with a reasonable amount of effort.[45] However, broad categorical requests that make it impossible for the agency to reasonably determine what is sought are not permissible.[46] If the agency denies the initial request, the person seeking disclosure may file an action in a United States district court to compel disclosure after exhausting the applicable administrative procedures (including any appeal process) set forth in the agency's FOIA regulations.[47]

FOIA requests can be a means of expeditious, informal discovery to assist in the preparation of a claim. Even after an appeal or suit is pending, contractors and their counsel should consider the potential for appropriate contemporaneous FOIA requests and formal discovery requests. For example, many projects involve federal agencies other than the contracting agency. An appropriate FOIA request to the noncontracting agency may provide quicker access to records than the use of subpoenas on nonparty federal agencies. Similarly, in a case involving issues related to the performance by, or positions asserted by, an architect-engineer firm, an FOIA request to view the records on other projects designed or administered by the same firm might reveal contradictory views and positions.

22.4 CONTRACTOR CLAIMS

The Act states that "[a]ll claims by a contractor against the government relating to a contract shall be in writing and shall be submitted to the contracting officer for a decision."[48] Claims may be either monetary or nonmonetary. In that regard, the Act further provides that monetary claims by a contractor in excess of $100,000 must be

---

[42] *Hamilton Securities Group, Inc. v. Department of Housing and Urban Development*, 106 F. Supp. 2d 23 (D.D.C. 2000); *Television Wis., Inc. v. NLRB*, 410 F. Supp. 999 (W.D. Wis. 1976).

[43] If the requesting party is not sure of the cost (scope) associated with the FOIA request, it is possible to advise the agency to contact the party making the request prior to conducting a search that it is expected to cost more than a stated amount.

[44] H.R. Rep. No. 93-876, 93d Congress, 2nd Sess. (1974).

[45] 5 U.S.C. § 552(a)(3)(A). *See Jimenez v. F.B.I.*, 910 F. Supp. 5 (D. D.C. 1996).

[46] S. Rep. No. 93-854, 93rd Congress, 2d Sess. (1974). *See Jimenez, supra* note 45; *Fonda v. Central Intelligence Agency*, 434 F. Supp. 498 (D.D.C. 1977).

[47] 5 U.S.C. § 552(a)(6)(c); *Oglesby v. United States*, 920 F.2d 57 (D.C. Cir. 1990).

[48] 41 U.S.C. § 605(a).

certified.[49] The existence of a claim in dispute and the submission of that claim to the contracting officer for a decision are prerequisites to the contractor's ability to invoke the disputes-resolution procedures of the CDA. Until a claim is submitted, the contracting officer has no obligation to issue a final decision and the contractor has no right of access to either a board of contract appeals or the Court of Federal Claims. If a contractor initiates either a board or court proceeding prior to the submission of a proper claim, the proceeding will either be dismissed or stayed, depending upon the deficiency in the contractor's claim submission. Even though a dismissal would be without prejudice to the right of the contractor to reinitiate the process,[50] the contractor must begin the process by resubmitting the claim to the contracting officer for a decision.[51] This costs time and money. CDA interest does not begin to accrue on a proposal or request for an equitable adjustment until the submission qualifies as a claim under the Contract Disputes Act. Failure to understand and to follow the requirements of the CDA can be very costly.

22.5 WHEN MUST A CLAIM BE SUBMITTED?

The CDA now states that "each claim" relating to a contract shall be submitted "within six years after the accrual of the claim."[52] This 1994 amendment to the Act failed to define the term "accrual"; however, the final implementing regulations addressed the need for a definition of that term and also addressed the application of the six-year limitation to contracts in effect at the time of the passage of the 1994 amendment to the Act.

The final regulations[53] stated that the six-year period did not apply to contracts awarded prior to October 1, 1995. For purposes of the CDA, "accrual of a claim" was defined as follows:

> [T]he date when all events, which fix the alleged liability of either the Government or the contractor and permit assertion of the claim, were known or should have been known. For liability to be fixed, some injury must have occurred. However, monetary damages need not have been incurred.[54]

The implementing regulations made the term "accrual" applicable to claims by either the contractor or the government, except for government claims based on a contractor claim involving fraud. This definition may still stimulate questions of

---

[49] 41 U.S.C. § 605(c). When the CDA was enacted, the threshold for certification was any amount greater than $50,000. This threshold was increased to $100,000 in 1994.

[50] *Thoen v. United States*, 765 F.2d 1110, 1116 (Fed. Cir. 1985).

[51] *Skelly & Loy, Inc. v. United States*, 685 F.2d 414, 419 (1982); *Technassociates, Inc. v. United States*, 14 Cl. Ct. 200, 212 (1988); T.J.D. *Servs., Inc. v. United States*, 6 Cl. Ct. 257, 260 (1984).

[52] 41 U.S.C. § 605(a).

[53] 60 Fed. Reg. 48, 225 (1995).

[54] *Id.*

what constitutes "injury" when no monetary damages have been incurred. Contractors also need to bear in mind that there is a distinction between a CDA claim and a proposal or a request for an equitable adjustment (REA). Submission of the latter may not satisfy the six-year submission requirement if it is later determined that the equitable adjustment proposal or REA was not a "CDA claim."[55]

Even if the six-year statute of limitations is not applicable, a prolonged delay in the submission of a claim by a contractor may provide the basis for the government to assert a defense on the basis of "laches." In that context, the claim may be denied if the prolonged passage of time substantially prejudiced the government's ability to defend against the claim.[56] Similarly, failure to submit a claim for relief due to a mistake in bid until several years after award may be the basis for rejection of the claim on the grounds of waiver by the contractor, even though the government failed to demonstrate any prejudice and no statute of limitations had expired.[57]

22.6 NOTICE REQUIREMENTS

Lack of timely notice of a potential claim can be a costly omission for contractors. Factual and objective notice is good business. It provides an opportunity for the agency to address a problem before it becomes a costly dispute. To assist with the identification of notice requirements, the staff responsible for the day-to-day management of a project should prepare a notice checklist for each project. That checklist should be based on a thorough review of the prime contract, the subcontracts, and purchase orders. The checklist should identify the clause, the time requirements for notice, the subject matter of the notice, whether the notice must be in writing, and the stated consequences for failing to give timely notice.

Regardless of a contractor's general familiarity with the standard clauses found in government construction contracts, each contract should be reviewed in detail, as "standard" or "boilerplate" contracts may contain special requirements regarding notification and documentation of delays, extra work, and so on. Generally, a notice checklist can be easily summarized on a single sheet of paper, which should be three-hole-punched and retained in the operations manual for the project. A few hours of review time at the project's start may save the contractor thousands of dollars later. While a notice checklist can take various formats, Table 22.1 reflects a summary of the provisions of three of the standard government contract clauses with critical notice requirements. This format can be readily modified for any contract, subcontract, or purchase order.

---

[55] See *Reflectone, Inc. v. Dalton*, 60 F.3d 1572 (Fed. Cir. 1995).

[56] *Anlagen und Sanierungstechnik GmbH*, ASBCA No. 49869, 97-2 BCA ¶ 29,168.

[57] *Turner—MAK (JV)*, ASBCA No. 37711, 96-1 BCA ¶ 28,208.

Table 22.1 Notice Checklist—Government Construction Contract

Clause Reference	Subject Matter of Notice	Time Requirements for Notice	Writing Required	Stated Consequences of a Lack of Notice
Differing Site Conditions— FAR 52.236-2	Existence of unknown or materially different conditions, affecting the contractor's cost	From the time such conditions are identified, notice must be furnished "promptly" and before such conditions are disturbed.	Yes	Claim not allowed. Lack of notice may be waived until final payment.
Suspension of Work— FAR 52.242-14	Proposal for adjustment	20 DAYS of act or failure to act, causing suspension, delay, or interruption.	Yes	Claim not allowed, but notice requirement does not apply to a claim resulting from a suspension order.
Changes— FAR 52.243-4	Proposal for adjustment	30 DAYS from receipt of a written change order from the government or written notification of a constructive change by the contractor	Yes	Claim may not be considered; requirement may be waived until final payment.
Constructive Changes— FAR 52.243.4	Date, circumstances, and source of the order and that the contractor regards the government's order as a contract change.	No starting point stated, but notice within 20 DAYS of incurring any additional costs due to the constructive change fully protects the contractor's rights.	Yes	Costs incurred more than 20 DAYS prior to giving notice cannot be recovered, except in the cast of defective specifications.

22.7 WHO MAY SUBMIT A CLAIM?

Generally, under the CDA, only a prime contractor may assert claims against the government. The Act refers to "contractor claims"[58] and states that the term "contractor means a party to a government contract other than the government. . . ."[59] Similarly,

[58] 41 U.S.C. § 605(a).
[59] 41 U.S.C. § 601(4).

FAR § 33.201 defines a claim as a demand or assertion "by one of the contracting parties."[60] This requirement for "privity of contract" denoting a contractual relationship is strictly enforced in government contracts. Generally, subcontractors are not considered to be one of the contracting parties and are not in privity of contract with the government. Accordingly, subcontractors may not assert claims directly against the government under the Act.[61] Only in rare situations does privity of contract exist between a subcontractor and the government, such as when the government utilizes an agent to enter into a contract "by and for" the government, or there is an assignment of a subcontractor's contract to the government pursuant to a clause such as the "Termination for Convenience" clause.[62] Similarly, a noncompleting performance bond surety is not a contractor for the purposes of the CDA.[63] However, a surety that expressly or implicitly assumes contract performance is in privity with the government and may assert claims under the Act.[64] Finally, unless the government is a party to the assignment transaction, the assignee of a contractor's rights under a government contract does not attain the status of a contractor and is not in the position to assert a claim under the CDA.[65]

Given the nature of most construction projects, subcontractor performance is often a key issue and subcontractor claims are common. While subcontractors do not have the right to directly assert a claim against the government, subcontractor claims are routinely considered in the context of the disputes process. With the prime contractor's consent and cooperation, a subcontractor claim can be submitted to the contracting officer for decision and appealed through the disputes process. In that situation, the prime contractor acts as a "sponsor" for the subcontractor's claim.[66] However, a prime contractor must recognize that only it can certify a subcontractor's claim when it is submitted under the CDA. *See* **Section 22.18** *infra.*

---

[60] 48 C.F.R. § 33.201 (all references are to the 2003 edition of the Code of Federal Regulations).

[61] *Lockheed Martin Corp. v. United States*, 50 Fed. Cl. 550 (2001); *Erickson Air Crane Co. of Wash., Inc. v. United States*, 731 F.2d 810, 813 (Fed. Cir. 1984); *United States v. Johnson Controls, Inc.*, 713 F.2d 1541 (Fed. Cir. 1983); *G. Schneider*, ASBCA No. 333021, 87-2 BCA ¶ 19,865.

[62] *Kern-Limerick v. Scurlock*, 347 U.S. 110 (1954); *Deltec Corp. v. United States*, 326 F.2d 1004 (Ct. Cl. 1964); *Lockheed Martin Corp., supra* note 61; *Globex Corp. v. United States,* 54 Fed. Cl. 343 (2002); *Marine Contractors, Inc.*, ASBCA No. 54017, 03-1 BCA ¶ 32, 240; *Coastal Drilling, Inc.*, ASBCA No. 54023, 03-1 BCA ¶ 32,241.

[63] *See Universal Surety Co. v. United States*, 10 Cl. Ct. 794, 799–800 (1986).

[64] *See Fireman's Fund Ins. Co. v. United States,* 909 F.2d 495, 499 (Fed. Cir. 1990); *Balboa Ins. Co. v. United States*, 775 F.2d 1158, 1161 (Fed. Cir. 1985).

[65] *See Fireman's Fund/Underwater Constr., Inc.*, ASBCA No. 33018, 87-3 BCA ¶ 20,007.

[66] *Erickson Air Crane Co. of Wash., Inc., supra* note 61, at 813–814; *Planning Research Corp. v. Dept. of Commerce,* GSBCA No. 11286-COM, 96-1 BCA ¶ 27,954. However, if a prime contractor refuses to authorize prosecution of a claim in its name, the claim will be dismissed. *See Divide Constructors, Inc.*, IBCA No. 1134-12-76, 77-1 BCA ¶ 14,430.

22.8 WHAT CONSTITUTES A CLAIM?

The Contract Disputes Act states that all claims "shall be in writing and shall be submitted to the contracting officer for a decision."[67] However, the Act does not define a claim. Moreover, while it would seem that the definition of a "claim" would be uniform in government contracts, there is a marked lack of uniformity. There are differing definitions of a claim for the purpose of the disputes clause,[68] the disallowance of certain costs associated with the prosecution of a "claim" against the government,[69] and for the purpose of contractor liability under the False Claims Act.[70]

FAR § 33.215 provides that absent specific circumstances, each government contract must contain the disputes clause set forth at FAR § 52.233-1.[71] The disputes clause provides, in pertinent part, the following definition of a claim.

> (c) Claim, as used in this clause, means a written demand or written assertion by one of the contracting parties seeking, as a matter of right, the payment of money in a sum certain, the adjustment or interpretation of contract terms, or other relief arising under or relating to this contract. . . . [A] written demand or written assertion by the Contractor seeking the payment of money in excess of $100,000 is not a claim under the Act until certified as required by subparagraph (d)(2) of this clause. . . .
>
> (d)(1) A claim by the Contractor shall be made in writing and, unless otherwise stated in this contract, submitted within 6 years after accrual of the claim to the Contracting Officer for a written decision.

Thus, in order for a contractor's claim to be properly filed under the CDA, there must be submitted to the contracting officer in writing within six years after accrual of the claim:[72] (1) a demand or assertion, (2) which seeks, as matter of right, the payment of money in a sum certain, the adjustment or other interpretation of contract terms or other relief arising under or related to the contract, (3) with respect to which a contracting officer's written decision is requested, (4) and which is certified if the amount involved exceeds $100,000.

In *Reflectone, Inc. v. United States*,[73] the Federal Circuit held that the FAR definition of a "CDA claim" distinguishes between "routine" requests for payment—that is, a voucher or a progress payment invoice—and "nonroutine" claims for payment. A routine request for payment is not a CDA claim until it is converted into a claim.

---

[67] 41 U.S.C. § 605(a).

[68] FAR § 52.233-1, 48 C.F.R. § 52.233-1. *Reflectone, Inc. v. United States,* 60 F.3d 1572 (Fed. Cir. 1995).

[69] *Bill Strong Enters., Inc.,* ASBCA Nos. 42946, 43896, 93-3 BCA ¶ 25,961.

[70] 18 U.S.C. § 287; *United States v. Neifert-White Co.,* 390 U.S. 228 (1968).

[71] 48 C.F.R. § 33.215

[72] The six-year statute of limitations applies to contracts awarded on or after October 1, 1995. *Motorola, Inc. v. West,* 125 F.3d 1470 (Fed. Cir. 1997).

[73] *See* note 68.

Therefore, the CDA time limits for consideration by the contracting officer do not apply to routine requests for payment. CDA interest does not accrue on a routine request for payment. A routine request for payment can be converted into a CDA claim by written notice to the contracting officer if it is disputed as to liability or dollar value or if it is not acted upon in a reasonable time. In those circumstances, the conversion to a CDA claim occurs because the otherwise routine payment request is in dispute.

A nonroutine payment request does not have to be "in dispute" in order to be considered a CDA claim. However, the analysis does not stop with the distinction between a "routine" and "nonroutine" request for payment. For example, a termination for convenience proposal that was not accompanied by a request for a final decision did not become a CDA claim until after the subsequent negotiations failed and the contractor impliedly requested a final decision.[74] Given this uncertainty surrounding nonroutine payment requests, contractors should not assume that a change order proposal will be treated as a CDA claim absent notice to the contracting officer and the submission of any necessary certification.

22.9   Written Submission to the Contracting Officer

As indicated by the language of the disputes clause quoted above, the claim for the purposes of the CDA must be in writing and must be submitted to the contracting officer for a written decision. Accordingly, oral demands or assertions seeking compensation are not claims for the purposes of the CDA. Similarly, a written demand or submission that is submitted to a person who is not the contracting officer is not a claim for the purposes of the Act. The CDA defines a contracting officer as "[a]ny person who, by appointment in accordance with applicable regulations, has the authority to enter into and administer contracts and make determinations and findings with respect thereto."[75] This definition also includes an authorized representative of the contracting officer, acting within the limits of that person's authority.

Under certain circumstances, the submission of a written claim to a subordinate of the contracting officer has been held to be ineffective for the purposes of the Act.[76] A contractor should be able to avoid the problem of misdirected claims by ascertaining at the outset of performance these specific individuals, in addition to the contracting officer, who are authorized to receive claims. Moreover, if there is any doubt regarding whether the submission to the contracting officer's subordinate will be deemed appropriate under the Act, the contracting officer should be copied on the submission. This removes any doubt regarding the date when the contracting officer received the submission for the purposes of the Act.

---

[74] *Ellett Constr. Co. v. United States*, 93 F.3d 1537 (Fed. Cir. 1996).

[75] 41 U.S.C. § 601(3).

[76] *Lakeview Constr. Co. v. United States*, 21 Cl. Ct. 269 (1990); *but see West Coast Gen. Corp. v. Dalton*, 39 F.3d 312 (Fed. Cir. 1994); *Gardner Zemke Co.*, ASBCA No. 51499, 98-2 BCA ¶ 29,997.

22.10   Elements of a Claim

In submitting a claim, a contractor is not required to use any particular wording or format.[77] However, the contractor is required to give the contracting officer sufficient information that the contracting officer has adequate notice of the basis for, and the amount of, the claim.[78] Therefore, there are basically two elements of any claim: *entitlement* and *quantum*.

The entitlement portion establishes the factual and contractual basis supporting the contractor's right to recover from the government. For example, in a claim involving the alleged misinterpretation of a specification by the government, the entitlement portion would describe how the government misinterpreted the specification as contrasted to the contractor's reasonable understanding of the contract's requirements. In addition, that section would also describe the extra work and delay, if any, caused by the misinterpretation.

The second part of the claim is quantum. At a minimum, the quantum portion of a monetary claim requires that the contractor state a "sum certain" under the Act and the disputes clause.[79] In that part of the claim, the contractor describes the amount of money or time to which it is entitled and attempts to relate cause (act by the government) to effect (expenditure of money). The relation of cause and effect can be quite difficult, as it often encompasses issues of scheduling, cost accounting, and the support for estimates. As with any contract, project documentation is often critical to establishing cause and effect. The evaluation of a contractor's claims for time or money can be significantly affected by the nature and quality of the contemporaneous records maintained by the contractor. For example, some government contracts expressly require that the contractor document on a daily basis the specific critical path activities affected by delays such as adverse weather.[80] Even if there is no specific contract requirement for contemporaneous documentation of the extra time or expense incurred by the contractor, the absence of such documentation can create a substantial hurdle to recovery.[81]

There is no simple test to determine the degree of detail necessary to constitute a claim. In general, the boards and Court of Federal Claims have adopted a standard similar to notice pleadings. That is, the contractor must provide the contracting officer with adequate notice of the basis and the amount of the claim and a request for the contracting officer to render a final decision.[82] In other words, the contractor

---

[77] *Contract Cleaning Maintenance, Inc. v. United States*, 811 F.2d 586, 592 (Fed. Cir. 1986); *Clearwater Constructors, Inc. v. United States*, 56 Fed. Cl. 303 (2003).

[78] *Mitcho, Inc.*, ASBCA No. 41847, 91-2 BCA ¶ 23,860; *Holk Dev., Inc.*, ASBCA No. 40579 *et al.*, 90-3 BCA ¶ 23,086; *Gauntt Constr. Co.*, ASBCA No. 33323, 87-3 BCA ¶ 20,221.

[79] FAR § 52.233-1(c); *MDP Constr. Inc.*, ASBCA Nos. 52769, *et al.*, 01-1 BCA ¶ 31,359.

[80] *Consolidated Const., Inc.*, ASBCA No. 46498, 99-1 BCA ¶ 30,148.

[81] *Bechtel Nat'l, Inc.*, NASA BCA No. 1186-7, 90-1 BCA ¶ 22,549; *Centex Bateson*, VABCA No. 4613 *et al*, 99-1 BCA ¶ 30,153 (number of RFIs and changes are not enough by themselves to demonstrate loss of productivity); *Hensel Phelps*, ASBCA 49270, 99-2 BCA ¶ 30,531.

[82] *Metric Constr. Co. v. United States*, 1 Cl. Ct. 383, 392 (1983); *I.B.A. Co.*, ASBCA No. 37182, 89-1 BCA ¶ 21,576.

should assert specific rights and request specific relief. Ultimately, whether a contractor's submission constitutes a claim depends upon the totality of the circumstances and communications between the parties.[83] For example, the following submissions have been found to be claims:

(1) A letter in which a contractor specified various items that a government audit had disallowed but to which the contractor claimed entitlement. The letter was viewed together with a prior letter from the contractor giving a detailed breakdown of the additional amounts to which the contractor believed it was entitled and referring to the contractor's previous request for "funding of [a] back-wage demand."[84]

(2) A letter sent by a company having a contract for transportation services at an Air Force base stating that the company viewed certain newly demanded bus service as beyond the contract's requirements and specifically seeking "compensation of $11,000.04 per year, to be billed at $916.67 per month."[85]

(3) A letter from the contractor's attorney to the contracting officer that "expressed interest" in a final decision with respect to the contractor's request for contract reformation and that stated that the contractor was seeking a decision so that it could pursue its appeal routes under the CDA, if necessary.[86]

(4) Letters that, when taken together, showed the contractor protesting the payment of additional sums under a contract to purchase crude oil from the government and demanding that certain identified wire transfer payments comprising those sums be returned to the contractor.[87]

(5) A contractor's cover letter that attached a detailed argument by a subcontractor setting forth the basis of the subcontractor's disagreement with the government regarding the effect of a contract modification.[88]

However, the claim must be made "by the contractor"; accordingly, a letter from the contractor's lawyer to the contracting officer has been held to be insufficient to establish a claim.[89] The burden is on the claimant to identify, specify, and perfect its claims. For example, in *Mingus Constructors, Inc. v. United States*,[90] the contractor had complained of malicious harassment by the government's project representative

---

[83] *Transamerica Ins. Corp. v. United States*, 973 F.2d 1573 (Fed. Cir. 1992); *Penn Envtl. Control, Inc.*, VABCA No. 3599, 93-3 BCA ¶ 26,021; *Atlas Elevator Co. v. General Servs. Admin.*, GSBCA No. 11655, 93-1 BCA ¶ 25,216; *Winding Specialists Co.*, ASBCA No. 37765, 89-2 BCA ¶ 21,737.

[84] *Contract Cleaning Maintenance, Inc. v. United States*, 811 F.2d 586, 592 (Fed. Cir. 1986).

[85] *Tecom, Inc. v. United States*, 732 F.2d 935, 937 (Fed. Cir. 1984).

[86] *Paragon Energy Corp. v. United States*, 645 F.2d 966, 976 (Ct. Cl. 1981).

[87] *Alliance Oil & Refining Co. v. United States*, 13 Cl. Ct. 496, 499–500 (1987).

[88] *Clearwater Constructor's, Inc.*, supra note 77.

[89] *Construction Equip. Lease v. United States*, 26 Cl. Ct. 341 (1992). In contrast, the bankruptcy trustee for a contractor in bankruptcy has been held to be the proper party to assert a prebankruptcy claim against the government. *See Jerry Dodds d/b/a Dodds & Assocs.*, ASBCA No. 51682, 02-1 BCA ¶ 31,844.

[90] 812 F.2d 1387 (Fed. Cir. 1987).

during the construction of a road and had stated an intention to claim the added costs resulting from the alleged harassment. These general complaints were set forth in various letters. At the conclusion of the project, the contractor executed a standard final release form and added a notation to the release that it did not apply to "claims" stated in the earlier correspondence. The Federal Circuit affirmed the summary judgment granted to the government, finding that the contractor had never properly identified, specified, or perfected its claims. As the claims were never properly made, the release barred the contractor from making a valid claim after it was executed.

Some decisions of the Claims Court and the Federal Circuit have emphasized the need for an explicit request for a final decision as part of the submission of a claim. However, in *Transamerica Insurance Corp. v. United States*,[91] the Federal Circuit expressly rejected a rule that a "claim" must include a specific request for a final decision. In particular, a formal demand for final decision has been held to be unnecessary if the claim gave a clear indication that a decision was desired.[92]

Even though there is case law that there is no absolute requirement for a specific request for a final decision, there is a risk that the failure to make a specific request for a final decision will be viewed as evidence that there was no dispute between the parties sufficient to constitute a "claim" under the Act. For this reason, correspondence from a contractor that contains information detailing costs and, rather than demanding or requesting that the contracting officer issue a final decision, merely expresses a willingness to reach an agreement may not constitute a claim.[93] Similarly, the passage of time may not convert a proposal into a CDA claim. In *Santa Fe Engineers, Inc. v. Garrett*,[94] the contractor's certified proposal had been pending for more than two years, during which time the parties met on several occasions to discuss the proposal and the contractor submitted additional information for the government's consideration. During that period of time, the contractor never asked for a contracting officer's final decision. The Federal Circuit affirmed the board decision,[95] which had concluded that the failure to ask for a contracting officer's final decision was an indication that the parties had not reached an impasse in their negotiations and that the matter was not sufficiently in dispute to constitute a CDA claim.

Often the decision whether a particular submission is a claim depends upon the totality of the circumstances. For example, in one case, a certified request for an equitable adjustment accompanied by a letter requesting a final decision did constitute a valid claim even though the letter also suggested the possibility, or hope, of a

---

[91] 973 F.2d at 1572 (Fed. Cir. 1992).

[92] *Cable Antenna Sys.*, ASBCA No. 36184, 90-3 BCA ¶ 23,203; *Ellett Constr. Co. v. United States, supra* note 74.

[93] *Hoffman Constr. Co. v. United States*, 7 Cl. Ct. 518, 525 (1985). *See also Technassociates, Inc., supra* note 51, at 209–10 (letters contractor sent in order to get contracting officer to negotiate "on the future direction of the contract" did not constitute claims).

[94] 991 F.2d 1579, 1583–84 (Fed. Cir. 1993). However, in *D.H. Blattner & Sons, Inc.*, IBCA Nos. 2589, 2643, 89-3 BCA ¶ 22,230, the board held that a properly certified letter using the term "proposal" was not a claim. The Federal Circuit reversed this decision in an unpublished decision. *See Blattner & Sons, Inc. v. United States*, 909 F.2d 1495 (Fed. Cir. 1990).

[95] *Santa Fe Eng'rs, Inc.*, ASBCA No. 36292, 92-2 BCA ¶ 24,795.

negotiated resolution to the dispute.[96] In contrast, a letter sent to the contracting officer during negotiations on a proposal requesting that the matter be referred to an auditor did not qualify as a claim, because a contracting officer had not been asked to issue a decision.[97]

Finally, the contractor may not submit a claim in an unspecified amount or in an amount that is open-ended.[98] A proper claim and request for a final decision exists only when the amount sought is either set forth in a "sum-certain"[99] or is determinable by a simple mathematical calculation or from the information provided by the contractor.[100]

22.11   Certification Requirement

The CDA currently requires that a claim in excess of $100,000 be certified.[101] The accepted purpose of the certification requirement is to discourage the submission of unwarranted or inflated contractor claims, to decrease litigation, and to encourage settlements.[102] Prior to an amendment to the CDA in 1992, proper compliance with the certification requirement was a prerequisite to invoking the disputes-resolution procedures of the Act.[103] If the requirements for a properly certified claim were not satisfied, any final decision on that claim was a nullity, and any appeal or suit was subject to dismissal.[104]

---

[96] *Isles Eng'g & Constr., Inc. v. United States*, 26 Cl. Ct. 240, 243 (1992).

[97] *G.S.&L. Mechanical & Constr., Inc.*, DOT BCA No. 1856, 87-2 BCA ¶ 19,882; *see also Huntington Builders*, ASBCA No. 33945, 87-2 BCA ¶ 19,898, at 100,654–655 (letters to contracting officer that, when taken together, alleged defective specifications and requested a 30-day time extension to contract and release of monies withheld for liquidated damages did not constitute a claim because no specific monetary relief was requested for costs incurred as a result of contractor's having to comply with allegedly defective specifications).

[98] *Metric Constr. Co. v. United States*, 14 Cl. Ct. 177, 179–80 (1988) (contractor's submissions made it clear that contractor was seeking to recover extended home office overhead and third-party indemnification fees, but the submissions did not constitute a claim because the amount was not specified).

[99] Disputes clause ¶ (c), FAR § 52.233-1, 48 C.F.R. § 52.233-1. A claim for a "sum certain" that reserved the right to include additional line items to "modify the presentation" was, in fact, deemed to be a predicate for negotiations, rather than a CDA claim. *McElroy Mach. & Mfg. Co., Inc.*, ASBCA No. 39416, 92-3 BCA ¶ 25,107. The sum certain requirement is determined when the claim is filed, not when the complaint is filed. *Morgan & Son Earthmoving, Inc.*, ASBCA No. 53524, 02-2 BCA ¶ 31,874; *MDP Constr. Inc., supra* note 79. If the monetary claim does not explicitly state a sum certain, it may be acceptable if the amount could be determined from the submission by simple arithmetic. *Mulunesh Berhe*, ASBCA No. 49681, 96-2 BCA ¶ 28,339; *J&J Maintenance, Inc.*, ASBCA No. 50984, 00-1 BCA ¶ 30,784.

[100] *Metric Constr. Co., supra* note 82, at 392.

[101] 41 U.S.C. §§ 605(c)(1) & 605(c)(2).

[102] *Paul E. Lehman, Inc. v. United States*, 673 F.2d 352, 354 (Ct. Cl. 1982).

[103] *Id.* at 352.

[104] Prior to 1992, if a claim in excess of the monetary threshold was not properly certified, interest did not accrue, *Fidelity Constr. Co. v. United States,* 700 F.2d 1379, 1382-85 (Fed. Cir. 1983); no valid final decision could be issued, *Paul E. Lehman, Inc., supra* note 102, *Conoc Constr. Corp. v. United States*, 3 Cl. Ct. 146, 147-48 (1983); and the contractor had no right of access to either a board of contract appeals or a court, *Skelly and Loy v. United States*, 685 F.2d 414 (Ct. Cl. 1982); *W. M. Schlosser Co. v. United States,* 705 F.2d 1336, 1338-39 (Fed. Cir. 1983).

Section 907(a) of the Federal Courts Administration Act significantly modified many of the more rigid formalities of the CDA pertaining to the certification of claims while leaving intact the basic policy safeguards underlying the requirement for the certification.[105] This amendment made the following changes to the law regarding the requirements for a proper CDA claim certification and the consequences if the certification was "defective" or improper in some manner.

(1) Broadened the class of individuals who could properly certify a claim to include anyone who was authorized to bind the contractor with respect to the claim.

(2) Expressly stated that a "defective" certification would not deprive a board or court of jurisdiction over that claim.

(3) Required that a "defective" certification be cured before a board or court could render a decision on that claim.

(4) Excused a contracting officer from issuing a final decision on a defectively certified claim if the contracting officer advised the contractor in writing of the basis for the conclusion that the certification was inadequate within 60 days of the date of the contracting officer's receipt of the claim.

(5) Allowed CDA interest to accrue on a claim even though the certification was defective.

These changes clearly liberalized the rules related to CDA claim certification. However, the fundamental requirement for the certification as an element of a claim in excess of $100,000 remains in effect. Consequently, the total absence of a required certification will not be treated as the equivalent of a "defective" certification.[106] If a claim is submitted without the required certification, and a final decision is issued, that omission cannot be cured by the submission of a retroactive submission. The claim submission and the certification must occur at the same time.[107] The certification must be separately signed, as at least one board has ruled that the failure to sign the certification is "more akin" to a failure to certify.[108] Moreover, the failure to properly certify a claim most likely will delay its resolution and increase the cost of resolving the dispute.

Therefore, it remains important to understand the monetary threshold at which a claim must be certified, how it must be certified, who can certify it, and the relationship of that certification to other government contract certifications.

---

[105] Pub. L. No. 102-572.

[106] *Golub-Wegco Kansas City I, LLC v. General Services Administration*, GSBCA No. 15387, 01-2 BCA ¶ 31,553. *Westar Engineering, Inc.*, ASBCA No. 52484, 02-1 BCA ¶ 31,759. In *Westar*, the board dismissed an uncertified claim labeled as a request for an interpretation upon concluding that it was a veiled quantum claim in excess of $100,000; *Schnider's of OKC Inc.*, ASBCA No. 53947, 03-1 BCA ¶ 32,160.

[107] *Golub-Wegco Kansas City I, LLC v. General Services Administration*, *supra* note 106; if a claim and its certification are separately submitted, it is treated as a new claim at the time of the certification. *See J&J Maintenance, Inc.*, *supra* note 99.

[108] *Hawaii Cyberspace*, ASBCA No. 54065, 04-1 BCA ¶ 32,455.

22.12 Monetary Threshold for Certification

The Act requires a certification when the contractor asserts a claim exceeding $100,000. Therefore, it is not possible to bypass a certification requirement by breaking a claim into a series of separate claims each of which is $100,000 or less.[109] The test is whether there exists a "single, unitary claim based upon a common and related set of operative facts," which the contractor, unintentionally or otherwise, divided into separate and distinct claims.[110] However, if the claims are distinct and independent, with one claim having no relationship to the operative facts of the other claim, each independent claim of $100,000 or less need not be certified.[111] Even if the contractor submits a single letter to the contracting officer that reflects claims totaling more than $100,000, the certification is not required unless the claims arose from a common or related set of operative facts and are therefore truly a unitary claim.[112] In other words, does the claim or claims submitted by the contractor arise from the same or different events or causes of action?[113]

The following examples illustrate the application of this test. In one case, the contractor alleged that one differing site condition gave rise to three separate claims: one for additional paving costs; one for additional insurance, supervision, and maintenance costs; and one for loss of interest on funds spent to perform additional work. The court concluded that, in fact, there was just one claim.[114] Similarly, when a contract was terminated for the convenience of the government, the court concluded that a contractor's demand for "pre-termination and post-termination items" constituted one claim because both items were directly related to the government's termination of the contract, and the resolution of both items depended upon what, if any, liability the government incurred as a result of its action.[115] Similarly, in a case where the

---

[109] *Fidelity & Deposit Co. of Md. v. United States*, 2 Cl. Ct. 137, 143–43 (1983). Initially, the certification threshold was $50,000, and this amount is referenced in the earlier CDA decisions. While the monetary threshold has been increased, that statutory amendment did not affect the basic analysis in those decisions regarding efforts to avoid the certification requirement by dividing the claim into separate parts, each less than the threshold amount for a certification. *See also, Columbia Constr. Co., Inc.*, ASBCA No. 28536, 96-1 BCA ¶ 27,970; *D&K Painting Co., Inc.*, DOT BCA No. 4014, 98-2 BCA ¶ 30,064.

[110] *Warchol Constr. Co. v. United States*, 2 Cl. Ct. 384, 389 (1983). *See also LDG Timber Enters., Inc. v. United States*, 8 Cl. Ct. 445, 452 (1985).

[111] *Little River Lumber Co. v. United States*, 21 Cl. Ct. 527 (1990); *Walsky Constr. Co. v. United States*, 3 Cl. Ct. 615, 619 (1983); *Reliance Ins. Co. v. United States*, 27 Fed. Cl. 815, 822 (1993); *C.B.C. Enters., Inc.*, ASBCA No. 43496, 92-2 BCA ¶ 24,803.

[112] *Placeway Constr. Corp. v. United States*, 910 F.2d 835 (Fed. Cir. 1990); *Spirit Leveling Contractors v. United States*, 19 Cl. Ct. 84 (1989).

[113] *Zinger Constr. Co.*, ASBCA No. 28788, 86-2 BCA ¶ 18,920; *J.S. Alberici Constr. Co., Inc., and Martin K. Eby Constr. Co., Inc., a Joint Venture*, ENG BCA No. 6178, 98-2 BCA ¶ 29,875.

[114] *Warchol Constr. Co., supra* note 110.

[115] *Palmer & Sicard, Inc. v. United States*, 4 Cl. Ct. 420, 422–23 (1984).

contract involved security guard services at five different locations in Boston, the court held that the contractor could not fragment its total dollar claim into separate claims based upon each of the different locations. The rationale was that the amounts claimed from the various locations were based upon the same operative facts (a total number of hours of services performed for which a total number of dollars allegedly was due).[116] In another case, however, the Armed Services Board of Contract Appeal determined that when 18 different claims arose from different causative events and were brought under different legal theories, such as differing site conditions and defective specifications, it was proper to separate the claims.[117]

22.13 Modification of Claim Amount

Sometimes a claim that initially does not exceed $100,000 (and therefore is not certified) increases in amount after a contracting officer's decision is issued. In these circumstances, the question arises whether the contractor can still proceed on the basis of the increased claim before the court or board of contract appeals, or whether it is necessary for the contractor to certify the claim in the increased amount and resubmit it to the contracting officer for a decision.

This question was addressed in *Tecom, Inc. v. United States,*[118] In *Tecom,* the contractor's claim was less than the threshold value for certification when it was submitted to the contracting officer. However, by the time the company filed its complaint before the Armed Services Board of Contract Appeals, the amount of the claim exceeded the monetary threshold for a certification. This increase was the result of two events that occurred after the contracting officer's decision: a reevaluation of the claim by the contractor and the government's exercise of an option to extend the contract for an additional year. Under these circumstances, the court held that it was not necessary for the contractor to certify and resubmit its claim.

Tecom stands for the proposition that a monetary claim properly considered by a contracting officer "need not be certified or recertified if that very same claim (but in an increased amount reasonably based on further information) comes before a board or a court."[119] The Federal Circuit stated that it would be disruptive of normal litigation procedures "if any increase in the amount of a claim based on matters developed in litigation before the court [or board] had to be submitted to the contracting officer before the court [or board] could continue to final resolution on the

---

[116] *Black Star Sec., Inc. v. United States*, 5 Cl. Ct. 110 (1984).

[117] *Zinger Constr. Co., supra* note 113.

[118] 732 F.2d 935 (Fed. Cir. 1984).

[119] *Id.* at 938.

claim."[120] In a footnote, however, the *Tecom* court pointed out that its decision should not be taken as an invitation to seek to evade the certification requirement.[121] Thus, a contractor that deliberately understates the amount of its original claim (with the intention of raising the amount on appeal on the basis of information that was readily available at the time the claim first was submitted) may well find its subsequent suit in the Court of Federal Claims or its board appeal dismissed for lack of any certification.[122] Dismissal occurs because the total absence of a certification is different from a defective (or inadequate) certification.

22.14   CDA Certification Language

The CDA sets forth the language to be used in the certification. The contractor must certify "that the claim is made in good faith, that the supporting data are accurate and complete to the best of [the contractor's] knowledge and belief, and that the amount requested accurately reflects the contract adjustment for which the contractor believes the Government is liable."[123] The procurement regulations,[124] as well as the disputes clause utilized in contracts covered by the CDA,[125] contain identical language. The 1992 Amendment to the Act added a fourth element to the disputes clause certification. This element requires that the person signing the certification state that "the certifier is duly authorized to certify the claim on behalf of the contractor."[126]

---

[120] *Id.* at 937–38 (quoting *J. F. Shea Co. v. United States*, 4 Cl. Ct. 46, 54 (parentheticals in *Tecom*)). *See Kunz Constr. Co. v. United States*, 12 Cl. Ct. 74, 79 (1987) (stating that contractor can enlarge dollar amount of its claim in court over what was presented to contracting officer under two conditions: (1) if increase is based on same set of operative facts previously submitted to contracting officer, and (2) if court finds that contractor neither knew, nor reasonably should have known, at time when claim was presented to contracting officer of factors justifying increase). *See also E. C. Schleyer Pump Co.*, ASBCA No. 33900, 87-3 BCA ¶ 19,986 (costs that were merely an additional area of damages from same facts alleged in claim could be brought before board though not presented to contracting officer). Also, in *Glenn v. United States*, 858 F.2d 1577, 1580 (Fed. Cir. 1988), the contractor submitted a claim to the contracting officer in the amount of $31,500. Because the claim was less than $50,000 (the applicable threshold for certification at that time), the contractor did not certify it. The contracting officer issued a final decision denying the claim, which the contractor appealed to the Armed Services Board of Contract Appeals. Thereafter, the contracting officer issued a second final decision. In that decision, the contracting officer stated that he was withholding $66,570.32 from the contractor (consisting of the $31,500 that the contractor previously had sought to recover and an additional $35,070.32). Relying on its prior decision in *Tecom,* the Federal Circuit held that it was not necessary for the contractor to certify its $66,570.32 claim before bringing suit in the Claims Court. "Because Glenn was not required to certify his $31,500 claim before the C.O., he need not have certified the $66,570.32 resulting from the denial of his initial claim . . . and [the] additional setoffs."

[121] 732 F.2d at 938, n.2. *See D.E.W., Inc.*, ASBCA No. 35173, 89-3 BCA ¶ 22,008.

[122] *Id.* Even the reduction of a claim below the applicable threshold at the board will not eliminate the need for a certification if the claim, as submitted to the contracting officer, exceeded the certification threshold. *Building Sys. Contractors*, VABCA Nos. 2749 *et al.*, 89-2 BCA ¶ 21,678.

[123] 41 U.S.C. § 605(c)(1).

[124] FAR § 33.207(a), 48 C.F.R. § 33.207(a).

[125] FAR § 52.233-1, 48 C.F.R. § 52.233-1.

[126] 41 U.S.C. § 605(c)(7).

Under the pre-1992 statutory language, the boards, the United States Claims Court, and the Federal Circuit developed strict rules defining a defective or inadequate certification. These rules, in conjunction with the holding that the submission of a proper certification for any claim in excess of the monetary threshold was a jurisdictional requirement,[127] created extensive problems for claimants and their counsel. While the 1992 Amendment eliminated the rule that the submission of a valid certification was a jurisdictional requirement that could not be waived, potential problems for a contractor regarding the form of the certification remain. To the extent that the cases interpreting the preamendment Act provide guidance regarding the proper wording of a certification, it is possible that these decisions will still be relied upon by the boards and the courts in determining whether a certification is "defective."

Prior to the 1992 Amendment, there was a split in authority regarding the contractor's obligation to strictly track the statutory certification language in order to submit a valid certification. One line of cases took a very formalistic view and held that any deviation from the statutory language would be subject to strict scrutiny. In those cases, a contractor's attempt to deviate from the statutory language by substituting alternate language was usually held to invalidate the certification.[128] A second line of cases held that substantial compliance was sufficient and the inadvertent omission of a few words in the certification and the omission of the claimed amount, which was stated elsewhere in the claim, were not fatal defects.[129] In general, any certification must simultaneously state all elements of the statutory requirements, and an effort to satisfy the certification requirement by reference to multiple letters or by piecemeal submissions has not been deemed to be sufficient to satisfy the statutory requirement.[130]

In endorsing the substantial compliance approach, the GSBCA accepted a certification that omitted any reference to "knowledge or belief." The board held that this unqualified certification "more fully exposed [the contractor] to potential liability" for false statements than "if it had mimicked the words of the statute."[131] In contrast,

---

[127] *Environmental Specialists, Inc. v. United States*, 23 Cl. Ct. 751 (1991); *Skelly & Loy v. United States*, 685 F.2d 414, 419 (Ct. Cl. 1982); *Paul E. Lehman v. United States*, 673 F.2d 352 (Ct. Cl. 1982); *Kaco Contracting Co.*, ASBCA No. 43066, 92-1 BCA ¶ 24,603; *Guilanani Contracting Co.*, ASBCA No. 41435, 91-2 BCA ¶ 23,774.

[128] *Centex Constr. Co.*, ASBCA No. 35338, 89-1 BCA ¶ 21,259; *Liberty Envtl. Specialties, Inc.*, VABCA No. 2948, 89-3 BCA ¶ 21,982.

[129] *United States v. General Elec. Corp.*, 727 F.2d 1567, 1569 (Fed. Cir. 1984); *Young Enters., Inc. v. United States*, 26 Cl. Ct. 858, 862 (1992); *P. J. Dick, Inc.*, GSBCA No. 11847, *et al.*, 93-1 BCA ¶ 25,263. In *Metric Constructors, Inc.*, ASBCA No. 50843, 98-2 BCA ¶ 30,088, the ASBCA held that a signed termination for convenience settlement proposal on Standard Form 1438 contained certification language sufficiently similar to the CDA to constitute a correctable certification. However, in *Keydata Systems, Inc. v. Dept. of Treasury*, GSBCA No. 14281-TD, 97-2 BCA ¶ 29,330, the GSBCA held that the 1992 Amendment did not authorize contractors to cure defective certifications resulting from fraud, bad faith, or "negligent disregard" of the certification requirements.

[130] *W. H. Moseley Co. v. United States*, 677 F.2d 850, 852 (Ct. Cl. 1982); *Black Star Sec., Inc. v. United States*, 5 Cl. Ct. 110, 117 (1984); *Parriono Enters. v. United States*, 230 Ct. Cl. 1052 (1982).

[131] *P. J. Dick, Inc.*, *supra* note 129 at 126,605.

the ASBCA has held that a failure to state that the contractor "believes" the government is liable invalidates the certification.[132] In addition, the following certifications have been held to be defective:

(1) A certification that varied from the language of the statute and the disputes clause by referring to "all data used" instead of the "supporting data" for the claim (thereby restricting the certification to "unidentified data [which the contractor] chose to use while the statute requires certification of all data that support the claim").[133]

(2) A certification that omitted the assertion that the supporting data was accurate and complete.[134]

(3) A certification in which the contractor stated that it would not assume any legal obligations that it would not have without the certification, that the data submitted was "as accurate and complete as practicable," and that the contractor was not demanding a "particular amount."[135]

By contrast, in another case, a contractor whose certification did not contain the amount of the claim involved and did not have the words "the amount requested accurately reflects the contract adjustment for which the contractor believes the government is liable" still was found to be in substantial compliance with the certification requirement. The statement in which the certification was contained did have the remainder of the elements required by the Act; and, when the statement was read in its entirety and together with documents that accompanied it, all of the information and statements required by the statute were found to be present.[136] Notwithstanding the degree of flexibility that may be allowed by the liberalized amendment to the Act, the prudent course is to track the language of the Act when certifying a claim.

22.15 Supporting Data

A contractor that certifies its claim by tracking the language of the statute still may find itself confronted with the argument that the data supporting its claim is inadequate for purposes of the certification requirement. For the most part, though, neither the courts nor the boards have taken an overly stringent attitude with respect to the extent of the supporting data.

In *Metric Construction Co. v. United States*,[137] the government argued that the contractor's certification was defective because the contractor had failed to attach

---

[132] *C. F. Elecs.*, ASBCA No. 4077, 91-2 BCA ¶ 23,746.

[133] *Gauntt Constr. Co.*, ASBCA No. 33323, 87-3 BCA ¶ 20,221 at 102,412.

[134] *Raymond Kaiser Eng'rs, Inc./Kaiser Steel Corp., a Joint Venture*, ASBCA No. 34133, 87-3 BCA ¶ 20,140, at 101,940–41.

[135] *Cochran Constr. Co.*, ASBCA No. 34378, 87-3 BCA ¶ 19,993 at 101,280-81, *aff'd on reconsideration*, 87-3 BCA ¶ 20,114.

[136] *General Elec. Corp.*, *supra* note 129, at 1569.

[137] 1 Cl. Ct. 383 (1983).

copies of the pertinent change order modifications to its claim. In rejecting the government's argument, the court observed that the certification requirement "was not intended, nor should it be so construed, to require a full evidentiary presentation before the contracting officer."[138] The court noted that the contracting officer had not denied the contractor's claim for lack of supporting data and that the data that had been presented had assisted the contracting officer "in making a meaningful determination on the dispute before him."[139]

The Department of Energy Board of Contract Appeals took a similar position and cited *Metric* with approval in *Newhall Refining Co.*[140] In response to the government's argument that the contractors involved had not submitted accurate and complete supporting data when they certified their claims, the board noted that, on their face, the certifications met the requirements of the Act, that the claims were "articulated in a clear and concise fashion," that the contractors had notified the contracting officer of the basis for their claims prior to submitting them, and that the contracting officer already was in possession of information relating to the claims.[141] The board also noted the fact that the claims before it involved a legal issue of contract interpretation, and it found "highly persuasive" the fact that the contracting officer had not requested additional information from the contractors.[142] Under these circumstances, the board determined that the data submitted with the claims was "adequate."[143]

These cases suggest that, when the language of the contractor's certification meets the requirements of the Act, and the contracting officer is provided with the needed information to render a final decision and has issued a final decision, the contractor probably does not have to worry about having its case derailed by a government assertion at the board or court that it failed to submit adequate supporting data. However, adequate supporting data for the purposes of a claim submission may not be sufficient to prevail on the merits.

22.16   Who May Certify the Claim?

The 1992 Amendment to the CDA effectively eliminated the prior questions regarding the authority of the person signing the certification and the extent of the personal knowledge that the person certifying the claim needed to have regarding the underlying facts set forth in the claim.

With the enactment of the 1992 Amendment to the CDA,[144] questions of a person's authority to certify a claim should be minimal, so long as the certifier follows the language of the amended Act, which requires an express representation that the

---

[138] *Id.* at 391.

[139] *Id.*

[140] EBCA Nos. 363-7-86, *et al.,* 87-1 BCA ¶ 19,340.

[141] *Id.* at 97,583.

[142] *Id.*

[143] *Id.*

[144] 41 U.S.C. § 605(c)(7).

person signing the certification is authorized to do so. In that context, it is not necessary for the person certifying the claim to have personal knowledge of the facts and data supporting the claim. Rather, it is sufficient for the person certifying the claim to rely upon data and facts developed by others within the contractor's organization.[145]

22.17   OTHER CERTIFICATION REQUIREMENTS

The complexity of the CDA certification is only compounded by the fact that there are at least two other claim-related certifications that a contractor may be required to submit under other statutes. Contracts with agencies of the Department of Defense are subject to an additional statutory certification requirement.[146] This law requires that any request for equitable adjustment to the contract terms or request for relief under Public Law 85-804 that exceeds the "simplified acquisition threshold"[147] may not be paid unless it is certified by a person authorized to bind the contractor at the time of submission. This certification must state that the request is made in good faith and that the supporting data are accurate and complete to the best of that person's knowledge and belief. The DFARS Regulation implementing this law expands the scope of the certification.[148] The certification must state that the request for an equitable adjustment includes only the cost for performing the change, does not include any costs that have already been reimbursed or separately claimed, and that all claimed indirect costs are properly allocable to the change.

A third certification is required by the Truth in Negotiations Act.[149] There are significant differences between the Truth in Negotiations certificate and the two certificates previously discussed. Under the Truth in Negotiations Act, the certificate is not provided until the parties reach agreement on a price—at the time of the handshake. The threshold for a Truth in Negotiations certificate is $550,000 for contracts, as well as subcontracts under such contracts and modifications to any contract.[150] The Truth in Negotiations Act provides a specific remedy when the data does not meet the requirements of accuracy, currency, and completeness. Under the Act and the related regulations, the government is entitled to a price reduction if the data is found to be defective—that is, inaccurate, not current, or not complete.[151]

---

[145] *Fischbach & Moore Int'l Corp. v. Christopher*, 987 F.2d 759, 762 (Fed. Cir. 1993).

[146] 10 U.S.C. § 2410(a).

[147] $100,000 as of 02/20/04. *See* 48 C.F.R. § 2.101.

[148] DFARS § 252.243-7002 (July 2003).

[149] 10 U.S.C. § 2306a. This statute applies only to the Department of Defense and the National Aeronautical and Space Administration (NASA). By regulation, the requirements of this statute have been extended to the civilian agencies. 48 C.F.R. § 15.804; 48 C.F.R. § 52.215-22; 48 C.F.R. § 52.215-2; 48 C.F.R. § 52.215-24 and 48 C.F.R. § 52.215-25.

[150] 10 U.S.C. § 2306a; 41 U.S.C. § 2546 ; 48 C.F.R. § 15.403-4.

[151] 48 C.F.R. § 15.407-1.

These certification requirements overlap to some extent. However, there are sufficient differences that confusion can develop. Table 22.2 contains a chart comparing the current requirements set forth in each of these statutes and their implementing regulations.

Table 22.2   Comparison of Certifications

	Contract Disputes Act (CDA)	DOD Contracts	Truth in Negotiations Act
Language:	(1) Claim made in good faith. (2) Supporting data accurate and complete to best of contractor's knowledge and belief. (3) Amount requested accurately reflects adjustment for which contractor believes government liable. (4) Certifier is duly authorized to certify the claim on behalf of the contractor.	(1) Claim made in good faith. (2) Supporting data accurate and complete to best of contractor's knowledge and belief. (3) Amount requested accurately reflects adjustment for which contractor believes government liable.	Data in support of proposal is accurate, current, and complete.
$ Threshold:	Claim > $100,000.	Claim or request for adjustment > $100,000.	Price or adjustment: Over $550,000 (subject to adjustment for inflation to nearest $50,000 every five years).
Certified by:	"Any person duly authorized to bind the contractor with respect to the claim."	"Any person duly authorized to bind the contractor with respect to the claim."	"The contractor" is anyone authorized to sign contractual documents.
Date Required:	When submitted as a "claim" under CDA.	Upon submission of a request for equitable adjustment, or request for extraordinary relief.	Any time of agreement ("handshake") on price.

22.18   SUBCONTRACTOR CLAIM CERTIFICATION

Submission and CDA certification of subcontractor claims can present problems for prime contractors. To varying degrees, the prime may not fully agree with the positions asserted by the subcontractor. In addition, it is likely that the prime contractor must, to some extent, rely on data and information developed outside of its organization. Notwithstanding these practical problems, both the boards and the courts have held that the certification of a subcontractor's claim must be signed by the prime contractor and contain all of the required elements.[152]

The prime contractor is not entitled to qualify its certificate by stating that it is "based on" a certificate provided by the subcontractor[153] or that it was "subject to review."[154] Absolute agreement with the subcontractor's claim is not essential, as the prime contractor may certify a claim with which it does not fully agree, if it concludes the subcontractor's claim is made in good faith and is not frivolous.[155] In *Arnold M. Diamond, Inc. v. Dalton,*[156] the prime contractor, which had previously rejected its subcontractor's claim, certified it on the order of a federal bankruptcy court. The Federal Circuit reversed an earlier board decision that refused to accept the contractor's certification as being in good faith. In the Federal Circuit's opinion, certification of a claim upon the direction of a federal bankruptcy judge satisfied the Act's requirements.

22.19   GOVERNMENT CLAIMS

The CDA also covers government claims. The Act provides that "[a]ll claims by the Government against a contractor relating to a contract shall be the subject of a decision by the contracting officer."[157] While most government claims are the subject of a final decision, a government withholding of a "sum certain" due a contractor,[158] an

---

[152] *United States v. Johnson Controls, Inc.,* 713 F.2d 1541 (Fed. Cir. 1983); *Century Constr. Co. v. United States,* 22 Cl. Ct. 63 (1990) (prime may not substitute subcontractor's name for itself); *Lockheed Martin Tactical Defense Sys. v. Dept. of Commerce,* GSBCA No. 14450-COM, 98-1 BCA ¶ 29,717; *Harrington Assoc., Inc.,* GSBCA No. 6795, 82-2 BCA ¶ 16,103.

[153] *Cox Constr. Co.,* ASBCA No. 31072, 85-3 BCA ¶ 18,507.

[154] *Alvarado Constr., Inc., v. United States,* 32 Fed. Cl. 184 (1994).

[155] *United States v. Turner Constr. Co.,* 827 F.2d 1554 (Fed. Cir. 1987).

[156] 25 F.3d 1006 (Fed. Cir. 1994).

[157] 41 U.S.C. § 605(a). Some cases indicated that the boards may decline jurisdiction over government counterclaims where the counterclaims were never presented to the contractor nor given an opportunity to comment on it. *See Osborn Eng'g Co.,* DOT CAB No. 2165, 90-2 BCA ¶ 22,749; *Instruments & Controls Serv. Co.,* ASBCA No. 38332, 89-3 BCA ¶ 22,237. *But see Security Servs., Inc.,* GSBCA No. 11052, 92-1 BCA ¶ 24,704. In *Security Services,* the GSBCA concluded that the contracting officer had the discretion to either first negotiate the claim *or* issue a final decision. Similarly, a contracting officer's refusal to negotiate a government claim before issuing a final decision did not negate the finality of that decision. *See also Siebe North, Inc. v. Norton Co.,* ASBCA No. 34366, 89-1 BCA ¶ 21,487.

[158] *Sprint Communications Co. v. General Servs. Admin.,* GSBCA No. 14263, 97-2 BCA ¶ 29,249. *But see McDonnell Douglas Corp.,* ASBCA No. 50592, 97-2 BCA ¶ 29,199.

assessment of liquidated damages,[159] or a default termination action[160] may constitute an appealable final decision even though no formal final decision is issued. The one clear exception to the requirement for a final decision is the situation where the government asserts a fraud claim against a contractor. Such a claim need not be the subject of a contracting officer's final decision.[161] Moreover, such claims are generally beyond the jurisdiction of the boards or the Court of Federal Claims.[162]

All government demands are not government claims. For example, the ASBCA has refused to consider an appeal of a government demand that a contractor repair defective work. Although the government directed the contractor to perform the work, and the contractor disputed that it was required to do so without additional compensation, the board held that there was no government claim that could be appealed until the government either defaulted the contractor or the contractor did the work and submitted a claim.[163]

The question of when a claim is a government claim or a contractor's claim requiring certification to obtain a final decision has not been answered consistently by the boards and the courts. Several boards have held that the government's withholding of payment due a contractor is a government claim that does not require contractor certification.[164] Similarly, a demand for repayment of money allegedly paid to the contractor by mistake is a government claim, and no contractor certification is required.[165]

While the assessment of liquidated damages has been characterized as a government claim,[166] the decisions addressing this question are not consistent. Certain boards have held that where a contracting officer assesses liquidated damages in a final decision, a government claim exists and no contractor certification is required.[167] One board has indicated that the burden of proof determines whose claim it is.[168]

In the context of an appeal of a termination for default, the Armed Services Board of Contract Appeals has ruled that it did not have jurisdiction over the contractor's claim for a partial remission of liquidated damages because the contractor had never submitted a claim seeking remission of the liquidated damages.[169] The Claims Court,

---

[159] *Midwest Properties, LLC v. General Services Administration, supra* note 29.

[160] *K&S Constr. v. United States*, 35 Fed. Cl. 270 (1996).

[161] *Martin J. Simko Constr., Inc. v. United States*, 852 F.2d 540 (Fed. Cir. 1988).

[162] *Comada Corp.*, ASBCA No. 26599, 83-2 BCA ¶ 16,681; *Warren Beaves d/b/a/ Commercial Marine Servs.*, DOT CAB No. 1324, 83-1 BCA ¶ 16,232. *But see Martin J. Simko v. United States, supra* note 161.

[163] *H. B. Zachry Co.*, ASBCA No. 39209, 90-1 BCA ¶ 22,342.

[164] *General Dynamics Corp.*, ASBCA No. 31359, 86-3 BCA ¶ 19,008; *Perkins & Will*, ASBCA No. 28335, 84-1 BCA ¶ 16,953; *TEM Assocs., Inc.*, NASA BCA No. 33-0990, 91-2 BCA ¶ 23,730; *Mutual Maintenance Co., Inc.*, GSBCA No. 7496, 85-2 BCA ¶ 18,098; *Alaska Lumber & Pulp Co., Inc.*, AGBCA No. 83-301-1, *et al.*, 91-2 BCA ¶ 23,890.

[165] *PX Eng'g Co., Inc.*, ASBCA No. 40714, 90-3 BCA ¶ 23,253.

[166] *Midwest Properties, LLC, v. General Services Administration, supra* note 29.

[167] *Evergreen Intern. Aviation, Inc.*, PSBCA No. 2468, 89-2 BCA ¶ 21,712.

[168] *Equitable Life Ins. Society of the U.S.*, GSBCA No. GS-7699R, 87-2 BCA ¶ 19,733.

[169] *AEC Corp., Inc.*, ASBCA No. 42920, 03-1 BCA ¶ 32,071.

however, has required a contractor to certify a claim for the return of liquidated damages that the government withheld from payments due a contractor, apparently because acknowledged delays occurred that the contractor claimed were caused by the government.[170] Thus, although the government generally withholds the liquidated damages, a contractor's claim to recover such amounts withheld as liquidated damages must be certified.[171]

Even if the contractor is not required to submit or certify a claim because it is considered to be the government's claim, the contractor should recognize that the submission of a claim by the contractor is probably needed in order to create the basis to recover CDA interest on the funds held by the government. Many government claims—for example, the assessment of liquidated damages or deductive changes—may result in the government withholding funds that are otherwise due under the contract. Even if the government's position is eventually determined to have no merit, the contractor is not entitled to receive CDA interest on those funds unless it submits a CDA claim.[172] When responding to a government claim and deduction of monies for liquidated damages or a deductive change order, the contractor's more prudent course of action is to submit a CDA claim.

22.20 CONTRACTING OFFICER'S DECISION

Once a claim meeting all the requirements of the CDA has been submitted, the next step in the dispute-resolution process is the issuance of a contracting officer's decision. The issuance of a valid contracting officer's decision, or the failure to issue such a decision within the time allowed by the Act, is a prerequisite to bringing suit on the claim in the Court of Federal Claims or filing an appeal with an agency board of contract appeals.[173]

22.21 Time Allowed for Issuing the Decision

The CDA provides that, in the case of claims of $100,000 or less, the contracting officer will issue a decision within 60 days of receipt of a written request from the contractor that a decision be issued within that period.[174] For claims over $100,000, the Act provides that, within 60 days of receipt of a certified claim, the contracting officer will issue a decision or notify the contractor of the time within which a decision will be issued.[175] If the claim's monetary value requires a contractor certification,

---

[170] *Warchol Constr. Co., supra* note 110, at 392–93.

[171] *Sun Eagle Corp. v. United States*, 23 Cl. Ct. 465 (1991).

[172] *General Motors Corp.*, ASBCA No. 35634, 92-3 BCA ¶ 25,149.

[173] *Milmark Servs., Inc. v. United States*, 231 Ct. Cl. 954, 956 (1982). As noted in **Section 22.19** *supra,* an assessment of monies by the government may constitute an appealable final decision even though the assessment was not labeled as a "final decision."

[174] 41 U.S.C. § 605(c)(1).

[175] 41 U.S.C. § 605(c)(2).

the contracting officer has no obligation to render a decision on a claim accompanied by a defective certification so long as the contracting officer notifies the contractor in writing of the basis for the conclusion that the certification is defective within 60 days of the date of receipt of the claim.[176]

The Act states that contracting officer's decisions are to be issued "within a reasonable time" in accordance with agency regulations, taking into account such factors as the size and complexity of the claim and the adequacy of the information in support of the claim.[177] Thus, although the CDA does not require a full evidentiary submission in order to recognize a claim,[178] it is in a contractor's interest to make its claim submission clear, persuasive, and understandable.

The CDA also provides that, in the event of undue delay on the part of the contracting officer in issuing a decision, a contractor may request the appropriate agency board of contract appeals or the Court of Federal Claims to direct that a final decision be issued in a specified period of time.[179] In making such a request, the contractor should be sure that it has provided the contracting officer with all the information reasonably necessary for a proper review of the claim and the issuance of a decision.

Any failure by a contracting officer to issue a decision on a claim within the period required by the Act or directed by a board or the Court of Federal Claims is deemed to be a decision by the contracting officer denying the claim ("deemed denied" decision), and such failure authorizes the commencement of suit in the Court of Federal Claims or an appeal to the appropriate board.[180] The fact that the contracting officer fails to issue a decision, however, does not mean that the government is barred from contesting the claim in subsequent proceedings. Failure to issue a decision is deemed a denial and not a default that precludes the government from contesting the merits of the claim at the board or court.[181]

A contractor should be aware, however, that even when a claim is properly submitted and the contracting officer fails to issue a decision, the Court of Federal Claims or a board of contract appeals still has the option of staying proceedings for the purpose of obtaining a decision on the claim.[182] It is reasonable to expect, however, that the Court of Federal Claims or a board will not be inclined to exercise this option in the situation where the contracting officer involved has been directed to issue a decision but has failed to do so, or in a situation where the contracting officer gave no reason for the failure to issue a decision.

---

[176] *See supra* note 105.

[177] 41 U.S.C. § 605(c)(3); *Dillingham/ABB-SUSA,* ASBCA Nos. 51195 *et al.,* 98-2 BCA ¶ 29,778; *Suburban Middlesex Insulation, Inc.,* VABCA No. 4896, 96-2 BCA ¶ 28,841; *VECO, Inc.,* DOT BCA No. 2961, 96-1 BCA ¶ 28,108. *But see Defense Supply Co., Inc.,* ASBCA No. 50534, 97-2 BCA ¶ 28,981 (nine months to review $71 million claim not unreasonable).

[178] *Metric Constr. Co., supra* note 82, at 391.

[179] 41 U.S.C. § 605(c)(4).

[180] 41 U.S.C. § 605(c)(5).

[181] *Maki v. United States,* 13 Cl. Ct. 779, 782 (1987).

[182] 41 U.S.C. § 605(c)(5).

22.22   Contents of the Decision

The CDA requires that each contracting officer's decision "state the reasons for the decision reached and . . . inform the contractor of his rights as provided in [the Act]. Specific findings of fact are not required, but, if made, shall not be binding in any subsequent proceeding."[183]

FAR § 33.211[184] also sets forth the procedure that the contracting officer is to follow if a claim by or against a contractor cannot be settled by mutual agreement. In preparing the final decision, the contracting officer is directed to include the following:

(1) Description of the claim or dispute;

(2) Reference to pertinent contract terms;

(3) Statement of the factual areas of agreement and disagreement;

(4) Statement of the final decision, with supporting rationale; and

(5) In the case of a final decision that the contractor is indebted to the government, a demand for payment in accordance with FAR § 32.610(b).

As a practical matter, the extent of the findings of fact and the rationale provided in the final decision can vary greatly, depending upon the nature of the dispute and the specific contracting officer. While the degree of detail and explanation may vary, every final decision is required by regulation[185] to contain a paragraph that reads substantially as follows:

> This is the final decision of the Contracting Officer. You may appeal this decision to the agency board of contract appeals. If you decide to appeal, you must, within 90 days from the date you receive this decision, mail or otherwise furnish written notice to the agency board of contract appeals and provide a copy to the Contracting Officer from whose decision this appeal is taken. The notice shall indicate that an appeal is intended, reference this decision, and identify the contract by number. With regard to appeals to the agency board of contract appeals, you may, solely at your election, proceed under the board's small claims procedure for claims of $50,000 or less or its accelerated procedure for claims of $100,000 or less. Instead of appealing to the agency board of contract appeals, you may bring an action directly in the United States Court of Federal Claims (except as provided in the Contract Disputes Act of 1978, 41 U.S.C. 603, regarding Maritime Contracts) within 12 months of the date you receive this decision.[186]

While a final decision that fails to contain this paragraph is considered defective,[187] a defective statement of the contractor's appeal rights does not automatically toll

---

[183] 41 U.S.C. § 605(a).

[184] 48 C.F.R. § 33.211.

[185] *Id.*

[186] *Id.*

[187] *Pathman Constr. v. United States*, 817 F.2d 1573, 1578 (Fed. Cir. 1987).

(stop) the period for filing an appeal or suit. To excuse a late appeal, the contractor must demonstrate detrimental reliance on the defective statement of its appeal rights.[188] Since the receipt of the final decision triggers the time periods for an appeal or filing of a suit, the FAR directs the contracting officer to furnish the contractor a copy of the decision by certified mail, return receipt requested, or any other method that provides evidence of receipt.[189]

Notwithstanding the statutory requirement that the contracting officer act on claims within specific time frames, a contractor and its counsel must consider whether to petition the board to set a deadline for a final decision or to commence formal proceedings by filing an appeal or a suit on a deemed denied basis if the contracting officer fails to act on the claim.[190] One practical consideration is that a board or the court may stay the proceedings to await the issuance of a final decision,[191] particularly if there is an indication that the agency is attempting to comply with the Act's requirements.

In order to provide the necessary foundation to appeal or file an action from the lack of a final decision or petition a board to set a deadline for the issuance of a final decision, certain basic documentation should be available to clearly establish the key events and their dates. This would include a letter notifying the agency that the matter is in dispute and that a final decision is requested. If the claim is in excess of $100,000, the request for a final decision must be certified. If the proposal in excess of $100,000 has been previously certified and nothing has occurred that would require a new certification,[192] a basic request for a final decision is sufficient.

Once it is apparent that no final decision will be received, it is necessary to decide whether to petition the board or Court of Federal Claims to set a date by which the contracting officer is required to issue a final decision[193] or file an appeal (institute a suit). The latter involves making an election regarding the forum that will eventually decide the matter. Regardless of whether a petition or appeal (suit) is filed, it is important to set forth the history of the efforts to obtain a final decision. While this approach is more detailed than notice pleadings, a detailed event-by-event statement of the facts with supporting documents enables the board or court to quickly evaluate the reasons why an action was instituted prior to the receipt of a final decision.

---

[188] *Florida v. United States*, 81 F.3d 1093 (Fed. Cir. 1996); *Decker & Co. v. West*, 76 F.3d 1573 (Fed. Cir. 1996); *TPI Int'l Airways, Inc.*, ASBCA No. 46462, 96-2 BCA ¶ 28,373 (reliance shown); *but see Medina Contracting Co.*, ASBCA No. 53783, 02-2 BCA ¶ 31,979; *and American Renovation & Constr. Co.*, ASBCA No. 54039, 03-2 BCA ¶ 32,296.

[189] 48 C.F.R. 33.211; *David Grimaldi Co.*, ASBCA No. 49795, 97-2 BCA ¶ 29,201; *Select Contracting, Inc. v. VA Medical Ctr.*, VABCA No. 4541, 95-2 BCA ¶ 27,830; *National Interior Contractors, Inc.*, VABCA No. 4561, 95-2 BCA ¶ 27,695.

[190] *Boeing Co. v. United States*, 26 Cl. Ct. 257 (1992); *Mitcho, Inc.*, ASBCA No. 41847, 91-2 BCA ¶ 23,860.

[191] *Continental Maritime*, ASBCA No. 37820, 89-2 BCA ¶ 21,694; *Titan Group, Inc.*, ASBCA No. 28584, 83-2 BCA ¶ 16,803.

[192] *Santa Fe Eng'rs, Inc.*, *supra* note 95.

[193] 41 U.S.C. § 605(c)(4).

22.23   APPEAL DEADLINES

The CDA provides that a contracting officer's final decision on a claim (whether a contractor or a government claim) is "final and conclusive and not subject to review by any forum, tribunal, or Governmental agency unless an appeal or suit is timely commended as provided in the [Act]."[194] Once a contractor receives a contracting officer's final decision, it has two possible alternatives. The contractor can take no action on the appeal, in which event it becomes binding on both parties; or it can appeal the decision.

Under the CDA, a contractor has two avenues of appeal from a contracting officer's final decision. Within 90 days of the date of receipt of the decision, the contractor may appeal the decision to the appropriate board of contract appeals.[195] Alternatively, within 12 months of the date of receipt of the decision, the contractor may initiate an action in the Court of Federal Claims.[196]

With respect to either an appeal to a board of contract appeals or an action in the Court of Federal Claims, it is important to consider three basic points. First, there can be no appeal or suit unless there has been a valid contracting officer's final decision or the failure to issue such a decision within the period required under the Act. Second, once a valid final decision has been issued, it is essential that a board appeal, or Court of Federal Claims suit, whichever the contractor wishes to pursue, be filed within the required time frames. Third, the contractor should realize that, once it has elected either a board or the Court of Federal Claims as the forum in which to challenge the contracting officer's decision, it may not switch to the other forum.

As noted above, the contracting officer is directed to obtain evidence of the date on which the contractor received a final decision.[197] This regulatory directive reflects the requirement for strict compliance with the time limits set forth in the CDA for appealing to boards and the Court of Federal Claims. Neither a board nor the court can consider an appeal that is not timely presented to it,[198] as the periods for challenging a contracting officer's decision set forth in the CDA are jurisdictional and cannot be waived.[199]

---

[194] 41 U.S.C. § 605(b). The government may not appeal a final decision of its own contracting officer. *Douglas Indus., Inc.,* GSBCA No. 9630, 90-2 BCA ¶ 22,676. However, a final decision favoring a contractor can be rescinded and a new final decision denying the claim may be issued so long as it is done within the CDA appeal period. *Daniels & Shanklin Constr. Co.,* ASBCA No. 37102, 89-3 BCA ¶ 22,060.

[195] 41 U.S.C. § 606.

[196] 41 U.S.C. § 609(a)(1), (a)(2). *See Opalack v. United States,* 5 Cl. Ct. 349, 361 (1984).

[197] *See* note 189. When the government alleges that an appeal is untimely, it bears the burden of proving the date of the contractor's receipt of the final decision. *Alco Mach. Co.,* ASBCA No. 38183, 89-3 BCA ¶ 21,955; *Atlantic Petroleum Corp.,* ASBCA No. 36207, 89-1 BCA ¶ 21,199.

[198] *Cosmic Constr. Co. v. United States,* 697 F.2d 1389 (Fed. Cir. 1982); *Gregory Lumber Co. v. United States,* 229 Ct. Cl. 762 (1982); *L. C. Craft,* ASBCA No. 47351, 94-2 BCA ¶ 26, 929; *Contract Servs. Co.,* ASBCA No. 34438, 87-2 BCA ¶ 19,850.

[199] *Id.*

The boards' rules typically provide that filing of the appeal occurs when it is mailed or otherwise furnished to the board.[200] "Mailing" has been interpreted as meaning the United States Postal Service. Thus, an appeal that was submitted to a commercial carrier before the expiration of the 90-day appeal period but received after that period expired was untimely.[201] Sometimes contracting officers send out a copy of the final decision by facsimile, followed by a copy sent via certified mail. Unless the facsimile copy clearly indicates that it is an "advance" copy, the 90-day period has been calculated from the date of receipt of the facsimile.[202]

Often counsel participate directly in the transmission of a claim and may correspond with the agency regarding the claim. If the contracting officer sends the final decision to the contractor's attorney, that attorney may be treated by the boards or the court as the contractor's representative for the purpose of receiving the final decision. Accordingly, the time period for filing an appeal or suit would begin to run upon the attorney's receipt of the final decision.[203] Even if the real party in interest is a subcontractor, and the prime contractor is only sponsoring the subcontractor's claim, the period for an appeal or suit begins to run when the prime contractor receives the final decision.[204]

A contracting officer cannot waive the filing deadlines.[205] However, reconsideration of final decision by a contracting officer can have the effect of starting a new appeal period, which would allow the board to assume jurisdiction over a timely appeal of the second final decision[206] or, under certain circumstances, even the lack of a second final decision.[207] However, relying upon postfinal decision communications to extend the appeal period is very risky, as such communications do not revive appeal rights unless they clearly constitute a reconsideration of the final decision.[208] If both parties are interested in further negotiations after a final decision is issued, a

---

[200] *See* ASBCA Rule 1(a). Some boards, but not all, will accept facsimile notices of appeal. *See J. C. Equip. Corp.*, IBCA No. 2885–89, 91-3 BCA ¶ 24,322.

[201] *Tiger Natural Gas, Inc., v. General Services Administration*, GSBCA No. 16039, 03-2 BCA ¶ 32,321; *C. R. Lewis Co.*, ASBCA No. 37200, 90-2 BCA ¶ 23,152; *North Coast Remanufacturing, Inc.*, ASBCA No. 38599, 89-3 BCA ¶ 22,232; *Associated Eng'g. Co.*, VABCA No. 2673, 88-2 BCA ¶ 20,709. The AGBCA has held that the notice of appeal must be mailed to the board, not the contracting officer, within the appeal period in order to be timely. *Doris Bookout*, AGBCA No. 89-147-1, 89-1 BCA ¶ 21,750.

[202] *Tyger Constr. Co.*, ASBCA No. 36100 *et al.*, 88-3 BCA ¶ 21,149.

[203] *Structural Finishing, Inc. v. United States*, 14 Cl. Ct. 447 (1988).

[204] *Colton Constr. Co., Inc.*, ASBCA No. 30313, 85-3 BCA ¶ 18,262.

[205] *Watson Rice & Co.*, AGBCA No. 82-126-3, 82-2 BCA ¶ 16,009 at 79,359.

[206] *Summit Contractors v. United States*, 15 Cl. Ct. 806 (1988); *Nash Janitorial Serv., Inc.*, GSBCA No. 7338-R, 89-2 BCA ¶ 21,615.

[207] *Westland Builders*, VABCA No. 1664, 83-1 BCA ¶ 16,235.

[208] Ongoing negotiations without clear evidence of an agreement to reconsider the decision will not prevent the appeal period from running. *Compare Colfax, Inc.*, AGBCA No. 89-159-1, 89-3 BCA ¶ 22,130, *and Birken Mfg. Co.*, ASBCA No. 36587, 89-2 BCA ¶ 21,581, *with Royal Int'l Builders Co.*, ASBCA No. 42637, 92-1 BCA ¶ 24,684.

safer course is to file an appeal or suit and then mutually seek a brief stay to explore a negotiated resolution unless there is a clear written record that the decision is being "reconsidered" by the contracting officer.

Although strict compliance is required with the appeal limitation periods set forth in the CDA, the limitation periods are not triggered when the contractor's right to proceed to either a board or the Court of Federal Claims arises because the contracting officer has failed to issue a decision on a proper claim within the period of time required by the Act and the claim therefore is deemed denied.[209]

Finally, in the case of a termination for default, the circumstances may be such that the time the contractor has to challenge the termination does not begin to run when the contracting officer issues the final decision terminating the contract, but at a later date. This exception to the general basic requirement for strict compliance with the appeal deadlines reflects the continuing application of the doctrine set forth in *Fulford Manufacturing Co.*[210] The proposition embodied by the Fulford Doctrine is that when a contractor makes a timely appeal to an assessment of excess reprocurement costs, the propriety of the default termination can be challenged even though the default termination was not appealed.[211] The Fulford Doctrine has not been altered by the CDA.[212] Thus, in most cases, the limitation periods set forth in the CDA do not "bar a contractor from contesting the propriety of a default termination in an action appealing a contracting officer's decision assessing excess reprocurement costs" if such an action is filed within 90 days (a board appeal) or 12 months (Court of Federal Claims) of the decision assessing excess costs.[213] Failure to seek review of a default termination within the 90-day or 12-month period, however, bars a contractor from challenging the default termination if excess costs are not assessed.[214]

---

[209] *Pathman Constr. Co. v. United States*, 817 F.2d 1573 (Fed. Cir. 1987).

[210] ASBCA Nos. 2143, 2144 (May 20, 1955), Cont. Cas. Fed. (CCH) ¶ 61,815 (May 20, 1955) (digest only) (timely appeal of the default action will also preserve right to contest excess cost assessment even though second final decision is not appealed in timely manner). *See also T. E. Deloss Equip. Rentals*, ASBCA No. 35374, 88-1 BCA ¶ 20,497; *El-Tronics, Inc.*, ASBCA No. 5457, 61-1 BCA ¶ 2961. However, one board has held that the failure to timely appeal a default termination final decision will preclude a challenge to the default in a subsequent appeal from a government claim for recovery of unliquidated progress payments or property damages. *See Dailing Roofing, Inc.*, ASBCA No. 34739, 89-1 BCA ¶ 21,311. *See also Guidance Sys.*, ASBCA No. 34690, 88-3 BCA ¶ 20,914.

[211] *D. Moody & Co. v. United States*, 5 Cl. Ct. 70 (1984).

[212] *D. Moody & Co.*, supra note 211; *Southwest Marine, Inc.*, DOT BCA No. 1891, 96-1 BCA ¶ 27-895; *Tom Warr*, IBCA No. 2360, 88-1 BCA ¶ 20,231. However, in *Ace Forestration, Inc.*, AGBCA No. 87-272-1, 87-3 BCA ¶ 20,218, the Department of Agriculture Board of Contract Appeals declined to follow the Fulford Doctrine.

[213] *D. Moody & Co.*, supra note 211.

[214] *Id.*

22.24 CHOOSING A FORUM: BOARD OR U.S. COURT OF FEDERAL CLAIMS

When it becomes apparent that the agency will or is likely to issue an adverse final decision, it is essential that the contractor and its counsel give careful consideration to the election of the forum (board or Court of Federal Claims). The CDA gives the contractor the basic right to seek a *de novo*, or complete, review of a final decision in either forum.[215] When considering whether to elect to go to the board or to the court, there are a number of factors to consider, such as:

(1) *Time and Money*: Ordinarily, board proceedings are believed to be less time-consuming and costly than court proceedings. Often this perception reflects the fact that the boards' formal rules of procedure are not as extensive as the rules in the Court of Federal Claims. However, some board judges issue extensive prehearing orders that mirror, to a great degree, orders issued by a federal district court or the Court of Federal Claims.

(2) *Judicial Background and Experience*: In accordance with the CDA, board judges must have at least five years of experience in government contract law. Typically, they have much more than that minimum level of experience in government contracting.[216] There is no parallel specialized experience requirement for Court of Federal Claims judges. Board judges hear only government contract cases. Judges on the Court of Federal Claims hear a wide range of matters besides contract cases.

(3) *Case Issues*: If the case involves a particular issue or contract provision, it is important to learn how that board or the court views that issue. For example, a board or the court may have recently issued a decision reflecting its views on the proof of delay and the use of a CPM to demonstrate delay. If the case warrants the investment, this type of research should be conducted as part of the forum selection process.[217]

(4) *Agency Involvement*: If a case is appealed to a board, the agency will provide the government trial counsel. Accordingly, the counsel representing the government may be the same person who advised the contracting officer when the claim was being denied. When a case is filed in the Court of Federal Claims, the Civil Division of the Justice Department represents the government. Under certain circumstances, the Justice Department can, in theory, settle a case over the procuring agency's objections.

---

[215] 41 U.S.C. §§ 606, 609(a)(1) & 609(a)(2).

[216] 41 U.S.C. § 607(b)(1).

[217] For example, a comparison of the decisions of the ASBCA and the Claims Court (now the Court of Federal Claims) concerning the interpretation of essentially the same specification illustrates the value of this type of research. *Compare Western States Constr. Co. v. United States*, 26 Cl. Ct. 818 (1992), *with Tomahawk Constr. Co.*, ASBCA No. 41717, 93-3 BCA ¶ 26,219.

(5) *Hearing/Trial Location*: All of the boards and the Court of Federal Claims are located in Washington, DC. In practice, the boards and the court can and often do hold hearings outside of Washington. Location usually depends upon the convenience of all of the parties.

(6) *Representation by Legal Counsel*: Board practice permits an officer of the corporation to represent it. At the Court of Federal Claims, a corporation must be represented by an attorney admitted to practice before that court.[218]

Once a contractor has elected either a board or the Court of Federal Claims as the forum in which to challenge a contracting officer's final decision, it may not switch to the other forum. In this regard, a contractor that is poised to proceed to either a board or the court should be aware of the Election Doctrine. The term "Election Doctrine" refers to the body of law related to the contractor's right to initially select the forum in which to challenge a contracting officer's decision. However, the Act does not allow the contractor to pursue its claim in both forums.[219] Thus, once a contractor makes a binding election to appeal a contracting officer's decision to the appropriate board of contract appeals, the contractor cannot change course and pursue its claim in the court.[220] The converse is also true.

A binding election takes place when a contractor files an appeal or initiates a suit in a "forum with jurisdiction over the proceeding."[221] This means that when a contractor initiates proceedings on its claim before a board of contract appeals in a timely manner, it has made a binding election to proceed before the board and it is barred from initiating suit in the court. Any suit it files in the court will be dismissed.[222] However, the filing of an appeal with the appropriate board of contract appeals is not a binding election if it is determined by the board that the contractor's appeal was untimely; hence the subsequent filing of a claim in the Court of Federal Claims is not barred.[223] The rationale is that a contractor's choice of forums in which to contest the contracting officer's decision is a binding election only if that choice is truly available, which it is not if resort to a board of contract appeals is untimely.[224] In those circumstances, the untimely appeal to the board was an absolute nullity and the Election Doctrine is not applicable.[225]

---

[218] *Alchemy, Inc. v. United States*, 3 Cl. Ct. 727 (1983).

[219] *Tuttle/White Constructors, Inc. v. United States*, 656 F.2d 644, 649 (Ct. Cl. 1981); *Marshall Associated Contractors, Inc. v. United States*, 31 Fed. Cl. 809 (1994).

[220] *Tuttle/White Constructors, Inc.*, *supra* note 219. However, a notice of appeal to a board that was retrieved before docketing did not constitute a binding election. *Blake Constr. Co., Inc. v. United States*, 13 Cl. Ct. 250 (1987).

[221] *Tuttle/White Constructors, Inc.*, *supra* note 219.

[222] *National Neighbors, Inc. v. United States*, 839 F.2d 1539, 1541–42 (Fed. Cir. 1988).

[223] *Id.*

[224] *Id.*

[225] *Id.*

22.25   TRANSFER AND CONSOLIDATION OF CASES

The CDA provides that if two or more suits arising from one contract are filed in the Court of Federal Claims and with one or more boards, the court is authorized to order the consolidation of the suits before it or to transfer suits to or among the boards involved "for the convenience of parties or witnesses or in the interest of justice."[226] In deciding whether a case should be consolidated or transferred, the court will take into account a number of factors: whether the disputes in the different forums arise out of the same contract, whether the cases present overlapping or the same issues, whether the plaintiff initially elected to initiate proceedings at the board, whether substantial effort in the case already has been expended in one forum but not the other, which proceeding involves the most money, and which proceeding presents the more difficult and complex claims.[227]

22.26   ADR AND FEDERAL GOVERNMENT CONTRACT DISPUTES

There has long been a need for alternatives to the traditional manner in which government contract disputes are resolved. The Administrative Conference of the United States ("Conference"), whose purpose is to promote efficiency and fairness in federal agency procedures, has been a major proponent of ADR in government contracts. The Conference has strongly supported alternative dispute resolution (ADR) and has several publications that discuss the contract disputes dilemma and various ADR efforts.[228]

FAR § 33.214[229] states that the objective of using ADR procedures is to increase the opportunity for relatively inexpensive and expeditious resolution of issues in controversy. Essential elements of ADR include: (1) existence of an issue in controversy, (2) a voluntary election by both parties to participate in the ADR process, (3) an agreement on alternative procedures and terms to be used in lieu of formal litigation, (4) participation in the process by officials of both parties who have the authority to resolve the issue in controversy, and (5) contractor certification of claims in excess of $100,000.

ADR procedures may be used at any time that the contracting officer has authority to settle the issue in controversy and may be applied to a portion of a claim. When

---

[226] 41 U.S.C. § 609(d). *See Glendale Joint Venture v. United States*, 13 Cl. Ct. 325, 327 (1987); *Multi-Roof Sys. Co. v. United States*, 5 Cl. Ct. 245, 248 (1984); *E.D.S. Fed. Corp. v. United States*, 2 Cl. Ct. 735, 739 (1983).

[227] *Glendale Joint Venture, supra* note 226; *Multi-Roof Sys., supra* note 226; *E.D.S. Fed. Corp., supra* note 226, at 739.

[228] *See generally 1987 Sourcebook: Federal Agency Use of Alternative Means of Dispute Resolution (Office of the Chairman 1987)* and its report on Appealing Government Contract Decisions: "Reducing the Cost and Delay of Procurement Litigation"; DOD Directive 5145.5.

[229] 48 C.F.R. § 33.214.

ADR procedures are used subsequent to issuance of a contracting officer's final decision, their use does not alter any of the time limitations or procedural requirements for filing an appeal of the contracting officer's final decision and does not constitute a reconsideration of the final decision. In the event that the contracting officer rejects a request by a small business to use ADR, the contracting officer is required by regulation to set forth a written explanation for that decision and to provide it to the contractor.[230]

The CDA states that the boards shall provide, to the fullest extent practicable, informal, expeditious, and inexpensive resolution of disputes, and this is the authority for their use of ADR.[231] The boards of contract appeals have implemented ADR procedures and issued a Notice Regarding Alternative Methods of Dispute Resolution that strongly endorses the use of ADR and suggests several techniques. Many of the procedures outlined by that notice come from the recommendations made by the Administrative Conference of the United States. The boards routinely provide a notice of the availability of ADR procedures when the docketing notice is sent out to the parties together with a copy of the board's rules of procedure. In addition, most boards will seek to assist in the resolution of claims prior to the issuance of a final decision by making a judge available to mediate a claim. Similar to ADR after an appeal is filed, this voluntary process requires a joint request by the contractor and the government.

The decision to use ADR is made jointly by the parties, and a board will not accept a unilateral request. However, the board may take the initiative in suggesting ADR as an option in dispute resolution. There are a number of ADR methods, and both the parties and the board may agree to the use of any of these methods, such as settlement judge, mini-trial, summary trial with binding decision, and other agreed methods. The United States Court of Federal Claims has formally approved the voluntary use of ADR. As described in the *Deskbook for Practitioners* published by that court's bar association,[232] the court is sensitive to rising litigation costs and the delay often inherent in the traditional judicial resolution of complex legal claims. Accordingly, General Order 13 established two alternative methods of dispute resolution: the settlement judge and the mini-trial.

These techniques are voluntary and both parties must agree to their use. The court expects the techniques to be invoked in complex cases where the amount in controversy exceeds $100,000, the parties anticipate a lengthy period of discovery, and a trial is expected to consume more than one week.

When both parties agree to utilize one of these alternative methods of dispute resolution, they notify the presiding judge as early as possible in the proceedings or concurrently with the submission of a joint preliminary status report.

If the presiding judge agrees, the case will be referred to the clerk, who will assign the case to another court judge, who will preside over the procedure and who will

---

[230] *Id.*

[231] 41 U.S.C. § 605(d).

[232] The United States Court of Federal Claims, *A Deskbook for Practitioners*, United States Court of Federal Claims Bar Association.

exercise final authority, within the general guidelines adopted by the court, to determine the form and function of each method. If the ADR method utilized by the parties fails to produce a satisfactory settlement, the case will be returned to the docket of the presiding judge. All representations made in the course of utilizing a method of ADR are confidential, and except as permitted by Federal Rule of Evidence 408, may not be utilized for any reason in subsequent litigation.

22.27 RECOVERY OF ATTORNEYS' FEES IN GOVERNMENT CONTRACT CLAIMS

Generally, the FAR disallows the recovery of attorneys' fees and expenses, as well as claim consultants' fees and expenses associated with the preparation and prosecution of government contract claims.[233] However, with the passage of the Equal Access to Justice Act (EAJA),[234] Congress provided a statutory basis for certain eligible contractors to recover some or all of their legal costs and expenses of litigation with the government.

An EAJA application for recovery of legal fees and expenses is filed within 30 days after the conclusion of the primary appeal or suit.[235] To recover its fees and expenses, the claimant must meet the following criteria:

(1) Have a net worth of not more than $7,000,000;

(2) Have no more than 500 employees;[236] and

(3) Be the prevailing party in the litigation with the government.[237]

The government will not be held liable for the claimant's legal fees and expenses if it can demonstrate that its position in the litigation was substantially justified.[238] Even though the contractor recovers less than it claimed or prevailed on fewer than all of the issues, the claimant may still be deemed to be the prevailing party.[239]

---

[233] FAR § 31.205–33; *Plano Builders Corp. v. United States*, 40 Fed. Cl. 635 (1998). If the contractor can convince the board or court that these costs were incurred in aid of contract administration, rather than claim preparation or prosecution, these costs can be recovered to the extent they are reasonable and allocable. *See Bill Strong Enters., Inc. v. United States*, 49 F.3d 1541 (Fed. Cir. 1995); *Betancourt & Gonzalez, S.E.*, DOT BCA Nos. 2785 *et al.*, 96-1 BCA ¶ 28,033.

[234] 5 U.S.C. § 504.

[235] *Id.; see Southern Dredging*, ENGBCA No. 6236-F, 97-2 BCA ¶ 29,014; *AIW-Alton, Inc.*, ASBCA No. 474, 39, 96-2 BCA ¶ 28,399.

[236] 5 U.S.C. § 504(b)(1)(B). These requirements apply to corporations, partnerships, or unincorporated businesses.

[237] 5 U.S.C. § 504(a)(1).

[238] *Oneida Constr., Inc./David Boland, Inc., Joint Venture*, ASBCA Nos. 44194 *et al.*, 95-2 BCA ¶ 27,893; *Labco Constr., Inc.*, AGBCA No. 95-104-10, 95-2 BCA ¶ 27,667; *ABC Health Corp.*, VABCA No. 2462E, 94-3 BCA ¶ 27,013; *Sun Eagle Corp.*, ASBCA No. 45985, 94-2 BCA ¶ 26,870.

[239] *Midland Maintenance, Inc.*, ENGBCA Nos. 6080-F, 6092-F, 97-1 BCA ¶ 28,849; *Jackson Elec. Co.*, ENGBCA No. 6238-F, 97-1 BCA ¶ 28,848; *Tayag Bros. Enters., Inc.*, ASBCA No. 42097, 96-2 BCA ¶ 28,279.

The size and net worth criteria must be satisfied by the prime contractor. Even though the real party in interest is a subcontractor, it is not in privity of contract with the government and is not eligible to recover EAJA legal fees and expenses.[240]

The EAJA limits the amounts that can be recouped for legal fees to a maximum hourly rate[241] plus out-of-pocket expenses. Expert witness rates can be no higher than those paid by the government to its expert witness.[242]

> ## ➤ POINTS TO REMEMBER

- While the Contract Disputes Act (CDA) addresses the procedures for the processing of claims on a government contract, it is essential that you understand your obligations and rights under the standard clauses, such as the Changes, Differing Site Conditions, and Suspension of Work clauses.
- Compliance with the contract's notice provisions, as well as consideration of the six-year statute of limitations, is essential to preserving your right to recovery on a claim.
- Every request for an equitable adjustment is not necessarily a claim. A "claim" is a nonroutine written submission or demand that seeks, as a matter of right, the payment of money in a sum certain.
- Every claim in excess of $100,000 must be certified by an authorized representative of the prime contractor in order to be considered a "claim" and entitle you to recover CDA interest.
- Prime contractors must provide unqualified certifications of their subcontractors' claims. In that context, consider obtaining an appropriate indemnity agreement.
- A defective claim certification may delay action by the contracting officer, a board of contract appeals, or the Court of Federal Claims.
- The CDA specifies time frames for action by the contracting officer on all claims and provides a means for a contractor to compel consideration of the claim if the contracting officer is unreasonably slow in acting.
- Once a final decision is received, you have 90 days to file an appeal at the board of contract appeals or one year to file a suit in the Court of Federal Claims. If these periods are allowed to pass, the final decision is, in almost all cases, final and binding.

---

[240] *SCL Materials & Equip. Co.*, IBCA No. 3866-97F, 98-2 BCA ¶ 30,000.

[241] 5 U.S.C. § 504(b)(1)(A). For actions or appeals awarded on or after March 29, 1996, the maximum rate for legal fees is $125 per hour. For actions or appeals commenced prior to that date, the maximum rate was $75 per hour.

[242] *Techplan Corp.*, ASBCA Nos. 41470 *et al.*, 98-2 BCA ¶ 29,954.

- Carefully consider whether you wish to have your appeal heard at a board of contract appeals or in the Court of Federal Claims. Once an election is made, it is, in almost all cases, binding on the parties.
- Whether you appeal the final decision to a board of contract appeals or file a suit in the Court of Federal Claims, the claim receives *de novo* consideration. That means that no presumption of correctness is attached to the decision—even those portions favorable to the contractor.

ABOUT THE CD-ROM

INTRODUCTION

This appendix provides you with information on the contents of the CD that accompanies this book. For the most current information, please refer to the ReadMe file located at the root of the CD.

SYSTEM REQUIREMENTS

- A computer with a processor running at 120 Mhz or faster
- At least 32 MB of total RAM installed on your computer; for best performance, we recommend at least 64 MB
- A CD-ROM drive

USING THE CD WITH WINDOWS

If the opening screen of the CD-ROM does not appear automatically, follow these steps to access the CD:

1. Click the Start button on the left end of the taskbar and then choose Run from the menu that pops up.
2. In the dialog box that appears, type *d:\setup.exe*. (If your CD-ROM drive is not drive d, fill in the appropriate letter in place of *d*.) This brings up the CD Interface described in the preceding set of steps.

WHAT'S ON THE CD

This companion CD-ROM contains sample contract documents from the following organizations:

- American Institute of Architects®—29 sample contracts
- Associated General Contractors of America®—61 sample contracts
- Engineers Joint Contract Documents Committee—92 sample contracts

The following applications are on the CD:

Adobe Reader

Adobe Reader is a freeware application for viewing files in the Adobe Portable Document format.

CUSTOMER CARE

If you have trouble with the CD-ROM, please call the Wiley Product Technical Support phone number at (800) 762-2974. Outside the United States, call 1(317) 572-3994. You can also contact Wiley Product Technical Support at **http://www.wiley.com/ techsupport**. John Wiley & Sons will provide technical support only for installation and other general quality control items. For technical support on the applications themselves, consult the program's vendor or author.

To place additional orders or to request information about other Wiley products, please call (877) 762-2974.

INDEX

CUSTOMER NOTE: IF THIS BOOK IS ACCOMPANIED BY SOFTWARE, PLEASE READ THE FOLLOWING BEFORE OPENING THE PACKAGE.

THIS SOFTWARE CONTAINS FILES TO HELP YOU UTILIZE THE MODELS DESCRIBED IN THE ACCOMPANYING BOOK. BY OPENING THE PACKAGE, YOU ARE AGREEING TO BE BOUND BY THE FOLLOWING AGREEMENT:

THIS SOFTWARE PRODUCT IS PROTECTED BY COPYRIGHT AND ALL RIGHTS ARE RESERVED BY THE AUTHOR, JOHN WILEY & SONS, INC., OR THEIR LICENSORS. YOU ARE LICENSED TO USE THIS SOFTWARE ON A SINGLE COMPUTER. COPYING THE SOFTWARE TO ANOTHER MEDIUM OR FORMAT FOR USE ON A SINGLE COMPUTER DOES NOT VIOLATE THE U.S. COPYRIGHT LAW. COPYING THE SOFTWARE FOR ANY OTHER PURPOSE IS A VIOLATION OF THE U.S. COPYRIGHT LAW.

THIS SOFTWARE PRODUCT IS SOLD AS IS WITHOUT WARRANTY OF ANY KIND, EITHER EXPRESS OR IMPLIED, INCLUDING BUT NOT LIMITED TO THE IMPLIED WARRANTY OF MERCHANTABILITY AND FITNESS FOR A PARTICULAR PURPOSE. NEITHER WILEY NOR ITS DEALERS OR DISTRIBUTORS ASSUMES ANY LIABILITY FOR ANY ALLEGED OR ACTUAL DAMAGES ARISING FROM THE USE OF OR THE INABILITY TO USE THIS SOFTWARE. (SOME STATES DO NOT ALLOW THE EXCLUSION OF IMPLIED WARRANTIES, SO THE EXCLUSION MAY NOT APPLY TO YOU.)